BARRON'S

GMAT®

BOBBY UMAR, M.B.A.
GMAT Instructor and Consultant
President, Raeallan
Leadership Speaking and Training
Toronto, Canada

CARL S. PYRDUM, III, M.A., Ph.D.
GMAT Tutor
Ivory Tower Tutoring
Atlanta, Georgia

BARRON'S

® GMAT and Graduate Management Admissions Test are registered trademarks of the Graduate Management
Admission Council (GMAC). The GMAC does not endorse, and is not affiliated with this product.

About the Authors

Bobby Umar, MBA is a highly sought after GMAT instructor in North America. For almost 15 years, he has taught GMAT prep courses for Veritas Prep and Kaplan, global test prep companies, and his own company, Raeallan. In 2009–2010, he was awarded the "Worldwide Instructor of the Year" for Veritas out of 500+ instructors from 130 countries.

During his MBA studies at Degroote School of Business in Hamilton, Ontario, Bobby was President of the MBA Association, received awards in case competitions, academics, and leadership, and graduated at the top of his class as co-valedictorian. With a background in brand marketing, engineering, and the performing arts, he also draws on his diverse career to lead Raeallan, a transformational training and speaking company (*www.raeallan.com*). A four-time TEDx speaker, Bobby speaks about leadership, personal branding, networking, and social media. With his expertise about the GMAT, he has helped thousands of young leaders get into the best business schools.

You can connect with Bobby via Twitter, Linkedin or *www.GMATBobby.com*

Carl Pyrdum is a long-time GMAT tutor, who opened his own tutoring company, Ivory Tower Tutoring in Atlanta, Georgia. He has worked as a teacher, tutor, and content developer for the GMAT, GRE, LSAT, SAT, and ACT for Barron's as well as for Kaplan. He has helped more than a thousand students improve their test scores and reach their undergraduate, graduate, and professional school goals.

Acknowledgment

The authors would like to acknowledge the valuable contribution of Sophia Glisch, who helped formulate a number of questions and answers in the book.

All inquiries should be addressed to:
Barron's Educational Series, Inc.
250 Wireless Boulevard
Hauppauge, New York 11788
www.barronseduc.com

ISBN: 978-1-4380-0231-6 (book)
ISBN: 978-1-4380-7334-7 (book with CD-ROM)

Library of Congress Control Number: 2013954776 (book)
Library of Congress Control Number: 2013954775 (book with CD-ROM)

PRINTED IN THE UNITED STATES OF AMERICA
9 8 7 6 5 4 3 2

10% POST-CONSUMER WASTE
Paper contains a minimum of 10% post-consumer waste (PCW). Paper used in this book was derived from certified, sustainable forestlands.

CONTENTS

PART 4: VERBAL

Introduction

→ **PRACTICAL MATTERS**

→ **THE TEST'S STRUCTURE**

→ **YOUR 10 (YES, 10!) TEST SCORES**

→ **WHAT THE CAT IS AND WHAT IT MEANS TO YOU**

→ **WHAT THE GMAT *REALLY* TESTS . . . AND WHAT IT DOESN'T**

→ **GATHER YOUR MATERIALS**

→ **REGISTER FOR THE TEST, ALREADY!**

Officially, GMAT is an acronym that stands for The Graduate Management Admissions Test, the standardized computer-based test that the vast majority of business schools use in admissions decisions for their MBA programs.

The GMAT dates back to 1953, when deans from the most prestigious business schools asked the maker of the SAT, the Education Testing Service (ETS), to create an objective, national entrance exam for graduate business programs. The first test, which went by the less pronounceable acronym ATGSB (Admissions Test for Graduate Study in Business) was given in February of 1954 to a few more than 4,000 hopeful business students. Believe it or not, the questions those students faced were quite similar to the ones you'll be facing now, nearly 60 years later, even though the format of the test has changed a good bit over time.

Currently, the test is administered at Pearson VUE test sites and the questions are written by ACT, an assessment and reporting company.

The latest change in guard has, thankfully, done little to change the overall nature of the core test and its questions. True, some sections and question types have been dropped over the years, some added (the most recent, the Integrated Reasoning, added in 2012), but the underlying logic behind the test remains the same—and that's good news for prospective test takers like you! With the right guidance and a bit of hard work, the GMAT *can* be mastered, no matter how strange and difficult it might seem at the outset. There's not just a method to the GMAT's madness; there's a system of hidden rules and expectations that it always operates by that you can learn in order to secure the score you need to meet your admissions goals.

PRACTICAL MATTERS

There are many places to find the nuts-and-bolts information about registering for and scheduling the test, but there is no place better than the website of the test maker. So if you haven't already, now would be a good time to visit and sign up for an account.

The official website: http://www.mba.com/

Nevertheless, here are the high points:

> **How do I register for the test?** Once you have an account at mba.com, you will find the link to the registration page on your personal mba.com home page.
>
> **When is the GMAT offered?** It is offered almost every day, excluding public holidays, but including Saturday and Sunday. And on any given day, multiple time slots are available, so if you're a morning person, you can usually schedule it for 8:00 A.M. If you like to sleep in, some centers offer tests as late as 4 or 5:00 P.M.
>
> **How often can I take the GMAT?** There are two limitations: you may only take the GMAT once every 31 calendar days and no more than five times in 12 calendar months.
>
> **How much does the GMAT cost?** At the time of this book's printing, the GMAT will set you back a cool $250. Alas, the price is subject to increases from time to time; however, oddly, it never decreases.
>
> **Can I use a calculator?** Nope. No slide rules, either. In fact, they're awfully touchy about what they let you bring into the test room. They'll provide you with a yellow spiral-bound wet erase noteboard and two or three wet erase pens for scratch work and there will be headphones at each computer for those worried about noise; otherwise, all your possessions must be locked away outside the testing area until after you're done.

THE TEST'S STRUCTURE

When you sit down in front of your assigned computer on test day, you will face four scored sections in this order:

1. **ANALYTICAL WRITING ASSESSMENT SECTION (THE AWA).** In the AWA, you are given 30 minutes to write a response to an essay prompt, typing it into a simplified word processing interface. The prompt asks you to produce an "Analysis of an Argument," presenting a brief, fictitious argument from a made-up source and asking you to critique it.

2. **INTEGRATED REASONING SECTION (THE IR).** Here, you will be given 12 questions and 30 minutes to complete the section. IR questions ask you to use multiple sources of information—graphs, tables, charts, and short reading passages—and to employ both your math and your verbal knowledge and skills. Four types of questions are attached to these different sources of information: Graphics Interpretation, Two-Part Analysis, Table Analysis, and Multisource Reasoning.

3. **QUANTITATIVE SECTION (AKA "THE MATH" OR "THE QUANT").** The Quantitative Section contains 37 questions written in two different formats, Problem Solving and Data Sufficiency (aka "the weird ones"). The questions will alternate between the two formats more or less at random. According to the test maker, both types of questions will require familiarity with arithmetic, elementary algebra, and "commonly known" concepts of geometry. You will have 75 minutes—an hour and a quarter—to answer all the questions.

4. **VERBAL SECTION.** As with the Quantitative Section, you have 75 minutes, but here you'll face 41 questions in three different formats (Reading Comprehension, Sentence Correction, and Critical Reasoning), also in no particular order. The Verbal questions require a basic understanding of the "rules" of arguments, the ability to read and organize information presented in both long (350- to 400-word) and short (100-word) passages, and familiarity with the grammatical rules of standard written English.

A few extra things to keep in mind:

- In addition to the scored sections, you will also be given the opportunity at the very beginning of the test to take a short computer tutorial to familiarize yourself with the machine you've been assigned and the test interface.
- After the first two 30-minute sections and between the Math and Verbal sections you are allowed, but not required, to take a short 10-minute break.
- The test maker slips a few "experimental" or unscored questions in with the scored ones in order to fine-tune them for future test takers. There's no real way to know which ones aren't scored, though, and they look just like normal, scored questions, so it's probably best to just pretend that all the questions are scored.

Section	# of Questions	Time	Question Types
AWA	1 essay prompt	30 minutes	Analysis of an Argument
Integrated Reasoning	12	30 minutes	Graphics Interpretation, Two-Part Analysis, Table Analysis, Multisource Reasoning
Short Break—up to 10 minutes			
Quantitative Section	37	75 minutes	Problem Solving, Data Sufficiency
Short Break—up to 10 minutes			
Verbal Section	41	75 minutes	Critical Reasoning, Sentence Correction, Reading Comprehension

TIP

If you're asking yourself, "What about the other essay?", there is good news! As of June 5, 2012, the GMAT no longer asks you to write an "Analysis of an Issue" essay. It was dropped to make room for the Integrated Reasoning section.

TIP

As far as we know, there's no AKA for the Verbal: Everyone just calls it "the Verbal."

YOUR 10 (YES, 10!) TEST SCORES

When all is said and done, you will receive a lot of different scores for the GMAT—ten in total! Usually, people will just refer to one, the Overall Score (as in "I got a 720" or "I heard you need a 712 to get into Harvard" or "You get 200 points just for writing your name down!"). In actual practice, your score will come back with a little chart that looks like this:

Test Date	Verbal	Quantitative	Total	Analytical Writing	Integrated Reasoning
23 June 20XX	40/90%	50/89%	690/89%	6/91%	7/82%

Actually, the scores you receive on the day of the test are considered Unofficial Scores, only becoming Official Scores when your score report appears in your email inbox and on the Graduate Management Admissions Council (GMAC) website. It is rare for the numbers to change in between, so in practice most people don't use the "Official" and "Unofficial" distinction. Note, however, that most schools require you to have an Official Score to report *before* their application deadline!

Eight of your scores are calculated automatically on site, so you'll find them out on the day of your test. You have to wait a few weeks for the essays to be graded to receive the final two.

1. **OVERALL SCORE (YOUR SCALED SCORE).** This is that famous three-digit number, the first score in the Total column. It ranges from 200 to 800, in increments of 10. Two-thirds of test takers score between 400 and 600, and the median score is usually between 540 and 570. The scores are arranged on a bell curve, so scores below 300 or above 700 are relatively rare. This score is produced by a weighted average of your performance ONLY in the Quantitative and Verbal sections. (The AWA essay and the IR sections are tracked independently.) The average's weight skews toward the Math score, though the exact amount is a trade secret closely guarded by the test maker.

2. **OVERALL PERCENTILE SCORE.** The second score in the Total column, this one is actually more important than the three-digit number, although admittedly less iconic. It tells you what percentage of recent test takers your score bests. Thus, a 75th percentile scorer did better than 75 percent of people who've taken the test over the last three years. This score can change from year to year as the test taking population changes, though in practice it rarely moves more than a single point in either direction.

3. **QUANTITATIVE SUBSCORE.** Your performance in both the Math and Verbal sections is also tracked separately, on a range from 0 to 60, with increments of 1 point. Quantitative Subscores are typically in the 7 to 50 range (again, because of the test's built-in bell curve).

4. **QUANTITATIVE PERCENTILE SUBSCORE.** Like the Overall Score, your Quantitative Score will also be expressed as a percentile (the second score in the Quantitative column) and it, too, can change slightly from year to year. In most years, it takes a subscore of at least 52 to break into the 99th percentile.

5. **VERBAL SUBSCORE.** The first score in the Verbal column, this one's just like the Quantitative, but for Verbal: 0–60, 1 point increments. Most test takers will score between 9 and 44, which is, you might have noticed, a good bit smaller a range than in Math, with a lower top-end score as well.

6. **VERBAL PERCENTILE SUBSCORE.** The Verbal column's second score works just like the other percentiles, though the bell curve here is slightly more forgiving. A 99th percentile score can be had for the low, low price of a subscore of 45.

7. **INTEGRATED REASONING SCORE.** Calculated completely separately from any other section, the first score in your IR column will range from 1 to 8, with increments of one point. That means there are only eight possible scores for all people taking the test, and most of those scores are between 3 and 7, with a mean of 4. Interestingly, even though a score of 1 is theoretically possible, most years no one receives one.

8. **INTEGRATED REASONING PERCENTILE SCORE.** The second score in your IR column is also calculated only from your performance on the 12 IR questions and is also variable from year to year. The numbers here have jumped around quite a bit over this section's short history, although it seems to have stabilized around 94% as the top score, 46% the mean, and 17% the bottom.

> Because the scores only come in 10-point increments, it's impossible to get a 712; only a 710 or a 720—no matter what that guy at work told you he got. When you see a number in between the tens—say, on a list of scores needed for the top schools—it means multiple students' scores have been averaged to produce it.

9. **AWA SCALED SCORE.** Your essay scores will be calculated independently of all the other sections. The Scaled Score, first in the Analytical Writing column, has a theoretical range of 0–6, with increments of 0.5 (meaning it's possible to get a 4, a 4.5, or a 5, but not a 4.1 or a 4.8; however, in practice 0's are never given and more than 90% of test takers receive a score between 2 and 5.5. So, even though there are 11 possible scores in their range, the test maker only uses 7 regularly.

TIP
2013's 85th percentile might be 2014's 86th percentile.

10. **AWA PERCENTILE SCORE.** Your final percentile score works like all the rest, though the top score of 6 translates to only the 91st percentile most years.

> If you'd like to see the full charts of scores and their percentiles, you can find them at the Official GMAT website—at the time of this printing found at http://www.gmac.com/gmat/learn-about-the-gmat-exam/gmat-scoring-by-exam-section.aspx
>
>

Of all these many scores, the one most important to your business school admissions goals remains that three-digit Overall Score. Though they are loathe to admit it, it's still the case that many schools have an Overall Score cutoff they use to winnow down the mountain of applications they receive each year. Fall under it, and your application goes to the circular file. Accordingly, the bulk of this book is dedicated to the principles and techniques that will allow you to raise that Overall Score to vault over whatever arbitrary bar you face.

WHAT THE CAT IS AND WHAT IT MEANS TO YOU

Now that you've got the basic who, what, where, and why of the GMAT down, it's high time we moved onto the how—as in, "How am I going to improve my score on the test?" The first step is to understand how this test differs from other tests you might have taken elsewhere, not the mundane details like number of questions and how to register but the real nitty-gritty that separates the GMAT from the SAT, GRE, and ABCs: the CAT.

The C in CAT is easy enough to understand, as is the T: we all know the GMAT is a **T**est that's only offered on a **C**omputer. It's that A that bears explaining. What does it mean for a test to be "**A**daptive"?

Back when the GMAT was administered on paper, every student in the room taking it faced exactly the same questions in exactly the same order. In general, the questions were organized with the easiest ones up front and the hardest toward the end, the idea being that a student who "deserved" a 540 would be able to work only a certain percentage of the test's questions, whereas one destined for a 740 would be able to work a much higher percentage, all but a few questions, and future 800s would be able to do them all.

The paper test could be administered only a few times a year because each administration requires the test makers to write an entirely new set of questions to keep those who took the February exam from telling those taking the test in April what questions they'd see. So if there were 100 questions on a test, each sitting meant a fresh 100.

Adaptive Features

An adaptive test is, instead, built from a single pool of questions much larger than the 41 Verbal and 37 Math questions a single student sees, and it's almost impossible that any two test takers would see the exact same 78 questions as any other. The pool of possible questions is organized into "tiers" of questions of similar difficulty. The first question the test taker sees is drawn from the middle tier of questions, ones that the test maker has designed to be doable by students who will end up with a score right in the fat part of the test's bell curve (and all those who exceed it) but not by those below it.

The next question drawn from the pool is determined by how the test taker performs on that first question. If the correct answer was picked, the next question will be from a slightly higher tier, and if one of the four incorrect choices picked, a slightly lower one. Another correct answer will mean the next question is more difficult still, while an incorrect one will dial the difficulty back a notch. As the test progresses, the jumps or falls in difficulty decrease in magnitude, so missing a question in the first ten will have a greater impact on the tier your questions are drawn from than missing one of the last ten.

TIP

"Tier" is just a term of convenience. There is no official category system for questions on the GMAT.

The idea is that the test will be able to home in very quickly on the test taker's true skill level and only offer questions appropriate to that skill level. Whenever test takers get enough questions right to raise the difficulty up into a tier that's too hard for them, they'll start missing questions, lowering it right back down to their true skill level.

If the system worked perfectly, eventually test takers should expect to reach a point where they miss every other question, wobbling back and forth around their true skill level. In practice, as you might imagine, that sort of precision is seldom the case.

NO SKIPPING AROUND

On a paper test you're free to flip back and forth from page to page, doing whichever questions strike you as easiest and quickest, leaving yourself more than an average question's allotted time to tackle the hardest ones. On the *adaptive* portions of the GMAT (Quantitative and Verbal), you have to answer all the questions in front of you before you are given the next.

EVERYONE GETS A HARD TEST

No matter what your skill level, eventually the test will throw you questions that make you work a bit more, ones that take more time or employ more difficult or complicated concepts. Once you start struggling, the questions' difficulty might dip a bit, but a question or two later you'll be right back doing the questions that give you a hard time.

Thus, if your true skill in math is in the 600 range, most of the questions you'll face will be drawn from the very top end of that range, where the questions you find most difficult live. You'll see very few "gimme" questions, and those will only appear early in the test.

YOU HAVE TO FINISH THE TEST

Because of the way GMAT's special proprietary score-calculation algorithm works, failing to complete a question counts against your score more than missing it does. Suppose two students missed exactly the same questions in the Math section and in their Verbal section up until question 39. If one student never answers question 40 and never sees question 41 whereas the other tries both but gets them both wrong, the second will get the higher score on the test. But wait, you might protest, maybe the first student was just being careful, and the second one rushing, shouldn't the careful student get more points? Not according to the GMAT's algorithm, and the algorithm's is the only opinion that counts.

THE EARLY QUESTIONS ARE THE LEAST PREDICTABLE . . . BUT THAT'S ABOUT IT

There are many superstitions about the adaptive test, and many of these superstitions have been attached to the early questions. You've probably heard that the first five questions are the most important or that they "count the most"—or maybe it was the first seven or the first ten. Consequently, you've probably also heard that you should spend an extra 30 seconds on those questions—or an extra minute, or even twice as long! The important thing, these superstitions hold, is that you make sure you get the early questions right. If you're going to miss a question, miss one of the last few.

In truth, such advice is based on a misunderstanding of how the difficulty jumps between questions work. It is true that the difficulty jumps are bigger earlier in the test, so that missing an early question will have more of an immediate effect on the tier from which your next few questions are drawn, but this does not mean that they have a larger overall effect on your score. But no matter how high you climb in the difficulty tiers by giving special attention to these early questions, you would still fall right out of that tier if you were unable to continue answering questions in that tier consistently. Your fall might be slower, but it will still happen, and the remaining 32 (or 30 or 28) questions are more than sufficient for you to bottom out in the tier you're least comfortable doing.

Such advice is also based on the idea that more time is the secret to getting a question correct and that with the proper amount of time allocated to those early questions you'll be able to "make sure" that you don't miss them. But, as we all know, you might get a question wrong for any number of reasons. Maybe you misread and thought that they wanted you to calculate the final percent instead of the percent change. Maybe you thought that verbs that end in -ing are always wrong on the test (another superstition) and eliminated the right answer out of hand. Heck, maybe you just never studied the particular concept being tested in the question. If you encounter one of these sorts of questions in the first five, no amount of extra time would "make sure" that you got it right.

Indeed, in trying to make sure that they do those first five to ten questions correctly, many students end up without enough time to keep doing well on the later questions and find themselves rushing through the last ten, missing most of them and risking not finishing at all.

NEVERTHELESS, YOU MUST START STRONG AND BE CAREFUL

All that said, we must admit that people are absolutely correct when they say that the early questions are often the key to your performance on the GMAT. It just has little to do with the amount by which the difficulty changes from question to question. Rather, it's mostly about making sure your stress level remains low and that, consequently, you are able to shake off mistakes or confusing questions and thereby maintain momentum.

Suppose you were worried about time and rushed through the first question. Likely you wouldn't feel the best about your answer; you'd know you were cutting corners, pushing through, and that maybe you missed something—even if it was a question that you knew how to do and could do well under less stressful circumstances. When the second question pops up on the screen, you have a new challenge to attack, but you'll have to attack it burdened by the doubts and anxiety your rushing through the first question left you with. If that stress makes the second question harder than it should be, when you roll into the third, you're now doubly weighted down by the anxiety generated from the first question compounded by the uneasiness from the second. Lather, rinse, and repeat. By the middle of the test you're so out of sorts that you're missing easy questions that you know how to do, and that ever-ticking clock just keeps counting lower and lower. It's the anxiety snowball effect.

This series of little mistakes that compound each other could happen at any point in a test, of course, but if those first questions go well you have a much greater chance of being able to halt the anxiety snowball before it rolls out of control. Being careful early gives you something to fall back on. Just don't spend time on early questions merely for the sake of spending extra time. If you're certain you isolated the right variable, double and triple checking your work isn't going to make that question count for any more than it already does, but it might steal away time you're going to need to get a harder question later on.

YOU MUST MAINTAIN AN EVEN, CONSISTENT PACE

Because the test soon learns the level of difficulty liable to give you the most trouble, the temptation to slow down and give more time to each subsequent question grows as the test goes on. Beware of the "just *one* more minute" trap because one minute can easily become two or three. You have to be willing to give the occasional question more than the one and a half or two minutes you have, on average, for each question, but put emphasis on the word *occasional*. The GMAT isn't a test suited to either tortoises or hares: slow and steady fails just as surely as quick and careless. Aim instead for brisk but careful. As St. Augustine famously wrote, "Hurry, but hurry slowly."

YOU CAN'T AFFORD TO LOOK OVER YOUR OWN SHOULDER

Because test takers know that the test is adapting to their performance, many end up trying to gauge their performance on the test with each question. If a new question feels difficult, they silently fist-pump, but if it feels easier, they start to sweat, worried that means that they missed the question they just hit "confirm answer" on. The first problem with this approach is that the more time you spend assessing your performance, the less time you're spending on the question that's actually in front of you, the one that, because there's no going back or skipping ahead, is the only question that can actually improve your performance.

The other problem is that it's actually tricky determining the difficulty of a question because there's actually no such thing as an objectively easy question or an objectively hard one. When we speak about a question's difficulty, we have to use the only ranking tool that test makers have available to them: the percentage of students who, when given the question as an experimental question on a past GMAT, answered it correctly. We say a question is "hard" when a sizable number of those past GMAT students got the question wrong; when most of them got it right, it's an "easy" question. But the reason we put scare quotes in that last sentence is that no one, not even the master test makers employed by the GMAC, has any way of knowing why any particular student got a given question right or wrong.

So what if 88% of beta-testing students got a question wrong. If you were in the 12% of students who got it right, it probably felt pretty easy to you. The same goes for easy questions. Even if 94% of people knew how to solve an equation, the 6% who didn't would probably rank the question it appeared in as hard.

Nobody aligns perfectly with the statistical average, so the reason the question in front of you feels easier than the last may have absolutely nothing to do with your performance so far.

TO DO WELL, YOU MUST KNOW YOUR COMFORT ZONE (AND WHEN YOU'VE LEFT IT)

Even though an individual question may feel easy or hard for esoteric or personal reasons, after taking a few practice exams and studying for a while, you actually should be able to get a pretty good feel for whether you're headed toward the score you've gotten in the past over a stretch of about six or seven questions (instead of from question-to-question).

As we said before, the test is designed to feel hard for everyone, regardless of their ability level. With a little reflection, you should be able to recognize how it feels to do a stretch of hard questions and how that feeling differs from doing several easy ones in a row. Thus, when the test starts to consistently "feel hard," when you've left your comfort zone—that is, once you're in the difficulty tier that is just at the edge of your ability—you know you're on track. The better you get at the test, the later this feeling will kick in, the later you'll enter what we might call your "discomfort zone."

Moreover, how well you can recognize and manage your discomfort zone will determine how high your score can go. If you consistently "freak the heck out" (to use the clinical phrase) when the test gets to an uncomfortable level of difficulty, you'll fall back into your comfort zone, just as you would if you calmly executed a triage strategy to deal with a question you didn't understand, but after a freak out you'll probably also fall further, missing a couple of hard but still manageable questions that are on the high end of your comfort zone. That means you'll have to spend a few more questions climbing back to the edge of the zone, and you won't be able to climb as high in the end, leaving you 20 points shy of your peak performance.

 TIP

If 20 points doesn't seem like that big a deal, ask yourself, would you be satisfied with an Official Score of 680 when you'd gotten 700s and 720s on practice exams?

WHAT THE GMAT *REALLY* TESTS . . . AND WHAT IT DOESN'T

Hopefully, it's becoming clear that the GMAT isn't like most of the tests you've taken before, and consequently the study habits and test-taking strategies you've used on other tests might not be as useful to you here. That's where the book in your hands comes in. Before we go any further, let's clear up one final misconception about the test. The GMAT tests your ability to take the GMAT. It's that simple.

The GMAT is not a test of your business knowledge. There are many successful executives and managers who would absolutely fail the test, and many has-beens and never-beens who could post near perfect scores.

The GMAT is also not an intelligence test. MENSA won't let you use it to prove your IQ, and securing a 740 doesn't mean you're smarter than your friend with the 700.

The GMAT isn't a very good predictor of your ultimate success in business school, either. Even though there is some positive correlation between a high GMAT score and good grades in the first year of business school, the correlation falls away after that.

The GMAT isn't even much of a math or English test. Certain mathematical concepts appear on the test, as do certain grammatical rules and basic principles of formal logic. Ultimately, however, neither your math skills nor your deftness with the subjunctive mood will translate directly to an impressive GMAT score. So what will affect your score?

Patterns and Predictability: The Keys to GMAT Success

It's often said that the key to sales is telling the buyers what they want to hear. That jaded platitude works for the GMAT, too, when you get right down to it. The key to a higher score is learning what it is that the test makers want to hear. Test makers have certain ways of thinking that are thoroughly predictable because they've employed them time and time again on previously administered tests. Beneath every question lies a handful of patterns that have appeared in different combinations in other questions.

GMAT test takers just beginning their studies often feel as though the testmakers always have another trick up their sleeve, that there's always an exception or an additional rule that they can whip out to make a weird looking statement in a Data Sufficiency question turn out to be sufficient or an answer choice in a Critical Reasoning passage look wrong when it's actually right.

The good news is that there actually is a limit to the things the test makers can spring on you. The GMAT is a small world. Indeed, odds are that any trick you fall for probably has popped up in a dozen different questions over the past year. Once you learn to spot their tricks, the little tells that are peppered throughout the GMAT, the test makers may even start to seem a little bit pathetic. "Oh, silly test makers," you'll find yourself saying instead, "the only reason to put absolute value in an equation in a Data Sufficiency question like this one is so one statement can be sufficient on its own once I plug the answers back in."

How Can We Be So Sure the Test Hasn't Changed Recently?

That's easy. Both of the authors of this book (who tend to write in the royal "we") make their living as professional GMAT tutors, drawing clients from many different backgrounds and with score goals that run the gamut from 500 all the way to the top. The book you hold in your hands represents nearly 25 combined years of experience with the test in all its subtle nuances. What's more, with this brand new edition of the *Barron's GMAT,* the book has been completely revamped and written from the ground floor up, unlike some of those other books in your stack, which just change the number on the cover every year and call it a day. And it's loaded with helpful strategies for answering the various question types.

Let's face it: no book could cover every single facet of the test or provide the instruction to overcome every student's particular challenges—not if you want it to fit in a backpack, at least. So, think of this book as your comprehensive guide to GMAT preparation. While preparing, you'll still probably need to consult other sources for help on particular topics.

> We know people tend to buy half-a-dozen prep guides and get hand-me-downs from all their friends, too. That's OK. This book will help you understand how to use whatever resources you have access to by explaining the fundamental patterns and principles found on the GMAT.

GATHER YOUR MATERIALS

As we all know, sometimes the difference between success and failure boils down to having the right tools for the job. In this, the GMAT is no different. You'll want to lay your hands on the following as soon as you can:

A Legal-sized Wet Erase Pad

For security reasons, the test center won't let you use paper for your scratch work. Instead, you get a noteboard, a spiral-bound booklet of six double-sided yellow legal-sized laminated sheets of graph paper. As much of a pain as it might be, you need to get used to working problems and taking notes on boards like these. Mock-ups are available from various online retailers (Amazon and the like); however, you can always have a print shop photocopy some graph paper lines onto appropriately sized pages, then laminate and spiral bind them. Either option will set you back less than $10.

A Stockpile of Wet Erase Pens

You also need the pens to go with your board, naturally. If you want to make your practice work as close to the test day experience as possible, you can even purchase the exact model that the testing centers all stock: the Staedtler Lumocolor Non-permanent #3119 Superfine black pen.

A Reliable Digital Timer

While there is great value to be had in working practice questions in untimed conditions, eventually you have to bite the bullet and add the pressure of the ticking clock to your efforts. Digital is preferable to analog, as the timer on the day of the test (found in the upper left corner of the GMAT's computer interface) will be digital.

Some Real Live People to Study With

Forget those dubious groupwork assignments from your undergrad days. Finding a study group of similarly dedicated future business school students can do wonders for your preparation. Even if you end up as the person in the group with the most advanced math knowledge, the one everyone's always asking to explain why it's important that pies aren't square, you'll still find that the very process of explaining it to someone else will further cement and deepen your own understanding of the material.

Simulate Test Day as Often as Possible

There's a reason we asked you to get a practice noteboard. On the day of the test, it's all you'll have to write on. Remember, too, that you should use it as you answer the questions in this book. Although it's perfectly acceptable for you to take notes as you study, the first time you work a question, resist the temptation to write on the page. You won't be able to underline a telling phrase in a Reading Comprehension passage on the day of the test, so don't give yourself that luxury in practice.

Likewise, it's very easy to inadvertently provide yourself with convenient excuses for why you're having trouble with the test. Chief among these is taking practice exams and doing practice problems in loud public places or in front of the TV. You might not realize you're doing it, but by putting distractions in your environment, you're tacitly providing yourself with a fallback: you can always say, "Yeah, I was kind of distracted, that's why I missed this question." (This might be an accurate explanation, but it might also be true that you would still have missed the clue in the question stem, and you won't figure that out if you stop at distraction.) The same can be said of doing questions too late at night or when you haven't eaten.

REGISTER FOR THE TEST, ALREADY!

It's all too easy to delay taking the GMAT, to give yourself "just a few more weeks" of study, to wait until after a looming deadline, an upcoming vacation, the end of the semester exam week, Christmas break, and the list can go on forever to "really get serious about the test." There's always a theoretical better time to study that's just a few weeks away. I'll study tomorrow, next week, some day. The problem is, to quote John Fogerty, "Someday never comes." When one someday rolls around, there's always another one, just a few weeks away.

The best way to forestall this stalling is to give yourself a deadline and put some money on the line. At $250, the GMAT isn't cheap. Schedule your GMAT for an appropriate time in the future; for most students, that's two or three months from now. Go ahead, you can sign up for the test right now. We'll wait here while you do.

Back? Good. Now you have a deadline and a $250 bet with yourself, a good reason to turn to the next chapter, where you'll begin learning about those predictable GMAT patterns and how best to turn them to your advantage. Sure, you could wait until later, but there's no time like the present . . .

PART 1

Analytical Writing Assignment

The Analytical
Writing Assignment

1

→ **INTRODUCTION**
→ **ANATOMY OF AN AWA PROMPT**
→ **OVERALL STRATEGY FOR THE AWA**
→ **THE FOUR(ISH)-STEP METHOD FOR ANALYTICAL WRITING**
→ **THE PLAN IN ACTION**
→ **STRATEGY TIPS, TWEAKS, AND OTHER CONSIDERATIONS**

INTRODUCTION

After you've navigated the testing center's security protocols and been ushered to a seat, the first test content you'll see will be the 30-minute Analytical Writing Analysis, also known as the GMAT's essay section.

The main reason that business schools had been demanding a writing section actually had little to do with writing directly. The late 1980s and early 1990s saw a huge boom in the number of applications to business schools, particularly applications from abroad, places where English was not the primary spoken or written language. Those years also saw a not-so-coincidental rise in the number of applications in which the admissions essays, writing samples, and personal statements had clearly been written by a hired gun and not the applicant in question. The best way to sort out the cheaters from the honest-to-goodness writers in the applying crowd was to get another sample of their writing on file, one produced in a controlled, secure setting, and thus the AWA was born.

Of course, it should be admitted, a good many business schools also desired a clearer picture of their applicants' writing ability. The AWA also fills this role. Admissions professionals are quite interested in your ability to write, it's just that they have many other excellent ways to gauge that: your cover letter, your TOEFL scores, the number of writing courses on your transcript and the accompanying grades in them, whether the job descriptions on your CV seem to indicate much experience writing outside of academia, samples of your previous written work, essays specific to their institution, etc.

How Schools *Actually* Use the AWA

If you're an applicant from a country where English isn't the native tongue, there's some bad news. Your AWA essay will be scrutinized a bit more heavily than an applicant hailing from the United States or the United Kingdom because business schools want to make sure you're up to the challenge presented by courses conducted entirely in English. The AWA still won't overrule more important indicators—your TOEFL score chief among them—but it will be considered.

If, on the other hand, you're a native English speaker, your AWA score is likely to get the most cursory of glances, unless your academic career or your career experience suggests some sort of deficiency in your writing skills. In that case, the AWA does allow you the opportunity to answer some of those lingering questions.

What Does an AWA Score Look Like?

As discussed in the first chapter of this book, you'll receive two scores for the AWA, and you'll have to wait about three weeks to find out what they are. Your AWA Score and its accompanying percentile score will arrive only with your Official Score Report. Your primary AWA Score will be a number from 0 to 6, either a whole number or something point five—that is, in half-point increments. The test maker almost never awards a score of .5 to 1.5, and 0 is reserved for students who simply do not write anything. Most business school applicants' scores fall between 4 and 5.5, or across only 4 different possible scores—not a lot of room to distinguish one candidate from the next.

This score, as well as the actual essay you type on the day of the test, is made available to every business school that receives your overall score.

How High an AWA Score Do I Need?

As a rule of thumb, once your AWA score is above 4, you're in the clear. If it's 4 or below, the schools will probably look more closely at your application and possibly even at the essay you wrote itself.

How Is the AWA Score Generated?

The best indication of how much schools should value your AWA score is how the score is generated. If you have images of panels of old professorial types in tweed jackets with leather elbow patches all sitting around a table in a well-appointed study discussing the relative merits of your essay, which they all have annotated heavily with red pen, congratulations, you have an excellent imagination. Alas, the truth is, unless there's some sort of problem, your essay will be read by two graders only. One of them will be a part-time employee of ACT working in a massive cubicle farm. Your essay will pop up on their computer screen for 2 minutes total. At the end of that 2 minutes, the reader—usually a current or former humanities graduate student—will enter a score for the essay, from 0 to 6 in half-point increments.

During the typical work day, these human essay graders will see about 30 essays every hour over an 8-hour shift. You don't have to have a perfect Verbal Subscore to know that means about 240 essays each day and 1200 a week.

The E-Rater (or "I, for One, Welcome Our New Robot Overlords")

If you find it weird that that last paragraph used the phrase "human essay graders," you're in for another shock, for the other grader is one who reads your essay and assigns it a score from 0 to 6 without remorse and without reading it for anything like 2 minutes. Indeed, this grader will spit out your score before a human essay grader could get through the first sentence. This grader never takes coffee breaks because this reader is . . . a robot! And the robot grader has been on the job since 1999, when it stole the job away from the less-efficient second human grader that used to read GMAT essays.

Or, to put it more accurately, this reader is a computer algorithm, much like the one that governs the grammar check on your word processing program of choice. This algorithm is called the E-Rater. If the E-Rater and the human grader's assessment differ by more than a point, then the essay is sent to a third grader, another human, to make the final call.

What the GMAT AWA Really Doesn't Test . . .

According to the GMAC's *Official Guide*, the best essays are those that exhibit:

- Exemplary critical thinking skills
- An organized argument with well-developed support
- Mastery of the language and diction of the professional English vernacular

But are those really things that you can tell about an essay that (1) is read for no more than 2 minutes and (2) is graded partially by a computer program nowhere near as sophisticated as the one that beat Kasparov? We don't think so, either.

There is, however, a silver lining underneath this cloud. All you need to do is learn the formula, and you will be the proud owner of a robot-approved AWA score between 4.5 and 6.

The vaunted E-Rater is only going to scan your essay looking at the following:

- Structural keywords and phrases that indicate organization
- Spelling and grammar mistakes
- The general difficulty of vocabulary used
- The number and average length of phrases, sentences, and paragraphs

Attempting to match the E-Rater's assessment, the human graders will be looking for mostly the same things. So, instead of the GMAC's impressive-looking list of requirements, your essay will instead be aiming for two main things:

> **Length:** The essay has to be long enough to give the impression that it covers the topic thoroughly and in detail.
>
> **Appropriate Vocabulary:** Words that might strike your college English teacher as superfluous are absolutely essential, so you're going to need lots of transition words like *first*, *next*, *consequently*, *on the other hand*, *moreover*, and *in conclusion*.

Also, a liberal (but not excessive) dusting of "five-dollar words" can make your fluency with English rate higher with both man and machine. There is one grain of salt this advice does need to be taken with. Since one-half of the grading team actually is a person, you can bolster your chances for a score over 4 by making sure that the essay is also:

> **Easy to Read:** Their job is not an easy or glamorous one; do the readers a favor and make sure your essay, particularly the first paragraph, glides easily from point to point.
>
> **On Topic:** Though the computer algorithm can't tell lightning from a lightning bug, human readers can, and so make sure the essay actually is on the topic indicated at the top of the computer screen.
>
> **Palatable:** If you think something might be offensive or alienating, then err on the side of caution. You want your essay to be easy, breezy, and comfortable for the grader.

TIP

Famously, an analysis of high-scoring essays performed by the large test prep companies found that the main commonality shared was simply length: the number of words on the screen.

Note the one big thing left out through all of this: content. As long as you don't write an essay about how much you love your dog when the prompt calls for an analysis of whether a particular code of ethics is likely to bring about a change in the corporate culture at Company X, *what* you say is almost insignificant compared to *how* you say it.

Indeed, it's an open secret in the test prep industry that graders of GMAT essays like to talk about essays in terms of what they call "fourness." As long as an essay *looks* like one that answers the question without having anything else to say for it—a mediocre but acceptable by-the-numbers essay—then it gets a 4. If it has any easily spotted plus, that bumps it up to a 4.5 or 5. Sixes get reserved for essays that make a great first impression and don't look at a further glance like they've committed any big errors of style or diction.

On the other hand, if there's something weird or hard to follow in the first few lines, only then do the 2's and 2.5's come out.

Take It Seriously

Here is one final word of warning before we delve deeper into an actual AWA question. Don't get clever. We don't mean that you should try to write a boring essay or one that lacks thought. Rather, we know that there are all sorts of urban legends floating around about essay questions, and some of them have attached themselves to the GMAT AWA. You've perhaps heard of the philosophy professor who asked his students, "Why?" and gave an A+ to the only student brave enough to write, "Why not?" and turn his paper in. Those are the sorts of urban legends we mean. Believe us when we say that this is not the place to get clever, if for no other reason than to prevent yourself from wondering, "Did I go too far this time?"

ANATOMY OF AN AWA PROMPT

When you finally hit that Begin Test button on test day, you'll be greeted with something that looks like this on your computer screen:

> The following appeared as part of a newspaper editorial:
>
> > "Five years ago the teachers at Bellville Heights Technical School introduced interactive computer displays to their refrigeration and air conditioning classes. The proportion of students enrolled at the school who later failed their licensing exams dropped substantially. What's more, the decline followed almost immediately upon the program's introduction. Clearly, if we wish to improve education throughout our post-secondary educational system, we must allocate a greater portion of our education budget to bringing innovative technological approaches to learning into all of our classrooms."
>
> Discuss how well reasoned you find this argument. In your discussion be sure to analyze the line of reasoning and the use of evidence in the argument. For example, you may need to consider what questionable assumptions underlie the thinking and what alternative explanations or counterexamples might weaken the conclusion. You can also discuss what sort of evidence would strengthen or refute the argument, what changes in the argument would make it more logically sound, and what, if anything, would help you better evaluate its conclusion.

Notice that, much like Critical Reasoning questions, there are essentially three parts to an AWA question:

The Three Parts of an AWA Prompt

1. **THE SOURCE.** Every AWA question includes a single short line ending in a colon that gives a purported source for the argument that follows. This isn't filler, exactly, though you don't have to consider the source in making your essay if you prefer. The source does give you a handy way to reference the argument, however. "As the editorial states," "the editorialist's position," or "the argument in the editorial" would all be handy to have.

2. **THE ARGUMENT.** Usually the argument is fewer than 100 words long and generally presents either a plan to accomplish something, a recommendation of a course of action, or an abstract evaluation of whether one thing is more important than another (both in a general way that extends to many different circumstances or in a specific, given circumstance).

3. **THE INSTRUCTIONS.** Read them now, commit them to memory soon, and once you have, never look at them again. They're not going to change, and it'll save you precious seconds on test day.

Writing to the Instructions

By far, the most important part of the AWA prompt is the instructions. It's your job to make sense of the argument, and in that quest, the instructions are your best tool.

Keep in mind that the arguments in the AWA are never well reasoned. If one seems like it might be, you need to look away from the screen, take a couple of deep breaths, and look again. Why? Because if the argument in the question were well reasoned, there wouldn't be much for you to write. There are only so many ways you could write that you think the argument is perfectly reasonable.

In fact, the arguments found in AWA questions are usually much worse than the ones you'll see in the Critical Reasoning prompts. And it's a good thing that they are! The test maker very thoughtfully provides you with all kinds of juicy unwarranted assumptions, logical flaws, and vaguely used terms with which to fill out your essay. It's a target-rich environment.

In your discussion be sure to analyze the **line of reasoning** and the **use of evidence** in the argument. By "line of reasoning," the GMAT means "terms used in the chain of evidence and the conclusion." And, inevitably, there will be big gaps between the terms. These gaps will usually form the core of your essay. The usual flaws from Critical Reasoning are well represented in these prompts. You'll see a lot of broad conclusions drawn from too narrow a survey or test case (**representativeness**), speakers acting like the only two possibilities to explain or consider are the two mentioned in the prompt (**false dichotomies**), and clear counterevidence dismissed out of hand (**unexamined alternatives**).

The "use of evidence" will be a boon to your test day essay. Unlike in Critical Reasoning questions, you can feel free to question the motives of those who provide the evidence or discuss the limitations of a certain type of data. Even though the evidence still has to be taken as true, you have more leeway to examine it here.

For example, you may need to consider

1. **WHAT QUESTIONABLE ASSUMPTIONS UNDERLIE THE THINKING . . .** All that time spent learning how to spot assumptions in Critical Reasoning really pays off here in the AWA. These AWA speakers' arguments are full of slipshod assumptions, uncovered bases, and clear, glaring misuses of critical terms. The only thing wrong with the test maker's advice here is that *may*. There's no *may* about it. If your essay is to work well, it will definitely need to consider the arguments' assumptions.

2. **WHAT ALTERNATIVE EXPLANATIONS OR COUNTEREXAMPLES MIGHT WEAKEN THE CONCLUSION . . .** This half-sentence tips us off to the major difference between Critical Reasoning and the AWA. In the Critical Reasoning section, your main job was to analyze whether a given answer choice did or did not provide an alternative explanation or weaken the conclusion. In the AWA, you'll need to come up with these possible weakeners or possible counterexamples yourself.

It is important that these weakeners and counterexamples be *possible* and not definitive, however. The task the test maker sets before you is to analyze the argument, not to disprove it. The speaker isn't generally displaying bad faith, trying to pull the wool over someone's eyes, being evasive, or purposely misleading anybody in the assumed audience. Thus, you'll be writing in the subjunctive a fair amount. There will be more "*if it were the case that*" rather than "*because this is the case*" in an effective AWA essay.

3. **WHAT SORT OF EVIDENCE WOULD STRENGTHEN OR REFUTE THE ARGUMENT . . .** Consider "can" or "should" in your quest for an effective essay. This is also how you'll manage to meet your goal of making sure your essay is long enough to seem like a comprehensive, well-thought-out response. Take the case of a prompt in which the speaker assumes that remedial training being proposed for teachers is actually effective. You'd want to demonstrate how that assumption leaves the situation up for grabs in a way that the speaker doesn't clear up. For example:

> While it's certainly possible that the proposed remedial training will prove effective, few details of the nature of this training are presented and thus left for the speaker's audience to speculate about. Were it to turn out that the remedial instructors are competent and well-qualified and that the material presented in their classes is well designed and thorough, then clearly there would be no problem accepting the author's overall claim that the problem of teachers in the ABC-ville schools who do not know their subject area would be reversed by implementing the new requirements. It would be inadvisable to simply assume that the programs are effective. Many college courses fail to convey the information its title promises. Indeed, these teachers presumably were already trained in their respective areas of concentration. If these remedial courses are no more effective than those, then it is unlikely that the problem will be ameliorated simply through additional course requirements.

All that text came simply from taking one assumption—that the proposed courses will work as advertised—and exploring the possibilities, both weakening and strengthening, and how they might affect our ability to accept the assumption.

4. **WHAT CHANGES IN THE ARGUMENT WOULD MAKE IT MORE LOGICALLY SOUND ...** Now the test makers are just repeating themselves. What changes would make an argument more logically sound? Why, such changes could only be ones that took questionable, unwarranted assumptions and made them less questionable and more warranted. It's rare to find an argument that's truly 100 percent logically off its rocker. (Because bees give us honey, we should use them to power our rockets that explode when they come into contact with honey.) The soundness lies in the problematic assumptions.

5. **WHAT, IF ANYTHING, WOULD HELP YOU BETTER EVALUATE ITS CONCLUSION ...** Funny, there must be an echo at GMAT HQ, as they have now said the same thing three different ways. What would help you better evaluate a conclusion? If you said, "evidence that shores up questionable or unwarranted assumptions," give yourself a gold star!

If they say it three times, the test makers must clearly mean it. They are going to provide you with an argument replete with holes. Your job is to point out said holes and explain that they could be filled if certain evidence were true and that certain other evidence would confirm that the speaker is wrong and that we're certain to fall into that metaphorical hole the speaker doesn't see.

OVERALL STRATEGY FOR THE AWA

The Speaker and You

The voice of the fictitious speaker who gives the argument in the AWA question is precisely the opposite of how you want to appear to your readers, human and robot alike. These AWA speakers aren't merely confident about their conclusions, they're overconfident, almost absurdly so. Is there a problem? The speaker has the answer! Will it work? By Jiminy, of course it will work! Is there a choice between two options? It's hardly a choice at all, and the speaker is willing, wanting, and waiting to tell you why!

In your evaluation of the speaker's argument, you—while still confident—are measured, fair, generous, and even-handed. You don't know all the facts that are pertinent to the situation. If only you did, you'd be able to say, but the speaker didn't give you what you needed. You don't know if the plan will work because there are key components the speaker left unaddressed.

In your essay, don't confuse an evaluation with a response. It's not your job to prove that the speaker is wrong or to prove that the argument's conclusion is incorrect, only to point out that the speaker failed to sufficiently establish the conclusion with the appropriate evidence. It's completely possible that the speaker will turn out to be correct about the conclusion in the long run, if the necessary evidence is provided and the open questions are decided the way they need to be for the speaker to be correct. Think loose ends, not damning omissions.

At the same time, the speaker is a useful character to have in your essay, a foil for your points. You can avoid overly complex ways of referencing the argument like "the proposal to eliminate school lunchroom waste by recycling food into casseroles" with a simple "the speaker's proposal" or "as the speaker indicates."

Slow Down. 30 Minutes Is Longer Than You Think

When most students hear that the test's graders value length, they often worry that they'll not have enough time to write the entire essay. "So much typing!" they complain, thinking of the test like an all-night essay writing session that ends the morning the paper is due from their undergrad days.

TIP

The source tag will tell you how to refer to the speaker. They are editorial writers, city councilpersons, scientists, and business leaders. "Speaker" is just the generic we use for convenience here.

Relax. Length does not mean you'll be producing *War and Peace*—not even a book report on *War and Peace*. This essay should be closer in length to the good old five-paragraph essays from high school.

In fact, it's critical that you allow yourself time up front and at the end so that you can follow our next bit of advice.

Plan Ahead and Proofread After

Again, because you're so conscious of the time limit, you may feel the temptation to start typing the moment you've finished reading the question. Don't let yourself! You need to budget at least 5 minutes before you start writing for the single most important part of your AWA success: planning. Depending on where your high school English teacher studied, you may be used to calling this "preplanning," "outlining," or "brainstorming." Whatever the handle, you need to make sure you know what you're planning to type before you set your fingers to flying across the keyboard. Some students stretch this time to 7 and even 10 minutes, and there's absolutely no problem doing so.

The reason that long essays tend to correlate well with high scores isn't simply because more is always better. A long, rambling, aimless discussion of a topic that's 1000 words long will generally receive a lower score than a shorter piece that is well-organized and sticks to the subject at hand. Rather, the reason that long essays tend to produce higher scores is that test takers who produce long essays have generally thought through the topic and consequently have more to say about it. It's much harder to think up supporting examples on the fly than it is to come up with a quick jot list beforehand.

On the same note, you need to leave yourself time at the end of the essay to do some quick, light proofreading. It's all too easy to start a sentence thinking you're going one way only to change your mind midway and take the sentence in a different direction. If you don't look back and fix the sentence's first half, you're left with gibberish. And don't forget that the lack of an autocorrect or a spell check does tend to lead to more little slips of the finger. You can catch them if you give yourself the time to catch them.

THE FOUR(ISH)-STEP METHOD FOR ANALYTICAL WRITING

Prepare to have your earth shattered and your world rocked by our fundamentally revolutionary and entirely unprecedented method for writing—

Wait, hold that thought. We've been informed that our method for approaching AWA essays isn't much different from what you probably have already learned to do in the writing courses you have under your belt. Indeed, it's probably a bit of a simplification of your existing method.

It may even feel like a return to your high school days and the old five-paragraph essay that your college instructors spent two or three semesters teaching you not to write.

Identify	Step 1: Assess the Argument
Process	Step 2: Brainstorm
Plan	Step 3: Outline Your Main Points
Attack	Step 4: Write the Essay
	Proofread and Tidy Up

Step 1: Assess the Argument

As we will soon see, a thorough assessment of an AWA argument is a lot like untangling a Critical Reasoning question. Identify the speaker's conclusion and make a jot list of all the points of evidence the speaker employs. Unlike in the Critical Reasoning section, you're almost certainly going to want to jot this information down. You can use the note board or the question's response box.

While assessing the argument, take note of the usual suspects, particularly differences in the words used in the evidence and the conclusion. If a survey, study, or sample group appears (and they often do), make sure to compare every piece of information given about them and line those pieces up with the group the conclusion concerns.

Finally, don't forget that source note that comes at the top of the page. Context is always useful.

TIP

Just be sure to delete all your notes if you use the actual interface!

Step 2: Brainstorm

Now that you have the moving parts of the argument arrayed before you and understand the gaps in the author's reasoning, it's time to come up with all the points you think you might want to make. Though the general direction of the AWA essay is almost always the same (the speaker's argument is not convincing), be careful not to prejudge which bits of the argument will make the best hay for your essay. Very often, you'll find that something that initially seems like it might anchor one of your body paragraphs turns out to be a dud, and the point you only wrote down for completion's sake turns out to barely fit in a single paragraph once you've thought it over.

Nothing is off limits during your brainstorm. Let your mind wander free. Your essay will be the better for it.

Step 3: Outline Your Main Points

Here's a spot of good news: the outline you write for a GMAT AWA essay response will likely be shorter than one that you'd write for a paper for college credit. Forget all that old business about Roman numerals, capital letters, and so on. This can be as detailed or as scanty as you need. Keep your eyes on the prize. No one but you will ever see the outline. The essay's the only thing that can influence your score.

There is one part of the GMAT AWA outline that will differ from other essays you've written, the prewriting. Since the readers are unlikely to give careful or prolonged attention to your prose, you want to make sure that the places they will actually look are as polished and powerful as you can make them. As you finish up your outlining, you will want to convert your notes into fully completed first sentences for each of your main paragraphs. If you reach for clever turns of phrase or powerful hooks, they'll be wasted buried any further in your work, so now's the time to work them out.

Step 4: Write the Essay

All told, you'll probably only spend about 15–20 of your 30 minutes typing out your essay, with the remainder devoted to the other steps, with the bulk of that time devoted to planning out the essay. Once you're all planned up, it's time to get those fingers dancing across the keys—just remember, there's no spellcheck and auto-correct, so perhaps finger-dance a slightly slower tempo than you would at home.

Proofread and Tidy Up

Always, always, always leave yourself time at the end of the essay to look back over what you've produced. Any number of tiny errors can creep into your essay. You can catch and correct a lot of them in only a minute or two of effort.

THE PLAN IN ACTION

Let's analyze the familiar prompt on page 18 step by step.

Step 1: Assess the Argument

Since AWA arguments follow the same rules as Critical Reasoning arguments in terms of structure, the first heavy lifting you'll have to do with an AWA prompt will be finding the argument's conclusion.

Here, the argument's conclusion is clearly flagged for us with the concluding keyword "clearly":

> "Five years ago the teachers at Bellville Heights Technical School introduced interactive computer displays to their refrigeration and air conditioning classes. The proportion of students enrolled at the school who later failed their licensing exams dropped substantially. What's more, the decline followed almost immediately upon the program's introduction. Clearly, if we wish to improve education throughout our post-secondary educational system, we must allocate a greater portion of our education budget to bringing innovative technological approaches to learning into all of our classrooms."

Whenever you're surveying the information in an argument, a good test of whether you've got it down is to reword the pieces in your own words. How would you rewrite this conclusion?

Write your rephrasing here:

_____

_____

One possible way you could have gone would be something like this:

> If you want to make all colleges/technical schools in the area better, spend higher % of $ in budget on classroom "technology"

Note a couple of key points:

The conclusion has a **qualification** attached; in other words, it's an **if/then** conclusion. We will need to be careful that we don't overstep the argument's conclusion in the essay and imply that our editorialist thinks that we have to follow this plan, period. It's only if we want to make the schools better that we need to spend this money. (Of course, it's not much of a qualification. Who doesn't want to make schools better?)

The scope of the argument is not just a greater **amount** of money, but a greater **percent** of the money in the budget. So, however big that budget becomes or however much it should shrink, the speaker is committed to the percentage increasing.

TIP

As always, rephrasings are personal and individual. The important question is not, "Do my words match the sample?" but "Did I capture all the points the sample captures?"

The reason we placed "technology" in scare quotes is that it's a relatively **vague term**. There's no way the author's evidence could possibly encompass all technological innovations, so this is an assumption waiting to happen.

Once you have the conclusion well in hand, it's time to characterize and track the evidence the author employs. With the argument less than 100 words, and so much of that taken up on that kind of lame qualification, there's not going to be much room to support the claim. That's intentional on the part of the test maker. If the argument were supported, what would you write?

Again, write your jot list of evidence points down. If you have your notes from when you took the diagnostic quiz, all the better:

_____

_____

A possible jot list might look something like this:

> Sample group: one school, type of class: AC/Refrig, 1 type of tech: interactive student displays, effect: lisc exams
> Effect is % of entire school; tech only in AC/Refrig. "substantial" decr
> Timeframe: Incr *immediately* after tech; 5 years of history

There's a lot going on here in the evidence; or, it might be more accurate to say that there are so many places where not enough is going on in the evidence.

The argument, like so many on the AWA, draws a conclusion from a **sample group**, raising the issue of **representativeness**.

There are numerous ways the sample group can be characterized (and none of them appear in the conclusion specifically). The test case is **one school** in the district and only **one type of class** offered at that school. Likewise, as we should have expected, only **one type of technology** was involved: "interactive student displays." The **timeframe of the survey** is also specified. We're only talking about 5 years of data here. Is that enough?

An even more interesting discrepancy crops up in the editorialist's description of the effect this tech had on the school. Only one type of improvement was tracked, naturally, but note that the effect is not calculated directly from the sample group. Instead of telling us that the qualifying exam scores improved for the AC and Refrigeration students—the ones in the class with the computer screens—the evidence concerns the school's students as a whole! Since we don't know how big a percent of the student body the AC students are, the possibility of both a **percent versus number** problem and an **alternate cause** emerges.

The extent of the effect is characterized as "substantial," a fairly **vague term**, all things considered. How much of an improvement will the school board or regents of this district be purchasing with their increased budget allocation?

And finally, the **timeframe** is a bit suspicious. Were the students in these classrooms that received the computers all on the verge of taking their licensing exam?

TIP
Whenever *representativeness* rears its head, be sure to check the sample group's correspondence with the conclusion group point by point.

As is always the case with GMAT arguments, once you have the evidence laid out (either in your head, as is usually the case in Critical Reasoning, or on paper, as here), the argument's assumptions become clear, and we have highlighted them by bolding the words above. In order for this argument to be true, we need to believe a lot that we're not told explicitly. Jot your thoughts down below and compare against the model:

_____

_____

_____

_____

The following is not meant to be an absolutely exhaustive list, but it covers the high points. For AWA prompts, our analysis of the assumptions need not be complete in any case, as we're only going to have room to write one or two as it is.

The assumptions in play:

- Bellville Heights Technical School must be similar enough to a substantial proportion of the schools in the district; otherwise, it's not going to be a good test case for making educational decisions in general.
- The students and classwork in the AC & Refrigeration courses also need to be typical, both of Bellville Heights' student body and of students in the district in general.
- These "interactive computer displays" must be sufficiently similar to the types of educational technology the editorialist believes will be purchased. And whatever their role in that AC & Refrigeration classroom, it has to be similar enough to how technology could be used in other courses throughout the district. In short, there's nothing special about these displays.
- The timeframe cited requires us to take an awful lot on faith. We must assume that the displays caused the increase in passing scores on the licensing exams and that there's nothing suspicious about how soon after their introduction the scores went up.
- We must also be content to accept that 5 years of evidence is good enough to make a recommendation as large as the editorialist makes.
- When the editorialist says "substantial" decreases in the licensing board failure rate is a big enough benefit to count as an improvement, particularly of the sort that would change the way classes should be conducted in however many schools there are in Belleville's area.
- Since the author never discusses the actual dollar amounts, we're left to assume that however much new technology costs, it's within the budget's ability to accommodate and that moving the money around won't cause some sort of indirect harm.

TIP

"Wow. Do I have to have written all of that?" Absolutely not! One or two of those assumptions would do for our purposes. Only write as much as you need to get the job done.

The speaker in this argument sure did leave a lot of bases uncovered. And that's excellent news for us, as there are so many ways we could go with this essay. Indeed, we'd best be careful not to try chasing down each and every one of them in the next step. Though 30 minutes is a good long while to write an essay in, it's still only 30 minutes.

On a scale of 1 to 10, rank how well you spotted the elements that appear in the diagnostic question discussed above.

_____ Finding argument conclusions in general

_____ Qualifications and if/then conclusions

_____ Amount versus percent distinction

_____ Vagueness of terms in the conclusion

_____ Representativeness as main issue in evidence

_____ Completeness of representativeness analysis (school, class, tech, effect, timeframe)

_____ Percent versus number in the evidence

_____ Alternate cause in the evidence

_____ Vague terms in evidence

_____ Timeframe for improvement/effect

_____ Keywords (clearly, what's more)

_____ Completeness of assumption analysis

Total: _____ / 120

Step 2: Brainstorm

We've done so much in Step 1, how much could there be for us to do now? That's kind of the point, actually. If we take enough time to understand the argument, we really won't have much difficulty with the points we're going to raise in the essay.

On your whiteboard or in the text field of the GMAT CAT interface, you'd pick some assumptions and consider how best to frame them for the purposes of writing a 15- to 20-minute 500–1000 word essay.

When you wrote the essay during the diagnostic quiz, you might have focused on any number of issues. Here, we'll just go through a quick sample of a few.

> Representativeness! How big is Bellville? The AC dept? The school system? What types of schools? Are the same sort of places, students disciplines, etc.?
> Too soon? How could computers turn AC around? How do we know it's relevant at all? Maybe just happy to have $ thrown at them, happy students.
> Representativeness #2 What do "displays" do for AC? How useful in lit, history, brain surgery, law, race car mechanics?
> Show me the $$$ — How much do they have? How big a % of budget? Room to spare? Throwing $ at problem . . .

When you brainstorm an essay for the AWA, you're now moving beyond the things the speaker brought up to consider the sorts of facts that might change your ability to accept or cause you to reject the assumptions you've identified. Reach for specifics! You're going to need them as we enter Step 3.

_____ Brainstorming: Enough to help you later?

_____ Notes in general easy to work with?

Total: _____ / 20

Step 3: Outline Your Main Points

If you wrote your notes on your dry erase board, it's now time to move them up to the text field of the CAT interface. If you wrote your notes there on the computer, now would be the time to start deleting the lines of thought that proved less promising and to polish up the ones that you're going to go with. Of course, before you do either, you'll also need to make some decisions. What are you going to structure your essay around? Look for related points, points that will be easy to explain, and points that will flow into one another easily as you move from body paragraph to body paragraph in Step 4.

If you'd produced something like the sample brainstorming notes from Step 2, the direction is clear. If you're aiming for three body paragraphs, then the line item labeled "Too Soon" might be the one to drop, as it's a bit complicated an explanation to make in limited space and time and doesn't necessarily mesh with the other points.

If you're shooting for two body paragraphs, or an essay structured around two major points, then representativeness is clearly the way to go. Let's say that's the direction we decided to head. Our essay will be primarily about how the sample group is in many and varied ways not necessarily the best group to use to make comprehensive educational reform decisions.

Remember also that this is the part of our essay where we'll be writing out the first sentence of each of the paragraphs we're going to have in our final essay. It may seem a little bit like a cheat, but let's face it, the readers aren't likely to read past that first line anyway, and they certainly won't want to if the first lines aren't compelling.

Before we produce a sample outline here, though, we need to discuss what sort of essay we're aiming to produce, not just here with the computers at Belleville but on any prompt we might encounter in the AWA.

A Sample Essay Template

Writing is, in general, a very personal thing. Your writing style is as unique as your thumbprint, so we could hardly tell you precisely what your essay would look like if you were to give the essay your best effort and if you had the time to fully draw upon your individual gifts.

But then again, you won't have the time or space on the AWA to craft a truly personalized essay. Then there's the matter of effort. The AWA comprises the first 30 minutes of your 3-hour GMAT ordeal. Unless writing GMAT essays is the sort of thing you could do in your sleep, you simply can't afford to expend the effort to create a unique essay.

Thankfully, uniqueness and perfection aren't necessary on the AWA. Serviceable and functional will do just fine. With that in mind, it's time to consider an essay format you probably abandoned long ago, the much maligned (but in our case highly useful) five-paragraph essay.

A famous Ivy League professor of writing once described the five-paragraph essay as follows:

> Paragraph 1: In this essay, I will demonstrate to you that the cat is on the mat.
>
> Paragraph 2: There is a cat.
>
> Paragraph 3: There is a mat.
>
> Paragraph 4: Guess where the cat is? Precisely! She's on the mat.
>
> Paragraph 5: See? I told you the cat was on the mat the whole time.

We can even condense this to just three parts.

> First Paragraph: Let me tell you the essay's **main idea**.
>
> Body Paragraphs: Here are some examples that **support** my idea.
>
> Final Paragraph: In **conclusion**, I think I've pretty much proven what I said I'd prove in my First Paragraph.

Or, to put it even more succinctly: (1) Main Idea, (2) Support, (3) Conclusion. We'll flesh this template out a bit as we proceed through Step 4, but this is the underlying base we'll be building upon.

Now, let's see how we would slot our brainstormed ideas into such a template. Paragraph 1 is where we will orient our reader to the question we're discussing and where we'll announce what we think of the argument in question. Each of the body paragraphs will discuss a different type of representativeness, and we will need to take special care that the points in each are different enough that they don't blend together into a disorganized mess. That would certainly turn our reader off. Our final paragraph will give the argument in précis and end with the suggestion of what could be done to make the argument stronger.

Drawing from our note pile, we'll likely create an outline along these lines:

> P1: Intro of argument: editorial recommending change in $ in budget to buy more tech.
> Evidence is drawn from 1 school's AC program that got some computer screens.
> Not convincing, because too much has to be taken on faith. Lots of possible differences btwn single school and district, use of single technology and tech in general.
> P2: Belleville's AC prog. Size not specified. How big is B'ville, even? Are there lots of tech colleges, or lots of lib arts, too? Students might vary school to school.
> P3: Tech. How does computer work in AC? For that matter, how does tech work in all classes? Same tech across board? Golf class and comp lit, anatomy? If not same tech, how decided? Where will money be taken from for tech?
> P4: Conclusion, holes in argument, hard to accept. Need extra info: details, prices, demographics.

Once the structure is there, it's time to write the first sentences of each paragraph. As we'll be giving three possible versions of the essay in the discussion of Step 4, the big reveal of what a hypothetical student might have written here will have to come below. Let's get writing!

Step 4: Write the Essay

To make sure that the reader understands the issue, the first paragraph should begin with a restatement of the argument and the situation it arises in—both should be given in your own words, though don't strain too hard to produce synonyms for every single word in the original question. There's bound to be some overlap in terminology, as there are some concepts that are hard to express any other way. After the issue has been clearly presented, it's time for the big reveal: you don't think the argument is a good one, and here's a quick sketch of why you don't.

Here are three sample first paragraphs we could write for this essay, arranged from "not quite good enough" (under 4) to "meh" (4–5), to "that'll do nicely" (6)—or, to put it in the test's argot: well under 4, 4–5, 6.

> This argument is not a good one. Its assumptions are weak and the evidence it gives is insufficient.

The good: OK, so there's not much good here. But this scant little two-sentence introductory paragraph does manage to accomplish one of our goals. It clearly lays out what the essay's main point will be: this isn't a good argument.

The bad: The biggest problem is there's no explanation of just what argument we're talking about. While there's no need for us to pretend that we're writing about school systems all through history or the higher truths of education itself, we should still take the effort to inform our reader of what we think the argument in the question says. At this rate, our hypothetical AWA writer is cruising for a 2 at best.

> This argument, an anonymous editorial's recommendations for educational policy, asks us to believe that the evidence drawn from a single school is enough to make big decisions about how a school district should spend its entire budget. It supports this claim by asking us to believe without adequate support that the many differences between the pilot program's specifics and the district are inconsequential. Further, its recommendations are based only on a single type of technology. Without the addition of serious extra support, the argument should not be taken as valid.

The good: We're getting closer, but we're not there just yet. The introduction gives more specifics about the situation and the argument, and is also clear about the overall thrust of the essay. This has the whiff of "fourness" about it, though it might have an outside shot at a 5 if there's something eye-catching to follow.

The bad: The presentation of the argument and the essay's thesis statement kind of bleed together, as the hypothetical essayist seems to want to say both things at once. Hopefully, this essayist doesn't intend to call the editorial writer out for vague terminology, as this introductory paragraph is general and vague where it could easily be specific. (Pots should not call kettles black.)

TIP

All of the sample essay pieces will contain English prose that's up to the minimum standards of the GMAT. No fake typos to prove how much you should proofread, either.

This editorialist's argument recommending that an unnamed school district drastically change the allocation of money within its educational budget in order to incorporate more technology into the classrooms in its colleges and technical schools fails to convince. The main evidence offered to support the claim is quite limited, requiring us to assume that the educational improvement of students in a single schools' air conditioning and refrigeration program following the introduction of interactive computer displays will be repeated throughout the district so long as those in charge of its educational budget are willing to spend extra money on technology. No regard is given to possible differences in kinds of program, sizes of school, or even the type of technology that will be purchased as the program moves from its pilot school to the entire district.

The good: Obviously, this hypothetical student's essay is going to end up longer than the other two, but notice how that length is accomplished: specific references and concrete detail. The author gives the essay's main point in the first line, fleshes out the argument in the middle of the paragraph, and then returns at its end to a preview of the sorts of issues that will be raised in the body paragraphs. It's also clear that this writer took the time to make sure that the first line of the essay was well written back in their version of Step 3.

The bad: This test taker's version of the argument is so tightly condensed into just a few phrases that it might be a little hard for the grader to grab onto. The level of diction and overall organization will probably mitigate that, however, so it's not that big a problem.

Now it's time for all three of our students to tackle the body paragraphs. Granted, it'd be hard to believe that all three of them are working from the same outline as we produced. Student 1's introduction is probably scantier, Student 3's is more developed, but not necessarily. One skill that separates the 4's from the 5.5's is the ability to take an outline and run with it.

Let's check back in with Student 1:

To begin, how do we know whether the students in the first school are like the students all over the district? It could be that the increases in passing scores weren't even that impressive. And even if they are, that's not reason to believe that these students aren't different somehow. They're AC & Refrigeration majors, after all, and that's not exactly brain surgery. Until we know more about these guys, it's not a good idea for us to accept the editorial's argument. I mean, how do we even know that this editorialist is good at telling real educational successes from what just looks like a success after five years. You can spend ten years thinking you're doing the right thing, and only later find out that you weren't. There are too many examples of this sort of thing to list, and that's not even considering the possibility that there are a lot of schools in this district where people study all kinds of things, not just how to make sure your house is cool in the summer and your cold cuts don't spoil.

That's not the biggest problem with this argument, though. We need to know a lot more about how those computer screens were used in the AC classes even. What does "interactive" even mean, and how would it help you figure out which part of the air conditioner you need to bang on when it doesn't work. And it's not like you bang on the same part when you're doing brain surgery, at least I'd hope not.

TIP

"Don't all introductory paragraphs have to end with a three part thesis statement?" That's one way to do it, and an easy way to remember, but there is no rule demanding it.

The good: Even with an inauspicious beginning, this student is managing to bring up specific reasons why the argument's underlying assumptions might not be valid. The occasional bit of color like the cold cuts in paragraph two isn't a bad idea, truth be told, though banging on the brain might be a little *too* colorful.

Also, notice that the student does manage to use transitional keywords to make sure the reader knows when the subject is being changed.

The bad: A tendency to meander and lose sight of the paragraph's purpose is this student's main flaw. The language is a bit loose, yes, but disorganization will do much more to lower a score than a casual tone. The student's body paragraphs likely mean that a 3 is not out of the question, though it is likely the essay's ceiling.

Over at Student 2's computer, body paragraphs are coming along, too:

> The program that saw the "substantial" results that so impress the editorial writer and motivate the entire proposal seems far too specific and esoteric a subject matter to use to make any drastic or far-reaching decisions about educational spending priorities. Nothing against Air Conditioning and Refrigeration Repair students, but this doesn't tend to be the program that draws the best and brightest, even at a technical school like Belleville Heights Technical. It's not clear that the results of a technical college are even relevant to collegiate education in general. Whatever the new technological improvements did for the tech school students' licensing exams, we should not be so quick to change course on the basis of their example. It is certainly within the realm of possibility that the AC Repair program at BH Technical is a comparatively small program, even at the school itself. If this were the case, it would be inadvisable for a school board to make too much of their success, however "substantial."
>
> A more compelling issue is the exact nature of the technology and the question of whether it could be usefully applied in other programs at BHT and elsewhere. The drama majors at Belleville Heights Fine Arts Academy might not know what to do with an interactive computer display, even if the business majors at a different school could use them for PowerPoint presentations that were miles above the ones they'd been able to do with noninteractive displays.

The good: The introduction of the appropriately named Fine Arts Academy is a nice touch, as is the PowerPoint example in the second paragraph. Whenever you can incorporate specific, relatable examples into your discussion, your essay will be the better for it. Student 2 is also doing a fair job of showing how the unwarranted assumptions aren't necessarily wrong, and that it will all come down to specifics that the editorial writer doesn't provide in the argument.

The bad: The problem of different points getting a bit mixed together in this student's presentation continues here. Putting the focus on the technology itself in the middle of paragraph two does mean that paragraph three is a clear extension of the overall line of thought, the original point about the HVAC students' representativeness is getting overshadowed. When writing an AWA essay, it's imperative that you finish making one point before moving on to the next.

And what sort of masterpiece has our 6-bound student produced while these last two students were sweating away?

The first and most glaring flaw with the editorial's argument is how little is told about the students in the pilot program. If the school district that contains Belleville Heights Technical is full of similar technical colleges that focus on subjects similar to air conditioning repair, we can be more confident that attempts to duplicate its success throughout the district will be met with success. On the other hand, if Belleville Heights is the only technical college in a sea of liberal arts schools, things might be different. Moreover, it is not even a certain thing that air conditioning repair itself represents a large proportion of the study body at the school in where the new computer technology was introduced. Though the drop in failure rates was substantial for students at the school in general, it is possible that the gains were found more in automobile repair or electrical engineering. The performance of the air conditioning repair students may well have gone down, for all the editorialist reveals.

This brings another problem to mind. There is very little information in the editorialist's writings about how the new "interactive computer screens" were used in the air conditioning and refrigeration repair classrooms. Without such knowledge, there is no way to determine how big a part of the increased performance was due to the computers. It could even be the case that they weren't used at all, only introduced and left to gather dust in the corner. Similarly, without knowing if there exist comparable technological advancements that could enhance the other programs in the school district, it is not possible to say whether allocating more funds to purchasing technology will bring about any increase in performance there. What helps an air conditioning repair student pass a qualifying exam might hinder a poet from creating a portfolio to send out to graduate programs.

The good: Again, it's easy to tell this essay is going to do well from the length alone, even though it is not the length alone that will determine its fate. Rather, Student 3 has clearly taken the time to think through several different points within the larger topics that serve as the focus for each of the two body paragraphs. There is little to no repetition in this student's delivery, instead detail upon detail added to flesh out the specifics of the essay's argument.

The bad: There's not much to criticize, though do notice how hard this student is having to work to keep from using personal pronouns. One wonders whose mind the problem is being brought to in the second body paragraph. At other points the diction gets a little obtuse. Great pains are being taken to keep even from abbreviating "air conditioning." This likely will not drag the essay lower than a 5.5, but if the essay seems too off putting to the human grader, it may just block the possibility of a 6.

It's time for our three students to sum their positions up in a concluding paragraph. We return to Student 1 first:

In conclusion, this argument cannot be accepted simply on the evidence that the editorial gives because we do not know enough about the other schools or about the computers the AC program used.

The good: Don't let the brevity sway your assessment too much. This is a perfectly serviceable conclusion. It wouldn't elevate an essay from a 3 to a 3.5, but it also wouldn't lower one from a 3.5 to a 3, either. In fact, Student 1 finally shows signs of clarity and focus, very cleanly reprising the two points of the body paragraphs—more clearly than the topics were presented originally, in fact.

The bad: We could easily wish for a longer conclusion, particularly one that mentions some way in which the editorialist might be able to improve the argument or answer the student's objections. Your essay on test day should avoid simply attacking the speaker's position.

Now back to Student 2, who was teetering on the edge of the acceptable score range with a rambling middle section.

> Until more information about the scarcity or abundance of other, nontechnical colleges in the editorial writer's school district, and until more can be learned about the kinds of technology that fall within the potentially expanded budget, it will be hard for anyone to go along with the proposal in the editorial. Whenever someone suggests moving money around, but can only provide one limited example to back their suggestion up, we are right to be skeptical. Otherwise, we might end up with a ballet classroom full of VR helmets but no pointe shoes.

The good: Once again, Student 2 manages to rescue a substandard paragraph with a final flourish. Though beginning with the possible strengtheners as this paragraph does is a solid way to begin bringing an AWA essay to a close.

The bad: Resisting the temptation to go meandering for a sentence or two is still this student's greatest challenge. Often these shifts in subject are accompanied by shifts in tone, so that the essay oscillates unevenly between formal and casual. It would be better if this hypothetical essayist were to write an entirely casual essay than to haphazardly attempt more professional or academic sounding diction.

In the final analysis, the occasional flourishes and sparks of wit might convince the human grader to bump this essay up to 4.5 or even 5 if feeling generous. The E-Rater would probably not be as impressed and would likely suggest a 4, meaning the student's 4.5 is all but secured. It's not the most impressive AWA score, but it is good enough.

Back at Student 3's terminal, we might expect that the keystrokes have all but died down as the student dutifully follows this book's advice and is proofreading away. But what is there to show for the effort?

> The holes in this argument are too many and too substantial that it remains difficult to take the editorialist seriously. Without further evidence confirming the representative quality of the air conditioning program and explaining how different technologies might improve the educational outcomes in all of the district's programs, whatever they may be, the proposal to reallocate funds to technology should be greeted with the utmost skepticism.

The good: This conclusion is perfectly serviceable, too, though not much more so than the short little conclusion that Student 1 gave. This is simply the wordy version, which is perfectly OK to do. The reader is adequately reminded of the essay's earlier points, and some suggestion for improvement is given, but there is also nothing particularly interesting or eye catching. The 6 is probably not going to happen, though Student 3 will almost certainly not score lower than a 5.5.

Step 5: Proofread

The sorts of things that our three hypothetical essayists might find on their proofreading runs won't be typos or spelling mistakes, but that does not mean that their essays could not have benefited from the time. Even Student 3's very polished essay could be further enhanced, little inconsistencies of language could be ironed out or the vocabulary choices touched up here and there. And at the very least, the time allocated to proofreading will ensure that no one's essay cuts off abruptly.

The Final Template

Our experience with the three essayists allows us to suggest a final, fleshed out version of the potential essay template. Feel free to use it as you will. Tweak it to your own strengths and tastes, but remember that you don't have to reinvent the wheel in order to secure an excellent AWA score.

> **Introductory Paragraph**
> - Present the argument from the question in your own words.
> - Clearly announce that the argument is flawed and indicate why.
> - Sketch out briefly the points that form the core of the essay body.
>
> **Body Paragraphs**
> - In each, develop a single idea, most often a single assumption or type of assumption.
> - Begin with a clear statement of the assumption to be discussed.
> - Provide specific details of how certain unknown facts could weaken, others strengthen the assumption.
> - Transition to the remaining body paragraphs, if any.
>
> **Concluding Paragraph**
> - Begin with some indication of the sorts of evidence that might strengthen the argument.
> - Proceed to reiterate your claim that the argument, as currently stated, is unconvincing.

STRATEGY TIPS, TWEAKS, AND OTHER CONSIDERATIONS

Relax!

There's no such thing as an advanced or difficult AWA question. There's nothing adaptive here and you get only one per test. And, as we've seen, all AWA prompts are more or less the same. So, instead, consider these following pointers with some tricks and flourishes you can focus on once you've got your basic standardized test essay format down as well as a couple of pertinent reminders of small points.

The "Fourth" Part of the AWA: the Interface

In general, we haven't spent too much time in this book discussing the GMAT CAT's interface, as it's not too hard to figure out that you use the mouse to move the cursor and the left-hand button to click on the answer buttons.

But with the AWA, many students do struggle a bit, spoiled by the robustness of the word processing software that they've become accustomed to using at home, at school, or on the job. The GMAT's AWA is not your old reliable word processor. You'd have to go back to the days when word processors were single-function devices that looked like fancy typewriters to find an interface this basic. It's got fewer features than Microsoft Notepad!

The most glaring lack is that function we most disdain day to day: the spellcheck. No helpful red lines will appear under misspelled words, and no button will autocorrect them for you. The only buttons you'll have access to will be Cut, Copy, Paste, Undo, and Redo.

Does spelling count?!? Officially, no, spelling does not count. But do remember that one of your readers is only human, and you are trying to make a good impression; the grad students grading essays can't help but be influenced by your spelling to some degree. It might be the difference between a 5 and a 5.5.

The lack of your computerized spelling coach is very important to keep in mind when following the advice elsewhere to pepper your essay with a reasonable number of high syllable count words. You should only elevate your vocabulary to words that you are comfortable spelling. Misspelling those sorts of words will quickly give the reader the impression you're trying to manipulate them and may even assume your true facility with the language is lower than the rest of the essay might demonstrate.

You won't need to use those buttons if you don't want, however, as there are a few shortcuts "under the hood" that are nice to know about. The interface designers even decided to make their bare-bones word processor agnostic to the PC versus Mac divide. Windows types will recognize these shortcuts:

Ctrl + X = Cut	Ctrl + V = Paste	Ctrl + Y = Redo
Ctrl + C = Copy	Ctrl + Z = Undo	

And Mac aficionados will welcome this complementary set:

Alt + T = Cut	Alt + A = Paste	Alt + R = Redo
Alt + C = Copy	Alt + U = Undo	

The AWA prompt will always take up a good bit of your screen real estate, while you'll be left to make do with the lower half. If you don't want to move your hands from the keyboard to scroll that tiny window up and down, don't forget the helpful [Page Up] and [Page Down] keys.

TYPING MATTERS AND MATTERS OF TYPING

While typing isn't supposed to matter in a big way to the graders, who've all been given explicit instructions to ignore the occasional "trasnposition," "inadvvertantly reppeated" letter, or "stra!y" punctuation mark, they will likely hurt your case if occasional becomes more than once or so a paragraph.

Moreover, you might actually be a worse typist than you believe yourself to be, thanks to the autocorrect feature in most modern word processors. But so long as you slow down just a smidge to make sure you watch the letters and words that actually appear on the screen, your typing is probably sufficient to the task.

But if you're one of those holdouts who's somehow managed to hunt and peck your way into the Digital Age, it's time to bite the bullet and learn to type.

In Conclusion, Conclude

The 30 minutes you have for the AWA essay is a hard limit. There's no way to signal the computer that you need just one more second to finish your last sentence. When the timer in the upper right-hand corner of your screen hits 0:00, the word processing interface closes itself and punts you right into the Integrated Reasoning instruction screen. So in actual practice, you have about 29 minutes and 50 seconds in which to write your essay.

Essays that break off mid-sentence or mid-paragraph do take a grading hit from the computer and human readers alike. Prepare for this by knowing what your conclusion is going to be and, if possible, have it typed out at the bottom of your essay screen *before* you've written some of the middle paragraphs. It's easy to delete a supporting paragraph if you realize you don't have time to finish it, and so long as you've got other supporting paragraphs, they can compensate for the loss. A lost conclusion sinks the essay.

The Last 30-Second Failsafe

Sometimes, even with all the best intentions and foreknowledge, we still slip up and find we've spent too long on the last body paragraph. Now there are only 30 seconds left, and no real conclusion to speak of. Whatever can we do?

Before test day, you should practice typing this sentence (or your own reworded version of the same):

> In conclusion, because it lacks the necessary evidence to substantiate its claim, the speaker's argument is unconvincing.

If you find yourself in the situation above, your escape hatch is that sentence or one like it. Quickly finish the sentence you're writing, truncating it as much as you need to, hit Enter, Tab, and type the boilerplate conclusion. No matter what the topic happens to be, you know the speaker (whoever he or she happens to be) has failed to prove the case because evidence that would substantiate the unstated assumptions were left out. Essays with conclusions score higher than those without, even when the conclusion is a perfunctory one-line statement.

I Didn't Forget the Other Side—It's Just Wrong

Here's a simple but effective way to make your essay seem more well-reasoned and convincing with minimal extra effort on your part. You'll always be lacing your essay with pieces of information that will both strengthen and weaken particular unwarranted or under-warranted assumptions in the argument. Simply include a gracious acknowledgment that the side you find most likely is not the only possible outcome and that, indeed, many thoughtful people have disagreed.

It all boils down to one magic phrase: "There are [those/many/some] who would [say/argue/contend]…"

 TIP

"But I only have 30 minutes!" Worry not. Successful essays, even long ones, aren't much more than 1000 words.

Consider the following:

> Industry alone is not sufficient to spur job growth. The Soviet political machine learned this in the last quarter of the past century, when their single-minded focus on industrial growth left villages of starving and diseased men and women who once could have entered the workforce. If only the central planners realized that if agricultural development does not keep pace with industrial, the proportion of the workforce simply unable to work will surely swell, erasing job gains in the industry.

Now, back off of that stance just a touch:

> While there are certainly economists who contend that industry alone is always sufficient to spur job growth, such an approach has often proven inadequate, as those advising the Soviet political machine learned in the last quarter of the past century, when a single-minded focus on industrial growth left villages of starving and diseased men and women who once could have entered the workforce. If only the central planners realized that if agricultural development does not keep pace with industrial, the proportion of the workforce simply unable to work will surely swell, erasing job gains in the industry.

Just one minor tweak and the author of the argument seems more engaged and even-handed, without a single jot of extra evidence!

It's possible to take the acknowledgment of other sides so far that it becomes the complete rejection of your own authority on the subject. Remember that the whole reason you're acknowledging the other side is to prove to your reader that you considered *but rejected* it.

When in Doubt, Space It Out

As many high schoolers also know, one sure way to make an essay seem longer than it is is to refrain from paragraph breaks unless they're absolutely necessary. On the GMAT, this rookie technique will likely end with your human grader's eyes glazing over. The appearance of length is important, yes, but so is making the essay as easy on the reader as possible. The human grader can be your best ally, affording you an extra bite at the apple by overruling the computer and sending you on to the final human grader, so long as you cater to them. Put an extra carriage return at the end of each paragraph. Make sure that you start your paragraphs with a full tab's worth of room, don't just hit the spacebar three times. And most importantly, if you're uncertain whether a thought belongs in its own paragraph or not, default to breaking it up.

Take a hint from the dinosaur media. Newspaper reporters have known this one for years, and even though the essay isn't as limited as their column inches, the essay is still displayed on a narrow field to the reader. Paradoxically, that means that an essay with shorter paragraph breaks seems longer than one with long chunks of text.

Don't Repeat Your Evidence

Don't repeat your evidence.

In the ever-present quest for an essay that is long enough for a 6, it can be tempting to belabor points because doing so does make the page so nice and full and paragraphs so nice and long. The problem is that human reader again. You don't want your one possibility of a sympathetic soul to turn his or her head in disgust the fourth time you pound out your example. So don't repeat your evidence.

That doesn't mean you should never repeat a structural point, however. The three phases of every successful essay boil down to the mantra *Tell them what you're going to tell them; tell them; then tell them you told them.* The structural glue of your essay might seem too repetitive, all that "first, second, third" and "for this reason, too, the argument fails to convince" isn't how the writers on the New York Times' best-seller list operate—but it is how the successful GMAT AWA essayist works.

Exterminate Weasel Words

A "weasel word" is a little qualifying tweak that adds wiggle room to an otherwise straightforward statement. This is not the same as saying, "There are those who say"; rather, it's putting those squishy little asides like "sort of," "kind of," "of a sort," "so to speak," and "seems to." No responsible reader assumes that direct, forthright sentences mean that the author is some sort of pig-headed absolutist unable to see nuance, and overworked as they may be, the graders the GMAT employs are still responsible readers.

High schoolers use weasel words because they think that they make their case more compelling. Journalists do it to avoid recrimination and libel. They're both wrong, and in this you should not seek to join them.

BUT BEWARE PHANTOM WEASELS

This section has mentioned high schoolers a lot, and that's because high school is the source of a lot of our superstitions about writing. Perhaps you've heard of these two pieces of advice:

> Never use "I" or the first person in an essay.
> Always avoid the passive voice.

Each of these maxims can be traced back to a nugget of wisdom and the difficulty of teaching high schoolers (or anyone else with no experience writing longform) to write an essay. The reason that your high school English teacher wouldn't let you use the word "I" way back then is that, unchecked, I turns into "I think," "I feel," and "I believe" tacked onto every single sentence in the essay. The untrained writer feels that they simply must qualify their thoughts with the admission that they're not making universal statements.

What your teacher probably should have said was this:

You don't have to tell the reader you think, feel, or believe the things in your essay. It's your essay. An essay is expected to reflect the views of its author.

and

Only interject yourself into the essay with good reason—and there *are* good reasons to interject yourself, particularly when avoiding *I, me,* or *mine* requires unnatural linguistic contortions.

But, then again, those explanations lack the punch of the often-recited and incorrect maxims, and the high school you was probably not paying attention after the first ten words, anyway. When followed inflexibly, this first-person rule produces sentences like this:

> **In the experience of the writer of this essay, one's first job can prove to be a great learning experience, as the example of this writer's brother proves.**

Particularly when what you are trying to convey is a personal detail about your life, avoiding I is all but impossible if you wish to write well. Personal details are definitely welcome in your essay. You shouldn't shun the rich experiences that have given you the opinions and understanding you bring to the essay.

In a similar vein, the second "rule" that labels the passive voice as some kind of unnatural aberration or plague upon the language easily produces terrible sentences.

As you will learn in the Sentence Correction chapter, the standard word order for English sentences is Subject-Verb-Object. If one sentence ends with an object, it is often to your reader's benefit to start the following sentence with that object, to better link the thoughts and avoid a choppy presentation. The passive voice allows you to do that. In fact, you probably use the passive voice that way all the time. It's only when writing that the old high school worry comes back to haunt you.

And once again it's those first-time essayists who are to blame. Just as with the "I" rule, if left unchecked, the untrained writer tends to begin sentences with placeholder subjects, easing into them, as if trying not to disturb the reader. Each paragraph becomes a long series of sentences beginning "It is" and "There are" and "It can be seen." Nobody wants that, but it's not the passive voice that's to blame.

Relax. The AWA Is Just One Part of the GMAT

Nobody is kept from business school by a low AWA score. At worst, the admissions department might suggest some remedial business writing courses, but that's it.

The only truly important thing about the AWA is that you don't let it tire you out or distract your focus from the sections to follow, the ones that actually have a demonstrable effect on your admissions chances. The AWA needs to feel like a warm-up, a little bit of writing to get the juices flowing, nothing more.

Where to Go from Here

Now that you have an essay template to work from, examples of possible essays to draw upon, and an understanding of the actual standards that will be used to evaluate your writing, you should begin to feel a bit more confident about this small essay that begins the test. If you're still worried, or simply want extra help, there are a few extra resources readily available to you that will undoubtedly meet your needs.

Additional Practice

If you are wondering why this chapter has no final selection of targeted quizzes, unlike all the other ones in this GMAT guide, it's because there is no reason to look for simulated questions for the AWA. In a departure from their normal reticence to share test questions, the good folks at the GMAC have made available *every single possible AWA prompt*. And if you find yourself without Internet access, the GMAC's *Official Guide* contains dozens of sample topics drawn from that very same pool.

It'd be folly to try writing an essay for each of the prompts in advance and committing them all to memory, but that doesn't mean that *some* practice isn't in order. After an essay or two under simulated test conditions, you'll find that any previous reservations will swiftly dwindle. But if any last doubts remain, you could always follow the next and final piece of advice.

www.mba.com/~/media/files/mba/newthegmat/analysisofanargument100606.pdf

Pay Off the E-Rater

If the thought that maybe, just maybe, your personal writing style is somehow so eclectic or unconventional that the E-Rater won't know what to do with it, you can submit a single essay to the E-Rater service (for a fee) and in return you'll receive the numerical score that the E-Rater would have awarded.

www.mba.com/store/store-catalog/gmat-preparation/gmat-write.aspx

PART 2

Integrated Reasoning

Integrated Reasoning 2

→ **OVERALL STRATEGIES**
→ **THE FOUR QUESTION TYPES**
→ **GRAPHICS INTERPRETATION**
→ **TABLE ANALYSIS**
→ **TWO-PART ANALYSIS**
→ **MULTI-SOURCE REASONING**

The Integrated Reasoning section has a 30-minute time limit and 12 questions. Some of the questions may have several parts. A special online calculator is available for use only on this part of the GMAT. The Integrated Reasoning section will be scored separately from your GMAT score (from 200–800) and from your AWA score (from 0–6). This section will be scored on a scale from 1–8, in intervals of 1. There are no partial points given, which means, for example, that if a question has three Yes/No statements, you need to get all three correct in order to get credit.

The Integrated Reasoning section is designed to measure your ability to review data in multiple formats using various methods, to identify key issues and trends, to apply high-level reasoning, and to organize information in order to make an informed decision. For this, you will need to be comfortable with synthesizing information from charts, tables, graphs, spreadsheets, e-mails, and letters in paragraph form. As with the rest of the GMAT, you will not need prior business knowledge to answer Integrated Reasoning questions. The Integrated Reasoning section can be best summarized as a blend of the GMAT Quantitative and Critical Reasoning sections along with some argumentative logic, thus the use of the term integrated.

Note that the Integrated Reasoning section is not computer adaptive like the quantitative and verbal sections, which become easier or more difficult in response to your performance. This means the questions are preselected, just like in a simple paper and pencil test. Therefore, you should expect a diverse mix of question types and difficulty levels.

OVERALL STRATEGIES

The Integrated Reasoning section requires some of the same skills you will use on the overall GMAT. It also has a similar structure and format. Therefore, you can apply many of the strategies.

1. **INVEST TIME TO UNDERSTAND THE QUESTION:** For every GMAT problem, including those in the quantitative and verbal sections, you must ask yourself "What's going on?" before you dive into solving the question. Make sure you understand the question and the information given. Get a general sense of what the question is asking. Think about how you might set up your solution. Investing time up front to review the data and key insights before diving into the questions will save you from losing time by backtracking.

2. **AVOID THE TWO MOST COMMON ERRORS:** The most common errors that test takers make on the GMAT are misreading the question and making unnecessary calculation errors. Make sure you review the questions, the information, the passages, and the answer choices quickly but carefully. When you make calculations, be sure to keep your scratch work clean, structured, and error free.

3. **KNOW HOW EVERYTHING RELATES:** Try to get a sense of how all the pieces of information—variables, numbers, and text—relates to each other. The GMAC writers don't expect you to look at all the data in great detail. Therefore, look for certain themes or trends within the data that are obvious. Most of the information given in the questions tells you the "what." Your job is to figure out the "so what." Ask yourself, "What does this tell me?" and "Why is this so important?"

4. **YOU DON'T ALWAYS NEED THE CALCULATOR:** The Integrated Reasoning section provides a calculator, but that doesn't mean you should always use it. It is an awkward tool. Most of the time, you can set up your questions to keep its use to a minimum. Most GMAT math problems can be solved conceptually and with minimal calculations. Even though you can solve all quantitative problems with a step-by-step process, there are always shortcuts. Do some mental calculations, simplify your work, and estimate whenever possible. You will be surprised by how little you need the online calculator.

5. **DON'T SKIM, SYNTHESIZE INSTEAD:** Skimming will not help you in this section. You are being tested on your ability to analyze and synthesize the data. That doesn't mean you have look at every single detail. However, you do need to watch for important key words, note titles, headings, labels, and subject lines, along with units and key numbers.

6. **PRACTICE DATA SHUFFLING:** Since much of the navigation in Integrated Reasoning requires using tabs, scrolling, and sorting, you can practice much of this using spreadsheet software like Microsoft Excel. You can also try using a calculator on your computer for practice. Don't let the need to navigate slow you down.

7. **LEVERAGE CURRENT GMAT STRATEGIES:** Use the theory and strategies you learned in the Quantitative and Verbal sections of this book to help you. Many of the typical GMAT strategies use processes and methodologies that are transferable to the Integrated Reasoning section. You can apply similar skills to answering all the questions—quantitative analysis, algebra, deductive reasoning, argumentative logic and structure, identifying conclusions, and anticipating questions.

8. **LOOK FOR ALL THE HIDDEN CLUES:** The GMAT test developers like to hide clues to questions in many places. You need to know where these clues are. Start with the questions and answer choices themselves. They can give you an idea of where to look in a question and what to look for. You can also use your work from previous questions within a section; you can use your work cumulatively to solve the next problem. Don't forget to look within the charts, tables, graphs, and paragraphs. They contain key numbers, labels, and words that provide more insight to the problem than you might originally realize. Digest every piece of the puzzle. With practice, you will begin to know what you should look for and what you can ignore.

9. **YOU DON'T NEED TO MEMORIZE:** Since you are given so much data and information, the test writers at the GMAC cannot expect you to memorize everything, nor should you try. Devote your time and energy to understanding the problem, navigating effectively, outlining a solution path, and getting to the answer. If you need to refer back, the data is always available.

10. **CONFIDENCE IS KEY:** Just like with the rest of the GMAT, confidence goes a long way to your success. When you are confident, you look at problems as a fun challenge and have the determination to solve them correctly. When you lack confidence, you second-guess yourself and you spend too much time focused on the wrong things. You use many of the skills tested on the Integrated Reasoning section every day in your professional and personal lives. Approach problems knowing that the theory, structure, and strategies you have internalized will help you succeed on the Integrated Reasoning section and on the rest of the GMAT.

TIP

The IR section goes by very fast. If you can't keep up, try giving yourself a "free pass" to completely skip one question. Your time management will benefit, especially when avoiding a question with 5 or 6 answers you need to get all correct in order to get any credit.

THE FOUR QUESTION TYPES

The new Integrated Reasoning section contains four types of questions:

1. **GRAPHICS INTERPRETATION:** You will analyze a graphical image and then select options in a drop-down menu in order to create accurate statements.

2. **TABLE ANALYSIS:** You will receive a sortable table of information, similar to a spreadsheet, that you must analyze to answer questions in true/false, yes/no, or other formats.

3. **TWO-PART ANALYSIS:** You will receive a paragraph of information and then answer a question in a two-part format. This requires you to look at data in two different ways in order to solve the question.

4. **MULTI-SOURCE REASONING:** You are given two to three sources of information presented in various forms—including text, charts, and graphs—on tabbed pages. You then have to answer questions in either a yes/no format or in a select one out of five format.

Following are the four Integrated Reasoning question types, along with strategies and sample questions for each.

GRAPHICS INTERPRETATION

True to its name, this section will require you to interpret graphics. The basic idea is this:

Look at this graph. Understand what it is trying to say. Extract some key information.

You will be given a graphical image—scatter plot, graph with variables, Venn diagram, bar chart, statistical curve distribution, or pie chart—and some explanatory text. There will be several statements you will need to complete using choices from a drop-down menu.

SKILLS TESTED

- Assimilating, analyzing, and interpreting data in graphical forms
- Identifying and extracting key information
- Interpreting past events and predicting future outcomes

Graphics Interpretation Strategies

1. **START WITH WHAT YOU KNOW:** As with any GMAT question, ask yourself "What's going on?" before attempting to answer. Invest the time to get the gist of the graph. Try to look at it from a high-level perspective and to understand the information it is trying to convey. Think of an appropriate title for the graph in your own words (IYOW) if none is given.

2. **MAKE SURE YOU CATCH EVERYTHING:** Now focus on the details. Look at any titles, axis labels, symbols, legends, or units of measurements given. Is the graph displaying data in thousands or millions, in inches or feet, and so on? Investing time up-front to understand the graph thoroughly will save you from having to analyze everything again later.

3. **IDENTIFY TRENDS AND RELATIONSHIPS:** Look for any key trends or relationships among the variables, the *x*-axis, and *y*-axis. Are there any direct or indirect relationships? Do certain areas of the graph have spikes, a greater concentration of points, or either a positive or a negative slope? This is where we interpret the data and extract the key information.

4. **USE THE STATEMENTS TO HELP YOU:** Just like in the rest of the GMAT, the answer choices can provide you with some great insights. If the statements talk about slope, familiarize yourself with the slopes of any lines shown on the graph. The statements will mention certain key words that are relevant to answering the question. If you identify enough, you will be able to "connect the dots" and solve the puzzle. In other words, you can piece together all the different aspects of the graph and what it is trying to say.

5. **ANTICIPATE THROUGHOUT THE QUESTION:** Throughout your first read of the material, try to anticipate the relevant information and what the questions are going to ask. Once you see the questions, you can try to figure out the answer before you open up the drop-down menu. It's a great confidence booster if you see the answer you anticipated in the drop-down menu. If you don't see your answer there, it's a good indicator that you may have made some oversights.

The following two graphs show economic data from 1999–2000.

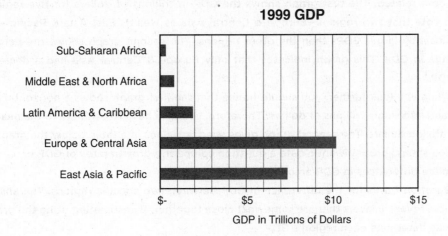

1999 GDP

GDP in Trillions of Dollars

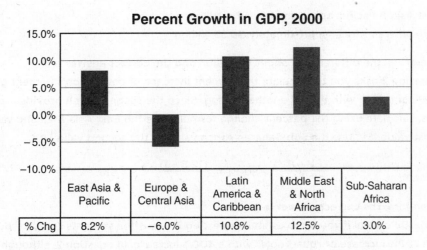

Percent Growth in GDP, 2000

% Chg	East Asia & Pacific	Europe & Central Asia	Latin America & Caribbean	Middle East & North Africa	Sub-Saharan Africa
% Chg	8.2%	−6.0%	10.8%	12.5%	3.0%

Complete each statement according to the information presented in the diagram.

1. In 1999, by approximately how much did the East Asia and Pacific GDP surpass Sub-Saharan Africa's GDP?

    (A) $4.5 trillion
    (B) $5.0 trillion
    (C) $6.0 trillion
    (D) $7.0 trillion

2. In the year 2000, the Middle East and North Africa's percent growth in GDP was approximately what percent greater than Sub-Saharan Africa's percent growth in GDP?

    (A) 225%
    (B) 317%
    (C) 367%
    (D) 417%

SOLUTION AND STRATEGY REVIEW

The first thing you should notice is that you are given two graphs, not one, and that they are both related. The first graph shows the GDP in trillions of dollars for five regions. Also note that two regions—Europe & Central Asia as well as East Asia & Pacific—had significantly larger GDPs than the other regions. The second graph shows the percent change in GDP. This graph indicates that only Europe & Central Asia had a decrease in GDP.

When you look further, you should notice that the first graph shows a horizontal axis divided into single trillions of dollars. Therefore, you may have to estimate to the nearest half-trillion dollars. The second graph gives specific values in a table below the graph.

You should probably anticipate a question comparing growth rates of GDP or absolute differences in GDP among the regions.

Question 1 asks for the difference in GDP between two specific regions. The answer choices reveal answers that are somewhat close together. By estimating using the graph, we can determine each region's GDP.

East Asia & Pacific: approximately $7.4 trillion
Sub-Saharan Africa: approximately $0.33 trillion

Therefore, the difference is about $7 trillion **and the correct answer is D**.

Question 2 asks you to calculate the percent increase of one region's percent growth in GDP compared with that of another region. Since the second graph provides specific values, calculate using the percent change formula. Use the East Asia & Pacific value as the first value, *FV*. Use the Sub-Saharan Africa value as the second value, *PV*.

$$\frac{(FV - PV)}{PV} \times 100\% = \frac{(12.5 - 3)}{3} \times 3 = 316.7\%$$

Therefore, **the correct answer is B**.

Note: Be careful if you try to estimate question 2. Too often students confuse "double" with a 200% increase or "quadruple" with a 400% increase. In question 2, although 12.5% is a little over four times 3.0%, this actually means that it is a little over a 300% increase.

TABLE ANALYSIS

In this section, you will be required to analyze tables. The basic idea is this:

Look at this detailed table. Sort the information to answer questions about it.

You will be given a table or spreadsheet that has sorting ability, much like a Microsoft Excel worksheet. Some text will be included to explain the table. The questions will have varying types of statements—yes/no, true/false, would help to explain/would not help to explain, or inferable/not inferable. You will have to select one choice for each statement. Every column in the table is sortable either numerically or alphabetically.

SKILLS TESTED

- Assimilating, analyzing, and interpreting data tables
- Sifting through and organizing a mass of information
- Identifying trends and patterns
- Extracting meaningful information to make decisions
- Understanding how data can be used to satisfy certain conditions or support either a hypothesis or principle

Table Analysis: Strategies

1. **START WITH WHAT IS GIVEN:** Look at the table and the headings. Invest the time up-front to get the gist of the table. Get a sense of the data given, sorting options, rankings, columns, and highest and lowest items in the table. Think of an appropriate title for the table in your own words (IYOW) if none is given.

2. **USE THE QUESTIONS OR STATEMENTS TO HELP YOU FOCUS:** The questions will give you a good idea of what kind of information needs to be extracted from the table. Yes/no and true/false are usually easy to figure out. However, watch out for the more abstract "would help explain" questions. Ask yourself if sorting a particular column would point you toward a solution.

3. **IDENTIFY TRENDS AND RELATIONSHIPS:** Look for any key trends or relationships among the numbers given. Look at how the numbers or rankings change among columns. Do you see some obvious disparities? Are there direct, indirect, or inverse relationships? This is where you interpret the data and extract the key information. Do not spend an undue amount of time going through each piece of data. Rather, you need to get an overall sense of the table. Remember, you can always look back at the table for reference, so there is no need to memorize anything.

4. **DON'T OVERANALYZE; BE EFFICIENT:** These questions contain a lot of information. You can easily get lost on some of the larger spreadsheets and forget about the clock. If you practice sorting beforehand using a spreadsheet program, you can get a better understanding of how sorting works. When you look at numbers, you can **estimate** or use very rough numbers (for example, $23,846 is better thought of as $24k). Remember again that the questions will refer you to which columns to look at. So take the time to determine what would be the best sort to find the answer.

The table below displays data of the Best Picture Oscar winners from 1996-2010.

Movie	Year of Release	Month of Release	Cost to Produce (in millions $)	Rank of Cost	Box Office Gross (in millions $)	Rank at Box Office
The English Patient	1996	Nov.	$27	8	$64	12
Titanic	1997	Dec.	$200	1	$496	1
Shakespeare in Love	1998	Dec.	$25	9	$73	10
American Beauty	1999	Other	$15	11	$108	8
Gladiator	2000	Other	$103	2	$187	3
A Beautiful Mind	2001	Dec.	$58	5	$155	4
Chicago	2002	Dec.	$45	6	$134	5
The Lord of The Rings: The Return of The King	2003	Dec.	$94	3	$364	2
Million Dollar Baby	2004	Dec.	$30	7	$65	11
Crash	2005	Other	$7	15	$53	14
The Departed	2006	Other	$90	4	$132	6
No Country for Old Men	2007	Nov.	$25	9	$64	12
Slumdog Millionaire	2008	Nov.	$15	11	$98	9
The Hurt Locker	2009	Other	$15	11	$15	15
The King's Speech	2010	Nov.	$15	11	$114	7

For each of the following statements, select *True* if the statement can be shown to be true based on the information in the table. Otherwise, select *False*.

True **False**

○ ○ Best Picture winners have frequently been released very late in the year, often in December, but a recent trend has been to release Best Picture winners earlier in the year.

○ ○ Best Picture winners are always profitable at the box office.

○ ○ The median box office gross of Best Picture winners is greater than the average box office gross of Best Picture winners.

SOLUTION AND STRATEGY REVIEW

The first things you should notice are the column headings. In particular, the year of release and the month of release suggest that you may get a question on trends over time. Note also that month of release has only three options: December, November, and other. Columns are also included for both production cost and box office grosses. This may lead to a question on profitability. Lastly, since you are given rankings, you may encounter a statement that refers either to the ranking specifically or to the median.

The questions are true or false. One GMAT trick is to have double statements where you are given two pieces of information to prove true or false. The GMAT will often have one portion that is true while the other portion is false, so beware. Let's now look at the statements to help determine the path to a solution.

(i) The first statement discusses release date. Therefore, sort by either release year or release month. Since December is a key word in the statement, you should use the month of release column. Note that the question is also asking for a yearly trend, so your best sorting option is by year of release. December release dates happen in the early years. In the years past 2004, half the release months were November and the other half were other. Therefore, the trend described in the questions is correct. **The answer is True.**

(ii) The second statement is all about profitability, as you had anticipated! You can sort either by cost to produce or by box office gross. Every single movie was profitable EXCEPT *The Hurt Locker*. Therefore, **the answer is False**.

(iii) This statement refers to both the median and the average box office gross. So you should sort by box office rank or by box office gross. Since there are 15 items in the list, the median is at 8, which is *American Beauty*. Its box office gross was $108 million. Calculating the average will clearly take a long time, so there has to be an easier way. If you look at the top-ranked movies, *Titanic and Lord of the Rings: The Return of the King* made $496 million and $364 million, respectively. These two movies will skew the average higher than the median. **The answer is False.**

Note that you might not use all the data or columns, especially when the table is very large. That is why it's better to use the questions to determine your approach.

TWO-PART ANALYSIS

This section requires you to do two-part analysis. The basic idea is this:

Analyze a problem with two components and solve for two components.

You will be given a problem that is structured with two components. The question could be either a typical GMAT quantitative problem (two-variable, rate, or work problems), a verbal problem (two opinions on an issue, two separate aspects of research), or a combination of both. The problem will have two issues, variables, or aspects under consideration. The question will also have two components, usually as columns in a chart, with several possible answers in rows. These answer components may or may not be related. Your job is to select the one correct answer for each column.

SKILLS TESTED

- Solving complex or multilayered problems
- Recognizing relationships between two entities
- Solving simultaneous equations
- Thinking and reasoning
- Weighing trade-offs and making decisions with more than one aspect

Two-Part Analysis: Strategies

1. **START WITH WHAT YOU KNOW AND UNDERSTAND:** Write down what you know from the question, especially for multilayered or complex problems. This includes what you know and what is implied by the statements in the question. This is your starting point and helps you figure out what's going on before diving deeper.

TIP

Two-Part Analysis questions are similar to typical GMAT quantitative and verbal problems. Therefore, many of the strategies and theory you learn in the other sections of this book will apply to this question format.

2. **STRUCTURE WITH CHARTS OR DRAWINGS:** Typically, the more complex a GMAT problem, the more important it is to add structure to it. Lay out the data in a more organized form or use a drawing to visualize the information. Imposing structure also keeps your scratch work clean, makes your scratch work easy to follow, and helps you to extract key aspects of the problem.

3. **ALGEBRA IS YOUR BEST FRIEND:** In many of the more quantitative problems, algebra is a great tool. Algebra is the language of math. It can help you simplify the problem, understand what's going on, and unlock keys to the solution.

4. **DETERMINE THE KEY ISSUES:** In complex problems, several issues, aspects, or constraints are at play. Spend some time identifying and understanding what they are. Then you might be able to look at the answer choices and see which ones meet the question's criteria.

5. **PLUG AND PLAY:** Once you have a strong understanding of the problem, you can start trying some of the answer choices given. Many of the Two-Part Analysis problems have dependent variables. Plugging in one answer may lead to what the other answer should be. If the other answer choice is there, that is great. If not, try another answer choice and see if you can find a match.

TWO-PART ANALYSIS: SAMPLE PROBLEM

Mackintoshies, a raincoat company, sells three different types of raincoats: vinyl, wool, and polyester. Due to an economic downturn, the company has reduced its spending budget on materials to $250,000 for the next year. The company recently acquired 10,000 meters of vinyl fabric for $7 per yard. The best supplier price that Mackintoshies could find sells wool for $10 per yard and polyester for $8 per yard.

In the table below, determine the amount of wool and polyester that Mackinoshies should spend so that the total amount spent on materials is exactly $250,000. Choose only one option in each column.

Wool	Polyester	Number of Yards
○	○	4,000
○	○	6,000
○	○	9,000
○	○	12,000
○	○	15,000

SOLUTION AND STRATEGY REVIEW

Start by writing down everything you know, both direct and implied.

Coat types: vinyl, wool, and polyester
Budget: $250,000
Money recently spent: 10,000 yards of polyester at $7 per yard = $70,000 spent
Costs for wool and polyester: $10/yard and $8/yard, respectively
Amount left to spend: $250,000 – $70,000 = $180,000

This problem looks like an ideal one for your best friend algebra. Use algebra to create a cost equation.

Let W = the amount in yards of wool bought

Let P = the amount in yards of polyester bought

$$10W + 8P = \$180{,}000$$

Since you do not have another equation to solve this algebraically, your best bet is to look at the answer choices. You can solve either by inspection (looking at the numbers and see which pair fits) or by plugging answer choices into the cost equation. Remember that GMAT math typically works out quite cleanly, so the $10W$ is very easy to fit in. Note that any of the answer choices multiplied by 10 (as in the $10W$) would give a number that ends in 0,000. So a shortcut would be to find a number that also multiplies by 8 (as in the $8P$) to give four zeros. The only answer choice that would do that is 15,000. So try 15,000 as the amount of polyester bought.

$$8(15{,}000) + 10W = 180{,}000$$
$$120{,}000 + 10W = 180{,}000$$
$$10W = 60{,}000$$
$$W = 6{,}000$$

Since that answer is in the chart, it's clear. **The answer is 6,000 yards of wool and 15,000 yards of polyester.**

MULTI-SOURCE REASONING

For the final question type in the Integrated Reasoning section, you will be required to use multi-source reasoning. The basic idea here is:

Look at multiple sources of information, and pull the relevant data to solve problems.

You will be given two or three tabs that contain a large amount of information, either in text form (such as e-mails and research articles) or in table form. The idea is to give you more information than you need. Your job is to pull the relevant information from the sources and solve problems. Some of the more wordy problems resemble GMAT Reading Comprehension or lengthy Critical Reasoning questions. You may be required to use quantitative skills, verbal skills, or both. You will also have to use either deductive or inductive reasoning. Questions may be in a yes/no or a multiple-choice format.

SKILLS TESTED

- Assimilating a voluminous amount of data and extracting relevant content
- Using both deductive and inductive reasoning
- Integrating various types of information from different sources to make a decision
- Dealing with information overload
- Using both quantitative and qualitative information simultaneously
- Analyzing a case study

Multi-Source Reasoning: Strategies

1. **DETERMINE THE SCOPE OF THE QUESTION:** First determine whether the question is more quantitative or verbal, as this will determine which strategies and tactics are appropriate for the question. If the question is more verbal, first think about what the key aspect or topic is of the entire case study. Then look at each tabbed section and identify its key aspect or topic. This will help you get a better understanding of the pieces of the puzzle and the puzzle as a whole. If the question is more quantitative, make sure you know what the basic objective of the question is and what variables are at play.

2. **DETERMINE THE "SO WHAT?":** Each section, particularly for the verbal-type questions, will have conclusions, inferences, and purposes from which you can extract deductions or use inductive reasoning. Think about each section's purpose and what the writer is trying to conclude. Again, you should do this both in context and in your own words (IYOW). Most of these questions will ask you to draw a conclusion, so understanding each section is key. The writer of each section will give you the "what," but you need to determine the "so what?"

3. **USE EACH QUESTION FOR DIRECTION:** Each question will give you a good idea of what issues or areas to focus on. The question should align with the scope and purpose you have already identified. If you are confused with all the information, you can first determine the main gist of the information and then look at the question. Depending on the question, you should be able to determine which section will be the best place to start.

4. **STRUCTURE YOUR INFORMATION:** Whether the question is qualitative, quantitative, or both, you will have to digest a lot of information. Write down the key pieces of information from each section, or create a chart that helps you sort out the issues or the math. Take the time to determine which would be the best tab to find the answer.

5. **LOOK AT THE STATEMENTS, AND ASK YOURSELF WHETHER OR NOT THAT IS TRUE:** For every inference or conclusion you have to make, you will find support in the content. As a quick check, you can try two options. The first is to find the specific support from the statements. If you can find support, then you know the answer is correct. However, if you cannot find the support, the answer cannot be correct. The second option is to ask yourself whether or not the answer is true based on the statements. If you can find a plausible alternative inference, perhaps the statement is false or the answer is no.

E-mail 1: E-mail from **HR manager** to prospective employee

Oct 19, 2011, 4:45 P.M.

I have just spoken with the finance director, and we are pleased to offer you the position of Analyst, Financial Services within our organization. Your starting salary will be $55,000 prorated to the date that you start. Your full health and dental benefits will take effect within three months of your start date. I have attached a standard contract that outlines everything in our official offer.

We are anxious to get you going, so we are hoping you are willing to start right away this upcoming Monday, October 24, 2011. We look forward to your early confirmation so that we can start the paperwork before your first day.

If you have any questions, please do not hesitate to contact me.

E-mail 2: From **prospective employee** in response to HR manager's
Oct 19, 2011, 4:45 P.M. message

Oct 21, 2011, 8:30 A.M.

Thank you so much for your offer. I am very pleased that you responded so promptly and are anxious to have me join your team. I want to ask for some more time to consider this offer, as I have been looking for a job externally over the past three months and now have other similar offers on the table.

Additionally, I would like to propose a later start date of November 14, 2011, because I would love to have some time to spend with my family on a vacation to celebrate the new position. My work-life balance is important to me since my wife and I had a baby last year and I have been working long hours over the past two years in my current role.

Lastly, I would like to ask for a higher starting base salary. The current industry rate, $55,000, is within the median range of salaries. However, your organization is well-known to be a Tier-1 company, so I would expect a salary more comparable to a top-quartile range. Additionally, I already have two years of experience in my current role as an analyst. I currently make $53,500 and thus would want a more senior role.

I look forward to your response.

TIP

On the actual GMAT, multiple documents (in this case, e-mails), will be in a document similar to an Excel document. You will be able to click back and forth between tabs containing different documents and sort information in multiple ways. However, for the sake of this book, the documents are presented one after another.

E-mail 3: E-mail from **HR manager** in response to the prospective employee's message.

Oct 21, 2:57 P.M.

Thank you for your e-mail. We understand your concerns and appreciate the time and energy you have put into your response.

At this time, I can offer you only a starting bonus of $6,000 if you start with us this coming Monday, October 24, 2011. I am authorized to also offer a new title of Senior Analyst, which will put you in the next higher salary grade, which will give you more room to grow with wage increases and bonuses. Finally, instead of our normal benefits package, I can offer additional room for more extended health and dental benefits, totaling approximately $2,000.

This offer is now final, conditional on your acceptance and nonnegotiable. We need to have a decision from you by Friday, October 21, 2011 at 5 P.M. Please confirm at your earliest convenience.

Consider each of the following statements. Does the information in the three sources support the inference as stated?

Yes	No	
○	○	The HR manager addressed the majority of the employee's demands.
○	○	The most important issue for the company is the starting date.
○	○	Both parties are in agreement over the starting salary and benefits.
○	○	If given similar offers from other companies, the prospective employee will likely favor a company that has a more flexible starting date.
○	○	If given similar offers from other companies, the prospective employee will likely not accept this current offer.

SOLUTION AND STRATEGY REVIEW

First, you should determine the gist of the question. This situation is basically a contract negotiation for employment. The person doing the hiring is negotiating the terms of the contract with the potential employee. More specifically, the first e-mail is the offer, which includes the title, salary, benefits, and start date. The second e-mail brings up issues surrounding the starting date and the salary. The third e-mail offers a starting bonus and extra benefits but remains firm on the starting date.

If you look at the purpose of each section, you can identify that the potential employee goes into some detail about the starting date. You can infer that this issue is quite important to him. He also mentions salary and puts together a cogent argument about his current salary, the industry, and his two years of experience.

What is really interesting is the last section. The person doing the hiring clearly has not directly addressed the potential hire's concerns and is not very flexible on the starting date.

You now have enough information and understanding to look at the questions.

(i) The employee's demands were starting time, base salary, and title. The HR manager offered a bonus, extra benefits, and a better title. Although there was accommodation on the job title, the HR manager did not meet the majority of the demands. **Therefore, the answer is No.**

(ii) The HR manager mentions expediting the process several times and has remained firm on the starting date, despite the employee's request. You can see key words such as "anxious," "early confirmation," and the entire last paragraph of the final e-mail saying that the offer was now "final." The company wants him to start right away. **Therefore, the answer is Yes.**

(iii) Although the HR manager offered extra benefits and the employee has needs for his new family, they are both still in disagreement over the starting salary. **Therefore, the answer is No.**

(iv) The key here is the "similar offers" from other companies. The employee has made it clear that a later starting date is important. If given the same offer, the employee "will likely" (another key phrase) accept an offer with a more favorable starting date. **Therefore, the answer is Yes.**

(v) This question is a little bit tougher, as you need to use some inductive reasoning here. The employee did mention that he was shopping around other offers. He also has been clear about the importance of a flexible starting date. Additionally, the HR manager has not addressed the potential employee's major concerns. Since other offers are at play, you can infer that he will "likely not" accept this offer. **Therefore, the answer is Yes.**

Note how important it is to understand the gist—subject, purpose, and conclusion—of the overall situation and each section. Understanding what drives each person and the main aspects of the case study are essential to doing well in this qualitative example of Multi-Source Reasoning.

PART 3

Quantitative

Quantitative Section: An Introduction

3

→ **PROBLEM-SOLVING DIRECTIONS FROM THE GMAT**

→ **PROBLEM-SOLVING STRATEGY, METHODS, AND TACTICS**

→ **DATA SUFFICIENCY DIRECTIONS FOR THE GMAT**

→ **DATA SUFFICIENCY STRATEGY, METHODS, AND TACTICS**

The good news about the quantitative or math section of the GMAT is that you've seen it before, probably in grade 11 or earlier. The chapters ahead review the fundamentals along with some of the more commonly tested topics. Go through at your own pace, making sure you have a solid understanding of each section because the learning is cumulative. The further you go, the more you build up a GMAT quantitative bag of tricks. Eventually, you will have several tools and tactics in your arsenal to defeat the GMAT—and isn't victory fun?

PROBLEM-SOLVING DIRECTIONS FROM THE GMAT

According to the GMAC, the following directions will appear on your screen just before your first problem-solving question.

> **DIRECTIONS:** Solve each problem, and indicate the best of the answer choices given.
>
> **Numbers:** All numbers used are real numbers.
>
> **Figures:** A figure accompanying a problem-solving question is intended to provide information useful in solving the problem. Figures are drawn as accurately as possible EXCEPT when it is stated in a specific problem that its figure is not drawn to scale. Straight lines may sometimes appear jagged. All figures lie on a plane unless otherwise indicated.

Problem-Solving Sample Question

1. A packer at M&M Nuggets Inc. wrapped boxes weighing 24, 16, 31, 6, 20, and 4 pounds. What was the median weight in pounds of the packages that the packer wrapped?
   (A) 16.67
   (B) 17
   (C) 18
   (D) 27.5
   (E) 31

PROBLEM-SOLVING STRATEGY, METHODS, AND TACTICS

We will cover several comprehensive strategies and tools for conquering the GMAT problem-solving questions. Below is a summary of what we will explore in more detail in the problem-solving chapter.

Problem-Solving Fundamentals

- Careless errors be gone!
- The secret is out about minimal or no calculations.
- The math is clean.
- Know how they deceive you.

Problem-Solving Strategies

- You need strong fundamentals.
- Invest in your immediate future.
- Harvest the garden of answer choices.
- Try this concept—conceptual thinking!
- Simplicity is the Ultimate Sophistication.
- Carry 3 big sticks—picking numbers, algebra, and number properties.

Problem-Solving Methods

Use the know-want-approach method:

1. What do you know?
2. What do you want?
3. What is your approach?

Problem-Solving Tactics

1. Pick numbers . . . wisely.
2. Use your best friends (algebra and number properties) . . . forever.
3. Don't break your back solving, try backsolving.
4. Construction, construction, what's your function?
5. Break it down!
6. Estimate, guess-timate, approximate to elucidate.
7. Process of elimination (POE): return of the friend.
8. Don't get tricked. Become a trickster.
9. Stop staring!
10. Let it go.

DATA SUFFICIENCY DIRECTIONS FOR THE GMAT

Below are the official directions from the GMAC that appear before your first data sufficiency problem on the GMAT.

DIRECTIONS: This problem consists of a question and two statements, labeled (1) and (2), in which certain data are given. You have to decide whether the data given in the statements are sufficient for answering the question. Using the data given in the statements plus your knowledge of mathematics and everyday facts (such as the number of days in July or the meaning of counterclockwise), you must indicate whether:

A. Statement (1) ALONE is sufficient, but statement (2) alone is not sufficient to answer the question asked;
B. Statement (2) ALONE is sufficient, but statement (1) alone is not sufficient to answer the question asked;
C. BOTH statements (1) and (2) TOGETHER are sufficient to answer the question asked, but NEITHER statement ALONE is sufficient;
D. EACH statement ALONE is sufficient to answer the question asked;
E. Statements (1) and (2) TOGETHER are NOT sufficient to answer the question asked, and additional data specific to the problem are needed.

Numbers: All numbers used are real numbers.

Figures: A figure accompanying a data sufficiency problem will conform to the information given in the question but will not necessarily conform to the additional information in statements (1) and (2).

Lines shown as straight can be assumed to be straight, and lines that appear jagged can also be assumed to be straight.

You may assume that positions of points, angles, regions, etc., exist in the order shown and that angle measures are greater than zero.

All figures lie in a plane unless otherwise indicated.

Note: If the data sufficiency problem asks you for the value of a quantity, the data given in the statements are sufficient only when it is possible to determine exactly one numerical value for the quantity.

SAMPLE QUESTION OVERVIEW

Question Stem	What is the value of x?
Statement 1	(1) The square of x is 25
Statement 2	(2) $x(x - 5) = 0$

DATA SUFFICIENCY STRATEGY, METHODS, AND TACTICS

We will cover several comprehensive strategies and tools for conquering the GMAT data sufficiency section. Below is a summary of what we will explore in more detail in the data sufficiency chapter.

1. **INVEST UP FRONT, AND MAKE IT COUNT.**
   - Avoid misreading the question and statements
   - Understand the macroquestion, and know what data sufficiency type it is
   - Determine what you know, want, and need.

2. **MANAGE THE INFORMATION IN A STRATEGIC AND TIMELY WAY**
   - Every statement implies something.
   - Know what you *know,* both direct and implied.
   - Avoid making assumptions.
   - Do not carry information from statement 1 into statement 2.

3. **LEVERAGE THE CONSTRUCT TO YOUR ADVANTAGE.**
   - Do not do calculations unless you have to.
   - Start with the easier statement.
   - Statements 1 and 2 never contradict.
   - Determine sufficiency by proving insufficiency.

4. **DON'T LET THE GAME FOOL YOU.**
   - The tests put the same info in each statement.
   - Do not forget that "no" can mean sufficient.
   - Watch out for the easy C.
   - When the tests asks for $a + b$, you do not need individual values.

5. **USE YOUR KNOWLEDGE OF GMAT THEORY, STRATEGIES, AND METHODOLOGIES TO SIMPLIFY.**
   - Manipulate the equations.
   - You always have your two BFF's (algebra and number properties).
   - Do not forget about 0 (zero).
   - Pick numbers.

Arithmetic

4

→ **ARITHMETIC DEFINITIONS AND OPERATIONS**
→ **STRATEGIES FOR CALCULATION SHORTCUTS**
→ **FRACTIONS**
→ **DECIMALS**
→ **FACTORS AND MULTIPLES**
→ **PROPERTIES OF NUMBERS**
→ **PERCENTS**
→ **RATIOS**

DIAGNOSTIC SKILL QUIZ

DIRECTIONS: Before continuing, try your hand at these arithmetic questions to assess your level of understanding. The answers will be explained throughout this chapter.

1. What is $\dfrac{0.375 \cdot 0.444 \cdot 0.75 \cdot 0.888}{0.333 \cdot 0.833 \cdot 0.8 \cdot 0.5} = ?$

    (A) 0.2
    (B) 0.333
    (C) 0.5
    (D) 0.75
    (E) 1

2. The sum of prime numbers that are between 110 and 125 is

    (A) 113
    (B) 119
    (C) 232
    (D) 240
    (E) 353

3. What is the value of the integer K?

    (1) K is a 3-digit prime number.
    (2) $88 \le K \le 102$

4. What is the lowest positive integer that is divisible by each of the integers 1 through 8, inclusive?

(A) 420
(B) 840
(C) 2520
(D) 5040
(E) 40,320

5. If S is an integer, which of the following must be odd?

(A) $S + 1$
(B) $2S - 1$
(C) $S^2 + 2$
(D) $S + 2$
(E) $2S$

6. If $abc > 0$, then which of the following must be true?

(A) $\dfrac{a}{b} < 0$
(B) $a > 0$
(C) $\dfrac{ab}{c} > 0$
(D) $bc < 0$
(E) $a > bc$

7. The selling price of a computer part is equal to the cost of the computer part plus the markup. The markup on computer part XZ-700 is what percent of the selling price?

(1) The selling price of the original computer is $1,000.

(2) The cost of computer part XZ-700 is exactly $\dfrac{1}{2}$ of its markup.

8. Karl and Alex were avid comic book collectors. The number of comic books that Karl and Alex owned was in the ratio of 5:3, respectively. After Karl sold Alex 10 of his comic books, the ratio of the number of comic books Karl had to the number that Alex had was 7:5. As a consequence, Karl had how many more comic books than Alex did?

(A) 30
(B) 40
(C) 60
(D) 90
(E) 150

> **CONTENT SUMMARY/CHECKLIST**
>
> By the end of this chapter, you should have enough information to review and understand the following topics:
>
> ☐ Arithmetic definitions and operations
> ☐ Strategies for calculation shortcuts
> ☐ Fractions
> ☐ Decimals
> ☐ Factors and multiples
> ☐ Properties of numbers
> ☐ Percents
> ☐ Ratios

INTRODUCTION

The best way to deal with math is to have fun with it. One of the reasons why the quantitative section proves challenging for students is that they likely have not done this kind of math in several years. If you do a practice test and score less than the 25th percentile on the quantitative section, you are probably missing many fundamental math skills. Even if you score above the 80th percentile, you may still have some gaps in basic definitions. Regardless, know that the math concepts on the GMAT are mostly grade 11 level or earlier. You have already "been there, done that" with success. Now you can do it again and hopefully have fun in the process. This section will introduce you to the basic definitions and arithmetic fundamentals that you need for your GMAT quantitative journey.

ARITHMETIC DEFINITIONS AND OPERATIONS

INTEGER: Any whole number that is not a fraction or decimal. It can be positive or negative. For example, –1200, –43, –2, –1, 0, 1, 2, 28, and 1462 are integers, and –0.6, $\frac{1}{2}$, and π are not integers.

EVEN INTEGER: Any integer that, when divided by 2, gives you another integer. For example, –4, –2, 0, 2, 4, 6, 8, and 10 are even integers.

ODD INTEGER: Any integer that, when divided by 2, gives you a noninteger. For example, –3, –1, 1, 3, 5, and 7 are odd integers.

REAL NUMBER: Any number on the number line. This includes (but is not limited to) positives and negatives, integers, rational and irrational numbers, roots, and π (pi). For example, –4.5, $-\frac{1}{3}$, 0, 2, $\frac{7}{37}$, $\sqrt{139}$, and 3.2 • 10^{87} are real numbers. The only numbers that are not real are called complex or imaginary numbers (e.g. $\sqrt{-1}$), and they are not tested on the GMAT.

DIVISOR OR FACTOR: For an integer N, the divisor is a positive integer that can divide into N without creating a remainder. For example, 1, 2, 3, 4, 6, and 12 are divisors of 12 while 0, 1.5, 5, and 10 are not divisors of 12.

MULTIPLE: A multiple of integer N results from multiplying N with another integer. For example, –7, 0, 7, 140, and 28,007 are multiples of 7 while –5, 1, 8, 139, and 28,005 are not.

PRIME NUMBER: An integer that is divisible by **only** itself and 1. Prime numbers have exactly 2 factors. For example, 2, 3, 5, 7, 29, and 31 are prime numbers while 4, 10, 15, and 35 are not prime numbers. Note that 0 and 1 are not prime numbers. Note also that 2 is the smallest prime number and the **only** even prime number.

DIVISION: If we look at the simple expression $\frac{7}{3} = 2$, r1, we find several terms used in division: 3 is the **divisor**, 2 is the **quotient**, 7 is the **dividend**, and 1 is the **remainder**.

STRATEGIES FOR CALCULATION SHORTCUTS

Test takers often make computational errors on the GMAT. You are expected to know all aspects of mathematical calculations and operations including addition, subtraction, multiplication, and division of integers, decimals, and fractions. You also have to do these computations quickly and efficiently but without sacrificing accuracy. The good news is that most GMAT quantitative questions require a conceptual approach with little need for calculations. Still, it is important that you master the beginner concepts.

Calculation Shortcuts

Many students have trouble with time management. Although most questions in the GMAT math section require few calculations, you can expect some. These provide you with an opportunity to save time by employing shortcuts. The seconds that you shave off each calculation will add up to minutes of extra time that you can apply to the harder questions. For example, if you can reduce your average time per question by even 20 seconds, you will save $37 \cdot 20 = 740$ seconds $= 12\frac{1}{3}$ minutes saved on the quantitative section!

MULTIPLICATION TABLES: To save time, you should **memorize** the classic times table.

x	1	2	3	4	5	6	7	8	9	10
1	1	2	3	4	5	6	7	8	9	10
2	2	4	6	8	10	12	14	16	18	20
3	3	6	9	12	15	18	21	24	27	30
4	4	8	12	16	20	24	28	32	36	40
5	5	10	15	20	25	30	35	40	45	50
6	6	12	18	24	30	36	42	48	54	60
7	7	14	21	28	35	42	49	56	63	70
8	8	16	24	32	40	48	56	64	72	80
9	9	18	27	36	45	54	63	72	81	90
10	10	20	30	40	50	60	70	80	90	100

You should also **memorize** these commonly seen multiples.

Perfect Squares		Powers of 2	Cubes and Fourths
$1^2 = 1$	$11^2 = 121$	$2^3 = 8$	$3^3 = 27$
$2^2 = 4$	$12^2 = 144$	$2^4 = 16$	$3^4 = 81$
$3^2 = 9$	$13^2 = 169$	$2^5 = 32$	$4^3 = 64$
$4^2 = 16$	$14^2 = 196$	$2^6 = 64$	$4^4 = 256$
$5^2 = 25$	$15^2 = 225$	$2^7 = 128$	$5^3 = 125$
$6^2 = 36$	$20^2 = 400$	$2^8 = 256$	$5^4 = 625$
$7^2 = 49$	$25^2 = 625$	$2^9 = 512$	$6^3 = 216$
$8^2 = 64$		$2^{10} = 1024$	
$9^2 = 81$			
$10^2 = 100$			

Multiplying and Dividing Larger Numbers

Remember that the mathematical operations on the GMAT are generally clean. That is, you will not be expected to manipulate complicated numbers. Instead, the numbers can usually be broken down for simpler computations. You can also use certain tricks to help you do the math in your head.

What is 32 • 15?

Solution: You can break this down to 30 • 15 = 450 plus 2 • 15 = 30 and add them together to get 480. You can also break this down to 32 • 10 = 320 plus 32 • 5 = 160 and add them together to get 480. Note that 32 • 5 is half of 32 $\times$ 10.

What is 651 ÷ 7?

Solution: To break this down, think of the multiple of 7 closest to 651 that you can quickly figure out in your head. In this case, 7 $\times$ 90 = 630. What is left over is 21 = 7 • 3. Therefore, the answer will be 90 + 3 = 93.

Simplify when you can: Look to simplify mathematical expressions whether at the beginning, middle, or end of a calculation.

$$144x = \frac{12y}{5}$$

Simplification: Instead of multiplying 5 • 144, divide 12 out of both sides to get $12x = \dfrac{y}{5}$, which simplifies to $y = 60x$.

Estimate where you can: Sometimes the answer choices are such that you don't need to calculate everything, you can just estimate.

701 • 52

The correct answer is going to be just a little bit more than $700 \times 50 = 35,000$, so look for that value among the choices. Furthermore, we know the correct answer will have a unit digit of 2 due to properties of numbers (discussed later in this book).

LEVERAGE FRACTIONS: Since you don't have a calculator, many decimal and percent calculations are much easier when you use fractions.

$$33.3\% \text{ of } 24 \text{ multiplied by } 0.25 \text{ becomes } \frac{1}{3} \cdot 24 \cdot \frac{1}{4} = \frac{24}{12} = 2.$$

---

1. What does $\dfrac{0.375 \cdot 0.444 \cdot 0.75 \cdot 0.888}{0.333 \cdot 0.833 \cdot 0.8 \cdot 0.5} = ?$

   (A) 0.2

   (B) 0.333

   (C) 0.5

   (D) 0.75

   (E) 1

Solution: The two quickest ways to answer this question are either by using fractions or by estimating. Fractions are much easier to manage. Since we know (or should know) all the decimal/fraction equivalents, we get $(\frac{3}{8} \cdot \frac{4}{9} \cdot \frac{3}{4} \cdot \frac{8}{9})/(\frac{1}{3} \cdot \frac{5}{6} \cdot \frac{4}{5} \cdot \frac{1}{2})$

Everything cancels out, which means the answer is about 1.

The alternative method would be to estimate. You might notice that

0.375 is a little more than 0.333   0.444 is a little less than 0.5

0. 888 is a little more than 0.833   0.75 is a little less than 0.8

This means you should get an answer close to 1.

The answer is E.

FRACTIONS

In GMAT math, using fractions is especially important since no calculators are allowed. A fraction is made up of 2 numbers: the numerator divided by the denominator.

$$\frac{\text{numerator}}{\text{denominator}}$$

Definitions and Properties

PROPER FRACTION: When the numerator is less than the denominator. For example,

$\frac{1}{2}, \frac{4}{5}, \frac{5}{13}$, and $\frac{15}{114}$.

IMPROPER FRACTION: When the numerator is greater than the denominator. For example, $\frac{2}{1}$, $\frac{5}{4}$, $\frac{13}{5}$, and $\frac{114}{15}$.

MIXED NUMBER: When a whole number and a fraction are combined. For example, $2\frac{1}{2}$, $3\frac{3}{4}$, and $7\frac{1}{3}$.

A fraction cannot have 0 as a denominator because this would make the number undefined. Integers can be expressed as fractions. For example, $12 = \frac{12}{1}$ and $5 = \frac{5}{1}$.

Fraction Operations

ADDITION AND SUBTRACTION

Fractions need to have the same or common denominator. You can multiply all the denominators together to find a common denominator. Instead, you can find the least common multiple (LCM) for all denominators, which is sometimes easier depending on the complexity of your calculations.

$$\frac{1}{2} + \frac{1}{8} - \frac{1}{5}$$

In this case, the common denominator is 2 • 8 • 5 = 80. However, you may notice that the least common denominator is 40, so let's use that.

$$\frac{20}{40} + \frac{5}{40} - \frac{8}{40} = \frac{(20+5-8)}{40} = \frac{17}{40}$$

Multiplication and Division

When multiplying 2 fractions, multiply the two numerators on top and then the two denominators on the bottom. When dividing 2 fractions, convert the equation to a multiplication problem by flipping the 2nd fraction.

$$\frac{3}{4} \cdot \frac{2}{7} = \frac{(3 \cdot 2)}{(4 \cdot 7)} = \frac{6}{28} = \frac{3}{14}$$

$$\frac{3}{4} \div \frac{2}{7} = \frac{3}{4} \cdot \frac{7}{2} = \frac{(3 \cdot 7)}{(4 \cdot 2)} = \frac{21}{8}$$

Fraction Conversions

On the GMAT, you will often need to convert decimals or percents into fractions. You will also need to convert fractions from one form to another.

$$225\% = 2.25 = 2\frac{1}{4} = \frac{9}{4}$$

All of these numbers are expressing similar values.

TIP

In most cases, you will need to convert mixed numbers into fractions to make your calculations easier.

CONVERTING MIXED NUMBERS

The following diagram shows the basic process.

$$3\frac{3}{5} = \frac{18}{5}, \text{ but how?}$$

$$3 \overset{\text{add}}{\underset{\text{multiply}}{\rightleftarrows}} \frac{3}{5}$$

1. Multiply the denominator by the integer of the fraction: $5 \cdot 3 = 15$.

2. Add this result to the numerator: $15 + 3 = 18$.

3. Set this result above the numerator: $\frac{18}{5}$.

CONVERTING DECIMALS

Each fraction is a division problem, one number divided by another or one numerator divided by a denominator. The GMAT is not going to give you very complicated decimals that require conversion. However, learning to convert either way is helpful in calculations. So it's much easier simply to **memorize** the most commonly occurring decimal/fraction equivalents. Some of the following are approximations.

$\frac{1}{5} = 0.5$	$\frac{1}{6} = 0.167$	$\frac{4}{9} = 0.444$
$\frac{1}{3} = 0.333$	$\frac{5}{6} = 0.833$	$\frac{5}{9} = 0.555$
$\frac{2}{3} = 0.666$	$\frac{1}{7} = 0.143$	$\frac{7}{9} = 0.777$
$\frac{1}{4} = 0.25$	$\frac{1}{8} = 0.125$	$\frac{8}{9} = 0.888$
$\frac{3}{4} = 0.75$	$\frac{3}{8} = 0.375$	$\frac{1}{10} = 0.1$
$\frac{1}{5} = 0.2$	$\frac{5}{8} = 0.625$	$\frac{3}{10} = 0.3$
$\frac{2}{5} = 0.4$	$\frac{7}{8} = 0.875$	$\frac{7}{10} = 0.7$
$\frac{3}{5} = 0.6$	$\frac{1}{9} = 0.111$	$\frac{9}{10} = 0.9$
$\frac{4}{5} = 0.8$	$\frac{2}{9} = 0.222$	$\frac{1}{11} = 0.0909$

Note that we left out such fractions as $\frac{2}{6}$ or $\frac{4}{10}$ because they reduce to $\frac{1}{3}$ and $\frac{2}{5}$, respectively. We also didn't include all of the sevenths as you will likely need only the first $\frac{1}{7}$ fraction.

Reducing Fractions

To simplify your calculations, you will often have to reduce a fraction. A fraction is reduced to its lowest term when the numerator and denominator have no common factors.

$$\frac{1000}{1200} = \frac{10}{12} = \frac{5}{6}$$

The 5 and 6 have no common factors, so you cannot reduce further.

The key to reducing fractions with large numbers is to find large common factors. In the example above, we could have divided by 2 a few times, but that would've taken more time. Instead, we divided by 100 right away to save time.

If you aren't sure if there are any common factors, you can either break down each number into prime factors or memorize and use divisibility rules. Here is a list of the most common divisibility rules.

DIVISIBILITY RULES FOR NUMBERS

Number	Divisibility Rule	Example
2	The number is even	108 is even, 108 = 54 • 2
3	The sum of the digits is divisible by 3	108, sum of digits is 1 + 0 + 8 = 9, which is a multiple of 3, 108 = 3 • 36
4	The last 2 digits represent a number that is divisible by 4	108, last 2 digits are 08, which represents a number divisible by 4, 108 = 4 • 27
5	The last digit of the number is either a 0 or a 5	1050 ends with a 5, 1050 = 5 • 210
7	Take the last digit of the number, double it, and then subtract it from the rest of the digits of the original number; if the result is divisible by 7, the original number is divisible by 7	1050, last digit is 0, double it we get 0, subtract that from the rest of the digits, we get 105 – 0 = 105, since 105 = 7 • 15, then 1050 is divisible by 7, 1050 = 7 • 150
10	The last digit of the number is a 0	1050, last digit Is 0, 1050 = 10 • 105
11	Take the difference between sums of alternate digits; if the result is divisible by 11, the original number is divisible by 11	4,862, we get 4 + 6 = 10 and 8 + 2 = 10; 10 – 10 = 0, which is divisible by 11; so 4,862 = 11 • 442
25	The last 2 digits of the number are divisible by 25	1050, last digits are divisible by 25, 1050 = 25 • 42

TIP

Note that we don't need divisibility rules for 6, 8, or 9 because we already have them for 2 and 3.

Another shortcut is to find the closest multiple that is easy to calculate. For an awkward number like 7, this works nicely. For example, what if we want to determine if 1050 is divisible by 7? We know that 700 is divisible by 7. If we subtract 1050 – 700, we get 350. We know that 350 is a multiple of 7; therefore 1050 is divisible by 7.

2. The sum of prime numbers that are between 110 and 125 is

    (A) 113

    (B) 119

    (C) 232

    (D) 240

    (E) 353

Solution: Using our divisibility rules, we can quickly determine which numbers are prime. The first step is to list out all the odd numbers that do not end in 5 since we already know that even numbers this high will not be prime and neither will multiples of 5. This gives us 111, 113, 117, 119, 121, 123. From this list, we know that 111 and 123 are multiples of 3 because the sums of their digits are multiples of 3. The next prime number to look at is 7. Since $7 \cdot 10 = 70$ and 119 is 49 away, we know that 119 is a multiple of 7. We know 121 is 11^2, so that is out. Now we are down to 113 and 117. If you look at the answer choices, there is no choice for 230, which is the sum of these two numbers. Therefore, 113 must be the only prime. If we had used the prime number 13, we would have seen that $13 \cdot 10 = 130$, which is 13 away from 117. Therefore 117 is a multiple of 13.

The answer is A.

DECIMALS

Although fractions are easier to use in GMAT calculations than decimals, you still need to understand decimals. Some of the most common things to remember are below.

TERMINATING DECIMAL: Any decimal that has a finite number of nonzero digits. For example, $\frac{2}{5} = 0.4$.

NONTERMINATING DECIMAL: Any decimal that has an infinite number of nonzero digits. For example, $\frac{3}{11} = 0.2727\ldots$

ADDITION OR SUBTRACTION OF DECIMALS

When adding or subtracting two numbers with decimal places, make sure you line up the decimal points. You may need to add zeros to help you.

$$134.6 - 3.547 = ?$$

$$\begin{array}{r} 134.600 \\ - 3.547 \\ \hline 131.053 \end{array}$$

MULTIPLICATION OF DECIMALS

When multiplying two numbers with decimal places, the number of decimal places in the answer must equal the sum of all the decimal places in the numbers being multiplied. Be sure to place the number with the fewest digits on the bottom.

What is 1.8 × 0.1212?

$$
\begin{array}{r}
0.1212 \\
\times\ \ \ 1.8 \\
\hline
9696 \\
+\ 12120 \\
\hline
0.21816
\end{array}
$$

DIVISION OF DECIMALS

When dividing numbers that have decimal points, always remove the decimal points before calculating. Determine which number has the most decimal places. Then move the decimal point to the right in both numbers as many times as is necessary to remove the decimal places.

Divide 0.0024 by 0.008.

Since 0.0024 has the most decimal places, we need to move the decimal point to the right 4 times in each number. This gives us $\frac{24}{80} = 0.3$

FACTORS AND MULTIPLES

Prime Numbers

Understanding prime numbers is essential for GMAT questions that involve factorization, fractions, and properties of numbers.

> **PRIME NUMBER:** Any positive number that has exactly 2 factors, itself and 1. For example, 2, 3, 5, 7, 11, 13, 17, 19, 23, 29, 31, 37, 41, 43, and 47 are prime numbers.

> **COMPOSITE NUMBERS:** Numbers greater than 1 that are not prime numbers.

You should memorize all the prime numbers less than 50. They show up often on the GMAT and this will save you time.

If a number is not prime, it can be expressed as a multiple of 2 or more prime factors.

30 = 2 • 3 • 5.

Factor (or Divisor)

> **FACTOR:** A positive integer that can be evenly divided into another integer, N, resulting in another integer.

30 has the factors 1, 2, 3, 5, 6, 10, 15, and 30.

Factors are always positive. Remember that 1 is a factor of all integers and 0 is never a factor.

TIP

0 and 1 are not prime numbers.

2 is the only even prime number. The GMAT will have many questions involving prime numbers. The trick is often to remember the number 2.

The quickest way to determine the factors of a number, whether prime factors or all the factors, is to use a factor tree.

[30 broken down into 6, 5 and then the 6 broken down into 2, 3]

[280 broken down into 14, 20, then 7, 2 and 5, 2, 2, then 7, 2, 2, 5, 2]

When you factor a number, first try to break it down into factor pairs that are close to the square root. Note that the 280 above could have been broken down into 140 • 2, but the process would have taken longer.

---

3. What is the value of the integer K?
   (1) K is a 3-digit prime number.
   (2) $88 \leq K \leq 102$

Solution: This is a data sufficiency problem type known as a straight solve, where we are looking for only one value in order to have sufficiency. Statement 1 tells us that K can be any 3-digit prime number. Since there are definitely more than one 3-digit prime numbers, this is insufficient. Statement 2 tells us that K can be any integer between 88 and 102 inclusive. This means we have multiple possible values, therefore this is insufficient. When we combine the 2 statements, K can only be a 3-digit prime number and the number is 100, 101, or 102. Since we know 100 and 102 are not prime numbers, 101 must be a prime number.

The answer is C.

If you are still unsure, you could check to see if 7 divides into 101, but it doesn't. There is no need to check 11 as a possible factor because $11^2 = 121$, a number greater than 101. This means that in order for 11 to be a factor of 101, it would have to be multiplied by a number smaller than itself. Since we know no other numbers less than 11 are factors except for 1, 101 must be a prime number.

GREATEST COMMON FACTOR (GCF): The largest number that divides evenly into each of the numbers given. The best way to determine the GCF is to look at the prime factors. The GCF is the product of all the prime factors the numbers have in common.

> The GCF of 42 (which is 2 • 3 • 7) and of 70 (which is 2 • 5 • 7)
> is 2 • 7 = 14

TIP

By definition,
0 is a multiple
of all integers.

Multiples

MULTIPLE: A multiple of any number is that number multiplied by an integer.

> 6, 9, 12, 15 are all multiples of 3 because $3 \times 2 = 6$, $3 \times 3 = 9$,
> $3 \times 4 = 12$, and $3 \times 5 = 15$.

Note that if we multiply 2 and 3 to get 6, then 6 is a multiple of both 2 and 3. Conversely, 2 and 3 are factors of 6.

LEAST COMMON MULTIPLE (LCM): The smallest nonzero number that is a multiple of 2 or more given numbers. The key to finding the LCM involves prime factorization. You need to look at each individual number and make sure that the LCM includes the minimum required prime factors for each number.

> The LCM of 42 (which is $2 \cdot 3 \cdot 7$) and of 56 (which is $2 \cdot 2 \cdot 2 \cdot 7$)
> is $2 \cdot 2 \cdot 2 \cdot 3 \cdot 7 = 168$.

42 has 2, 3, and 7 as factors. 56 has 2, 2, 2 and 7 as factors. This means that the LCM must have at least one 7, one 3, but most importantly, it must have at least three 2s in order to be a multiple of 56.

---

4. What is the lowest positive integer that is divisible by each of the integers 1 through 8, inclusive?

(A) 420

(B) 840

(C) 2520

(D) 5040

(E) 40,320

Solution: Break down the integers into their prime factors. Then multiply the terms. You would get $1 \cdot 2 \cdot 3 \cdot 2^2 \cdot 5 \cdot (2 \cdot 3) \cdot 7 \cdot 2^3$. What we are looking for is the least common multiple (LCM). The rule for LCM is that we need to have the minimum required prime factors for each number. Therefore, there needs to be at least one 7, one 5, one 3, and three 2s. This gives us $2 \cdot 2 \cdot 2 \cdot 3 \cdot 5 \cdot 7 = 840$. Note that the quick way to do this calculation is

> $5 \cdot 2 = 10 \; \rightarrow \; 10 \cdot 3 = 30 \; \rightarrow \; 30 \cdot 7 = 210 \; \rightarrow \; 210 \cdot 2 = 420 \; \rightarrow \; 420 \cdot 2 = 840$

The answer is B.

PROPERTIES OF NUMBERS

Number properties determine how numbers work—how they increase, decrease, or change in value. For example, when you multiply two negative numbers, the result is a positive number. When you square a positive proper fraction, the number becomes smaller. Understanding number properties is essential for doing many GMAT questions. You will need them mostly on data sufficiency questions. However, with certain problem-solving questions, especially those that seem to require far too many calculations, you can use number properties to reduce your calculations and more quickly find a solution.

Even and Odd Integers

EVEN INTEGERS: Integers that are divisible by 2. For example, the integers {. . . –6, –4, –2, 0, 2, 4, 6, . . . } form the set of even integers.

ODD INTEGERS: Integers that are not divisible by 2. For example, the integers { . . . –5, –3, –1, 1, 3, 5 . . . } form the set of odd integers.

You should understand and **memorize** the following rules.

- The sum and difference of two even integers is even: $2 + 4 = 6$ and $6 – 4 = 2$.
- The sum and difference of two odd integers is even: $3 + 5 = 8$ and $5 – 3 = 2$.
- The sum and difference of an odd integer and an even integer is odd: $2 + 3 = 5$ and $5 – 2 = 3$.
- The product of two even integers is even: $2 \cdot 4 = 8$.
- The product of two odd integers is odd: $3 \cdot 5 = 15$.
- The product of an odd integer and an even integer is even: $3 \cdot 2 = 6$

TIP

If you forget the rules, you can always pick numbers as we did above to demonstrate the rules.

5. If S is an integer, which of the following must be odd?
   - (A) $S + 1$
   - (B) $2S – 1$
   - (C) $S^2 + 2$
   - (D) $S + 2$
   - (E) $2S$

Solution: Since we see the key word "odd," this is a properties of numbers question. We can look at each answer choice and determine if its answer can be even. If yes, then eliminate the choice from contention.

   - (A) If $S = 3$, then this would be even. Not true.
   - (B) $2S$ will always be even. When we subtract 1, we will get an odd integer. True.
   - (C) If S is even, then S^2 will be even. When we add 2, it will stay even. Not true.
   - (D) If S is even, then $S + 2$ will remain even. Not true.
   - (E) $2S$ must be even. Not true.

The answer is B.

Positive and Negative

Just like with odd and even numbers, positive (+) and negative (–) numbers have specific rules.

TIP

Note that zero by definition is an even integer that is neither positive nor negative.

Multiplication	**Division**
$(–) \cdot (+)$ or $(+) \cdot (–) = (–)$	$(–) \div (+)$ or $(+) \div (–) = –$
$(–) \cdot (–) = (+)$	$(–) \div (–) = +$
$(+) \cdot (+) = (+)$	$(+) \div (+) = +$

6. If $abc > 0$, then which of the following must be true?

(A) $\dfrac{a}{b} < 0$

(B) $a > 0$

(C) $\dfrac{ab}{c} > 0$

(D) $bc < 0$

(E) $a > bc$

Solution: If abc is positive, that means that either all 3 values are positive or 1 value is positive and the other 2 values are negative. The best way to answer this question is to look at each choice in turn and find numbers to prove whether or not it is possible. Alternatively, you can use your understanding of properties of numbers to eliminate answer choices.

(A) Since a and b can be positive, this is not necessarily true.

(B) Since a can be positive or negative, this is not necessarily true.

(C) If all three values are positive, then this works. If two values are negative and one is positive, it still works. If $a = 1$, $b = 2$, $c = 3$, then $\dfrac{ab}{c} = \dfrac{2}{3}$. If $a = -1$, $b = -2$, and $c = 3$, you still get $\dfrac{ab}{c} = \dfrac{2}{3}$.

(D) Since 2 values can be positive, this is not necessarily true.

(E) This is not necessarily true because we don't know the values of a, b or c.

The answer is C.

Units Digit

As we saw in the section on decimals, the units digit of a number is the number just to the left of the decimal point and just to the right of the tens place. Understanding how the unit digit works can greatly increase your computation speed.

What is the unit digit of 6,797 • 13,473?

The GMAT does not expect you to do the long calculation. Rather, you can use properties of numbers. The first number has the unit digit 7, and the second number has the unit digit 3. Because $7 \cdot 3 = 21$, we know that the resulting number, no matter how huge it is, will end in a unit digit of 1.

Since you have already memorized your basic times table, you can calculate the unit digit for any multiple of large numbers.

PERCENTS

Understanding percent calculations will greatly increase your computation speed and minimize mindless errors. Your ability to maneuver quickly among fractions, decimals, and percents will be a key to success on test day.

Percent, Fraction, and Decimal Conversions

Percent	Fraction	Decimal
40%	$\frac{40}{100} = \frac{2}{5}$	0.4
320%	$\frac{320}{100} = \frac{16}{5}$	3.20
0.4%	$\frac{0.4}{100} = \frac{1}{250}$	0.004

"Percent" means per 100. For example, 20% means 20 per 100. Percents are used to measure or report the change in an amount. You hear it all the time in statements like "X stock rose 22% today in massive trading" or "24% of students failed that course." To determine percent increases and decreases quickly you need to know the basic formula:

$$\text{Percent change} = \left(\frac{(\text{Future value} - \text{Present value})}{(\text{Present value})} \right) \cdot 100$$

If you let FV mean "future value" and PV mean "present value" you can write the formula like:

$$\% \text{ change} = \left(\frac{(FV - PV)}{(PV)} \right) \cdot 100$$

$$\text{The percent change from 12 to 15 is } \left(\frac{(15 - 12)}{12} \right) \cdot 100 = 25\%.$$

You should also be able to calculate quickly percent increases and decreases algebraically using the formula:

$$\text{Increase or decrease of a number} = \left(1 + \frac{(\text{percent increase or decrease})}{100} \right) \cdot (\text{The number})$$

If x increases by 30%, then you get $(1 + 0.3)x$ or $1.3x$.
If x decreases by 30%, then you get $(1 - 0.3)x$ or $0.7x$.

TIP

When we increase and then decrease a number by the same percentage, the resulting number is always lower than the original number.

> Stock x goes up by 80% in year 1 but then decreases by 80% in year 2. By what percentage did the value of the stock change from the beginning to after year 2?

Solution: There are many ways to do this problem, but let's try using algebra.

We start at $x \rightarrow 1.8x$ after year 1 $\rightarrow (1.8) \cdot (0.2)x$ after year 2.

$1.8 = \frac{9}{5}$ and $0.2 = \frac{1}{5}$. Therefore we get $\frac{9}{5} \cdot \frac{1}{5}x = \frac{9x}{25}$, which is a decrease of $\frac{16x}{25}$ or 64%.

TIP

Make sure you know the difference between "percent change" and "percent of."

Another great strategy with percent questions is to pick numbers, especially 100. For this example, we would do the following.

We start with $100 \rightarrow 180$ after year 1 $\rightarrow 180 \cdot 0.2 = 36$ after year 2 or a 64% decrease.

Note that we would have gotten the same answer had the stock decreased first and then increased.

7. The selling price of a computer part is equal to the cost of making the computer part plus the markup. The markup on computer part XZ–700 is what percent of the selling price?
   (1) The selling price of the original computer is $1,000.
   (2) The cost of computer part XZ-700 is exactly ½ of its markup.

Solution: In this data sufficiency question, you need a relationship or an equation between the cost and markup of the computer part XZ-700. We know that price (P) equals cost (C) plus markup (M) or $P = C + M$. We are trying to find the value of M/P as a percent. Statement 1 gives us useless information (by itself); therefore, it is insufficient. Statement 2 tells us that $C = 0.5M$. By substitution we get $P = 0.5M + M \rightarrow P = 1.5M \rightarrow M/P = 1/1.5$, so statement 2 is therefore sufficient.

The answer is B.

RATIOS

Ratio: A proportional relationship that compares two or more numbers. The ratio of x to y is written as $x:y$ or $\dfrac{x}{y}$, which is read as "x to y." It is a relationship of a part to a part or a part to a whole. Interpreting ratios properly is critical.

> In a GMAT class, the ratio of females to males is $\dfrac{1}{3}$.
> What proportion of the class is female?

Solution: Be careful when you write this out. You should get $\dfrac{\text{F:M:Total}}{1:3:4}$.

Note that we often need to keep track of the total of all the parts in order to interpret the question properly. In this case, the sum of the parts is 4. The proportion is now $\dfrac{1}{4}$ and not $\dfrac{1}{3}$ as many students might think.

> If the ratio of dogs, cats, and mice in a pet store is $\dfrac{\text{D:C:M:Total}}{2:3:5:10}$,
>
> then the percentage of dogs in the store would be $\dfrac{2}{10}$ = 20%.

STRATEGIES FOR RATIOS

1. Do not forget about the sum of the parts when writing out the ratio. Note also that the total actual amount will be a multiple of this number. Multiples are a big factor in ratio problems.
2. Try to line up the ratios when doing calculations in order to keep a clear structure.
3. When you are given a ratio and you multiply or divide any of its parts, you can determine the new ratio. However, if you add or subtract any of the parts, you cannot determine a new ratio without having a clear reference amount.
4. When dealing with humans or animals, you cannot have ratios that are not whole numbers. This can be a clue in determining the minimum numbers of people or animals. For example, if the ratio of men: women, is 7:13 then minimally the room has 20 people.
5. When determining the exact number for any ratio, you need to have only a specific reference number to calculate the rest.
6. If the numbers are small, sometimes you can solve ratio problems just by writing out the first few possibilities.

---

8. Karl and Alex were avid comic book collectors. The number of comic books that Karl and Alex owned were in the ratio of 5:3, respectively. After Karl sold Alex 10 of his comic books, the ratio of the number of comic books Karl had to the number that Alex had was 7:5. As a consequence, Karl had how many more comic books than Alex did after the sale?

(A) 30
(B) 40
(C) 60
(D) 90
(E) 150

Solution: If we represent the before and after ratios using algebra, we would get

Before: $\dfrac{K}{A} = \dfrac{5}{3} \rightarrow 3K = 5A.$ Multiplying by 5 gets $\rightarrow 15K = 25A.$

After: $\dfrac{(K-10)}{(A+10)} = \dfrac{7}{5} \rightarrow 5(K-10) = 7(A+10) \rightarrow 5K - 50 = 7A + 70 \rightarrow 5K = 7A + 120.$

Multiplying by 3 gets $15K = 21A + 360$. By combining the 2 equations, we get

$25A = 21A + 360 \rightarrow 4A = 360 \rightarrow A = 90.$ Thus $K = 150.$

The difference is 60, but when Karl sold his 10 comics, the difference became 40.

The answer is B.

1. If y is an integer, is $\dfrac{3^y}{10,000} > 1$?

   (1) $\dfrac{100}{3^y} < 0.01$

   (2) $\sqrt{3^y} = 243$

2. At a business superstore, Stephen spends $\dfrac{1}{3}$ of his money on software, $\dfrac{1}{7}$ on accessories, and $\dfrac{1}{10.5}$ on paper products. If he spends the remaining $90 on gift cards, how much did Stephen spend at the business superstore?

   (A) $90
   (B) $110
   (C) $140
   (D) $210
   (E) $260

3. If r and s are positive integers and $900s = r^3$, which of the following must be an integer?:

   I. $\dfrac{s}{\left(3 \cdot 5 \cdot \left(2^3\right)\right)}$

   II. $\dfrac{s}{\left(\left(3^2\right) \cdot 5 \cdot 2^2\right)}$

   III. $\dfrac{s}{\left(3 \cdot 2^2 \cdot \left(5^2\right)\right)}$

   (A) I only
   (B) II only
   (C) II and III only
   (D) I and II only
   (E) None of the above

4. If x is an odd integer and y is an even integer, which of the following must be true?
   (A) y is not a factor of x.
   (B) xy is an odd integer.
   (C) x^2 is an even integer.
   (D) $y - x$ is an even integer.
   (E) x is a prime number.

5. In Centreville High School, 20 percent of the student body are athletes. In Smallville High School, 25 percent of the student body are athletes. If Smallville has 60 percent more students than Centreville, then the number of athletes in Smallville is what percent of half of the athletes in Centreville?

(A) 25%

(B) 50%

(C) 100%

(D) 200%

(E) 400%

6. What is the tens digit of the 2-digit positive integer x?

(1) x divided by 20 has a remainder of 17.

(2) x divided by 11 has a remainder of 0.

7. A terminating decimal is defined as any decimal that has only a finite number of nonzero digits such as 0.25, 100, and 6.375. If x and y are positive integers, is $\frac{x}{y}$ a terminating decimal?

(1) $190 < x < 210$

(2) $y = 8$

8. A world-famous blogger writes about only 3 topics—health and wellness, entrepreneurship, and cars. The ratio of health and wellness blogs to car blogs is 3 to 2. The ratio of car blogs to entrepreneurship blogs is 4 to 3. If the total number of blog posts is greater than 500, which one of following can be the total number of blog posts?

(A) 501

(B) 504

(C) 507

(D) 508

(E) 509

9. The ratio of the number of fine-dining restaurants to the number of fast-food restaurants in country X is the same as in country Y. What is the ratio of the number of fast-food restaurants in country X to the number of fast-food restaurants in country Y?

(1) The ratio of the number of fine-dining restaurants to the number of fast-food restaurants in country X is 1 to 10.

(2) There are 5,000 more fast-food restaurants in country X then there are in country Y.

SOLUTIONS

1. **(D)** We can manipulate the original question stem to ask if $3^y > 10,000$.

   Statement 1 can be manipulated by multiplying both sides by 3^y, which gives us $100 < 0.01(3^y) \rightarrow$ Multiply both sides by 100 to get $10,000 < 3^y$, which is exactly what the question is asking for. *Sufficient*

   Statement 2 tell us that if we square both sides, we will get $3^y = 243^2 = (3^5)^2$, which means we can solve for y and that $y = 10$. *Sufficient*

   Each statement alone is sufficient.

2. **(D)** This is a fraction question. The key to doing this quickly is to recognize the common denominator. We get $\frac{1}{3} + \frac{1}{7} + \frac{1}{10.5} = \frac{7}{21} + \frac{3}{21} + \frac{2}{21} = 12/21$ of the total. The rest of the amount, $90, represents $\frac{9}{21}$ of the total. Therefore the total is $90 \cdot \frac{21}{9} = \$210$.

3. **(E)** This question tests your knowledge of prime factors. If we break down $900s$, we get
$$90 \cdot 10 \cdot s = 9 \cdot 10 \cdot 5 \cdot 2 \cdot s = 3 \cdot 3 \cdot 5 \cdot 2 \cdot 5 \cdot 2 \cdot s = r^3$$

   Since s and r are positive integers and $r^3 = 2 \cdot 2 \cdot 3 \cdot 3 \cdot 5 \cdot 5$, then each side of the expression is a perfect cube. Therefore, s must have minimally $2 \cdot 3 \cdot 5$ as factors in order for the expression to remain a cube. It could, for example, have $2 \cdot 3 \cdot 5 \cdot 7^3$ as factors because it is still a cube. However, we should look at the least possible value. If s was $2 \cdot 3 \cdot 5$, then none of the three expressions given would be an integer.

4. **(A)** One way to solve this properties of numbers question is to pick numbers to prove four of the statements false. Alternatively, you should be able to leverage your thorough understanding of number properties, especially since you should know the theory anyway.

   (A)   If y is even, it cannot be a factor of x, which is odd. True

   (B)   Odd • even is always even, just like $3 \cdot 2 = 6$. False

   (C)   An odd number squared is still odd, e.g., $3^2 = 9$. False

   (D)   Even – odd = odd, just like $6 - 3 = 3$. False

   (E)   Most prime numbers are odd, except for 2. Regardless, if x is odd, it is not necessarily a prime number. False

5. **(E)** This question can confuse test takers. Be sure to read and sort the information carefully. Percent questions are often simplified with the picking numbers tactic. Let's say the number of students in Centreville High School (CHS) is 100. Then the number of athletes at CHS is 20% or 20 students. Smallville High School (SHS) has 60% more students than CHS, so the number of students at SHS is $100(1.6) = 160$ students. Since 25% of SHS students are athletes, SHS has $160 \cdot (25\%) = 40$ athletes. Watch the wording of the problem. We are comparing the 40 athletes at SHS to **half** the athletes at CHS, or $\frac{1}{2} \cdot 20 = 10$. 40 is what percent of 10? It's 400%.

6. **(C)** Start with what we **know**—x is a positive integer and has 2 digits. Then determine what we **want**—the tens digit and only one possible answer. Let's look at the statements to see if they give us what we **need**.

Statement 1 tells us that x could be 17, 37, 57, 77, or 97. 17 is here because when we divide 17 by 20, we get 0 and a remainder of 17. Regardless, we have multiple values for x. *Insufficient*

Statement 2 tells us that x could be any 2 digit multiple of 11, which means $x = 11, 22, 33, 44, 55, 66, 77, 88$ or 99. *Insufficient*

When we combine the statements, we now know that x could only be 77. *Sufficient*

Both statements together are sufficient.

7. **(B)** We know that x and y are positive integers, and we know the definition of a terminating decimal. Statement 1 gives us no information about the denominator; therefore it's impossible to tell what the decimal would be when you divide.

Example: $200 \div 3 = 66.666\ldots$ or $\dfrac{200}{400} = 0.5$ *Insufficient*

Statement 2 gives us a value for the denominator, but we have no value for the numerator. The GMAT test makers want us to think that the answer is obviously C. However, if you try a few numbers, you'll see that when you divide any integer by 8, you always get a terminating decimal.

$\dfrac{3}{8} = 0.375 \qquad \dfrac{10}{8} = 1.25 \qquad \dfrac{17}{8} = 2.125 \qquad \dfrac{40}{8} = 5$ *Sufficient*

Statement 2 alone is sufficient.

8. **(C)** This is a common ratio problem set up where we have two different ratios and a common element between them. The best way to solve this is to line up the ratios side by side and find a common multiple to relate them to each other.

$\underline{H : C} \qquad \underline{C : E} \rightarrow$ need a common multiple for C $\rightarrow \qquad \underline{H : C} \qquad \underline{C : E}$
$\,3 : 2 \qquad\;\; 4 : 3 \rightarrow$ multiply the 1st ratio by 2 $\qquad\qquad\quad 6 : 4 \qquad\quad 4 : 3$

Thus the full ratio of blog posts is H : C : E : Total $\rightarrow$ don't forget about the total
$$6 : 4 : 3 : 13 \rightarrow \text{the total is 13}$$

Since the total of the ratios is 13, the total number of blog posts must be a multiple of 13. Only one of the answer choices can work, so try to find a multiple of 13 that is close to 500.

130 is a multiple   390 is a multiple $390 + 130 = 520$ $520 - 13 = 507$

9. **(E)** Let's use the know-want-need approach.

Know: $\dfrac{FD_x}{FF_x} = \dfrac{FD_y}{FF_y} \rightarrow$ we also know that $\dfrac{FD_x}{FD_y} = \dfrac{FF_x}{FF_y}$

$\rightarrow FD_x$ and FF_x are the number of fine-dining and fast-food restaurants, respectively, in country X.

$\rightarrow FD_y$ and FF_y are the number of fine-dining and fast-food restaurants, respectively, in country Y.

Want: $\dfrac{FF_x}{FF_y}$

Need: FF_x and FF_y or $\dfrac{FD_x}{FD_y}$ or enough equations or relationships with the 4 variables in order to solve for $\dfrac{FF_x}{FF_y}$

Statement 1 tells us that $\dfrac{FD_x}{FF_x} = \dfrac{1}{10}$ → Since $\dfrac{FD_x}{FF_x} = \dfrac{FD_y}{FF_y}$ then $\dfrac{FD_y}{FF_y} = 1/10$. From this we get $FF_x = 10\,FD_x$ and $FF_y = 10FD_y$.

When we plug this into the "want" expression, we get $\dfrac{FF_x}{FF_y} = \dfrac{10FD_x}{10FD_y}$

However, we still don't know the values of FD_x or FD_y. *Insufficient*

Statement 2 tells us that $FF_x = FF_y + 5{,}000$ → This gives $\dfrac{FF_x}{FF_y} = \dfrac{\left(FF_y + 5{,}000\right)}{FF_y}$

However, we still don't know the value of FF_y. *Insufficient*

When we combine statements 1 and 2, we still don't have all the information that we need to solve. We can try picking numbers to understand this better.

If $FF_y = 5{,}000$ then $FF_x = 10{,}000$ → $\dfrac{FF_x}{FF_y} = \dfrac{10{,}000}{5{,}000} = \dfrac{2}{1}$.

If $FF_y = 1{,}000$ then $FF_x = 6{,}000$ → $\dfrac{FF_x}{FF_y} = \dfrac{6{,}000}{1{,}000} = \dfrac{6}{1}$.

Both statements together are still not sufficient.

Algebra

5

→ **ALGEBRAIC TRANSLATION**
→ **ABSOLUTE VALUE**
→ **EXPONENTS AND ROOTS**
→ **ALGEBRAIC CALCULATIONS AND OPERATIONS**
→ **ALGEBRAIC EQUATIONS**
→ **INEQUALITIES**
→ **FUNCTIONS, SYMBOLS, AND SEQUENCES**

ALGEBRA: DIAGNOSTIC SKILL QUIZ

DIRECTIONS: Before continuing, try your hand at these algebra questions to assess your level of understanding. The answers will be explained throughout this chapter.

1. Fred's age is 5 more than twice Janet's age. In 20 years, Janet's age tripled will be 7 more than Fred's age doubled. How old will Fred be 10 years from now?

   (A) 21
   (B) 24
   (C) 30
   (D) 31
   (E) 62

2. If $27^{x+2}25^y = 3^9 5^{x-3}$, what is the value of y?

   (A) −3
   (B) −2
   (C) −1
   (D) 0.5
   (E) 2

3. What is $\left(\left(\sqrt[3]{\left(\sqrt[4]{256}\right)}\right)^3\right)^2$?

   (A) $\sqrt{2}$
   (B) $2\sqrt{2}$
   (C) 8
   (D) $8\sqrt{2}$
   (E) 16

4. A radio interviewer goes to the streets and randomly selects 60 people to find out who is going to watch the Super Bowl. How many are going to watch the Super Bowl?

   (1) From the sample, the number of people who are not watching the Super Bowl is 12 less than the number who are watching it.

   (2) From the sample, twice the number of people who are watching the Super Bowl is 3 times the number of people who are not watching it.

5. Which of the following equations is NOT equivalent to $9a^2 = (b-3)(b+3)$?

   (A) $a^2 = (b^2 - 9)/9$

   (B) $(3a - b)(3a + b) = -9$

   (C) $18a^2 - 2b^2 + 18 = 0$

   (D) $27a^2 = (3b - 9)(b + 3)$

   (E) $3a^2 + 6 = b^2$

6. Is $xy > 5$?

   (1) $2x - y > 6$

   (2) $x + 3y < 17$

7. The function $f(x)$ is equal to the square of a number lessened by 5. The function $g(x)$ is equal to a number tripled. What is $f(g(2))$?

   (A) 4

   (B) 7

   (C) 13

   (D) 22

   (E) 31

8. In the infinite sequence $a_1, a_2, a_3 \ldots, a_n$, each term after the first is equal to triple the previous term. If $a_4 - a_3 = 36$, what is the value of a_1?

   (A) $\dfrac{6}{7}$

   (B) 1

   (C) 2

   (D) $\dfrac{24}{7}$

   (E) 4

ALGEBRA: CONTENT SUMMARY/CHECKLIST

By the end of this chapter, you should have enough information to review and understand the following topics:

☐ Algebraic translation
☐ Absolute value
☐ Exponents and roots
☐ Algebraic calculations and operations
☐ Algebraic equations
☐ Quadratic Equations
☐ Factoring
☐ Inequalities
☐ Functions, symbols, and sequences

INTRODUCTION

Algebra intimidates many GMAT math students. It is often the topic that separates the strong from the weak. Remember, though, that you were exposed to algebra concepts in high school and now you are much smarter! We've said before that your two best friends in GMAT math are algebra and properties of numbers. Why? Algebra is the language of math. It's how we translate problems, unlock keys, and simplify our process to solve even the toughest of questions. Although the GMAT categorizes 25% of the quantitative questions as algebra, you will find that you can you can apply algebra more than 60% of the time. Mastering algebra will give you the largest gain in your GMAT studies. So why not get to know algebra and be good friends with it?

Simply put, algebra uses variables or symbols, such as letters, to represent values in math. At the basic level:

Let x = whatever it is we are looking for

In most cases, you should let the variable equal exactly the above—what you are looking for or the unknown. From there, you can build the algebraic equation that needs to be solved. You are tested in many ways. The most common questions ask you to solve for one or more unknowns, usually in a word problem or a data sufficiency problem. Other times, you will have to work with specific equations, expressions, exponents, or roots.

ALGEBRAIC TRANSLATION

Often the biggest obstacle in algebra is translating word problems. Here are some of the common key words that you might see on the GMAT.

ALGEBRA TRANSLATION KEYWORDS

Addition	Increased by, more than, combined, together, total of, sum, added to
Subtraction	Decreased by, minus, less, difference between/of, less than, fewer than
Multiplication	Of, times, multiplied by, product of, increased/decreased by a factor of
Division	Per, out of, ratio of, quotient of, percent (divide by 100)
Equals	Is, are, was, were, will be, gives, yields, sold for

"Billy is three years older than twice Megan's age 5 years ago" translates to

$$B - 3 = 2(M - 5)$$

A rope 40 cm in length is cut into two pieces, a short piece and a long piece. The short piece is 8 cm shorter than the long piece. What is the length of the long piece?

Solution: We could let the variables be x and y or, better, s and l. However, the simplest way is to have just one variable, which we'll call L for the long piece of rope. The short piece of rope we can call $40 - L$. By using the 8 cm difference, we get:

$$L - 8 = 40 - L \;\rightarrow\; 2L = 48 \;\rightarrow\; L = 24 \text{ cm}$$

TIP

When you are translating key words in an algebraic expression, the phrases "less than" and "greater than" do not translate in the same order as they are written in the sentence. For example, when you are translating the expression "five less than twelve," the correct expression is 12 – 5, not 5 – 12.

1. Fred's age is 5 more than twice Janet's age. In 20 years, Janet's age tripled will be 7 more than Fred's age doubled. How old will Fred be 10 years from now?

   (A) 21
   (B) 24
   (C) 30
   (D) 31
   (E) 62

Solution: We have to be careful when we translate the algebra, but here is what we should get:

$$F - 5 = 2J \;\rightarrow\; F - 2J = 5 \;\rightarrow\; 2F - 4J = 10$$

$$(F + 20) \bullet 2 = (J + 20) \bullet 3 - 7 \;\rightarrow\; 2F + 40 = 3J + 60 - 7 \;\rightarrow\; 2F - 3J = 13$$

By subtracting the two equations, we get $-J = -3 \;\rightarrow\; J = 3$. Thus $F = 11$.

Note that the first trick here is that we never really suspect Fred and Janet to be so young. The second trick is that the question asks for Fred's age 10 years from now, which is 21.

The answer is A.

ABSOLUTE VALUE

The absolute value of a number is its value without regard to its sign. Another way to look at it is that the absolute value of a number is the measure of its distance to 0 on the number line.

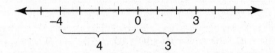

The absolute value of −4, denoted as |−4|, is 4. Similarly, |+3| = 3.

Strategies for Absolute Value

- When given multiple absolute value parentheses, start inward and work outward.

$$| \, 6 - (| -10|) \, | = | \, 6 - 10 \, | = | -4 | = 4$$

- Solving an equation with absolute value requires you to consider two cases. In case 1, you open the bracket normally and set everything equal. In case 2, you open the bracket and change the expression in the absolute value brackets to its negative form. (Do not change the side of the equation that isn't in absolute value brackets).

$$| \, x - 10 \, | = 20, \text{ solve for } x$$

Case 1: $x - 10 = 20$ $\rightarrow$ $x = 30$

Case 2: $-(x - 10) = 20$ $\rightarrow$ $-x + 10 = 20 \rightarrow x = -10$

- To avoid confusion when you have absolute values on both sides, try breaking down the equation by looking at the left-hand side (LHS) and the right-hand side (RHS) separately.

$$| \, x \, | = - | \, -x \, |, \text{ solve for } x$$

Try picking numbers. If $x = 2$, LHS = 2, RHS = −2. Doesn't work!

If $x = -2$, LHS = 2, RHS = −2. Doesn't work!

Don't forget about zero! If $x = 0$, LHS = 0, RHS = 0. This works. Therefore, $x = 0$.

Later on, we will see how to solve absolute value inequality problems.

EXPONENTS AND ROOTS

Exponents are involved in a large portion of the algebra questions on the GMAT. Let's look at the most common definitions and rules for exponents.

$$x^y = 16$$

In the above expression, x is called the **base** and y is the **exponent**. Sometimes we say "x to the **power** of y." In this particular example, if both x and y are positive integers, then either $x = 2$ and $y = 4$ or $x = 4$ and $y = 2$.

BREAKING DOWN EXPONENTS

Exponent	Expanded Expression	Base	Exponent	Value
5^3	$5 \cdot 5 \cdot 5$	5	3	125
2^6	$2 \cdot 2 \cdot 2 \cdot 2 \cdot 2 \cdot 2$	2	6	64
10^9	$10 \cdot 10 \cdot 10 \cdot 10 \cdot 10 \cdot 10 \cdot 10 \cdot 10 \cdot 10$	10	9	1,000,000,000

EXPONENT RULES

$x^0 = 1$	Any number, except zero, to the zero power equals 1.
$x^1 = x$	Any number to the 1 power equals that number.
$x^{-n} = \dfrac{1}{x^n}$ $\quad$ $4^{-2} = \dfrac{1}{4^2} = \dfrac{1}{16}$	A negative exponent changes sign when you move it between the numerator and denominator.
$2^4 \cdot 2^2 = 2^6$ $2^{(4+2)} = 2^6$	Add the exponents when multiplying two powers of the same base.
$2^6 \div 2^2 = 2^4$ $2^{(6-2)} = 2^4$	Subtract the exponents when dividing a power by another power of the same base.
$(2^2)^3 = 2^6$ $2^{(2 \times 3)} = 2^6$	Multiply the exponents when you raise a power to a power via parentheses.
$6^3 = (2 \cdot 3)^3 = 2^3 \cdot 3^3$	The exponent can be distributed among the factors of a base.
$\left(\dfrac{10}{2}\right)^3 = \dfrac{10^3}{2^3} = 5^3$	When a fraction is raised to a certain power, you can distribute the exponent to the numbers or variables in the fraction.

PROPERTIES OF EXPONENTS

$\left(\dfrac{1}{3}\right)^2 = \dfrac{1}{9}$ $\left(\dfrac{2}{3}\right)^3 = \dfrac{8}{27}$	When you apply any positive exponent to a positive proper fraction, the number becomes smaller. In this case, $x^2 < x$.
$(-3)^2 = 9$ $(2)^6 = 64$	Any positive or negative number with an even exponent is always positive. In this case, $x^2 > 0$ and $x^6 > 0$
$(-3)^3 = -27$ $(3)^3 = 27$	Any positive or negative number with an odd exponent could be positive or negative depending on the sign of the original number.
$x^3 = x$ $\quad$ $0^3 = 0$ $x^2 = x$ $\quad$ $0^2 = 0$	When $x = 0$ and x is the base, raising it to any positive power always results in 0, which is neither positive nor negative.
$2^1 = 2,$ $\quad$ $2^5 = 32,$ $\quad$ $3^1 = 3$ $2^2 = 4,$ $\quad$ $2^6 = 64,$ $\quad$ $3^2 = 9$ $2^3 = 8,$ $\quad$ $2^7 = 128,$ $\quad$ $3^3 = 27$ $2^4 = 16,$ $\quad$ $2^8 = 256$ $\quad$ $3^4 = 81$	There is a repeating pattern for all unit digits raised to a certain power. For powers of 2, the unit digit pattern is 2, 4, 8, and 6 repeating. For powers of 3, the unit digit pattern is 3, 9, 7, and 1 repeating and so on.

STRATEGIES FOR EXPONENTS

1. When multiplying or dividing numbers with exponents, always reduce each base to its lowest common prime number base.

   If $25^x = 125^{x-3}$, what is x?

   This should become $(5^2)^x = (5^3)^{x-3}$, which leads to $5^{2x} = 5^{3x-9}$. Once the bases are equal, we can set the exponents equal to each other. This gives $2x = 3x - 9$, therefore x = 9.

2. When adding or subtracting exponents, factor out the highest possible value and combine like terms.

   $3^7 - 3^6 + 3^5 - 3^4 = ?$

   We can factor out 3^4 from all the terms to get

   $3^4(3^3 - 3^2 + 3^1 - 3^0) = 3^4(27 - 9 + 3 - 1) = 3^4(20) = 3^4 \cdot 2^2 \cdot 5.$

3. As mentioned in the arithmetic section, you should memorize all the basic powers to speed up your calculations.

TIP

Your ability to manipulate exponents quickly and apply several rules in the same problem is a critical skill for GMAT test day.

---

2. If $27^{x+2} \cdot 25^y = 3^9 \cdot 5^{x-3}$, what is the value of y?

   (A) −3
   (B) −2
   (C) −1
   (D) 0.5
   (E) 2

Solution: We need to bring every base down to its lowest prime base, either 3 or 5 in this example. We first need to convert the 27 to 3^3 and the 25 to 5^2. Then we will solve the exponent on the base of 3 because on the right hand side of the equation the base 3 has an actual number for the exponent and not a variable. We get

$$(3^3)^{x+2} \cdot (5^2)^y = 3^{3x+6} \cdot 5^{2y} = 3^9 \cdot 5^{x-3} \rightarrow \text{ Thus } 3x + 6 = 9, \text{ and } x = 1.$$

By substituting $x = 1$ and looking at the exponents on base 5, we get

$$5^{2y} = 5^{1-3} = 5^{-2} \rightarrow \text{ Thus } 2y = -2 \text{ and } y = -1.$$

The answer is C.

Roots are similar to exponents because they can be expressed in the same way. Therefore, the rules will also apply the same way to roots as they do to exponents.

$$\sqrt{x} = x^{\frac{1}{2}}$$

In the above equation, 1 represents the exponent of x and the 2 represents the root of x.

You should be able to move back and forth between the radical form and the exponent form.

$$x^{\frac{2}{3}} = \sqrt[3]{x^2}$$

Note that by definition if no number is in the root, a square root is implied. Secondly, the root sign implies a positive value.

Multiplication and Division of Roots

When you multiply and divide roots, you can treat them like regular numbers.

$$\sqrt{2} \cdot \sqrt{3} = \sqrt{6} \quad \text{and} \quad \frac{\sqrt{10}}{\sqrt{2}} = \sqrt{5}$$

$$\sqrt{\left(\frac{x}{y}\right)} = \frac{\sqrt{x}}{\sqrt{y}} \quad \text{and} \quad \sqrt{(x \cdot y)} = \sqrt{x} \cdot \sqrt{y}$$

Addition and Subtraction of Roots

When you add or subtract roots, you generally need to remember two things:

1. As with variables and with adding or subtracting like terms, you can only add or subtract like roots.

$$\sqrt{2} + 3\sqrt{2} + 4\sqrt{3} - \sqrt{3} = 4\sqrt{2} + 3\sqrt{3}.$$

You cannot simplify this any further.

2. Certain roots can be reduced, which can help you find like roots. The key is to find a factor that is a perfect square and then take it out of the root.

$$\sqrt{2} + \sqrt{8} + \sqrt{98} = \sqrt{2} + \sqrt{4 \cdot 2} + \sqrt{49 \cdot 2} = \sqrt{2} + 2\sqrt{2} + 7\sqrt{2} = 10\sqrt{2}$$

You should **memorize** the most commonly occurring roots that can be reduced.

$$\sqrt{8} = 2\sqrt{2} \qquad \sqrt{12} = 2\sqrt{3} \qquad \sqrt{20} = 2\sqrt{5} \qquad \sqrt{27} = 3\sqrt{3}$$

$$\sqrt{50} = 5\sqrt{2} \qquad \sqrt{75} = 5\sqrt{3} \qquad \sqrt{98} = 7\sqrt{2}$$

ROOTS IN A DENOMINATOR: It is considered bad form to have roots in a denominator. Therefore, you may need to remove the root by multiplying the numerator and the denominator by the root found in the denominator. Example: $\frac{8}{\sqrt{2}}$ is not in standard form, so we need to remove the root in the denominator.

$$\frac{8}{\sqrt{2}} \cdot \frac{\sqrt{2}}{\sqrt{2}} = \frac{8\sqrt{2}}{2} = 4\sqrt{2}$$

> **TIP**
>
> Sometimes the best way to deal with a complicated root is to change it into exponent form.

PROPERTIES OF ROOTS

$\sqrt{16} = 4$ $\sqrt[6]{64} = 2$	All even roots of positive numbers result in another positive number. You cannot take an even root of a negative number. For example, you cannot solve $\sqrt{-16}$.
$\sqrt[3]{-27} = -3$ $\sqrt[5]{32} = 2$	Odd roots of real numbers can be negative, positive, or zero.
$\sqrt{\left(\dfrac{4}{9}\right)} = 2/3$ $\sqrt{25} = 5$	When you take the square root of a number between 0 and 1, the result is greater than the original number. When you take the square root of a number greater than 1, the result is less than the original number.

3. What is $\left(\left(\sqrt[3]{\left(\sqrt[4]{256}\right)}\right)^3\right)^2$?

(A) $\sqrt{2}$

(B) $2\sqrt{2}$

(C) 8

(D) $8\sqrt{2}$

(E) 16

Solution: The simplest way to solve this equation is to convert everything to parentheses form. We get

$$\left(\left(\left(256^{\frac{1}{4}}\right)^3\right)^{\frac{1}{3}}\right)^2 \rightarrow (256)^{\frac{1}{2}} = 16$$

Alternatively, if you didn't know that 16 is the square root of 256, you should have remembered from the arithmetic chapter that 256 is a power of 2.

$$256 = 2^8, \text{ so we get } \left(2^8\right)^{\frac{1}{2}} = 2^4 = 16.$$

The answer is E.

ALGEBRAIC CALCULATIONS AND OPERATIONS

Not only must you be very comfortable working with algebraic equations, expressions, and inequalities, you need to be quick with your calculations and flexible in applying the rules. These rules include simplifying, factoring, expanding, combining like terms, eliminating variables, and so on.

Order of Operations

TIP

A common mnemonic device to memorize this order of operations is "Please Excuse My Dear Aunt Sally"

The order in which you carry out calculations can be critically important in reaching the correct answer. For example, $3 + 5 \cdot 2$ may, at first glance, be seen as equivalent to $8 \cdot 2$. However, it is not. The correct simplification is $3 + 10$. PEMDAS is a useful acronym for remembering the correct order.

1. **P**arentheses: Work from the innermost to the outermost parentheses
2. **E**xponents: Work from left to right.
3. **M**ultiplication and **D**ivision: Work from left to right.
4. **A**ddition and **S**ubtraction: Work from left to right

$$3 + 4^2 \cdot 2 - 10 \div (5 - 3) = 3 + 16 \cdot 2 - 10 \div 2 = 3 + 32 - 5 = 30$$

Parentheses

The biggest challenge for test takers when dealing with parentheses occurs when you open them up. You might forget to change the sign or multiply an outside number by all of the terms in a set of parentheses.

Rule: $a(b + c) = ab + ac$

$$-2(x + (-6)) = -2x + 12$$

Rule: $(a + b)(c + d) = ac + ad + bc + bd$

You can use **FOIL** (**F**irst, **O**utside, **I**nside, **L**ast) to make sure you multiply every term of an expression in parentheses with every other term in the other set of parentheses.

$$(2x + y) \cdot (x - 3) = 2x^2 - 6x + xy - 3y$$

ALGEBRAIC EQUATIONS

There are three main types of algebraic equations.

1. **LINEAR EQUATIONS WITH ONE VARIABLE:** The variable has an exponent of degree 1.

2. **LINEAR EQUATIONS WITH MULTIPLE VARIABLES:** Every variable has an exponent of degree 1.

3. **QUADRATIC EQUATIONS:** One or more variables has an exponent of degree 2.

Linear Equations with One Variable

The following example shows the algebraic equation in its most basic form:

$$x + 7 = 3$$

To solve these equations, you generally need to isolate the variable. You follow several general steps to do this.

1. Eliminate any parentheses
2. Get rid of any fractions or denominators
3. Put all numbers on one side and all terms with the variable on the other side
4. Combine like terms
5. Isolate the variable by dividing by its coefficient (if there is one).

Solve for the expression $x + 2(x - 3) = \dfrac{2(x + 1)}{3} - 4x$

Solution:

$x + 2x - 6 = \dfrac{2x}{3} + \dfrac{2}{3} - 4x$	(Open the parentheses)
$3x + 6x - 18 = 2x + 2 - 12x$	(Multiply both sides by 3 to eliminate the denominator)
$9x - 2x + 12x = 2 + 18$	(Gather all terms with the x variable on one side and all numbers on the other side)
$19x = 20$	(Combine like terms)
$x = \dfrac{20}{19}$	(Divide by 19 and solve)

Linear Equations with Multiple Variables

Most GMAT problems have more than one variable. When you have two variables in algebra, you need to have more than one equation in order to solve. The general rule is that you need N distinct equations for N unknowns. Therefore, if you have to solve for 5 variables, then you need 5 equations. This concept is often tested in data sufficiency type questions.

There are two ways to solve multiple equations, **substitution** and **addition/subtraction**.

SUBSTITUTION METHOD

1. Express one variable in terms of everything else in the equation.
2. Plug this expression into one of the other equations.
3. Keep repeating until you solve for one of the variables. You can then substitute the solved value into the other equations. If possible, substitute into one of the original equations.

$$(1)\ x + y = 6$$
$$(2)\ x - y = 2$$

Solution:

Express equation (1) in terms of x	$\rightarrow$ (3) $x = 6 - y$
Substitute equation (3) into equation (2)	$\rightarrow$ $(6 - y) - y = 2$
Solve for the variable y	$\rightarrow$ $6 - 2y = 2$, $-2y = -4$, $y = 2$
Substitute $y = 2$ into equation (1)	$\rightarrow$ $x + 2 = 6$, $x = 4$

TIP

If you have 3 unknowns and 3 equations, look for a way to eliminate 2 variables simultaneously through addition/ subtraction.

ADDITION/SUBTRACTION METHOD

1. Line up the equations on top of each other.
2. Look for a variable to eliminate by adding or subtracting the two equations. You may have to multiply one or more equations by a constant number so that the variables will have the same coefficient but with opposite signs.
3. Add or subtract the equations so that the variables with the same coefficients will cancel out.
4. Solve for the variable that remains.
5. Substitute the solved variable back into one of the original equations if possible and repeat until you have all the variables.

$$(1)\ x + y = 6$$
$$(2)\ x - y = 2$$

Solution: This is the same question as the one we used in the substitution method above. Since the variables all have coefficients of 1, we can easily eliminate either x or y. Let us add and so we get

$$2x + 0 = 8, \text{ therefore } x = 4$$

Substitute back into equation (1) to get $y = 2$.

TIP

So the big question is which method is better? The answer really depends on which equations are given to you. GMAT math usually works out cleanly, so one method is likely to be more obvious than the other.

TIP

Make sure that the equations you are solving are *distinct* and not the same equation. This is a common GMAT trap, especially in data sufficiency problems.

4. A radio interviewer goes to the streets and randomly selects 60 people to find out who is going to watch the Super Bowl. How many are going to watch the Super Bowl?

   (1) From the sample, the number of people who are not going to watch the Super Bowl is 12 less than the number who plan to watch it.

   (2) From the sample, twice the number of people who plan to watch the Super Bowl is 3 times the number of people who are not watching it.

Solution: Let y be the number of people who said yes to watching the Super Bowl, and let n be the number who said no. We know that $y + n = 60$. If the statements give us another distinct equation, we will have sufficiency.

Statement 1 gives us the algebraic equation $n = y - 12$. Now we can solve for both variables by plugging this 2nd equation into the 1st equation to get $y + y - 12 = 60 \rightarrow 2y = 72 \rightarrow y = 36 \rightarrow$ Sufficient

Statement 2 gives us the algebraic equation $2y = 3n$. Now we can solve for both variables by plugging this 2nd equation into the 1st equation to get $2y = 3(60 - y) \rightarrow 2y = 180 - 3y \rightarrow 5y = 180, y = 36 \rightarrow$ Sufficient

The answer is D; each statement alone is sufficient.

Quadratic Equations

A quadratic equation takes the form $ax^2 + bx + c = 0$, where a, b, and c are numbers of any value.

These equations are solved by **factoring**, where you break apart the equation into two or more separate parts or factors.

> $x^2 + 7x + 12 = 0$ factors into $(x + 3)(x + 4) = 0$, which means that
> $x = -3$ and $x = -4$.

In the previous example, –3 and –4 are also known as the **roots** of the equation. When you plug them into the original equation, the left side will equal zero. Although this equation has two distinct roots, some quadratic equations have only one distinct root. For example, $x^2 + 6x + 9 = 0$ breaks down into $(x + 3)^2 = 0$. Therefore the only root is $x = -3$.

You can use three ways to solve a quadratic equation on the GMAT:

There are 3 ways to solve a quadratic equation on the GMAT.

1. **You can factor the equation by inspection**, which is likely the preferred and quickest way.
2. **You can plug in the answer choices**, which is not preferable as it is generally time consuming.
3. **You can use the quadratic equation**, but do this only as a last resort.

HOW TO FACTOR

How did we solve the equation $x^2 + 7x + 12 = 0$ in the example above so quickly by inspection? The basic idea is to look for a pair of factors of +12 (because the number could be negative) that will add up to +7. The factors of 12 are 1 and 12, 2 and 6, 3 and 4. Note that we look at the factors in pairs. In this method, 3 and 4 stand out. We can then set up the factors as $(x + 3)$ and $(x + 4)$.

QUADRATIC FORMULA

The **quadratic formula** is $x = \dfrac{-b \pm \sqrt{b^2 - 4ac}}{2a}$ for any equation in the form $ax^2 + bx + c = 0$. In most quadratic equations, x usually has two solutions. Note that if $b^2 - 4ac < 0$, there is no real solution and if $b^2 - 4ac = 0$, the equation has only one solution. Sometimes you should check the value of $b^2 - 4ac$ before solving the entire formula. This check may solve you time.

Algebraic Factoring

As with any algebraic expression, you need to move back and forth between expanding expressions and factoring them. In other words, you can use FOIL to expand an expression and use factoring to bring the equation back to its pre-expanded form.

To help with your algebraic manipulation, you should **memorize** the 3 most common algebraic identities that are easily factored. You must be able to recognize these three factored forms and work quickly with them.

> $(a + b)^2 = (a + b)(a + b) = a^2 + 2ab + b^2$
> $(a - b)^2 = (a - b)(a - b) = a^2 - 2ab + b^2$
> $(a + b)(a - b) = a^2 - b^2$ Also known as the **difference of two squares**

5. Which of the following equations is NOT equivalent to $9a^2 = (b-3)(b+3)$?

    (A) $a^2 = (b^2 - 9)/9$

    (B) $(3a - b)(3a + b) = -9$

    (C) $18a^2 - 2b^2 + 18 = 0$

    (D) $27a^2 = (3b - 9)(b + 3)$

    (E) $3a^2 + 6 = b^2$

Solution: When $b = 3$ or $b = -3$, the equation becomes $9a^2 = 0$, which means that $a = 0$. You can plug these values into the answer choices to see which ones work. In other words, let $a = 0$ and see which equations give you $b = 3$ or $b = -3$. Alternatively, you can try to manipulate the original equation into the given answer choices. Either way, answer choice (E) does not work.

The answer is E.

INEQUALITIES

Inequalities compare two statements with different values. They are very similar to typical algebraic expressions except that the equal sign (=) is replaced by several other possible symbols. There are five main types of inequalities:

x	$>$	y	x is greater than y
x	$\geq$	y	x is greater than or equal to y
x	$<$	y	x is less than y
x	$\leq$	y	x is less than or equal to y
x	$\neq$	y	x is not equal to y

Almost all of the rules for algebraic equations also apply to inequalities. Remember this key difference:

> **INEQUALITIES GOLDEN RULE**
>
> If both sides of an inequality are multiplied or divided by a negative number, then you must flip the inequality sign.

What is fascinating is that the inequalities golden rule drastically increases the difficulty level of inequalities for test takers. Most of this difficulty is just confusion about the rules and how to apply them. Note that the general rule above does not apply to addition or subtraction. So let's look at the main ways you need to address inequalities.

Addition and Subtraction of Inequalities

When you add or subtract a number to both sides of the inequality, the sign is not affected.

$$2x - 3 > x - 10$$

Subtract x from both sides and add -3 to both sides

$$x > -7$$

Note that the unknown variable and the negative number have no effect on the inequality sign.

Multiplication or Division of Inequalities

This is where the golden rule of inequalities comes into play. Remember these three tips.

1. If you multiply or divide by a positive number, there's no sign change. Treat the inequality as you would an equation.
2. If you multiply or divide by a negative number, change the direction of the inequality symbol.
3. If you multiply or divide by a variable, you need to ask the question, "Is this number positive, negative, or I don't know?" Once you confirm, then proceed according to the first two tips above.

$$\text{Is } x > y?$$

(1) $\frac{x}{y} > 1$ If this were an equation, you might try to multiply the y on both sides to get $x > y$. However, this is an inequality. You don't know if y is positive or negative. Therefore, you cannot manipulate this inequality to solve it. Insufficient

Solving Multiple Inequalities

As with equations, you can solve two or more inequalities together by adding or subtracting inequalities, or by using substitution. The key difference is that the inequality signs must be pointing in the same direction.

$$x + y > 12 \text{ and } x - y < 6. \text{ Solve for } x \text{ and } y.$$

Solution: Set up the inequalities so that their signs are facing the same direction.

(1) $x + y > 12$

(2) $\underline{+ \quad -x + y > -6}$ (We did this by multiplying both sides by –1, thus changing the sign.)

$2y > 6 \rightarrow y > 3$ This means that $x > 9$ (via substitution into equation 1).

Inequalities with Absolute Value

The GMAT frequently increases the difficulty of problems by combining two separate concepts. Inequalities are often combined with absolute values, but the process to solve these is the same. You will again have to solve two separate cases.

$$| x - 5 | > 3, \text{ solve for } x$$

Solution: We need to look at two cases.

Case 1: $x - 5 > 3 \rightarrow x > 8$

Case 2: $-(x - 5) > 3 \rightarrow -x + 5 > 3 \rightarrow x - 5 < -3 \rightarrow x < 2$

So we get $x < 2$ or $x > 8$. If you have time, you can check numbers just to be sure.

6. Is $xy > 5$?

    (1) $2x - y > 6$

    (2) $x + 3y < 17$

Solution: Each statement by itself is insufficient because there are 2 unknowns. Because these are inequalities, we need to solve them for this data sufficiency problem. Note that when you solve 2 distinct inequality expressions, you need to make sure that the signs are pointing in the same direction. Let's start by taking the 1st equation and multiplying it by –3. This will both change the sign and align the coefficients of y.

$-6x + 3y < -18$

$\underline{x + 3y < 17}$ Subtracting gives $-7x < -35 \rightarrow$ which gives $x > 5$

If we take the 2nd equation and multiply it by –2, this will align both the sign and the coefficients of x.

$-2x - 6y > -34$

$\underline{2x - y > 6}$ Adding gives $-7y > -28 \rightarrow$ which gives $y < 4$

Since y could be positive or negative, there's no way to determine if $xy > 5$. Thus this problem is insufficient.

The answer is E; both statements together are still not sufficient.

FUNCTIONS, SYMBOLS, AND SEQUENCES

Functions are simply an alternate way to write an algebraic expression with one variable. Test takers find functions confusing because they are more abstract. A function comes in the form

$$f(x) = 2x + 3 \rightarrow \text{This is the same as saying} \rightarrow y = 2x + 3$$

The two expressions above are identical. In each case, when we have a specific value for x we simply plug it into the equation and solve. So if $x = 1$, then

$$f(1) = 2(1) + 3 = 5 \quad \text{OR} \quad y = 2(1) + 3 = 5$$

You can solve for functions in almost the same way as you solve for algebraic expressions. To illustrate further how similar they are, let's create a T-chart for a function and an equation.

$$g(x) = x^2 - 3 \rightarrow \text{which again is the same as} \rightarrow y = x^2 - 3$$

T-charts for both

$g(x)$	x		y	x
6	–3		6	–3
1	–2		1	–2
–2	–1		–2	–1
–3	0		–3	0
–2	1		–2	1
1	2		1	2
6	3		6	3

As you can see, functions are the same as algebraic equations. Just as we would say $y = -2$ when $x = -1$ or $x = +1$, we can also say $g(-1) = -2$ or $g(1) = -2$.

The **domain** of a function is the set of all possible values for the variable.

$$g(x) = \frac{\sqrt{x-3}}{x-5}$$

The variable x cannot be 5 because the denominator would be undefined. x also cannot be less than 3 because the radical would be undefined. Therefore, the domain of $g(x)$ is all values of x, as long as $x \geq 3$ and $x \neq 5$.

---

7. The function $f(x)$ is equal to the square of a number lessened by 5. The function $g(x)$ is equal to a number tripled. What is $f(g(2))$?

(A) 4

(B) 7

(C) 13

(D) 22

(E) 31

Solution: When we translate the algebra, we get the following functions:

$$f(x) = x^2 - 5 \text{ and } g(x) = 3x$$

There are two ways to calculate $f(g(2))$.

The 1st way is to calculate $g(2)$ and then plug this value into $f(x)$.

$$g(2) = 3(2) = 6 \rightarrow \text{Plugging 6 into } f(x) = (6)^2 - 5 = 36 - 5 = 31.$$

The 2nd way is to take the expression for $g(x) = 3x$ and plug that directly into $f(x)$ for every value of x that $f(x)$ has and then input $x = 2$.

$$f(g(x)) = (3x)^2 - 5 = 9x^2 - 5 \rightarrow \text{Plugging in } x = 2 \text{ gives us } 9(2)^2 - 5 = 36 - 5 = 31.$$

The answer is E.

Function Symbol Problems

Symbol problems are challenging because of the use of unfamiliar symbols to define an expression. Despite this abstract nature, you just need to "plug and play" by inputting the values and carrying out the operations as you normally would. One effective strategy is to separate all the steps and operations with a clear and structured chart.

If the operation ¥ is defined for all a and b as the equation

a ¥ $b = \dfrac{ab}{2}$, then what is 2 ¥ (3 ¥ 4)?

Solution: It's important to understand what the definition is. Simply put, whatever values of a and b we have, we plug them into the expression as defined. Using a chart can help here.

	a	b	a ¥ $b = \dfrac{ab}{2}$
3 ¥ 4	3	4	$\dfrac{3 \times 4}{2} = 6$
2 ¥ (3 ¥ 4) = 2 ¥ 6	2	6	$\dfrac{2 \times 6}{2} = 6$

Sequence Functions

Sequence problems are a particular kind of function question on the GMAT. In general, you are given a formula that defines the sequence, the domain, and some of the terms of the sequence. The formula is of the form: a_n = (some equation with n as a variable). The terms of the sequence are: $a_1, a_2, a_3 \ldots a_n$.

$a_n = n^2 - 1$, where $n > 1$. What is the value of a_5?

Solution: The quickest way to do this is to input $n = 5$ for a_5 to get $a_5 = 5^2 - 1 = 24$.

The GMAT asks 3 common types of sequence questions:

- **Sequence type 1**: Find the nth term of the sequence. (Solve by inputting values into the definition.)
- **Sequence type 2**: Find the nth term of the sequence when given two or more values for terms. (Solve using the definition to find the link.)
- **Sequence type 3**: Find the 1000th term of the sequence. (Solve by finding a pattern with the definition to figure out the far away term.)

SEQUENCE STRATEGY

1. Make sure you understand the definition of the sequence.
2. Line up the terms in order vertically.

   - If you are given the value of a few terms, make sure to leave gaps for the terms that you do not know but may need to solve.
   - If you are not given any terms, try to input the first 3–5 terms of the sequence.
   - If you can't find any terms to put in, use algebraic terms.

3. Use the definition to fill in the gaps and solve.
4. If that doesn't work, try to find a pattern to help you solve the problem.
5. Make sure you do not violate any given domain.

---

8. In the infinite sequence $a_1, a_2, a_3 ..., a_n$, each term after the first is equal to triple the previous term. If $a_4 - a_3 = 36$, what is the value of a_1?

   (A) $\dfrac{6}{7}$

   (B) 1

   (C) 2

   (D) $\dfrac{24}{7}$

   (E) 4

Solution: This sequence is defined by tripling the next term. Another way of understanding this definition is that each subsequent term adds twice the amount of the current term. We aren't given any values nor are there any we can put in. Therefore, let's use algebra and let $a_1 = x$. We can build from there.

$a_1 = x \rightarrow a_2 = 3x \rightarrow a_3 = 9x \rightarrow a_4 = 27x \rightarrow$ since we know $a_4 - a_3 = 36$, we get

$27x - 9x = 36 \rightarrow 18x = 36$, thus $x = 2$ and $a_1 = 2$.

Alternatively, we know that 36 represents twice the value of the current term, a_3. This means that $a_3 = 18$, which allows us to solve backward for $a_2 = 6$ and $a_1 = 2$.

The answer is C.

1. If $3^x - 3^{x-2} = 2^3 \cdot 3^{17}$, what is x?

   (A) 15
   (B) 17
   (C) 19
   (D) 20
   (E) 23

2. If the operation £ is defined by $q \text{ £ } p = \dfrac{(q-p)}{(q+p)}$ for all non-zero integers q and p, then $3 \text{ £ } (-4 \text{ £ } 5)$ is

   (A) −9
   (B) −4.5
   (C) −2
   (D) 1.5
   (E) 6

3. What is the sum of x, y, and z?
   $$2x + y - z = 10$$
   $$x - 2y + 2z = 15$$
   $$4x + y - 2z = 28$$

   (A) −5
   (B) −2
   (C) 0
   (D) 3
   (E) 11

4. A convenience store bought an item for C dollars, then sold it for D dollars. The cost of the item was what percent of the gross profit that the convenience store realized?

   (1) $\dfrac{D}{C} - 1 = \dfrac{2}{3}$
   (2) $D - C = 8$

5. For which of the following functions S is $S(t) = S(1 - t)$ for all t?

   (A) $S(t) = 1 + t$
   (B) $S(t) = t^2(1 - t)^2$
   (C) $S(t) = 2 + t^2$
   (D) $S(t) = t^2 - (1 - t)^2$
   (E) $S(t) = t / (1 + t)$

6. If the sequence S has 1000 terms, what is the 777th term of S?

   (1) The 4th term of S is −26.
   (2) The 977th term is 16,515, and each preceding term of S before the last is 17 less than the current term

7. If a and b are integers and $a = |b + 11| + |12 − b|$, does a equal 23?

   (1) $b < 12$
   (2) $b > -11$

8. If x is a product of all integers from 2 to 24, inclusive, what is the greatest integer y for which 35^y is a factor of x?

   (A) 2
   (B) 3
   (C) 5
   (D) 7
   (E) 9

ANSWER KEY

1. **(C)**   3. **(A)**   5. **(B)**   7. **(C)**

2. **(C)**   4. **(A)**   6. **(B)**   8. **(B)**

SOLUTIONS

1. **(C)** When you first look at this question, you may second-guess yourself because you're wondering why there is a 2 on the right side of the equation. The rules and tactics for exponent manipulation are the same, which are to reduce everything to a prime factor base (already done) and to factor out like terms when you see addition or subtraction. So in this question, let's take out 3^x from each term on the left-hand side

$$3^x(1 - 3^{-2}) = 3^x(1 - \frac{1}{3^2}) = 3^x(1 - \frac{1}{9}) = 3^x(\frac{8}{9}) = 3^x(\frac{2^3}{3^2})$$

Now we know where the 2^3 comes from. This gives us

$$3^x 2^3 3^{-2} = 2^3 \bullet 3^{17} \rightarrow 3^{x-2} 2^3 = 2^3 3^{17} \rightarrow \text{Thus } x - 2 = 17, x = 19.$$

2. **(C)** This is a symbol problem. The key is to make sure to structure it clearly, plug in the numbers correctly, and follow the order of operations.

$$q \pounds p = \frac{(q-p)}{(q+p)} \rightarrow \text{Thus } -4 \pounds 5 = \frac{(-4-5)}{(-4+5)} = -\frac{9}{1} = -9$$

$$3 \pounds -9 = \frac{(3-(-9))}{(3+(-9))} = \frac{(3+9)}{(3-9)} = \frac{12}{-6} = -2.$$

3. **(A)** Whenever you're presented with 3 equations, first be sure to label them. Then you should try to eliminate 2 variables at a time instead of one if you can:

$$① \ 2x + y - z = 10 \quad ② \ x - 2y + 2z = 15 \quad ③ \ 4x + y - 2z = 28$$

Using the tactic of addition and subtraction, we can double equation ① and add equation ②

$$2 \bullet ① + ②$$

$$\begin{array}{l} 4x + 2y - 2z = 20 \\ + \ x - 2y + 2z = 15 \\ \hline 5x \qquad\qquad = 35 \ \rightarrow \ x = 7 \end{array}$$

We can also do the same by doubling equation ① and subtracting equation ③

$$2 \bullet ① - ③$$

$$\begin{array}{l} 4x + 2y - 2z = 20 \\ - \ 4x + y - 2z = 28 \\ \hline \quad\ y \qquad\quad = -8 \ \rightarrow \ y = -8 \end{array}$$

Substituting $x = 7$, $y = -8$ into equation ① gives

$$4(7) + 2(-8) - 2z = 20 \rightarrow 28 - 16 - 2z = 20 \rightarrow 12 - 20 = 2z \rightarrow z = -4$$

The sum of x, y, and z is $x + y + z = 7 - 8 - 4 = -5$.

4. **(A)** What we want in this question is the proportion of cost to gross profit on the item or $\frac{(D-C)}{D}$ or $1 - \frac{C}{D}$. So what we need is either 2 distinct equations or the ratio $\frac{C}{D}$.

Statement 1 tells us, with a bit of manipulation, that $\frac{D}{C} = \frac{5}{3}$. This is sufficient, because we can plug into $1 - \frac{C}{D}$ and get $1 - \frac{3}{5} = \frac{2}{5}$. *Sufficient*

Statement 2 gives us a distinct equation. However, there's no other information, such as another distinct equation, to help us solve or to manipulate in order to get the ratio $\frac{C}{D}$.

Insufficient

Statement 1 alone is sufficient.

5. **(B)** There are 2 ways to handle this type of function question. You can take the value $1 - t$ and substitute it into each of the answer choices given and see which one works. However, this can involve messy calculations. Another way to do this is to create a chart and pick numbers to see which answer choice works. Let $t = 1$ and $1 - t = 0$. Calculate the functions accordingly.

	$S(t) = S(1)$ **What is $S(1)$?**	$S(1 - t) = S(0)$ **What is $S(0)$?**	**Are They Equal?** **Is $S(1) = S(0)$?**
$S(t) = 1 + t$	2	1	No
$S(t) = t^2(1 - t)^2$	0	0	Yes
$S(t) = 2 + t^2$	3	2	No
$S(t) = t^2 - (1 - t)^2$	1	−1	No
$S(t) = t\,/\,(1 + t)$	1/2	0	No

6. **(B)** In order to determine the 777th term of sequence S, we either need the definition of the sequence or some way to find a pattern.

Statement 1 gives us only one term. Therefore, there is no way to determine the pattern for the definition. *Insufficient*

Statement 2 gives us a term and a definition. This means we could take the number 16,515 and subtract 17 as many times as needed in order to get to the 777th term. The GMAT test makers don't expect you to calculate this number. You just have to know that you can. *Sufficient*

Statement 2 alone is sufficient.

7. **(C)** The best way to do this question is to pick numbers and prove insufficiency by finding one example that works and one that does not.

Statement 1 $\rightarrow$ If $b = -20$, then $a = |-20 + 11| + |12 - (-20)|$ $= |-9| + |32| = 9 + 32 = 41$

$\rightarrow$ If $b = 11$, then $a = |11 + 11| + |12 - 11|$ $= |22| + |1| = 22 + 1 = 23$

Insufficient

Statement 2 → If $b = 20$, then $a = |20 + 11| + |12 - 20|$ $= |31| + |{-}8| = 31 + 8 = 39$

          → If $b = 11$, then $a = |11 + 11| + |12 - 11|$ $= |22| + |1| = 22 + 1 = 23$

Insufficient

When we combine statements 1 and 2 together, we know that $-11 < b < 12$. Pick numbers.

    If $b = 11$, then $a = |11 + 11| + |12 - 11|$ $= |22| + |1| = 22 + 1 = 23$

    If $b = -10$, then $a = |{-}10 + 11| + |12 - (-10)|$ $= |1| + |22| = 1 + 22 = 23$

Try a 3rd number if you are not convinced.

    → If $b = -1$, $a = |{-}1 + 11| + |12 - (-1)| = 10 + 13 = 23$

Both statements together are sufficient

8. **(B)** Make sure you understand the definition of x. Let's break it down into its factors:

$x = 2 \cdot 3 \cdot 4 \cdot 5 \cdot 6 \cdot 7 \cdot 8 \cdot 9 \cdot 10 \cdot 11 \cdot 12 \cdot 13 \cdot 14 \cdot 15 \cdot 16 \cdot 17 \cdot 18 \cdot 19 \cdot 20 \cdot 21 \cdot 22 \cdot 23 \cdot 24$. This is a very big number!

What was the question really asking? If, say $y = 3$, then 35 goes into the big number x 3 times. Since we want to maximize the integer y, what we really want to know is how many times does 35 divide into x? We can break down $35 = 7 \cdot 5$. We know that within x are a whole bunch of 5s and 7s. There are likely fewer 7s than there are 5s. So the amount of 7s within the big number x would be the limiting factor as to how many 35s would go into it. So let's track the number of 7s within the factors of x.

There is a   7 $14 = 7 \cdot 2$ $21 = 7 \cdot 3$ → a total of three 7s within the factors of x.

Therefore, there are three 35s. The greatest integer y would be 3.

Note that whenever you see a question dealing with factors or prime factors, you should try breaking it down into such factors or prime factors.

Geometry

6

→ **LINES AND ANGLES**

→ **TRIANGLES**

→ **QUADRILATERALS**

→ **OTHER POLYGONS**

→ **CIRCLES**

→ **VOLUMES AND 3-D FIGURES**

→ **COORDINATE GEOMETRY**

GEOMETRY: DIAGNOSTIC SKILL QUIZ

DIRECTIONS: Before continuing, try your hand at these geometry questions to assess your level of understanding. The answers will be explained throughout the chapter.

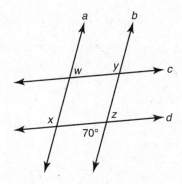

1. In the figure above, $a \parallel b$ and $c \parallel d$. What are the measures of angles w, x, y and z, respectively?

   (A) 70°, 70°, 110°, 110°

   (B) 110°, 110°, 70°, 70°

   (C) 110°, 70°, 70°, 110°

   (D) 110°, 70°, 110°, 70°

   (E) None of the above

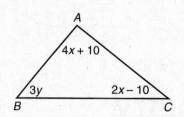

2. Given triangle *ABC*, what is the value of *y*?

(1) Angle *BAC* is 90°.

(2) Side *AC* is twice the length of side AB.

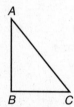

Note: Figure NOT drawn to scale.

3. Triangle *ABC* is shown in the figure above. What is its perimeter?

(1) *BC* is half of *AB*.

(2) *AB* is of length 6 and is perpendicular to *BC*.

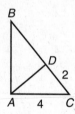

4. In triangle *ABC* above, angle *BAC* is a right angle and *DC* is 2 units long. What is the length of *BC*?

(A) 8

(B) 10

(C) $6\sqrt{3}$

(D) 12

(E) $12\sqrt{3}$

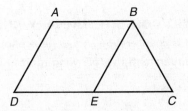

5. Within quadrilateral *ABCD* there is rhombus *ABED*, and *D*, *E*, and *C* are all on the same line. If we drew a line segment *AE*, is quadrilateral *ABCE* a rhombus?

   (1) *BC* is parallel to *AE*.
   (2) Angle *ADE* is 60°.

6. What is the radius of the circle that circumscribes a triangle whose sides measure 41, 40, and 9?

   (A) 9
   (B) 20
   (C) 20.5
   (D) 41
   (E) 45

7. A rectangular box of width *a*, length *b*, and height *c* has a solid cylinder of height *c* and of diameter *a* placed within it. If *a* = 4, *b* = 5, and *c* = 6, how much volume is left in the rectangular box?

   (A) $60 - 12\pi$
   (B) $240 - 96\pi$
   (C) $120 - 24\pi$
   (D) $120 - 12\pi$
   (E) 96

8. Line *M* is perpendicular to line *N*, whose equation is $3y = 4x + 12$. Lines *M* and *N* intersect at (a, b). Is $a + b > 0$?

   (1) The *x*-intercept of line *M* is less than that of line *N*.
   (2) The *y*-intercept of line *M* is less than that of line *N*.

INTRODUCTION

Geometry is fun! Now you may wonder where our enthusiasm comes from. Simply put, geometry is all about making drawings and a bunch of rules. In other words, you get to doodle! Some students, having forgotten most of the rules, decide to skip geometry altogether, thinking they can make up their score with the other questions. This is a bad idea. As mentioned before, there is a finite amount of underlying theory on the GMAT. There is an end in sight. In addition, the tested quantitative theory is from high school or earlier. Geometry is often taught even earlier, likely in junior high or middle school (oh those fun, awkward years). So you may find it more difficult than other quantitative topics because you were exposed to it so long ago. Geometry makes up about 10% to 15% of the quantitative questions. This represents at least 4 to 6 GMAT questions that you should be getting right!

Basic Geometry Strategy

1. **KNOW ALL THE RULES:** Geometry is rule based. To solve geometry problems, you need to know the rules and be able to recognize which ones apply. You already know most of the rules, such as the area of a circle or the angles of a triangle. The key to success is to know the more obscure rules as well as the common ones.

2. **ALWAYS MAKE A DRAWING:** Visualizing will help you greatly in geometry. Even if the GMAT provides a diagram, you should draw it again on your scratch pad. Draw it neatly and large enough to work with effectively. In many cases, you will need to draw more than what you are given.

3. **LEVERAGE SPECIAL TRIANGLES:** Most quantitative problems have a key insight that helps you understand and solve the problem efficiently. In geometry, you will often find that the key insight involves special triangles such as isosceles triangles, equilateral triangles, Pythagorean right triangles, 30-60-90 triangles, and 45-45-90 triangles.

TIP

Be careful when you see "Figure NOT drawn to scale" on a problem-solving question. This means the drawing has been intentionally manipulated to prevent you from using it. If the drawing doesn't say this, then you can use the drawing to estimate or eyeball. On data sufficiency problems, you cannot assume anything is drawn to scale, ever.

LINES AND ANGLES

A **line** is defined as a geometric object that is straight and can be either finite or infinite.

A fixed portion of a line is often called a **line segment**, as is AB in the diagram below.

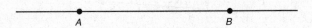

When 2 lines intersect, we create 2 pairs of angles. The angles opposite each other are equal. The sum of the angles on one side of the line is 180°.

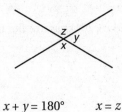

$$x + y = 180° \qquad x = z$$

Parallel and Perpendicular Lines

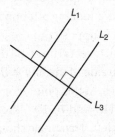

Parallel lines are those in the same plane that never intersect. As shown in the diagram, $L1$ and $L2$ are parallel.

Perpendicular lines are those that intersect, creating 90° angles. In the diagram, $L3$ is perpendicular to $L1$ and $L2$.

When two parallel lines are intercepted by a third line, as shown below, we create two sets of four identical angles. Again this case, $x + y = 180°$.

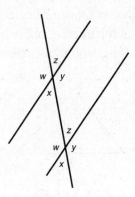

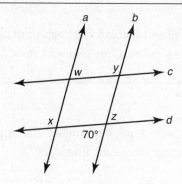

1. In the figure above, $a \parallel b$ and $c \parallel d$. What are the measures of angles w, x, y, and z, respectively?

    (A) 70°, 70°, 110°, 110°
    (B) 110°, 110°, 70°, 70°
    (C) 110°, 70°, 70°, 110°
    (D) 110°, 70°, 110°, 70°
    (E) None of the above

Solution: Sometimes with geometry questions, it's important to know what rules are at play. In this question, we are looking at opposite angles and parallel lines. The measure of angle $z = 70°$ since it is opposite to the given angle. Right away, we know that answer choices A and C are incorrect. The angle directly above the 70° must be 110° because the sum of angles on one side of the line is 180°. Both angles y and x are equal to 110° because of the parallel lines. At this point, none of the answer choices gives us a combination that ends with 110, 110, and 70. If you're really curious about the measure of angle w, look to the angle to its left. That angle should be 110° because of the parallel lines with angles x and y. Since w is on the same side of the line as the 110°, $w = 70°$.

The answer is E.

TRIANGLES

The GMAT test makers love to use triangles. In fact, you will find triangles in the majority of geometry questions. Special triangles are often the key to solving more difficult problems.

In the triangle below, the sum of the interior angles is always 180°, no matter what the shape. Therefore, when you know 2 angles, you can determine the 3rd angle.

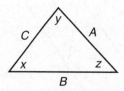

$$x + y + z = 180°$$

The perimeter of a triangle is the sum of the length of its sides. $P = A + B + C$

The area of a triangle is its base multiplied by its perpendicular height divided by 2.

$$A = \frac{B \times H}{2}$$

Note that any side can be the base. However, you must make sure that you use the perpendicular altitude from that base for the height.

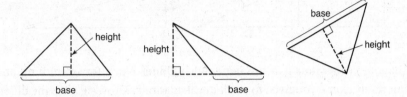

The shortest side of a triangle is opposite the smallest angle. The longest side is opposite the largest angle.

The sum of any 2 sides of a triangle must always be greater than the 3rd side.

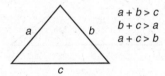

$$a + b > c$$
$$b + c > a$$
$$a + c > b$$

The exterior angle of a triangle is equal to the sum of the 2 interior angles of a triangle that are not next to that exterior angle.

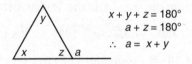

$$x + y + z = 180°$$
$$a + z = 180°$$
$$\therefore \quad a = x + y$$

Right Triangles

The most important triangle in the GMAT quantitative section is the right triangle. In a right triangle, one angle measures 90°. This angle is opposite the longest side of a triangle, which is known as the hypotenuse. We can calculate the length of the third side of a right triangle when given the length of the other two sides using Pythagoras's famous formula:

PYTHAGOREAN THEOREM

$$a^2 + b^2 = c^2$$

where c is the hypotenuse while a and b are the other two sides of a right triangle

The most well known Pythagorean triangle identity is the 3-4-5 triangle. Not only should you know this right triangle, but you should also know common multiples of it such as 6-8-10, 9-12-15, 15-20-25. There are also a few other common Pythagorean triangle identities shown below.

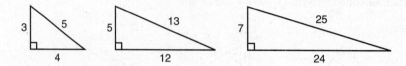

The Pythagorean theorem is a fundamental building block for everything about right triangles, but rarely would you need to use it in calculations. Knowing all of the different right triangle identities you will save time on your calculations.

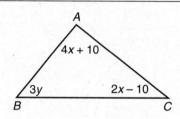

2. Given triangle *ABC*, what is the value of *y*?

(1) Angle *BAC* is 90°.
(2) Side *AC* is twice the length of side *AB*.

Solution: We know to start that the sum of all the angles is 180°. Therefore we get

$$3y + 4x + 10 + 2x - 10 = 180° \rightarrow 3y + 6x = 180° \rightarrow \text{Reduces to } y + 2x = 60°$$

Statement 1 tells us that $4x + 10 = 90$; therefore $4x = 80$, $x = 20$. We can solve for *y*, which equals 20. *Sufficient*

Statement 2 tells us that side *AC* is twice that of side *AB*, but angle *ABC* need not be twice that of angle *ACB*. This is not enough information to solve for *y*. *Insufficient*

The answer is A.

Special Triangles

There are 4 special triangles that are critical to success in GMAT geometry:

1. **EQUILATERAL TRIANGLES**

2. **ISOSCELES TRIANGLES**

3. **45-45-90 TRIANGLES**

4. **30-60-90 TRIANGLES**

Equilateral Triangles

All sides of an equilateral triangle are the same length. All angles in an equilateral triangle are the same—60°. An equilateral triangle is also by definition an isosceles triangle. If you cut an equilateral triangle in half, you create 2 identical 30-60-90 right triangles. What is not commonly known about this special triangle is that you need only one side length to calculate the area by using the following formula.

$$A = \frac{s^2 \sqrt{3}}{4}$$

These properties of equilateral triangles are key in both problem solving and data sufficiency type questions.

Isosceles Triangles

Isosceles triangles have 2 angles and 2 sides that are the same. So if 2 sides of a triangle have the same length, then the 2 opposite angles are also equal to each other and vice versa. Sometimes you will find isosceles triangles cleverly hidden in circle problems where the radius is involved. This is because 2 radii are of equal length and thus can be used to create isosceles triangles.

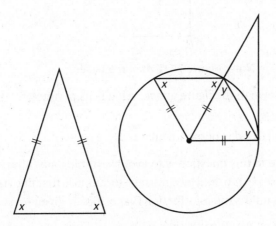

30-60-90 and 45-45-90 Triangles

These triangles are special because they have specific proportions for each side. You need to know only the length of one side in order to find the length of the other 2 sides. This is especially important to know for data sufficiency type problems.

In a 30-60-90 triangle, the ratio of the lengths is fixed at $1 : \sqrt{3} : 2$. This means if the side opposite the 30° angle measures 1, the side opposite the 60° angle measures $\sqrt{3}$, and the hypotenuse measures 2. Note that you can also create this triangle when you split an equilateral triangle in half. When dealing with this type of triangle, the best way to calculate the other sides is to use a chart as shown on the next page.

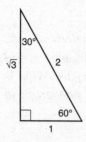

EXAMPLE   EXAMPLE

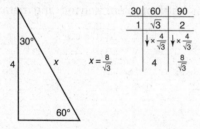

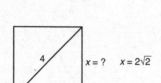

In a 45-45-90 triangle, the ratio of the side lengths is fixed at 1:1:$\sqrt{2}$. This means that if either leg measures 1, the hypotenuse measures $\sqrt{2}$. This triangle is also an isosceles right triangle. Note that 45-45-90 triangles are created when you split a square in half by the diagonal. You should also be familiar with common multiples of this ratio such as $\sqrt{2}$, $\sqrt{2}$, and 2.

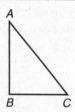

Note: Figure NOT drawn to scale.

3. Triangle *ABC* is shown in the figure above. What is its perimeter?

   (1) *BC* is half of *AB*.

   (2) *AB* is of length 6 and is perpendicular to *BC*.

Solution: The challenge in this question is to avoid assuming anything in the drawing since it is not drawn to scale. It would be a mistake to suppose that line *AB* is the height. We cannot assume this unless the information is specifically given to us.

Statement 1 tells us the ratio of the two sides *BC* and *AB*. Since we do not know for sure that angle *ABC* is 90°, we cannot determine the values of the sides.

Statement 2 tells us that angle *ABC* is 90° and the height of the triangle is 6. Make sure to treat this new information separately from statement 1, otherwise, you may think statement 2 is sufficient by itself. With only the angle and the height, we cannot determine the perimeter.

When we combine the two statements, we now know that this is a 30-60-90 triangle because of the ratio and the right triangle. We can calculate all the sides using the ratios. *Sufficient*

The answer is C; both statements together are sufficient.

Similar Triangles

Over the years, the GMAT has become more sophisticated and complex. The test makers use a variety of ways to complicate questions whether through tricky wording or by using advanced concepts more frequently. Similar triangles are one such area where savvy test takers need to have a better understanding.

When two triangles are similar, they share the same angles and thus share similar proportional properties. In other words, any two triangles with the same angles have their sides and heights in proportion.

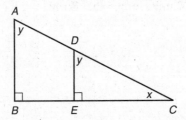

Triangles *ABC* and *DEC* are similar because they both have one right angle and they share the same angle at *C*. Note that we need only two pairs of equal angles to know that the third pair is also equal. If we take any ratio of two sides of one triangle, it must be the same for the other triangle.

$$\frac{AB}{AC} = \frac{ED}{DC}, \frac{BC}{AB} = \frac{EC}{ED}, \text{ and } \frac{BC}{AC} = \frac{EC}{DC}$$

There are three standard ways to determine that triangles are similar.

- **AAA (ANGLE, ANGLE, ANGLE):** If the angles are the same, then the triangles are similar. This is the most common type found in the GMAT.
- **SAS (SIDE, ANGLE, SIDE):** If the triangles share two sides with corresponding ratios and the angle in between those two sides is the same in both triangles, these triangles are similar. This type is less frequent on the GMAT.
- **SSS (SIDE, SIDE, SIDE):** If there are constant ratios of corresponding sides for two triangles, then the triangles are similar. This type is rarely seen on the GMAT, usually because most geometry questions won't give you that much information (all the lengths of six different sides!).

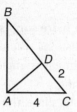

4. In triangles *ABC* and *ADC* above, angle *BAC* is a right angle and angle *ADC* is a right angle. Also, *DC* is 2 units long. What is the length of *BC*?

(A) 8
(B) 10
(C) $6\sqrt{3}$
(D) 12
(E) $12\sqrt{3}$

Solution: The two triangles are similar. You know this because they both contain a right angle and they share angle *B*. As soon as two triangles share two same angles, they must, by process of elimination, share the third angle too.

The sides of similar triangles are proportional. The shortest side of triangle *ADC* is 2. The shortest side of triangle *ABC* is 4. Therefore, the ratio of sides between these two triangles is 2 to 1. So if the longest side or hypotenuse of triangle *ADC* is 4, then the longest side of triangle *ABC* must be twice that, or 8.

The answer is A.

The most common similar triangle identity you might see is the following.

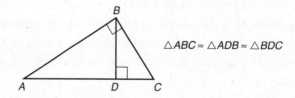

QUADRILATERALS

Quadrilaterals are 4-sided polygons. The four most commonly occurring quadrilaterals on the GMAT are the square, rectangle, parallelogram, and trapezoid.

TIP

Another important shape to note is a rhombus. It is a special type of parallelogram that has four equal sides.

QUADRILATERAL TYPES AND PROPERTIES

	Square	Rectangle	Parallelogram	Trapezoid
Properties	All opposite sides are parallel; All sides are the same length; All angles are 90°; Diagonals are the same length, intersect at 90°, and bisect each other; interior angles add up to 360°	All opposite sides are parallel; Opposite sides are the same length; All angles are 90°; Diagonals are the same length and bisect each other; interior angles add up to 360°	All opposite sides are parallel; Opposite sides are the same length; Opposite angles are equal; Diagonals bisect each other; interior angles add up to 360°	2 sides are parallel; Interior angles add up to 360°
Area	$A = s^2$	$A = l \cdot w$	$A = b \cdot h$	$A = \frac{1}{2}(b + c)h$ or (Avg. base) $\cdot h$
Perimeter	$P = 4s$	$P = 2l + 2w$	$P = 2a + 2b$	$P = a + b + c + d$
Key shapes	Diagonals create two 45-45-90 isosceles right triangles	Diagonals create 2 right triangles	Right triangle needed to find the height	Right triangle needed to find the height

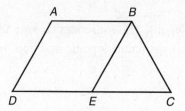

5. Within quadrilateral *ABCD* there is rhombus *ABED*, and *D*, *E*, and *C* are all on the same line. If we drew a line segment *AE*, is quadrilateral *ABCE* a rhombus?

(1) *BC* is parallel to *AE*.

(2) Angle *ADE* is 60°.

Solution: In order to determine if *ABCE* is a rhombus, we need to know that all four of the sides are equal and that the opposite angles are equal. Let's first label the entire diagram with sides and angles.

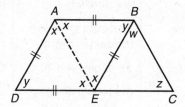

Statement 1 tells us that angles *w* and *z* are both equal to *x*. This means that *BE* and *EC* are equal, which are also equal to *AB*. We still don't know the lengths of *AE* and *BC*. *Insufficient*

Statement 2 tells us that *y* = 60; therefore, *x* = 60 and triangles *ADE* and *ABE* are equilaterals. So now *AE* is equal to all the other sides of quadrilateral *ABED*. By itself, we cannot be sure of the length of *BC* or the measure of angle *w*. *Insufficient*

When we look at statements 1 and 2 together, we have 3 equilateral triangles and all the sides are equal to each other. Therefore, *ABCE* is a rhombus.

The answer is C; both statements together are sufficient.

OTHER POLYGONS

Polygons are two-dimensional, closed plane figures that are bound by straight lines. You may see other polygons on the GMAT besides triangles and quadrilaterals such as pentagons, hexagons, or more complicated figures. You need to know a few things about polygons.

1. The sum of the interior angles of any polygon is $(n - 2) \cdot 180°$, where *n* is the number of sides.

2. A regular polygon is one where all sides are the same measure and all angles are the same measure.

3. All polygons can be broken down into smaller triangles, which can be a quick way to determine the sum of all interior angles.

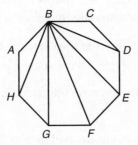

Here we have a regular octagon, with all sides and angles equal.

Sum of angles is (8 − 2) • 180° = 1080°.

You can also see that we can draw 6 triangles within the octagon. Since triangles have interior angles that add up to 180°, then octagons have 6 • 180 = 1080°.

When you see an irregular polygon on the GMAT, the key is to break the shape down into polygons that you recognize and can solve. For example, a shape like the front of a house can be broken down into rectangles and triangles.

CIRCLES

A circle is an infinite set of points that are all equidistant from a point called the center. Circles are often involved in some of the harder geometry problems on the GMAT, mostly because test makers combine circles with other geometric shapes such as triangles and quadrilaterals. Circles also have a large number of properties that can be used for a variety of GMAT questions. Let's first understand the basic definitions.

Definitions

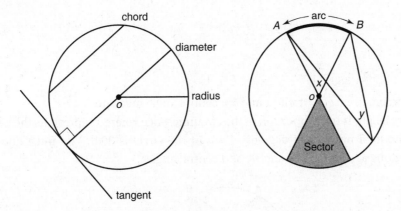

RADIUS: The distance from the center of the circle to the outside edge. The radius is usually the most important piece of information that you need for circle problems.

DIAMETER: The largest distance from one side of a circle to the other, going through the center. The diameter is twice the length of the radius.

CHORD: A line that connects any 2 points on the circle. Note that the diameter is also a chord.

CIRCUMFERENCE: The distance around the circle, which has a standard formula $C = 2\pi r$, where r is the radius.

ARC: Any portion of the circumference. The points *A* and *B* on the diagram create 2 arcs, which are the minor arc (shorter length) and the major arc (longer length).

CENTRAL ANGLE: An angle with its vertex at the center of the circle. These angles are used to calculate arc lengths and sector areas. This is angle *x* in the diagram.

INSCRIBED ANGLE: An angle with its vertex on the circumference of the circle. This is angle *y* in the diagram.

SECTOR: A portion of the area of a circle, defined by 2 radii and an arc.

TANGENT: A line that touches a circle at just one point. This tangent line is perpendicular to the radius at the point of tangency.

Circle Formulas and Properties

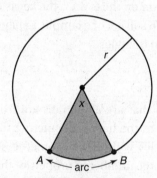

Your ability to connect the dots among all the geometry rules is a key factor to success. Therefore, you should know the main formulas in some of the commonly tested properties and relationships of circles. Know the following three most commonly used formulas for GMAT circles:

1. $A = \pi r^2$
2. $C = 2\pi r$
3. Arc length $= 2\pi r \left(\dfrac{x}{360°} \right)$

A = area, *C* = circumference, *r* = radius, and *x* = central angle measure.

Note that arc length is the proportion of the circumference where *x* represents the angular proportion. The total number of degrees of arc in the circle is 360°. You must know the relationship among arcs, inscribed angles, and central angles.

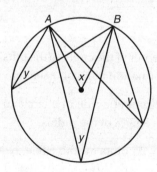

- **SIMILAR INSCRIBED ANGLES:** All inscribed angles that extend to the same arc or same 2 points on a circle are equal to each other. This can be seen with angles *y* in the previous diagram.

- **CENTRAL ANGLE VS. INSCRIBED ANGLE:** Any central angle that extends to the same arc or the same two points on a circle as does an inscribed angle is twice the size of the inscribed angle. Therefore as shown in the diagram, $x = 2y$.

- **TRIANGLES INSCRIBED IN A SEMICIRCLE:** Any triangle that is inscribed in a semicircle where the longest length is the diameter of the circle is always a right triangle.

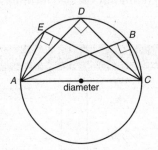

- **RADII CREATE ISOSCELES TRIANGLES:** Note that in some difficult circle problems, you can sometimes use 2 radii to create isosceles triangles and thus create 2 angles that are equal to each other.

---

6. What is the radius of the circle that circumscribes a triangle whose sides measure 41, 40, and 9?

   (A) 9
   (B) 20
   (C) 20.5
   (D) 41
   (E) 45

Solution: The 1st step is to draw this. Start by drawing a triangle, noting that one side is much shorter than the other two. Then draw a circle around the triangle.

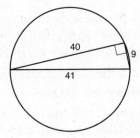

If you're unsure of this problem, look for special triangles. In this particular example, the triangle 9-40-41 is a right triangle and, more specifically, a Pythagorean right triangle identity. Remember the GMAT math is clean or works out smoothly. Since this is a right triangle embedded in a circle, the hypotenuse is the diameter. Note that the question asks for the radius. So if the diameter is 41, the radius is 20.5.

The answer is C.

VOLUMES AND 3-D FIGURES

The most common three-dimensional (3-D) figures in the GMAT geometry are cubes, rectangular solids, and cylinders. You may also see spheres, cones, or figures that are a combination of these. You will need to understand volumes, surface areas, and line segments within 3-D figures. A simple way to think of most volumes is that you are multiplying an area by a new dimension.

$$\text{Volume} = (\text{Area of 2-D surface}) \times (\text{Height})$$

The chart below outlines the most commonly needed formulas and properties of 3-D figures on the GMAT.

	Cube	Rectangular Solid	Cylinder	Sphere
Visualize as	Dice	Box	Soda Can	Ball
Definitions	Faces, edges, vertices, bases, and heights	Faces, edges, vertices, bases, lengths, widths, and heights	Bases, heights, radius	Radius, surface
Volume	$V = s^3$	$V = lwh$	$V = \pi r^2 h$	$V = \left(\dfrac{4}{3}\right)\pi r^3$
Surface area	$SA = 6s^2$	$SA = 2lw + 2lh + 2hw$	$SA = 2(\pi r^2) + 2\pi rh$	$SA = 4\pi r^2$
Longest length within	$L = \sqrt{(3s^2)}$	$L = \sqrt{(l^2 + w^2 + h^2)}$	$L = \sqrt{(4r^2 + h^2)}$	$L = 2r$

Note that a sphere would be considered a more unusual shape, as would be cones. However, we've added it to the above chart because there have been a few sphere questions where the volume formula was not given. In general, the GMAT test makers will give you the formulas required for unusual shapes. If the question gives you a more complex figure, look for ways to break it down into more common 3-D shapes.

With your knowledge of basic geometry and areas, you should be able to calculate the volume of most 3-D figures such as the triangular solid below.

TIP

Sometimes it helps to visualize unusual 3-D figures as 2-D figures, e.g., seeing the triangles within the cone shape.

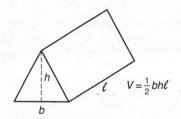

$V = \frac{1}{2}bh\ell$

7. A rectangular box of width a, length b, and height c has a solid cylinder of height c and of diameter a placed within it. If $a = 4$, $b = 5$, and $c = 6$, how much volume is left in the rectangular box?

(A) $60 - 12\pi$

(B) $240 - 96\pi$

(C) $120 - 24\pi$

(D) $120 - 12\pi$

(E) 96

Solution: This is a classic geometry problem where you have a geometric shape within another. The "break it down" tactic applies here. First, try to draw this out—visualize a soup can in a box. Then calculate the volume of the box, which is abc. Next calculate the volume of the solid cylinder, which is normally $V = \pi r^2 h$. In this case, we get

$$V = \pi \left(\frac{a}{2}\right)^2 c$$

since the radius is $\left(\frac{a}{2}\right)$ and the height is c. Finally, we subtract the volume of the cylinder from the volume of the box to get the volume left over.

$$\text{Volume left in box} = abc - \pi \left(\frac{a}{2}\right)^2 c \rightarrow 4 \cdot 5 \cdot 6 - \pi 2^2 \cdot 6 = 120 - 24\pi.$$

The answer is C.

Take some time to draw the 3-D figures correctly when you attempt the problem. This extra 5 to 10 seconds will help your visualization tremendously.

COORDINATE GEOMETRY

Coordinate geometry is simply the mapping of points, lines, and shapes on a coordinate plane. It has become more important in recent years. Coordinate geometry questions are often combined with algebraic equations. Below we review the basic equations and properties of coordinate geometry.

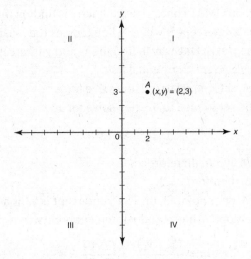

The figure above is called the **coordinate plane**. The horizontal line is called the **x-axis**, and the vertical line is the **y-axis**. The point O is the **origin**. The axes divide the planes into four quadrants, 1, 2, 3 and 4 as shown above. Every point in the plane has an **x-coordinate** and a **y-coordinate**, which is expressed (x, y).

Linear Equations

The line drawn in the diagram can be expressed using an algebraic equation. In coordinate geometry, the equation of a line is usually expressed using the slope-intercept formula.

TIP

When the linear equation is a horizontal line or a vertical line, then the equation of the line is simply $y = a$ or $x = b$, where a and b are constants.

> **SLOPE-INTERCEPT FORMULA**
>
> $$y = mx + b$$
>
> where m is the slope, b is the y-intercept, and $\frac{-b}{m}$ is the x-intercept

Slope

The slope of a line is an expression of its steepness. In the slope-intercept formula, it is m. We can think of the slope from left to right as a hill, where uphill is positive and downhill is negative. A straight horizontal line, which would be no hill at all, has a slope of 0. A straight vertical line has an undefined slope. The slope of a line can be found by calculating the following:

$$\frac{\text{Change in } y\text{-coordinate}}{\text{Change in } x\text{-coordinate}} = \frac{\Delta y}{\Delta x} = \frac{(y_2 - y_1)}{(x_2 - x_1)} = \frac{rise}{run}$$

Note that the slope is the same for all lines that are parallel to each other.

Lines with the equations $y = 2x$, $y = 2x + 7$, and $y = 2x + 11$ all have a slope of 2.

Lines that are perpendicular to each other will have slopes that are the negative reciprocals of each other.

The lines $y = 3x - 1$ and $y = -\frac{1}{3}x + 7$ intersect at 90° because 3 and $-\frac{1}{3}$ are negative reciprocals of each other.

x- and y-Intercepts

TIP

You don't always have to spend time converting the equation to the standard $y = mx + b$ form to find the x-intercepts.

The most important skill on GMAT coordinate geometry is finding the x- and y- intercepts of an equation quickly. The x-intercept is where a line crosses the x-axis and the y-intercept is where the line crosses the y-axis. One way to find the x- and y-intercepts is to use the formula $y = mx + b$. The other way is to set x or y equal to 0.

To find the y-intercept, set x equal to 0. Then solve for y.

To find the x-intercept, set y equal to 0. Then solve for x.

$$2x + 3y = 6$$

Solution: Set x equal to 0. $3y = 6$, therefore $y = 2$.

Set y equal to 0. $2x = 6$, therefore $x = 3$.

So, the x-intercept is 3, or at point $(3, 0)$. The y-intercept is 2, or at point $(0, 2)$. If needed, we can also calculate the slope using x- and y-intercept points.

$$m = \frac{(y_2 - y_1)}{(x_2 - x_1)} = \frac{(2-0)}{(0-3)} = -\frac{2}{3}$$

8. Line M is perpendicular to line N, whose equation is $3y = 4x + 12$. Lines M and N intersect at (a, b).

Is $a + b > 0$?

(1) The x-intercept of line M is less than that of line N.
(2) The y-intercept of line M is less than that of line N.

Solution: The first thing you must do is draw the graph.

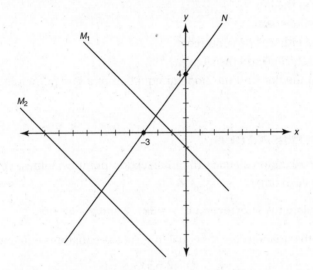

The other thing is to consider what the question is really asking. Lines M and N intersect at (a, b), which could be anywhere along either line. In order to figure out if $a + b > 0$, the point of intersection would have to be in either quadrant 1 (both positive) or quadrant 3 (both negative). Now let's look at the statements.

Statement 1 says the x-intercept of line M is less than that of line N. This means that the x-value of line M must be to the left of the x-intercept of line N. Therefore, line M will intersect line N in quadrant 3. Both values of a and b will be negative. Now we know that $a + b$ cannot be positive. *Sufficient*

Statement 2 says the y-intercept of line M is less than that of line N. In the previous statement, the x-intercept was already in the negative section and going further to the left, thus remaining negative. In this situation, the y-intercept of line N is positive. If the y-intercept of line M needs to be less, it could cross the y-axis above or below 0. If it's above 0, $a + b$ could be positive. If it's below 0, $a + b$ could be negative. Therefore, we can't be certain. *Insufficient*

The answer is A; statement 1 alone is sufficient.

Other Formulas and Properties

You will often be asked other types of coordinate geometry questions on the GMAT.

CALCULATE THE EQUATION OF THE LINE

Often in GMAT, coordinate geometry problems will ask you to determine the equation of the line. To do this, you will need any of the following:

1. Any 2 points on the line
2. Both x- and y-intercepts
3. The slope and either x- or y-intercept
4. One point on the line and the slope
5. One point on the line and the slope or equation of a line perpendicular or parallel to that line

CALCULATING INTERSECTIONS

Whenever you are asked to calculate the intersection point of 2 lines, you need to set the equations equal to each other.

Calculate the intersection of $y = 3x - 2$ and $y = 5x - 6$.

Solution: Since both equations are set equal to y, set the equations equal to each other.

$$3x - 2 = 5x - 6$$

We get $4 = 2x$. Therefore $x = 2$. Now substitute $x = 2$ into either of the original equations.

$$y = 3(2) - 2 = 6 - 2 = 4$$

So $y = 4$.

If you use the other equation, you get the same answer.

$$y = 5(2) - 6 = 10 - 6 = 4$$

The intersection is at (2,4).

DISTANCE FORMULA

When you have 2 points on a coordinate plane, you can usually find the distance between them using the Pythagorean theorem. (You can't use this formula for 2 points on the same axis.) The distance is found by drawing a right triangle between the 2 points.

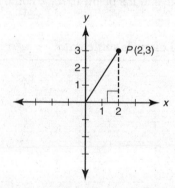

Distance between any 2 points (x_1, y_1) and (x_2, y_2) = $\sqrt{(\Delta x)^2 + (\Delta y)^2} = \sqrt{(x_1 - x_2)^2 + (y_1 - y_2)^2}$

MIDPOINT FORMULA

When you have 2 points in the coordinate plane, you can find their midpoint, which can save you time on some of the more complex geometry questions. The basic idea is to calculate the average of the x- and y-coordinates.

$$\text{Midpoint} = \left(\frac{(x_1 + x_2)}{(2)}, \frac{(y_1 + y_2)}{(2)} \right)$$

Nonlinear Equations—Curved Lines and Circles

Sometimes on the GMAT you will see quadratic equations and circles in the coordinate plane. In these cases, your knowledge of intercepts and algebraic manipulation will be most useful.

$$y = x^2 - 3x + 2 \qquad\qquad \text{or} \qquad\qquad x^2 + y^2 = 100$$

When $x = 0$, the y-intercept is 2.

When $y = 0$, we get
$(x - 2)(x - 1) = 0$; thus the
x-intercepts are 1 and 2.

Note that this equation creates a circle of radius 10.

Using algebra, we can also calculate the x- and y-intercepts to be at ± 10.

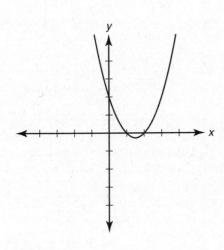

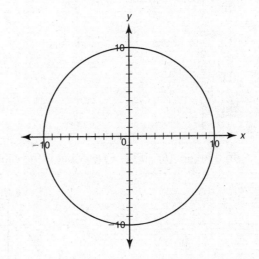

As you can see, graphing quadratic equations creates curved lines. If you still have trouble, try using a T-chart to get a better visual understanding. You can also use your knowledge of algebraic manipulation to simplify the equation.

1. If $\ell1$ is perpendicular to $\ell2$ and $\ell2$ is perpendicular to $\ell3$ in a three-dimensional space, what do we know about the relationship between $\ell1$ and $\ell3$?

    I. $\ell1 \parallel \ell3$
    II. $\ell1 \perp \ell3$
    III. $\ell1$ equal to $\ell3$

    (A) I only
    (B) II only
    (C) I and III only
    (D) II and III only
    (E) None of the above

2. Cylindrical container x has a height of h and a radius of r. Cylindrical container y has a height 3 times and a radius one-half that of cylinder x. If cylinder y is half-full of water and all of this is poured into empty cylinder x, how full is cylinder x?

    (A) $\dfrac{1}{8}$

    (B) $\dfrac{1}{4}$

    (C) $\dfrac{3}{8}$

    (D) $\dfrac{5}{8}$

    (E) $\dfrac{3}{4}$

3. In triangle ABC, if $BD = DC$, what is the value of angle BAD?

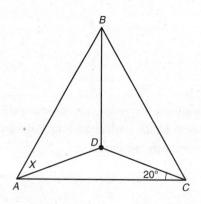

    (1) Triangle ABC is equilateral.
    (2) AD bisects BDC.

4. If x and z are the centers of 2 circles x and y, respectively, what percent of the area of circle x is the area of circle z?

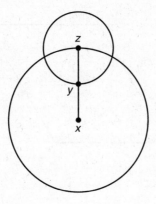

(1) $yz = \left(\dfrac{1}{2}\right)xz$

(2) The circumference of circle x is 49.

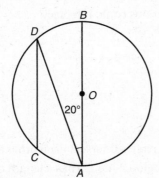

5. The circumference of the circle above is 18π, and AB is parallel to CD. What is the length of minor arc CD?

(A) $\left(\dfrac{9}{2}\right)\pi$

(B) 5π

(C) 12π

(D) 18π

(E) $\left(\dfrac{27}{2}\right)\pi$

6. Rhombus *ABCD* of side 6 has perpendicular line *ED* intersecting side *AB*. What is the area of trapezoid *BCDE*?

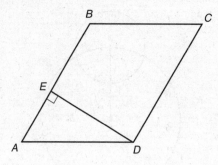

(1) $\dfrac{AE}{EB} = \dfrac{1}{1}$

(2) Angle *EDA* is 30°.

7. A line segment in the coordinate plane begins at the point (1, 4) and then continues past both the *x*- and *y*-axes. If the product of its *x*-intercept and *y*-intercept is negative, which of the following equations could intersect?

(A) $x = 3$

(B) $y = 13$

(C) $y = -1.25x + 10$

(D) $y = 1.25x + 10$

(E) $y = -0.1x + 6$

8. In the diagram below, the 4 circles intersect each other at a point tangent to their centers, forming a shaded region. Line *BD* has a length of $8\sqrt{2}$. What is the area of the shaded region?

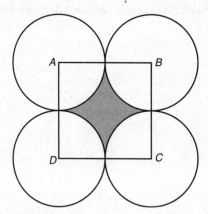

(A) $16 - 4\pi$

(B) $64 - 16\pi$

(C) $128 - 32\pi$

(D) $128 - 16\pi$

(E) 128

SOLUTIONS

1. **(E)** The best way to solve this question is to visualize it with a drawing.

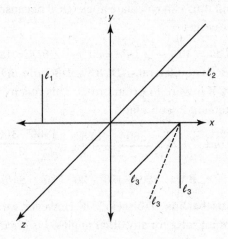

The trick here is to understand that perpendicular lines are not necessarily in the same surface plane. In other words, you should consider 3 dimensions instead of 2 dimensions. As you can see from the drawing, $\ell 3$ is not necessarily parallel to or perpendicular to $\ell 1$. It is also not necessarily the same length.

2. **(C)** Let's draw out both cylinders X and Y to visualize better.

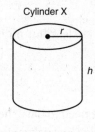
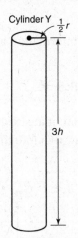

We can solve this question algebraically or by picking numbers. Let's try algebraically.

The volume of cylinder X = $V_X = \pi r^2 h$.

The volume of cylinder Y = $V_Y = \pi(0.5r)^2(3h) = \left(\dfrac{3}{4}\right)\pi r^2 h$.

So the volume of cylinder Y is three-quarters that of cylinder X. If cylinder Y were half-full of water, the volume of the water would be $\dfrac{1}{2} \bullet \left(\dfrac{3}{4}\right)\pi r^2 h = \left(\dfrac{3}{8}\right)\pi r^2 h$. Since we know the volume of cylinder X and we know the volume of water, we know that cylinder X would be $\frac{3}{8}$ full.

3. **(A)** In data sufficiency questions, we cannot assume that figures are drawn to scale. Even though it may look like an equilateral triangle, we cannot be certain unless information tells us so. We do know angles *DBC* and *DCB*.

   Statement 1 confirms for us that the triangle *ABC* is an equilateral triangle. We are given angle *DCA* and thus can calculate angle *DCB* because the entire angle *ACB* must equal 60°. From this we get

   $$\angle DCB = \angle DBC = 40° \ \rightarrow \ \angle DBA = 20° \ \rightarrow \ \angle BDC = 180° - 40° - 40° = 100°$$

   Since triangle *ABC* is equilateral, $\angle DCB = \angle DBC$ and $BD = DC$. The point *D* is at the midpoint of line *BC* if it were to extend to *D*. This means that the line *AD* will bisect $\angle BDC$ (making statement 2 redundant).

   $$\angle BDA = \angle ADC = \frac{(360° - \angle BDC)}{2} = \frac{(360° - 100°)}{2} = 130° \ \rightarrow$$

   $$\angle BAD = 180° - 130° - 20° = 30° \quad \textit{Sufficient}$$

   Statement 2 tells us that line *AD* bisects *BDC*. However, we don't know what $\angle DCB$ and $\angle DBC$ are so we cannot solve for any other angles. *Insufficient*

   Statement 1 alone is sufficient.

4. **(A)** What we know is there are two circles, *x* and *z*. What we want is $\frac{A_z}{A_x}$. What we need is A_z and A_x, $\frac{A_z}{A_x}$, r_z and r_x, or $\frac{r_z}{r_x}$ because the radius will also give us the area.

   Statement 1 tells us that the radius of *z* is half the radius of *x*, giving us $\frac{r_z}{r_x} = \frac{1}{2}$. *Sufficient*

   Statement 2 gives us information about circle *x* but no information about circle *z*. *Insufficient*

   Statement 1 alone is sufficient.

5. **(B)** In order to find the minor arc length, we need to have the central angle going to *CD*. Therefore, we should draw that into the circle to visualize the problem better.

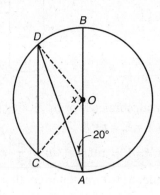

Let x be the central angle. In order to find x, we need to get $\angle DOB$ and $\angle OAC$. Another method would be to find $\angle ODC$ and $\angle OCD$. We are given the angle 20°, which is also the inscribed angle for arc BD. This means that the central angle going to the same arc BD would be double the measure of the inscribed angle; therefore $\angle DOB = 40°$. Because lines AB and CD are parallel, $\angle ADC$ is also 20°. $\angle ADC$ is an inscribed angle to the arc AC, which means $\angle AOC$ is a central angle going to the same arc AC. Therefore $\angle AOC = 40°$. We now know that $x = 180° - 40° - 40° = 100°$. The circumference was given as $C = 18\pi = 2\pi r$; thus the radius is 9. To calculate the arc length of CD,

$$\text{arc length} = \left(\frac{\text{central angle}}{360°}\right) \bullet 2\pi r = \left(\frac{100}{360}\right) \bullet 2\pi 9 = \left(\frac{10}{36}\right) \bullet 2\pi 9 = 5\pi$$

6. **(D)** Since this figure is a rhombus, we know that all four sides are of length 6. What we need to solve for the trapezoid is the length of the two bases EB and CD as well as the height ED. We already have $CD = 6$.

Statement 1 gives us the ratio of sides AE and EB, which means $AE = 3$ and $EB = 3$. Since triangle AED is a right triangle (and a 30-60-90 one too), we can also calculate the length of ED using the Pythagorean theorem.

$6^2 - 3^2 = ED^2 \rightarrow ED = \sqrt{36-9} = \sqrt{27} = 3\sqrt{3} \rightarrow$ We could have used the 30-60-90 ratios.

To find the area of a trapezoid, $A = (\text{average base})(\text{height}) = \left(\frac{(3+6)}{2}\right) \bullet 3\sqrt{3} = \frac{27\sqrt{3}}{2}$ *Sufficient.*

Statement 2 tells us that triangle AED is a 30-60-90 right triangle. Since we have the length of the hypotenuse, we can determine the other two sides using the ratio $1\text{-}\sqrt{3}\text{-}2$. Sides AE and ED would be 3 and $3\sqrt{3}$, respectively. Now we can solve for the trapezoid as we did in statement 1 above. *Sufficient*

Each statement alone is sufficient.

7. **(D)** When we draw this out, we should note how far the line segment from the point can possibly extend. It must cross both the x-axis and y-axis.

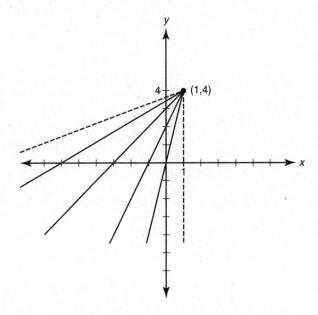

Clearly, answer choices A and B will not intersect. For the other equations, we can just plug in *x*- and *y*-intercepts.

Equation	*x*-intercept	*y*-intercept	Will it intersect?
$y = -1.25x + 10$	$\dfrac{10}{1.25} = 8$	10	No
$y = 1.25x + 10$	$-\dfrac{10}{1.25} = -8$	10	Yes
$y = -0.1x + 6$	$\dfrac{6}{0.1} = 60$	6	No

8. **(B)** When a geometry problem seems complex, it's important to break it down into easier-to-manage steps. In order to calculate the shaded region, you need to take the area of the square and subtract the area of each sector of the 4 circles. More simply put, you just need to subtract the area of one circle from the area of the square. The problem gives the diameter of the square as $8\sqrt{2}$. Using the 45-45-90 right triangle ratio of 1-1-$\sqrt{2}$, you know that a hypotenuse of $8\sqrt{2}$ means you have a side of 8. Thus the radius of the circle is 4. This gives:

$$\text{area of square} - \text{area of the circle} = s^2 - \pi r^2 = 8^2 - \pi 4^2 = 64 - 16\pi$$

Statistics

7

→ **AVERAGE (ARITHMETIC MEAN)**
→ **SETS OF NUMBERS**
→ **MEDIAN**
→ **RANGE**
→ **MODE**
→ **STANDARD DEVIATION**

STATISTICS: DIAGNOSTIC SKILL QUIZ

> **DIRECTIONS:** Before continuing, try your hand at these statistics questions to assess your level of understanding. The answers will be explained throughout this chapter.

1. In a class of 25 students, 3 students did not submit any book reports for extra credit, 8 students each submitted 1 book report, 6 students each submitted 2 book reports, and the rest of the students each submitted at least 3 book reports. If the average (arithmetic mean) number of book reports submitted per student was 2, what is the maximum number of book reports that any individual student could have submitted?

   (A) 4
   (B) 5
   (C) 7
   (D) 9
   (E) 30

2. What is the sum of all consecutive, positive, even integers between –200 and 200, inclusive?

   (A) 0
   (B) 9,900
   (C) 10,000
   (D) 10,100
   (E) 20,200

3. 5 children's books have an average (arithmetic mean) length of 18 pages and a median length of 17 pages. If three times the length of the shortest book is one page less than the longest book, what is the longest possible length, in pages, of the longest book?

    (A) 22
    (B) 34
    (C) 41
    (D) 43
    (E) 54

4. Set S consists of the integers –7, 5, 3, 11, and x. Set T consists of the integers –3, 5, 0, 7, –7, and y. If M is the median of set S, if K is the mode of set T, and if M^K is a factor of 35, what is the value of y if x is negative?

    (A) –6
    (B) 0
    (C) 1
    (D) 2
    (E) 6

5. Set x consists of five consecutive even integers. Set y consists of consecutive prime numbers between 30 and 50. Set z consists of the following numbers: {120, 111, 109, 130, 108}. If we increase the value of each element in set x by 50% and we increase the value of each element in set y by adding 10, what is the order of magnitude of their standard deviations from least to greatest?

    (A) z, y, x
    (B) y, z, x
    (C) x, z, y
    (D) x, y, z
    (E) Cannot be determined

STATISTICS CONTENT SUMMARY/CHECKLIST

By the end of this statistics chapter, you should have enough information to review and understand the following topics:

☐ Average (arithmetic mean)
☐ Sets of numbers
☐ Median
☐ Range
☐ Mode
☐ Standard deviation

INTRODUCTION

Statistics is a topic that was very relevant to you even before you become a business school student. We see statistics cited every day in our professional and personal lives. Now here is your chance to appreciate them even more! If you are unfamiliar with statistics theory, know that you have to learn it for your MBA anyway, so you might as well start learning now. Mastering statistics will increase your confidence and will help you on some of the harder problems. The GMAT has lately been including more statistics problems. However, the depth of theory is not too complex. For example, you don't need to know how to calculate standard deviation, just how to maneuver it or understand its magnitude. You should expect to see at least a couple of statistics questions if not more.

AVERAGE (ARITHMETIC MEAN)

The **average** or the **mean** is the most common statistical concept on the GMAT. The basic formula is straightforward.

$$\text{Average} = \text{arithmetic mean} = \text{mean} = \bar{x} = \frac{\text{the sum of the terms in the set}}{\text{the number of terms in the set}}$$

Billy's marks this term were 80, 85, 90, 95, and 60. What was his average mark?

Solution: There are five terms. If we plug them into the formula, we get

$$\frac{(60+80+85+90+95)}{5} = \frac{410}{5} = 82.$$

Note that you may see the words **average**, **arithmetic mean**, and **mean** used interchangeably on the GMAT. They all mean the same thing. The test makers are not likely to give you the sum of the terms and the number of terms. That would be way too easy. If you do get that, then you're probably doing pretty badly on the test. What you will likely see is any of the following:

- An average and a way to find the sum of the terms
- An average and a given number of terms
- An abstract mix of the sum of the terms and the number of terms

Strategies for the Arithmetic Mean

1. **LOOK AT THE ANSWER CHOICES FIRST.** The answer choices tend to give clues for many GMAT quantitative problems, but this is especially true for questions involving the mean.

2. **THINK CONCEPTUALLY.** Although this advice applies to most quantitative problems, it is particularly important for questions involving the mean. Look for a way to solve without calculations, especially if you see the key word "approximately" or "estimate" in the question stem.

3. **USE YOUR "BEST FRIENDS": ALGEBRA AND NUMBER PROPERTIES.** Understanding arithmetic mean problems may require you to set up algebraic equations or leverage number properties to unlock a shortcut or key insight.

1. In a class of 25 students, 3 students did not submit a book report for extra credit, 8 students each submitted 1 book report, 6 students each submitted 2 book reports, and the rest of the students each submitted at least 3 book reports. If the average (arithmetic mean) number of book reports submitted was 2, what is the maximum number of book reports that any individual student could have submitted?

   (A) 4
   (B) 5
   (C) 7
   (D) 9
   (E) 30

Solution: If we apply the standard equation for averages to this question we will get

$$\text{average number of book reports submitted} = \frac{(\text{total number of reports submitted})}{(\text{total number of students})}$$

We know that $3 + 8 + 6 = 17$ students submitted at most 2 book reports. What we don't know is how many reports the other 8 students submitted. The key insight here is that we have to maximize the number of book reports that any student could have submitted. We can do this by letting 7 of the students each submit 3 reports. The 8th student would then submit the maximum number of reports possible. Our equation will look like this:

$$\text{average} = 2 = \frac{(3(0 \text{ reports}) + 8(1 \text{ report}) + 6(2 \text{ reports}) + 7(3 \text{ reports}) + 1(x))}{25}$$

The sum of all the reports must equal $2 \cdot 25 = 50$. So we get

$$8 + 12 + 21 + x = 50 \;\rightarrow\; 41 + x = 50 \;\rightarrow\; x = 9 \text{ reports (which is pretty nerdy)}$$

The answer is D.

SETS OF NUMBERS

A **set** is a collection of things. In math, a set usually refers to a set of numbers.

An **element** is one of the things or numbers in a set. A set can have a finite or an infinite number of elements.

If we take part of a set made up of elements, we have a **subset**.

> If set $S = \{-3, 2, 7, 10, 100\}$, and if set $T = \{2, 7, 10\}$, then T is a subset of S

Remember these few things about sets of numbers:

1. Rearrange the order of elements from smallest to largest. Not every set is given to you in the proper order. The first step when you see any set of numbers is to fix this.

2. When you multiply or divide a set by a constant, you must multiply or divide every element in the set.

3. Several commonly seen sets of numbers appear on the GMAT. Be familiar with them. Remember n is any interger.

   - **CONSECUTIVE INTEGERS:** $\{-3, -2, -1, 0, 1, 2, 3)$. This can be written as $n, n+1, n+2, \ldots$
   - **CONSECUTIVE EVEN INTEGERS:** $\{-10, -8, -6, -4, -2\}$. These can be written as $2n, 2n+2, 2n+4, \ldots$
   - **CONSECUTIVE ODD INTEGERS:** $\{1, 3, 5, 7, 9, \ldots\}$. These can be written as $2n+1, 2n+3, 2n+5, \ldots$
   - **PRIME NUMBERS:** $\{2, 3, 5, 7, 11, 13, 17, \ldots\}$
   - **CONSECUTIVE MULTIPLES** of any number: e.g., $\{7, 14, 21, 28, 35\}$

4. To find the number of elements in a larger set of consecutive numbers, you can do the following calculation: (largest number) – (smallest number) + 1

   How many numbers are between 50 and 175, inclusive?

   Solution: $175 - 50 + 1 = 126$ numbers

   Note that if we wanted the numbers between 50 and 175 but not including 50 and 175, we would take (largest number) – (smallest number) – 1 → $175 - 50 - 1 = 124$ numbers.

5. To find the number of multiples in a set, use $\dfrac{(\text{largest number}) - (\text{smallest number})}{\text{multiple}} + 1$.

   Be careful that the largest and smallest numbers are actual multiples themselves so that they fit the criteria.

   How many even integers are between 520 and 300, inclusive?

   Solution: $\dfrac{(520 - 300)}{2} + 1 = 111$ even integers.

   If the question above had asked about even integers between 521 and 299, we still would need to use 520 and 300 in the equation. What if the questions wanted the number of multiples of 3 between 520 and 300 exclusive? You would get

   $$\frac{(520 - 300)}{3} + 1 = \frac{220}{3} + 1 = 73\frac{1}{3} + 1$$

   In this case, take $73 + 1 = 74$ multiples of 3.

2. What is the sum of all consecutive, positive, even integers between –200 and 200, inclusive?

(A) 0
(B) 9,900
(C) 10, 000
(D) 10,100
(E) 20,200

Solution: Note that the question stem threw in the word "positive," hoping that you might miss it. The question is really asking about the sum of all even integers from 2 to 200, inclusive. To find the sum, we need to take the average of all the terms and multiply by the number of terms. Since we have consecutive numbers, the average is simply

$$\frac{(200-2)}{2} + 2 = 101.$$

(We will explain this concept later in the chapter.) To find the number of terms, find the difference between the highest and lowest number, divide the result by 2 because we are looking only at even integers, and then don't forget to add one. We get

$$\frac{(200-2)}{2} + 1 \rightarrow \frac{198}{2} + 1 \rightarrow 99 + 1 = 100 \text{ terms}$$

The sum of all the numbers is now $101 \cdot 100$. Without doing any calculations, you should realize that the answer will be a little over 10,000.

The answer is D.

MEDIAN

The **median** is the middle value of a set of numbers when the numbers are arranged in order. If the set has an even number of terms, it is the average of the two middle terms in the set.

> The median of the set {2, 3, 5, 7, 11} is 5 because it is the middle term. The median of the set {2, 3, 5, 7, 11, 13} is 6 because the average of the two middle terms, 5 and 7, is 6.

Median and Mean

For consecutive sets, otherwise known as evenly distributed sets, the median and the mean are equal. This statistics concept is tested often on the GMAT. One great tactic to determine the mean and median of a consecutive set quickly is by taking the average of the first and last number.

> What is the mean and median of set Z: {6, 12, 18, 24, 30, 36, 42, 48}?

Using the first and last elements $\rightarrow \dfrac{(48+6)}{2} = 27$

3. 5 children's books have an average (arithmetic mean) length of 18 pages and a median length of 17 pages. If three times the length of the shortest book is one page less than the longest book, what is the longest possible length, in pages, of the longest book?

(A) 22
(B) 34
(C) 41
(D) 43
(E) 54

Solution: Let A, B, C, D, and E be the number of pages of each book from shortest to longest, respectively. We know that $C = 17$ and $3A + 1 = E$. In order to maximize the length of E, we need to maximize the length of A. This means that the shortest 2 books also need to be the same length; therefore $A = B$. We now have A, A, 17, D, and $3A + 1$ as our 5 books. Because we have a fixed average, D needs to be the lowest possible value so that we can maximize the length of the 5th book; therefore $D = 17$. Since the average is 18 and there are 5 books, we can use the formula for arithmetic mean to get

$$A + A + 17 + 17 + 3A + 1 = 18 \bullet 5 \ \rightarrow \ 5A + 35 = 90 \ \rightarrow \ 5A = 55.$$

Thus $A = 11$ and the longest book is $3A + 1 = 34$ pages long.

The answer is B.

RANGE

The **range** is the difference between the largest value of a set and the smallest value of a set.

> The range of the set {-7, -2, 6, 9, 10} is 17, which we get from
> 10 - (-7) = 17.

Remember a few things about the range of a set.

1. The range is always a positive number.
2. If you add numbers to a set that are between the highest and lowest numbers, the range is not affected.
3. A range of zero means that all numbers in the set are the same, e.g. {3, 3, 3, 3}.

MODE

The **mode** is the most frequently occurring number in a set. A set can have multiple modes. If all the numbers in a set are distinct from each other, then there is no mode.

> A: {2, 4, 4, 8, 8, 10, 10, 12} has three modes: 4, 8, and 10.
> B: {2, 4, 4, 8, 10, 12} has only one mode: 4.
> C: {2, 4, 8, 10, 12} has no mode.

On their own, each statistics concept is relatively straightforward. So then how can the test makers create difficult questions? Often the GMAT will present statistics problems that combine concepts from mean, median, mode, and range.

4. Set S consists of integers -7, 5, 3, 11, and x. Set T consists of integers -3, 5, 0, 7, -7, and y. If M is the median of set S, if K is the mode of set T, and if M^K is a factor of 35, what is the value of y if x is negative?

(A) -6
(B) 0
(C) 1
(D) 2
(E) 6

Solution: This is one of those question types that students tend to stare at too long. Don't panic, just breathe and focus. The best start here is to write everything down, making sure that you reorder the sets.

$$S: \{x, -7, 3, 5, 11\} \qquad T: \{-7, -3, 0, 5, 7, y\}$$
$$M = \text{Median of } S \qquad K = \text{Mode of } T \qquad M^K \text{ is a factor of } 35$$

Note that we placed x and y arbitrarily in their respective sets, not forgetting that x is negative. From this we can determine that $M = 3$. This gives us 3^K as a factor of 35. You're probably asking yourself how this is possible. The catch, of course, is that K must be zero so $3^0 = 1$, making that a factor of 35. If K represents the mode of set T, then y must be 0 in order for that set even to have a mode.

An alternative, super shortcut is to notice the answer choices compared with the numbers in set T. All the numbers in set T are distinct, which means that y must be one of those numbers in order to have a mode. None of the answer choices, except B, have any numbers that are in set T. Thus $y = 0$.

The answer is B.

STANDARD DEVIATION

Standard deviation is a measure of the **spread** of numbers in a set. Another way to say this is that it is the **dispersion** or **deviation** of numbers. More specifically, the standard deviation looks at how closely terms in a set are spread out around the set's mean. You will not have to calculate standard deviation on the GMAT. However, you should know how it is calculated, what exactly it stands for, and what aspects are tested on the GMAT.

1. Analyze and compare magnitudes of different sets and their standards deviations
2. Determine what happens to a standard deviation when changes are made to the elements of the set

Calculating Standard Deviation

The steps to calculating the standard deviation are in the following example.

Set S: {2, 4, 9, 10, 15}.

1. Calculate the mean of the set: $\frac{40}{5} = 8$.

2. Find the difference between each term and the mean. Then square that difference.

Term	Difference from Mean	Square of Difference
2	$(2-8) = -6$	$(2-8)^2 = 36$
4	$(4-8) = -4$	$(4-8)^2 = 16$
9	$(9-8) = 1$	$(9-8)^2 = 1$
10	$(10-8) = 2$	$(10-8)^2 = 4$
15	$(15-8) = 7$	$(15-8)^2 = 49$

3. Calculate the sum of the differences between each value and the mean squared:

$$36 + 16 + 1 + 4 + 49 = 106$$

4. Divide the previous sum by the number of terms:

$\frac{106}{5} = 21.2 \rightarrow$ This is also known as the **variance, or the mean of the squares**.

5. Take the square root of the previous value:

$$\sqrt{21.2} = 4.604$$

Here are some other things to keep in mind about the standard deviation.

- Standard deviation is never negative. If it is zero, this means that all numbers in the set are equal, such as in the set {2, 2, 2, 2, 2}.
- Adding or subtracting a constant to each number in a set does not change the standard deviation.
- If you multiply each term in a set by a number greater than 1, the standard deviation will increase. Conversely, if you divide each term in a set by a number greater than 1, the standard deviation will decrease.
- The variance is the square of the standard deviation.
- Numbers that are tightly clustered around an average have a smaller standard deviation than numbers that are spread out.
- When analyzing the standard deviation among sets, the first thing to look at is the relative spread of the numbers. This usually is enough. If you are still not sure, look at the range of the set as a tiebreaker. If you still aren't sure, then you may have to calculate the average and look at how spread the numbers are around the mean.

5. Set x consists of five consecutive even integers. Set y consists of consecutive prime numbers between 30 and 50. Set z consists of the following numbers: {120, 111, 109, 130, 108}. If we increase the value of each element in set x by 50% and we increase the value of each element in set y by adding 10, what is the order of their standard deviations from least to greatest?

(A) z, y, x

(B) y, z, x

(C) x, z, y

(D) x, y, z

(E) Cannot be determined

Solution: From the information above, we initially have the following sets. Note that set x was constructed by selecting a random set of even integers.

$$x: \{2, 4, 6, 8, 10\} \qquad y: \{31, 37, 41, 43, 47\} \qquad z: \{108, 109, 111, 120, 130\}$$

We have rearranged the elements in the sets in their proper order. Note that we could have chosen any series of values for set x. With the changes mentioned, the sets become

$$x: \{3, 6, 9, 12, 15\} \qquad y: \{41, 47, 51, 53, 57\} \qquad z: \{108, 109, 111, 120, 130\}$$

The quickest way to observe the magnitudes of standard deviations is to look at the spread of numbers in the set. Set x has a spread of 3. Set y has a spread of 6, 4, 2, and 4. Set z has a spread of 1, 2, 9, and 10. If you're unsure, take a look at the ranges, too. The range of x is 12, the range of y is 16, and the range of z is 22. Therefore, z has the largest standard deviation and x has the smallest standard deviation.

The answer is D.

1. The table shows the maximum and minimum recorded temperatures for City X.

	April	May	June	July	Aug.	Sept.
Minimum	29	30	31	33	31	30
Maximum	42	54	65	70	63	53

Which of the following measures is greater for the maximum recorded temperatures than for the minimum recorded temperatures during the months shown for City X?

  I: The average (arithmetic mean)

 II: The range

III: The standard deviation

(A) I only

(B) III only

(C) I and II

(D) II and III

(E) I, II, and III

2. Is the standard deviation of set X greater than the standard deviation of set Y?

  (1) Set X has no mode, and set Y has consecutive terms.

  (2) The range of set X is greater than the range of set Y.

3. A waitress serving customers throughout the day keeps track of the number of people she serves each hour. On Monday, the number of people she served in each of the hours during her shift was 6, 7, 5, 10, 7, 6, S, and T. If there is only one mode for the number of customers served in an hour on Monday, how many different numbers could be the mode?

(A) 2

(B) 3

(C) 4

(D) Greater than 4

(E) It cannot be determined from the information given

4. The median monthly rental income of a commercial real estate property with 17 different stores is $5,000. If the average rental income increases by 20% in the next month, what will the median rental income in the real estate property be next month?

(A) $5,000

(B) $5,500

(C) $6,000

(D) $6,500

(E) It cannot be determined from the information given

5. What is the standard deviation of the 4 integers a, b, c, and d?

   (1) $b = a + 2$, $c = b + 2$, and $d = a + 6$
   (2) $a = 6$, $b = 8$, and $d = 12$

6. For set T: {100, 102, 101, 103, 102, 100, 101, 103, Y}, which of the following values would increase the standard deviation the most?

   (A) 100
   (B) 101
   (C) 102
   (D) 103
   (E) 104

7. The median of the four terms a, b, $a + b$, and $b - a$ is 3. If $a > b > 0$, what is the arithmetic mean (average) of the four terms?

   (A) 4
   (B) $\dfrac{(2b+a)}{2}$
   (C) $\dfrac{3b}{2} + a$
   (D) $3 + \dfrac{(b-a)}{4}$
   (E) $4 + \dfrac{(b+a)}{2}$

8. Rakesh took 5 engineering midterms during his course last semester. Each of his scores was between 1 and 100, inclusive. What was Rakesh's median score for these 5 engineering midterms?

   (1) Rakesh's scores on the first 3 midterms were 66, 77, and 63, respectively. Rakesh's average (arithmetic mean) on all 5 midterms was 76.
   (2) Rakesh's scores on the first 4 midterms were 66, 77, 63, and 86, respectively. Rakesh's average on the last 3 midterms was 79.

ANSWER KEY

1. **(E)**	3. **(C)**	5. **(A)**	7. **(D)**
2. **(E)**	4. **(E)**	6. **(E)**	8. **(B)**

SOLUTIONS

1. **(E)** Let's look at each statement carefully one at a time.

I: The average temperature for the maximum recordings is clearly greater than that for the minimum recorded temperatures. There is no need to calculate when it is so obvious from the chart. True

II: The range of the maximum temperatures is $70 - 42 = 28$. The range of the minimum temperatures is $33 - 29 = 4$. True

III: Remember that standard deviation is simply the spread or dispersion of numbers and you do not need to know how to calculate it. If you look at the spread of numbers for the maximum temperatures, they are far more spread out than those of the minimum temperatures. True

2. **(E)** What we really want to know in this question is if the numbers in set X have a larger spread or dispersion than the numbers in set Y. The statements talk about modes, consecutive terms, and range, which may or may not affect the standard deviation. Our best bet is to come up with examples of sets in order to disprove sufficiency for each of the statements.

Statement 1 essentially implies that neither set X nor set Y has a mode. We can come up with 2 examples.

$$X: \{2, 4, 5\} \text{ and } Y: \{2, 3, 4\} \text{ or } Y: \{3, 6, 9\}$$

These 2 different sets of Y have standard deviations less than or greater than that of set X. *Insufficient*

Statement 2 suggests that a greater range will always lead to a greater standard deviation, but this is not true. Again, let's come up with a specific example.

$$X: \{2, 4, 6, 8\} \text{ and } Y: \{2, 3, 4, 5, 6, 7\} \text{ or } Y: \{2, 7\}$$

Again we come up with 2 different sets of Y where both have a smaller range than X. The first set has a smaller standard deviation, and the second set has a larger standard deviation. *Insufficient*

When we combine statements 1 and 2, we can take the example we just used above to disprove sufficiency. *Insufficient*

Both statements together are still not sufficient.

3. **(C)** In order to have only one mode, one of the numbers in the set must occur the most frequently. Currently, both 6 and 7 occur twice, but we don't know what S and T are. They could be anything. Let's write out the possible scenarios to see how many unique modes we can create

Case 1: $S = 7$, $T = 7$ → 7 is the mode
Case 2: $S = 6$, $T = 6$ → 6 is the mode
Case 3: $S = 5$, $T = 5$ → 5 is the mode
Case 4: $S = 10$, $T = 10$ → 10 is the mode

If S and T were two other numbers, say $S = 8$ and $T = 8$, this would violate the fact that there can be only one mode. Therefore, we have 4 possible modes.

4. **(E)** Often our assumptions can trip us up. For example, just because the average rental increase was 20% doesn't mean that each property had a 20% increase on its rent. We are given 17 properties, so the median would be ranked 8th among the rental incomes, leaving us with 7 rental incomes on either side of the set. We could increase all the rental incomes by 20% and the median would become $6,000. However, we could also increase fewer or even one rental income by a much larger amount to give us the same average increase. So we really don't know what the exact rental distribution is. There is no way to determine the answer to this problem.

5. **(A)** In order to determine standard deviation, we need to know the spread of all the numbers. If we jump ahead to statement 2, we don't have any value for c; therefore we cannot determine the standard deviation. *Insufficient*

   Statement 1 gives us enough information to determine that the integers in the set are a, $a + 2$, $a + 4$, and $a + 6$. Even though we don't have specific values, we do have the spread of numbers. No matter what the value of a is, the four integers will have the same distribution. *Sufficient*

   Statement 1 alone is sufficient.

6. **(E)** Standard deviation is a measure of the spread of numbers and, more specifically, the distribution of numbers around the mean. When we put the set above in correct order, we have {100, 100, 101, 101, 102, 102, 103, 103, Y}. Of the answer choices, the only number outside our current group is 104. Just to be sure, we can check the mean of this set, which is 101.5. The number that is most likely to affect the standard deviation will be the one that's farthest from the mean. The number 104 will make this set as widely distributed as possible.

7. **(D)** The first thing we need to figure out is how these numbers rank in value. We know that a and b are both positive and that $a > b$. This means that $a + b$ is the largest number and that $b - a$ is a negative number and thus the smallest. This gives us the ordered set $\{b - a, b, a, a + b\}$ Since the median is 3, we know that it is the average between a and b so

$$\frac{(a+b)}{2} = 3 \;\rightarrow\; a + b = 6$$

The arithmetic mean is the (sum of terms)/(number of terms), which give us

$$\frac{((b-a)+(b)+(a)+(a+b))}{4} \rightarrow \frac{((b-a)+(a+b)+(a+b))}{4} \rightarrow \text{substitute } a+b=6$$

$$\frac{(b-a+6+6)}{4} = \frac{(12+b-a)}{4} = 3 + \frac{(b-a)}{4}$$

8. **(B)** Statement 1 gives you the scores for the first 3 midterms and an average of all 5 scores. From this, you can find the sum of scores for midterms 4 and 5.

$$66 + 77 + 63 + \text{midterm 4} + \text{midterm 5} = 76 \cdot 5 = 380 \rightarrow$$
$$\text{midterm 4} + \text{midterm 5} = 380 - 206 = 174$$

If Rakesh's last two midterm scores were 100 and 74, then his median score would be 74. However, if Rakesh's last 2 midterm scores were 96 and 78, then his median score would be 77. Therefore, we can't say for certain what his median score would be. *Insufficient*

Statement 2 gives you the first 4 midterm scores and the average of the last 3 scores. The sum of the last three scores is $79 \cdot 3 = 237$, which means the last test score is $237 - 86 - 63 = 88$. This means we know the median is 77. *Sufficient*

Statement 2 alone is sufficient.

Data Sufficiency

8

→ **WHAT IS DATA SUFFICIENCY?**

→ **WHY DATA SUFFICIENCY?**

→ **DATA SUFFICIENCY DIRECTIONS FOR THE GMAT**

→ **DATA SUFFICIENCY BREAKDOWN**

→ **DATA SUFFICIENCY STRATEGIES**

→ **DATA SUFFICIENCY TIPS**

DATA SUFFICIENCY: DIAGNOSTIC SKILL QUIZ

DIRECTIONS: Before continuing, try your hand at these data sufficiency questions to assess your level of understanding. The answers will be explained throughout the chapter.

1. Team A won 30 basketball games. What percent of its basketball games did Team A win?

   (1) Team B won 40 games, which represents $\frac{4}{7}$ of the games it played.

   (2) Team A played 10 fewer games than Team B did.

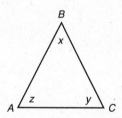

2. Is triangle *ABC* isosceles?

   (1) Side *BC* = 6

   (2) *x* = *y*

3. If *a* is an integer, what is the value of the unit digit of a^3?

   (1) $\sqrt{a}$ is an integer.

   (2) *a* is a multiple of 6.

4. A manuscript containing 225,000 words is to be reviewed by a copy editor. How many hours will it take the copy editor to review the entire manuscript once?

    (1) The rate at which all manuscripts are first reviewed by the copy editor is 86 words per minute.
    (2) The copy editor's reviewing speed increases upon the second review of the manuscript by 30%.

5. What is the value of integer x?

    (1) $9^{\frac{x}{2}} = 81$
    (2) $x(x-1) = 12$

6. Is $9^{a+b} = 27^{10}$?

    (1) $\dfrac{2b}{a} - \dfrac{1}{2} = \dfrac{b}{a} - \dfrac{1}{4}$
    (2) $a - b = 5$

7. Is $y + z > 6$?

    (1) $yw + xz = 35 - wz - xy$
    (2) $x + w = 7$

8. Jonathan has a cell phone plan that charges 70 cents per minute for all international long-distance calls and 20 cents per minute for all domestic long-distance calls. If Jonathan used his cell phone for 180 minutes last month, how many of those minutes were for international calls?

    (1) The total charges on Jonathan's cell phone bill totaled $76.00.
    (2) The total charges of long-distance domestic calls on Jonathan's cell phone bill was $20.00.

WHAT IS DATA SUFFICIENCY?

Data sufficiency problems ask a simple question: are the data provided sufficient to solve the problem? Determining the answer may not be so simple. Data sufficiency problems test your mathematical knowledge in a unique way. Because the setup is somewhat abstract, many students are intimidated by this section. The good news is that once you understand the structure, data sufficiency problems are easy to break down. In addition, you don't always have to perform calculations in order to solve them. You only have to know whether you **can** solve a problem via calculations. Therefore, data sufficiency questions generally take less time to answer than problem-solving questions.

WHY DATA SUFFICIENCY?

It's important to understand why business schools want to test you on data sufficiency. As a future manager or leader, you will be required to do several things:

1. Sort through information or data
2. Identify key issues
3. Make decisions

Data sufficiency is designed to measure your ability to think critically, identify relevant information, extract key insights, and know when you have enough information to solve a problem. These skills are important for any business school graduate and future manager.

DATA SUFFICIENCY DIRECTIONS FOR THE GMAT

Below are the official directions from the GMAC that appear before your first data sufficiency problem on the GMAT.

DIRECTIONS: This problem consists of a question and two statements, labeled (1) and (2), in which certain data are given. You have to decide whether the data given in the statements are sufficient for answering the question. Using the data given in the statements plus your knowledge of mathematics and everyday facts (such as the number of days in July or the meaning of counterclockwise), you must indicate whether:

A. Statement (1) ALONE is sufficient, but statement (2) alone is not sufficient to answer the question asked;
B. Statement (2) ALONE is sufficient, but statement (1) alone is not sufficient to answer the question asked;
C. BOTH statements (1) and (2) TOGETHER are sufficient to answer the question asked, but NEITHER statement ALONE is sufficient;
D. EACH statement ALONE is sufficient to answer the question asked;
E. Statements (1) and (2) TOGETHER are NOT sufficient to answer the question asked, and additional data specific to the problem are needed.

Numbers: All numbers used are real numbers.

Figures: A figure accompanying a data sufficiency problem will conform to the information given in the question but will not necessarily conform to the additional information in statements (1) and (2).

Lines shown as straight can be assumed to be straight, and lines that appear jagged can also be assumed to be straight.

You may assume that positions of points, angles, regions, etc., exist in the order shown and that angle measures are greater than zero.

All figures lie in a plane unless otherwise indicated.

Note: If the data sufficiency problem asks you for the value of a quantity, the data given in the statements are sufficient only when it is possible to determine exactly one numerical value for the quantity.

SAMPLE QUESTION OVERVIEW

Question Stem	What is the value of x?
Statement 1	(1) The square of x is 25.
Statement 2	(2) $x(x - 5) = 0$

Solution (in case you were curious)

We are looking for one value of x. In statement 1, the value of x could be either 5 or −5; therefore, it is not sufficient. In statement 2, the value of x could be either 0 or 5; therefore, it is also not sufficient. When we combine the two statements, the value of x could only be 5. Since we have only one value for x, we have sufficiency.

The correct answer is C.

DATA SUFFICIENCY BREAKDOWN

Based on the structure, format, and directions of data sufficiency questions, there are a few things you need to know:

- Data sufficiency accounts for at least 15 of the 37 quantitative problems. However, in recent years, test takers have seen nearly half the questions as data sufficiency, depending on how well they are doing. The better you are doing on the quantitative section, the more data sufficiency questions you will get.
- Your job is to determine when you have enough information to solve the problem. However, you rarely need to solve the problem.
- The format of the answer choices is the same, so you should memorize what each answer choice represents to save time.
- Data sufficiency tests all the same math theory that problem-solving does—arithmetic, algebra, geometry, properties of numbers, probability, statistics, and combinatorics.
- For each statement, you have to ask yourself, "Do I have enough information to determine sufficiency?" This is very similar to the real world where business leaders ask, "Do we have enough information to make a decision?" The major difference here is that in the real business world, managers rarely make decisions with 100% of the information required (usually anywhere from 20%–80%) because getting all of the information would take too long. However, the principle remains the same.
- Data sufficiency questions have a fixed format and set rules. Knowing the rules and how to exploit them is key.

There are two types of data sufficiency questions: straight solve and yes/no. The chart below describes both.

DATA SUFFICIENCY QUESTIONS—STRAIGHT SOLVE VS. YES/NO

	Straight Solve	Yes/No
Description	The question asks you to solve for something.	The question asks you to answer either Yes or No.
Key words	Solve, find, calculate, what? e.g., "What is x?"	Is, does, can, will? e.g., "Is $x > y$?"
Key insight	You need only one quantity for sufficiency; multiple quantities would be insufficient	You may have multiple quantities but just need to answer either "Yes definitively" or "No definitively."
Example	Q. What is x? (1) $x^2 = 9$ Since x = 3 and –3, statement 1 is not sufficient.	Q. Is $x > 0$? (1) $(x + 3)(x + 2)(x + 1) = 0$ Since x = –3, –2, –1 and x is always negative, we can answer "No definitively," and therefore statement 1 is sufficient.

DATA SUFFICIENCY STRATEGIES

Strategy 1: Decision Tree Method

The most common strategy is to use a decision tree to answer the following questions:

1. Is statement 1 sufficient by itself to solve the problem?
2. Is statement 2 sufficient by itself to solve the problem?
3. Are statements 1 and 2, when taken together, sufficient to solve the problem?

Depending on your answer for each question, you can follow the decision tree below to determine the proper answer choice. Notice that you only have to ask the third question approximately 40% of the time. Make sure you understand why you answered "yes" or "no" to each question.

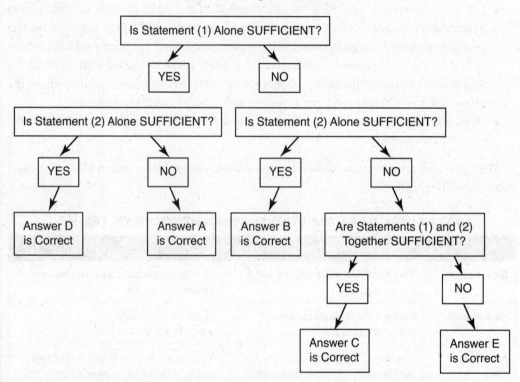

Data Sufficiency Decision Tree

Let's look at a question that uses this approach.

1. Team A won 30 basketball games. What percent of its basketball games did Team A win?

   (1) Team B won 40 games, which represents $\frac{4}{7}$ of the games it played.

   (2) Team A played 10 fewer games than Team B did.

Solution: Use the decision tree to ask each question.
   1. Is statement 1 alone sufficient?
      No, we don't have any information about Team A.

   2. Is statement 2 alone sufficient?
      No, we don't know how many total games that either Team A or Team B played.

   3. Are statements 1 and 2 together sufficient?
      Yes, statement 1 gives the total number of games Team B played and statement 2 gives us the total number of games that Team A played. From this, we can calculate Team A's percent of games won.

The correct answer is C.

Strategy 2: Know-Want-Need Method

Another key strategy is to use the know-want-need method. It works well for a variety of quantitative topics—number properties, algebra, geometry, probability, weighted average, mixture, and word problems.

KNOW: What information do you know or have that is either directly given or implied? Do the statements themselves give you any extra insight about the problem?

WANT: What does the question ask for (i.e., what is the macro question)? Are there any specific units? Is this a straight solve or a yes/no question type? Do you need to be aware of any key words (ratio of, percent of, number of, etc.)?

NEED: This is the link between what we know and what we want. Data sufficiency, while seemingly complex at times, can always be simplified. You are looking for a statement that gives you what you need either directly or indirectly. Every quantitative problem has a key insight, and here is where you should try to extract it. Some common things you might need include:

- x or y
- x and y
- A relationship between x and y
- Other items such as two equal sides, the number of games played (as above in question 2), the rate that Alice ran, the height of Billy, etc.

The reason why the know-want-need method works well is that it helps you to **understand**, **focus**, and be **efficient**. When you identify clearly what you need, the statement will often jump out at you in an obvious way that it is either sufficient or not. This can be a nice boost to your confidence and save you time.

Let's look at some questions that use the know-want-need approach.

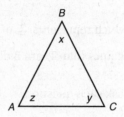

2. Is triangle *ABC* isosceles?

   (1) Side *BC* = 6

   (2) *x* = *y*

Solution: Using know-want-need gives:

Know: We have triangle *ABC* with angles *x*, *y*, and *z*
Want: Isosceles triangle
Need: 2 equal sides or 2 equal angles

Statement 1 gives only one side, therefore it is not sufficient. Statement 2 gives two equal angles, which is what you need. So it is sufficient.

The answer is B.

---

3. If *a* is an integer, what is the value of the unit digit of a^3?

   (1) $\sqrt{a}$ is an integer

   (2) *a* is a multiple of 6.

Solution: Using the know-want-need method gives:

Know: *a* is an integer.
Want: Unit digit of a^3.
Need: Either the numeric value of *a* or the unit digit of *a*.

Statement 1 implies that *a* is a perfect square. However, it doesn't give what you need as *a* could be any number. *Insufficient*

Statement 2 gives several values of *a* such as 6, 12, 18, and 24. So you cannot determine a specific value or unit digit. *Insufficient*

    When you combine the statements, you know that *a* can be 36, but it also can be 144 (which is a multiple of 6). Again, you have two different values for *a*, so you cannot solve. *Insufficient*

The answer is E.

DATA SUFFICIENCY TIPS

TIP 1. INVEST UP FRONT AND MAKE IT COUNT

As with many GMAT questions in both the verbal and quantitative sections, you should invest the time up front to understand the problem. The extra 15–30 seconds you invest to "get it" before you dive in can save you considerable time and mental energy. Make sure you:

- Avoid misreading the question and statements
- Understand the macro question and know what data sufficiency type it is
- Determine what you know, want, and need

---

4. A manuscript containing 225,000 words is to be reviewed by a copy editor. How many hours will it take him to review the entire manuscript once?

   (1) The rate at which all manuscripts are first reviewed by the copy editor is 86 words per minute.

   (2) The copy editor's reviewing speed increases upon the second review of the manuscript by 30%.

Solution: This is a work rate problem, where the amount of work is the number of words to be reviewed. In order to determine how long it will take, you need the rate at which the copy editor can review the manuscript. Be careful to avoid misunderstanding the question by noting keywords such as "once" in the question stem and "second" in statement 2.

Statement 1 gives exactly what you are looking for, the copy editor's reviewing rate. *Sufficient*

Statement 2 gives a rate of review, but note that it is for the 2nd review of the manuscript. *Insufficient*

The answer is A; statement 1 alone is sufficient.

TIP 2. MANAGE THE INFORMATION IN A STRATEGIC AND TIMELY WAY

You can mine plenty of information from data sufficiency questions. The challenge is to know what to extract, when to extract it, and what not to extract. Keep in mind the following:

- **EVERY STATEMENT IMPLIES SOMETHING.** Determine the "what" and the "so what" for each statement. Ask yourself, "What is this telling me?" or "Why are you here?"

  (1) $x^5 y^2 > 0$

  This statement implies that $x > 0$ because $y^2 > 0$.

- **KNOW WHAT YOU KNOW, BOTH DIRECT AND IMPLIED.** The question often has information embedded within it.

- **AVOID MAKING ASSUMPTIONS.** Use only explicit information from the question and statement. What's given is given, and what's not given is not given.

If y is an integer and xy = 150, is y a 2-digit number?

Note that the question stem mentions y to be an integer but makes no mention of x. You can be sure the test makers will try to make you assume that x is an integer, so be careful. Insufficient

- **DO NOT CARRY INFORMATION FROM STATEMENT 1 INTO STATEMENT 2.** You first need to look at each statement with a clean slate.

---

5. What is the value of integer x?

(1) $9^{\frac{x}{2}} = 81$

(2) $x(x-1) = 12$

Solution: This is a straight solve type, so you are looking for one distinct value for x.

Statement 1 implies that 9 to the power of $\frac{x}{2}$ will yield 81. So 9 must be squared. Therefore

$$\frac{x}{2} = 2 \rightarrow x = 4. \; Sufficient$$

Statement 2 implies that two consecutive integers multiplied together will give 12. So either it's going to be two positive numbers ($3 \cdot 4$, thus $x = 4$) or two negative numbers ($(-3) \cdot (-4)$, thus $x = -3$). Since you have two possible values for x, and since the question stem didn't say anything about x being only positive or only negative, you have two values for x. *Insufficient*

The answer is A.

TIP 3. LEVERAGE THE CONSTRUCT TO YOUR ADVANTAGE

Data sufficiency questions have a certain construct. The test makers have to follow the logic and process of this structure. Therefore, if you know how they set up the questions, having this insight can give you certain advantages on test day.

- **DO NOT DO CALCULATIONS UNLESS YOU HAVE TO.** Many data sufficiency questions are conceptual and do not require solving. You just have to know that you can. Often the test makers will make you think you need to do calculations when you don't have to.

  Drake's taxes were what portion of his salary?
  (1) Drake received a year-end bonus of 7% of his salary.
  (2) Drake's salary was $72,000.

Conceptually, you need to know Drake's tax rate. Since no information about the tax rate is given in either statement, you can't solve this. *Insufficient.*

The answer is E; both statements together are still not sufficient.

- **START WITH THE EASIER STATEMENT.** Since most test takers like to do things in order, the test makers will make statement 1 more complex than statement 2. Doing statement 2 first will not only eliminate some answer choices, but it might give you further insight into the problem and dealing with statement 1. (See sample question 6 below.)

- **STATEMENTS 1 AND 2 NEVER CONTRADICT.** For example, in a straight solve type, if you find for statement 1 that $x = 2$ and for statement 2 that $x = 3$, you have made an error and need to redo your calculations. You could also use this information to gain extra insight.

> What is the value of x?
> (1) x is negative
> (2) $x^2 = 49$

If you thought here that $x = 7$, this would contradict what you learned in statement 1. This reminds you that $x = -7$ as well!

The answer is C.

- **DETERMINE SUFFICIENCY BY PROVING INSUFFICIENCY.** Sometimes you can focus on proving insufficiency by picking numbers to find both a scenario that works and another that doesn't work, thus proving insufficiency.

---

6. Is $9^{a+b} = 27^{10}$?

   (1) $\dfrac{2b}{a} - \dfrac{1}{2} = \dfrac{b}{a} - \dfrac{1}{4}$

   (2) $a - b = 5$

Solution: By manipulating the equation in the question stem, you can determine what this question is really asking.

$$(3^2)^{a+b} = (3^3)^{10} \rightarrow 3^{2a+2b} = 3^{30} \rightarrow 2a + 2b = 30 \rightarrow \text{Does } a + b = 15?$$

Let's look at statement 2 first. Statement 2 tells you that $a - b = 5$. Do not be fooled into thinking that this is sufficient because you have two equations and two unknowns. This question is not asking you to find specific values for a and b. You can actually find values for a and b that both work and don't work.

If $a = 10$ and $b = 5$, then $a + b = 15$. $\rightarrow$ If $a = 11$, $b = 6$, then $a + b \neq 15$. *Insufficient*

You can rearrange statement 1 to get $\dfrac{b}{a} = \dfrac{1}{4}$. This tells you that $4b = a$. Again, let's look to prove insufficiency.

If $b = 3$ and $a = 12$, then $a + b = 15$. $\rightarrow$ If $b = 4$, $a = 16$, then $a + b \neq 15$. *Insufficient*

Given the two statements, you have two equations ① $a - b = 5$ and ② $a = 4b$. You can substitute the second equation into the first to get

$$4b - b = 5 \rightarrow 3b = 5. \rightarrow b = \frac{5}{3}, a = \frac{20}{3}$$

$a + b = \dfrac{20}{3} + \dfrac{5}{3} = \dfrac{25}{3}$. This does not equal 15. Remember, though, that you are dealing with a yes/no type data sufficiency question. Since you know that the answer to the macro question is "No definitively," then you have sufficiency. *Sufficient*

The answer is C; both statements together are sufficient.

TIP 4. DON'T LET THE GAME FOOL YOU

Given the previous tip, the construct of data sufficiency also gives the test makers a variety of ways to trick you. There is almost a game to how the GMAT is tested or played. Arm yourself with the knowledge of some of the traps the test makers set up for you.

- **THEY PUT THE SAME INFO IN EACH STATEMENT.** It is very easy in math to say the same thing in completely different ways (e.g., positive integer, whole number, nondecimal number greater than zero, etc.). So if you were the GMAT test maker, why not do this in data sufficiency as a way to trick test takers? If this does happen, the answer can only be either D or E. If one statement works, the other has to work. If statement 1 doesn't work, then statement 2 won't work. Putting them together adds no new information.

  > Solve for x.
  > (1) $x - 3y = -7$
  > (2) $21 + 3x = 9y$

  The equation in statement 2 is a manipulated version of the equation in statement 1. Therefore, we essentially have one equation and two unknowns. The equation cannot be solved. *Insufficient*

  The answer is E.

- **DO NOT FORGET THAT "NO" CAN MEAN "SUFFICIENT."** A common thought process is to associate "No" with "Not sufficient." For yes/no data sufficiency questions, remember that if the answer to the macro question is "no, definitively," then that is sufficient.

  > Is $x > 0$?
  > (1) $(x + 3)(x + 2)(x + 1) = 0$

  The statement tells us that $x = -3, -2,$ or -1. We know definitively that x is not greater than 0. *Sufficient*

- **WATCH OUT FOR THE EASY C.** If the question seems to lead you to think that both statements together are sufficient, think again! You should expect the same difficulty level of questions, so getting an easy one doesn't make sense. It is likely that one (or both) of the statements have some information embedded in them or there is something in the question stem that you missed. Alternatively, there may be a hidden reason why the statements don't work even when taken together.

  > If $2x + y = 5z$, what is the value of y?
  > (1) $3x = -1.5 + 7.5z$
  > (2) $x = 2$

  Upon first glance, statement 2 doesn't work. When combined with statement 1, though, you can plug in $x = 2$ and then solve for z and y because you have 2 equations and 2 unknowns. If you look closely at the question stem and statement 1, both can be manipulated to get ① $y = 5z - 2x$ and ② $7.5z - 3x = 1.5$, respectively. If we divide $7.5z - 3x = 1.5$ by 1.5, we get $5z - 2x = 1$. We can substitute this into ① and get an actual value for y. *Sufficient*

  The answer is A.

■ **WHEN THE TEST ASKS FOR *a* + *b*, YOU DO NOT NEED INDIVIDUAL VALUES.** Some data sufficiency questions seem to have too many algebraic variables, but you don't always need to solve for every variable. As long as you know what $a + b$ equals, you do not need to know what a and b are individually.

---

7. Is $y + z > 6$?

    (1) $yw + xz = 35 - wz - xy$

    (2) $x + w = 7$

Solution: First, given the question stem, you should be looking to isolate $y + z$ in the statements. Second, jump ahead to statement 2, which doesn't tell you anything about y or z. *Insufficient*

Given the simplicity of statement 2, you have to ask yourself why the test makers provided that information. The only reason would be that it might be used in the other statement. Therefore, you should try to isolate x and w because of statement 1 and because of the question stem. Statement 1 can be manipulated to get

$$yw + yx + xz + wz = 35 \;\to\; y(w + x) + z(w + x) = 35 \;\to\; (w + x)(y + z) = 35$$

By itself, each statement is insufficient. However, when combined, you know that $w + x = 7$. When substituted into statement 1, you get $7(y + z) = 35 \;\to\; y + z = 5$. Therefore $y + z$ is not greater than 6. Remember again that "no definitively" is sufficient in a yes/no data sufficiency question type.

The answer is C; both statements together are sufficient.

TIP 5. USE YOUR KNOWLEDGE OF GMAT THEORY, STRATEGIES, AND METHODOLOGIES TO SIMPLIFY

Everything you learn in this book and externally is ammunition for beating the GMAT. All the skills and tips we share throughout the book will help you better process, understand, and approach all data sufficiency problems. You just have to leverage them when needed and be flexible whether doing data sufficiency questions conceptually or mathematically.

■ **MANIPULATE THE EQUATIONS.** Just because an equation is given to you in a certain way, whether it is in the question stem or in the statement, this does not mean you can't manipulate it to serve your needs.

    Is *x* − *y* > 0?

This is the same as asking if $x > y$

■ **YOU ALWAYS HAVE YOUR TWO BFFs.** As we said earlier in the book, algebra and properties of numbers are your two "best friends forever" in data sufficiency as well as in all the quantitative questions. You can set up equations, simplify your work, unlock keys, break down the statements via conceptual understanding, and so much more!

- **DO NOT FORGET ABOUT 0 (ZERO).** It's so easy to forget about zero. It has unique qualities in terms of both usage and how it can change the dynamics of a question. Be wary of zero when dealing with inequalities, absolute value, and properties of numbers. Zero can also be a powerful number to use when picking numbers.

> Is $x > 0$?
> (1) $|x| = -x$

This implies x is negative but also zero. *Insufficient*

- **PICKING NUMBERS.** We've saved the best for last and so can you (although you can try it first sometimes, too). This is the universal strategy taught by every test prep company in the world. We all can't be wrong! It helps you to understand the question better and to simplify the process. In a straight solve question type, you pick numbers to find more than one value. In a yes/no type problem, you pick numbers to find both a yes and a no answer.

> If x and y are distinct prime numbers, is $x(y - 5)$ odd?
> (1) $x < 3$

Statement 1 tells us that $x = 2$. Try any prime number for y ($y = 3, 5, 7, 11$, etc.). The equation $x(y - 5)$ is always even. *Sufficient*

---

8. Jonathan has a cell phone plan that charges 70 cents per minute for all international long-distance calls and 20 cents per minute for all domestic long-distance calls. If Jonathan used his cell phone for 180 minutes last month, how many of those minutes were for international calls?
   (1) The total charges on Jonathan's cell phone bill totaled $76.00.
   (2) The total charges of long-distance domestic calls on Jonathan's cell phone bill was $20.00.

Solution: First use our good friend algebra to sort out information in the question stem. $I + D = 180$, where I = total international minutes used and D = total domestic minutes used.

Statement 1 gives us the total bill. Since we have the per-minute charges for both international and domestic calls, $70I + 20D = 7600$ → Since we have 2 equations and 2 unknowns, we can solve. *Sufficient*

Statement 2 gives us the total domestic charges, and we get $20D = 2000$ → Since we can solve for D, we can now solve for I. *Sufficient*

As a check, we have $D = 100$. Therefore $I = 80$. If we plug these values into our statement 2 equation, the number should work out because the statements cannot contradict each other.

$$70(80) + 20(100) = 5600 + 2000 = 7600 \rightarrow \text{It checks out!}$$

The answer is D; each statement alone is sufficient.

1. If t is the tens digit and u is the units digit of a two-digit number, what is the value of this number?

   (1) $t + u = 9$

   (2) $t - u = -5$

2. An organization is showcasing an outdoor play in a park. If over the course of a two-week run, it sells $3,200 worth of tickets, all at the same price, what is the price of one ticket?

   (1) If the price of each ticket were $1 more, the total revenue would be $800 more.

   (2) If the organization decreases the ticket price by $1 and sells 25% more tickets as a result, the total revenue would remain the same as before.

3. If x and y are positive integers, is $\sqrt{2x+2y} > 2\sqrt{2x}$?

   (1) $3x - y < 0$

   (2) $x + y > 3x$

4. Milk carton A and milk jug B each contain milk. The capacity of jug B is 40% greater than that of carton A. How much more milk is in carton A than in jug B?

   (1) When full, container B holds 7 L of milk.

   (2) Container A is 4/5 full, and container B is 2/7 full.

5. If Aloysius had an appointment with his lawyer on a certain day, was his appointment on a Thursday?

   (1) The appointment was between 11 A.M. and 4 P.M.

   (2) Exactly 58 hours before the appointment, it was Tuesday.

6. If x_1 and x_2 are the number of schoolchildren and y_1 and y_2 are the number of schools in Country A and Country B, respectively, the ratio of the number of schoolchildren to the number of schools is greater for which of the two countries?

   (1) $y_1 > y_2$

   (2) $x_1 < x_2$

7. If the vertices of triangle ABC have coordinates $(0, 1)$, $(0, -4)$, and $(x, 0)$, is the area of the triangle greater than 13?

   (1) $x < 3$

   (2) Triangle ABC is a right triangle.

8. If a, b, c, and d are positive prime numbers and the product of $abcd = 210$, what is the value of b?

   (1) $b + c = d$

   (2) $c + d = a^2$

ANSWER KEY

1. **(C)** 3. **(A)** 5. **(C)** 7. **(B)**
2. **(D)** 4. **(C)** 6. **(C)** 8. **(B)**

SOLUTIONS

1. **(C)** You know that *tu* is a two-digit number. You want the value of both *u* and *t*. You need either *u* AND *t* (which of course test makers are not likely to give directly) or two equations with *u* and *t* that you can solve algebraically.

   Statement 1 means that the number could be 18, 27, 36, 45, 54, 63, 72, 81, or 90. *Insufficient*

   Statement 2 means that the number could be 16, 27, 38, or 49.

   When you combine both statements, you have two distinct equations that can be solved for *u* and *t*. Furthermore, you know that the only possible value satisfying both statements is 27. *Sufficient*

   Both statements together are sufficient.

2. **(D)** Using algebra, you know that $P \cdot n = 3200$, where P = the price of a ticket and n = the number of tickets. You want P. What you need is either P, or n, or another distinct equation with P and n.

   Statement 1 means that $(P + 1)n = 3200 + 800. \rightarrow (P + 1)n = 4000$. This is another equation with P and n, thus giving you what you need. *Sufficient*

   You don't have to solve this, rather just know that you can. However, just by inspection you know that a \$1 increase per ticket leads to an \$800 increase in overall sales. Therefore, the organization sold 800 tickets.

   Statement 2 means that $(P - 1)(n \cdot 1.25) = 3200$. Again, this is another distinct equation with P and n. Therefore, you can solve it. *Sufficient*

   Each statement alone is sufficient.

3. **(A)** Whenever you see inequalities and variables in data sufficiency questions, you can try picking numbers, algebraic manipulation, or number properties. Let's manipulate the equation in the question stem.

   By squaring both sides of $\sqrt{2x+2y} > 2\sqrt{2x}$, you get $2x + 2y > 8x$. This is allowed because both x and y are positive integers, which means that the numbers under the radicals were not fractions less than 1. This gives $y > 3x$. So what you really want to know is if $y > 3x$.

   Statement 1, when manipulated, gives $y > 3x$, which is exactly what you need. *Sufficient*

   Statement 2 gives $y > 2x$, which is not what you need. Just to be sure, you can plug in numbers.
   If $x = 1$ and $y = 3$, then $\sqrt{2x+2y} > 2\sqrt{2x}$ becomes $\sqrt{2+6} > 2\sqrt{2} \rightarrow 2\sqrt{2} > 2\sqrt{2}$. This doesn't work!

   Yet if $x = 1$ and $y = 4$, you would get $\sqrt{2+8} > 2\sqrt{2} \rightarrow$ (which is also $\sqrt{8}$) $\rightarrow$ $\sqrt{10} > \sqrt{8}$. This works! *Insufficient*

   Statement 1 alone is sufficient.

4. **(C)** Let's use the know-want-need method along with algebra.

know: $C_B = 1.4C_A \rightarrow$ Jug B's capacity is 40% more than carton A's capacity.

want: $A - B \qquad \rightarrow$ The amount of milk in A minus the amount of milk in B

need: A and $B \quad$ or a relationship among A, B, C_B, and C_A

Statement 1 means that $C_B = 7$. The trick here is that the statement says "when full" and does not say that the container is actually full. You still don't know the amount of milk in either container. *Insufficient*

Statement 2 tells how full the containers actually are. $A = \left(\frac{4}{5}\right)C_A$ and $B = \left(\frac{2}{7}\right)C_B$. However, you

don't know the actual capacities of either container. Make sure you do not mistakenly take information from statement 1 and apply it to statement 2 by itself. *Insufficient*

When you combine both statements, you know the capacities of both containers and the amount of milk in each container. Therefore, you can solve. *Sufficient*

$$C_B = 7 \text{ and } C_B = 1.4C_A \text{ which means } 7 = \left(\frac{7}{5}\right) \cdot C_A \rightarrow C_A = 5$$

$$A = \left(\frac{4}{5}\right)C_A \rightarrow A = 4\text{L} \qquad B = \left(\frac{2}{7}\right)C_B \rightarrow B = 2\text{L} \rightarrow A - B = 4 - 2 = 2\text{L}$$

Both statements together are sufficient.

5. **(C)** The main trick on this GMAT question is that some test takers will forget about the 24-hour clock when it comes to determining the current day.

Statement 1 doesn't tell you anything about the day, so you cannot solve. *Insufficient*

Statement 2 says that 58 hours before the appointment was a Tuesday. This could be 11 P.M. Tuesday night, making the appointment fall on Friday at 9 A.M. Instead, the appointment could be 58 hours after 9 A.M. on Tuesday, making it fall on 7 P.M. on Thursday. Since you have no idea when on Tuesday the 58 hours before was, you cannot solve. *Insufficient*

When you combine both statements, you know that it is impossible to have an appointment on Friday between 11 A.M. and 4 P.M. You know this from statement 2 above where you looked at Tuesday at 11 P.M. in the late evening. Even if you went to 11:59 P.M. on Tuesday night, the latest you can extend it, the Friday appointment could be only as late as 9:59 A.M. Therefore, the appointment has to be on Thursday. *Sufficient*

Both statements together are sufficient.

6. **(C)** What you want to know is if $\dfrac{x_1}{y_1} > \dfrac{x_2}{y_2}$ or if ratio 1 > ratio 2.

Statement 1 says that the denominator of ratio 1 is larger than the denominator of ratio 2. This is not helpful because you don't know the numerators. Try picking numbers to visualize this.

If $y_1 = 10$ and $y_2 = 5$ and if $x_1 = x_2 = 1$, then $\dfrac{x_1}{y_1} < \dfrac{x_2}{y_2}$ because $\dfrac{1}{10} < \dfrac{1}{5}$.

If $y_1 = 10$ and $y_2 = 5$ and if $x_1 = 100$ and $x_2 = 1$, then $\dfrac{x_1}{y_1} > \dfrac{x_2}{y_2}$ because $\dfrac{100}{10} > \dfrac{1}{5}$.

Insufficient

Statement 2 gives you the same dilemma as above. Now you know the numerators of ratio 1 and ratio 2, but you don't know the denominators. Thus you cannot compare the ratios. *Insufficient*

When you combine both statements, you know that $y_1 > y_2$ and $x_1 < x_2$. Ratio 2 now has both the larger numerator and smaller denominator. This means that it must be greater than ratio 1. Again, you can use numbers to verify this.

If $y_1 = 10$ and $y_2 = 5$ and if $x_1 = 5$ and $x_2 = 10$, then $\dfrac{x_1}{y_1} > \dfrac{x_2}{y_2}$ because $\dfrac{10}{5} > \dfrac{5}{10}$. *Sufficient*

Both statements together are sufficient.

7. **(B)** First of all, you need a diagram

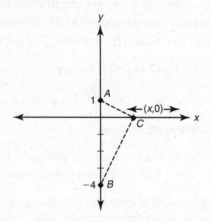

As you can see, the unknown point on the *x*-axis can be anywhere on the number line. So you cannot be sure of the size of the triangle.

Statement 1 says that $x < 3$. However, that means x could be 2, giving a small triangle, or x could be −100, giving triangle *ABC* a very large area. *Insufficient*

Statement 2 says that *ABC* is a right triangle, which definitely limits the possibilities. This statement also implies that the right angle is at the point $(x, 0)$ and that the hypotenuse is 5. Thus, you would have a 3-4-5 right triangle. There are only two possible values for *x*, one on either side of the *y*-axis (i.e., positive or negative). However, the absolute value of *x* must be the same. So the area of the triangle *ABC* will also be the same. Since you can calculate the area of one triangle, then you will be able to answer the macro question. *Sufficient*

If you wanted to calculate the value of the point, you could break down the triangle into two right triangles separated by the *x*-axis. The top triangle would have a short side of 1 and a hypotenuse of 3. Therefore, the side on the *x*-axis would be

$$b^2 = c^2 - a^2 = b^2 = 9 - 1 = 8 \;\rightarrow\; b = 2\sqrt{2}$$

Statement 2 alone is sufficient.

8. **(B)** Let's use the know-want-need method here.

Know: Direct: a, b, c, and d are positive prime numbers

                         $abcd = 210$

       Indirect: 2, 3, 5, and 7 are the prime numbers that a, b, c, and d must be

                         because $2 \cdot 3 \cdot 5 \cdot 7 = 210$

Want: The value of b

Need: The value of b

       The values of a, c, and d.

       Three distinct equations with a, b, c, and d.

       A relationship or number property describing a, b, c, and d that allows
          you to determine b.

Statement 1 tells you that $b + c = d$, which means that $d = 7$ and b or c could be 2 or 5, although you don't know which one specifically. You do not know the value of b. *Insufficient*

Statement 2 says that $c + d = a^2$. The only way this equation could work with the given prime numbers is if you had $2 + 7 = 3^2$. So for a, c, and d the values are 3, 2, and 7, respectively. Therefore, $b = 5$. *Sufficient*

Statement 2 alone is sufficient.

Problem Solving

PROBLEM SOLVING: DIAGNOSTIC SKILL QUIZ

DIRECTIONS: Before continuing, try your hand at these problem-solving questions to assess your level of understanding. The answers will be explained throughout this chapter.

1. A packer at M&M Nuggets Inc. wrapped boxes weighing 24, 16, 31, 6, 20, and 4 pounds. What was the median weight in pounds of the packages that the packer packed?

   (A) 16.67

   (B) 17

   (C) 18

   (D) 27.5

   (E) 31

2. What is the square root of 3969?

   (A) 49

   (B) 57

   (C) 63

   (D) 69

   (E) 73

3. The tires of a car have a diameter of y inches, and the spare tire has a diameter of x inches. The front tires cover a distance of z feet in 1000 revolutions. How many revolutions does the spare tire make in covering z feet?

(A) $1000xy$

(B) $1000x - y$

(C) $1000y - x$

(D) $\dfrac{1000x}{y}$

(E) $\dfrac{1000y}{x}$

4. The angles in a triangle are x, $2x$, and $3x$ degrees. If P, R, and S are the lengths of the sides opposite to angles x, $2x$, and $3x$, respectively, then which of the following must be true?

  I. $S > P + R$

  II. $S^2 > P^2 + R^2$

  III. $S/P/R = 10/6/2$

(A) I only

(B) II only

(C) I and III only

(D) II and III only

(E) None of the above

5. Chuck, Jean-Claude, and Dolph take their pal Arnold out for a fancy dinner and offer to pay Arnold's bill. Chuck contributes 2 dollars more than $\dfrac{1}{5}$ the cost of Arnold's bill. Jean-Claude contributes 1 dollar less than $\dfrac{1}{2}$ the cost. Dolph contributes the remaining 14 dollars. What is the cost of Arnold's bill?

(A) $42

(B) $50

(C) $55

(D) $61

(E) $70

6. Ricky and Bobby both work for the same sales company. Ricky's commission rate is 20%, and Bobby's commission rate is 30%. If Ricky sold $55,000 worth of goods and Bobby sold $80,000 worth of goods, what is their combined average commission rate?

(A) 15%

(B) 24.1%

(C) 25%

(D) 25.9%

(E) 35%

7. Students in Mrs. Tisdale's class took a geometry test. The girls' scores in the class averaged 90%, the boys' scores in the class averaged 82%, while the overall class average was 85%. What is the ratio of boys to girls in the class?

    (A) 3 : 5
    (B) 9 : 8
    (C) 5 : 4
    (D) 8 : 5
    (E) 5 : 3

8. Ned has 10 L of a 30% solution of salt in water. He adds enough salt to create a 50% solution. How much water will Ned need to add to the solution in order to get it back to a 30% solution?

    (A) 7 liters
    (B) 10 liters
    (C) $11\frac{1}{3}$ liters
    (D) $13\frac{2}{3}$ liters
    (E) 15 liters

9. Samantha is traveling from Philadelphia to New York City, a distance of 80 miles, at a rate of 25 mph. Fred is traveling from New York City to Philadelphia at a rate of 35 mph but leaves 60 minutes after Samantha starts her trip. They're both traveling on the same route. How long will Fred have traveled by the time he passes Samantha?

    (A) 48 minutes
    (B) 55 minutes
    (C) 1 hour
    (D) 1 hour 20 minutes
    (E) 1 hour 40 minutes

10. An apartment building has 200 tenants, 80% of whom use the amenities. Of the people who use the amenities, 90 use the indoor pool and 130 use the fitness room. How many tenants use both the indoor pool and the fitness room?

    (A) 40
    (B) 60
    (C) 90
    (D) 110
    (E) 130

11. The owner of a unique pet store keeps only cats and dogs. Of the 60 pets in the store, 38 are cats, 28 have black fur, and 14 are neither black furred nor cats. What percentage of the store's dogs are black furred?

    (A) 13.3%
    (B) 23.3%
    (C) 36.4%
    (D) 57.1%
    (E) 63.6%

12. Philip has a collection of 54 DVDs, some movies and some television shows. If exactly $\frac{3}{4}$ of the movies and exactly $\frac{1}{3}$ of the television shows are comedies, what is the greatest possible number of Philip's DVDs that could be comedies?

   (A) 9
   (B) 23
   (C) 36
   (D) 38
   (E) 48

13. Chelsea invests $1200 at 5% interest. How much additional money must she invest at 8% so that her total annual income will be equal to 6% of her entire investment?

   (A) $500
   (B) $600
   (C) $1200
   (D) $1500
   (E) $1800

14. A leather goods manufacturer produces leather purses at a cost of $20 per purse. The manufacturer's fixed costs are $7200 per month, regardless of how many purses are produced. If the manufacturer produces 240 purses per month and shipping costs are $2 per unit, at what price does the manufacturer need to sell the purses in order to break even?

   (A) $52
   (B) $55
   (C) $60
   (D) $67
   (E) $72

15. The following table shows the gross domestic (U.S.) revenue and gross overseas revenue of 5 movies. Which movie had the most success internationally versus domestically in terms of gross revenue?

Movie	Studio	Domestic Gross (In Millions of $)	Overseas Gross (In Millions of $)
The Avengers	Buena Vista	623.4	888.4
The Dark Knight Rises	Warner Bros.	448.1	632.9
Skyfall	Sony	304.2	804.1
The Hobbit: An Unexpected Journey	Warner Bros.	301.0	679.6
Ice Age: Continental Drift	Fox	161.3	714.0

   (A) *The Dark Knight Rises*
   (B) *The Hobbit: An Unexpected Journey*
   (C) *Ice Age: Continental Drift*
   (D) *Skyfall*
   (E) *The Avengers*

INTRODUCTION

Problem solving accounts for up to 22 of 37 questions in the quantitative section of the GMAT. In recent years, some test takers have likely seen more data sufficiency questions if they were doing well. Based on this information, the number of problem-solving questions you face could reduce to about half. Problem-solving questions cover all of the theoretical topics including arithmetic, algebra, geometry, statistics, number properties, probability, and combinatorics. In this chapter, we will review the strategies, methods, and tactics for problem solving. Then we will dive deeper into the major word problems and question types.

PROBLEM SOLVING: CONTENT SUMMARY/CHECKLIST

By the end of this problem-solving chapter, you should have enough information to review and understand the following topics:

☐ Problem-solving directions from the GMAT
☐ Problem solving: winning the war
☐ Conversion problems
☐ Weighted averages
☐ Mixture problems
☐ Rate problems
☐ Venn diagrams and matrix boxes
☐ Minimum/maximum problems
☐ Interest rate problems
☐ Profit and revenue
☐ Data interpretation

PROBLEM-SOLVING DIRECTIONS FOR THE GMAT

According to the GMAC, the following directions will appear on your screen just before your first problem-solving question.

DIRECTIONS: Solve each problem, and indicate the best of the answer choices given.

Numbers: All numbers used are real numbers.

Figures: A figure accompanying a problem-solving question is intended to provide information useful in solving the problem. Figures are drawn as accurately as possible EXCEPT when it is stated in a specific problem that its figure is not drawn to scale. Straight lines may sometimes appear jagged. All figures lie on a plane unless otherwise indicated.

Note that if a problem-solving question includes a figure, it is considered drawn to scale unless you're told otherwise. If you see "NOT DRAWN TO SCALE" on a figure, then it has been intentionally distorted to prevent you from using it to help you solve the problem.

Problem-Solving Sample Question

Question Stem: 1. A packer at M&M Nuggets Inc. wrapped boxes weighing 24, 16, 31, 6, 20, and 4 pounds. What was the median weight in pounds of the packages that the packer packed?

Answer choices: (A) 16.67
                          (B) 17
                          (C) 18
                          (D) 27.5
                          (E) 31

Solution: If you look at the set of numbers in order from least to greatest, you would get {4, 6, 16, 20, 24, 31}. The median is the middle number of the set. If there is an even number of elements in the set, you need to take the average of the middle two numbers. Here, 16 and 20 are the middle two numbers. So the average is $\frac{(16+20)}{2} = 18$.

The answer is C.

Note above that if the question gives specific numbers for answer choices, the answer choices are given in increasing numerical order. This will become useful when applying any back-solving strategies.

PROBLEM SOLVING: WINNING THE WAR

The general strategy for problem solving is common among most test prep books.

1. **READ THE PROBLEM CAREFULLY.**
2. **MAKE SURE YOU ANSWER THE PROPER QUESTION.**
3. **PICK THE BEST APPROACH.** There are also dozens of tools and tactics you can use. These weapons are a significant part of your arsenal when dealing with GMAT problems. You need to be flexible, creative, and swift enough to handle any question. Below are some fundamentals, key strategies, methods, and tactics to keep in mind for problem solving on the GMAT.

Problem-Solving Fundamentals

Understanding how the GMAT test makers structure problem-solving questions will help you to process the question better and come up with a plan that works.

- **CARELESS ERRORS BE GONE!** The two most common errors test takers make are misreading and computational error. By being aware of these common errors and the fact that the test makers will try to exploit this, you can make every effort to try to avoid them.
- **THE SECRET IS OUT ABOUT MINIMAL OR NO CALCULATIONS.** Most GMAT problem-solving questions can be done conceptually or with several shortcut tactics that will be presented later in this chapter. This means that you should not have to do many calculations. You can often do calculations. However if you don't have to, you would be better off just selecting your answer and moving on.

- **THE MATH IS CLEAN.** If calculations are necessary, they will not be very complex. The numbers will work out smoothly. If they don't, you either have made a calculation error or have missed a shortcut such as simplifying, estimating, or algebra.
- **KNOW HOW THEY DECEIVE YOU.** The GMAT test makers can trick you in many ways. The most common are using clever wordplay, including misleading answer choices, and making you do unnecessary calculations. After going through all of the advice in this book, you should be able to spot the deceptions.

---

2. What is the square root of 3969?

    (A) 49

    (B) 57

    (C) 63

    (D) 69

    (E) 73

Solution: There is a long process for calculating square roots of large numbers, but the GMAT test makers don't expect you to do this. Most questions require minimal or no calculations. All questions are set up so that they can be done in less than 3 minutes, sometimes in much less time than that. Note also in the answer choices that you have whole numbers, suggesting a pretty clean calculation. If you use conceptual thinking, you can eliminate calculations and thus errors. One concept is number properties, particularly unit digits. The number 3969 ends with the unit digit of 9. Therefore, whatever number is squared must end with a 3 or a 7. This leaves you with answer choices B, C, or E. Furthermore, you know that $60^2 = 3600$ and $70^2 = 4900$. Thus, you can extrapolate that 57 is too low and 73 is too high while 63 is about right.

The answer is C.

Problem-Solving Key Strategies

- **YOU NEED STRONG FUNDAMENTALS.** If you want to get a competitive MBA score, you must have a solid understanding of fundamentals. If you struggle to reduce fractions, manipulate exponents, or translate algebra, this will slow you down big time. The information covered in the first few chapters of this book (arithmetic, algebra, geometry) provides an essential foundation for your success.
- **INVEST IN YOUR IMMEDIATE FUTURE.** Many test takers dive right into the questions by doing calculations and then quickly get lost. However, you know that many questions require minimal or no calculations. You must invest the time up front to understand the question thoroughly before attempting to solve it. You should do this for all GMAT questions, both verbal and quantitative. Don't spend too much time, though. You have 15–30 seconds to understand the question and come up with a plan of attack. This investment will save you time in the immediate future (the next 1–2 minutes).
- **HARVEST THE GARDEN OF ANSWER CHOICES.** The answer choices provide more information than you realize. They narrow the field down to five possibilities. They tell you what kind of response is required. They give you extra insight into the question. For example, if every answer choice has a π or a $\sqrt{3}$ in it, this may tell you to exploit your knowledge of

circles or special triangles. If you eliminate an answer choice, you may be able to eliminate another choice or two for the same reason, allowing you to get rid of two or three answer choices at the same time.

- **TRY THIS CONCEPT—CONCEPTUAL THINKING!** As mentioned before, conceptual thinking is a big part of doing problem solving questions quickly and with minimal calculations. Most test takers, though, have not practiced this enough. So they go back to doing small calculations on the side. We know this is hard at first. However, the more you exercise your brain, the smarter, faster, and more confident you become.

- **"SIMPLICITY IS THE ULTIMATE SOPHISTICATION."** Leonardo da Vinci said it best. Sophisticated test takers simplify problems in many ways by leveraging conceptual thinking, algebra, and number properties and by breaking down the question. Simplify your calculations, your processes, and your thinking.

- **CARRY 3 BIG STICKS—PICKING NUMBERS, ALGEBRA, AND NUMBER PROPERTIES.** Although we will discuss these tactics below, leveraging these three biggest weapons in your arsenal really counts as a strategy on its own. Every GMAT test prep book, course, and successful student will champion picking numbers, algebra, and number properties. You should too.

---

3. The tires of a car have a diameter of y inches, and the spare tire has a diameter of x inches. The front tires cover a distance of z feet in 1000 revolutions. How many revolutions does the spare tire make in covering z feet?

(A) $1000xy$

(B) $1000x - y$

(C) $1000y - x$

(D) $\dfrac{1000x}{y}$

(E) $\dfrac{1000y}{x}$

Solution: The GMAT test makers have complicated the question with algebra. None of the answer choices include z. This means one option would be to set up an equation with x, y, and z and then solve for z. Perhaps there is a simpler way via a conceptual approach and picking numbers. If you can't figure out a shortcut, you can still do the algebra. Let's try picking numbers.

Say $y = 20$ inches and $x = 10$ inches	→ Each revolution is the circumference, $C = 2\pi r$ or $C = \pi d$. So we get
Circumference of tire $Y = 20\pi$	→ z = distance of 1000 revolutions = $1000 \cdot 20\pi$ = $20{,}000\pi$
Circumference of tire $X = 10\pi$	→ How many revolutions to get a distance of $z = 20{,}000\pi$?
$\dfrac{20{,}000\pi}{10\pi} = 2000$ revolutions	→ So what value of the answer choices gives 2,000?

Since $y = 20$ and $x = 10$, only choice E gives us $\dfrac{1{,}000 \cdot 20}{10} = 2000$.

The answer is E.

Notice that for this problem, we needed the fundamentals of algebra and distance/rate/time. We had to think conceptually and combine it with a simplified approach to our calculations. Had we harvested the answer choices more deeply, we would have determined that the answer would have to be a multiple, thus eliminating B and C. Later in this chapter, we will spend time understanding how to find the best approach.

Problem-Solving Methods

We introduced this chapter with a basic three-step approach. We will now discuss a variety of methods and processes for some of the more common problem-solving question types later in the chapter. The main methodology you should use is the **know-want-approach method.**

When you encounter a problem-solving question on the GMAT, ask yourself the following questions:

1. **WHAT DO YOU KNOW?** You need to extract and digest everything you read.

   - What information has been given to you directly in the problem?
   - What extra information is implied?
   - What do the answer choices tell you about the question?

2. **WHAT DO YOU WANT?** You need to understand the scope clearly.

   - What is the problem specifically asking for?
   - Are there any particular keywords or hints to be aware of?
   - Are there any defined units in the question?

3. **WHAT IS YOUR APPROACH?** You need to come up with a plan of attack. For every problem-solving question, you should be able to identify the necessary components quickly.

   - What theory is being tested?
   - What relevant strategies, methods, and tactics do you have in your arsenal?
   - What is the key insight or catch of the problem? (Most quantitative questions require a special insight for doing the problem most effectively.)
   - Based on the above, what is the best approach, or mix of approaches, for you to apply?

The idea behind the **know-want-approach** method is a solid **understanding**, a strategic **focus** of your time and effort, and overall **efficiency**. In the initial stages of your GMAT studying, you may want to write down everything. Eventually, with practice, this method will become instinctive.

---

4. The angles in a triangle are x, $2x$, and $3x$ degrees. If P, R, and S are the lengths of the sides opposite to angles x, $2x$, and $3x$, respectively, then which of the following must be true?

   I. $S > P + R$
   II. $S^2 > P^2 + R^2$
   III. $S/P/R = 10/6/2$

   (A) I only
   (B) II only
   (C) I and III only
   (D) II and III only
   (E) None of the above

Solution: Break down this question via the know-want-need approach to get:

Know: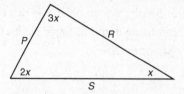

A triangle with angles x, $2x$, and $3x$ and sides P, R, and S
Implied: $x + 2x + 3x = 180$
Therefore $6x = 180$, $x = 30$
The angles are 30º, 60º, 90º

Want: Determine the truth of the given statements.
Other observations: 2 statements are inequalities.
Statement III gives a ratio.

Approach: Theory: Geometry of triangles and algebra
Strategy 1: Algebra
Strategy 2: Conceptual thinking
Key insight 1: 30-60-90 triangle rules
Key insight 2: Third side rule of triangles
Approach: Solve algebraically and input directly in the 3 options given.
Draw a triangle to visualize better.
Evaluate each statement by trying to prove it false.

In the beginning of your GMAT studies, you may want to write down everything. Eventually once this thought process and methodology are in your head, you may write less or nothing at all. By drawing out the triangle below and looking at the statements, we get the following.

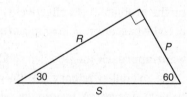

I: The side of a triangle cannot be greater than the sum of the other two sides. This is the direct opposite of the third side rule. False

II: Since we know this is a right triangle, the square of one side cannot be greater than the sum of the squares of the other 2 sides. This would violate the Pythagorean theorem. False

III: Since we know this is a 30–60–90 right triangle, the ratios of the sides S, P, R would be $2/1/\sqrt{3}$, which does not equal 10/6/2. False

The answer is E.

Problem-Solving Tactics

We've already mentioned a few tactics above in our fundamentals, strategies, and methods. However, let's look at some of the more effective and popular tactics for GMAT problem solving.

TACTIC 1. PICK NUMBERS . . . WISELY

Picking numbers is one of the oldest tricks in the book. But it still remains one of the wisest tricks in the book. Almost every GMAT prep guide in the universe (OK, at least on planet Earth), with the ironic exception of the official guide, mentions this tactic. When you begin to work out your solution, you can pick numbers to understand the question better and to simplify your approach. As you proceed, you can pick numbers to make your calculations easier. Lastly, you can pick numbers to check your work. Just make sure you pick numbers that make sense for the question.

- In general, use simple numbers such as 2 or 3. You can also use 0 and 1 for certain problem types (such as inequalities and absolute value), although be mindful of their special properties. Don't forget about fractions, such as $\frac{1}{2}$ or $\frac{1}{3}$, or about negative values if the question allows for them.
- If the question involves a fraction with $\frac{1}{3}$, use a large multiple of 3 such as 30, 60, or 120. Similarly, if you see a $\frac{x}{5}$ or $\frac{y}{7}$ in a question, you should pick a number that is a multiple of 35.
- If the question involves percent changes in a stock, you might try using 100.
- The most likely questions where picking numbers can be a good tactic include percents, mixtures, ratios, or problems where algebraic expressions are in the answer choices.

> Company X's stock rose 30% in year 1 and declined 10% in year 2. How much did the stock increase from the beginning of year 1 to the end of year 2?

Solution: Pick 100 as your starting number $\rightarrow$ After year 1, you get $100 + 30 = 130$. After year 2, you get $130 - 13 = 117$. $\rightarrow$ The increase is 17%.

TACTIC 2. USE YOUR BEST FRIENDS (ALGEBRA AND NUMBER PROPERTIES) . . . FOREVER.

As we have said before, algebra and properties of numbers are indeed your BFFs in math because they are always there to support you and bail you out of a messy situation. Algebra is the language of math, helping you to translate problems, unlock key insights, and simplify calculations on the majority (that's right, over half!) of quantitative questions. Properties of numbers are like the letters and words of math. These properties are how numbers work together and how they react to mathematical situations. Properties of numbers are often the key insight to questions that seem to require 10+ minutes of calculations, letting you figure things out in less than a minute.

> What is the unit digit of 2^{23}?

Solution: Clearly, multiplying the number 2 by itself 23 times is not the answer, as it would take an excessive amount of time. Properties of unit digits tell us that powers of 2 have a pattern of 2-4-8-6 as unit digits, looping every fourth power. This means that 2^4, 2^8, and thus 2^{24} have a unit digit of 6. Therefore, the looping pattern tells us that 2^{23} has a unit digit of 8.

TACTIC 3. DON'T BREAK YOUR BACK SOLVING, TRY BACKSOLVING

If you get stuck on a problem and have already spent over a minute to no avail, backsolving or working backward from the answer choices can be a good last resort option (along with POE and guess-timating below). Start with answer choice C because almost all GMAT answer choices are in ascending order and you can likely get to the right answer within three tries. On certain GMAT questions, you should consider backsolving:

- If the problem gives you an end result and asks you to find the starting number
- When the answer choices are simple, clean, and thus easy to plug into the question
- When the math seems to get a bit too labor intensive
- When the algebra in a word problem is more complex than plugging in the answer choices or logically reasoning them out in the question

5. Chuck, Jean-Claude, and Dolph take their pal Arnold out for a fancy dinner and offer to pay Arnold's bill. Chuck contributes 2 dollars more than $\frac{1}{5}$ the cost of Arnold's bill. Jean-Claude contributes 1 dollar less than $\frac{1}{2}$ the cost. Dolph contributes the remaining 14 dollars. What is the cost of Arnold's bill?

(A) $42
(B) $50
(C) $55
(D) $61
(E) $70

Solution: This problem could be solved with algebra. Let's say you weren't sure how to set it up and decided to go with a backsolving approach. Start with answer choice C.

$55 → Chuck pays $2 more than $\frac{1}{5}$ the bill, which gives $\frac{1}{5} \cdot 55 + 2 = 11 + 2 = \$13$.

→ Jean-Claude pays $1 less than $\frac{1}{2}$ the bill, which gives $\frac{1}{2} \cdot 55 - 1 = 27.5 - 1 = \$26.50$.

→ Since Dolph pays $14, the total bill is $14 + $13 + $26.50 = $53.50.

Dolph's contribution is a constant, so we need Chuck and Jean-Claude's portions to equal $55 – $14 = $41. Note that since the math is meant to work out cleanly, answer choices A and D are likely not going to work. Let's try $50.

$50 → Chuck pays $2 more than $\frac{1}{5}$ the bill, which gives $\frac{1}{5} \cdot 50 + 2 = 10 + 2 = \$12$.

→ Jean-Claude pays $1 less than $\frac{1}{2}$ the bill, which gives $\frac{1}{2} \cdot 50 - 1 = 25 - 1 = \$24$.

→ Since Dolph pays $14, the total bill is $12 + $24 + $14 = $50.

To solve algebraically, you would let the total bill be x. From this, you would get

$$x = \frac{1}{5}x + 2 + \left(\frac{1}{2}\right)x - 1 + 14 \rightarrow x - \frac{1}{5}x - \left(\frac{1}{2}\right)x = 15 \rightarrow \left(\frac{3}{10}\right)x = 15 \rightarrow x = 15 \cdot \frac{10}{3} = \$50$$

The answer is B.

TACTIC 4. CONSTRUCTION, CONSTRUCTION, WHAT'S YOUR FUNCTION?

The more complicated a question, the more important it is for you to add structure to the problem. There are many ways you can organize the information—charts, drawings, lists, arrows, matrix boxes, Venn diagrams, and headings such as before/after or year 1/year 2/year 3, etc. Adding structure allows you to see and process things more clearly. It can also provide a great method for solving a problem (e.g., distance-rate-time charts, seen later in this chapter). Lastly, if your scratch work on the given GMAT yellow pad is structured, clean, and easy to follow, you can easily track your work if the answer you get is not among the 5 choices.

TACTIC 5. BREAK IT DOWN!

This is an excellent GMAT tactic, aside from being one of the most common expressions sung by numerous musical artists over the years (MC Hammer leaps to mind). However, these words ring true for many questions, especially those that require structure as described in tactic 4. When you set up your approach to a problem, a high-level view shows you 2, 3, or sometimes even 4 steps to solve it. When you break down a problem, you separate each section into more easily solved pieces.

TACTIC 6. ESTIMATE, GUESS-TIMATE, APPROXIMATE TO ELUCIDATE

This tactic is not used enough. We know that most calculations are minimal. Therefore, some questions may test your ability to make reasonable approximations. You can approximate to simplify your calculations. You can estimate if the answer choice values are quite far apart from one another. You can guess-timate (intelligently of course!) if you are running out of time. For example, in geometry if you're stumped but you have a diagram drawn to scale, you can eyeball and guess the closest answer.

TACTIC 7. POE: RETURN OF THE FRIEND

As we saw in the critical reasoning chapter, process of elimination (POE) is a very helpful tactic. Eliminating answer choices that are clearly incorrect increases the probability that any guesses, should you make them, will be correct. If you can get down to 2 possible answer choices, your chances are now 50% versus 20% had you not eliminated choices. While eliminating choices, you might just gain further insight to solve the problem. Again, this tactic should be considered among the last resort options. After all, we're hoping you will learn and retain all the theory and strategies to beat the GMAT.

TACTIC 8. DON'T GET TRICKED: BECOME A TRICKSTER

GMAT test makers have an unusually large bag of tricks from which to conjure smoke and mirrors and throw you off the scent of the correct answer. If you understand how and when they do this, you can become a magician yourself! You can then finesse any tricky question and pull that rabbit out of the hat. Watch for some of the common GMAT traps:

- Incorrect assumptions made when reading questions quickly
- Units of measurement that confuse you
- Wordy questions that ramble on to make you overthink
- Mixing a percent increase with an absolute percent, or misunderstanding the percent of a whole versus the percent of a part

- Good-looking answer choices that seem too easy but are meant to lead you astray
- Mistaking the distance remaining with the distance traveled
- Equation types that you are prone to set up incorrectly
- In geometry, confusing the area inside a figure with the area outside a figure
- Wasting time looking for the shortcut when sometimes you just have to do the math

TACTIC 9. STOP STARING!

Many students will gaze at a question in bewilderment, trying to process where to begin. Meanwhile, an entire minute has gone by and they've done nothing. Write down what you know, redraw the diagram, put down a relevant question, and/or map out your know-want-approach method. Just get something on paper. You might find something in the visual scratch work.

TACTIC 10. LET IT GO

This is one of the hardest things for even the most advanced test takers to do. Letting go of a question is hard because you want so badly to get it right. You might even know that you're pretty close. There is no reason to ever spend more than 3 minutes on a question. Sometimes it's not working out. Sometimes you are just not getting it. It's OK. This happens. You can still get several questions wrong and earn a great score. So focus on the questions you know you can get right and let go of the ones you can't get right. Make sure you really let go of a question and aren't dwelling on it 5 questions later. You need the time and energy to get the doable questions right.

CONVERSION PROBLEMS

Some questions are categorized as conversion problems. In most cases, when other questions require you to make some type of the conversion, the conversion will be given to you in the problem. However, you should be quite familiar with a few conversions, especially converting imperial to metric units.

$$1 \text{ kg} = 2.2 \text{ lbs. (pounds)} \quad 1 \text{ mile} = 1.61 \text{ km} \quad 1 \text{ inch} = 2.54 \text{ cm}$$
$$1 \text{ kilometer} = 1,000 \text{ meters} \quad 1 \text{ meter} = 100 \text{ cm} = 1000 \text{ mm}$$

You should also know how to calculate conversions. The key is to figure out the end result and then determine which units you need to get rid of. Keep track of numerators and denominators. Use conversion equivalents to get rid of or change units.

20 mph is how many meters per second?

Solution: 20 miles/hour • 1 hour/60 min • 1 min/60 s • 1.61 km/1 mile • 1000 m/1 km

Note all the different units that cancel out (miles, hour, minutes, km)

$$\left(\frac{20 \cdot 1.61 \cdot 1000}{3600} \right) \text{m/s} = \left(\frac{20 \cdot 1.61 \cdot 10}{36} \right) \text{m/s} = \left(\frac{50 \cdot 1.61}{9} \right) \text{m/s} = 8.944 \text{ m/s}$$

WEIGHTED AVERAGES

The idea behind weighted averages is that sometimes the components that you are averaging are not equal. One or more components may have significantly more weight than the others. Consider the following example.

---

6. Ricky and Bobby both work for the same sales company. Ricky's commission rate is 20%, and Bobby's commission rate is 30%. If Ricky sold $55,000 worth of goods and Bobby sold $80,000 worth of goods, what is their combined average commission rate?

(A) 15%
(B) 24.1%
(C) 25%
(D) 25.9%
(E) 35%

Solution: Let's make a chart.

	Ricky	Bobby
Sales this year	$55,000	$80,000
Commission rate	20%	30%
Total commission		

You could calculate this just by adding up their total commission and dividing by their total sales. If you look at the answer choices, though, both 15% and 35% are not logically possible. Furthermore, we know that Bobby's sales give his commissions more weight. Thus the commission rate should be closer to 30% than to 20%.

Therefore, the answer is D.

This example illustrates how weighted averages work. The numbers with more weight have greater pull or influence on the overall average. Most weighted average problems are arithmetic or algebra questions that can be solved conceptually like the above example. There's also a clever shortcut method called the weighted average line graph. We will demonstrate it in the next example.

---

7. Students in Mrs. Tisdale's class took a geometry test. The girls' scores in the class averaged 90%, the boys' scores in the class averaged 82%, while the overall class average was 85%. What is the ratio of boys to girls in the class?

(A) 3 : 5
(B) 9 : 8
(C) 5 : 4
(D) 8 : 5
(E) 5 : 3

Solution: You can do this algebraically, or you can use the weighted average line graph.

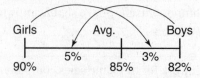

According to the graph above, the number that corresponds to the boys is 5 and the number that corresponds to the girls is 3. Therefore the ratio of boys to girls = 5:3.

Had you used algebra, you could let B = the number of boys and G = the number of girls. Use the formula

$$\text{Average} = (\text{Sum of scores})/(\text{Number of kids in class})$$

The sum of scores for the girls would be $90G$ (average score • number of girls) and for the boys it would $82B$. This gives us

$$85 = \frac{(90G + 82B)}{(B + G)} \rightarrow 85B + 85G = 90G + 82B \rightarrow 3B = 5G \rightarrow \frac{B}{G} = \frac{5}{3}$$

The answer is E.

MIXTURE PROBLEMS

Most mixture problems involve two or more solutions mixed together or a solution with two or more parts going through changes. Often you'll need to create algebraic expressions to solve these problems. However, there are many shortcuts and tactics you can use.

1. **ALGEBRA.** If you can set up an algebraic equation to start, then do it. If the answer choices are in algebraic form, then this is a pure algebra question. You'll likely have to manipulate the equations.

2. **DRAWING.** It's easy to do mixture problems if you can visualize them with a drawing.

3. **TRACK EVERYTHING.** In many mixture problems, you need to keep track of units, amounts, percentages, total volumes, or a mix of all of them.

4. **CHARTS.** For mixtures that go through changes (e.g., adding 2 L of water to an existing solution), a chart is a good way to lay out the information clearly.

5. **WEIGHTED AVERAGE LINE GRAPH.** If two solutions are mixed together, the resulting solution may have a weighted average mixture. Thus, you can use the line graph to your advantage.

6. **MEASUREMENT PROBLEMS ARE OFTEN CONCEPTUAL.** Whenever you see a classic measurement problem, which is a form of mixture problem where "Jar A is half-full and half of it is poured into Jar B," your best bet is to solve conceptually by visualizing and using logic and reason to figure it out.

8. Ned has 10 L of a 30% solution of salt in water. He adds enough salt to create a 50% solution. How much water will Ned need to add to the solution to get it back to a 30% solution?

(A) 7 liters

(B) $9\frac{1}{3}$ liters

(C) 10 liters

(D) $13\frac{2}{3}$ liters

(E) 15 liters

Solution: This question should be broken in 3 parts—the original state, the middle state, and the desired end result. Let's break this down into a chart and keep track of all units.

	Salt		Water		Total Liters
	Amount in Liters	% of Solution	Amount in Liters	% of Solution	
Beginning	3	30%	7	70%	10 L
Middle	7	50%	7	50%	14 L
End	7	30%	x	70%	y

If you look closely, the change from beginning to middle requires the amount of salt to change and the amount of water to stay the same. Going from middle to the end, the amount of salt stays the same and now only the amount of water will change. By using algebra, you get:

$$\frac{x}{7} = \frac{7}{3} \rightarrow x = 7 \cdot \frac{7}{3} = \frac{49}{3} = 16\frac{1}{3} \text{ L of water} \rightarrow \text{You need to add } 18\frac{1}{3} - 7 = 9\frac{1}{3} \text{ L.}$$

The answer is B.

RATE PROBLEMS

Rate problems include mostly work/rate and distance/rate questions. The basic formula is

$$\text{Work} = \text{Rate} \cdot \text{Time or } W = RT$$

where W is the amount of work done, R is the speed or rate at which the work is done, and T is the time it takes to do the amount of work.

> Robert peels potatoes at a rate of 3.5 per minute. How many potatoes will he peel in 1 hour?

Solution: W = (3.5 potatoes/min) • (60 min) Note that we converted 1 hour to 60 min = 210 potatoes

Whenever you deal with rate problems, here is what you need to know:

1. **KEEP TRACK OF UNITS.** Often in work/rate problems, several units are at play, which can often get lost in your calculations.

2. **ALWAYS CONVERT TO UNIT RATES OF COMPLETE JOBS.** If you're told that a machine can produce 300 papers in 2 hours, you should convert that to 150 papers per hour. For rate questions, the unit rate means you are converting to per hour (or per days, minutes, or seconds) or converting to per job. If you are given the time for a partial job, calculate the rate for the complete job.

3. **YOU CAN ADD RATES TOGETHER.** If you know the unit rates of 2 different people or 2 different machines, you can add them to come up with a combined rate of the 2 people or the 2 machines. This is another reason why it's important to convert to unit rates.

4. **WHEN STUCK, USE *W = RT*.** If the rate problem is unfamiliar to you, try starting with the basic equation and look for the pieces.

5. **CHART IT OUT!** For more complex rate problems and most distance/rate/time (DRT) problems, a chart is a great method for sorting the information and solving. We'll visit this further in the DRT section.

Work/Rate Problems

There are 3 main types of work/rate problems—single jobs, batch jobs, and triple aspect types. We will explore them all and work for a sample problem for each type.

WORK/RATE TYPE 1: SINGLE JOBS

> Hose A fills a pool in 3 hours, and hose B fills the pool in 4 hours. How long will it take hose A and hose B, working together, to fill the pool?

Solution: For this type of problem, there are 2 methods. We will show them side by side.

Method 1: Combine Unit Rates

Calculate the unit rates for each hose.

Hose *A*: unit rate = $\frac{1}{3}$ pool/hr

Hose *B*: unit rate = $\frac{1}{4}$ pool/hr

Add the rates to get the combined rate:

$\frac{1}{3} + \frac{1}{4} = \frac{7}{12}$ pool/hr

Flip the equation to get the total time

$\frac{12}{7}$ hours/pool.

Method 2: Use the Work/Rate Formula

The standard work/rate formula is

$$\frac{1}{A} + \frac{1}{B} = \frac{1}{\text{Both}}$$

where A = the time A takes to do something

B = the time B takes to do something

Both = the time both A and B take to do something

Plugging in we get $\frac{1}{3} + \frac{1}{4} = \frac{1}{x}$ $\frac{7}{12} = \frac{1}{x}$

Therefore $x = \frac{12}{7}$ hours/pool.

The big question is which method is better? Unfortunately the answer is, as always, it depends. The formula method is quicker if the test makers give you specific times for all the people or machines in the question. For more complex rate questions, tracking and combining unit rates might be better.

> **TIP**
>
> Note that you should not forget to flip the rate in order to get the total time.

> **TIP**
>
> This equation is also additive, which means that if there were 3 hoses and we wanted to calculate them, we would use $1/A + 1/B + 1/C = 1/x$.

WORK/RATE TYPE 2: BATCH JOBS

> Machine A prints 350 newspapers in 7 hours, and machine B prints 2400 newspapers in 6 hours. How long will it take both machines working together to print 1800 newspapers?

Solution: For this type of question, you need to calculate unit rates. Depending on the question, you would either calculate a rate per hour or rate per thing, such as, per newspaper. Given the way that the question is laid out, you should calculate the hourly rate.

Machine A: unit rate = 50 newspapers/hr
Machine B: unit rate = 400 newspapers/hr

Therefore, the combined rate is 450 newspapers/hr. You should be able to see that the math works cleanly and the total number of hours is 4 hours. However, if you cannot see this, then use the formula

$$W = RT \rightarrow 1800 \text{ newspapers} = (450 \text{ newspapers/hr}) \bullet T \rightarrow T = \frac{1800}{450} = 4 \text{ hours}$$

WORK/RATE TYPE 3: TRIPLE ASPECT

A common format for this type is *"X people can do Y things in Z hours. How long will it take A people to do B things?"*

Here you have three aspects at play in the question, which makes it a bit harder. Let's look at a specific example.

> 10 people can paint 6 houses in 5 days. How long would it take 2 people to paint 3 houses?

STRATEGY FOR TYPE 3 WORK/RATE PROBLEMS

1. **FOCUS ON 2 ASPECTS AT A TIME.** The work/rate problem asked above has 3 aspects. Look at 2 aspects, and decide which one you want to adjust. In this example, you may want to change the 10 people down to 5 people. When you do that, keep the 3rd aspect the same and calculate how the 2nd aspect changes.

10 people	paint 6 houses	in 5 days	becomes
↓ ÷2	↓ ÷2	↓	
5 people	paint 3 houses	in 5 days	

   Notice that we changed the number of houses and people but kept the time constant.

2. **BE CAREFUL OF THE INVERSE RELATIONSHIPS.** In the previous step, the number of people and the number of houses had a direct relationship. So when we reduced the people by half, the number of houses also reduced by half. The amount of time, however, has an inverse relationship with both the number of people and the number of houses. At this point in the example, we have the correct number of houses but now we want to change the people from 5 to 2.

5 people	paint 3 houses	in 5 days	becomes
↓ $\bullet \frac{2}{5}$	↓	↓ $\bullet \frac{5}{2}$	
2 people	paint 3 houses	in 12.5 days	

Since the number of people versus days has an inverse relationship, we multiplied the second number by the inverse. In order to get from 5 people to 2 people, we had to multiply by $\frac{2}{5}$. Therefore, for the number of days, we had to multiply by $\frac{5}{2}$, which is the inverse (or the reciprocal).

3. **UNIT RATES CAN HELP.** Sometimes if the question is a bit more complex, it can be worthwhile to bring 2 of the 3 aspects to a unit rate. (It is unlikely you can get all 3 rates equal to 1). Using unit rates can be an easier starting point for your calculations. In the example, bringing two aspects to a unit rate would mean finding how many days it would take for 1 person to paint 1 house. Had we calculated this (feel free to have fun trying to calculate this), we would get 8.33 days.

Distance-Rate-Time (DRT) Problems

The basic formula for distance/rate problems is an offshoot of the work/rate formula:

$$\text{Distance} = \text{Rate} \cdot \text{Time} \rightarrow D = RT$$

> If Jill travels 5 hours by car at a speed of 50 mph, the total distance she travels is $D = RT = (50 \text{ mph}) \cdot (5 \text{ hours}) = 250$ miles.

Most DRT problems will not be this simple. Instead, they will be broken down into 2 and sometimes 3 sections. Here are the 3 most common setups.

1. **THE MEET UP:** Alice travels from the west, and Billy travels from the east. They are a certain distance apart. When do they meet?
2. **THE OVERTAKE:** Alice travels from a certain point in a certain direction. Billy travels from the same point and same direction but a little bit later and at a faster speed. When will Billy overtake Alice?
3. **THE MIXED SPEEDS:** Alice travels at a certain speed during part of a trip but then travels at a different speed during another part of the same trip. What was Alice's average speed?

So how do the GMAT test makers make these questions more difficult?

- They make one or both persons start at different times.
- They make one or both persons have to stop or go slower for a short period of time.
- They throw in algebraic variables instead of actual numbers.
- They mix up the units, thinking that you might forget to convert them.

DRT METHOD: THE DiRTy CHART

Regardless of the setup, the best way to deal with DRT problems is to use the "DiRTy chart method." Here's how it works.

	Route A	Route B	Total
D			
R			Average rate
T			

STEP 1 If it helps, you may want to draw a diagram to understand the question better.

STEP 2 Draw the DiRTy chart as per the diagram. Note that some DRT problems may split into 3 parts.

STEP 3 Input the values given in the question.

STEP 4 Determine what value you need to find, and let the variable equal this value. Input that variable into the chart.

STEP 5 Fill in the rest of the chart using your chosen variable.

STEP 6 Determine the key relationship that will help you create an equation to solve. In most cases, it will be:

- Total distance = $D_A + D_B$
- Total time = $T_A + T_B$
- D_A is equal to or is related to D_B
- T_A is equal to or is related to T_B
- Average rate = Total distance/Total time (The chart has been grayed out above so that you don't think that box might represent total rate, because it doesn't.) Calculating average rate is a special subtype of DRT problems that requires you to calculate total distance and total time in order to figure it out.

STEP 7 Solve for the equation or relationship to get your answer.

Some of these steps you can do at the same time. Let's use an example to show how the DiRTy chart method works.

---

9. Samantha is traveling from Philadelphia to New York City, a distance of 80 miles, at a rate of 25 mph. Fred is traveling from New York City to Philadelphia at a rate of 35 mph but leaves 60 minutes after Samantha starts her trip. They're both traveling on the same route. How long will Fred have traveled by the time he passes Samantha?

(A) 48 minutes

(B) 55 minutes

(C) 1 hour

(D) 1 hour 20 minutes

(E) 1 hour 40 minutes

Solution:

STEP 1 Try a diagram

Samantha   Fred
25 mph → Philadelphia ———————————— NYC ← 35 mph, 60 min later

STEP 2 and

STEP 3 Draw the chart and input the values given. We have Samantha's rate of 25mph and Fred's rate of 35 mph. The total distance is 80 miles. (Note that we keep track of units.)

STEP 4 We need to find Fred's time, so we let that be T.

STEP 5 We fill in the rest of the chart using this variable. Samantha's time becomes $T + 1$ because she spent 1 extra hour on the road. Samantha's distance is input as $25(T + 1)$ and Fred's distance is input as $35T$.

At this point, your DiRTy Chart should look like this

	Sam	Fred	Total
D	25 (T + 1)	35 T	80 miles
R	25 mph	35 mph	
T	T + 1	T	

Note that we didn't fill in the total time because in this question, it is not relevant.

STEP 6 and
STEP 7 The key relationship here is that Samantha's and Fred's distances will add up to the total. So we get

$$25(T+1) + 35T = 80 \;\rightarrow\; 25T + 25 + 35T = 80$$

$$60T = 55 \;\rightarrow\; T = \frac{55}{60} \text{ hours} = 55 \text{ minutes}$$

The answer is B.

In this example, we had to account for Fred leaving 60 minutes later and we had to convert 60 minutes into one hour. Sometimes a question is complex enough that you may need to use the chart twice. That's OK because the chart works quickly once you get the hang of it. The DiRTy chart method is effective for many DRT problems because it sorts out information in a clear and understandable way. It also helps you to determine the key equation to solve.

VENN DIAGRAMS AND MATRIX BOXES

Venn Diagrams and Matrix Box problems are very similar because they are a form of set theory. Simply put, these questions require you to organize information that relates to each other. They are almost like fun word puzzles! In many of these cases, when there are 2 sets of information, both of these methods work. What is important is to find the best method to use for the question in front of you. How do we tell them apart?

- Use Venn diagrams for overlapping groups and matrix boxes for complementary groups (parts add up to 100%). For example, if the group is made up of red and nonred boxes, this is a complementary group and should be solved with matrix boxes.
- For Venn diagrams, you will see key words such as "only," "exactly," "both," or "neither."
- If there are 3 sets or groups of information, you should use Venn diagrams.

In most cases, test takers seem to prefer the matrix box.

1. It tends to involve less work.
2. It has more spaces and so can represent more quantities explicitly.
3. Its rows and columns are nicely aligned for automatic addition/subtraction.

However, if you can fully grasp how Venn diagrams work, they are a much more powerful tool for the tougher problems. Of course, we recommend that you master both methods. Let's first look at Venn diagrams.

The Venn Diagram Method

The basic setup for Venn diagrams is as follows:

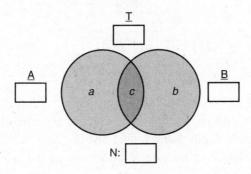

Venn formula 1: $T = a + b + c + N$
Venn formula 2: $T = A + B - c + N$

Depending on the question, you will be given values for either formula 1 or formula 2. Note that the c in formula 2 is subtracted because it was counted twice.

STEP 1 Fill in the total number of elements in the question if given. Label the 2 groups in the question.

STEP 2 Input values in the boxes or inside of circles only if they are specifically given.

STEP 3 Don't forget to consider the value of "neither" in the question. Quite often, this value is zero.

STEP 4 Determine which Venn formula is appropriate. If you are given a value for "a only," then you would use formula 1. If you are given a value for "all of A," then you would use formula 2. Make sure it is clear from the precise wording what the values are.

STEP 5 Manipulate the equation to solve.

Let's use an example to show how the Venn diagram method works.

---

10. An apartment building has 200 tenants, 80% of whom use the amenities. Of the people who use the amenities, 90 use the indoor pool and 130 use the fitness room. How many tenants use both the indoor pool and the fitness room?

    (A) 40
    (B) 60
    (C) 90
    (D) 110
    (E) 130

Solution:

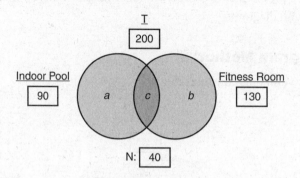

STEP 1 You can label the Venn diagram "Indoor Pool" for box *A* and "Fitness Room" for box *B*. You can also input the total number of elements in question as 200.

STEP 2 You can input 90 for box *A* and 130 for box *B*.

STEP 3 You can also input 40 for box *N* since 20% of the tenants do not use the amenities.

STEP 4 In this question, you are using formula 2 → $T = A + B - c + N$.
You get $200 = 90 + 130 - c + 40$

STEP 5 We can solve to get $c = 260 - 200 = 60$.

The answer is B.

The Matrix Box Method

For the matrix box, we use a similar input approach as we did for the Venn diagrams. Essentially, we create a 2 × 2 box to input our values. This is why it's often referred to as a double matrix. We also have a third column and a third row for our totals. When we combine that with another row and column for descriptive headings, we get the following matrix box.

MATRIX BOX

	Description *A*	Description *B*	Total
Aspect *X*			
Not aspect *X*			
Total			100%

MATRIX BOX TACTICS

- You can have 2 separate descriptions, *A* or *B* (e.g. the animals are either dogs or cats). You can instead have aspect *X* and its complementary opposite (e.g., the animals are black or not black).
- The column and row headings have to be mutually exclusive. In other words, they cannot occur at the same time. Therefore, using our previous example, we cannot have a dog and a cat at the same time nor can we have a black and a nonblack animal at the same time.

- If the question gives you awkward percentages or fractions, try the Picking Numbers tactic. Start with a total number that makes sense, such as a number that is divisible by all the denominators, if you were given fractions in the question.
- Remember that the right-most columns must equal the sum of the columns to the left of them. Similarly, the bottom rows must equal the sum of the number above them.

Let's demonstrate the matrix box method with a sample problem.

11. The owner of a unique pet store keeps only cats and dogs. Of the 60 pets in the store, 38 are cats, 28 have black fur, and 14 are neither black furred nor cats. What percentage of the store's dogs are black furred?

   (A) 13.3%
   (B) 23.3%
   (C) 36.4%
   (D) 57.1%
   (E) 63.6%

Solution: When you label and fill in the chart with what you know, you get what is in **bold**. With that information, you can fill in the rest of the table (*in italics*).

	Cats	Dogs	Total
Black fur	20	8	28
Not black fur	18	14	32
Total	38	22	60

Now that you have all the information, you can easily calculate the percentage of black-furred dogs. Don't forget that the question specifically asks for the proportion of black-furred dogs to total dogs, **not** total animals. You get:

$$\text{(Black-furred dogs)} / \text{(total dogs)} = \frac{8}{22} = \frac{4}{11} = 0.3636 = 36.4\%$$

The answer is C.

MINIMUM/MAXIMUM PROBLEMS

A common requirement on GMAT problems is to find the maximum or minimum value. This can also be written as "least," "smallest," "most," and "largest" to name just a few synonyms.

> Harry is running for President of his club against two others, Stephen and Gillian. If 31 people are in the club, including Harry, what is the minimum number of votes with which he could actually win?

Solution: To find the minimum number of votes Harry needs, we need to find the minimum number of votes that Stephen and Gillian could get such that Harry would need only one extra vote. Ironically, if we think about the maximum spread of votes, we should just divide $\frac{31}{3}$ and get a spread of $10\frac{1}{3}$. This means that the maximum spread of votes would be 10, 10, and 11. Therefore, Harry needs a minimum of 11 votes.

Minimum/Maximum Strategies

- Figure out first whether you need to maximize or minimize and what variables are at play in the question.
- If you're asked to maximize something, you will usually need to minimize the remaining variables in the problem. If the problem asks you to minimize something, you will usually need to maximize the remaining variables.
- Even though most of the time you can use logic to understand these abstract questions better, you still should do the math and look at the scenarios that exploit the minimum or maximum values.

---

12. Philip has a collection of 54 DVDs, some movies and some television shows. If exactly $\frac{3}{4}$ of the movies and exactly $\frac{1}{3}$ of the television shows are comedies, what is the greatest possible number of Philip's DVDs that could be comedies?

  (A) 9
  (B) 23
  (C) 36
  (D) 38
  (E) 48

Solution: You need to maximize the number of comedies. Another way of looking at this problem is that you need to minimize the number of noncomedies. Since the movies have a much larger proportion of comedies than do television shows, you should try to maximize the number of movies. In other words, you should try to maximize the $\frac{3}{4}$ of the movies. You can also try to minimize the $\frac{1}{3}$ of the television shows. You can use a chart and pick numbers.

Total DVDs	TV Shows	$\frac{1}{3}$ of TV shows	Movies	$\frac{3}{4}$ of Movies
54	3	1	51	$51 \cdot \frac{3}{4} \rightarrow$ not an integer
54	6	2	48	$48 \cdot \frac{3}{4} = 36 \rightarrow$ This works!

The total number of DVD comedies would be 36 + 2 = 38.

The answer is D.

INTEREST RATE PROBLEMS

GMAT math questions involving interest rates fall into two categories: simple interest and compound interest. These are calculated on a starting loan or investment called the principal. Let's first understand the definitions.

INTEREST: The amount paid for the use of lent or invested money, usually given as a percentage.

PRINCIPAL: The amount of the loan or investment.

SIMPLE INTEREST: Interest that is calculated on only the original principal.

COMPOUNDED INTEREST: Interest that is calculated on the original principal *plus* all accumulated interest.

SEMIANNUAL: Twice a year.

BIANNUAL: Every other year.

SEMIMONTHLY: Twice a month.

BIMONTHLY: Every other month.

Simple Interest Rate Problems

Simple interest is the most basic type of interest rate question tested on the GMAT. The formula is

$$\text{Interest earned} = (\text{Principal invested}) \bullet (\text{interest rate}) \bullet (\text{Time}) = Pit$$

If you invest \$2000 at an annual interest rate of 8%, your interest earned at the end of year is 2000 • 0.08 • 1 = \$160

Another way of looking at this calculation is using the more formal equation

$$A = P(1 + In)$$

where A = amount, P = principal, I = interest rate, n = number of periods

Total amount of investment = Principal • (1 + (Interest) • (number of time periods))

INTEREST RATE TACTICS

1. Make sure you express the rate of interest in decimals rather than percentage.
2. Make sure you are clear about whether you are solving for the interest or for the new amount due to the interest. These two different things can be easily confused.
3. When you deal with periods of the loan or investment that are not full years and if you adjust the time period, do not adjust the rate of interest or vice versa. For example, if the calculation is to be made on a semiannual basis, then adjust either the time period or the rate of interest, not both.
4. Know how to interpret between simple interest and compound interest. The key is to see how many periods the interest is paid. If interest is paid in one period, that is simple interest. If interest is paid on interest in multiple periods, that is compound interest.
5. Some questions can be solved conceptually by applying concepts such as weighted average or by backsolving.

13. Chelsea invests $1200 at 5% interest. How much additional money must she invest at 8% so that her total annual income will be equal to 6% of her entire investment?

   (A) $500
   (B) $600
   (C) $1200
   (D) $1500
   (E) $1800

Solution: If you tried to solve this question algebraically, you should have recognized that it's essentially just a giant weighted average problem. Try using the weighted average line graph.

Let x = the amount invested at 8%. Chelsea's total amount invested will be $1200 + x$. The interest income of 5% on the $1200 plus the interest income of 8% on x will give you the interest income from both investments. This gives you algebraically

$$0.08x + 0.05(1200) = 0.06(1{,}200 + x) \rightarrow 0.08x + 60 = 72 + 0.06x \rightarrow 0.02x = 12$$

$$x = \frac{12}{0.02} = \frac{1200}{2} = \$600$$

Alternatively, you could have also used the weighted average line graph here as a nice shortcut.

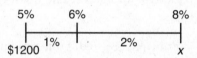

$$\frac{1200}{2} = \frac{x}{1} \rightarrow x = 600$$

The answer is B.

Compound Interest Rate Problems

Often interest rates are compounded monthly, quarterly, or semiannually. This means that the interest at each period of compounding is added to the original principal. Compounded interest will yield a bigger return than does simple interest at the same rate. The standard formula is:

$$A = P(1 + \frac{r}{n})^{nt}$$

where

A = Amount currently in the investment (principal plus interest)

P = Original principal amount

r = Interest rate (yearly) in decimal format (i.e., 8% = 0.08)

n = Number of times per year the interest is compounded

t = Number of years

There are some common question types when it comes to compound interest rate problems.

TYPE A EXAMPLE

> If Alice invests $2000 at an interest rate of 10%, how much
> money will she have at the end of a year?

Answer: $2000 • 1.10 = $2200

TYPE B EXAMPLE

> If Alice invests $2000 at an interest rate of 10%, compounded
> semiannually, how much money will she have at the end of
> a year?

Since the annual interest rate is compounded twice during the year, you need to calculate interest at $\frac{10}{2}$ = 5% every 6 months. This is how compounding gets you more money on your investment than does simple interest.

STEP 1 At 6 months, the principal becomes $2000 • 1.05 = $2100.

STEP 2 At 12 months, the new principal balance of $2100 earns another 5% interest, or $2100 • 1.05 = $2205.

TYPE C EXAMPLE

> If Alice invests $2000 at an interest rate of 12%, compounded
> quarterly (or bimonthly or monthly), how much money will she
> have at the end of a year?

You can take the step-by-step approach to solve for the 4 quarters, but it will take you time. The calculating would be even more time consuming for bimonthly or monthly compounding questions. This is where using the formula helps. Remember that 12% = 0.12.

$$\text{Quarterly compound: } A = P\left(1+\frac{r}{n}\right)^{nt} \rightarrow A = 2000 \cdot \left(1+\frac{0.12}{4}\right)^{4\cdot1} = 2000 \cdot (1.03)^4$$

   The GMAT test makers won't require you to make lengthy calculations, so look for the answer choices to be in the format above.

PROFIT AND REVENUE

Profit, revenue, and cost questions are relatively common on the GMAT, usually in the form of arithmetic or algebra word problems. You need to know two main equations:

Profit = Revenue – Costs   or $\pi = R - C$
Revenue = Price • (Number of units sold)   or $R = P \cdot Q \rightarrow$ Note that $P = R/Q$

P stands for price, while π stands for profit, just so you can avoid any confusion. Other terms you might hear about include the following.

BREAK-EVEN POINT: The point when the profit is zero. If $\pi = 0$, then $R = C$.

GROSS PROFIT: This is Selling price – Cost, usually on a per unit basis.

PER UNIT: This is the most important GMAT trick to understand on these questions. Sometimes the test makers will give you values in cost per unit while revenue is expressed in total number of unit sales. Make sure you convert to per unit revenue or convert the unit cost to a total cost value.

---

14. A leather goods manufacturer produces leather purses at a cost of $20 per purse. The manufacturer's fixed costs are $7200 per month, regardless of how many purses are produced. If the manufacturer produces 240 purses per month and the shipping costs are $2 per unit, at what price does the manufacturer need to sell the purses in order to break even?

   (A) $52
   (B) $55
   (C) $60
   (D) $67
   (E) $72

Solution: Since you are looking at the break-even point, $\pi = R - C = 0$. Therefore, $R = C$. Let's calculate the total cost.

Cost = $20/unit + $2/unit + $7200 → You can convert $7200 into a cost per unit, using the 240 units

$\dfrac{7200}{240}$ = $30/unit → The total cost per unit is now $20 + $2 + $30 = $52/unit

Price = Revenue/Unit and Revenue/Unit = Cost/unit in a break-even scenario. You already have an answer of $52 for the price of each purse.

The answer is A.

DATA INTERPRETATION

Data interpretation questions are occurring less frequently on the GMAT. This is because some of the core skills are now being tested on the graphical interpretation section of integrated reasoning. However, you still may see some. If you do, here are some strategies to keep in mind.

- **FIRST, ANALYZE THE DATA CAREFULLY:** Note labels, units, and trends. Avoid misreading.
- **BE QUESTION DRIVEN:** Use the question given in the stem to ask yourself, "What data do I need to solve?"
- **ESTIMATE WHEN POSSIBLE:** Just as in the integrated reasoning section, the GMAT test makers don't expect you to make lengthy or precise calculations. Estimating will simplify your process and reduce the time you spend.

15. The following table shows the gross domestic (U.S.) revenue and gross overseas revenue of 5 movies. Which movie had the most success internationally versus domestically in terms of gross revenue?

Movie	Studio	Domestic Gross (In Millions of $)	Overseas Gross (In Millions of $)
The Avengers	Buena Vista	623.4	888.4
The Dark Knight Rises	Warner Bros.	448.1	632.9
Skyfall	Sony	304.2	804.1
The Hobbit: An Unexpected Journey	Warner Bros.	301.0	679.6
Ice Age: Continental Drift	Fox	161.3	714.0

    (A)   *The Dark Knight Rises*
    (B)   *The Hobbit: An Unexpected Journey*
    (C)   *Ice Age: Continental Drift*
    (D)   *Skyfall*
    (E)   *The Avengers*

Solution: You need to be clear about what the table says and what the question is asking for. The table shows how each movie did in the U.S. and overseas. The information about the studio is irrelevant. The question wants to know which movie benefited the most from the overseas gross revenues. What this question is really asking is which movie has the largest ratio of overseas to domestic grosses. If you estimate the values, you would get

$$\text{Avengers: } \frac{9}{6} \quad \text{Dark Knight: } \frac{6.5}{4.5} \quad \text{Skyfall: } \frac{8}{3} \quad \text{Hobbit: } \frac{7}{3} \quad \text{Ice Age: } \frac{7}{1.5}$$

Clearly *Ice Age* has the best ratio. Be careful of the answer choices because they are not listed in the same order as the chart. (They've been changed to reflect overseas ranks in ascending order.)

The answer is C.

RATE PROBLEMS

1. Daniel can paint the fence in 10 hours. When Mr. Miyagi helps, they can both paint the fence in $3\frac{1}{3}$ hours. How long would it take Mr. Miyagi to paint half the fence by himself?

   (A) $2\frac{1}{3}$

   (B) $2\frac{1}{2}$

   (C) 3

   (D) 5

   (E) $6\frac{1}{6}$

2. Machine 1 produces 1000 bolts in 5 hours, while machine 2 can complete 75% of the same job in 3 hours. How much time is required for both machines to produce 1750 bolts if machine 2 stops producing after 3 hours?

   (A) 5

   (B) 5.75

   (C) 6

   (D) 7.5

   (E) 8

3. 24 computer hackers can scan and infect 10 computers in 5 hours. If this group of hackers wants to scan and infect 20 computers in 8 hours, how many new computer hackers do they need to recruit and join their team in order to accomplish this task, assuming all hackers work at the same rate?

   (A) 0

   (B) 6

   (C) 8

   (D) 10

   (E) 16

4. Sam and his friends go on a fishing trip. In order to get to the lake, they have to portage from their base camp for x miles at a speed of r. Once at the lake, they take their canoes y miles out, going twice the speed as when they were portaging. When Sam is injured, his friends call for help. The helicopter arrives, taking them back to their camp at a speed 3 times that their boat went. Not including the time spent fishing, what is Sam and his friends' average rate from the camp to their fishing location and back?

(A) $\dfrac{r(2x+2y)}{(7x+4y)}$

(B) $\dfrac{r(7x+4y)}{(2x+2y)}$

(C) $4.5r$

(D) $\dfrac{(2x+2y)}{6r}$

(E) $9r$

VENN DIAGRAMS

5. 500 dormitory residents eat daily in a campus cafeteria with a prepurchased meal plan. On an average day, 320 residents have soup with their meal and 160 residents have salad with their meal. If at least 100 residents have neither soup nor salad, then the number of residents who have both soup and salad must be between:

(A) 40 and 100
(B) 80 and 120
(C) 80 and 160
(D) 100 and 160
(E) 160 and 320

6. Molly's high school focuses on the performing arts. In her year, 40 students can sing, 60 students can dance, and 24 students can act. No student is a triple threat (someone who can sing, dance, and act). However, 16 students can sing and dance, 12 students can dance and act, and 8 students can sing and act. How many students have only one performing talent?

(A) 44
(B) 52
(C) 60
(D) 66
(E) 72

MIXTURE/MEASUREMENT

7. In a lab experiment, the number of bacteria cells produces double the amount of new bacteria cells each day for each of the 4 days since initiation. If the total number of bacteria cells after 4 days is 54 million, how many bacteria cells did the experiment begin with?

(A) 1.5 million
(B) 2 million
(C) 4 million
(D) 5.5 million
(E) 7 million

8. London, the beloved German Shepherd of Luke, is fed 150 grams of a mixture of two foods, food A and food B. Food A contains 10 percent protein, and food B contains 15 percent protein. If the dog's diet provides exactly 18 grams of protein daily, how many grams of food A are in the mixture?

(A) 50
(B) 60
(C) 75
(D) 90
(E) 120

MATRIX BOXES

9. At *A Magazine's* Oscar party, $\frac{7}{12}$ of the guests are its employees, and $\frac{1}{2}$ of the guests at the Oscar party are men. If $\frac{1}{5}$ of the guests are men who are not employees of *A Magazine*, what percent of the guests are male employees of *A Magazine*?

(A) 12%
(B) 20%
(C) 24%
(D) 30%
(E) 36%

MINIMUM/MAXIMUM

10. On a hot day in July, an ice cream man sold an average of 14 ice cream products per hour over 5 consecutive hours. If during each hour, this ice cream man sold at least 7 ice cream products, what is the greatest possible range of the number of ice cream products sold in any hour?

    (A) 14
    (B) 28
    (C) 35
    (D) 42
    (E) 49

INTEREST RATES

11. Kumar's parents bought him a $5000 GIC investment that paid interest at an annual rate of 6 percent compounded semiannually. What was the total amount of interest paid on the investment in one year?

    (A) $150
    (B) $300
    (C) $304.50
    (D) $618
    (E) $10,300

12. During a trip, Terry traveled Y percent of the total distance at an average speed of 30 mph and traveled the rest of the distance at an average speed of 20 m/s. In terms of Y, what was Terry's average speed for the entire trip?

    (A) $\dfrac{100}{(Y+45)}$

    (B) $\dfrac{(200-Y)}{2}$

    (C) $\dfrac{6000}{(300-Y)}$

    (D) $\dfrac{9000}{(200-Y)}$

    (E) $\dfrac{9000}{(200+Y)}$

13. Just Lamps Inc. sells only lamps and bulbs. Lamp sales revenue was 8% higher in 2011 than in 2010 while bulb sales revenue was 12% lower. If Just Lamps Inc. saw its overall revenue decline by 2% during the same period, what was the ratio of lamp revenues to bulb revenues in 2010?

    (A) 2 : 3
    (B) 3 : 4
    (C) 1 : 1
    (D) 3 : 2
    (E) 5 : 3

ANSWER KEY

1. **(B)**	5. **(C)**	9. **(D)**	13. **(C)**
2. **(A)**	6. **(B)**	10. **(C)**	
3. **(D)**	7. **(B)**	11. **(C)**	
4. **(A)**	8. **(D)**	12. **(E)**	

SOLUTIONS

1. **(B)** Use the $\dfrac{\text{work}}{\text{rate}}$ standard formula:

$\dfrac{1}{10} + \dfrac{1}{M} = \dfrac{1}{\frac{10}{3}}$, where M is the number of hours Mr. Miyagi takes to paint the fence

$$\dfrac{1}{M} = \dfrac{3}{10} - \dfrac{1}{10} = \dfrac{2}{10} \rightarrow M = \dfrac{10}{2} = 5 \text{ hours}$$

However, you need Mr. Miyagi's time to paint half the fence, which is 2.5 hours.

2. **(A)** First determine unit rates

Machine 1 unit rate = $\dfrac{1000}{5}$ = 200 bolts/hr

Machine 2 unit rate = $(75\%) \cdot \dfrac{(1000)}{3} = \dfrac{750}{3}$ = 250 bolts/hr

The two machines' combined rate is 200 + 250 = 450 bolts/hr
Now break down this problem into the first 3 hours and the rest of production.
In 3 hours, the machines produce 450 • 3 = 1350 bolts → leaving 1750 – 1350 = 400 bolts.

Machine 1 can produce the rest of the 400 bolts in 400 bolts/200 bolts/hr = 2 hours.
The total time is 2 + 3 = 5 hours.

3. **(D)** First, you need to get this 3-aspect work/rate problem to the desired task, focusing on only two tasks at a time. Start by changing the hours from 5 to 8 and adjusting the appropriate number of hackers while keeping the number of computers constant.

24 hackers	10 computers	5 hours
$\downarrow \cdot \dfrac{5}{8}$	$\downarrow$	$\downarrow \cdot \dfrac{8}{5}$
$24 \cdot \dfrac{5}{8}$ = 15 hackers	10 computers	8 hours

Notice that we multiplied the number of hackers by the inverse of what we multiplied the number of hours by. This is because if we had more time, we would need fewer hackers. Now let's change the number of computers from 10 to 20, adjusting the appropriate number of hackers but keeping the number of hours constant.

15 hackers	10 computers	8 hours
$\downarrow \cdot 2$	$\downarrow \cdot 2$	$\downarrow$
30 hackers	20 computers	8 hours

The number of extra hackers is 30 – 20 = 10.

4. **(A)** Use a DiRTy chart to sort out this information.

	To Lake	To Spot	Back to Camp	Total
D	x	y	x + y	
R	r	2r	6r	
T	x/r	y/2r	(x + y)/6r	

The average rate is calculated by $\dfrac{\text{Total distance}}{\text{Total time}}$

Using the chart, you can sum up the total distance to be $2x + 2y$. You can also find the total time to be

$$\frac{x}{r} + \frac{y}{2r} + \frac{x}{6r} + \frac{y}{6r} = \frac{(6x + 3y + x + y)}{6r} = \frac{(7x + 4y)}{r}$$

Therefore, the average rate will be $\dfrac{r(2x + 2y)}{(7x + 4y)}$.

Note that you should never calculate average rate by finding the average of the rates given. Otherwise you would incorrectly answer C.

5. **(C)** Let's start by drawing a Venn diagram.

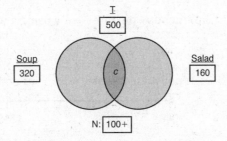

In this case, use the formula $T = A + B - c + N$, which gives

$500 = 320 + 160 - c + (100+)$ → By isolating the c, you get $c = 480 - 500 + (100+)$

$c = 80+$ → The range is limited by the number of people who can have salad, which is 160.

6. **(B)** Because you have overlapping sets, this is a Venn diagram problem. However, this is a triple diagram since there are 3 different performing disciplines. Don't get too stressed out. The process is the same and the GMAT test makers typically make these triple Venn diagrams easier than the standard ones. First, fill in what you know

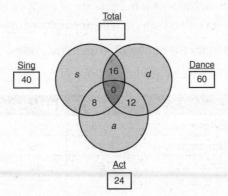

Now calculate the number of students with a single performing talent by subtracting the double threats from the whole of each performance type.

Singing: 40 – 16 – 8 = 16   Dancing: 60 – 16 – 12 = 32   Acting: 24 – 12 – 8 = 4

This gives 16 + 32 + 4 = 52 students with a single performing talent.

7. **(B)** Given that you are looking for a starting point number, this question could best be served by backsolving. Start with answer choice C.

Day 1	Day 2	Day 3	Day 4	Total	
4	+ 8 = 12	+ 24 = 36	+ 72 = 108	108	→ Too high!
					Try a lower number
2	+ 4 = 6	+ 12 = 18	+ 36 = 54	54	→ On target!

Algebraically, you could have let the starting amount be x, which would give you

$$x + 2x + 6x + 18x = 54 \rightarrow 27x = 54 \rightarrow x = 2 \text{ million}$$

The algebra here is relatively straightforward. In a harder question, though, it's good to have two different tactics up your sleeve.

8. **(D)** You can typically solve mixture problems either algebraically or with a weighted average line graph. If the dog gets 18 grams of protein, you first need to calculate what percentage of the total mixture this represents.

$\frac{18}{150} = \frac{6}{50} = \frac{12}{100} = 12\%$ of the total mixture $\rightarrow$ By using a weighted average line graph, you get

The ratio of food A to food B is $A{:}B = 3{:}2 \rightarrow$ This ratio can also be expressed as $A{:}B{:}$Total = 3:2:5.

Therefore food A represents $\frac{3}{5}$ of the mixture, which gives $\frac{3}{5} \cdot 150 = 90$ grams.

If we solved this algebraically, you would get two equations ① $A + B = 150$ and ② $0.1A + 0.15B = 18$. Multiplying equation ② by 10 gives ③ $A + 1.5B = 180$. Subtracting ③ – ① gives

$$0.5B = 30 \rightarrow B = 60 \rightarrow A = 150 - 60 = 90 \text{ grams of Food } A.$$

9. **(D)** This is a matrix box problem because there are 2 • 2 elements at play and there is no overlap. Guests are either male/female or employee/nonemployee. Also, because of the fraction $\frac{7}{12}$, let's pick the number 120 total. Your box should look like this (**bold** is for original values: *italics* are calculated values):

	Male	Female	Total
Employee	36	34	70
Nonemployee	24	26	50
Total	60	60	120

From the matrix box, you can see that the number of male employees is 36 out of 120 or $\frac{36}{120}$, which reduces to $\frac{3}{10}$ or 30%.

10. **(C)** In order to find the greatest number of ice cream products sold in any hour, you need to minimize the number sold in all the other hours. This means that you should let the ice cream man sell 7 ice cream products in each of 4 different hours, or $7 \cdot 4 = 28$ ice cream products sold. You also need to look at the average for the 5 hours.

$$\text{Average} = \frac{(\text{Sum of terms})}{(\text{Number of terms})} \rightarrow 14 = \frac{(28+x)}{5}$$

$70 = 28 + x \rightarrow x = 42 \rightarrow$ You want the range, though, which is $42 - 7 = 35$.

11. **(C)** You can use the formula $A = P\left(1 + \frac{r}{n}\right)^{nt}$, where

A = the amount of money after t or 1 year
P = the principal amount invested of \$5,000
r = the annual interest rate of 6% or 0.06
n = the number of times compounded, which is 2

$$5000\left(\frac{1+0.06}{2}\right)^{(2)(1)} = 5000(1.03)^2 = 5000(1.0609) = \$5304.50$$

Therefore the interest paid is $5,304.50 - $5,000 = $304.50.

12. **(E)** First, you should note that the average speeds given in the problem are in different units and need to be converted. After converting 20 m/s to miles per hour, you would get

$$20 \text{ m/s} \cdot 3600 \text{ s/1 hr} \cdot 1\text{km}/1000\text{m} \cdot 1 \text{ mile}/1.6 \text{ km} = 20 \cdot 3.6/1.6 = 45 \text{ mph}.$$

Now you can use a DiRTy chart to sort the information. Since you don't have the total distance, pick a number that's easy to use, such as 100 and fill in the chart.

	Route A	Route B	Total
D	Y	$100 - Y$	100
R	30	45	Average rate
T	$\frac{Y}{30}$	$\frac{(100-Y)}{45}$	

The total time for Terry's trip was

$$\frac{Y}{30} + \frac{(100-Y)}{45} = \frac{3Y + 2(100-Y)}{90} = \frac{(3Y + 200 - 2Y)}{90} = \frac{(Y+200)}{90}$$

Since average rate = $\frac{\text{Total distance}}{\text{Total time}}$, you get $\frac{100 \cdot 90}{(Y+200)} = \frac{9,000}{(Y+200)}$

13. **(C)** Since you are given two different years, it's a good idea to sort out this information. Second, since you're dealing with percents and no actual numbers, picking numbers for one of the revenues would be a good tactic here. Use algebra for the rest. Use $100 for the starting bulb revenue in 2011 and x for the starting lamp revenue in 2011. When you draw a chart, you get

	2010	% chg	2011
Bulb revenue	100	–12	88
Lamp revenue	x	$+0.08x$	$1.08x$
Total revenue	$100 + x$	$-0.02(100 + x)$	$0.98(100 + x)$

Using the 2011 column gives the equation $88 + 1.08x = 0.98(100 + x)$

$$88 + 1.08x = 98 + 0.98x \rightarrow 0.1x = 10, x = 100$$

What this means is that in 2010, lamp revenues = bulb revenues, so the ratio is 1: 1.

You could also have used the weighted average line graph. Instead, you could have noticed that the overall decline of 2% (–2%) is exactly between +8% and –12%. It still is a good exercise to try this out and leverage algebra and picking numbers as a solid strategy.

Probability

10

→ **BASIC PROBABILITY OF A SINGLE EVENT**

→ **PROBABILITY OF ONE EVENT OR ANOTHER**

→ **MUTUALLY EXCLUSIVE AND COMPLEMENTARY EVENTS**

→ **PROBABILITY OF TWO OR MORE EVENTS**

→ **INDEPENDENT AND DEPENDENT EVENTS**

→ **MIRROR RULE PROBABILITY**

→ **PAIRS PROBABILITY**

→ **ADVANCED PROBABILITY**

PROBABILITY: DIAGNOSTIC SKILL QUIZ

DIRECTIONS: Before continuing, try your hand at these probability questions to assess your level of understanding. The answers will be explained throughout this chapter.

1. What is the probability of drawing a jack or a diamond from a deck of cards?

   (A) $\dfrac{1}{52}$

   (B) $\dfrac{1}{13}$

   (C) $\dfrac{1}{4}$

   (D) $\dfrac{4}{13}$

   (E) $\dfrac{17}{52}$

2. What is the probability of rolling 2 sixes on two rolls of a die?

   (A) $\dfrac{1}{36}$

   (B) $\dfrac{1}{18}$

   (C) $\dfrac{1}{6}$

   (D) $\dfrac{7}{36}$

   (E) $\dfrac{1}{3}$

3. What is the probability of drawing 2 aces from a deck of cards with no replacement?

(A) $\frac{3}{676}$

(B) $\frac{1}{221}$

(C) $\frac{2}{52}$

(D) $\frac{2}{51}$

(E) $\frac{12}{221}$

4. A single coin is tossed four times. What is the probability that you will get at least one tail?

(A) $\frac{1}{16}$

(B) $\frac{1}{4}$

(C) $\frac{3}{8}$

(D) $\frac{5}{8}$

(E) $\frac{15}{16}$

5. Jenny has 7 pairs of shoes, each of a different design. If Jenny randomly selects 2 shoes without replacement from the 14 shoes, what is the probability that she will select 2 shoes of the same design?

(A) $\frac{2}{91}$

(B) $\frac{1}{14}$

(C) $\frac{1}{13}$

(D) $\frac{1}{7}$

(E) $\frac{3}{13}$

6. Joey and his friends played a new game that uses 20 playing cards made up of 2 suits of 10 cards each. The cards in each suit have values from 1 to 10. If Joey turns over 4 cards, what is the probability that he will find at least one pair of cards having the same value?

(A) $\dfrac{1}{5}$

(B) $\dfrac{99}{323}$

(C) $\dfrac{3}{5}$

(D) $\dfrac{224}{323}$

(E) $\dfrac{4}{5}$

7. Frances tosses a coin 10 times. What is the probability that she will get exactly 5 heads and 5 tails?

(A) $\dfrac{1}{32}$

(B) $\dfrac{63}{256}$

(C) $\dfrac{1}{4}$

(D) $\dfrac{1}{2}$

(E) $\dfrac{193}{256}$

The solutions to these questions are presented in the following pages along with a discussion of theory and strategies.

CONTENT SUMMARY/CHECKLIST

By the end of this chapter, you should have enough information to review and understand the following topics:

☐ Basic probability of a single event
☐ Probability of one event or another
☐ Mutually exclusive and complementary events
☐ Probability of two or more events
☐ Independent and Dependent events
☐ Mirror rule probability
☐ Pairs probability
☐ Advanced probability

INTRODUCTION

Probability is the likelihood that a certain event or multiple events will occur. The questions that show up on the GMAT range from easy to very difficult. This topic is broken down into three main probability formulas along with several key topics that are used to increase the difficulty. Some basic elements to remember are the following:

- Probability values range from 0% to 100%, inclusive. You cannot have a probability of 150% to win a game (no matter what Kobe Bryant or other professional athletes might tell you).
- Probability can be measured in decimals, fractions, or percents. Be sure to check the answer choice format before starting to solve.
- Many probability questions use decks of cards, coin tosses, or dice rolls. So if you're not a card shark and have no idea how many aces or spades are in a deck of cards, you should probably buy a set or watch some Texas hold'em poker on TV.

Things That Won't Be Tested

Depending on how well you are doing on the GMAT, you should expect to see all levels of probability topics. However, you won't see experimental probability or linear regression theory.

BASIC PROBABILITY OF A SINGLE EVENT

The simplest probability question would ask, "What is the probability of rolling a six on one roll of a die?"

The answer, of course, is $\frac{1}{6}$. This realization stems from the basic formula for probability of a single event.

$$P(A) = \text{(The number of outcomes where } A \text{ occurs)} / \text{(The total number of possible outcomes)}$$

This is the starting point for all probability questions. The difficulty of the questions is increased by adding further obstacles such as multiple events or restrictions.

PROBABILITY OF ONE EVENT OR ANOTHER

Although we gave you the basic formula for probability, there is also the general case formula for probability of one event or another.

$$P(A \text{ or } B) = P(A) + P(B) - P(A \text{ and } B)$$

Let's look at an example.

1. What is the probability of drawing a jack or a diamond from a deck of cards?

   (A) $\frac{1}{52}$

   (B) $\frac{1}{13}$

   (C) $\frac{1}{4}$

   (D) $\frac{4}{13}$

   (E) $\frac{17}{52}$

Solution: $P(\text{jack or diamond}) = P(\text{jack}) + P(\text{diamond}) - P(\text{jack and diamond})$

This gives $\frac{4}{52} + \frac{13}{52} - \frac{1}{52} = \frac{16}{52}$ which reduces to $\frac{4}{13}$.

The answer is D.

In this example, we had probability values for drawing a jack and a diamond. However, it was also possible to get a value for drawing a jack and a diamond at the same time. Often in the general case formula, the third part of the equation goes to zero. This is because many questions are mutually exclusive or complementary.

MUTUALLY EXCLUSIVE AND COMPLEMENTARY EVENTS

The best way to explain and compare mutually exclusive and complementary events is with a chart.

MUTUALLY EXCLUSIVE AND COMPLEMENTARY EVENTS

Aspect	Mutually Exclusive Events	Complementary Events
Definition	Events that can never occur together; the occurrence of one event eliminates the possibility of the other event occurring	Events are complementary if one or the other must occur but they can never occur together
Examples	<ul><li>Scoring both 780 and 800 score on the same GMAT test</li><li>Coming in 1st and 3rd place in an Olympics marathon</li><li>Getting both heads and tails on the same coin toss</li><li>The Miami Heat and the LA Lakers winning the NBA Championship in the same year</li></ul>	<ul><li>Getting into the MBA school of your dreams or not</li><li>Winning the Olympics marathon or not</li><li>Getting heads or tails on the same coin toss</li><li>Winning at least one game of the NBA Championships or not winning any games</li></ul>
Why is this important?	If events are mutually exclusive, then you simply add the probabilities of each event.	The probability of complementary events always adds to zero, you can use the mirror rule to solve some difficult problems

Aspect	Mutually Exclusive Events	Complementary Events
How does this affect the general case formula?	$P(A \text{ and } B) = 0$	$P(A \text{ and } B) = 0$ $P(A \text{ or } B) = 1$
Other tips to consider	<ul><li>Note that the probability of heads and tails in coin tosses is both complementary and mutually exclusive.</li><li>All complementary events are, by definition, also mutually exclusive</li></ul>	

PROBABILITY OF TWO OR MORE EVENTS

When you are trying to determine the probability of 2 or more events occurring, use this third formula. It is applicable to a large proportion of GMAT probability questions.

$$P(A + B) = P(A) \cdot P(B)$$

Let's look at two examples.

---

2. What is the probability of rolling 2 sixes on two rolls of a die?

(A) $\dfrac{1}{36}$

(B) $\dfrac{1}{18}$

(C) $\dfrac{1}{6}$

(D) $\dfrac{7}{36}$

(E) $\dfrac{1}{3}$

Solution: $P(6 \text{ and } 6) = P(6) \cdot P(6) = \dfrac{1}{6} \cdot \dfrac{1}{6} = \dfrac{1}{36}$.

The answer is A.

---

3. What is the probability of drawing 2 aces from a deck of cards with no replacement?

(A) $\dfrac{3}{676}$

(B) $\dfrac{1}{221}$

(C) $\dfrac{2}{52}$

(D) $\dfrac{2}{51}$

(E) $\dfrac{12}{221}$

Solution: $P(\text{ace, ace}) = P(\text{ace}_1) \cdot P(\text{ace}_2) = \dfrac{4}{52} \cdot \dfrac{3}{51} = \dfrac{1}{(13 \cdot 17)} = \dfrac{1}{221}$

The answer is B.

Notice that in question 2, the second 6 we rolled had the same probability as the first. However in question 3, the second ace drawn had a different probability than the first. This illustrates the difference between **independent** and **dependent events**.

INDEPENDENT AND DEPENDENT EVENTS

The best way to explain and compare independent and dependent events (also known as conditional probability) is with a chart.

INDEPENDENT AND DEPENDENT EVENTS

Aspect	Independent Events	Dependent Events
Definition	Events where the occurrence of one event does not affect the probability of the other	Events where the occurrence of one event affects the probability of another
Examples	■ Coin tosses ■ Dice rolls ■ Winning money at the casino and getting hit by a truck on the way home ■ Picking balls out of jars/boxes with replacement ■ Picking cards out of a deck with replacement	■ Picking balls out of jars/boxes without replacement ■ Picking cards out of a deck without replacement ■ The probability of getting the 3rd prize in a raffle after the first two prizes are given out
Why is this important?	If events are independent, then you can easily multiply events together to calculate probability	With dependent events, you need to determine how the new probabilities are conditional to previous outcomes
How does this affect the 3rd formula?	No effect	$P(A + B) = P(A) \cdot P(A/B)$ or $P(A + B) = P(A) \cdot P_A(B)$
Other tips to consider	■ Watch for whether the question specifies "with" or "without" replacement when selecting objects ■ Dependent events can sometimes create two or more scenarios to consider ■ Whenever multiple events are said to be simultaneous, you can look at each event in turn	

MIRROR RULE PROBABILITY

Often the GMAT will ask you the probability of something "not happening" or of "at least one" thing happening. By using the complementary rules for probability, we get two equations that make the mirror rule.

$$P(A \text{ happens}) = 1 - P(A \text{ doesn't happen})$$
$$P(\text{at least one of } B \text{ happens}) = 1 - P(\text{no } B \text{ happens})$$

Let's look at the mirror rule strategy in an example.

4. A single coin is tossed four times. What is the probability that you will get at least one tail?

(A) $\dfrac{1}{16}$

(B) $\dfrac{1}{4}$

(C) $\dfrac{3}{8}$

(D) $\dfrac{5}{8}$

(E) $\dfrac{15}{16}$

Solution:

P(at least one tail) $= 1 - P$(no tails) $= 1 - P$ (4 heads) $= 1 - \dfrac{1}{2} \cdot \dfrac{1}{2} \cdot \dfrac{1}{2} \cdot \dfrac{1}{2} = 1 - \dfrac{1}{16} = \dfrac{15}{16}$

The answer is E.

Be sure you understand the complementary opposites of "will happen" and of "at least one happens."

In question 4, we could still have used conceptual thinking to help us narrow the choices. You are more likely to get at least one tail out of four tosses as opposed to three tails. Therefore, we can reason that the correct answer will be closer to 1 than it is to zero, leaving us with choices D and E as our possible picks.

PAIRS PROBABILITY

What if you are asked, "If you roll a die twice, what is the probability you will end up with a pair?" Let's draw.

P(die #1)   **P(die #2)**

?/?   ?/?

A common mistake is to make the probability of the first die roll $\dfrac{1}{6}$. The first roll can actually be any number from 1 to 6. The question is asking the probability that the second roll will match the first. This second probability is dependent on the first roll. No matter what the first die roll is, the probability of the second roll is the same. So we would actually get:

Die #1   **Die #2**

6/6   1/6

Probability(getting a pair in two die rolls) $= \dfrac{6}{6} \cdot \dfrac{1}{6} = \dfrac{1}{6}$

TIP

Often in complementary questions, the answer choices will add up to 1. If only one pair does, you should narrow down your choices to those two options.

TIP

A good way to visualize some tougher probability problems is to draw them!

Let's illustrate this concept in another example.

---

5. Jenny has 7 pairs of shoes, each of a different design. If Jenny randomly selects 2 shoes without replacement from the 14 shoes, what is the probability that she will select 2 shoes of the same design?

(A) $\frac{2}{91}$

(B) $\frac{1}{14}$

(C) $\frac{1}{13}$

(D) $\frac{1}{7}$

(E) $\frac{3}{13}$

Solution: The probability of the first shoe is irrelevant. It is expressed as

$$P(\text{shoe \#1}) = \frac{14}{14} = 1$$

$$P(\text{shoe \#1}) \bullet P(\text{shoe \#2}) = \frac{14}{14} \bullet \frac{1}{13} = \frac{1}{13}$$

There is only one shoe out of the 13 left that will match the first shoe she picked.

The answer is C.

ADVANCED PROBABILITY

The GMAT creates more difficult and advanced questions by simply adding different elements of theory to the question. For example, the test makers have a probability question combined with algebra or take two probability concepts and put them both in the same question. So even though we've reviewed all the main topics of probability, the GMAT test makers will require your cumulative knowledge and adaptability in order to solve the tougher questions.

6. Joey and his friends played a new game that uses 20 playing cards made up of 2 suits of 10 cards each. The cards in each suit have values from 1 to 10. If Joey turns over 4 cards, what is the probability that he will find at least one pair of cards having the same value?

   (A) $\dfrac{1}{5}$

   (B) $\dfrac{99}{323}$

   (C) $\dfrac{3}{5}$

   (D) $\dfrac{224}{323}$

   (E) $\dfrac{4}{5}$

Solution: This question is tough because it combines the mirror rule with pairs probability. Let's draw it out first.

Card 1	Card 2	Card 3	Card 4

Note that this question uses the key phrase "at least one," which tells you to use the mirror rule. So you would get:

$$P \text{ (at least one pair)} = 1 - P(\text{getting no pairs})$$

To solve P (getting no pairs), you need to make sure that for every card that gets picked, the next card cannot match the previous cards. This means you are going to have fewer cards to pick and a smaller number of cards to pick from each time.

$$\frac{20}{20} \cdot \frac{18}{19} \cdot \frac{16}{18} \cdot \frac{14}{17} = \frac{224}{323}$$

Finally, $1 - \dfrac{224}{323} = \dfrac{99}{323}$

The answer is B.

7. Frances tosses a coin 10 times. What is the probability that she will get exactly 5 heads and 5 tails?

(A) $\dfrac{1}{32}$

(B) $\dfrac{63}{256}$

(C) $\dfrac{1}{4}$

(D) $\dfrac{1}{2}$

(E) $\dfrac{193}{256}$

Solution: This is taking the probability of two or more events to a higher level! You can look at this question using your advanced knowledge of combinatorics. To simplify, use the basic equation of probability, which is

$$P(A) = \dfrac{\text{(The number of outcomes where } A \text{ occurs)}}{\text{(The total number of possible outcomes)}}$$

The denominator, or the total number of possible outcomes, is based on each coin toss. Every time the coin tosses, you multiply another 2 possibilities. So the denominator will be $2^{10} = 1024$.

For the numerator, you want to know how many ways Frances can get 5 heads and 5 tails in a particular order. For example, one order could be HHHHHTTTTT. Note that 5 heads and 5 tails can occur in many different orders (e.g., HTHTHTHTHT), where order matters. The real challenge is that the 5 H's and 5 T's are repeating elements in this problem. Therefore, you can use your knowledge of the calculation of permutation with repeated elements, which has the formula

$N!/(A!B!...)$, where N is the total number of elements (10) and A, B are the total number of repeats (5).

So you get $\dfrac{10!}{(5!5!)} = 252$.

The answer is $\dfrac{252}{1024} = \dfrac{63}{256}$

The answer is B.

1. In a raffle that sells 3200 tickets, there is only one prize. What is the probability that a man who bought 40 tickets will win the prize?

   (A) $\dfrac{1}{3200}$

   (B) $\dfrac{1}{320}$

   (C) $\dfrac{1}{80}$

   (D) $\dfrac{3}{80}$

   (E) $\dfrac{1}{8}$

2. On a certain Little League baseball team, one player is to be selected at random as the leadoff hitter. What is the probability that a boy will be the leadoff hitter?

   (1) The total number of baseball players is 30
   (2) There are 20 boys on the Little League baseball team

3. There are 12 pens, each of which is yellow, green, white, or red. If a person selected one pen randomly, is the probability that the pen selected will be yellow or green greater than $\dfrac{1}{4}$?

   (1) $P(\text{yellow pen}) = \dfrac{1}{12}$

   (2) $P(\text{red pen}) = \dfrac{1}{2}$

4. Teams A, B, and C compete in a baseball league but in separate divisions. Each team is vying to win at least 100 games against division rivals in the season. The probability of each team doing so is $\dfrac{1}{3}$, $\dfrac{2}{5}$, and $\dfrac{3}{8}$, respectively. What is the probability that teams A and B will win 100 games against division rivals while team C will not?

   (A) $\dfrac{1}{40}$

   (B) $\dfrac{1}{20}$

   (C) $\dfrac{1}{12}$

   (D) $\dfrac{2}{15}$

   (E) $\dfrac{5}{8}$

5. The Savoy Society executive council consists of an Imperial Monarch, a Lord High-Everything-Else, a Count of the Sacred Largess, and a Keeper of the Royal Script. Samantha is one of 12 members of the club. If each position is chosen at random from the members starting with the Imperial Monarch, the Lord High-Everything-Else, the Count of the Sacred Largess, and the Keeper of the Royal Script, what is the probability that Samantha will be chosen as either Lord High-Everything-Else or a Count of the Sacred Largess?

(A) $\dfrac{1}{12}$

(B) $\dfrac{12}{121}$

(C) $\dfrac{1}{6}$

(D) $\dfrac{3}{12}$

(E) $\dfrac{1}{3}$

6. A number is selected from the first 40 positive 2-digit integers. What is the probability that the number is a multiple of 7 or 13?

(A) 2.25%
(B) 12.50%
(C) 20.25%
(D) 22.50%
(E) 25.25%

7. A jug contains balls with colors and numbers. Each ball has one of three colors and one of five numbers on it. If one ball is selected from the jug, what is the probability of selecting a white ball with a 3 on it.

(1) The probability of selecting a white ball or a ball with a 3 on it is $\dfrac{1}{5}$.

(2) P(a white ball) $- P$ (a ball with a 3 on it) $= \dfrac{1}{20}$

8. An Olympic team is getting ready to go to the Rio 2016 games. It is looking to select a flag bearer. The team consists of F females and M males. If 5 men and 7 women are added to the team and if 1 person is chosen at random to be a flag bearer, what is the probability that a woman will be selected?

(A) $\dfrac{F}{M}$

(B) $\dfrac{F}{(M+F)}$

(C) $\dfrac{(F+M)}{(M+5)}$

(D) $\dfrac{(F+7)}{(F+M+12)}$

(E) $\dfrac{(F+7)}{(F+M+5)}$

9. Sebastian draws x cards from a deck of cards. What is the probability that he draws at least one pair?

(1) The probability of selecting one pair is $\dfrac{1}{16}$.

(2) The probability of selecting no pairs is $\dfrac{5}{16}$.

ANSWER KEY

1. **(C)**	4. **(C)**	7. **(E)**
2. **(C)**	5. **(C)**	8. **(D)**
3. **(E)**	6. **(D)**	9. **(B)**

SOLUTIONS

1. **(C)** Using the basic formula for probability gives

$$\frac{40 \text{ tickets}}{(3200 \text{ tickets})} = \frac{4}{320} = \frac{1}{80}$$

2. **(C)** Statement 1 gives us the total number of players but doesn't give us the number of boys. (Don't forget that girls play baseball too!) Even if you got tricked by that, statement 2 should remind you that the team is not made up entirely of boys. *Insufficient*

   Statement 2 gives us the number of boys, but now we don't know the total number of players on the team. It's important not to take the information in statement 1 and apply it to statement 2. This is a classic GMAT trick. *Insufficient*

   When we put the statements together, we have enough information. *Sufficient*

$$P(\text{boy is a leadoff hitter}) = \frac{\text{Total number of boys}}{\text{Total number of players on the team}} = \frac{20}{30} = \frac{2}{3}$$

   Both statements together are sufficient.

3. **(E)** One way to look at this problem is to rephrase it. It is asking if the probability of yellow or green is greater than $\frac{1}{4}$. This means that the number of yellow or green pens is more than 3 because we have 12 total pens.

   Statement 1 tells us that there is one yellow pen, but we don't know how many green pens there are. *Insufficient*

   Statement 2 tells us that there are 6 red pens but nothing about the other three types of pens. *Insufficient*

   When we combine both statements, we still have 5 pens unaccounted for. The number of green pens could be 1 or 2 or could be more. Therefore, we still do not have enough information. *Insufficient*

   Both statements together are still not sufficient.

4. **(C)** Each team's probabilities are independent from each other. However, we should make sure that we use $\frac{5}{8}$ for team *C*'s probability of not winning 100 games. Thus the probability will be

$$\frac{1}{3} \cdot \frac{2}{5} \cdot \frac{5}{8} = \frac{1}{12}$$

5. **(C)** First let's calculate the probability that Samantha will be chosen as Lord High-Everything-Else.

P(not chosen as Imperial Monarch) • P (chosen Lord High-Everything-Else)

$$= \frac{11}{12} \cdot \frac{1}{11} = \frac{1}{12}$$

Second, calculate the probability that Samantha will be chosen as Count of the Sacred Largess.

P(not chosen as Imperial Monarch) • P(chosen Lord High-Everything-Else) •

P (chosen Count of the Sacred Largess) $= \frac{11}{12} \cdot \frac{10}{11} \cdot \frac{1}{10} = \frac{1}{12}$.

Add these two probabilities to get $\frac{1}{12} + \frac{1}{12} = \frac{1}{6}$.

6. **(D)** The set of numbers are 10 to 49 inclusive. There are 6 multiples of 7 and 3 multiples of 13 in this set. Therefore the probability is $\frac{9}{40} = 22.5\%$.

7. **(E)** If we use the classic probability formula, we will get

P(white ball or a ball with a 3)

$= P$(white ball) $+ P$(a ball with a 3) $- P$(white ball with a 3)

Statement 1 gives us only one part of this equation, and we are missing the other two pieces. *Insufficient*

Statement 2 gives us two parts of the equation that seem helpful. If we look closely, though, we are given a different setup (subtraction instead of addition). There is no way to manipulate the equation to solve for anything useful. *Insufficient*

Because of the awkward setup of statement 2, there is no way to solve this when you combine both statements. *Insufficient*

Both statements together are still not sufficient.

8. **(D)** Use the basic probability formula.
The total number of people on the team is $M + F + 5 + 7$.
The total number of females is $F + 7$.

Therefore, the probability is $\dfrac{(F+7)}{(F+M+12)}$.

9. **(B)** This question is a bit tricky because we don't know how many cards are drawn.

Statement 1 gives us the probability of selecting one pair, but we don't know how many pairs are actually drawn. *Insufficient*

Statement 2 gives us information that could be used with the mirror rule, which gives us

P (at least one pair) $= 1 - P$ (no pairs) $\rightarrow 1 - \frac{5}{16} = \frac{11}{16}$ *Sufficient*

Statement 2 alone is sufficient.

Permutations and Combinations

11

→ PERMUTATIONS VS. COMBINATIONS

→ REPEATING VS. NONREPEATING COMBINATORICS

→ PERMUTATIONS: BASIC AND WITH SELECTION

→ PERMUTATION WITH SCENARIOS

→ COMBINATIONS

→ COMBINATORICS METHOD

PERMUTATIONS AND COMBINATIONS: DIAGNOSTIC SKILL QUIZ

DIRECTIONS: Before continuing, try your hand at these permutations and combinations questions to assess your level of understanding. The answers will be explained throughout this chapter.

1. New York City wants to issue license plates with 4 letters and 3 numbers. If the numbers and letters are allowed to repeat, how many different license plates can be created?

   (A) 456, 976, 000
   (B) 258, 336, 000
   (C) 388,800
   (D) 26,000
   (E) Infinite

2. Billy goes to the movies with 5 of his friends. There are 6 seats left in the front row. How many different seating arrangements can Billy and his friends create?

   (A) 15,625
   (B) 7,776
   (C) 720
   (D) 30
   (E) 6

3. Billy goes to the movies again with 5 of his friends. There are only 3 seats available in the front row. How many different seating arrangements can Billy and his friends create?

   (A) 243
   (B) 125
   (C) 120
   (D) 60
   (E) 15

4. Alice is creating head tables for a wedding party of 14 people. Excluding the bride and groom, she is trying to decide whether to go with tables that seat 4 or 6 people. How many different seating arrangements can Alice have for the first table only?

   (A) $\dfrac{14!}{10!}$

   (B) $\dfrac{14!}{8!}$

   (C) $\dfrac{12!}{8!}$

   (D) $\dfrac{14!}{10!} + \dfrac{14!}{8!}$

   (E) $\dfrac{12!}{8!} + \dfrac{12!}{6!}$

5. Bobby is studying for the GMAT, and there are 8 other students in his class. He wants to create a study group with 3 others. How many different groups can he create?

   (A) 40,320
   (B) 336
   (C) 56
   (D) 24
   (E) 6

6. John has 8 friends and wants to have a series of dinner parties. How many ways can he have a dinner party with 1 guest, 2 guests, or 3 guests?

   (A) 12,544
   (B) 92
   (C) 56
   (D) 28
   (E) 8

CONTENT SUMMARY/CHECKLIST

By the end of this chapter, you should have enough information to review and understand the following topics:

☐ Permutations vs. combinations
☐ Repeating vs. nonrepeating combinators
☐ Permutations: basic and with selection
☐ Permutation with scenarios
☐ Combinations
☐ Combinatorics method

INTRODUCTION: WHAT IS COMBINATORICS?

Combinatorics is one of the more difficult topics in the math portion of the GMAT. Basically, combinatorics is the number of ways we can arrange things. A simple example would be the number of ways to arrange 5 different pictures in a display or to arrange 6 guests around a dinner table. Although this content is considered advanced material, some basic problems may show up for every student.

PERMUTATIONS VS. COMBINATIONS

There are two types of combinatorics: permutations and combinations. The basic difference is that in permutations, the order of the arranged objects matters. In combinations, the order does not matter. The chart below summarizes some of the main differences.

TIP

Think "pick" for permutations and "choose" for combinations!

PERMUTATION AND COMBINATION OVERVIEW

Aspect	Permutation	Combination
Does order matter?	Yes	No (anarchy!)
How do I check for order?	Switch two elements around and see if it creates a new arrangement. If it does, then you have a permutation	
Example of question types	Passwords, seating arrangements, license plates, anything where you arrange objects in a nonrepeating way	People in groups, sets of numbers
Key words	Arrangement, order, schedule, itinerary, display	Team, group, committee, set, numbers
Frequency of each type on the GMAT	Frequent	Not often
Standard formula where: N = the # of total elements K = the # of items being selected	$\dfrac{N!}{(N-K)!}$	$\dfrac{N!}{K!(N-K)!}$
Notation	$_N P_K$ or "N PICK K"	$_N C_K$ or "N CHOOSE K"

TIP

Use the key words to determine quickly if order matters.

REPEATING VS. NONREPEATING COMBINATORICS

By definition, permutations and combinations require that you cannot have repetition. For example, in a race, you cannot have someone finish in both 1st and 2nd place. For the permutation and combination section, we will assume that there is no repetition. If repetition is specifically allowed, then it is sometimes just easier to draw the problem and solve by inspection. License plates offer a perfect example:

TIP

Try drawing a problem and solving by inspection first.

1. New York City wants to issue license plates with 4 letters and 3 numbers. If the numbers and letters are allowed to repeat, how many different license plates can be created?

   (A) 456,976,000
   (B) 258,336,000
   (C) 388,800
   (D) 26,000
   (E) Infinite

Solution: Note that this question is by definition a nonpermutation problem. However, it is a combinatorics question because we are still counting the number of arrangements. If we draw it out and calculate the total *number of* possibilities for each group, we would get:

Now we just multiply them all together to get $26 \times 26 \times 26 \times 26 \times 10 \times 10 \times 10 = 456,976,000$ license plates. So it looks like New York has room to grow!

The answer is A.

Note that you should always try to solve all problems first by drawings and inspection. The majority of the problems in the rest of this chapter deal with nonrepeating combinatorics, otherwise known as permutations.

PERMUTATIONS: BASIC AND WITH SELECTION

The most basic permutation is the number of ways to arrange N items when order matters and there is no repetition. This is calculated as $N!$ or "N factorial," where N is the total number of elements in the question. Factorials are calculated by taking the number N and multiplying it by every whole number below it all the way down to the number 1.

$$10! = 10 \times 9 \times 8 \times 7 \times 6 \times 5 \times 4 \times 3 \times 2 \times 1$$

$$0! = 1 \quad 1! = 1 \quad 2! = 2 \quad 3! = 6 \quad 4! = 24 \quad 5! = 120 \quad 6! = 720$$

TIP

Note that 0! = 1 by definition. Don't ask why, just know that it is!

---

2. Billy goes to the movies with 5 of his friends. There are 6 seats left in the front row. How many different seating arrangements can Billy and his friends create?

   (A) 15,625
   (B) 7,776
   (C) 720
   (D) 30
   (E) 6

Solution: Since order matters, this is a permutation. The total number of elements is 6 people, so $N = 6$. The answer is $6! = 6 \times 5 \times 4 \times 3 \times 2 \times 1 = 720$.

The answer is C.

TIP

Memorizing the factorials up to 6! will save you time on the GMAT.

---

3. Billy goes to the movies again with 5 of his friends. There are only 3 seats available. How many different seating arrangements can Billy and his friends create?

   (A) 243
   (B) 125
   (C) 120
   (D) 60
   (E) 15

Solution: In this case, we are dealing with a selection from the larger group. We already know that $N = 6$. Since we are selecting 3 people to fill the seats, then $K = 3$. So the answer will be

$$_N P_K = {_6}P_3 = \frac{6!}{(6-3)!} = \frac{6 \times 5 \times 4 \times 3 \times 2 \times 1}{(3 \times 2 \times 1)} = 6 \times 5 \times 4 = 120$$

The answer is C.

PERMUTATION WITH SCENARIOS

If the combinatorics question uses the key word or phrases "or," "at least," or "at most," you may be dealing with scenarios. In this case, you will have different values for K. To resolve this type of question, you first need to determine the scenarios. For each scenario, calculate the total number of arrangements and then sum them up.

---

4. Alice is creating head tables for a wedding party of 14 people. Excluding the bride and groom, she is trying to decide whether to go with tables that seat 4 or 6 people. How many different seating arrangements can Alice have for the first table only?

   (A) $\dfrac{14!}{10!}$

   (B) $\dfrac{14!}{8!}$

   (C) $\dfrac{12!}{8!}$

   (D) $\dfrac{14!}{10!} + \dfrac{14!}{8!}$

   (E) $\dfrac{12!}{8!} + \dfrac{12!}{6!}$

Solution: This is a permutation because order matters with a seating arrangement. $N = 12$ because we do not include the bride and groom. The number we are selecting can be 4 or 6 so we are dealing with scenarios. For each scenario, the K will be different.

Scenario 1–4 person table	Scenario 2–6 person table
$N = 12$, $K = 4$	$N = 12$, $K = 6$
$_NP_K = {}_{12}P_4 = \dfrac{12!}{8!}$	$_NP_K = {}_{12}P_6 = \dfrac{12!}{6!}$

Now we add up the scenario totals, giving us $\dfrac{12!}{8!} + \dfrac{12!}{6!}$.

The answer is E.

COMBINATIONS

Combination calculations are very much the same as permutation calculations. The only differences are that order does not matter, and that the standard formula we use is different by a factor of $1/K!$

Combinations with Selection

5. Bobby is studying for the GMAT, and there are 8 other students in his class. He wants to create a study group with 3 others. How many different groups can he create?

   (A) 40,320
   (B) 336
   (C) 56
   (D) 24
   (E) 6

Solution: Order does not matter here because we are creating groups and the order in which the group members are selected does not matter (unless of course we are dealing with easily bruised egos).

$$N = 8, K = 3$$

$$_NC_K = {_8C_3} = \frac{8!}{(3!5!)} = \frac{(8 \times 7 \times 6)}{(3 \times 2)} = 56$$

The answer is C.

Combination with Scenarios

6. John has 8 friends and wants to have a series of dinner parties. How many ways can he have a dinner party with 1 guest, 2 guests, or 3 guests?

   (A) 12,544
   (B) 92
   (C) 56
   (D) 28
   (E) 8

TIP

Remember that the only time that you add or subtract in combinatorics is when you are dealing with scenarios. All other times you will be multiplying subgroups.

Solution: This is a combination since we are talking about people forming groups. Thus the order will not matter. As in permutations, the key word "or" says to us that we are dealing with scenarios. Since we are selecting from 8 guests, then $N = 8$.

Scenario 1: One Guest

$N = 8, K = 1$

$$_NC_K = {_8C_1} = \frac{8!}{(1!7!)}$$

$$= 8$$

Scenario 2: Two Guests

$N = 8, K = 2$

$$_NC_K = {_8C_2} = \frac{8!}{(2!6!)}$$

$$= 28$$

Scenario 3: Three Guests

$N = 8, K = 3$

$$_NC_K = {_8C_3} = \frac{8!}{(3!5!)}$$

$$= 56$$

Now we add up all the scenarios giving us $8 + 28 + 56 = 92$.

The answer is C.

COMBINATORICS METHOD

Follow this basic methodology for solving combinatorics problems:

1. **DRAW IT OUT:** If you can, use a drawing to set up the problem and understand it better.

2. **SOLVE BY INSPECTION:** Simpler problems, particularly ones that allow for repetition (and are not true permutations), can be solved by simply looking at the number of possibilities for each group and multiplying them together.

3. **CHECK FOR ORDER:** If you are not sure, you can use the check described in the first table in this chapter "Permutation and Combination Overview."

4. **DETERMINE _N_:** This is the total number of elements involved in the question.

5. **DETERMINE IF THERE IS A _K_:** In some examples, you will select a smaller amount from the larger amount _N_.

6. **CHECK FOR ANY SPECIAL CIRCUMSTANCES:** These are among the harder examples, so it's important to know which types will show up.

   - **CIRCLE:** Use $(N-1)!$
   - **REPEATED ELEMENTS:** Use $N!/A!B!...$, where _A_ and _B_ are the number of repeated elements in the question.
   - **COUPLES OR GROUPS:** Treat each subgroup as a single element. Then calculate the overall number of arrangements multiplied by the number of arrangements for each subgroup.
   - **SCENARIOS:** If the question uses the key word or phrases "or," "at least," or "at most," you need to calculate each combinatorics scenario separately and then add up the totals.
   - **SPECIAL CONSTRAINTS:** The key is essentially to break them down into separate portions and calculate each piece accordingly.

7. **SET UP THE BASIC EQUATIONS:** You can set up your equations in the form $_NP_K$ (_N_ Pick _K_) and/or $_NC_K$ (_N_ Choose _K_).

8. **PLUG IN FORMULAS AND SOLVE:** Use the memorized formulas to calculate the total. Remember to review the answer choices to determine whether the form of the answer will be a number or a combinatorics notation.

1. Dean and Deanna, a married couple, decide to invite all their single friends out to the movies in the hopes that there may be sparks. Dean and Deanna have to sit together and prefer a certain side, but the rest of the group can sit anywhere in the row with them together. How many different ways can the group sit together in the row?

    (1) Dean and Deanna decide to sit only on the left-most side of the group
    (2) Dean and Deanna invited 12 people, but only 75% showed up.

2. Wayne just received 5 vases in a set from his grandmother. Although he doesn't particularly like them, he decides to display them on the mantle behind his 50-inch plasma television. That way, he hopes they won't be noticed. All the vases look the same except that there are 2 vases colored green, 2 colored red, and the last one is colored blue. In how many ways can Wayne arrange the display in a row?

    (A) 6
    (B) 18
    (C) 30
    (D) 60
    (E) 120

3. Coach Will needs to get his glee team ready for sectionals by selecting a 6-person team of 3 men and 3 women. There are 5 men and 7 women vying for the spots. How many different ways can he arrange the teams?

    (A) 35
    (B) 120
    (C) 140
    (D) 280
    (E) 350

4. A business tycoon is bringing his team to the conference room to determine who is to be fired for screwing up a major fundraising project. Two of his team members are his daughter and son, between whom he always sits. He also makes sure that his 3 VP's never sit together so that they can be integrated within the team. How many different ways can the entire team be seated in the conference room?

    (1) The business tycoon has 21 members on his team.
    (2) The conference room has a large oval table.

5. Mario's Pizzeria is offering a special. Students can order a medium pizza for only $6.99 by choosing one topping from each of 4 categories: meats, veggies, cheese, and bread. Mario's has 5 different meats, 7 veggies, 4 types of cheese, and 3 varieties of bread. How many different combinations of pizzas can Mario make?

(A) 105
(B) 140
(C) 275
(D) 420
(E) 525

6. Billy and 10 of his friends are going to the movies. There are 2 couples who insist on sitting together and another group of 4 BFFs that always sit together. How many different ways can they arrange themselves in the front row of the movie theater?

(A) 11!
(B) $11! \times 2 \times 2 \times 3$
(C) $6! \times 2! \times 2! \times 3!$
(D) $6! \times 4!$
(E) $6! \times 4 \times 2$

7. Robin Hood and 4 of his Merry Men decide to see the Renaissance Festival evening show. There are 5 seats in the front row reserved for them. Little John has told the group that he has to sit on the end so that he can stretch his long legs. In how many ways can the Merry Men arrange themselves in the front row?

(A) 48
(B) 64
(C) 84
(D) 96
(E) 108

8. Brian, Ricky, Bobby, and Mike have 6 donuts to share. If any one of these men can be given any whole number of donuts from 0 to 6, in how many different ways can the donuts be distributed?

(A) 21
(B) 80
(C) 120
(D) 541
(E) 4400

9. The Stanley Cup hockey championship is one of the most grueling to win, as it pits two of the top teams against each other in a best-of-seven series. The first team to win 4 games wins the series and no subsequent games are played. What is the probability that the Stanley Cup will be won in 6 games or less?

(A) 12.5%
(B) 31.25%
(C) 47.75%
(D) 68.75%
(E) 75%

ANSWER KEY

1. **(C)**	4. **(C)**	7. **(A)**
2. **(C)**	5. **(D)**	8. **(B)**
3. **(E)**	6. **(C)**	9. **(D)**

SOLUTIONS

1. **(C)** We need the number of people N and also Dean and Deanna's specific seating preference in order to solve this permutation.

   Statement 1 gives us only the specific constraint to the problem but no total amount of people. *Insufficient*

   Statement 2 provides us with the number of people, which is 11, including Dean and Deanna. However, we are missing the specific seating preference of Dean and Deanna. *Insufficient*

   By combining both statements, we can now solve. If Dean and Deanna sit on the leftmost side of the group, they can arrange themselves in 2! = 2 ways. The other 9 people on the right side can arrange themselves in 9! ways. Thus the total number of ways the group can arrange themselves is 2!9! *Sufficient*

   Both statements together are sufficient.

2. **(C)** This is an example of permutations with repeated elements. The formula for repeated elements is $\dfrac{N!}{A!B!}$ ... where A and B are the repeated elements. In this case, the repeated elements are the red and green vases.

   So $N = 5$, $A = 2$, $B = 2$ and the answer is $\dfrac{5!}{(2!)(2!)} = 30$.

3. **(E)** This is a combination question since we are dealing with teams and we also have selection. We should treat the men and women as separate groups. For the men, $N = 5$ and $K = 3$. For the women, $N = 7$ and $K = 3$. So using the notation $_NC_K$ we get

Men		**Women**
$_5C_3$	*	$_7C_3$
$\dfrac{5!}{(3!)(2!)} = 10$	*	$\dfrac{7!}{(3!)(4!)} = 35 = 10 \times 35 = 350$ possibilities

4. **(C)** Despite all the complicated restraints in this question, one key piece of information we need to determine is N. However, we also need a bit more information about the seating arrangement (is it one row, many rows, a circle, etc.)?

   Statement 1 gives $N = 21$. However, we should not assume that the seating is in a straight line. Therefore we cannot solve. *Insufficient*

   Statement 2 tells us the table is an oval. By itself, we still do not have the total number of people on the team, so we cannot solve. *Insufficient*

When we combine both statements, we can solve the problem because the number of arrangements in a circle is $(N-1)!$ We have the constraints that complicate the problem. However, we can account for them. Again, we do not have to solve the complicated problem; we just need to know that we can. *Sufficient*

Both statement together are sufficient.

5. **(D)** Each ingredient can be treated as a separate piece in this simple combinatory problem. Since we are choosing only one ingredient from each category, the total number of pizzas is $5 \times 7 \times 4 \times 3 = 420$ pizzas.

6. **(C)** Normally we would say that $N = 11$. In this case, though, we treat each subgroup as a single element. We now have $N = 6$ (2 couples, 1 quartet, and 3 singles). We first calculate the number of ways to arrange the grouped elements, which is

$$N! = 6! = 720$$

We also have to calculate the number of arrangements within each subgroup.

Each couple is $2! = 2$. The quartet is $4! = 24$.

The total number of arrangements is $6! \times 2! \times 2! \times 3!$.

7. **(A)** In this problem, we have a constraint where Little John wants to sit only on the end. This results in 2 scenarios. Little John will be either on the left side or on the right side. Since the calculation for each scenario will be the same, we can just calculate one of the scenarios and multiply by 2.

Scenario 1: Little John is sitting on the left-hand side. To calculate the number of arrangements for the rest, $N = 4$, so it will be $4!$

The answer will be $2 \times 4! = 48$.

8. **(B)** The best way to answer this question is to track the different scenarios and add up the results. There are 4 scenarios here.

Scenario 1: One man gets all 6 donuts. There are 4 possibilities.

Scenario 2: Two men get all 6 donuts. The number of ways to have pairs of men without donuts is 1-2, 1-3, 1-4, 2-3, 2-4, and 3-4 or 6 ways. The number of ways for pairs to have donuts is 1-5, 2-4, 3-3, 4-2, and 5-1, which is 5 ways. Therefore, the total number of possibilities is $5 \times 6 = 30$ possibilities.

Scenario 3: Three men get all 6 donuts. Any of the four men can be the one without a donut, so we have four possibilities here. The three with donuts can split them in 10 different ways (411, 321, 312, 222, 231, 213, 114, 123, 132, and 141). This gives us $4 \times 10 = 40$ possibilities.

Scenario 4: All four men have donuts. The splits can be 2211, 2121, 2112, 1212, 1221, and 1122, so there are 6 possibilities. Total number of possibilities is $4 + 30 + 40 + 6 = 80$ possibilities.

9. **(D)** This question is very difficult because it combines combinatorics with probability. The best way to determine the probability that the series will last 6 games or less is by determining the probability that it will last exactly 7 games and then subtract this value from 1. This is known as the mirror rule.

This means that the first 6 games of the series must result in 3 wins and 3 losses for each team.

By arranging 3 wins and 3 losses is an example of a permutation with repeating elements, where $N = 6$ and the wins and losses repeat 3 times; we get $\frac{6!}{3!3!} = 20$ ways for the two teams to split the first 6 games.

There are 2 possible outcomes for the 7th game. Therefore, we have a total of $20 \times 2 = 40$ ways for a 7-game series.

This just gives us the number of occurrences for a 7th game. The total number of possible occurrences is a binomial property. Each win or loss is like heads or tails of a coin toss. Therefore, the total number of possibilities to get to a game 7 is $2^7 = 128$. So the probability of a 7th game is $\frac{40}{128} = 31.25\%$.

Finally, using the mirror rule, we get $1 - 31.25\% = 68.75\%$

PART 4

Verbal

Introduction to the Verbal Section

12

→ **THE GROUND RULES**

→ **PACING AND TIMING IN THE VERBAL SECTION**

→ **HOW TO TACKLE VERBAL QUESTIONS**

→ **THE THREE VERBAL QUESTION FORMATS**

→ **READING THE GMAT WAY**

→ **THE KEY TO KEYWORDS**

→ **THE PAYOFF**

THE GROUND RULES

In the Verbal section, you will have 75 minutes in which to answer 41 questions in three different formats: Sentence Correction, Critical Reasoning, and Reading Comprehension. All are multiple-choice questions and have five answer choices.

> **Sentence Correction:** These questions present you with a sentence that might or might not have a grammatical problem and four additional ways to phrase it; you have to pick the phrasing that contains no obvious errors.
>
> **Critical Reasoning:** These questions give you a very short passage to read (usually under 100 words), containing either (1) an argument for a conclusion that you're asked to evaluate or describe or (2) a loose collection of related facts from which you're asked to draw conclusions.
>
> **Reading Comprehension:** These questions give you a more substantial passage to read (either 100–200 words or 250–350 words). You're then asked a series of three or four questions about the passage's content, tone, and structure and the author's overall agenda.

There is no set order to the question formats, but the GMAT does keep track of the number of each format you have seen in a single test sitting, so that when all is said and done you will have seen about 12 Critical Reasoning questions, about 13 Reading Comprehension questions, and about 16 Sentence Correction questions.

We have to say "about," because the test maker slips a few questions into the 41 that don't count toward your score, "experimental questions" of each of the three formats that you're essentially beta-testing for future tests. Don't worry about trying to figure out whether a question is "experimental" or "real"—just know that it means you might have 14 Reading Comprehension questions and only 11 Critical Reasoning.

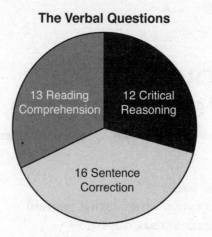

The Verbal Questions

13 Reading Comprehension

12 Critical Reasoning

16 Sentence Correction

What the GMAT *Says* the Verbal Section Tests

According the GMAC's official documents, the Verbal section of the GMAT tests your ability to do three things:

1. read and comprehend written material,
2. reason and evaluate arguments, and
3. correct written material to conform to standard written English.

But that's just an indirect way of saying, "There are three types of questions: Reading Comprehension, Critical Reasoning, and Sentence Correction." To be sure, these three broad conceptual areas are tested, just probably not in the way you expect.

What the Verbal Section Actually Tests and What it Doesn't

The most common complaint that test takers have with the Verbal section is that it is "boring." The passages are dense, the topics chosen are not all that interesting, the arguments all sound crazy, and the questions are worded in bafflingly obscure ways that make it a challenge to keep reading them.

This is all by design.

The Verbal section comes 2½ hours into the test; by that point, most test takers are starting to feel the strain. Exhaustion is creeping in. Stress levels are high. And then along comes a Reading Comprehension passage about the mating habits of this snail in Madagascar, and how they're different from those of the snails on the continent. Zzzz…

The test makers put the snails there not because snails are somehow secretly the key to success in business school, but rather because they hope you'll see something unfamiliar and kind of dry and just mentally check out. When you're bored, you don't proceed with care. You don't go back and check specific parts of the text. You read listlessly and haphazardly and end up picking the answers that "kind of sound right."

Thus, the GMAT Verbal section tests your ability to pay attention even when you'd rather not. If you want to raise your GMAT Verbal subscore, you must learn what the GMAT thinks is worthy of your attention and how to get yourself to focus on that, to the exclusion of all else. You're certainly not required to master every detail or logical nuance of the presented passages in the scant time you have to read them.

OK, we do have to admit that there are going to be *some basic grammar rules you'll need to remember*. And, yes, you'll also need to be able to recognize a couple of other technical things, like the fundamental parts of an argument. You might need to pick up your reading pace a little bit. But success on the GMAT is rarely a case of speed reading, grammatical wherewithal, or deductive brilliance; it's learning to avoid all the "easy outs," pushing aside the various things meant to distract or confuse, and finding the simple concept that lies at the core of the question.

The GMAT *doesn't* test depth.

People studying for the GMAT are often surprised to learn how short the passages actually are. The longest Reading Comprehension passages just barely top 400 words, which is shorter than the essays you were asked to write in high school. Critical Reasoning prompts are even shorter. You probably read more text in a Craigslist ad. And while there might always seem to be just one more grammar rule that you needed to know to get the right answer on a Sentence Correction question you missed, only about 30 grammar rules have ever been tested on the GMAT—not on a single test, mind you, but 30 rules tested across all GMATs ever.

So put your mind at ease. GMAT Verbal questions are shallow, although they masquerade as deep. The Verbal section can be tricky, but it consists of the same simple concepts and patterns throughout.

PACING AND TIMING IN THE VERBAL SECTION

If you were to split your 75 minutes time evenly among the 41 questions, you'd be able to spend a hair under 2 minutes on each question. However, spending equal time on all the questions would be a terrible idea. Reading Comprehension will require by far the largest share of your time. For this question type you will need to budget in the time needed to read the four passages that go with the questions—two long ones (about 300 words on average) and two short ones (about 150 words). That will take most people at least 10 minutes, and that's not counting the time needed to answer the questions themselves.

Where can you get the extra time? Critical Reasoning questions require a bit of reading themselves (and much more careful reading than Reading Comprehension questions), so it's best not to steal time away from them. That leaves only Sentence Correction questions. Because of the demands elsewhere on your time, you can afford to give no more than a minute a piece to the Sentence Correction questions.

Your overall time budget will look something like this:

Verbal Section Time Allocation

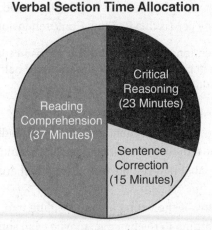

Though the most numerous question type, Sentence Correction questions will account for a fifth of your time, whereas more than half of the 75 minutes will be spent tackling the Reading Comprehension questions. As a rough guideline:

Type of Question	# of Questions	Average Time Per Question
Sentence Correction	15–16	1 minute
Critical Reasoning	11–13	2 minutes
Reading Comprehension	13–14	Questions: 1–1.5 minutes
		Long Passages: 3–4 minutes
		Short Passages: 2–3 minutes

1st Third	Q's 1–12
2nd Third	Q's 13–28
3rd Third	Q's 29–38
Last 5 minutes	Q's 39, 40, & 41

Two minutes per question can be useful, though, if used as a rough guide as you progress through the Verbal section. If you break your time into 25-minute thirds, you should be done with roughly the first 12 or so questions when 25 minutes have passed, and be on question 27 or 28 after 50 minutes. When the clock switches from counting down minutes to minutes and seconds (the 5:00 mark), you should be somewhere around question 39.

HOW TO TACKLE VERBAL QUESTIONS

Because the three big question types can appear in any order, it might seem like you're going to have to "change gears" frequently as you move through the section, but on a fundamental level the questions are a lot alike. Whether the question throws a handful of grammar rules at you, an argument against changing the zoning ordinances in Uzbekistan, or a catalog of the challenges faced by the earliest European colonists in Australia, each one consists of a discrete amount of information. Your job is to sort through that (often purposely disorganized) information to find the nugget that will allow you to pick the one point-bestowing answer choice from the available five.

Step 1: Identify the Task

Most questions in the Verbal section contain specific language, certain repeated phrases and ideas that both tell you how closely you're supposed to read the text you're working with and give you specific hints about what the right answer should sound like.

For example, say you came across this Reading Comprehension question:

> The author mentions the findings of Dr. Johnson's laboratory regarding the impact of the craters in the third half of the last ice age primarily in order to ...

The most important words of all are the last three: "in order to." That's your cue that you're dealing with a **Function** question. From that, you'll know immediately that the right answer will describe the role that the tediously described detail in the middle of the question (all that business about craters and labs) plays in the author's overall argument in the passage as a whole.

You'll also know that many of the wrong answers will be tempting because they contain information that is true according to the passage, maybe even some near-direct quotes from what you just read. Since the question is *why* the author said the detail, not *what* the author said, those can all be safely eliminated.

The same can be said of Critical Reasoning questions: Look in the right place for the right keywords, and you can tell immediately what you are supposed to do. If you saw

> **Which of the following, if true, most strongly supports the prediction that the plan will succeed?**

you'd know immediately that "most strongly supports" means your task is to Strengthen the argument by making one of its unstated assumptions more plausible. You would proceed to the big chunk of text and look for the argument's conclusion.

In the pages to come, you will learn how to spot those clues and what to do when you've spotted them. Master the clues, and your score will rocket upward.

Step 2: Process the Information

Everything that appears in a GMAT Verbal question is there for a reason—but that's not the same thing as saying that everything that appears in the question is necessary to finding the credited answer. Indeed, most of what's written exists either to distract you or to set up a trap that will make one of the wrong answers seem appealing.

Processing the information in a question doesn't just mean reading over the text to say you've read it. Every few lines you'll need to stop and ask yourself, "Do I understand what I just read?" and "How does this new bit relate to what I've already read?" and, most importantly, "How does this relate to the task at hand?"

Processing the information also means learning what bits of information the GMAT uses to make an answer right and what bits you should always pause to figure out. In each section that follows, you'll learn the most common ways the test makers tip their hand and how to quickly sort through the intentionally disorganized jumble of facts and claims.

Step 3: Plan Your Approach to the Answers

Before reading the answer choices, pause to ask yourself, "What is the right answer going to look like?" Lots of wrong answer choices are tempting because they are actually correct— they're just the right answer to a question you aren't currently being asked. Other times they're made to sound right because they remind you of something you just read or they remind you of something you know to be true in the real world.

In other words, the test maker wants you to have an "Aha!" moment for all the wrong reasons and miss what's actually going on. The best defense against this (and all the other little tweaks and twists you might encounter) is to know which "Aha!" you're aiming for.

Sometimes this will mean making a specific prediction to yourself, prephrasing the answer. "The flaw here is that the author confuses the cause with the effect" or "The author says the most important cause of the war was the economic depression in the years leading up to it." Other times it'll be a bit looser: "I know the right answer will have to mention 'contentment' or 'happiness'." In each case, though, you've got a target in mind as you read the answers. This alone will help you avoid a lot of the traps the GMAT has set for you.

Naturally, there are going to be times when your prediction is extremely tentative or a bit generic: "Uh… something about clay pots?" or "There's a lot of rules here, so I'm not sure what the inference they're looking for is." That's OK. It just means you'll have to be more careful with the answer choices. You still have some idea of what you're looking for, and that's better than just reading the answers and hoping something sticks out.

Step 4: Attack the Answers

One principle will guide you as you search for the right answer: There is no "best" answer.

Forget what you might have heard elsewhere about picking the better of two answer choices or weighing options that seem "kind of right" against each other. On the GMAT, right and wrong are all-or-nothing. There is no "kind of right." There are just four wrong answers and one right one.

Every wrong answer will have some sort of fatal flaw that the test makers could point to if an unhappy test taker were to challenge them on it, a poison pill that kills the answer choice dead, dead, dead. As you learn about the different types of questions, you'll get a better idea of what sorts of flaws kill answers in one type but not another and the things that are always deal breakers.

Be merciless with the answers, tearing into them until you find that fatal flaw that will let you eliminate it. And once an answer choice has been eliminated, you *stop reading* it. It's out. One down, three to go.

You must also be sure to use the same level of rigor with each answer choice you read. If you eliminate answer (A) because you don't like the word *surprising*, and (B) also contains *surprising*, you should either eliminate it, too, or go back and reconsider (A). Just because an answer is further down the page doesn't mean it gets more breaks than those that come before it. Be sure as well that you don't inadvertently change what you're looking for between answer choices.

Finally, it's OK to be unsure whether an answer is right or wrong. Nobody is 100 percent certain about every answer, not even those scoring perfect 800s. Knowing that you're unsure means you do still know something. If you can put a finger on exactly what part of the answer you're unsure about, all the better. You can keep even track of your evaluation of each answer on your center-provided wet erase noteboard like so:

In the end, the key is to turn those vague feelings about the answer into concrete ones. If you force yourself to verbalize why the answer you like is right or what your problem with another is, you can put an end to the potentially endless cycle of "Maybe I should go back and read it again (and again and again...)."

THE THREE VERBAL QUESTION FORMATS

Critical Reasoning

Each Critical Reasoning question you will see on the GMAT is composed of three parts: a **Prompt**, a brief question about that prompt (which we will call the **Question Stem**), and five **Answer Choices**.

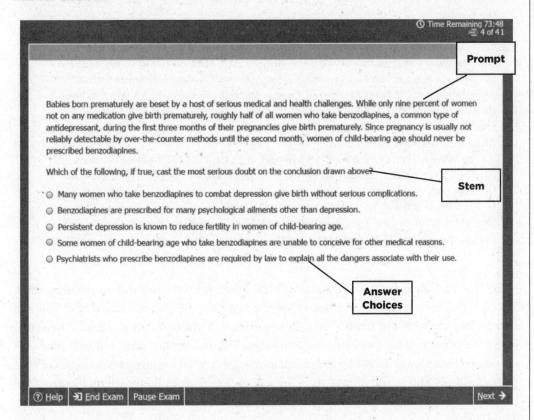

TIP

The Critical Reasoning question explanations in the *Official Guide* sometimes use the word "stimulus" instead of "prompt."

The **Prompt** contains a set of facts, opinions, and observations that create a scenario, a little self-contained world with only a handful of details sketching it out. For most of the questions, these details will be used to make an argument; for some, there will only be a series of related pieces of information. The only facts that you need to understand to find the answer can be found in the prompt. The test maker never asks you to rely on your outside expertise.

The typical Critical Reasoning prompt is about 100 words long, so you won't have to scroll to see the prompt all at once, although occasionally you will need to scroll down the page to see the fifth answer choice.

Unlike the Reading Comprehension questions, the Critical Reasoning questions will not reuse the same prompt to ask multiple questions. Each question has a unique scenario attached to it.

The information in the prompts is drawn from many different subject areas, including the arts, philosophy, the sciences, law, and business. You're not expected to know any of the material beforehand, and you should be careful if the subject happens to be one you're personally familiar with. There's no guarantee that the presented facts in these passages are actually true, and often the test maker will bend the truth in order to make the subject fit into the narrow constraints of a Critical Reasoning scenario.

TIP

Your reward for doing well on the Verbal section is harder questions, which can be longer than the standard 100-word average—though not by much.

BEWARE OF YOUR REAL WORLD INSTINCTS

The more you know about the subject of a CR prompt (or an RC passage), the more careful you must be not to let that knowledge color your understanding of the scenario presented. The prompts are often factually incorrect or ignore considerations that anyone with specialized knowledge about the field would immediately bring up were the subject broached in a real-life face-to-face debate on the matter.

In other words, if the test makers say that the ivory-billed woodpecker is extinct, you just have to take them at their word, even if you clearly remember the news story from a few years back about a pair of them being unexpectedly not extinct deep in the Big Woods of Arkansas—heck, even if you have a pet ivory-billed woodpecker waiting in the car to congratulate you on your stellar GMAT performance—for the purposes of finding the right answer, you must put that knowledge aside. As far as the question is concerned, the woodpecker is as dead as the dodo.

You will also never be asked whether an argument is true or false or even whether the situation described in the prompt is realistic or plausible. In order to make such judgments, you would need to employ some factual knowledge beyond what is given to you in the text of the question, and drawing on your outside knowledge is *explicitly forbidden* in Critical Reasoning questions (and, for that matter, in all the Verbal section questions).

TIP

Throughout this book, we will refer to the often unnamed imaginary person making the argument as the speaker.

The **Question Stem** that follows contains instructions from the test makers detailing what they expect us to do with the information in the prompt. In the chapters that follow, you will learn the language that test makers typically use to indicate the task they wish you to perform. Ninety-five percent of the questions reuse the same handful of phrasings, and with time and practice, you will almost always be able to tell immediately what the question demands of you.

The Answer Choices will always come in sets of five. Four of them will be incorrect for definite reasons, usually because of specific wording used in the original prompt. Only one will be correct.

Note: On the test, answer choices don't have letters (A), (B), etc. We'll use them in the printed questions, however, to avoid confusion.

CRITICAL REASONING QUESTION TYPES

All in all, there are 13 different types of Critical Reasoning questions, more types of questions than the number of Critical Reasoning questions you'll probably see in total on the day of your test! That's the bad news. But the good news is that these 13 questions are just slight variations on three far simpler questions:

1. What does this argument take for granted?
2. What is the structure of this argument?
3. If all of these facts are true, what else must be true?

Notice that the first two questions ask you about an **argument**. That's why we're going to classify them in the broad, cleverly named category, **Argument-Based Questions**, which we're going to immediately divide into the **Assumption Family** and the **Structure Family**, depending on whether the question asks you what the argument takes for granted (its **assumptions**) or how it's organized (its **structure**). The other Critical Reasoning questions ask you to work with a loose collection of facts, so we'll classify those as **Fact-Based Questions**.

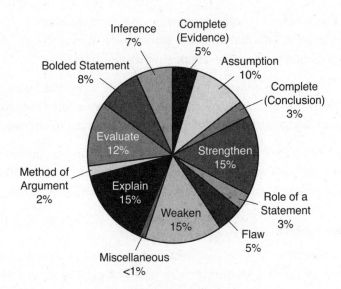

Critical Reasoning Question Frequency by Family

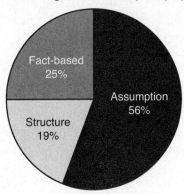

These question types will be discussed in detail in the Critical Reasoning chapter, but here's a quick rundown:

Argument-Based Questions

Argument-Based Questions make up about three-fourths of the questions on the GMAT, so you'll see about eight in a single test sitting. Your initial approach to all of these will be the same, breaking the information in the argument down into its component parts: its **conclusion** and its **evidence**.

The Assumption Family

ASSUMPTION—In Assumption questions, an argument is given, and you must identify something that the argument relies upon but that is not stated explicitly, something that, if not true, means the argument itself must not be true.

STRENGTHEN—Here, you go one step beyond the Assumption question to find a new piece of information in the answer choices that would make one of the argument's unstated assumptions more likely to be true or that would answer a possible objection to one of those unstated assumptions.

WEAKEN—The Weaken question is the flip side of the Strengthen question. Here you would find a piece of information in the answers that, if true, would call into question or present an objection to one of the arguments' assumptions.

EVALUATE—In Evaluate questions, which are closely related to Strengthen and Weaken questions, you must select an answer choice that describes some unknown information or a question that, if known, has the potential to either weaken or strengthen the argument.

FLAW—The stem of Flaw questions calls out the speaker in the argument prompt for making a mistake and asks you to find the answer choice that best describes it. Usually, the mistake is assuming something that shouldn't be assumed.

The Structure Family

BOLDED STATEMENT—Here, an argument is given, with two sentences or phrases in **bold type**, and you are asked to identify the part that each plays in the argument as a whole.

METHOD OF ARGUMENT—An argument is given, occasionally written as a dialogue between two people, and you must explain how the argument works (i.e., what sort of evidence the author uses such as invoking a general principle or providing a counter example) and whether that case is for or against something.

ROLE OF A STATEMENT—These questions are essentially Bolded Statement questions in which nothing is bolded. They, too, ask you to identify the role a particular part plays in the argument.

PARALLEL ARGUMENT—Very rare on the GMAT, this question contains five arguments for the price of one! You must match the argument in the prompt with the one in the answer choices that has the same structure.

Fact-Based Questions

The remaining quarter of Critical Reasoning questions do not ask about arguments. Their prompts almost always have no conclusion and no evidence. As Sgt. Joe Friday said, they want "Just the facts, ma'am." You'll probably see four or five of them in the Critical Reasoning section (SPOILER ALERT! **Inference** questions will make an appearance in the Reading Comprehension, too).

INFERENCE—These questions ask you to find the answer choice that must be true if the information in the prompt is true. (If the prompt tells you that *all dogs go to heaven* and that *Rusty is a dog*, then the correct answer could be that *Rusty will go to heaven*.)

EXPLAIN—The prompt that accompanies these questions contains an anomalous situation like "demand's up, but prices have stayed the same" or "after the law changed to require seatbelts, automobile injuries went up." The correct answer provides an additional fact that can explain why the *apparent* weirdness really isn't weird at all.

Complete the Argument Questions

Wait a minute, didn't we just say there were three categories? What's with this fourth? **Complete** questions are just a different way of asking you to do one of the two question types we've already discussed. They're easy to spot because their question stem is placed above their prompt, rather than below, and because there's a big empty blank (like this: _____) somewhere in the text. You're asked to insert something into the blank that will somehow complete the argument.

COMPLETE (EVIDENCE)—If an evidence keyword precedes the blank (e.g., *for example, because, since, after all)*, the **Complete** question is essentially a weirdly worded **Assumption** question. The only piece of evidence that could complete the argument is a piece that fills in the gap that is its unstated assumption.

COMPLETE (CONCLUSION)—If a conclusion keyword precedes the blank (e.g., *thus, therefore, hence, in conclusion)*, the Complete question can be treated as a form of the **Inference** question. The answer choice that fills the blank will be a certainty if all the information in the prompt is taken as true.

KEY POINTS TO REMEMBER ABOUT CRITICAL REASONING QUESTIONS

→ About 11 or 12 Critical Reasoning questions will appear on the GMAT.

→ *Every* fact needed to answer the question is found either in the prompt or in the answers.

→ The *only* facts allowed to answer the question are found either in the prompt or in the answers.

→ There are 13 different types of Critical Reasoning questions, but most consist of variations on three basic themes.

Sentence Correction

Each Sentence Correction question you see on the GMAT will look the same: a sentence will be either partially or completely **underlined** and followed by five **answer choices** that give different possible versions of the underlined section. Voila:

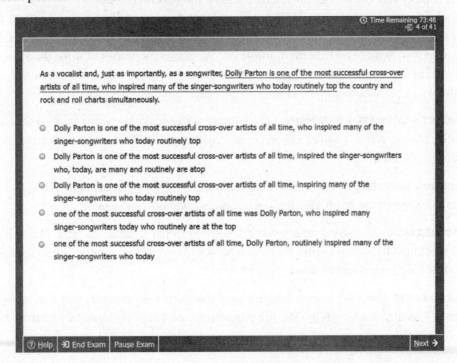

Note that the first answer choice is always a repetition of the sentence as originally written. If after analyzing the sentence and the other answer choices you conclude that there is absolutely nothing wrong with the underlined section, then you should select the first answer choice. A full fifth (20 percent) of Sentence Correction questions have no error as originally written.

Now take a moment to look at the answer choices. Don't worry about trying to find the right answer at the moment. Instead, notice how the answer choices are written. Most of the words are pretty much the same from answer choice to answer choice. Big changes tend to clump up into groups of two or three. For example, (A), (B), and (C) all start with Dolly Parton, whereas (D) and (E) move her to the middle.

TIP

Decision Points: Splits found in the answer choices of a Sentence Correction question; prime opportunities for the Process of Elimination.

In order to pick the right answer, you're obviously going to have to make a decision about where "Dolly Parton" should be. From here forward, we are going to refer to those points where the differences are clear as **Decision Points**.

There are also substantial portions of the answer choices that are identical or nearly so. The long modifying phrase *is one of the most successful cross-over artists of all time* doesn't change at all from answer to answer. Why bother to include something that big if they're not going to ask any grammatical question about it?

Usually, it's to distract you from some other grammatical question. Here, it interferes with your ability to see how Dolly is connected to that bit of the sentence that describes how influential she was. Successfully managing Sentence Correction questions requires you to identify and then ignore these **Distractors**.

SENTENCE CORRECTION QUESTION TYPES

TIP

Distractors: Grammatically correct stretches of text used to disguise the actual grammatical point being tested.

After the 14 Critical Reasoning variations, it should come as welcome news to learn that there is, strictly speaking, just the one type of Sentence Correction question. Sure, there's some variation in how much is underlined or where the underlined section is placed in relation to the rest of the sentence, but the fundamental task is still the same each time: eliminate the answer choices that contain an obvious error until you're down to one.

Thankfully, even though the English language has numerous multivolume textbooks filled with rules and variations on those rules, the GMAT limits itself to a very small collection of errors to test in Sentence Correction questions. Six major categories of error dominate the questions; at least one of them appears in just about every question, and most questions contain two or three of them. They are:

SUBJECT/PREDICATE AGREEMENT—The subject of the sentence (a noun) must match the predicate (the verb); singular subjects get singular predicates, and plural subjects take plural predicates.

PRONOUN REFERENCE—Pronouns must refer unambiguously to a single noun, and they must also match the noun they replace in number, gender, and case.

MODIFICATION—Modifying elements, such as adjectives, adverbs, and prepositional phrases, must be placed so that it's clear what they're supposed to modify and so that the modification makes logical sense.

PARALLELISM—Parts of a sentence that play the same role must be put into matching forms. This includes words in lists, in comparisons, and in other multipart constructions.

CLAUSES AND CONNECTORS—Clauses can be either independent or dependent. Linking them incorrectly can result in a run-on sentence or a sentence fragment.

IDIOMATIC CONSTRUCTION—Certain words are paired with other words in English not because of any logical rule but because that's just the way they're expected to be. Usually, this involves preposition choice (i.e., you sleep in a bed, not at a bed).

In the sections that follow, we will discuss each of these frequently tested errors, explaining both the formal rules and the ways that the rules tend to be tested in the context of a question. For now, let's see how to apply the Four-Step Verbal Method to all Sentence Correction questions, no matter what error they contain.

> **KEY POINTS TO REMEMBER ABOUT SENTENCE CORRECTION QUESTIONS**
>
> → About 15 or 16 Sentence Correction questions will appear on the GMAT.
>
> → 20 percent of them are correct as written [Answer Choice (A)].
>
> → Six types of error make up the vast majority of errors tested; if you are at a loss where to begin, start with these.
>
> → Certain parts of the sentence are grammatically correct in every answer choice and are used to distract your attention from the errors tested.

Reading Comprehension

You will know that you are dealing with a Reading Comprehension question set the moment the screen switches to a two-paned display with a scroll bar in the middle of the screen:

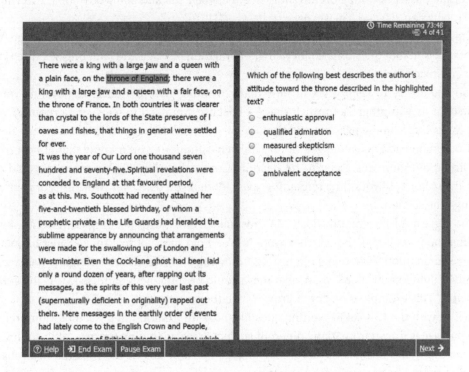

Like the other two formats, Reading Comprehension questions can appear at any point in the Verbal section, but they do cluster into sets every time. There's never a one-off single-question passage. Indeed, nearly every Reading Comprehension set is composed of three or four questions.

Thus, every Reading Comprehension set will be composed of a **passage** in the left-hand window on your screen and a **question** in the right. The **passage** will remain until all the questions in the set are completed. You can't skip questions; even though they're part of a set, they still appear one at a time. Each **question** is composed of a **stem** and **five answer choices**, four incorrect and one correct.

The lines of text are not numbered, as they are in a paper-and-pencil GMAT (such as those you'll encounter in the *Official Guides* and in this book). When a question makes a reference to a specific part of the passage, instead of line numbers, the interface will highlight that part of the passage in yellow for as long as the question is on your screen.

> There were a king with a large jaw and a queen with a plain face, on the throne of England; there were a king with a large jaw and a queen with a fair face, on the throne of France. In both countries it was clearer than crystal to the lords of the State preserves of l

The vast majority of test takers see four total passage and question sets during their test. Two of the passages will be on the short side, between 150 and 200 words long; two will be longer, between 250 and 350 words.

The number of questions doesn't necessarily correspond to the length of the passage. You might be asked four questions about a single-paragraph passage and later only get three with a passage twice that size.

You should try to keep track of how many Reading Comprehension questions you've seen so far as you progress through the test because you need to leave extra room in your time budget to read the passages. So if you're on question 25 but you've not seen any Reading Comprehension questions yet (a *very* unlikely situation), you'd know that almost every remaining question was going to be Reading Comprehension. To be on pace, you'd still have the majority of your time remaining, even though you'd be over two-thirds of your way through the section.

The biggest mistake that novice GMAT test takers make with Reading Comprehension is reading the passages as though they were just any old piece of text they've just happened to have come upon. "Oh, that's interesting," they might think while reading the passage, or "Really? I didn't know that," when what they should be thinking is "Whose side is the author on?" and "This example is meant to prove which theory, exactly?"

Just as with the Critical Reasoning questions, the information in a Reading Comprehension passage is drawn from many different subject areas, including the arts, philosophy, the sciences, law, and business. You're not expected to know any of the material beforehand, and you should be careful if the subject happens to be one you're personally familiar with because there's no guarantee that the things presented as facts in these passages are actually true.

Sure, the test maker generally starts with a journal article or a newspaper or magazine report, but in order to make it into a GMAT Reading Comprehension passage, the facts are tweaked and the descriptions of things changed so that the passage will fit into the specific logic they use to determine which of the five answers is right and to ensure that there are four tempting but wrong answers.

Thus, the key to mastering Reading Comprehension questions will be learning to organize the information in the passage in your head (or on your noteboard) in such a way that you can answer the sorts of questions the GMAT asks about these passages. You're not reading for fun or just to say you've read the passage. You're reading in preparation for a very narrow range of possible tasks you might be called upon to perform.

READING COMPREHENSION QUESTION TYPES

Remember the most important ground rule for the Reading Comprehension section: every answer must be based on **specific** pieces of **information found in the passage.** You are not required to know anything about the passages nor are you expected (or allowed) to justify picking an answer because of information you know from any other source.

Now, consider how limiting that is for the test makers and how hard it makes their job. They can present information from anywhere, from any source or subject under the sun, but they can only ask you to do things with that information that someone could reasonably be expected to do solely on the basis of that information and that information alone. Thus, a lot of the things that you're accustomed to doing with a piece of text or a chunk of an article are explicitly out of bounds. So what's left for them to do?

Recall Questions

One question the test maker can still ask is simply "Hey, what did this guy say about this particular subject?" Or, to put it in the context of the question, "Which of these five different things did the passage you just read actually say?" We call this general category of questions **Recall** questions because they ask you to do just that: recall a single piece of information from the passage. There are two ways this question can be asked:

DETAIL—These questions ask you to recall or locate a piece of information that was explicitly written in the text of the passage.

INFERENCE—These questions ask you to recall or locate a piece of information that was not explicitly written in the passage but that MUST BE TRUE if you take all the information in the passage as true.

Global Questions

The test maker can also ask you, "What was the reason this passage was written?" or, phrased another way, "What did the author do with this information? Was there some sort of point to it all? Or was it just a bunch of random facts?"

MAIN POINT—These questions ask you to identify the author's agenda or the overall point of the passage.

Nearly every single passage on the GMAT will have some sort of agenda or direction to it. Something is at stake. It might be as simple as, "People used to think this, but now they think that, **and it is right to think that instead of this for these reasons.**" Most often the author is explicitly siding with one of two parties or one of two interpretations. In this way, they're a lot more like Critical Reasoning questions than they might seem.

On the rare occasions that the passage does not have a point, then that means that the test maker is even more constrained than usual. The only questions in bounds would be **Detail** and **Inference** questions.

The other type of **Global** question singles out a specific piece of information presented in the passage and asks, "Why did the author mention this?" The answer to that question must always involve the author's overall goal.

FUNCTION—These questions ask you to identify the role that a particular piece of information plays in the author's overall agenda.

And that's it. There are just four questions.

RECALL QUESTIONS (ask you "What?")
   Detail: "Did the author say this or that?"
   Inference: "Which of these has to be true because of something the author said?"

GLOBAL QUESTIONS (ask you "Why?")
   Main Point: "Why did the author write this?"
   Function: "Why did the author say this here?"

Critical Reasoning Questions

Didn't we already cover Critical Reasoning questions two sections ago? Yes, but they also show up from time to time in the Reading Comprehension question sets. When one does pop up, you will treat it according to the method appropriate to whatever type of Critical Reasoning question it happens to be. If it's a **Weaken** question, then weaken; a **Strengthen** question, strengthen. That's that.

READING COMPREHENSION QUESTION FREQUENCY

There aren't any good numbers available for the number of each of these four question types (plus Critical Reasoning) that you can expect to see on the test. As a general rule, there are more Inference questions than any other type. Global questions aren't that frequent, but three of the four passages usually have one (and usually only one). Critical Reasoning questions are a little less common than Function questions, which are about as common as Detail questions. As a very rough guide:

Reading Comprehension Question Types

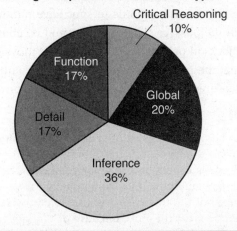

Critical Reasoning 10%

Function 17%

Global 20%

Detail 17%

Inference 36%

KEY POINTS TO REMEMBER ABOUT READING COMPREHENSION QUESTIONS

→ About 13–14 Reading Comprehension questions will appear on the GMAT.

→ The questions either ask you "What?" the passage says or "Why?" the passage says it.

→ As you work through the text, keep track of how many Reading Comprehension questions you've seen in a section; this will impact your time budget and pace.

→ Don't take notes summarizing the passage or copying directly from it.

→ Take notes that will help you with the four specific types of questions.

READING THE GMAT WAY

If it always seems like the GMAT question writers have got your number or that there's always *something* you missed or that a little detail should have been paid more attention to, you're probably letting the GMAT control your attention and dictate the flow of information. You're a passive audience member and they're the master stage magician, always getting you to look somewhere else in order to hide what they're actually doing.

Think of written material on the GMAT Verbal instead as a series of puzzles that demand one of a few specific processes in order to solve. You are always *doing* something, not just reading.

You're also not skimming. You read every word. But certain words are big flashing signals that tell you "Slow down and make sure you've got this part." Others will tell you, "Nothing to see here; move along." Take this piece of a passage, for example:

> Scientists have long known that the surface of the Earth is not static, as it appears to casual observation, but rather always in motion. Even the contours of the continents change, but the rate of change is usually too slow for us to perceive. These large-scale movements of the Earth's surface layer are the chief province of the theory of plate tectonics, which asserts that the continents drift apart because of the movement of solid plates atop a hidden liquid surface.
> Some early models of plate tectonics treated the motion of plates as though it were similar to a flat piece of lumber riding on top of a conveyor belt, the convection cells in

TIP

If you take nothing else from this book, take this to heart: don't ever "just read" a GMAT Verbal question.

Which words seem most important to you? What would you take note of?

On the GMAT, the most important words to spot have nothing to do with specifics of the content contained in the passage. The passage could be about Native American treaty negotiations during the Jackson presidency or, as here, the movement of tectonic plates—it really doesn't matter what the passage is *about*, it's what the author is *doing* that concerns us. Accordingly, to the seasoned GMAT test taker, the passage probably looks more like this:

> Scientists have **long known** that the surface of the Earth **is not** static, as it appears to casual observation, **but rather** always in motion. **Even** the contours of the continents change, **but** the rate of change **is usually** too slow for us to perceive. **These** large-scale movements of the Earth's surface layer are the chief province of the theory of plate tectonics, **which asserts** that the continents drift apart **because of** the movement of solid plates atop a hidden liquid surface.
>
> **Some early** models of plate tectonics treated the motion of plates **as though** it were **similar to** a flat piece of lumber riding on top of a conveyor belt, the convection cells in

Read for Structure and Function

Imagine that a power surge at the test center fried your monitor and all you could see were those words we highlighted.

	long known	**is not**
		but rather
Even		**but**
is usually		**These**
		which asserts
	because of	
Some early		
as though	**similar to**	

Obviously, there would be certain types of questions that you'd be unable to answer.

> According to the passage, the first theoretical model of tectonic plate movement relied on the analogy that

Notice that you would still, from just a few words, be able to tell where in the passage to start looking for the answer should the fritzed out computer monitor spontaneously start working again. It's either going to be the chunk of text following "long known" or the one after "some early."

Notice also that even without the content, you'd have a pretty good idea of how to describe the author's main point. At the least, you could eliminate some of the answer choices in a question like:

> Which of the following best describes the author's primary purpose?

Admittedly, your understanding of the passage would sound something like this:

> *Apparently, there is some phenomenon that somebody has known for a long time that can be described one way and not some other way.*
>
> *Then a bit later there's a definition of some sort of theory, probably one that describes the phenomenon they were just talking about.*
>
> *Then a little later still, there's a discussion of something else, probably a different theory, one that came before the one that was earlier described in the passage.*
>
> *This new theory or description treated the phenomenon as though it was like some other thing—and probably we'll find out later that treating it that way was wrong somehow.*

That is to say, you'd know an awful lot from only 19 of the passage excerpt's 113 words. You'd know both the **structure** of the passage and the **function** of most of the details. Many GMAT questions would be completely doable with only what we have now.

The models mentioned in the second paragraph serve primarily to

    (A) ~~present a point of view that the author later shows to have been discredited for insufficient reasons~~

     (B) contrast with the author's preferred interpretation of the details of an interpretation taken as incorrect

THE KEY TO KEYWORDS

As you read any chunk of GMAT text, you should be on the alert, waiting for **keywords** that will allow you to break the information contained in the text into smaller, more useful chunks. **Keywords** come in many different flavors, each with their own use.

Timing Keys	First, second, finally, in the end, in the 1850s, later, earlier, was once
Illustrating Keys	For example, to illustrate, this can be seen in, which shows, such
Emphasis Keys	Fortunately, crucially, most important, disastrously, even goes so far as
Concluding Keys	Therefore, thus, consequently, from this we can, in conclusion
Doubt Keys	Appears, seems, was even once, some critics contend, might be taken to
Continuing Keys	Moreover, additionally, also, as well as, and, further, not only
Contrasting Keys	However, nevertheless, despite, yet, although, but, rather
Place Holding Keys	This, that, these, those, such as, such a, the latter, the former

TIP

Always look out for "some people say." This is not how we talk about people we agree with.

Be careful! It's very easy to misuse keywords. When doing pencil-and-paper practice problems, people often underline and circle these words as they read them and stop there, treating the passage like some sort of word jumble search. *Finding* the keys is only the first step to understanding the passage. It's how you *use* them that counts.

So how do we use the keywords? When you see a keyword, pause long enough to figure out what the keyword tells you about the relationship between the pieces of information that surround it in the passage. GMAT questions are, at their core, built on the relationships between details. In action, the process would go something like this:

Scientists have **long known** that the surface of the Earth **is not** static, as it appears to casual observation, **but rather** always in motion. **Even** the contours of the continents change, **but** the rate of change **is usually** too slow for us to perceive. **These** large-scale movements of the Earth's surface layer are the chief province of the theory of plate tectonics, **which asserts** that the continents drift apart **because of** the movement of solid plates atop a hidden liquid surface.

Some early models of plate tectonics treated the motion of plates as though it were similar to a flat piece of lumber riding on top of a conveyor belt, the convection cells in

1 Sets up a contrast between old and new info? No new info in this ¶. Keep in mind for later.
2 Another contrast. What are the two parts? (1) appears static, but isn't and (2) is in motion (though slow). What's the contrast about? Earth's surface.
3 More info about (2) from before.
4 Contrast: actual vs. perceived. What's the contrast about? Movement of continents.
5 Hanging contrast. No exceptions given.
6 "these" what? Connect the dots ... this describes earlier "contours of continents changing."
7 Definition of what? The theory of plate tectonics.
8 What causes what? Drift caused by movement of solid on liquid.

If we could get inside the head of the GMAT test taker using this approach, we'd hear an inner monologue not too different from what we saw when we didn't know what the content was:

> OK, so there's a phenomenon that appears one way but is another: the Earth's surface appears still but actually moves. And now more about this: blah, blah, OK I get it, it seems still because of how slow it is. Hmmm hmmm—wait, **these** large-scale movements? Which ones were those? Ah, right, the ones that are hard to see because they're slow. The continent ones. So those movements are described by a theory. And now we get the theory's definition. And it's about a cause. Something about solids and liquids— another this versus that kind of thing.

Savvy GMAT readers are always asking questions, always double checking to make sure they understand the relationship between what they've already read and what they are reading at that moment. They're looking forward to what they're going to read in the future, waiting for the second half of two-part constructions, and noticing when questions are asked but left unanswered.

These readers aren't worried that they need to know exactly how the theory of plate tectonics works, though. They're confident that should they run across the question:

> **According to the passage, which of the following is a central claim of plate tectonics?**

All they will have to do is go back to the part of the passage where they know the definition lies and reread it to make sure they can recognize the correct answer when they read the answer choices.

THE PAYOFF

As we said earlier, the authors of this book have been working one-on-one with GMAT students for a long time now. The first time we force a student to slow down and read the passage in this way, the response is, inevitably, "How am I going to have time to do all of that? I'm already going too slow."

To this, we always respond: "The reason you're going too slow now is that you skim the passage, then get to the questions and realize you don't know what's going on, so all that time spent skimming was a waste. And you read again, but still without focusing on this stuff, so you end up reading the same part over and over. Your eyes flip back to the question. You read the answers. Because you still aren't sure what the author's overall goal was, you can't recognize the answer when you see it. Then you read the answers a few more times, but slower, hoping the right thing leaps out at you."

People who move too slowly in the Verbal section are going so slowly because they spend all their time trying to rush. To quote a certain green space muppet:

> "This one [...] all his life has he looked away [...] Never his mind on where he was. Hmm? What he was doing. Hmph. Adventure. Heh. Excitement. Heh. A Jedi craves not these things."

The reason we read passages this way is because of the way that the GMAT question writers build questions.

You know that one of the things they might ask you about a chunk of text is "Do you remember what the author said about X?" If they're going to ask that question, they're not going to make it easy to find that detail. They've got to hide the right answer in some way and make wrong answers somehow seem right. From the passage we've read so far, we might see this question:

> **According to the passage, the reason that the contours of the continents change**

The correct answer would likely not be anything written within two lines of that very recognizable phrase "contours of the continents." Instead, it would be:

> **(A)** is the influence of the molten layer beneath the Earth's solid surface

The savvier test takers already made that connection when they saw the place-holding keyword "these."

> Wait, **these** large-scale movements? Which ones were those? Ah, right, the continent ones. The theory says they're caused by this liquid stuff...

If the test maker wanted to make this question harder, they would go a couple of steps further in disguising that answer. In the part of the passage that we didn't excerpt above, the author introduces further ways to describe "the liquid stuff." If you're taking note of the connections between the jargon the passage is slinging around, you'd still be able to pick the right answer, even if it showed up as:

> (A) is the circulation of convection currents in the ductile material below the 1300°C isotherm

Wrong answers would be phrased to attract lazier or less aware test takers.

> (B) were once the chief province of the theory of plate tectonics

That answer would be great if not for the word "once." The passage does say that this movement of continents is what the theory of plate tectonics describes, but it doesn't indicate that there was a time when it was, and now it's not.

For people just reading for things that "sound right" or, worse yet, "sound like something the author talked about," this answer choice would certainly be tempting. It quotes the text of the passage almost verbatim. And there was something in the passage that was described as being one way for a while, then later another, the conveyor-belt theory from the second paragraph.

With only a vague understanding of the relationship between ideas, you might well fall for this trap answer choice.

These traps don't just appear in Reading Comprehension questions. Critical Reasoning and, yes, even Sentence Correction questions use these very same patterns to try to mislead you, and reading them in the way we've been describing in this section is, undoubtedly, the best way to avoid falling for the test maker's trickery.

Success on the GMAT isn't simply a matter of learning a collection of grammar rules or some formal logic. To succeed, you must learn how GMAT questions are designed to trap you and how to prepare yourself from the very beginning of a question to avoid those traps. Play by the GMAT's rules, know the GMAT's habits, and no score is out of your reach.

Critical Reasoning

13

→ **WHAT THE GMAT *SAYS* CRITICAL READING TESTS**

→ **ARGUMENTS AND FACTS**

→ **THE FOUR-STEP METHOD FOR CRITICAL REASONING QUESTIONS**

→ **THE ARGUMENT STRUCTURE FAMILY OF QUESTIONS**

→ **IDENTIFYING CONCLUSIONS AND EVIDENCE**

→ **COMMON WRONG ANSWER TRICKS AND TRAPS FOR ARGUMENT STRUCTURE QUESTIONS**

→ **THE ARGUMENT ASSUMPTION FAMILY OF QUESTIONS**

→ **VARIATIONS ON ASSUMPTION QUESTIONS**

→ **FACT-BASED QUESTIONS**

INTRODUCTION

The directions the GMAT provides for Critical Reasoning questions are so brief and unhelpful that it's almost silly:

> **DIRECTIONS:** Select the best of the answer choices given.

That's all she wrote. There is no hint as to what might make an answer choice "the best," no guidance of any sort. They might as well just write

> **DIRECTIONS:** Read our minds and select our favorite answer.

From a certain perspective, you *are* going to learn to read the GMAT question writer's mind. The master logicians back at GMAT HQ actually have a very narrow set of principles that they use to distinguish the credited answer from all the rest. Successful GMAT test takers often end up approaching a problematic answer choice asking not "What's the best answer?" but instead "Why does the GMAT think these four are wrong and this one is right?"

What the GMAT *Says* Critical Reasoning Tests

According to what GMAT and ACT say elsewhere, Critical Reasoning questions target three different cognitive skills:

ARGUMENT CONSTRUCTION: Questions of this type may ask you to recognize the basic structure of an argument, properly drawn conclusions, underlying assumptions, well-supported explanatory hypotheses, or parallels between structurally similar arguments.

ARGUMENT EVALUATION: Questions of this type may ask you to analyze a given argument, recognize factors that would strengthen or weaken an argument, reasoning errors committed in making an argument, or aspects of the methods by which an argument proceeds.

FORMULATING AND EVALUATING A PLAN OF ACTION: Questions of this type may ask you to recognize the relative appropriateness, effectiveness, or efficiency of different plans of action; factors that would strengthen or weaken a proposed plan of action; or assumptions underlying a proposed plan of action.

—"The GMAT—Test Structure and Overview—Verbal Section," *MBA.Com*

What Critical Reasoning Doesn't Really Test . . . and What It Does

Notice how much language is shared between the descriptions of the three skill areas in the official description. In truth, there isn't any difference between an argument's structure and how the argument proceeds. Nor is there really any difference between evaluating an argument and evaluating a plan of action. Plans in Critical Reasoning prompts are essentially just arguments that a proposed set of actions will be sufficient to bring about some stated goal.

In a nutshell, GMAT Critical Reasoning questions demand that you understand two things well:

ARGUMENTS—Understand their parts and how they work.

FACTS—Understand how to draw inferences from a collection of facts.

ARGUMENTS AND FACTS

Arguments

When the test makers use the word "argument," they mean the logician's definition: a series of connected premises meant to demonstrate the truth of a proposition.

Or, to put it another (less-jargony) way, all the arguments on the GMAT take the form of **someone making the case for something**, a contestable claim like *ABC Cola is the best cola in the world.* We call this claim the argument's **conclusion.** The conclusion will be accompanied by some information meant to prove the conclusion to be true, like, perhaps, *Studies have shown that 100 percent of people who drink ABC Cola find it to be delicious and refreshing.* This information we call the argument's **evidence**.

> **Argument**—An attempt to support a claim by giving reasons for it.
> **Conclusion**—The claim that an argument attempts to support.
> **Evidence**—The reasons given in support of an argument's conclusion.

The evidence explains the conclusion. The conclusion is explained by the evidence. When you have both, you have an argument.

Does that seem a little circular to you? It should. Logically speaking, **evidence** and **conclusion** only exist as a pair. If you don't have at least two pieces of information, it's impossible to have an **argument**. If you simply say *ABC Cola is the best cola in the world*, you have not made an argument. You've only made a claim.

And even when you have two pieces of information, if one doesn't explain why you should believe the other, that you *still* don't have an argument.

Add something explaining *why* to believe some particular *what*, and now you have an instant argument.

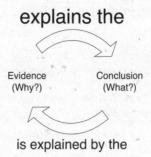

explains the

Evidence   Conclusion
(Why?)   (What?)

is explained by the

Thus, all arguments can be put into a very basic template:

[What] BECAUSE [Why]

[Conclusion] BECAUSE [Evidence]

[*ABC Cola is the best cola in the world*] BECAUSE [*Studies have shown that 100 percent of people who drink ABC Cola find it to be delicious and refreshing.*]

Evidence	Evidence	Conclusion
Socrates is a man.	All men are mortal.	Socrates is mortal.
Celery is gross.	You shouldn't eat gross things.	You shouldn't eat celery.
If it's Tuesday, we should eat by 12.	It's Tuesday, and it's 12:30!	We should have eaten by now.
Words in columns look cool.	These words are in columns.	How cool!

The arguments you'll encounter on the GMAT usually have only one or two pieces of evidence, and sometimes the test makers go out of their way to disguise the evidence, but whatever the trick being played, every single argument on the GMAT can be put into the form **conclusion** *because* **evidence**.

When you finish reading a Critical Reasoning prompt containing an argument, try to rephrase the argument into that basic template before going on to the answer choices. That's your spot check to make sure you understood what you just read.

Also, don't think that the argument's conclusion has to come at the end of the argument or the evidence at the beginning. You can scramble them up however you want. As long as there's something being explained and something doing some explaining, you have an argument.

You might not have a *good* argument, though, which brings us to valid and invalid arguments!

VALID AND INVALID ARGUMENTS

Valid Arguments

Once in a while (for Argument Structure questions), the GMAT lets you stop once you've identified the parts of the argument, but more often the test also asks you to say something about whether the argument is *good* or *bad*—or to use more formal-sounding words, *valid* or *invalid*. But what makes an argument valid?

Earlier we described an argument as a "series of connected premises meant to demonstrate the truth of a proposition." The keyword there was "connected." When an argument is valid, the evidence and conclusion form a chain, a series of reasonable little steps from one idea to the next.

> **FUN WITH SYNONYMS!**
>
> **Good arguments are** valid, properly drawn, supported, logical, sound, logically correct, convincing.
>
> **Bad arguments are** invalid, improperly drawn, flawed, unsound, illogical, unconvincing.

Consider this quick argument:

> Boston is a city in Massachusetts. Susan is in Boston. Massachusetts is in the United States. Therefore, Susan is in the United States.

We would call this a valid argument because it's possible to arrange it into a chain where one piece of evidence is directly connected to the next:

> Susan is in Boston. Boston is a city in Massachusetts. Massachusetts is in the United States.

If we believe each link in the chain, there's no doubt about it. Susan must be in the United States. Our argument is valid.

Invalid Arguments

There are lots of reasons an argument might be bad. Earlier, when we professed our undying love of ABC Cola, you probably found yourself thinking "Come on, no survey's going to show 100 percent agreement. That's crazy." In effect, you were thinking, "That's a pretty terrible argument." Maybe, getting into the spirit of this section's heading, you even thought, "That argument is invalid!" Not so fast! **Invalid** is not the same as **incorrect**.

Arguments aren't invalid because their evidence is wrong. They're invalid because their evidence, as stated, does not give enough reason *on its own* for you to believe the conclusion.

Assumptions

Earlier, you learned that arguments have two parts, evidence and conclusion. To this we add a final part that is never written out explicitly: the argument's **assumptions**. In one sense, assumptions are pieces of evidence that are left *unstated*. To put it another way, an argument's assumptions consist of everything else that needs to be true in order for the argument to be true.

When we say an argument is "convincing" or "well-formed" or "valid," we are actually passing judgment on the argument's assumptions. Good arguments don't require much beyond what is explicitly stated in order to be believed. Bad arguments, on the other hand—ones that fail to convince, aren't properly formed, or are invalid—require us to take too much on faith. Invalid arguments ask us to believe something that we know probably isn't the case (or that's actually impossible).

Don't take from this, however, that assumptions are always mistakes an argument makes.

If there's a question that needs an answer in order for us to be comfortable saying our evidence adds up to our conclusion, we've found an assumption. Assumptions answer questions. Assumptions bridge gaps in the evidence.

Susan's Boston — **ASSUMPTION** — Boston, MA

If it turns out that an assumption isn't true, then the argument will no longer be valid. Remember always:

$$\text{Evidence (+ Assumptions)} \rightarrow \text{Conclusion}$$

FACTS

What is a fact? In the world outside the GMAT, that's a thorny question, but for our purposes it couldn't be simpler: a fact is any piece of information that we are asked to take as true without being given an argument to explain why.

Every piece of evidence in a GMAT argument is something we'll be told to treat as though it were true. Thus, all GMAT arguments are built out of facts—but not all facts on the GMAT are found in arguments.

Paradoxically, that means that a lot of things that we think of in real life as opinions, on the GMAT we're going to be taking as facts. Other than the conclusion, everything found in a prompt is, to us, simply a fact.

DISTINGUISHING FACTS FROM ARGUMENTS

Consider these two simulated GMAT prompts:

No employee who works at a major corporation wishes to anger the boss, and all major corporations are arranged hierarchically. Bad news inevitably angers the boss who receives it. Those highest in the corporate hierarchy of major corporations are often the least informed about the problems their company is currently facing.

No employee who works at a major corporation wishes to anger the boss, and all major corporations are arranged hierarchically. Because bad news inevitably angers the boss who receives it, it is reasonable to believe that those highest in the corporate hierarchy of major corporations are often the least informed about the problems their company is currently facing.

What is the difference between the two?

The prompt on the left is presented as a series of facts. The prompt on the right is, instead, arranged into an argument. The only difference between them is that the one on the right has the words "because" and "it is reasonable to believe" added, but that is all it takes to turn a collection of facts into an argument: words that indicate which of them you are meant to accept as an explanation (i.e., the evidence) for why one of them (i.e., the conclusion) is true.

As we've already said, when the GMAT gives us an argument, we're expected to think about the argument's assumptions. But what does the GMAT ask us to do with facts?

MAKING INFERENCES FROM FACTS

Primarily, the GMAT expects us to be able to make valid **inferences** from facts.

In our day-to-day lives, we make a lot of inferences.

If someone comes back from vacation with a sunburn, we think, "I'll bet they went to the beach."

If we hear a crash in another room followed by the pitter pat of paws beating a hasty retreat, we think, "That darn cat broke something again."

When you start from something you know and make a guess or a prediction about something you don't know, you're making an inference.

However, if somehow these examples appeared in GMAT Critical Reasoning questions, we would have just missed these questions. Each of these inferences would be considered invalid according to the GMAT's rules for inferences.

On the GMAT, the only inferences allowable are those that are 100 percent certain, things that absolutely, positively, without a doubt and without any extra information beyond what is found in the prompt MUST BE TRUE.

Arguments preceded by *probably, possibly, maybe,* and *more than likely* all fail to make the GMAT inference cut.

> GMAT Inference—Something that MUST BE TRUE on the basis of something else taken to be true.

TIP

The same rules that apply to Critical Reasoning inferences also apply when the questions show up in Reading Comprehension!

Because of this narrow definition, most of the inferences you'll be asked to make on the GMAT might seem kind of pointless. For example:

> If someone comes back from a vacation sunburned, **on the GMAT** we think, "His or her skin has been damaged by the sun. It is not in the same condition it was in when it was not damaged. His or her skin has changed over the course of his or her life."

> If we hear a crash in another room followed by the pitter pat of paws beating a hasty retreat, **on the GMAT we think,** "The cat—or something that makes the same sound as the cat—has moved. I have just heard a sound that could have been caused by something breaking. The other room is not always quiet. Sometimes you can hear things that sound like a cat or like something breaking in it."

None of those inferences is interesting, but that's just it—GMAT inferences aren't interesting. They aren't clever. If we believe the first statement, we must believe all the others that follow. Very often, novice GMAT test takers miss Inference questions because they think, "But that's too obvious to be the answer!"

Too obvious is never a reason to get rid of a GMAT answer, but that is particularly true with Inference questions.

The GMAT gives us some facts that contain some categorical statements and ask us to say what follows from those statements.

Fact #1	Fact #2	Inference
Socrates is a man.	All men are mortal.	Socrates is mortal.
Celery is gross.	You shouldn't eat gross things.	You shouldn't eat celery.
If it's Tuesday, we should eat by 12.	It's Tuesday, and it's 12:30!	We should have eaten by now.
Words in columns look cool.	These words are in columns.	How cool!

OK, you caught us, we did just reuse the same table from a few pages ago. That's because inferences, arguments, and assumptions are not wholly unrelated concepts.

The conclusion to a valid argument is inferable on the basis of the evidence presented.

> If it is true that Socrates is a man and it is true that all men are mortal, then we can infer that Socrates is mortal.

If we are presented with an argument that we are told is valid, but there are gaps in the argument's evidence, then we may infer that the assumptions necessary to bridge those gaps are true.

> If it's true that Socrates is a man, and it's true that because Socrates is a man, Socrates is mortal, we can infer that all men must be mortal.

The GMAT will clearly indicate to you whether you need to make an inference of what must be true from a couple of facts or whether you need to look at some evidence and a conclusion and say what the conclusion assumes in order to be true.

But ultimately, making inferences and finding assumptions rely on a common skill set. You look at all the information you have and decide either what you need to get where you want to go (assumptions) or where you're going to end up given what you've started with (inferences).

THE FOUR-STEP METHOD FOR CRITICAL REASONING QUESTIONS

Time to see the **Four-Step General Verbal Method** in action on a Critical Reasoning question. We'll use the sample question from the Verbal Introduction:

> Babies born prematurely are beset by a host of serious medical and health challenges. While only nine percent of women not on any medication give birth prematurely, roughly half of all women who take benzodiazepines, a common type of antidepressant, during the first three months of their pregnancies give birth prematurely. Since pregnancy is usually not reliably detectable by over-the-counter methods until the second month, women of child-bearing age should never be prescribed benzodiazepines.
>
> Which of the following, if true, casts the most serious doubt on the conclusion drawn above?

Step 1: Identify the Question Type

The first step of the **Four-Step Verbal Method** is to **Identify the Task**. The task in a Critical Reasoning question always depends on the question **type**. The **question stem** will contain keywords that signal the question type and thus the task demanded.

After you've read the stem, first decide whether the question is **Fact-Based** or **Argument-Based**. Then narrow it down to the particular question type.

If we take a look at the stem of this question, three words allow us to decide:

> Which of the following, if true, casts the most serious doubt on the conclusion drawn above?

When a question asks us to *cast doubt* on an argument's *conclusion*, it's a **Weaken** question, part of the **Assumption** family of **Argument-Based** questions.

Step 2: Identify the Parts of the Argument (for Argument-Based Questions)

Because our question is **Argument-Based**, the best way to **Process** the information is to identify the parts of the argument.

The two basic parts of an argument are the **conclusion**, the idea that the speaker in the prompt is trying to prove, and the **evidence**, the reasons the speaker provides as proof. Start by locating the argument's conclusion.

TIP

Here's another good reason to read the stem first: sometimes that's where the question hides its conclusion.

TIP

The conclusion of an argument is not always placed at the end of the argument.

This argument's conclusion happens to be where you might expect conclusions to come, at the very end:

> [...] counter methods until the second month, women of child-bearing age should never be prescribed benzodiazepines.

Take note of how **absolute** is the argument's conclusion—by which we don't mean that it's provocative or the sort of thing an extremist might say, rather that this argument's conclusion is not qualified in any way. There is no hedging, no *maybe* this or *possibly* that. According to this speaker, there is absolutely no reason—none, nada, zero, zilch—why these benzodiazepines should be prescribed to women in the indicated age group. Such a far-reaching conclusion would require similarly far-reaching evidence to back up—indeed, far more evidence than you could ever fit in a 100-word GMAT prompt.

> **Absolute**—On the GMAT, something that applies to 100 percent of cases, without exception.

Once we have the conclusion, we need to take an **inventory** of the rest of the passage. After you've found the conclusion, what remains will almost always be some kind of **evidence**. Here, we should be able to tease out these pieces of evidence:

- ✔ It can sometimes be hard to tell a pregnancy has started.
- ✔ The drug whose name starts with a *b* is an antidepressant.
- ✔ The *b*-drug causes women to give birth prematurely.
- ✔ Being born prematurely is bad.

Your description of the evidence can be as general or as specific as you need; the important thing is to understand what things the speaker actually said and what was left to the speaker's audience to fill in. You can jot your evidence **inventory** down in a more abbreviated shorthand on your noteboard, or you could just keep it in your head.

Now, does all this **evidence** add up to a compelling case that benzodiazepines should *never* be prescribed to any women in this age group? Certainly not. The argument establishes only that there is *one disadvantage* associated with the drug and then makes a big leap to claim that the drug should *never* be prescribed. In other words, we've found a gap, the gap between *one disadvantage* and *never prescribing*.

Note: When you're doing a Fact-Based Question, this step is going to look a little different. Instead of breaking the argument down into parts, you'll be searching the prompt for the most definite pieces of information. See page 356.

Step 3: Prephrase the Answer

The third step of the **General Verbal Method** is to plan out your approach to the answers. Ideally, for Argument-Based questions we should have a concrete prediction in mind of what the right answer will look like.

For a **Weaken** question the right answer will contain new information about something in the argument that makes us less likely to believe the argument's **assumptions**.

We already know where this argument's assumptions lie, in that gap between finding out that this drug *has one disadvantage* and concluding that it should *never be used*. If the conclusion is correct, the speaker must assume that

> There are no possible advantages or other considerations that could outweigh the one disadvantage given.

So what sort of thing would make us less likely to believe that there are no other advantages? We might be moved by an answer choice that mentions an advantage the speaker neglected to bring up. Or perhaps information that defangs the disadvantage could change our mind, something showing that the disadvantage is not as bad as the speaker seems to think. As we move into the answer choices, we'll be looking for something that can change the **advantage/disadvantage balance**.

Step 4: Evaluate the Answer Choices

Let's take it from the top:

> (A) Many women who take benzodiazepines to combat depression give birth without serious complications.

This answer choice offers nothing new. The argument only claimed that the side effects were experienced by *roughly half of all women*, which is to say, not all of them. Thus, we already knew that there were some women who didn't experience the side effects (the roughly less than half). Something taken into account by the evidence already present can never weaken a GMAT argument. In other words, this is a **closed issue**. Eliminate.

> (B) Psychiatrists who prescribe benzodiazepines are required by law to explain all the dangers associated with their use.

This answer choice hopes to lead you astray by bringing up something **reasonable but irrelevant** to the situation presented in the prompt. You can probably think of several instances of required warning legislation that was passed in the real world. But there's no indication in the prompt that a patient's knowing about the dangers or not knowing would change the rate of negative outcomes significantly. (And that's why we try, whenever possible, to avoid **real-world thinking**. Limit yourself to the facts explicitly stated in the prompt.) Cross this one out.

> (C) Persistent depression is known to reduce fertility in women of child-bearing age.

But for the word *persistent*, this answer choice might require more thought. As it stands, we don't know anything about how benzodiazepines work or about what specific kinds of depressions they're used to treat or whether other treatments might be able to be used for the same thing. So how could we possibly say whether benzodiazepines could provide a benefit to people suffering this specific type of depression (the persistent kind)? Since we have to know more to know whether this answer choice would be relevant, we'd say it's **one step removed** from the argument we're dealing with. Out it goes.

> (D) Some of the women of child-bearing age who take benzodiazepines are unable to conceive for other medical reasons.

Aha! Finally, we have an answer choice that affects the balance of advantage and disadvantage because it both blunts the force of the disadvantage and suggests a possible advantage. The argument's conclusion, as stated, applies to all women of a certain age because of things that are dangerous only to a subset of those women—namely, the subset who can conceive. Those unable to conceive will not be directly affected by the cited disadvantage, so it might prove advantageous to allow benzodiazepines to still be prescribed, just only to those who cannot be harmed by their negative side effect. (D) is the correct answer.

(E) Benzodiazepines have been prescribed for many years by doctors for most common forms of depression.

There is one answer choice left, but we've already found one that must be right. On the day of the test, you might only spare (E) a courtesy glance to make sure you didn't misread something in answers (A) through (D).

After reading (E), we could be reasonably certain that we didn't make any mistakes earlier, as it's clearly a **closed issue** like (A). We already know that *benzodiazepines* are *a common type of antidepressant.*

Click the oval by the answer choice, hit Next and Confirm. It's on to the next question.

Speaking of questions. It's time for you to try some GMAT questions on your own . . .

> Remember these **common types of wrong answers**. You'll definitely see them again.
>
> **closed issue**—Something the evidence in the prompt already takes into account or which is explicitly excluded by the conclusion.
>
> **reasonable but irrelevant**—The answer choice test takers tend to default to when they don't understand the question, something that's reasonable or familiar from a different context.
>
> **one step removed**—Something that would be relevant to the argument, if a second fact unmentioned by the prompt was true.

Critical Reasoning Diagnostic Quiz

Try to complete the following 13 questions in 25 minutes or less. If you don't finish in that time, just take note of where you were when time was up so that you can get an idea of how long the questions currently take you, on average, to complete.

The questions are meant to be of average difficulty, targeted at test takers whose Verbal scores would be around the 50th percentile.

Answers and explanations follow the quiz. These questions will be used throughout the sections that follow to demonstrate various techniques and concepts vital to GMAT Critical Reasoning success.

DIRECTIONS: Select the best of the answer choices given.

1. Harry: Reducing our use of fossil fuels is a matter of national security; we cannot afford to allow foreign powers to threaten our economy by reducing production.

   Susan: You forget that most foreign oil is refined into gasoline and other usable products in domestic refineries. Your proposal would put thousands out of work when refineries close, and the result would be disastrous for our economy.

   Which of the following best describes a weak point in Susan's response to Harry?

   (A) Susan takes for granted that the refineries currently used to process foreign oil could not be refitted to allow the refining of other profitable commodities.
   (B) Susan doesn't take into consideration the political disadvantages of introducing a plan to reduce the use of fossil fuels.
   (C) Susan treats a possible reduction in foreign oil production as though it were inevitable.
   (D) Susan's response does not consider the concern of many environmentalists that believe fossil fuels cause ecological damage.
   (E) Susan wrongly assumes that Harry's proposal cannot be implemented unless new technology is developed.

2. While patients taking one 40-mg Zzzolution™ pill each night do sleep better than those who take the 20-mg pill, a new study has revealed that throughout the following morning those taking the 40-mg pill perform their daytime activities with much less efficiency and consistency than those taking the lower dose. Since the main reason people take pills to combat sleeplessness is to avoid the reduced productivity that typically follows a sleepless night, doctors now recommend their patients take no more than 20 mg of Zzzolution™ per night.

In evaluating the doctors' new recommendation, it would be most useful to determine which of the following about the study participants?

(A) Whether those taking the higher dose would have performed even worse if their dose had not been raised

(B) Whether those taking the lower dose would have experienced more sleeplessness taking the medicine less frequently

(C) Whether the lower dose would have been sufficient to reduce sleeplessness in the group taking the higher dose

(D) Whether the performance of those taking the lower dose varied more than that of those taking the higher dose

(E) Whether those taking the lower dose took their pills earlier in the evening than those taking the higher dose

3. Experts have long agreed that wearing a helmet can drastically reduce the most serious risks associated with skiing, but the recent experience of a California resort suggests otherwise. After High Hopes Family Resort made the wearing of helmets mandatory on all its slopes, the rate of skiing injuries at the resort did not go down; indeed, it actually rose a slight amount.

Which of the following, if true, most helps to explain the increase in the injury rate?

(A) The slopes at High Hopes Family Resort are much more heavily forested than those at other resorts.

(B) Helmets can only protect a skier from cranial trauma, concussions, and other head injuries.

(C) Before the new policy requiring helmets was implemented, High Hopes had a higher than average injury rate.

(D) Many of the accidents at High Hopes could be avoided if skiers were given adequate training before being allowed on the slopes.

(E) After helmets were made mandatory, many of the most skilled skiers stopped using the slopes at High Hopes.

4. Computech CEO: For over a decade, the M+ has been our flagship personal computer. But now that tablet sales are climbing, the M+ is losing market share, its sales down 25 percent in each of the past three quarters. In order to stop this decline, I propose we enhance the capabilities of the M+, doubling its processing power. Tablet computers are already underpowered, and **the difference will make the M+ obviously superior in the eyes of consumers, which is sure to increase sales**.

Consultant: The M+ is losing sales to tablets because people view tablets as cheaper alternatives to traditional desktop PCs. **Increasing the CPU's speed will raise the price of the M+**, causing even greater numbers of your customers to turn to tablets.

In the exchange above, the statements in **bold** play which of the following roles?

(A) The first presents a conclusion; the second is also a conclusion, but one that is irrelevant to the first.

(B) The first presents a conclusion; the second casts doubt on the conclusion by attacking the evidence on which that conclusion is based.

(C) The first presents a prediction; the second presents evidence that provides a reason to doubt the probability of that conclusion.

(D) The first is evidence that is provided in order to disprove the claim presented in the second.

(E) The first presents a conclusion opposite to the conclusion for which the second provides evidence.

5. Ironically, George Lucas's reputation as an artist has been hindered by the very technology that makes his films so dazzling. Many of the theaters that play his films lack top of the line projection machinery. Such machinery is absolutely vital to the full display of Lucas's artistic skill.

Which one of the following can be properly inferred from the statements above?

(A) Some theaters that play Lucas's films provide support for Lucas's reputation as an artist.

(B) All theaters that play Lucas's films and that possess top of the line projection machinery display Lucas's artistic skill fully.

(C) All of the showings of Lucas's films that do not display his full artistic skill lack top of the line projection machinery.

(D) If a theater possesses top of the line projection facilities, it will provide a full display of an artist's skill.

(E) At least some of the theaters that play Lucas's films fail to display fully Lucas's skills as an artist.

6. Which of the following answer choices, if true, best completes the argument below?

As violence in movies increases, so too do municipal crime rates in cities with large movie-going populations. To combat this, we must limit admission to violent films, only allowing those over the age of 18 because _____ and because it has been well-established that teenagers emulate the behavior they see in movies.

(A) those over the age of 18 are able to distinguish violence in movies from actual violence

(B) teenagers often lack the restraint necessary to refrain from crime when the opportunity presents itself

(C) laws restricting the display of violent films will damage the profits of the studios that produce them

(D) those under the age of 18 see more movies today than they did in the past

(E) teenagers are more likely to see movies if they contain objectionable content

7. Program Director: We designed this leadership training program specifically with your company in mind, so you can be certain that sending your employees on one of our weekend program retreats would lead to enhanced team-building and productivity in your business.

Human Resources Manager: While you may have designed it for us, your program is nevertheless poorly designed. Most of the companies that have attended your weekend retreat have seen no benefit at all, even those that are like our company in most respects.

The Human Resources Manager's response to the Program Director's pitch

(A) rebuts a central premise upon which the pitch is based by citing exceptions to it.

(B) rejects the pitch's conclusion by refuting each of its premises.

(C) accedes the pitch's conclusion, but rejects the evidence upon which the pitch is based.

(D) accepts that one of the premises on which the pitch is based may not be false.

(E) rejects the pitch on the grounds that its evidence cannot be proven.

8. The most famous protagonists in literature have always been at odds with societal norms, but it has been increasingly fashionable for postcolonial literature to glorify these iconoclastic protagonists much more than any previous genre of literature has. By presenting these characters as being worthy of emulation, postcolonial authors subtly endorse their outsider ethos and may convince their readers to adopt it. Thus, postcolonial literature can be harmful to at least some of its readers, and thereby to society itself.

Which of the following is an assumption on which the argument above depends?

(A) Some protagonists from earlier literature were better role models than any found in postcolonial literature.

(B) It is beneficial for some readers to avoid adopting an outsider ethos or to avoid emulating iconoclasts.

(C) Postcolonial protagonists who adopt an outsider ethos will harm readers more now than if they did not adopt that ethos.

(D) The aesthetic merit of some literary works cannot be judged without considering their moral implications.

(E) Postcolonial literature presents a greater number of outsider characters than did the literature of earlier eras.

9. Which of the following would best complete the argument?

Hymenoptera is the order of insects that contains all bees and most species commonly mistaken for them, such as wasps. Honey bees are the only Hymenoptera with a strongly barbed stinger, though the stingers of some wasps, such as the yellow jacket, have small barbs. Ants are also members of the order Hymenoptera, and many species of ants have stingers, and some of them, like honey bees and wasps, fly. To avoid confusing flying ants with honey bees, therefore, _____.

(A) one should not look at its stinger, unless the ant also resembles a wasp.

(B) one should determine whether all the members of that stinging ant species can fly.

(C) one could not look at the ant's stinger, unless it were strongly barbed.

(D) one could determine whether the ant's stinger is strongly barbed.

(E) one could determine whether the ant is an insect or a member of the order Hymenoptera.

10. As the old saying goes, if you wish to get to Carnegie Hall, you must practice. Paula practices her cello night and day, so she has at least part of what she needs to get to Carnegie Hall.

Which of the following exhibits a pattern of reasoning most similar to that in the argument above?

(A) Surviving the audition process at Julliard requires dedication like Trent's. All the same, Trent's lack of talent will prevent his being admitted to Julliard.

(B) As the old saying goes, if you love someone, set them free; if they do not come back, they were never yours to begin with.

(C) It just might be Spring, because when it is Spring, I can't stop sneezing, and I've not been able to stop sneezing all day.

(D) It is a truism that the sound of thunder moves more slowly than lightning's flash, but sometimes the lightning is so close that the two phenomena appear simultaneous; thus, the truism proves false.

(E) According to the architects, nothing short of an earthquake will cause this building to fall. Last night an earthquake struck the building, so it will surely fall soon.

11. Some managers believe that the hourly wage that an employee receives ought to be proportional to the effort required by that job's typical duties, but it would be terrible if a business actually followed this advice, as it would mean that those employees with the least ability to perform their jobs adequately would be entitled to the highest hourly wages, a perverse incentive.

The claim that employees with the least ability to perform their job adequately would be entitled to the highest hourly wages is used in the argument as

(A) a general principle that provides a reason in favor of adopting a disagreeable practice illustrated elsewhere in the argument.

(B) a potentially unpopular general principle that is illustrated by a list of reasons that its adoption would be favorable.

(C) an undesirable consequence that would follow from the adoption of a general principle described elsewhere in the argument.

(D) a piece of evidence that discredits a general principle under consideration by showing that the principle could not be uniformly applied.

(E) a possible consequence said to follow from a general principle's adoption that some incorrectly describe as inevitable.

12. Some say that the funding of a large high-energy particle accelerator will benefit only the few physicists who are given direct access to it. If society had listened to such naysayers, however, today we would not have such vital technologies as radio, nuclear power, and the Internet, as at one time the research necessary to bring these about would not have been seen as beneficial to society as a whole. Clearly, therefore, we should not hesitate to build the proposed large high-energy particle accelerator.

Which of the following principles, if accepted as true, would strengthen the argument above for the construction of a large high-energy particle accelerator?

(A) When there is a conflict between nonspecialists and specialists, such as physicists, the specialists ought to be trusted over the nonspecialists.

(B) When a proposed action is opposed only by those who are anonymous, the action should not be rejected because of their opposition.

(C) Unless experts agree about the benefit of a proposal to society as a whole, that proposal ought not be carried out.

(D) If a proposed action is to be considered, it must first be determined how beneficial the action will be to society as a whole.

(E) Whenever a proposed action is opposed by those who believe the action will have only minimal impact, that opposition ought to be ignored.

13. With recent cutbacks in educational funding, the state university must reduce its expenditures or risk bankruptcy. The university's president has proposed moving several introductory-level classes online in order to save money on building maintenance and energy costs associated with a normal classroom setting. Students enrolled in these proposed "virtual classrooms" would be taught by the same instructors who currently teach these classes, and the curriculum would not be changed. Lectures would be broadcast live, not prerecorded, and students would be able to interact with the instructors in real time through a private text-based chat program.

Which of the following, if true, would weaken the case for the adoption of the president's proposal?

(A) The university will be able to enroll more students in an introductory course taught in a virtual classroom than if the course were held in a traditional classroom.

(B) Much of the value of an introductory course stems from the spontaneous exchange of ideas between students in face-to-face discussions.

(C) Many students in the university's introductory classes have jobs and other demands on their time.

(D) The students at the university are accustomed to using computers to communicate with their instructors.

(E) Prerecorded lectures have been shown to have little negative impact on the ability of students to engage with their instructors.

Your Critical Reasoning Diagnosis

Congratulations on managing a full set of Critical Reasoning questions!

Before we go on, first check your answers against the following key.

ANSWER KEY

1. **(A)**	5. **(E)**	9. **(D)**	13. **(B)**
2. **(C)**	6. **(B)**	10. **(C)**	
3. **(E)**	7. **(D)**	11. **(C)**	
4. **(C)**	8. **(B)**	12. **(E)**	

There are 13 different types of Critical Reasoning questions, and it's no coincidence that there were 13 questions in the Diagnostic Quiz. Each question was drawn from a different one of the 13 types.

Obviously, you're not expected to have gotten all of the questions on the Diagnostic Quiz correct. But now that you've seen some GMAT questions up close and personal, you've got an excellent opportunity to figure out where your current strengths and weaknesses lie. Over the course of your GMAT Verbal studies, you'll need to do some work on all the different types of questions, even the ones you're already good at. As you read the following sections, which discuss the question types in more depth, use your performance on this Diagnostic Quiz as a guide to what you need to focus the most attention on initially.

In the discussion that follows, we're not going to focus solely on whether you got the question right or wrong. Picking the right answer is obviously important, but working with answers is only one of the skills you need for Critical Reasoning. It's also important for you to determine whether you understood the question as a whole, whether you were able to identify conclusions and evidence in the questions that involved arguments, and whether you were able to tell when a question was giving you an argument or when it was giving you a set of facts to make some inferences from.

Beneath each explanation below, you'll see a series of boxes to check. At the end of the discussion of the questions, you'll be asked to count up the number of boxes of each type you ticked off so that you can get a rough gauge of your ability at each of the skills indicated.

1. Because the stem asks us to find a *weak point* in an argument, we know this a **Flaw** question, part of the **Assumption** family of **Argument-Based** questions. The prompt is divided up between two speakers, Harry and Susan, and Susan's statement is the argument the stem indicates is flawed. All flaws are some kind of unwarranted assumption. Here, Susan's conclusion is that *Harry's proposal (reducing the use of fossil fuels) will be bad for the economy.* She cites as evidence one possible disadvantage, that *if refineries close, lots of people will lose their jobs.*

Susan makes a kind of argument that will become very familiar as you study for the GMAT: she's making a **net calculation** about a plan. Whenever such arguments are made, the person making them must assume that *there are no other relevant advantages or disadvantages* that might change the **advantage/disadvantage** balance. Answer Choice (A) describes this unwarranted assumption exactly. Susan's assuming that the one disadvantage she cites is inevitable, and this answer shows us how it might not be.

- ☐ **Recognized** as an Argument-Based Question
- ☐ **Identified** the Conclusion Correctly
- ☐ **Understood** the Evidence
- ☐ **Predicted** the Missing Assumption
- ☐ **Selected** the Right Answer

2. Zzzolution™ and the right dosage to prescribe was part of an **Evaluate** question, another member of the **Assumption** family of **Argument-Based** questions. In these questions, we're asked what piece of evidence would be "most useful to know" in order to "evaluate" the argument. We put those words in scare quotes because the wording makes it sound more complicated than it is. All the test maker wants you to do is to find an assumption in the argument and then pick an answer choice that would test whether the assumption was true or false.

The argument's conclusion is that *this hard-to-pronounce sleeping pill should only be prescribed at a dosage of 20 mg or less.* The evidence given for this recommendation is the result of a study that found, after comparing two groups, the group taking 20 mg was more efficient and consistent when doing their normal day-to-day activities than the group that took 40 mg. Whenever an argument invokes the authority of a **study**, it brings with it lots of assumptions. The relevant one for this question is that *there's nothing special about either group that's relevant to the conclusion.*

The correct Answer Choice (C) provides a way to test that assumption, on the issue of sleep. If the people taking the 40-mg dose wouldn't be able to sleep on the 20-mg dose, then that would be something special about one of the groups that would be relevant to the conclusion that everybody should take 20-mg doses.

- ☐ **Recognized** as an Argument-Based Question
- ☐ **Identified** the Conclusion Correctly
- ☐ **Understood** the Evidence
- ☐ **Predicted** the Missing Assumption
- ☐ **Selected** the Right Answer

3. This was your first question from the **Fact-Based** category of questions, one you'll soon learn to recognize as an **Explain** question. In these questions, instead of an argument with evidence and conclusion, you're given an information dump about a situation that, as presented, seems kind of weird. Something that ought to be happening isn't happening. With these questions, your first task is to **identify the two parts of the dilemma.** Here, the **dilemma** is an **expectation** that failed to come true. There's reason to think that (1) helmets should reduce the injury rate, but instead (2) the rate rose after helmets were made mandatory.

It's generally hard to predict what the right answer to an Explain question will look like, so once you have the dilemma's two parts in mind, you can proceed to the answer choices to perform a process of elimination. The right answer will bridge the gap between the two parts of the dilemma. Here, Answer Choice (E) does the trick: if the law requiring helmets made the ski resort less popular with the sorts of skiers who tend to know best how to avoid accidents—the experts—then it makes sense that the injury rate rose after the law. The helmets are still preventing accidents; the resort just has more accidents per capita because of the new composition of its population of skiers.

☐ **Recognized** as a Fact-Based Question
☐ **Identified** the Two Parts of the Dilemma
☐ **Understood** the Gap Between the Two Parts
☐ **Selected** the Right Answer

4. The **bolded** statements are the tipoff. This is a **Bolded Statement** question, part of the **Structure** family of **Argument-Based** questions. This question prompt presents a two-part argument. The CEO has a plan that the Consultant disagrees with. Your job is to say what role the bolded statements play in the exchange. Often, with these questions, it's easiest to pick one bolded statement and use it to do a process of elimination with the answer choices.

The second bolded statement is probably the easier of the two. We know the Consultant disagrees with the CEO's claim, so Answer Choice (E) is out. We also know that the Consultant's conclusion is the last line, that *even more customers will be lost if the plan is enacted.* The bolded statement is evidence in support of that conclusion, not a conclusion itself, so Answer Choices (D) and (A) would also go. Left with Answer Choices (C) and (B), we can eliminate (B), because the Consultant doesn't disagree with the CEO's evidence (though the Consultant does oppose the CEO's conclusion). The Consultant just states a fact that the CEO didn't take into account.

If we'd chosen instead to use the first statement, we could eliminate Answer Choice (D), but all the rest are probably OK. Describing a conclusion as a prediction is fine when that conclusion is actually a prediction, and the CEO's certainly is. He's concluding that *sales will rise.*

☐ **Recognized** as an Argument-Based Question
☐ **Identified** the Conclusion correctly (in both arguments)
☐ **Understood** the Evidence
☐ **Selected** the Right Answer

5. "Inferred" in the stem lets us know this is an **Inference** question, the most common kind of **Fact-Based** question. As with Explain questions, the information in the prompt is just a collection of facts; our job is to find an answer choice that must be true if we take those facts to be true. When you read through the prompt of an **Inference** question, look for the most definite pieces of information, the elements that are *always* or *never* the case, the things true of *everybody* or *anyone.* Here, there's one definite piece of information, the last sentence. Saying that something is *absolutely vital* is a way of saying that it is *required.* Thus, this fancy machinery is *required* for *the full display of Lucas's artistic skill.* Any theater that displays Lucas's full artistic skill must have this machinery, and any theater lacking it will be unable to display said artistic skill.

As luck would have it, the prompt also tells us something about *many theaters.* They lack this machinery. Thus, they will be unable to display Lucas's skill—and that's why Answer Choice (E) is the right answer. Apply the rule in the prompt and you get a close paraphrase of Answer Choice (E).

- ☐ **Recognized** as a Fact-Based Question
- ☐ **Identified** the Definite Information in the Prompt
- ☐ **Understood** How to Apply That Information
- ☐ **Selected** the Right Answer

6. Question 6 is one of those sneaky **Complete** questions that can either belong to the **Assumption** family or to the **Fact-Based** category, depending on what the keywords near the blank tell us is missing from the argument. Here, the word *because* tells us the blank is missing some *evidence*, which makes this a **Complete (Evidence)** question and a member of the **Assumption** family. Like all its familial cohorts, **Complete (Evidence)** questions require us to find the conclusion and see how the evidence is connected to it.

In this prompt, the conclusion is a **recommendation** about what *must* be done to solve a problem (that violent crime rates are going up in tandem with the increase in violent movies). The speaker recommends banning anyone younger than 18 from seeing the films and offers a single piece of evidence in support: *teenagers emulate the behavior they see in movies*. To complete the argument, we need to provide an extra piece of evidence that covers one of the argument's assumptions.

This argument does have a lot of assumptions! Just because teens tend to emulate what they see in movies doesn't necessarily mean that they're responsible for the increase in violent crime in the city. Maybe they just act violently towards each other, or play violent video games. To cover the assumption, we need information that makes it more likely the teens actually are up to no good. Answer Choice (B) works because it addresses the hanging *crime* issue. If teens are unable to resist criminal behavior, then it's more likely that their movie habits are the cause of the crime increase—as unlikely as that would be in the real world.

- ☐ **Recognized** as an Argument-Based Question
- ☐ **Identified** the Conclusion Correctly
- ☐ **Understood** the Evidence
- ☐ **Predicted** the Missing Assumption
- ☐ **Selected** the Right Answer

7. Because this question asks us *how* someone's argument works, it belongs in the **Structure** family of **Argument-Based** questions. It's a **Method of Argument** question, to be more specific. For these questions, the right answer will describe the way that the argument's evidence is used to support its conclusion.

The Manager's conclusion is to the point: *this program is poorly designed.* To support that claim, the Manager offers reasonable evidence, citing the terrible experiences with the program had by other companies similar to the Manager's company. The correct answer, (D), might have thrown the unwary, as it describes only a small part of the Manager's method of argument, the first few words in which the Manager accepts the Program Director's claim that the program was designed with the Manager's company in mind. Thus, (D) is the answer. Sneaky!

- ☐ **Recognized** as an Argument-Based Question
- ☐ **Identified** Both Conclusions Correctly
- ☐ **Understood** the Evidence
- ☐ **Selected** the Right Answer

8. The word *assumption* tells us, naturally, that this is an **Assumption** question. We'll be discussing this question in depth a bit later in this chapter. For now, the important thing is knowing whether you recognized it as an **Argument-Based** question and knew from that that you needed to find the argument's conclusion and characterize its evidence in order to find any gaps. The conclusion is stated in the last sentence: *postcolonial literature is harmful to its readers.* In support of this, the author provides no evidence that describes a harm, only some features of postcolonial literature. Thus, the argument assumes that *at least one of the things the evidence says that postcolonial literature does is harmful somehow.* Answer Choice (B) nails that assumption, though it does try to hide it under a layer of **double-negatives** (is beneficial to avoid = is bad to not avoid = is harmful).

- ☐ **Recognized** as an Argument-Based Question
- ☐ **Identified** the Conclusion Correctly
- ☐ **Understood** the Evidence
- ☐ **Predicted** the Missing Assumption
- ☐ **Selected** the Right Answer

9. Like Question 6, this is a **Complete** question, but the *therefore* before the blank classifies it instead as a **Complete (Conclusion)** question, a member of the **Fact-Based** category of questions. Because you'll be drawing a conclusion from some facts rather than identifying a conclusion, the task ahead is a lot like an Inference question. The right answer choice will follow if all the information in the prompt is taken to be true. When we read the prompt, we should be on the lookout for **definite** information, rules, and categorical statements, which are the things inferences are made of.

Here, there's a *lot* of definite information, and the challenge is just lining it all up to keep it straight. To fill the blank, we need a definite way to tell flying ants from honey bees. According to the rules above, honey bees are the *only* members of the order Hymenoptera that have *a strongly barbed stinger.* The prompt also tells us that flying ants are in the order Hymenoptera. Thus, a quick check of the ant's stinger will solve our problem. If the stinger of an insect in order Hymenoptera is not strongly barbed, then the insect in question is not a honey bee. Answer Choice (D) spells out this connection.

- ☐ **Recognized** as a Fact-Based Question
- ☐ **Identified** the Definite Information
- ☐ **Understood** How to Apply That Information
- ☐ **Selected** the Right Answer

10. When we see *a pattern of reasoning most similar* in the stem, we know we're dealing with a **Parallel Argument** question, a member of the **Structure** family that asks us to compare the argument in the prompt with five different arguments in the answer choices and find the prompt-answer pair that have the same structure. With these questions, you need to be able to describe the argument's structure in extremely abstract language, ignoring the content. The right answer choice almost never has anything to do with the original argument in subject matter, only in structure.

The argument in the prompt has a very safe conclusion: *Paula has at least part of what she needs.* It supports this conclusion with a rule that establishes a **requirement**: *in order to get to Carnegie Hall, practice is required.* It also provides information that lets us know that the requirement has been met: *Paula practices*. The correct answer, (C), has this precise structure. It has a safe conclusion (*It "might" be Spring*), which it backs up with a rule that establishes a requirement (*When it's Spring, I can't stop sneezing*) and information that the requirement has been met (*I can't stop sneezing.*)

When it's Spring, I can't stop sneezing might not have seemed like much of a requirement to you when you read the argument initially. In a later section, we'll discuss the basics of Formal Logic, the rules that govern requirements and guarantees. We won't get technical about it now, but the secret is to rephrase either statement and you'll see how they're the same:

If it is Spring, I cannot stop sneezing = If you are at Carnegie Hall, you must have practiced.

- ☐ **Recognized** as an Argument-Based Question
- ☐ **Identified** the Conclusion Correctly
- ☐ **Understood** the Evidence and the Argument's Structure
- ☐ **Selected** the Right Answer

11. Here we have another **Argument-Based** question from the **Structure** family. The stem tells us to describe how a part of an argument *is used*, meaning this is a **Role of a State-ment** question. To understand the role, you have to understand the argument, so identifying the conclusion and evidence is still your first step. This argument's conclusion follows a common pattern: **people who say X are wrong**—in this case, *managers who think that pay and effort should be proportional are wrong*. That conclusion is sup-ported, in part, by the piece of the argument about which the stem is asking us. Thus, the role of that statement is that it's a piece of evidence.

We usually have to be a smidge more specific with Role of a Statement questions, so we would also need to realize that this piece of evidence is a sort of **counterexample**, a prediction of an **undesirable consequence** that would follow if the argument were accepted. Answer Choice (C) describes that precisely.

- ☐ **Recognized** as an Argument-Based Question
- ☐ **Identified** the Conclusion Correctly
- ☐ **Understood** the Evidence and the Argument's Structure
- ☐ **Selected** the Right Answer

12. This question features another **people who say X are wrong** pattern to its reasoning, but the stem asks you to make the argument better, making it a **Strengthen** question, a member of the **Assumption** family of **Argument-Based** questions. Start by finding the conclusion. The *people who say X* are identified in the first line, those who *say that fund-ing this particle accelerator will only benefit a few physicists;* the *are wrong* doesn't show up until the last sentence, which goes one step further than just saying these people are wrong. They're wrong, and thus the argument concludes that *this accelerator should be built immediately*.

This conclusion is supported only by the evidence that other inventions that were ultimately beneficial also had "people who say" opposed to them, which means that the argument assumes that *the particle accelerator case is similar enough to the other cases that what is true of one is true of the other*. Soon, you'll learn to call this a **representative-ness** assumption, a very common GMAT argument pattern.

The stem also contains a common pattern, in this case a word that changes what we should expect from the answer choices: **principle**. When a GMAT question asks you for a principle, the right answer will be phrased as a **general rule** rather than as a description of the specific case at hand. The rule will still strengthen the argument in the same way as a specific description would, by supporting the unstated *representativeness* assumption. Answer Choice (E) does this exactly. If we follow this answer's principle, we will treat any case in which a potential action has naysayers the same, by going full steam ahead and doing the action.

- ☐ **Recognized** as an Argument-Based Question
- ☐ **Identified** the Conclusion Correctly
- ☐ **Understood** the Evidence
- ☐ **Predicted** the Missing Assumption
- ☐ **Selected** the Right Answer

13. Question 13 is Question 12's opposite number, a **Weaken** question, also part of the **Assumption** family of **Argument-Based** questions. Up until the final step, you'll treat Weaken questions the same as Strengthen questions, by finding the argument's conclusion, considering how the evidence is linked to the conclusion, and finding a gap that an unstated assumption is needed to cover. The only difference is that the correct answer will make the assumption *less* believable.

The stem tips off the argument's conclusion, the president's proposal to *move some intro classes online in order to save money*. When arguments present a proposal, the conclusion is almost always that *this proposal will work*. Such an argument inevitably assumes that *there are no disadvantages to the plan that would outweigh the advantages cited in the argument*, a kind of **net calculation** about the **advantage/disadvantage** balance (as we saw back in Question 1).

The advantages cited are that the online classes would be similar in a lot of ways but would still cost less overall. To weaken the assumption, we simply look for evidence in an answer choice of a possible disadvantage, and we find that in Answer Choice (B). If a lot of value will be lost, then the advantage of savings might be outweighed by the decrease in quality.

- ☐ **Recognized** as an Argument-Based Question
- ☐ **Identified** the Conclusion Correctly
- ☐ **Understood** the Evidence
- ☐ **Predicted** the Missing Assumption
- ☐ **Selected** the Right Answer

The Final Diagnostic Analysis

Use the boxes below to total what you did well in the section and the things you didn't and consult the information below for a better idea of how to improve these fundamental GMAT Critical Reasoning skills.

Recognizing the Task

In Argument-Based Questions _____ of 10 boxes checked
(Qs 1–2, 4, 6–8, 10–13)

In Assumption Family Questions _____ of 6 boxes checked
(Qs 1–2, 6, 8, 12–13)

In Structure Family Questions _____ of 4 boxes checked
(Qs 4, 7, 10–11)

In Fact-Based Questions _____ of 3 boxes checked
(Qs 3, 5, 9)

Overall _____ of 13 boxes checked
(all Qs)

Always read the stem first when attacking a GMAT Critical Reasoning question because it allows you to determine what you're supposed to be paying attention to when you read the information in the prompt.

In each of the sections that follows, the discussion will begin with a few sample stems. The keywords repeated across each type of question are relatively few in number and easily committed to memory. Note, however, that most successful GMAT test takers don't just memorize a list of keywords and apply them mechanically; instead, focus on how the keywords describe the *task* that each question demands.

For example, **Strengthen** questions and **Inference** questions use the same keywords to describe dramatically different tasks. A **Strengthen** question could ask *which of the following, if true, most supports the argument above?* An **Inference** question, on the other hand, could ask *which of the following is most supported by the argument above?* The *direction* of the support is more important than the word *support* itself. If the answers support the argument, it's a **Strengthen** question; if the argument/prompt supports the answers, then it's an **Inference** question.

Identifying the Conclusion
(Qs 1–2, 4, 6–8, 10–13) _____ of 10 boxes checked

In the sections that follow, you'll learn the three most powerful techniques for identifying an argument's conclusion.

LOOK FOR CONCLUSION KEYWORDS—Words like *thus*, *therefore*, and *in conclusion* usually—but not always!—indicate a conclusion. When you spot one, don't assume you've found what you're looking for; be sure to verify that what follows is actually the conclusion of the argument. For easy reference, you'll find a list of the most common GMAT argument keywords on page 307.

USE THE WHAT/WHY TEMPLATE—As we discussed in the previous section on **Arguments and Facts**, all arguments can be put into the form [CONCLUSION] because [EVIDENCE] or [WHAT] because [WHY]. If you think you've found the conclusion, but you're not sure, try rephrasing the argument so that it fits the template. If the thing you're identifying as the conclusion is never explained by the evidence, then you've probably got it the wrong way around.

RECOGNIZE THE MOST COMMON ARGUMENT PATTERNS—The more experience you get with the GMAT question writers' ticks and habits, the easier it will be to find the conclusion. While there is probably an infinite number of ways that an argument *could* be phrased, the GMAT tends to stick to only a few variations. You'll find these discussed starting on page 336.

Identifying Dilemmas and
Definite Statements (Qs 3, 5, 9)   _____ of 3 boxes checked

The most common difficulty test takers have with Inference and Explain questions is that they read the prompt thinking that there is no way to predict what the answer choices might bring up. On the one hand, they're right; the specific wording or new information you find in these answer choices is often designed to seem unfamiliar. On the other hand, you can't make a GMAT-approved inference with just any old piece of information. The inference must be supported by something definite, a rule or an otherwise categorical statement like *this always happens* or *this is required for that*.

Familiarize yourself with the most common Inference question setups (pages 357–364). You'll find as you work through GMAT practice problems, you're really being asked to do the same sort of inference process again and again.

The same can be said of Explain question prompts. It's true that the right answer will bring up something completely new, but you can prepare yourself for the answers by understanding what sort of information you're looking for. Practice finding the two sides of each little dilemma or paradox presented in these questions.

Understanding Information in the Prompt

In Fact-Based Questions   _____ of 3 boxes checked
(Qs 3, 5, 9)

In Argument-Based Questions   _____ of 10 boxes checked
(Qs 1–2, 4, 6–8, 10–13)

In Assumption Family Questions   _____ of 6 boxes checked
(Qs 1–2, 6, 8, 12–13)

In Structure Family Questions   _____ of 4 boxes checked
(Qs 4, 7, 10–11)

Overall   _____ of 13 boxes checked
(all Qs)

"Understanding Information" is a necessarily broad category that describes several GMAT skills. When you're practicing GMAT questions, be honest with yourself during the review process, after you've worked the question, and while you're reading over the answers and explanations. How much of the argument or fact pattern did you *really* understand, and how much of it did you just have a "feeling" about? Slow down as you read question prompts, and ask yourself, "OK, so what's going on here?" If you find you don't know what an argument says, either go back and reread it or sacrifice the question by guessing and move on.

You don't pick up speed on a standardized test by short-changing your understanding of the information in the questions. Clumsy, rushed, or otherwise too-swift strategies almost always lead to earning fewer points in the long run.

Predicting Missing Assumptions
(Qs 1–2, 6, 8, 12–13)   _____ of 6 boxes checked

The single most important key to understanding more than half of the Critical Reasoning questions on the GMAT is the ability to see the gap between the evidence and the conclusion *before you look at the answers.*

The most common reason that test takers fail to see the assumptions beneath an argument's explicit evidence is that they don't understand the definition of an assumption. That's why we've devoted an entire section to defining assumptions in the most helpful ways.

Depending on the argument, you might think of an assumption as *anything not stated that the argument needs to be true*, or as *the information that makes the evidence relevant to the conclusion*, or as *information that rules out any possible exceptions or roadblocks.* These are three different ways of saying the same thing: assumptions are the bare minimum extra information that the argument *needs* to cover a *lack of information* about a critical idea.

Lean heavily on the most common argument structures as well when searching for an argument's assumptions. Two arguments that share the same structure likely share a similar sort of assumption. For instance, whenever an argument relies on an **analogy**, we know that at least one of the assumptions is that the two items said to be similar in one way are also *similar in all the ways needed for the conclusion to be true.* Learn to spot the GMAT's patterns and you'll have a shortcut to knowing the assumptions being tested.

Selecting the Right Answer

In Argument-Based Questions   _____ of 10 boxes checked
(Qs 1–2, 4, 6–8, 10–13)

In Structure Family Questions   _____ of 4 boxes checked
(Qs 4, 7, & 10–11)

In Assumption Family Questions   _____ of 6 boxes checked
(Qs 1–2, 6, 8, 12–13)

In Fact-Based Questions   _____ of 3 boxes checked
(Qs 3, 5, 9)

Overall   _____ of 13 boxes checked
(all Qs)

The reason the GMAT frustrates so many is that even when you know the task you're supposed to do, and even when you understand everything in the argument, you can still end up picking the wrong answer choice. When you look at the Answers and Explanations, you think, "Oh! How did I not see that?" A better question would be, "What did this question do to *keep* me from seeing it?"

The question writers back at GMAT HQ aren't professional psychologists or sociologists, but they do employ psychological and sociological research in order to craft answer choices that seem right when they're not or that appeal to a certain sort of test taker or a certain type of mindset. Don't let yourself be satisfied with the explanation, "I just need to read more carefully," as you could *always* be more careful. Instead, keep a record of the ways you've been fooled and during subsequent reviews, compare your performance against the record. A diary or journal is often useful for this. You'll eventually come to understand what scenarios or tricks you're vulnerable to and how to recognize them during a test session.

Also, during the discussion of each type of question in the sections that follows, we'll be sure to outline the most common ways the test maker throws you off the scent of the right answer or makes you bite too soon on a wrong answer.

THE ARGUMENT STRUCTURE FAMILY OF QUESTIONS

Anatomy of an Argument Structure Question

Prompt

Some managers believe that the hourly wage that an employee receives ought to be proportional to the effort required by that job's typical duties, but it would be terrible if a business actually followed this advice, as it would mean that those employees with the least ability to perform their jobs adequately would be entitled to the highest hourly wages, a perverse incentive.

Stem

The claim that employees with the least ability to perform their job adequately would be entitled to the highest hourly wages is used in the argument as

Answer Choices

(A) a general principle that provides a reason in favor of adopting a disagreeable practice illustrated elsewhere in the argument.

(B) a potentially unpopular general principle that is illustrated by a list of reasons that its adoption would be favorable.

(C) an undesirable consequence that would follow from the adoption of a general principle described elsewhere in the argument.

(D) a piece of evidence that discredits a general principle under consideration by showing that the principle could not be uniformly applied.

(E) a possible consequence said to follow from a general principle's adoption that some incorrectly describe as inevitable.

Prompt

- All contain an **argument** that has a specific **conclusion** and one or more pieces of **evidence**.
- Keywords like *therefore* or *thus* are often absent or used misleadingly.
- Often the prompt contains more than one point of view—someone is **responding** to someone else or to a **commonly held** belief.

Stem

- Most include the actual word **argument** or a close synonym like **reasoning.**
- Will make reference to the **function, role**, or how a piece is **used in** or **factors into** the argument.

Answer Choices

- Abstract descriptive terms and answers that differ in only small ways are the norm.
- Can often be grouped into twos and threes that share the same part.

Identifying Argument Structure Questions

There are four different ways that a GMAT question might ask about an argument's structure. Sometimes, the question will ask only about a part of the argument and the role it plays in the argument as a whole. If the part is highlighted in **boldface**, we call it a **Bolded Statement** question. If there's no boldface, but you're still only looking at a part of the argument, then you're dealing with a **Role of a Statement** question. Most Bolded Statement questions are just two Role of a Statement questions stitched together. You're asked about two roles for the price of one argument.

The other two types of structural questions ask you to describe the argument as a whole, how it comes to its evidence is used to come to its conclusion. **Method of Argument** questions ask for that description directly, whereas **Parallel Argument** questions ask you to find the argument in the answer choices that has the same structure as the one in the prompt.

Because of the specific ways each of the four questions is phrased, you'll be able to identify the task just by looking at the stem.

ROLE OF A STATEMENT

A few ways Role of a Statement stems might be phrased:

- In the argument above, the statement that all wolves born in the wild are able to recognize their pack's leader plays which of the following roles
- The claim that the comptroller has overlooked the value of the finance department is used in the auditor's response as a
- In the passage above, the reference to a possible reduction in foreign oil production serves primarily to

Occasionally, a Role of a Statement question works in the opposite direction, naming a role and asking you to find the statement that plays that role:

- Which of the following states the main conclusion of the argument above?
- In defending the position above, the inspector offers which of the following as evidence?

METHOD OF ARGUMENT

The most common stems for Method of Argument questions include:

- In the passage, the author **develops** the **argument** by
- Which of the following best describes the **rhetorical strategy** used above?
- The statement that X **plays which role** in the **argument** above?
- In making his **claim**, the judge's use of Y **serves to**

A second style of Method of Argument stem usually occurs with prompts that contain more than one point of view and uses some synonym of the word *responds*:

- The farmer **responds** to the rancher's argument by
- The rancher **addresses** the issue by

BOLDED STATEMENT

Look for the **bolded parts**. Enough said!

PARALLEL ARGUMENT

Parallel Argument stems describe both the prompt and the answer choices as containing arguments and ask you to find the two that are *similar* or *parallel*:

- The reasoning above is most similar to that found in which of the following?
- The argument above contains reasoning most similar to which of the following answer choices?
- The argument above most closely parallels which of the following arguments?

Processing Argument Structure Prompts

Obviously there's always going to be an argument in the prompt, one composed of a conclusion and the pieces of evidence given in support of the conclusion. About half the time, there will be more than one argument present. Sometimes this is done explicitly, by dividing the prompt between two different speakers:

> Trina: Fish taste like squishy salt. We shouldn't serve fish tonight because our guests will be disgusted.

> Levon: But many of our guests are fishermen. They enjoy the taste of fish. The question isn't whether we should serve fish, but how many different types of fish to serve!

Other times, the second argument is presented by a speaker who intends to present an argument to the contrary:

> Chef: While some people may believe that fish tastes like "squishy salt," they are wrong to try to dictate the menu at a fine restaurant. Anyone who would describe the taste of fish in such a crass way clearly lacks a refined palate and should be ignored.

In other words, you'll see a lot of speakers in Argument Structure prompts arguing against other people, sometimes given titles or other descriptions like *environmentalists* or *the distinguished councilor*, but just as often left anonymous, merely *those who would say* or *some people*.

Pay careful attention if the question stem identified someone. Often, this means that the question will be about the method of argument of the person being argued *against*, rather than the argument's main speaker.

Whenever you see a speaker say something like, "But it would be wrong to think that" or "It is absurd to believe this," you've probably just been given the conclusion. Find what the *this* or *that* is referring to, and rephrase the conclusion into the author's position. For example:

> Critics often claim that the value of a work of art is inextricably linked to the circumstances in which it was created, but in this they are clearly mistaken, for [...]

"In this they are clearly mistaken" is the conclusion. What is "this" referring to? The claim that "the value of a work of art is inextricably linked to the circumstances in which it was created." Put the two together, and the conclusion of the speaker's argument becomes

> Art is not inextricably linked to the circumstances in which it was created.

Attacking Argument Structure Answer Choices

Recognizing the right answer choice will depend on your ability to describe the argument's parts using abstract terminology and descriptions rather than content. Answers, both wrong and right, will look more like

> The author rebuts a potential criticism to a general rule by showing the criticism to apply only to a small minority of instances in which that rule might be applied.

than

> The author argues that buying flea collars for your dog is still a good idea even though some particularly inbred poodles are allergic to flea collars.

The same argument is being described in each; the first is just using abstract vocabulary to do so.

IDENTIFYING CONCLUSIONS AND EVIDENCE

The first step to every Argument-Based question is to locate the conclusion of the argument given in the prompt. If you can't find the conclusion, you won't be able to identify the argument's structure, nor will you be able to consider the assumptions that underlie the argument. So how do you go about finding it?

Technique #1: Look for the Keywords

Sometimes, the speaker in the prompt just comes out and says, "Hey, lookie here, this is my conclusion." OK, so they don't put it that way exactly, but they might as well. Instead, speakers direct your attention to their conclusion by tagging it with "therefore," or "thus," or, our personal favorite, "in conclusion." These are conclusion keywords, and about half the arguments on the test have them.

TIP

Keywords are like road signs. When you spot one, it puts you on the lookout for something ahead.

THE MOST COMMON GMAT CONCLUSION KEYWORDS

thus	accordingly	may conclude
therefore	as a result	in conclusion
hence	for this reason	in the end
clearly	it follows that	from this
so	this shows that	
consequently	must be that	

Of course, not every prompt is so nice. Sometimes you can find the conclusion by looking for *evidence* keywords, eliminating everything following them; what you have left is likely your conclusion. This is most often the case when the conclusion comes at the beginning of the argument.

THE MOST COMMON GMAT EVIDENCE KEYWORDS

as	in that	as we know
because	given that	the studies found that
since	due to	this can be seen from/in
for	according to	we know this by
for example	as indicated by	

Using Keywords Drill

DIRECTIONS: Use the following short arguments to test your ability to spot keywords and to use them to identify an argument's conclusion and evidence. In each sentence, circle the keywords and underline the conclusion.

1. Our car is almost out of gas, so we need to find a gas station.

2. Since we're saving our money to buy a house, we must stop spending so much on impulse purchases.

3. The industry should focus its efforts on suing those who use the TorrentBit software, as these are the easiest pirates to catch and usually the most damaging.

4. Video games have a beneficial effect on society, overall. This can be seen from the lower incidence of youth crime in neighborhoods affluent enough that most young people own video game systems.

5. The economist's prediction, thus, cannot be accepted as given because it ignores key data.

6. "Therefore" is an excellent way to tell if an argument's conclusion is coming; thus, you should always be on the lookout for it.

DRILL REVIEW

1. "So" is the conclusion keyword that lets you know that "we need to find a gas station" is the argument's conclusion.

2. "Since" indicates evidence; the conclusion then is "we must stop spending so much on impulse purchases."

3. "As" is a subtle way of flagging evidence; the conclusion is found earlier: "the industry should focus its efforts on suing those who use the TorrentBit software."

4. "This can be seen from" is a two-way keyword, indicating evidence to come and a conclusion before, here "Video games have a beneficial effect on society."

5. "Thus" flags the conclusion and "because" the evidence. Either would lead to recognizing "The economist's prediction cannot be accepted as given" as the conclusion.

6. "Thus" here is the conclusion keyword that points to "you should always be on the lookout for it" as the conclusion. (And the "Therefore" was put there just to make sure you hadn't fallen asleep!)

Technique #2: The Types of Conclusion and Evidence

Suppose an argument lacks any identifying keywords (or that it has too many). What would you do then? One way to find the conclusion is to look for "the most conclusionary part."

While there's an infinite number of possible arguments that could be made in English, all argument conclusions can be sorted into a handful of categories that describe the *type* of claim the conclusion makes. Not just anything can be a conclusion.

THE MOST COMMON GMAT CONCLUSION TYPES

PREDICTION—A conclusion about what *will* happen, what *is going to* happen, what *ought to* occur, what *can be expected*, etc.

> The Hendersons will arrive tomorrow. Winning the bid will make a profit for the company. If Thomas enters the race, he will lose.

RECOMMENDATION—A conclusion about what someone *should* or *ought* to do, often phrased as a plan or proposal to meet a goal spelled out earlier.

> The company should invest in new machinery. People who want to be loved should learn to love others. The best way to get to Carnegie Hall is to practice.

BARE ASSERTION—A conclusion about what *is* the case, what *is true* about a situation or phenomenon, what someone *should believe* about a particular case. This is the most common type of conclusion.

> Petra is an excellent dancer. The building is structurally unsound. Hydrogen indicates contamination.

VALUE JUDGMENT—A conclusion about what is right or wrong and what is moral or immoral. These are relatively rare on the GMAT and can usually be treated as a more specific type of recommendation.

> One should never lie. Pol Pot was history's worst dictator.

CAUSAL CONNECTION—A conclusion that asserts that one thing *is responsible for, brought about*, or *caused* some other thing. These are usually established on the basis of a correlation between two things.

> Rain makes the flowers grow. The earthquake knocked the buildings down. Static electricity is responsible for your hair being so hard to manage.

Argument Structure questions in particular often turn on your ability to describe the argument's conclusion according to one of these categories.

But be careful when the answer choices to such questions further characterize conclusions as *recommendations, predictions,* etc., because it can be very easy to mistake one for the other. The verb used in the conclusion is the best sign as to what type of conclusion you have, but because of the way English plays fast and loose with the future tense (allowing *will*, *ought to*, and even *is to* as future indicators), even these can be misleading, particularly in distinguishing recommendations and predictions. As a rule of thumb, think of these examples:

> You will not shout in this room.
> You should not shout in this room.
> You cannot shout in this room.

The first is a **prediction** of what will happen. Regardless of whether shouting is allowed or not, it is not going to happen.

The second is a **recommendation**. While people might choose to ignore the rules and shout anyway, it's not *allowed* in the room.

The third is ambiguous. It *might* be a **recommendation**. You can't shout here because it isn't allowed. But it might be a simple **bare assertion**, too. You can't shout in this room because it is in outer space and there's no air (i.e., it's impossible). Sometimes, context is still necessary to decide what type of conclusion you're dealing with.

Just as with keywords, often you can narrow down to the conclusion by identifying things that are almost always evidence.

THE MOST COMMON GMAT EVIDENCE TYPES

STUDIES, POLLS, EXPERIMENTS, AND SURVEYS—Usually evidence because the conclusion is not an argument proving what the study *said* but rather how people are interpreting it or what it means.

> Recent research found a connection between …, 4 out of
> 5 dentists surveyed …, We asked our listeners …

LONG-HELD BELIEFS—Watch for arguments that tell you that something has been thought, believed, or considered for a long time. Usually, this will be evidence for a conclusion to come.

> Scientists have long known that …, History tells us that …, It is a
> truism that …

GOALS AND PLANS—Rarely will an argument try to convince you that something *is* the goal or that a plan *is being considered*; rather, the conclusion is usually that a goal will be met or a plan will succeed.

> The city has enacted an ordinance to …, In order to reduce
> costs …, In response to rising unemployment …

RECOGNIZING SETUP INFORMATION

All three of the most common types of evidence could be grouped under a heading that we've already used in passing earlier: **setup information**.

You know by now that the GMAT forbids you to use any information from the world outside the test in order to select the right answer. Because of this restriction, you can think of each new Critical Reasoning prompt as a little world unto itself.

Consider this argument prompt:

> Because they construct such elaborate and intricate nests, male
> weaver birds are often considered nature's avian artists. Because
> weaver nests share features with those built near them that they
> do not share with those built by males farther away, researchers
> have suggested that the style of nest that a male weaver bird
> builds is at least partially determined by information obtained
> during the lifetime of the individual bird and is not completely a
> function of a particular sequence of genes.

The first line isn't really direct evidence for the argument's conclusion, the researchers' hypothesis found later on. Instead, it establishes that, in the world of this particular Critical Reasoning prompt, there are birds and that they do this interesting thing with their nests.

But the first line also isn't being argued. It's not at stake, so it can't be the conclusion. The argument isn't trying to convince you that weaver birds do what they do. The conclusion is an *explanation* for why they do it.

Don't think of **setup information** as "fluff" or "filler." Very often, the difference between the credited answer and an incorrect but tempting one will be a little detail from the setup. Suppose the prompt above had a stem attached that asked you what the argument assumes. A wrong answer might well try to distract you by bringing up details from the setup.

> **(A)** Artistic species are seldom found in nature.

As stated, the argument doesn't require us to believe that the behavior of these birds is rare, even though it seems reasonable to believe it is. Reasonable but irrelevant answers, as always, are opportunities for the lazy reader to take an easy out.

The right answer might use vocabulary from the setup in order to disguise its correctness:

> **(B)** Elaborate or intricate features found in the work of
> geographically proximate species are unlikely to be similar
> purely by chance.

Answer Choice (B) is probably not how you would have prephrased the assumption, but a part of learning how to use your prephrased prediction is learning how to adapt it to the vocabulary used in the passage.

Types of Evidence and Conclusion Drill

> **DIRECTIONS:** Match the conclusion on the right with the type on the left that best describes it.

_____ Prediction

_____ Recommendation

_____ Bare Assertion

_____ Value Judgment

_____ Causal Connection

1. The best way to increase your car's performance is to use higher weight oil than the manual recommends.

2. The rain that we need to break this drought should arrive by the end of the week.

3. This is the worst drought in the last seventeen years.

4. Rudolph's nose was primarily responsible for Santa's success that year.

5. We should not long abide such behavior that is so antithetical to our country's principles.

DRILL REVIEW

1. Because the claim concerns what would be the best thing to do (what _should_ be done), this is a **recommendation**.

2. This conclusion makes a claim about what can be expected to happen in the future (what _will occur_), so it is a **prediction**.

3. Since it only states a fact, if this were the conclusion to an argument, it would be a **bare assertion** (what _is the case_).

4. Oh, Rudolph, your nose was the cause of Santa's successful night, so this conclusion is a **causal connection** (what _is responsible_ for something).

5. The moralizing tone and the denouncing of a specific behavior as being against someone's principles means this conclusion is a **value judgment**.

Technique #3: Further Characterizing the Evidence and Conclusion

Both **Role of a Statement** and **Bolded Statement** questions single out part of an argument and ask what role it plays. Since there is little to no fluff or filler in a GMAT Critical Reasoning prompt, everything that appears in the prompt of an Argument-Based question is either part of the **evidence** or part of the **conclusion**.

As you sort through answer choices, look for the words that indicate what type of evidence is used:

> finding, explanation, objection, judgment, standards, methods, data, etc.

or what type of conclusion:

> position, explanation, prediction, recommendation, hypothesis, interpretation, objection, contrary conclusion, implication, etc.

IS THE CONCLUSION POSITIVE OR NEGATIVE?

Sometimes the difference between the right answer and the wrong ones comes down to a simple word like *not*. Some authors arrive at positive conclusions; others reach negative conclusions.

HOW DEFINITE IS THE EVIDENCE OR CONCLUSION?

The basic parts of an argument can be **extreme** or **qualified**.

Extreme evidence takes the form of rules that are always true, characteristics that are never shared, things that are impossible or the only way to proceed:

> The shark, as scientists have long known, is **unable** to survive if it remains still.

> ... because there **can be only one** definition for a word in the Burundi language.

> **No** Ps are Qs, but **all** Qs are Js.

Qualified evidence leaves wiggle room:

> There was a forty percent **likelihood** that the participants would not survive.

> **Many** fields of study require specialized lingo or jargon.

> It **occasionally** can be seen from the north side of the mountain.

Extreme conclusions make all-encompassing claims that admit no exception:

> Therefore, **everything** in the universe is composed of either energy or matter.

> Thus, **all** the items on this table are edible.

> Hence, **there is only one** way to skin a cat.

Qualified conclusions hedge with weasel words like *some, probably, to an extent, in many cases*.

> So, the mail **will likely** be here by Tuesday.

> The researchers concluded that heart disease **is often** linked to diet.

> Consequently, **at least some of** the food in the refrigerator is rotten.

To determine whether the evidence and conclusion are qualified or definite, be on the lookout for keywords like:

> all, every, most, many, some, several, few, only, never, probably, not necessarily, rarely, etc.

IS THE SCOPE LIMITED?

Sometimes, the argument throws out a limitation on the applicability of its evidence or its conclusion, admitting that there are some cases to which it doesn't apply or some exceptions to the rule:

> This research, **if accurate**, suggests that people form opinions on such subjects immediately.

> **To the extent that** a species' range is limited, it will always adopt this behavior.

> **Inasmuch as** the goal of such programs is financial stability ...

> **If** you want to secure a seat by Tuesday, you must act now.

IS THE EVIDENCE USED TO PROVE OR DISPROVE SOMETHING?

Most of the time, evidence presented on the GMAT is positive.

> this shows, this confirms, an example would be, etc.

On the other hand, sometimes a fact is used as a counter example or an evidence to disprove a claim, often accompanied by keywords such as:

> but, yet, however, admittedly, by way of contrast, although, even still, whereas, despite this, in spite of, after all, and our favorite, on the other hand

HOW MANY PIECES OF EVIDENCE ARE USED?

Does the author cite only one rule or are multiple rules linked together? Does the author add a second premise that supports the conclusion indirectly, eliminates some possible misinterpretation, or answers an objection?

In these cases, you'll often see keywords like:

> furthermore, as well, besides, after all, moreover, in addition, what's more

HOW MANY CONCLUSIONS ARE THERE?

The most common way to complicate an argument in a Structure question is to present two arguments that oppose one another within the same prompt. This can be done implicitly:

> **There are those who say** that contentment is impossible if desire persists; **however, ...**

> **Some argue** that we always hurt the ones we love, **but ...**

> **A number of students** often maintain that they cannot arrive on time, **but ...**

Or explicitly:

> **The esteemed councilperson claims** that we should elect him to the judgeship, **but ...**

> **I oppose** the suggestion of **these environmentalists who believe** that we should limit its use.

Another way to throw more than one conclusion into an argument is to tack an **additional implication** or suggestion onto the **end** of an argument.

> **Because Chemical X harms small children, it should be banned.**
> **Further, those who developed it should be fined.**

Moreover, these extra conclusions are almost always present only to set up a wrong answer choice, not to be a part of the right one.

The final way an argument might have more than one conclusion is when the argument has a **complex** or **nested** structure. By this, we mean that it arrives at an **intermediate conclusion**, taking that conclusion as evidence for a **final conclusion** given later. An example:

> **Because no other military in the world possesses even a single "supercarrier," there exists no real threat to any naval operation. Consequently, the suggestion that we increase the Navy's budget to allow the purchase of three additional "supercarriers" is absurd.**

The first sentence presents a miniargument with both a conclusion and evidence:

> **Evidence: No one else has a supercarrier.**
> **Conclusion: No one can threaten our naval operations.**

This conclusion is itself used as evidence for the argument's final conclusion:

> **Evidence: No one can threaten our naval operations.**
> **Conclusion: We shouldn't buy three new supercarriers.**

If you're having trouble sorting evidence from conclusion because it seems like two different parts are being explained by evidence, you're likely facing a complex argument with a nested structure.

Characterizing Conclusions and Evidence Drill

DIRECTIONS: Identify whether each of the following is positive or negative, extreme or qualified, and indicate the type of evidence or conclusion it is.

1. Hence, everyone who comes to the beach party should contribute to the refreshments.

2. This is illustrated by the example of the platypus, an animal that seems to be an amalgam of many different species.

3. Consequently, it is unlikely to rain tomorrow.

4. The study proves that no more than 20 mg is needed in order for the pill to have a therapeutic effect.

5. If this were true, then the koala bear would eat many types of food, but it eats only eucalyptus leaves.

6. Therefore, tests for illicit substances will likely be phased out in the next year, perhaps sooner.

DRILL REVIEW

1. An extreme positive conclusion that asserts a fact.

2. A specific example used as evidence for a proposition.

3. A qualified negative prediction.

4. An extreme negative conclusion that makes a recommendation about what is needed, but limits its scope to one case (having a therapeutic effect).

5. An extreme, specific example used to counter some conclusion.

6. A doubly qualified (will likely, perhaps) positive prediction.

COMMON WRONG ANSWER TRICKS AND TRAPS
FOR ARGUMENT STRUCTURE QUESTIONS

There are always four wrong choices and one right choice; those four wrong choices display patterns of their own specific to each type of question. For Structure Family questions, whose answer choices tend to be abstract descriptions that are very similar from answer choice to answer choice, these tend to be the most common ways that wrong answers are constructed:

MISPLACED DETAIL—An element that is a feature of one part of the argument is used to describe the wrong part, usually a distraction written in language that is very similar to the actual language in the passage.

REASONABLE BUT WRONG—When an argument is confusing, unwary test takers gravitate toward descriptions that are sensible and easy to understand but don't correspond to the text of the argument. Beware of this "default answer choice." In structure questions, the reasonable but wrong answer choice is usually a description of the sort of argument that tends to be made when this subject is brought up but that isn't actually made in the prompt.

For example, an argument's subject might be global warming, and a tempting trap might say that the argument *seeks to establish the extent to which humans contribute to temperature change*, when the actual argument was just a debate over the applicability of one specific case to one specific principle.

EXACT OPPOSITE—This is perhaps the most frustrating trap to fall for. The conclusion was that a rule *should not* be applied, but you end up picking the answer choice that says that the rule *should* be applied. Often, these answer choices will use the language that "sounds better" than the real answer choice, which uses obfuscating synonyms that are nevertheless correct descriptions of what has occurred in the argument.

BUT FOR ONE WORD—A lot of answer choices that are **exact opposites** would qualify for this category as well (the tricky *no* or *not* you missed), but there are also answers that line up all the pieces correctly only to misdescribe a single element of the argument. For example, you might be looking for "The author uses a counterexample to disprove a suggested interpretation" and pick instead "The author employs a counter*conclusion* to disprove one interpretation of a given set of facts." But for the word *counterconclusion*, this answer would have been right.

HALF-RIGHT/HALF-WRONG—You see this trap in **bolded statement** questions most often. The first part of the answer choice correctly describes the first bolded statement and describes it in the way that feels most natural, the likely phrasing of a concept—but the description of the second statement goes off the rails. The test maker is counting on your having an "Aha!" moment when you read the first half, such a strong "Aha!" that you don't bother to read the full answer.

So read the full answer!

Argument Structure Quick Review Questions

DIRECTIONS: Try to complete the following question set in less than 8 minutes in order to test your proficiency with questions that require an understanding of argument structure.

1. At most chain jewelry stores, the person employed to assess the clarity of a diamond also works as a salesperson. This is a clear conflict of interest, since most of the salespeople at chain jewelry stores work on commission, and the higher the clarity of a diamond, the greater price it can command.

   In the argument above, the claim that there is a conflict of interest when someone is employed both as an assessor and a salesperson plays which of the following roles?

   (A) It is a piece of evidence used to advance the argument's main conclusion.
   (B) It is a counterexample to the principle the argument opposes and is enhanced by other evidence in the argument.
   (C) It is the argument's chief contention, for which support is subsequently given.
   (D) It is a premise that the author asserts in order to prove a claim made earlier in the argument.
   (E) It is the phenomenon for which the argument's conclusion provides an explanation.

2. In prehistoric times, the landmasses that today are separated by vast oceans—Europe, the Americas, Africa, etc.—were once a single massive continent, **if the explanations provided by continental drift theory are correct**. Though the theory was once controversial, it is hard to understand why, as **the shapes of the coastlines of South America and Africa clearly align with one another**, as any child with a globe can see for themselves.

In the argument above, the two portions in **bold** play which of the following roles, respectively?

(A) The first is an explanation that the author believes explains a phenomenon; the second is a counterexample that is later dismissed.

(B) The first is a hypothesis whose claims are tested; the second is the explanation of that test's results.

(C) The first is a hypothesis whose truth is taken conditionally; the second is a fact that would support the truth of that hypothesis.

(D) The first is a phenomenon whose explanation many believe to be settled; the second is the author's independent verification of that phenomenon.

(E) The first is an explanation for a phenomenon; the second is an unwarranted personal attack on those who criticize that explanation.

3. Professor: People often have unwarranted negative associations with words. The word "moist," for example, is often cited as the most disgusting word in the English language, yet moistness itself, as a concept, is not always considered disgusting.

Student: But in many cases moistness is extremely unpleasant. Most molds, for example, grow only in moist environments. Can't a few unpleasant exceptions affect our feelings towards something that is, in general, not objectionable?

Which of the following best describes the argumentative strategy employed by the student's response to the professor?

(A) The student uses an interpretation consistent with evidence that the professor presented in order to undermine the professor's conclusion.

(B) The student cites an exception to the professor's claim that is outside the scope of the argument the professor originally presented.

(C) The student advances a general rule that would counter the professor's explanation but which is not clearly related to the professor's evidence.

(D) The student accepts that the professor's conclusion is generally true, but challenges the evidence upon which the conclusion is drawn.

(E) The student rejects the professor's hypothesis but allows that more data could prove the hypothesis to be true.

4. Businesses that hire unpaid interns to do work that is extremely technical do so at their own peril; the only people willing to accept an unpaid internship are those who lack the technical skills necessary to secure jobs that would compensate them for their work.

The reasoning in the argument above is most similar to that found in which of the following?

(A) A mining company should not purchase used equipment unless there is no other alternative; businesses that purchase used equipment are generally seen as vulnerable to hostile takeovers by their competitors.

(B) A mining company should not purchase used equipment if that equipment is intended to be used in dangerous environments, as the only equipment sold used is equipment that the company selling it no longer considers to be safe to operate in dangerous environments.

(C) A mining company should not purchase used equipment because the investors most likely to fund future explorations are likely to believe that such a purchase indicates a lack of potential for growth.

(D) A mining company that purchases used equipment will surely face labor strikes; the miners that such companies rely upon are unlikely to continue working if forced to employ used machinery in dangerous mines.

(E) A mining company can purchase used equipment, but it is seldom a sound business practice to do so; used goods are often in such poor repair that they cannot be subsequently resold.

Answers and Explanations for these questions can be found at the end of the chapter.

THE ARGUMENT ASSUMPTION FAMILY OF QUESTIONS

Anatomy of an Argument Assumption Question

Prompt

The most famous protagonists in literature have always been at odds with societal norms, but it has been increasingly fashionable for postcolonial literature to glorify these iconoclastic protagonists much more than any previous genre of literature has. By presenting these characters as being worthy of emulation, postcolonial authors subtly endorse their outsider ethos and may convince their readers to adopt it. Thus, postcolonial literature can be harmful to at least some of its readers, and thereby to society itself.

Stem

Which of the following is an assumption on which the argument above depends?

Answer Choices

(A) Some protagonists from earlier literature were better role models than any found in postcolonial literature.
(B) It is beneficial for some readers to avoid adopting an outsider ethos or to avoid emulating iconoclasts.
(C) Postcolonial protagonists who adopt an outsider ethos will harm readers more now than if they did not adopt that ethos.
(D) The aesthetic merit of some literary works cannot be judged without considering their moral implications.
(E) Postcolonial literature presents a greater number of outsider characters than did the literature of earlier eras.

Prompt

- All contain an **argument** that has a specific **conclusion** and one or more pieces of **evidence**.
- You can usually trust a *thus* or *therefore* will point to the actual conclusion.
- Usually there's only one speaker in the prompt, although about a third of the time there's still a "those who say" that the speaker opposes.

Stem

- Look for *assumption* or an obvious stand-in like *unstated premise* paired with *required, necessary,* or *underlies.*

Answer Choices

- The answers to Assumption questions tend to bounce around from topic to topic; there's often no major theme or splits to grab onto. Prephrasing becomes key.

Assumption Questions

TIP

In general, we'll call both the family and the first type of question in it by the same name: Assumption.

Mastering the **Assumption** family of **Argument-Based** questions begins with the "pure" **Assumption** question, which asks you to recognize in the answer choices something that must be true if the argument in the prompt is taken to be valid.

IDENTIFYING ASSUMPTION QUESTIONS

A few examples of the way a "pure" **Assumption** question might be phrased:

- The argument depends on which of the following assumptions?
- Which of the following is an assumption made in drawing the conclusion above?
- The argument presupposes

PROCESSING THE ASSUMPTION PROMPT

Question 8 from your Diagnostic Quiz was an Assumption question, so let's practice with it. Begin by locating the conclusion. As you probably remember, in this prompt, the conclusion keyword *Thus* points the way:

> [...] postcolonial literature can be harmful to at least some of its
> readers, and thereby to society itself.

NOTE

Answer Choices (C) and (D) are both too *extreme* for our qualified conclusion.

Notice the ways in which the conclusion is **qualified**. The speaker doesn't claim that postcolonial literature is *always* harmful or that it harms *every* reader, just that it *can* be harmful to *some*. When a conclusion is qualified, there's almost certainly going to be some answer choices that are wrong because they're too **extreme**, offering us information that goes further than what we'd absolutely need in order to prove the modest *some* and *can*.

Now we take stock of the argument's evidence. When you're in the hunt for an argument's assumptions, always read the evidence with the conclusion in mind. Doing so here reveals that most of the argument is just **setup** information. We're told how literature *usually* works, and that's contrasted with how postcolonial literature works. A lot of specialized humanities major jargon gets tossed around. But we're not given much evidence for the argument's conclusion.

If we remember that the conclusion was not "postcolonial literature is the worst genre of literature ever," we can breeze over the comparison in the evidence, as we don't need information about postcolonial literature's relationship to modern literature. That is pure **setup information.** We do need to know why postcolonial literature is harmful, however. So what do we learn about postcolonial literature from the evidence? First, we learn that

> it has been increasingly fashionable for postcolonial literature
> to glorify these iconoclastic protagonists

and that

> postcolonial authors subtly endorse their outsider ethos

This is all well and good, but where's the harm? If the argument's conclusion is to be believed, *something* that postcolonial literature does has to harm its readers. But we're not told directly that either of these things is harmful. So does postcolonial literature do anything else?

> and may convince their readers to adopt it.

OK, postcolonial literature *may* convince people to act like protagonists from postcolonial literature. But where's the harm in that? It turns out that no harm is ever given, and thus we've found the gap between evidence and conclusion.

PREPHRASING AND PREDICTING ASSUMPTIONS

The speaker never told us *why* postcolonial literature is harmful.
Thus, the speaker's assumptions must include

> ✔ At least one of the things that postcolonial literature
> does—glorifying protagonists, endorsing their "outsider
> ethos" (whatever that is), getting people to emulate
> them, etc.—can harm readers.

Otherwise, the evidence that postcolonial literature does those things would be irrelevant to the argument's conclusion.

ATTACKING THE ANSWERS

Because of our specific prediction, as we read the answers, we'd be looking for the *harm* connection that the evidence never made. If an answer choice doesn't mention *harm*, it's probably not the right answer—like Answer Choices (A), (D), and (E).

As it turns out, only Answer Choice (C) uses the word *harm* itself, but it is not the right answer. Rather, it's a clever trap meant for people reading *solely* for the word *harm*.

If we look at the rest of the answer choice, we can see that it's confusing a detail from the evidence with the conclusion. The conclusion was not that postcolonial literature is "more harmful than ever" or "more harmful than anything" or even "more harmful than other types of literature." Instead, it was the qualified "postcolonial literature *can* harm." Answer Choice (C) would only be relevant to those more extreme conclusions.

The right answer, Answer Choice (B), addresses harm in a sneaky way, the **double-negative**. Instead of saying that acting like a postcolonial protagonist is bad, the answer says that *avoiding* acting like one is *good*. Untangle the double negative knot and we end up with what we wanted.

If it's good to avoid acting like them, it's *not* good to *not* avoid acting like them—thus, it's bad to act like them, exactly what we predicted.

IDENTIFYING ASSUMPTIONS

Ironically, the main reason that finding an argument's assumptions can be difficult is that, as reasonable people, we fill in the holes in an argument that makes no sense with reasonable information. Suppose someone were to come up to you in the hall at work and tell you that

> Anna is going to be fired tomorrow because Imran saw her
> stealing from the supply cabinet.

Though you might not necessarily think, "Oh, this person is making an argument," they are.

Conclusion:	Anna is going to be **fired** tomorrow.
	because
Evidence:	Imran saw her **stealing** from the supply cabinet.

TIP

Another way
to think about
assumptions
is that they're
information
that makes the
evidence relevant
to the conclusion.

Seems reasonable, right? Stealing is often the sort of thing that makes a company unhappy with you, and unhappy companies tend to fire employees. But the evidence did not explicitly tell us those things—we *assumed* that they were true because if they weren't, the person coming to us in the hallway would be kind of crazy to conclude that Anna's getting fired.

Put simply, then, assumptions are everything that needs to be true so that the person making the argument isn't crazy.

Technique #4: Look for the Three Main Types of Assumptions

We can divide these "non-crazy-making-things" into three basic categories: Connecting Assumptions, Defending Assumptions, and Feasibility Assumptions. When in doubt, use these three categories as a quick checklist of items an argument needs to assume in order for it to be valid.

CONNECTING ASSUMPTIONS

If an argument is valid, the reasons given as evidence are directly relevant to the conclusion. But unless an argument is just a tautology, there will be *some* difference between what the evidence states and what the conclusion claims. For Imran and Anna.

> Conclusion: Anna is going to be **fired** tomorrow.
>
> Evidence: Imran saw her **stealing** from the supply cabinet.
>
> Assumption: Stealing results in firing. (There is a connection between **stealing** and **firing**.)

Thus, when you are analyzing an argument in an Assumption family question, look carefully at the terms used in the conclusion and those used in the evidence. If they differ (and they usually will), then the argument assumes a connection between them.

DEFENDING ASSUMPTIONS

We defined arguments originally as "a series of connected statements that demonstrate the truth of a proposition." Connecting assumptions fill in the gaps where a connection is left unstated. Conversely, defending assumptions protect the connections against possible objections or weaknesses.

For example, if it's true that Anna is going to be fired because Imran saw her stealing, it needs to be the case that not only is stealing a fire-able offense, but also that Anna is the sort of employee who can get fired. There's nothing *special* about Anna that might protect her from what is generally the case.

> Assumption: Anna isn't exempt from normal rules about firing.

The test maker will generally test these assumptions by presenting specific scenarios in which the assumption would be tested and then ruling them out.

> Anna is not the only one at the company who can make firing decisions.
>
> Anna is not the daughter of a boss who never fires family members.
>
> If this is Anna's first offense, there is no "free pass" given to first time offenders.

TIP

When an argument's conclusion is the same as its evidence, you have a tautology. Spinach is green; therefore, spinach is green.

Defending assumptions also cover all the things that might render a piece of evidence irrelevant to the specific case at hand. For example, even if it's true that stealing does get you fired at this company and even if it's true that Anna is fire-able, we sill need to assume that

> Whoever does the firing at this company knows about what Imran saw.

If Imran never told anyone and is the only person who knows about what happened that day at the supply cabinet, then it doesn't matter whether stealing is punishable by firing.

FEASIBILITY ASSUMPTIONS

Feasibility assumptions concern unstated facts about the scenario presented that would make the argument possible. For example, if it's true that Anna is going to be fired *tomorrow*, then we must assume

> Anna is still working at the company today.

If Anna has already been fired for some other offense, then the argument that she'll be fired tomorrow is incorrect. In the same vein, we also must assume that

> Anna won't be fired tomorrow for cooking the books instead of stealing.

Remember, conclusions and arguments are not the same thing. If we found out that Anna is being fired for some reason other than what Imran saw, the argument that she'll be fired for stealing is incorrect. That argument's conclusion *is* correct, however. Anna's still getting fired. But the evidence presented in the original case does not explain why the conclusion is true anymore, so the argument based on that evidence is wrong.

Assumption Identification Drill

> **DIRECTIONS:** Below, you'll find arguments with certain assumptions listed beneath. Categorize each as a connecting, defending, or feasibility assumption.

TIP

Setup information often explicitly states things that, otherwise, would require a feasibility assumption.

CEO: The integrity of our employees is of foremost concern here at Innotech. Accordingly, even minor infractions are punishable by swift termination. It came to my attention that our receptionist, Eric, has been taking items from the break room refrigerator even when those items are clearly labeled, so I had Eric's case sent to our ethics board. We can reasonably expect that by tomorrow evening, Eric will no longer be a part of the Innotech family.

_____ 1. Taking items from the break room refrigerator is at least a minor infraction at Innotech.

_____ 2. The ethics board renders its decisions within a day or less after it is referred a case.

_____ 3. The facts of Eric's case, as understood by the CEO, have been communicated to the ethics board.

_____ 4. If Eric is away on vacation, the ethics board can render judgment in his absence.

The population of seagulls has been declining for many years, to the point that the species now qualifies as endangered in this area. In order to reverse this decline, steps must be taken to increase the number of seagull eggs that are successfully hatched each mating season. Thus, we must declare more of our local beaches as seagull preserves, banning any recreational use such as swimming, sunbathing, or boating.

_____ 5. Nonrecreational uses of the beach that are still permissible under the ban will not prevent the seagulls from hatching more eggs.

_____ 6. The reason that the seagull population has declined recently is largely a lack of sufficient protected territory.

_____ 7. Seagulls are able to expand into previously unprotected territory when such territory becomes available.

DRILL REVIEW

> **Note:** A given assumption might qualify for more than one category, depending how you are thinking about the gap that it is covering. Below are merely plausible understandings of the assumptions, not definitive ones.

1. **Connecting**. This links Eric's offense (taking items) with the rule about minor infractions.

2. **Connecting**. This links the timing of the referral to the timing mentioned in the conclusion.

3. **Defending**. This prevents the counterargument that the ethics board doesn't know enough to rule.

4. **Feasibility**. This establishes that one of the basic requirements for the evidence to add up to the conclusion is met, namely that Eric is *referable* to the board at present.

5. **Defending**. This protects the argument against the charge that other, unaddressed causes might still harm the gulls sufficiently to overcome the benefit of the plan.

6. **Connecting**. This connects the decline with the solution proposed to address it.

7. **Feasibility**. If seagulls have trouble taking advantage of the solution offered by the plan, the plan will not be able to address the harm.

Technique #5: The "Opposite Day" Test

NOTE

Some people call this the Denial Test or the Negation Test.

An assumption is something that MUST BE TRUE if the argument as a whole is true. Therefore, if you are uncertain about whether an answer choice contains something that MUST BE TRUE, you can ask yourself, "What if this answer choice *wasn't* true?"

Remember our argument about postcolonial protagonists?

> The most famous protagonists in literature have always been at odds with societal norms, but it has been increasingly fashionable for postcolonial literature to glorify these iconoclastic protagonists much more than any previous genre of literature has. By presenting these characters as being worthy of emulation, postcolonial authors subtly endorse their outsider ethos and may convince their readers to adopt it. Thus, postcolonial literature can be harmful to at least some of its readers, and thereby to society itself.

If on Opposite Day, the argument can still work, then the answer choice is not an assumption required for the argument. Consider tricky Answer Choice (C):

> Postcolonial protagonists who adopt an outsider ethos will harm readers more now than if they did not adopt that ethos.

What if that *wasn't* the case? Indeed, what if the *opposite* were the case? What if postcolonial protagonists who adopt an outsider ethos (whatever that is) don't harm readers *more*? What if they just harmed them *some*?

The argument's conclusion was that postcolonial literature *sometimes* harms its readers. On Answer Choice (C)'s Opposite Day, then, the readers still get harmed *some.* The argument can survive even when the opposite of Answer Choice (C) is true, so (C) fails the test. It's not required for the argument to be true, so it's not an assumption in the argument.

Practice the "Opposite Day" Drill

> **DIRECTIONS:** Unlike on the real GMAT, the questions below can have more than one right answer. In order to tell a necessary assumption from something extraneous, practice negating the answer choice and considering whether the argument can still hold. If it's Opposite Day for the answer choice and the argument still works, that answer choice is not a necessary assumption.

1. Advertisement: Chemically bonded gold is far superior to electroplated gold if you are looking for jewelry that is made from a substitute for 14k gold. Unlike electroplated chains, chemically bonded chains can be made into any length without betraying their artificial origin, and chemically bonded gold can be formed into much more delicate patterns than electroplated ever could. And because the chemical bonds are formed by cobalt-driven lasers, you can be sure that chemically bonded jewelry will never tarnish under normal wear.

Which of the following are assumptions required in order for the conclusion drawn to be valid?

(A) The easiest way to tell if a piece of jewelry is made of genuine gold is to watch whether it tarnishes under normal wear.

Opposite: _____

(B) Electroplated gold betrays its artificial origin if chains composed of it are cut into short lengths.

Opposite: _____

(C) The delicacy with which a metal can be shaped into a pattern contributes to its desirability.

Opposite: _____

(D) Electroplated gold tarnishes under some conditions that occur when jewelry made from it is worn regularly.

Opposite: _____

(E) Jewelry made from 14k gold is sometimes characterized by delicate patterns.

Opposite: _____

2. Clearly, the new owners of the magazine *OK, Go!* are influencing the content of the magazine by demanding less coverage of real news and more coverage of entertaining topics. In the five months since the takeover, the percentage of the magazine's covers devoted to movie stars and athletes has increased dramatically, yet over the same span, not a single politician has been featured.

(A) *OK, Go!* has never in the past featured models or athletes on its cover.

Opposite: _____

(B) The frequency with which entertainers appear on the cover of a magazine is determined by the content of the magazine.

Opposite: _____

(C) At least some of the people featured on previous *OK, Go!* covers were politicians and not models.

Opposite: _____

(D) The new owners of *OK, Go!* consider models and athletes more entertaining than politicians.

Opposite: _____

(E) Before the new owners took control of *OK, Go!* the covers of the magazine some-times corresponded with the magazine's content.

Opposite: _____

3. Our nation's economy has at long last cast off the prolonged recent recession and is entering a period of growth. All the signs point to such a transition: unemployment is down, and productivity, which lagged terribly over the past decade, has increased. The number of new bankruptcy filings since the start of the new year is also down compared to the year previous.

(A) Bankruptcy filings continue to increase as a recession deepens.

Opposite: _____

(B) Economies in recession do not experience dips in unemployment.

Opposite: _____

(C) Growth is considered likely in an economy in which several indicators have shifted.

Opposite: _____

(D) Productivity is not a more important indicator of economic health than bankruptcy.

Opposite: _____

(E) When productivity increases, it is impossible for an economy to be free of growth.

Opposite: _____

DRILL REVIEW

1. (A) Negate as "There are easier ways to tell if a piece of jewelry is made of 14k gold than looking for tarnish" to see this is *not* an assumption. So what if there are other ways to tell if a piece of jewelry is fake? As long as tarnish is relevant in some way, it can count as an advantage for the chemically bonded gold.

(B) On Opposite Day, "Electroplated gold still seems like gold when cut into short chains," and this, too, is *not* an assumption. It's not the specific length that matters, only that there is *some* length at which electroplated fails to convince.

(C) A possible denial: "There are easier ways to tell if a piece of jewelry is made of 14k gold than looking for tarnish." Again, this is *not* an assumption. So what if there are other ways to tell if a piece of jewelry is fake? As long as tarnish is relevant in *some* way, it can count as an advantage for the chemically bonded gold.

(D) On Opposite Day, "Electroplated gold doesn't tarnish under normal wear." If elec-troplated gold doesn't tarnish, then it's not to chemically bonded gold's advantage to do the same. Thus, this is an *assumption*.

(E) Negate as "Jewelry made from 14k gold is never characterized by delicate patterns," to see that this is also an *assumption*. If 14k gold jewelry is never delicate, it wouldn't matter that chemically bonded gold can be made into delicate patterns.

2. (A) On Opposite Day, "*OK, Go!* has sometimes featured models or athletes on the cover." Can the increase in the frequency of model and athlete covers still demonstrate something? Sure. Thus, this is *not* an assumption.

(B) Deny as "The content of a magazine doesn't have anything to do with who's on the cover." If so, then the argument makes no sense. Thus, (B) is an *assumption*.

(C) Negate as "There's never been a politician on the cover." If so, the evidence about politicians would be irrelevant. Thus, this is an *assumption*.

(D) On Opposite Day, "The new owners are more entertained by politicians." Close, but it doesn't matter what the owners *find* entertaining, only what they think constitutes an "entertaining topic" for people who read the magazine. Thus, this is *not* an assumption.

(E) Negate as "The cover of *OK, Go!* has never had anything to do with its content." If this is true, then why would the cover be a good way of telling that the editorial direction has changed? Thus, this is an *assumption*.

3. (A) On Opposite Day, "Bankruptcy filings don't always increase as a recession deepens." Close, but this is *not* an assumption. Bankruptcy could still be relevant to recession, even if it's not *always* true that they go up when things get worse.

(B) Deny as "Economies in recession sometimes see lessened unemployment" to see, again, close but *not* an assumption. The argument takes lessened unemployment as a *sign* of a bettering economy, not of a guarantee.

(C) On Opposite Day, "When several indicators shift in an economy, growth isn't likely," which shows that this is an *assumption*. The argument's evidence is that several indicators have shifted. If they could shift without foretelling growth, the argument would fall apart.

(D) Negate as "Productivity is a more important indicator of economic health than bankruptcy" to see that this is *not* an assumption. The argument doesn't depend on any of the factors being the most important or more important than any other.

(E) Deny as "When productivity increases, sometimes economies still don't grow." The argument doesn't depend on any *one* factor, just that there are *some* signs. Thus, this is also *not* an assumption.

Rules of Thumb for Assumption Question Answer Choices

#1: Give answers with *at least* and *some* a second look.

Because most Assumption questions ask for a *necessary* assumption, they are, in effect, asking you for the *bare minimum* that needs to be true for the argument to hold. Thus, answer choices that are limited in scope are often the credited response to Assumption questions. Remember, unless the conclusion's scope was extreme, necessary assumptions are limited and qualified.

#2: Check for stray *not*s and *no*s before confirming the answer.

This is particularly true when language from the prompt is directly repeated word for word in the answer choice. The test maker is counting on familiarity making you so sloppy that you won't notice the little negating word like *no* or *not* sitting right next to the verb at the very end of the answer choice.

#3: Be skeptical of comparisons

Be wary of comparisons unless the argument's conclusion involved a choice between two options, a comparison, or an extreme claim about something's quality, answer choices that use comparative language—*more* or *less, most, worst*—and those that single out a concept mentioned in the evidence as being the *most important* or the *most vital component*. Usually, the arguments only require the *at least* and *some* from Tip #1.

TAKE HOME POINTS FOR ASSUMPTION QUESTIONS

- **Understanding Assumptions** is the single most important skill for GMAT Critical Reasoning questions.
- An assumption is a piece of information that is **not stated explicitly** in the argument but that the argument **needs** or **requires** in order for its conclusion to be supported by its evidence.
- Many incorrect answers to assumption questions will present ideas that are reasonable, just not directly related to the argument's conclusion.
- Arguments can (and usually do) have more than one necessary assumption. Don't let the more obvious assumption keep you from seeing the one that actually shows up in the answer choices.

Assumption Quick Review Questions

1. As malaria is transmitted almost entirely by mosquito bites and mosquitos are most active at night, the easiest and most cost-effective way to dramatically reduce the malaria rate in a country is to cover all beds and other sleeping areas with mosquito-proof netting. The World Bank ought, therefore, to reallocate substantial funds to purchasing mosquito nets for the areas most affected by malaria, which include Sub-Saharan Africa and the South American interior.

   Which of the following is an assumption upon which the recommendation above depends?

   (A) Exposure to malaria can have beneficial effects in some, particularly the very young.
   (B) Malaria is the most serious disease that is transmitted by mosquitos.
   (C) There exist no vaccines for malaria which are effective in all populations.
   (D) World Bank efforts to reduce other diseases worldwide do not need the funds that would be reallocated.
   (E) The rate of malaria infection is not substantially higher in Sub-Saharan Africa than in the South American interior.

2. In European schools, young children are typically expected to master mathematics simply through practice. North American schools, on the other hand, frequently classify students as being "mathematically challenged" and privilege natural aptitude over applied effort. Not surprisingly, North American students' scores on standardized mathematics tests lag substantially behind those of their European peers. To reduce this gap in performance, North American schools must embrace the European attitude towards mathematic aptitude.

   Which one of the following is assumed in the argument above?

   (A) All children can achieve equal standardized mathematics test scores through applied effort.
   (B) All children can achieve better standardized test scores in mathematics if they are not classified as "mathematically challenged."
   (C) Most students who are classified as "mathematically challenged" possess some mathematical aptitude.
   (D) There are no ways to teach students mathematics except for ones that assume natural aptitude or expect applied effort.
   (E) The expectation that a subject can be mastered by practice alone is incompatible with a belief in natural aptitude.

3. A positive correlation has been established between the number of credits in educational theory classes a teacher has obtained and the degree to which elementary students report that they are satisfied with their teacher's performance. Clearly, an important factor in determining educational success is the competence of those who teach our children.

Each of the following is assumed by the argument above EXCEPT

(A) the number of credits a teacher has obtained in educational theory classes is a good measure of that teacher's competence.

(B) elementary school students would not report that they were equally satisfied by teachers of vastly different competence.

(C) students' reported satisfaction with a teacher will increase even further if the teacher is more than merely competent.

(D) when a positive correlation is found between components of an educational system, that correlation ought not be dismissed out of hand.

(E) educational success generally corresponds to the satisfaction levels of the students being educated.

4. Economist: The economy is headed into a dire recession. Recent sales of durable goods typically bought by consumers who expect economic growth in the near future are down substantially and have been for several quarters.

The economist's argument depends upon the truth of which of the following statements?

(A) An economy will not go into recession unless it has shown slow growth for several quarters in a row.

(B) Consumers who buy durable goods when they expect growth tend to save their money when they expect recession.

(C) When consumers do not expect economic growth in the future, a dire recession is all but inevitable.

(D) After a recession has run its course, sales of durable goods climb swiftly as consumers gain confidence.

(E) Consumer confidence is the most important factor that contributes to an economic recession.

Answers and Explanations for these questions can be found at the end of the chapter.

VARIATIONS ON ASSUMPTION QUESTIONS

The other five questions in the Assumption Family still require you to understand what the argument's assumptions are, but each goes one step further than the "pure" Assumption question and asks you to do a different thing with the assumptions you've found.

Weaken questions ask you to make the argument worse, which means making an assumption on which the argument relies less likely to be true. **Strengthen** questions are **Weaken**'s evil twins: find the answer choice that makes an assumption *more likely*. Note that neither requires you to absolutely prove or disprove the assumption, only to make it better or worse.

Evaluate questions are a little bit Weaken and a little bit Strengthen. The correct answer frames a question that, if it came out one way, would make an assumption more likely but, if it came out another, would make the assumption less likely. Still, these are Assumption Family questions because the only questions relevant to evaluating an argument are those questions that address the argument's assumptions. On the same note, **Flaw** questions ask you to find a problem in the argument's reasoning, but the only problems with reasoning found on the GMAT are problems with an argument's unstated assumptions—something was assumed that shouldn't have been.

And, finally, **Complete (Evidence)** questions ask you to fill in the blank with the answer choice that most logically completes the argument. On the GMAT, arguments are made more complete by providing additional evidence that *confirms* an unstated assumption.

Identifying the Question Type

It is important that you be able to distinguish these questions from one another, as the right answer to a **Weaken** question will be the wrong answer to a **Strengthen**, and so forth.

WEAKEN QUESTIONS

There are only a few ways to phrase a **Weaken** question stem, and almost all of them use that very word, *weaken*. Very rarely, the test maker will substitute *casts serious doubt* or *calls into question*.

Thus, you'll see stems like:

- Which of the following, if true, would most weaken the conclusion drawn above?
- Which of the following, if true about home heating costs, casts the most serious doubt on the conclusion drawn above?

STRENGTHEN QUESTIONS

A few examples of **Strengthen** stems:

- Which of the following, if true, most helps to justify Senior Calzoncillos's position?
- Which of the following, if true, would provide the most support for the prediction that bond prices will fall?
- Which of the following, if true, provides the strongest grounds for the doctors' conclusion?

EVALUATE QUESTIONS

Evaluate questions ask you what would be *most useful* to *determine, assess,* and *evaluate* arguments. Look for stems like these:

- Which of the following would be most important to know in determining whether Councilman Jamm's plan, if implemented, is likely to achieve its goal?
- In assessing the likelihood of the prediction given above, it would be most useful to know which of the following?
- In evaluating the argument, it would be most useful to compare

COMPLETE (EVIDENCE) QUESTIONS

The stems for these questions are always found above the prompt and will look something like these:

- Which of the following most logically completes the passage?
- Which of the following most logically completes the argument?
- Which of the following best completes the passage below?

The trick with these is making sure not to mistake them for **Complete (Conclusion)** questions. Look for the **evidence keyword** in front of the blank (or nearby).

FLAW QUESTIONS

You'll never see *if true* in a **Flaw** question stem because the flaw is present in the text **as written**. No additional information is needed to indicate that the argument is flawed. Contrast this with the **Weaken** question, which always includes *if true*, as the argument is not necessarily bad as written.

Common **Flaw** stems include:

- The argument is flawed primarily because the author
- The argument is most vulnerable to which of the following criticisms?

Occasionally, the stem will contain an indication of what the flaw actually is.

- The cheerleader's argument is flawed because it fails to consider the possibility that
- The argument above is vulnerable to the criticism that the rule provided

Technique #6: Use the Common Argument Patterns for Assumption Questions

Content is never king on the GMAT. The structure and function of the pieces of information is far more important to finding the right answer than the content itself. Consider these two arguments:

> The city council of Belleville has enacted a new ordinance allowing police officers to issue a ticket for loitering to anyone lingering longer than five minutes outside a storefront. We can expect a general decrease in crime to follow, as vagrants will now have less opportunity to commit street crimes such as mugging or vandalism.

> When salmon migrate from ocean to fresh water, they make a transition between environments few other aquatic species can manage. Significant energy resources are invested swimming upstream, and the salmon that mate after migration ultimately die. Yet the practice is to the species' advantage overall, as it allows the salmon to lay their eggs in streams unmolested by predators that threaten them in the ocean.

But for the content, they are essentially the same argument, a **net benefit** calculation: on balance, doing a thing would offer more good than harm (or harm than good). Consequently, you'll see big improvements in your GMAT Verbal subscore if you can learn to see the basic structures of arguments and the patterns that recur across many different types of question.

Obviously, since they ask you *directly* about an argument's structure, this skill is most vital in tackling Structure family questions, but the Assumption family draws heavily on it as well. If you recognize a common pattern to the evidence and conclusion, it is often a shortcut to the argument's assumptions.

PATTERN #1: THE APPLIED RULE

Evidence:	A general rule.	All men are mortal.
	A specific case.	Socrates is a man.
Conclusion:	The rule applies to the case.	Socrates is mortal.

In these arguments, the evidence will do two things: (1) present a **general rule** and (2) establish that there is a **specific case** to which the rule is said to apply—not necessarily in that order.

Granted, the test maker can sneak a rule into the evidence in a lot of ways so that it might not always feel "rule-like" on first reading. But the pattern is possible any time an argument presents evidence establishing either (1) a **guarantee** that something will happen (or is true) if that thing means one criterion or (2) a **requirement** that something is needed for something else to happen (or to be true). For example:

TIP

None of these arguments has a set order. Evidence and conclusion may appear at any point.

> Works of art that are designed to appeal to the senses cannot
> be made with an eye towards the utility of the work. There is no
> work of art that has more visual impact than the ceiling of the
> Sistine Chapel. [...]

According to the **general rule** stated in the first sentence, if I show you something that we can agree is *a work of art designed to the appeal to the senses*, then we will also have to agree that that work couldn't have been *made with an eye towards utility*. (In other words, if you set out to make some pretty art, you can't also set out to make something useful.)

The second sentence presents a **specific case**: the Sistine Chapel. If we can agree that the Sistine Chapel fits the criteria of the rule, that it is *a work of art designed to appeal to the senses*, then clearly the rule's **application** must apply, and we could safely conclude that *the Sistine Chapel was not made with an eye towards its utility*. The conclusion that would be attached to our example evidence above would likely read:

> Therefore, no matter what the current use to which Michelan-
> gelo's masterpiece is put in the Apostolic Palace, that use was
> not part of his original artistic conception.

If this argument had appeared in a **Structure** family question like the **Method of Argument** question, we might expect the right answer to be something like

> It proceeds from a general principle to make a claim about
> what is necessarily true in a particular instance to which that
> principle applies.

If you recognized this pattern in an **Assumption** family question, you would instantly know at least one of the argument's assumptions. If the argument above were true, we would need to assume that

> ✔ having lots of "visual impact" is the same as being "designed
>   to appeal to the senses," and

> ✔ an "original artistic conception" is the same as the "design"
>   of a work of art.

And thus, the right answer to an Assumption question about what the argument depends upon might be

> If a goal is not one that an artist originally intended an artwork
> to meet, that goal cannot be said to be part of the artist's con-
> ception of the work.

Departing from the specifics of the argument above, we could say that the main assumption that all arguments that follow the **applied rule** pattern will assume is

> ✔ There is nothing **special about the case** that would keep the
>   rule from applying or

> ✔ The rule applies to this case.

Thus, in **Weaken, Strengthen,** and **Evaluate** questions, correct answers would provide new information that addresses the link between case and rule, making it weaker, stronger, or just pointing out that it's an open question, respectively.

Flaw questions featuring invalid versions of this pattern usually involve someone mistaking a **guarantee** for a **requirement**.

> If all men are mortal, and my dog is not a man, he must not be mortal.

In other words, just because all men are mortal, it doesn't mean that men are the only things that are mortal. A possible correct phrasing for an answer choice pointing this out:

> (A) the argument treats a condition found among all members of a group as though it were exclusive to that group

You might also see a speaker sneakily swapping words as the argument moves from evidence to conclusion in a **Flaw** question, in essence assuming because a word sounds like another word or because two groups tend to be associated with each other that rules that apply to the first apply to the second:

> Car owners must register their cars with the city before they are allowed to park in this lot. Since many of the cars here clearly have expired registration stickers, their drivers should be ticketed.

In this case, the right answer could be that the argument is flawed because it

> (A) fails to establish that something true of one group is necessarily true of another.

The people who drove those cars are not necessarily the same people as the cars' owners.

PATTERN #2: CAUSE AND EFFECT

Evidence:	correlation:	1. X happened/is true	Fan sales rise during the summer.
		2. Y happened/is true	It is hot during the summer.
Conclusion:	causation:	3. X caused Y	The heat causes the increased fan sales.

From our discussion above, you already know that a **Causal Connection** is a type of conclusion. When you spot an argument concluding that something *is responsible for* something else or that one thing *brought about* another, you will find that the evidence is composed of two statements establishing only that two different things happened (or are true). The two events would be said to be **correlated**—they tend to happen at the same time or in the same place.

You've probably heard the maxim "correlation does not imply causation," often accompanied by a story like this one:

> According to folklore, there once was a czar who learned that the most disease-ridden province in his empire was also the province where the most doctors lived and worked. Accordingly, he ordered all doctors throughout his empire shot on sight in order to end the threat of plague once and for all.

Flaw questions often turn on "the czar's mistake," assuming that because there were more doctors in the diseased district (doctors and disease were correlated), it was the doctors who caused the spread of disease—and not that more doctors flocked to that district because of all the sick people to treat! Thus:

> Which of the following best describes the error in the czar's reasoning?
>
> (A) The evidence used to conclude one phenomenon is the cause of another is equally consistent with its occurrence being an effect of the other.

Certainly, there are cases where a causal connection is the likeliest explanation for two things occurring together, such as

> Runners often report that a feeling of euphoria follows a long run. When runners experiencing this heightened sense of well-being have submitted to blood tests, those tests have revealed an unusually high concentration of endorphins to be present. Therefore, it is reasonable to believe that some cases of such euphoria are brought on by the release of chemicals in the brain.

The difference between the flawed argument and the convincing one all comes down to a matter of assumptions. Causal arguments all assume:

✔ There is no other factor that might have been the cause.

✔ There is a plausible mechanism by which the cause could have brought about the effect.

✔ The correlation between the cause and effect is not coincidental.

If all these considerations check out, then the argument for a causal connection is strong. Thus, each of these answer choices would **Weaken** the argument:

TIP

X caused Y, so long as there is no Z.

> (A) Runners typically have heightened amounts of endorphins in their blood, as these chemicals are released when muscles regenerate from any sustained exercise.
>
> (B) Blood tests also reveal that runners who experience euphoria following a run have unusually high concentrations of certain minerals and nonchemical agents in their bloodstream.
>
> (C) Blood tests for endorphins are highly inaccurate.
>
> (D) Throughout the day, the body's concentration of mood-altering chemicals fluctuates wildly, particularly in runners.

And this one would **Strengthen** it:

> (E) Runners who report never experiencing postrun euphoria have been shown in MRI tests to lack a particular receptor in the brain that mediates the effect of endorphins.

Similarly, an **Assumption** question's correct answer often states the assumption directly:

> (A) It is unlikely that a blood test would record high concentrations of a mood-altering chemical in the blood unless the person tested had recently experienced a change in mood.

Spot a **causal connection** as an argument's conclusion and you can be certain that you know at least three of its assumptions.

PATTERN #3: REPRESENTATIVENESS

Evidence:	Something is true of one party.	Toy poodles present no threat to children.
Conclusion:	The same thing is true of another.	Dogs make safe pets if you have children.

In these arguments, the evidence establishes that there is a quality that members of one group have, like *all dogs go to heaven* or *participants in the survey were more likely to report satisfaction*. From this, the argument concludes that some other group shares this quality—usually a larger group, and often the group extends to "*everybody*" or "*people in general*." Other times, the conclusion group is a group of one, a single individual.

Any time an argument relies on an analogy between two things or the similarity between two groups, or uses as its evidence a poll, a survey, an experiment, or some other way of measuring a big effect by looking only at specific cases, the argument will contain an assumption that

> ✔ the evidence group is not different from the conclusion group in a way that would be relevant to the specific quality being discussed.

Thus, a prompt built on this pattern might look like this:

> Children who live within easy walking distance of a well-maintained public playground are much more likely to be physically fit than those who must be driven to a playground further from their homes, according to a new study of children's fitness nationwide. Thus, in order to combat obesity in the very young, more playgrounds ought to be built.

Were the question attached to this prompt an **Assumption** question, this would be a credited response:

> (A) There are no other significant demographic differences between the two groups of children that would account for their differing levels of fitness.

We might **Strengthen** it by eliminating a possible difference, like

> (B) Neighborhoods with public playgrounds do not typically have more recreational sports leagues for children than those without.

And to **Weaken** it, we could point out a difference, such as

> **(C)** Most often, it is only young parents vigorous enough to engage with their children in physical activities that walk their children to public playgrounds.

If asked to identify the **Flaw**, we might well see:

> **(D)** The argument relies on the overall similarity of two groups not shown to be similar in all relevant respects

Polls and surveys are, in particular, sticking points in Critical Reasoning prompts. Because we all know that polls need to be conducted in such a way that no unintended bias creeps in, we may often suspect bias where there is no evidence of it.

Whenever we employ statistical methods to draw conclusions, it is true that we must assume many things about the polls or surveys employed if we're going to believe those conclusions.

> ✔ The sample size of the poll (or survey, etc., was large enough to draw conclusions from.

> ✔ The people selected for polling were selected in a random enough fashion to avoid bias.

But we must be careful on the GMAT that we don't assume things about answer choices that they don't say. Suppose you saw an answer choice in a Flaw question that said

> **(A)** Because of the risk to participants' lives, only a dozen patients were involved in the clinical trial.

You might be tempted to choose it, as 12 doesn't sound like a very big sample size. But the keyword in each of the assumptions above is *enough*. The poll must be large *enough*, and random *enough*. You're not allowed to use outside information to make decisions in Critical Reasoning, and the answer choice doesn't explicitly tell you that 12 is not big *enough* to draw conclusions. Thus, it would NOT be the credited answer.

When the GMAT tests these two assumptions, they have to be very specific in their wording so that the *enough* is buried in there somewhere.

> **(B)** The incidence of the disease is one per ten thousand individuals, requiring at least one hundred trials to evaluate the vaccine's efficacy reliably.

The same goes for the original assumption, that the two groups are similar *enough with respect to the quality in question*. If you don't spot the *enough*, then just any old difference between the two groups is not sufficient to strengthen, weaken, or evaluate. In our original playground question, this would NOT be a credited answer:

> **(E)** Families that live near public playgrounds tend to be poorer, on average, than those who live further away.

Sounds reasonable, right? But the answer choice never hints at why wealth might affect a child's physical fitness, unlike the *recreational sports league* or the *young parents* who engage in other *physical* activities with their children. Thus, there's no way for you to know what effect wealth would have on the children's levels of physical fitness.

Just think, wealthy parents might be able to afford better coaches for their kids, but they also might tend to keep their children quiet by feeding them lots of expensive sweets and plying them with video games and other sedentary activities.

Finally, there's one special flavor of the **representativeness** pattern that often slips under the test taker's radar: **predictions**. Whenever you make a claim about what will happen in the future based on evidence about what has happened in the past, you are making a kind of **representativeness assumption**, namely that

> ✔ things that are true of the past can be taken as representative of things that will be true of the future.

Or put another way, you assume

> ✔ nothing on which the prediction is based will change materially in the future.

or

> ✔ the future will resemble the past in all relevant ways.

Thus, credited answer choices for questions involving a prediction often introduce information that indicates that the future will or won't resemble the past in some important way.

And don't forget, **plans** and **proposals** are often themselves claims about what *will* work or what *should* be done in the future—they're predictions, too! Thus, these arguments likewise assume that the conditions which the plan or proposal was built to address won't change in some material way in the future.

PATTERN #4: NET BENEFIT/NET HARM

Evidence:	Some **advantages** and **disadvantages**, **harms** and **benefits**, **costs** and **savings**, etc.	This brand of tuna is much cheaper than the one we currently eat.
Conclusion:	Something, on balance, is **good** or **bad**.	We will save money if we switch to it.

This is in all likelihood the most common argument pattern on the test. Remember the example we began with?

> The city council of Belleville has enacted a new ordinance allowing police officers to issue a ticket for loitering to anyone lingering longer than five minutes outside a storefront. We can expect a general decrease in crime to follow, as vagrants will now have less opportunity to commit street crimes such as mugging or vandalism.

The evidence in this argument is that **one factor** that contributes to crime **has been reduced** by the plan; therefore, the plan will bring about an **overall reduction**. But what about all the other factors that might increase or decrease crime? Will they remain the same? We must assume they will. Indeed, all arguments that fit this pattern must assume

> ✔ the thing said to be beneficial or harmful will not **indirectly** cause a harm or benefit that **outweighs** its stated effect.

Consider this the old law of unintended consequences. What if we found out, for instance,

> **(A)** Vagrants who usually spend their time loitering will, when unable to do so, often engage in criminal activity.

Exactly. The argument would be **Weakened**. On the other hand, we can **Strengthen** such an argument by eliminating a possible side effect that would **change the balance** between the plan's advantages and any possible disadvantages.

> **(B)** Reducing the number of people on the street outside a business will not make that business more likely to be the target of an armed robbery.

What does *armed robbery* have to do with anything? It's a crime that might have increased due to one of the effects of the new loitering law. Since the stated prediction was that crime would go down, any crime is within the argument's **scope**.

The pattern of a **net benefit** or a **net harm** can be found attached to virtually any type of conclusion, so in most arguments, we should be on the lookout for indirect effects that are clearly relevant to the goals stated by the speaker or the benefit said to accrue from a plan.

Patterns of Flawed Reasoning

Valid arguments are not the only commonly repeated patterns. We often see the same *invalid* argument patterns again and again as well. Part of the challenge of **Flaw** questions is lining up the way the answer choice describes a flaw with the way you typically phrase it when you spot it. As you work practice questions, take note of the different ways each flaw is phrased from question to question.

CONFUSING CORRELATION AND CAUSATION

(See Causal Arguments above)

As we've discussed, just because two things *happen around the same time, tend to be true of the same group*, or are otherwise *correlated* does not mean that one thing is responsible for the other. It could be coincidence, or it could be some other factor.

CONFUSING NECESSITY AND SUFFICIENCY

(See Applied Rules above)

Necessity and **sufficiency** describe the two ways that a pair of things or ideas can be linked conditionally. Some examples of statements expressing **necessity** would include:

> The car needs gas to run.
> (Gas is **necessary** for the car to run.)

> Without a credit score of 700, you will not be approved.
> (The credit score is **necessary** for approval.)

> You cannot be a man unless you are mortal.
> (Mortality is a **necessary** quality of men.)

TIP

Wrong answers can be particularly useful, as many do correctly describe a flaw, just not the flaw in *that* argument.

And some sufficient statements:

> If you goof off, you won't improve.
> (Goofing off is **sufficient** to ensure no improvement.)

> Every good boy does fine.
> (Being a good boy is **sufficient** to know that someone is a good boy.)

> When you buy S-Mart, you know you're buying quality.
> (Knowing something came from S-Mart is **sufficient** to know it is of high quality.)

All sufficient statements can be rewritten as necessary statements, and vice versa.

> If your car has no gas, it definitely won't run.
> (A lack of gas is **sufficient** to keep a car from running.)

> You cannot be a good boy unless you do fine.
> (Doing fine is **necessary** in order to be a good boy.)

Though sometimes, the thought expressed can get a little weird when you rephrase it:

> You cannot have a credit score that is less than 700 unless you aren't able to get approval.
> (The inability to get approved is **necessary** for anyone whose score is less than 700.)

Nevertheless, weird or not, you have to be careful when changing a sufficient statement into a necessary one. The two ways a flawed argument could mess this up:

1. Assuming that because something is a requirement for an event, once the requirement is met, the event has to happen.

> You cannot vote until you turn 18. But not every 18 year old can vote.
> (Some aren't registered; being 18 is not the only requirement, nor is it a guarantee you can vote.)

2. Assuming that if one way of doing something definitely brings about a result, it's the only thing that can bring that result about.

> Everybody who entered the race got a tee-shirt. Paul has a tee-shirt, but that doesn't mean he entered the race.
> (Maybe some shirts are sold to nonracers; entering the race wasn't required for the tee-shirt.)

CONFUSING PERCENTS AND TOTAL NUMBERS

Math, on the Verbal? Yes indeed. In **Flaw** questions, most often a rise or fall in the percentage of something (or the probability or risk) is taken as evidence that the overall amount of something rose or fell.

For example, you pour 8 ounces of coffee into a mug and add 2 tablespoons of cream, then later add another tablespoon of cream and another 10 ounces of coffee to the same mug. The amount of cream has increased, but the percentage of cream has decreased.

CONFUSING ONE THING FOR ANOTHER (AKA THE SCOPE SHIFT)

(See Representativeness on page 340)

Whenever the evidence asserts a fact about one sort of thing, but the conclusion is drawn about some other related thing, it's possible that the two things aren't, in fact, similar at all, or at least not similar in the way that the argument's conclusion claims. You often see this problem crop up when a representativeness assumption is present, but that's not the only way it might arise.

For example: *Gold is a good investment because gold has never been worth zero.* This argument takes "never being worth zero" as essentially the same thing as "being a good investment." But—regardless of what infomercials on cable news might tell you—there's a world of difference between the two. If gold used to be worth $1000 an ounce and has lost a couple of cents of value every decade or so, it's still true that it's never been worth zero, but such depreciation isn't the sign of a good investment.

CONFUSING THE POSSIBLE WITH THE INEVITABLE

An argument's evidence establishes reasonably that something *can* happen, but the conclusion is that it will *definitely* happen. For example, just because the lottery ticket ensures you have a chance of winning, that doesn't mean you're definitely going to win. Just because rain might break the drought, that doesn't mean that when it rains your water woes are over.

You could consider this flaw a subset of the previous two, as it is one way you could confuse necessity and sufficiency (i.e., something being possible is necessary for it to happen, but not sufficient to know it will happen), and it is also a way you could confuse one thing (possibility) with another (inevitability).

CONFUSING A BAD ARGUMENT WITH A FALSE CONCLUSION

As you no doubt remember, there is a difference between an argument for something being true and whether it is actually true or not.

For example, you might see that your friend's car is in the driveway and take that as evidence that your friend didn't go to work. If you later discover that your friend never drives to work, your argument for his being at home was a bad argument, but he might still have been at home that day. Maybe he was sick.

To borrow an old saying, *The absence of evidence is not evidence of absence.* Just because we have no reason to believe that Santa Clause is real doesn't mean he's definitely imaginary. He might exist, even if no one has ever seen him.

Argument Pattern Drill—Down to Two

Small children have more taste buds in the region of the tongue that detects sweetness and therefore tend to strongly prefer sweet treats to salty ones. If your children don't like the food you give them, you should try adding more sugar to your recipes, even ones that do not originally call for it.

1. Which of the following best describes the argumentative strategy above?

   (A) A quality held to be true among members of a group serves as the basis for a recommendation of the best way to address a problem experienced by the group.
   (C) A general rule that specifies the best way to bring about a result acceptable to members of a particular group is used to explain the preferences of that group.

2. The argument assumes that

   (B) recipes that do not originally call for sugar will never be made unpalatable if sugar is added to them.
   (E) the intensity with which a sensation is felt can influence the preferences of those feeling it.

3. Which of the following, if true, would most weaken the argument above?

   (A) Sugar in excess of what is typically found in a recipe will often mask or reduce salty flavors.
   (B) Sugar plays a structural role in many recipes, influencing other desirable qualities such as consistency and digestibility.

Editorial: If every dog has its day, then the distinguished congressperson may safely boast that she is no dog, for one has difficulty recalling any significant accomplishment for which she is responsible, nor any moment where her good judgment shined above that of her peers.

4. The editorialist's argument makes which of the following errors of reasoning?

   (D) It mistakes a quality found among all members of a group with a quality that must be present in that group.
   (E) It mistakes a condition that is necessary with one that is sufficient.

5. Which of the following, if assumed, would allow the previous conclusion to be properly drawn?

   (A) In order to be distinguished as exceptional amidst one's peers, one must be able to boast better judgment, if unable to take primary credit for at least one success.

   (C) Phrases used colloquially in one context would never be inappropriate if used in another.

6. The argument proceeds by

   (B) citing a general rule, then concluding on the basis of that rule that a person ought to be evaluated in a particular light.

   (C) citing a general rule, then concluding on the basis that all rules have exceptions that a person ought not be evaluated positively.

Physicians are rarely taught about pitfalls in cognition. During their training, they work as apprentices to senior doctors and learn largely by doing. In today's medical system, where there is intense pressure to see as many patients as possible, **quick judgment and snap decisions are often rewarded**. Such haste, however, will lead to errors in thinking that could impact the health of patients negatively, and for this reason, **practical training during a physician's residency should be supplemented with courses in critical thinking**.

7. Which of the following, if added to the premises above, would allow the conclusion to be more properly drawn?

   (C) The best way to ensure that someone is able to think critically is to require them to enroll in courses that teach the skills necessary for such thinking.

   (E) The demands on a physician's time during a residency program do not preclude additional coursework.

8. In the argument above, the portions in **bold** are best characterized by which of the following?

   (D) The first is a consideration in support of a conclusion; the second is a recommendation made on the basis of that conclusion.

   (E) The first is a preliminary conclusion that is used to draw a subsequent conclusion; the second is that subsequent conclusion.

9. The author's recommendation would be unlikely to bring about its intended result if

   (A) hospitals continue to require that physicians see as many patients as possible during their residency training

   (B) the curriculum of medical schools includes substantial time spent developing critical thinking skills

DRILL REVIEW

  1. (A) Method of Argument. The preference for sweet foods is used in the argument to make the recommendation to add sugar. It's not explained by the recommendation.

  2. (E) Assumption. The *never* kills (B), and (E) correctly describes a link between the argument's intermediate conclusion and the evidence given for it.

3. **(B) Weaken.** The argument presents a plan of sorts and advocates it on the basis of one (possible) advantage. Thus, it assumes no larger negative effects could come from the plan (adding sugar). If more sugar ruins these "desirable qualities," it might make the food less desirable to the babies, even if they have become more desirable in one respect.

4. The correct answer is neither—a trick question! **Flaw.** The instructions did say to pick the "best answer," but both of these are rotten. Though the sentiments are odd and oddly worded, the first sentence establishes a rule, the second brings up a specific case, and the remainder is the correct application of that rule.

5. **(A) Assumption.** Another *never* kills (C). Rephrased, (A) makes the connection between "having one's day" and "having accomplishments" and "displaying judgment."

6. **(B) Method of Argument.** (C) was a reasonable but wrong trap. Don't be fooled by the existence of clichés. This argument never made reference to an exception to the rule.

7. **(E) Strengthen.** *Best* ruins (C), but (E) correctly supports the argument's assumption that there is nothing standing in the way of the plan being put into effect.

8. **(D) Bolded Statement.** (E) uses a misplaced detail to try to lure you in. The argument *does* feature two conclusions, but the first bolded statement isn't one of them. It's evidence.

9. **(B) Weaken.** It's not clear whether "as many patients as possible" would interfere with the coursework. But if (B) were true, it would suggest that a lack of coursework is not the reason that physicians have underdeveloped cognitive skills.

Patterns of Flawed Reasoning Drill—Odd Man Out

> **DIRECTIONS:** In each set of three answer choices below, two are alternate descriptions of the same flaw; one is different from the other two. Eliminate the unpaired description.

1. The argument is flawed primarily because the author
   - (A) fails to consider that natural alternatives to diesel fuels could also address the problem.
   - (B) depends upon popular belief rather than on documented research findings.
   - (C) assumes that if one of a pair of options is impossible, the remaining one must be used.

2. The argument is most vulnerable to which of the following criticisms?
   - (A) It asserts that because a factor is known to bring about a result in some cases that it will always bring that result about.
   - (B) It takes one possible cause of a phenomenon to be the actual cause of that phenomenon without considering other possible causes.
   - (C) It does not rule out the possibility that the donkeys' arrival at the festival could have been unrelated to the actions of the monks.

3. The environmentalist makes which of the following errors of reasoning?

(A) Provides no reason to believe that hiring an "information agile" applicant will have only beneficial effects for a company.

(B) Overlooks the possibility that in reducing the problems at the production facility, those at the marina may be exacerbated.

(C) Confuses what is necessary for the most popular sport fish to survive with what is usually conducive to their survival.

DRILL REVIEW

1. **(B)** Questions an evidence's source (never kosher on the GMAT); the other two describe the flaw of **confusing necessity and sufficiency** by overlooking alternative requirements or paths to a goal.

2. **(A)** Describes an argument that confuses one thing (possibility) with another (inevitability); the other two describe **confusing correlation and causation**.

3. **(C)** Describes **confusing necessity and sufficiency**; the other two point to something being overlooked in the **net benefit/net harm** pattern.

Technique #7: Argument Diagramming

Remember, your wet erase noteboard isn't taken up after the break following the Quantitative section. It's still there for you to use during the Verbal section.

One thing you might consider doing with that board is using it to diagram tricky arguments in Critical Reasoning questions. You might just spot a common pattern you've missed or make a connection that you didn't realize already existed in the argument as stated.

Since the most important thing you need in order to understand an argument is to be able to state the conclusion (and distinguish the conclusion from the evidence), you'll need some symbol for keeping track of which is which.

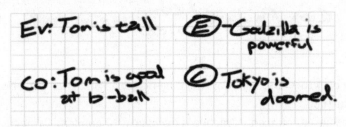

The next thing you'll need is some way to indicate "this is directly connected to that." Connections, after all, are what make an argument valid or invalid.

Ev: Soc → man
As: man ≈ mortal
Co: Soc → mortal

After that, you'll want to make sure you have a consistent shorthand for concepts that you see again and again. Here are a few to get you started:

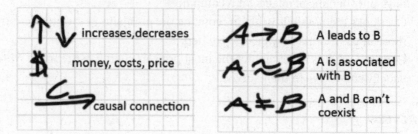

And now, here are a few final tips for diagramming:

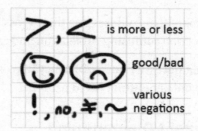

DON'T "PRONOUNCE" YOUR SYMBOLS IN YOUR HEAD

If you write something like this:

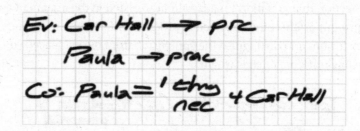

Don't read it back to yourself as "Car Hall then per-eck, Paula then per-eck, so Paula is one thig neck for Car Hall."

Instead, translate as you read. "Practice is necessary for going to Carnegie Hall; Paula has practiced; so, Paula has one thing necessary for Carnegie Hall." No caveman-speak, no gibberish—always use your diagrams as shorthand for your thoughts about the argument, not to replace those thoughts. If you let the notes take over, they become an extra step between you and understanding.

DON'T GET "ABBREVIATION HAPPY"

Because of the ever-ticking timer, you might be tempted to over-abbreviate. While it's true that you're the only person who has to be able to read your own diagrams, you still do need to be able to read them without wondering what the heck you meant only ten seconds ago. The time spent writing an extra letter or three won't cost you much, but avoiding doing so out of fear of lost time might itself end up costing you a lot more in the long term.

BE CONSISTENT

It might seem like a small thing, but using the same symbol to mean lots of different things can mean that if you get distracted while diagramming you might forget what your symbol meant *this time*, and thus miss the question in front of you.

Similarly, picking one symbol for a concept one time, another the next, and another the next will end up slowing you down as you struggle to recall "now what did the squiggle with the smiley over it mean again?"

As you practice, you're going to get a better feel for the concepts that the GMAT brings up over and over, and thus the concepts you need to have a handy way of representing symbolically.

Practice with Arguments You Understand First

You certainly won't be diagramming every argument you run across on the actual GMAT, only the ones that you need an extra hand untangling. During your practice work, however, you should force yourself to diagram some arguments you understand completely, just to practice the mechanical skill of diagramming. If you never practice it on the easy questions, you're still going to be shaky when you hit the hard ones.

Sample Diagrams:

The argument from question 12 on your diagnostic quiz:

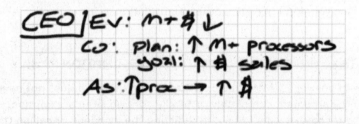

The CEO's half of the argument from question 4:

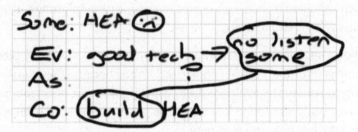

It even works for Inference! Question 9 from the diagnostic:

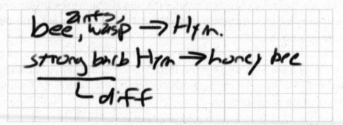

Common Wrong Answer Tricks and Traps

Assumption family questions include many of the same trap answer patterns found in the Structure family, particularly the **but for one word**, the **exact opposite**, and the **half-right/half-wrong**. But there are also a few new wrinkles to watch out for:

REASONABLE BUT IRRELEVANT—You know that the test maker is going to make the arguments difficult to read on purpose, hoping that rather than read, you'll just pick an answer choice that "seems right" or "seems reasonable" to someone who only knows the argument's broad subject. Often, these sensible answers are irrelevant to the *specific* conclusion drawn or the *specific* scenario the argument posits.

CLOSED ISSUE—If the evidence in the prompt already takes a potential gap in the argument or a particular objection into account, it still might show up in the answer choices to tempt you. Pay attention to subtle clues that certain common argument problems have been ruled out. For example, if the argument about highway fatalities specifically defines the increase as "per mile traveled," it's probably to set up an answer choice that acts as though the original claim was just that "the total number of accidents" had increased.

ONE STEP REMOVED—This is probably the most common type of wrong answer in an Assumption family question, a fact that is only relevant to the argument if something else is first assumed to be true. The missing step will be one that's reasonable to assume in general, but that the argument never specifically addresses. Lots of things might Strengthen or Weaken an argument if you were allowed to assume extra information, but since you're not, these answers are all incorrect.

EVIDENCE FOR THE EVIDENCE—Remember that you have to take every piece of evidence in the prompt as true. Many answer choices are wrong because they simply provide additional reason to believe the evidence itself, usually some sort of corroborating evidence like "a different study also found this to be true" or "this effect has been seen in multiple cities just like the one from the argument."

In real life, the more evidence we have for a given fact on which an argument is based, the more comfortable we are in saying the argument is correct. On the GMAT, once you've been told a fact, you don't need any other confirmation of it.

TAKE HOME POINTS ABOUT THE ASSUMPTION FAMILY

- The correct answer to a **Weaken** or a **Strengthen** question does not have to disprove the argument completely or totally contradict an assumption.
- If an answer choice seems to be contradicting the evidence or calling the author's motivations into questions, beware! Always take the evidence as true.
- If you would need to know an additional fact to know if an answer choice affects an argument, then it's not the right answer to an Assumption family question.
- Addressing a possible exception or eliminating a counterexample are both ways of supporting an assumption to strengthen an argument; the opposite weakens an argument.
- Corroborating evidence is almost always irrelevant. Since you've already taken the evidence as true, you don't need information that makes it *more* true.
- Evaluate questions have become more common since the GMAT switched from ETS to ACT, so be prepared!

Assumption Family Quick Review Questions

DIRECTIONS: Try to complete the following practice set in less than 10 minutes in order to assess your understanding of these closely related question types.

1. There is no animal whose cognitive faculties and abilities even begin to approach the complexity of a human's, and, sadly, once any of us become aware of this fact, he or she will most assuredly therefore no longer be content with activities that do not in some way connect to these faculties.

   Which of the following would be most useful to know in order to evaluate the truth of the position above?

   (A) Is it possible to separate one's desires and needs from one's awareness of a truth about his or her faculties?

   (B) Is it possible to fully satisfy someone who is not aware of the complexity of human faculties?

   (C) How far from human-like are the cognitive faculties of the more intelligent animals, such as whales?

   (D) Are there any people who enjoy physical pleasures more than they enjoy the pleasures of the mind?

   (E) Are there any people for whom contentment is not a goal?

2. Doctors, lawyers, scientists, and other experts are very unlikely to be selected for jury duty because both defense and prosecuting attorneys do not want the other jury members to be unduly biased by their expertise, particularly when the case relies on extremely technical information. Thus, jury trials will never be a fair means of judging disputes when extremely technical information is involved.

   Which of the following most weakens the argument above?

   (A) As the complexity of information presented to a jury increases, the likelihood that they will defer to an apparent expert increases.

   (B) The more expert a juror in one field, the more likely that juror will be biased when evaluating evidence of a technical nature.

   (C) Scientists who testify in complex cases often do not state their positions forcefully, causing jurors without scientific knowledge to doubt them.

   (D) When a case is found to be unsuitable for a jury trial, it is often sent to a panel of impartial experts for arbitration.

   (E) Most defense teams do not bother to acquire expert witnesses, as they believe such testimony is useless when no experts are present on the jury.

3. A diet high in saturated fat can substantially increase a person's risk of developing heart disease, but new research suggests that this risk can be mitigated by drinking one glass of red wine a day. In subsequent clinical tests, it was found that the presence of chemical compounds of a family known as "flavonoids" was chiefly responsible for the beneficial effect. Researchers are currently developing techniques to synthesize and distill the flavonoids found in red wine so that they can be added to other, nonalcoholic beverages.

Which of the following would strengthen the case for adding flavonoids to nonalcoholic beverages in order to combat heart disease?

(A) Saturated fat forms a plaque in the arteries that reduces the flow of blood to the heart, thereby damaging it.

(B) Many people who drink nonalcoholic beverages do so because they are opposed to drinking alcohol for religious reasons.

(C) Flavonoids are able to retain their beneficial health effects even when other compounds they are naturally found with are absent.

(D) The alcohol found in wine may also help reduce heart disease in some people, particularly those who suffer chronic stress.

(E) Children whose diets are high in saturated fat are often, later in life, found to have an increased risk of heart disease.

4. Editorial: The current proposal to close my neighborhood's only public pool should not be voted forward by the town council. There are no public pools that can easily be reached by pedestrians and cyclists in the neighborhood near ours, and currently nearly three-quarters of those who use our pool either walk or bike to get to it.

Which of the following, if true, would most weaken the editorial's argument?

(A) Children are among the most consistent users of the public pool, but only during the summer when school is not in session.

(B) There are many hours during the early morning and late evening during which the public pool is not used.

(C) Many of the most popular recreational activities among the neighborhood's residents do not require the use of a pool.

(D) Pools are often expensive to maintain, particularly in areas with high population densities.

(E) Many of those who walk or bike to the public pool only do so because it lacks parking spaces for their cars.

5. The critics of the CEO's plan to expand the business do not believe that she has adequately considered the risk that would come from doing so. But if the business is to thrive at all, it needs a CEO who is willing to take risks. So, since the CEO plans to expand, she must have considered all of the risks.

The reasoning in the argument above is in error because

(A) the reasons that the CEO believes the expansion is warranted are not presented.

(B) the CEO could be willing to take risks but still not have considered the risk of a particular strategy.

(C) other companies might also be considering expanding in spite of the risk involved.

(D) the CEO might well realize, if more facts were considered, that an alternate plan would be riskier.

(E) a thriving business can be expanded in many ways, some of which do not involve risks.

Answers and Explanations for these questions can be found at the end of the chapter.

FACT-BASED QUESTIONS

Anatomy of a Fact-Based Question

Prompt

Ironically, George Lucas's reputation as an artist has been hindered by the very technology that makes his films so dazzling. Many of the theaters that play his films lack top of the line projection machinery. Such machinery is absolutely vital to the full display of Lucas's artistic skill.

Stem

Which one of the following can be properly inferred from the statements above?

Answer Choices

(A) Some theaters that play Lucas's films provide support for Lucas's reputation as an artist.

(B) All theaters that play Lucas's films and that possess top of the line projection machinery display Lucas's artistic skill fully.

(C) All of the showings of Lucas's films that do not display his full artistic skill lack top of the line projection machinery.

(D) If a theater possesses top of the line projection facilities, it will provide a full display of an artist's skill.

(E) At least some of the theaters that play Lucas's films fail to display fully Lucas's skills as an artist.

Prompt

- There is more variation in Fact-Based prompts than Argument-Based prompts.
- Some are as short as a line and a half; others are quite long.

Stem

- Instead of using the word argument, stems often describe the prompt as "the passage" or "the statements."
- **Explain** and **Inference** questions work in opposite directions. Explain adds to the prompt; Inference deduces from it.

Answer Choices

- Pay attention to words that indicate that facts are qualified or extreme.
- Double-check the language of the answer choice to make sure you aren't glossing over a small detail.

Identifying Fact-Based Questions

Inference questions account for all but a tiny slice of the remaining Critical Reasoning questions, and they also show up among the Reading Comprehension questions.

Remember the test maker's definition of inference, which is something that **MUST BE TRUE** on the basis of some specific, definite piece of information. *Might be true, could be true,* and *really, really, really likely to be true* don't make the inference cut.

Complete (Conclusion) questions are just another form of **Inference**, as the only conclusion you are allowed to complete an argument with is one that is inferable (that MUST BE TRUE) from the facts presented.

For both, when you read the prompt, you are searching for the most definite, specific information present. Inferences come out of such information.

Explain questions rely on the same sorts of prompts—facts rather than arguments—but the task is different from that in **Inference** questions. Instead of adding the information in the prompt together to say what must be true, these questions ask you to add a piece of information *to* the prompt so that what seems like it can't possibly be true will be revealed to be sensible and sound.

As always, the stem will guide you. Possible stems for each follow.

INFERENCE QUESTIONS

- Which of the following conclusions can most properly be drawn from the information on the previous page?
- If the facts stated in the passage above are true, which of the following must be true on the basis of them?
- The claims above, if true, most strongly support which of the following conclusions?

COMPLETE (CONCLUSION) QUESTIONS

- The stems for these questions are always found above the prompt.
- Which of the following most logically completes the passage?
- Which of the following most logically completes the argument?
- Which of the following best completes the passage below?

Be sure not to mistake them for **Complete (Evidence)** questions. Look for the **conclusion keyword** in front of the blank (or nearby).

EXPLAIN QUESTIONS

- Which of the following, if true, most helps to explain the surprising finding?
- Which of the following, if true, does most to explain the phenomenon previously described?
- Which of the following, if true, best accounts for the race's anomalous results?

Processing the Prompts of Fact-Based Questions

In Argument-Based questions, your first step to untangling the prompt is to hunt for the conclusion. With Fact-Based questions, you're also on a hunt, just for different things.

INFERENCE PROMPTS

We begin with **Inference** questions, which require you to find the "most inference-y part" of the prompt—the definite rule, the principle, the thing that is *always true*, etc. The more you practice with Official Guide or GMATPrep questions, the more you will come to appreciate the way that the test maker sets up an inference question.

Technique #8: Recognize the Common Inference Keys

The content of an Inference prompt may vary, but there are certain things you learn to recognize as the test maker's way of saying "Hey, look here, we're going to build an Inference off of this!"

INFERENCE PATTERN #1: UNTANGLE THE DOUBLE NEGATIVES

The test maker loves hiding information under tortuously constructed double negatives. Or perhaps we should say instead, the test maker doesn't not love hiding it there.

Thus, you might see something like this in an Inference prompt:

> No one is incapable of everything.

What can you infer from that? Well, if *no one* is *incapable of everything*, then everyone (the opposite of no one) must be capable (i.e., not *in*capable) of something. Notice that negatives can be found both in little words like *no, not, nor,* and *none*, but also *inside* words through prefixes like *in-, un-,* and *im-*.

Combine the two, and you end up with all kinds of places in which to hide inferences.

> If everything that is not material is imperfect, then it's also true
> that everything that is immaterial is not perfect, and also that
> nothing that is not material lacks perfection.

INFERENCE PATTERN #2: KEEP TRACK OF "SO AND SO" AND "SUCH AND SUCH"

Another way to hide an inference is to separate two facts about the same thing in different parts of the prompt. The prompt starts out by talking about one thing:

> The detention of hostile combatants without specific charge
> has become commonplace during the modern struggle against
> fanaticism [...]

Then it switches gears to something else.

> [...] Throughout the era following the first two World Wars,
> nations generally fought other nations, rather than disparate
> loosely affiliated groups united only by ideology. [...]

Then sneakily switch back to the first topic.

> [...] These new methods, their proponents contend, are justified
> by the same principles that allow for nations to combat each
> other.

Take piece A and piece C, put them together, and you have the credited answer to an Inference question.

> (A) Established principles allow for some to defend the prac-
> tice of detention even when that detention is not accompa-
> nied by a formal charge.

Kind of silly, right? Just remember that the right answer to an Inference question must be 100 percent justified, not merely likely or sensible. The test maker's hands are bound by this limitation, so they have to resort to some pretty silly tactics to cloud your ability to see the credited answer.

Thus, look for demonstrative pronouns like *this, that,* and *these,* along with place holder words like *such, one, it, there,* or the *latter* and the *former*. Trace the pronoun back to its referent and you'll often have your Inference.

INFERENCE PATTERN #3: GROUP INFORMATION BY CATEGORY

Names are important. Sometimes, you're given two names for the same concept. Other times, you're told that two concepts can both be described by a single named. Either way, keeping track of what details are said to be true of which concepts is often the key to another sort of Inference. For example:

> Disruptive thinking challenges the status quo by advocating for change; some disruptive thinkers work within existing institutions, others from without. Regardless, in their efforts to bring about a new social consciousness, those intellectual elites who would break with the establishment are aided by the public's growing consensus that institutions no longer work as they should.

Keep track of which group is which. Here, we have one group, *disruptive thinkers*, who can also be called *intellectual elites* and *people who break with establishment.* That group is further subdivided into two groups, those who work *within* institutions, and those who work *outside* them. Nothing is told to us about the individual halves; rather, another two facts are added to the original group: they *try to bring about a new social consciousness* and when they do, they're *aided by the public's consensus that institutions are broken.*

The difference between a correct inference

> (A) The success of disruptive thinkers outside an institution can be influenced by attitudes toward that institution.

and an incorrect one

> (B) The public's distrust of institutions allows disruptive thinkers to form a consensus for social change.

is just lining up the details with the right party.

INFERENCE PATTERN #4: BUT THAT'S TOO OBVIOUS!

Take a look back at Answer Choice (A) above and notice how modest the claim contained in it is. Success *can* be influenced—not *will*, not *is always*, not *is never*, merely *can*. Sometimes Inference prompts contain little to no definite information, no rules, no conditional statements, nothing that will allow an impressive inference to be drawn.

In those cases—when the Inference prompt lacks concrete, definite information—the correct answer is most often phrased very weakly.

> (A) The atmosphere plays **some role** in the transmission of radio waves.
> (B) The success of a venture is determined, **in part**, by factors beyond a capitalist's control.
> (C) The ultimate temperature reached by a chemical reaction **is influenced by** the permeability of the outer valence.
> (D) Cholesterol **plays a part** in blood pressure assessment.
> (E) **At least one** of the factors that **contribute** to a gene's expression occurs after the organism has developed.

When the GMAT gives you lemons, make very small, very limited claims about those lemons, the sort of thing that's so bland and timid that it would be consistent with nearly any specific scenario.

INFERENCE PATTERN #5: FORMAL LOGIC PART 1—
INFERRING THE CONTRAPOSITIVE

We've told you throughout this chapter that you are not required to understand the complicated or arcane rules that logicians and philosophy professors concern themselves with, and we stand by that. The most complicated logical principle you're ever asked to handle on the GMAT is the sort of thing that's covered during the first week of a Symbolic Logic or Formal Logic class.

In truth, the only "formal logic" that appears on the test concerns **conditional statements** and what can be *inferred* from them. A conditional statement consists of two concepts, one of which is **sufficient** to bring the other about, the other of which is **necessary** for the other to occur. For example, there is a specific conditional relationship between automobiles with gasoline-powered engines and gasoline. If a car has no gas, then it will not run.

If we wanted to express this relationship formally, we would place the **sufficient condition** on the left side of an arrow and the **necessary condition** on the right side. Gas is necessary for your car to run, thus:

Sufficient	**Necessary**
If your car is running,	then it must have gas.
Run $\rightarrow$	Gas

Every conditional statement can be written two ways. If we call the way we just wrote it *the positive*, then the other way is called the *contrapositive*. The contrapositive of our statement above would look like this:

Sufficient	**Necessary**
If your car has no gas,	then it must not be running.
No Gas $\rightarrow$	No Run

If the positive is true, the contrapositive must also be true. Or, to put a finer point on it, they're the same statement just expressed two different but equally correct ways.

Transforming a simple conditional statement from the positive to the contrapositive (and back again), is a two-step process: (1) reverse the order the elements are written in, and (2) negate the elements. Thus:

Sufficient		Necessary
Positive:	If your car is running,	then it must have gas.
	Run	→ Gas
Step 1: Reverse	*Gas*	→ *Run*
Step 2: Negate	no Gas	→ no Run
Contrapositive:	If your car has no gas,	then it must not be running.
	no Gas	→ no Run

If the statement is complicated—that is, if it includes more than two connected ideas—then a third step is added: (3) any *and*s become *or*s and any *or*s become *and*s.

Here's a complicated formal logic statement:

Sufficient	Necessary
If you are not wearing shoes or not wearing a shirt,	then you will not be given service.
no Shirt or no Shoes →	no Service

To transform this complicated statement into its contrapositive, just follow the 3-step process:

Sufficient		Necessary
Positive:	If you are not wearing shoes or not wearing a shirt,	then you will not be given service.
	no Shirt or no Shoes	→ no Service
Step 1: Reverse	*no Service*	→ *no Shirt or no Shoes*
Step 2: Negate	*Service*	→ *Shirt or Shoes*
	(no no Service)	*(no no Shirt) (no no Shoes)*
Step 3: Or/And	*Service*	→ *Shirt and Shoes*
Contrapositive:	If you are getting service,	then you must be wearing a shirt AND shoes.

That's as difficult as the logic gets on the GMAT. But understanding how to do this little transformation does play into a sizeable minority of GMAT Critical Reasoning questions, particularly Inference questions. Whenever you see a definite, conditional rule in the prompt of an Inference question, the correct inference may just be as simple as recognizing the contrapositive—something *always* inferable from a conditional rule.

INFERENCE PATTERN #6: FORMAL LOGIC PART 2—CONNECTING CONDITIONALS

When two or more conditional statements appear in an Inference prompt, that's usually a clue that you should try to combine the two. For example:

> If it rains tomorrow, then the fair will be canceled. But since it's August, days when it doesn't rain are invariably so hot that cotton candy melts.

In shorthand, the statements and their contrapositives would look like this:

Rain → no Fair   no Rain → no Cotton Candy

Fair → no Rain   Cotton Candy → Rain

The necessary condition for one set becomes the sufficient condition for the other, and vice versa. Thus:

Fair → no Rain → no Cotton Candy

Cotton Candy → Rain → no Fair

What can we infer from these two linked conditionals? If the fair is open, then no one will be able to eat any cotton candy. Also, if people are able to eat cotton candy, they won't be eating it at the fair because the fair will be closed. Each way of phrasing this relationship between the fair and cotton candy is 100 percent true if the original two conditionals are true, the very definition of an Inference.

Recognizing Conditional Statements

If the test maker would always use the *if … then …* construction, then recognizing conditionals would be a lot easier. Alas, there are many ways to invoke a conditional relationship. Here are the most common:

If X, then Y.	X → Y	If you call me, then I'll be there. If I didn't come, then you didn't call me.
When X, Y	X → Y	When you call me, I'll be there. When I'm not there, you didn't call me.
Whenever X, Y	X → Y	Whenever you call me, I'll be there. Whenever I'm not there, you didn't call me.
Every X is Y.	X → Y	Every owl is able to fly. Every flightless thing (e.g., my desk) is not an owl.
All Xs are Ys	X → Y	All owls are birds. All nonbirds (mammals, for example) are not owls.
People who X, Y	X → Y	People who like birds like cool things. People who don't like cool things don't like birds.
Only Xs are Ys	Y → X	Only people who are cool like birds. Only people who don't like birds aren't cool.
X, only if Y	X → Y	You are cool only if you like birds.

X must Y	X → Y	Legal drivers must have a current license. Drivers who don't have licenses must not be legal.
X is required for Y	Y → X	Being 18 is required for voting.
X, unless Y	X → no Y	I will go to the store, unless it rains.
Can't be X unless Y	X → Y	You can't be a legal driver unless you have a license.
X, except Y	X → no Y	People are terrible, except for children.
X until Y	Y → no X	You can talk until the bell rings.
No X without Y	X → Y	You can't do well without studying. You can't (always) avoid studying without (later) failing.

Inference Patterns Drill—Logical Chains

DIRECTIONS: Write the positive and contrapositives of the statements below in formal logic, then connect any statements that connect (whose necessary results are themselves sufficient triggers for other rules). Note: some links may require double-negatives or other patterns to recognize.

1. The only way to get to Carnegie Hall is to practice.

2. Practice is impossible without dedication and support from one's family.

3. People who join the marching band spend too much time on their extracurricular activities.

4. Everyone whose family supports them has at least one advantage in their favor.

5. If you are unable to balance your schoolwork and your extracurriculars, you won't have time to practice.

6. Only members of the concert band will be allowed to take part in the marching band.

7. Whenever you fail to practice, you are letting your parents down.

Links:

DRILL REVIEW

1. Carnegie Hall → practice; no practice → no Carnegie Hall

2. no balance → no practice; practice → balance

3. marching band → no balance; balance → no marching band

4. support → advantage; no advantage → no support

5. practice → dedication and support; no support or no dedication → no practice

6. marching band → concert band; no concert band → no marching band

7. fail practice → parents let down; no parents let down → no fail practice

Links:

There are several ways these statements could be added together. For instance:

Carnegie Hall → practice → balance → no marching band or, in English, "If you make it to Carnegie Hall, you must have practiced, and in order to do that, you had to have a balanced approach to your extracurriculars, which means you weren't in the marching band."

marching band → no balance → no practice → no Carnegie Hall, or "People in the marching band can't balance the time they spend at extracurriculars, meaning they don't have time to practice in the way you have to practice if you hope to play at Carnegie Hall."

Carnegie Hall → practice → support → advantage, or "Playing Carnegie Hall takes practice, and practice requires the support of your parents, something that's always an advantage in your favor."

no advantage → no support → no practice → no Carnegie Hall, or "If you truly have no advantages in your favor, your parents must not support you, which means you'll never have time to practice, which means you'll never end up playing Carnegie Hall."

Alternately, you could have chosen to express the links in terms of starting point and ending point, like "Everyone who plays Carnegie Hall has at least one advantage in their favor," or "Nobody who's in the marching band ever plays Carnegie Hall."

EXPLAIN PROMPTS

Even though Inference prompts and Explain prompts both contain information, you are asked to treat as true at face value, what you do with that information differs greatly between the two. Remember, Explain questions ask you to *resolve* or *explain* an apparent dilemma. Your job when attacking these prompts will be to find the two "horns" of the dilemma. Called the "horns" from the idea that a bull has two horns, and the choice between being gored by one is no better than being gored by the other. After all, if you don't know what the two things that need to be brought together are, how are you ever going to find the answer that brings them together?

Technique #9: Finding the "Horns" of the Dilemma

Explain questions present you with all kinds of weird situations. The most common are:

THE RULE VIOLATION—The prompt presents two things: (1) a **general rule** and (2) a case that seems like the rule should be applied to it, but in which **the rule *seems* to be violated**. The correct answer will usually either show that the rule **doesn't actually apply** or that the violation is itself just **further demonstration** of the rule applying.

THE FLOUTED TREND—Similar to the rule violation, in these prompts (1) **a general trend** is cited but then (2) **a specific case** that seems **counter to the trend** is given. It, too, is usually solved by the introduction of information that shows that the trend **isn't relevant to this specific case**, or that, when another factor is considered, the specific case is just **further demonstration** of the general trend.

THE UNREALIZED EXPECTATION—These prompts present (1) an **expectation** or **prediction**, but then state that it (2) **never happened** or that the **opposite happened**. Usually, the right answer will show that the expectation was based on an **assumption that doesn't apply** in this case, sometimes by showing that there was an extra **unconsidered factor** that explains things.

THE REJECTED ADVICE—These prompts establish that, in general, (1) using **one strategy is a good idea**, but that some group or actor that has been given the facts has (2) **chosen otherwise**. These paradoxes are usually explained by answer choices that provide, again, an **unconsidered factor** that show that in *this case* the advice would be bad.

When you have identified an **Explain** question, read the prompt and then try to rephrase it into either

> (1), but (2) or on the one hand X, but on the other hand Y.

Only when you hold the two "horns" of the dilemma in your hand will you be able to bridge the gap between them.

Also, keep in mind that the wrong answer choices to explain questions usually fall into two camps, things that are **irrelevant to the dilemma**—that is, things that wouldn't change things at all if you knew them—or things that actually *worsen the dilemma*, by making the weirdness in the prompt even weirder.

Finding the Horns of the Dilemma Drill

> **DIRECTIONS:** Several dilemmas are given below. Classify them, and then pick the one answer choice out of the two given that resolves the dilemma.

1. The consumer price index has been down for three of the four prior quarters, but this quarter the index was flat. No increase was seen, even though there has been no indication of slowing inflation in any other indicator.

2. More people went to the movies last summer than in any previous summer, yet Hollywood's profits on the films shown last summer were down compared with the three preceding summers.

3. In order to keep its muscles in functional shape, an animal has to exercise at least a little; yet even though three-toed tree sloths merely hang upside down all day sleeping, they still have functioning muscles.

4. Since demand for Company Q's widgets shows no sign of declining, analysts recommend that those interested in adding stability to their portfolios purchase shares of Q; nevertheless, Mutual of Barbados, an investment vehicle that advertises itself as one of the most stable, has declined the opportunity to purchase such stock.

5. Since going to the gym, Sudesh has increased the number of calories he burns each day threefold, so he should be losing weight; yet at his last weigh in, he was the same weight as before he started his new workout regimen.

DRILL REVIEW

1. **Flouted Trend.** The most likely answer is that the consumer price index is a leading indicator, changing before other indicators catch up. Other ways to explain the change in the trend could include that there is something special in this month that affected only the consumer index, not other indicators.

2. **Rule Violation.** Any number of factors might influence the *profitability* of movies; only ticket sales are discussed. Possible explanations include that the recent movies were more expensive to make, or that the price of tickets has gone down, or that there was some new tax or other cost that had entered the calculation.

3. **Rule Violation.** The rule is stated explicitly, that muscles require exercise, but the rule doesn't seem to apply in the case of the sloth. Likely, the correct answer would explain that hanging from trees all day is actually pretty intense exercise.

4. **Rejected Advice.** It seems reasonable for Mutual of Barbados to purchase Q, yet they aren't going to. Presumably, there is a difference between showing signs of continued *demand* and *stability* in general, and the fund manager at Mutual of Barbados knows this.

5. **Unrealized Expectation.** Sudesh should be losing weight if he's burning calories, right? The correct answer would point to another factor that could overwhelm this expectation. Maybe Sudesh has increased the amount he eats, or maybe he has gained heavier muscle to replace lost fat.

Common Wrong Answer Traps and Tricks for Fact-Based Questions

You'll see variations on the wrong answer choices we've discussed for Argument-Based questions, such as:

REASONABLE BUT UNSUPPORTED—Often, answer choices to Inference questions are meant to tempt you by presenting things that are *true* in the real world, but that the prompt never specifically addresses.

POSSIBLE BUT NOT DEFINITE—Many answer choices are *consistent* with the information in the prompt; that is, the prompt doesn't *contradict* the answer choice, but it also doesn't prove it MUST BE TRUE.

TOO EXTREME—Inference questions in particular demand a close eye kept on the scope of the information presented.

For example, if you are told that *some people like cake*, you cannot infer from that that *all people like cake*, but you also can't rule out *all people like cake*. All people like cake is possible, but not definite, from the information that *some people like cake*.

On the other hand, if you are told that *most people like cake*, then you can infer that *some people like cake* and it's possible that *all people like cake*, but you can't say the latter for sure. You can be certain that *nobody likes cake* is flat wrong, however.

	implies	is implied by	allows as possible	is denied by
None	0	none	none	some, all, etc.
Only one	1	only one	only one	none, any number greater than one
Some, few, many	At least 1	most, all	some not, most, most not, all	none
Most not	50% minus 1	only one	some, some not, all not	most, all
Most	50% plus 1	all	some not, all	none, most not
All	100%	all	all, some, most	none, some not

All, *none*, and *exactly one* are **extremes** that require another extreme in order to be inferred. Specificity increases from some to all, with each level allowing certain inferences but denying others.

BUT FOR ONE WORD—These prompts come in two varieties, the standard "swap car *drivers* and car *owners between answer choice and prompt*" (and hope no one notices), and the **too extreme**, as above.

MIXED DETAILS—Two concepts from the prompt are connected in the answer choice in ways not supportable by the information in the prompt.

IRRELEVANT TO THE DILEMMA—In Explain questions, most answers are wrong because they cannot clearly be linked to the specifics given about the dilemma in the prompt.

WORSENS THE DILEMMA—The other sort of Explain trap, these answers are directly relevant to the dilemma, but they make the paradox or violation of expectations *even worse* than it was in the original.

TAKE HOME POINTS ABOUT FACT-BASED QUESTIONS

- Remember the GMAT's definition of an inference: Something that 100 percent MUST BE TRUE.
- Pay careful attention to how definite or how qualified the information in a Fact-Based prompt is.
- Seek the most definite information. This is the source of proper GMAT inferences.
- Don't bother reading Fact-Based prompts for conclusions. Most of the time, there won't be one, and when there is, it's usually just a distraction.
- Unless you have a handle on both sides of the dilemma in the prompt (the "two horns"), the answer choices are going to be useless at best.

Fact-Based Quick Review Questions

DIRECTIONS: Try to complete the following five questions in 10 minutes or less in order to test your understanding of questions that ask you to analyze a fact pattern on the GMAT.

1. People who lack health insurance are so worried about the possibility of accidents that they cannot be happy. Their unhappiness makes everyone close to them unhappy in turn. Only if they acquire health insurance can they and those close to them be happy.

   Which of the following can be inferred from the information above?

   (A) Only matters related to health make people unhappy.
   (B) People who are able to avoid worrying about accidents will be happy.
   (C) People who have health insurance are happy.
   (D) If people are unhappy, they must not have health insurance.
   (E) If people are happy, then they must not lack health insurance.

2. In the aftermath of the first Gulf War, investigators were surprised to discover that even though oil wells had been set ablaze and much oil deliberately spilled in order to keep it from being captured by enemies of the regime, the groundwater and soil in the Persian Gulf proved to be less contaminated by oil and oil byproducts than it had been shown to be by previous, prewar surveys.

Which of the following, if true, does the most to resolve the apparently surprising finding described above?

(A) Contaminants from oil and oil byproducts have a serious impact upon the health of those living permanently in a contaminated area.
(B) Contamination from oil and oil byproducts dissipate rapidly in regions like the Persian Gulf, where the arid ground does not absorb them readily.
(C) Contamination from oil and oil byproducts would not rapidly dissipate if the climate in the contaminated area had large amounts of rainfall.
(D) Oil production in the Persian Gulf before the war was plagued by accidents that often resulted in massive oil spills.
(E) The first Gulf War was far shorter than subsequent wars in the region, resulting in less damage to the civilian oil industry than many feared would occur.

3. The natural consequence of lowered speed limits is longer travel times. Recently, Nevada lowered the speed limit on Interstate 511 from 75 miles per hour to 55 miles per hour, yet in the months that followed, most drivers on I-511 found that their rush-hour travel times decreased substantially, 20% on average.

Which of the following, if true, most helps to explain the realized reduction in travel times on Interstate 511?

(A) During off-peak hours, travel times on Interstate 511 were unchanged in the months following the reduction of the speed limit.
(B) In the first week following the speed limit reduction, there was little to no change in the average speed of rush hour traffic on I-511.
(C) Few Nevada drivers whose daily commutes included Interstate 511 chose to take alternate routes after the speed limit reduction.
(D) The primary source of rush hour traffic delays prior to the speed limit reduction on I-511 was accidents caused by drivers travelling at 65 miles per hour or more.
(E) The Nevada State Patrol is notorious for its enforcement of the speed limit on I-511 and has been for many years.

4. There are no professors currently employed by the state's university system that are under the age of 35, the minimum age to be elected president. A great many intelligent people are full professors, and a great many intelligent people are eligible to be elected president. We should hope that our president would be intelligent, but it must also be remembered that many intelligent people are under the age of 35.

If the statements above are true, then which of the following may be inferred?

(A) No professors employed by the state are 35 years old exactly.
(B) All intelligent people are either professors, eligible to be president, or under the age of 35.
(C) Some people who are eligible to be elected president are not professors.
(D) Some professors are neither intelligent nor eligible to be elected president.
(E) Some intelligent people are neither professors nor eligible to be elected president.

5. When an economy enters an inflationary period, consumers tend to increase spending, fearful that by delaying major purchases, they will end up paying more for them. Yet after this initial increase in economic activity, the longer inflation wears on, the more consumer spending dips. Even though wages rise with persistent inflation, consumers will delay even routine trips to the grocery store or to the gas station in order to avoid spending until it is absolutely necessary.

Which of the following would, if true, contribute the most to an understanding of the consumer behavior described above?

(A) Savings tends to remain flat during recessions and other normal periods of inflation.
(B) Consumers tend not to recognize that an inflationary period has begun until after many economists do.
(C) No economic behavior can be described with 100 percent accuracy, even by the best economic principles and models.
(D) During periods of extended inflation, increases in wages tend to increase only slowly, while prices continue their steep climbs.
(E) After an inflationary period, prices tend to fall for most durable goods, though wages often remain at postinflation levels.

Answers and Explanations for these questions can be found at the end of the chapter.

Argument Structure

500- to 600-Level Argument Structure Practice Set

NOTE

Answers and Explanations to all Practice Set questions can be found at the end of the chapter.

1. The global increase in standard of living is the driving force behind the increased carbon dioxide emissions of the last three decades, and it is this increase that contributes the most to global climate change. As wages rise, more of the world's population can afford luxuries that, while agreeable, require substantially more energy to maintain, which causes more carbon dioxide to be emitted. Moreover, when the standard of living declined over the last few years because of the financial crisis, carbon dioxide emissions declined in turn.

   Which of the following best describes the role played in the argument above by the statement that the global increase in standard of living is the driving force behind increased carbon dioxide emissions?

   (A) It is a phenomenon whose existence is taken as evidence for a prediction later proposed.

   (B) It is the main conclusion that the remainder of the argument provides reasons to accept.

   (C) It is a phenomenon that can only be understood if all of the facts that follow are true.

   (D) It is a premise the argument presents in order to make a recommendation for conservation.

   (E) It is used to limit the extent of possible phenomenon to which a subsequent explanation can be applied.

2. In order to reduce the number of venomous cobra snakes in Delhi, the British colonial government offered a bounty for every dead cobra. Initially, this was successful, as large numbers of snakes were killed for the reward. Eventually, however, people discovered that breeding snakes to present to the government was easier than hunting them, and the cobra population rose, rather than fell. Thus, governments should not employ market-based solutions to combat biological problems.

   Which of the following best describes the method of reasoning employed in the argument above?

   (A) A potential solution to a problem is proposed and then discredited with the data provided.

   (B) A broad conclusion is drawn by applying a narrow principle to a specific circumstance.

   (C) A specific instance of a strategy in practice is taken as sufficient evidence that it ought never be used.

   (D) A principle applicable to many cases is applied to a single case to make a prediction about its future application.

   (E) Two potential solutions to a problem are presented, and one is discredited by data provided.

3. Despite what they profess to believe, **atheists clearly believe in a higher power**. A prominent religious activist has posted a bounty on his website offering $10 to anyone who would sign a piece of paper that says that he owns their soul, and yet after many months, there have been no takers. Why would anyone be unwilling to part with something that they do not believe exists to begin with?

Which of the following best describes the role played in the argument by the portion in **bold**?

(A) It is a statement that the author believes is valid to hold for reasons given later.

(B) It is an observation that the author uses to support a position given later.

(C) It is a pattern of cause and effect that the author believes holds true for reasons given later.

(D) It is a conclusion that the author presents in order to discredit later.

(E) It is a relationship that the author does not believe holds true in a case described later.

4. There is no need for me to take the recycling to the curb tonight. Even though our typical pickup is early Tuesday morning, and although today is in fact Monday, today is also a federal holiday. After any federal holiday, the city delays recycling pickups by one full day.

Which of the following best describes the argumentative strategy employed above?

(A) Treating several irrelevant observations as though they amounted to support for a given proposition

(B) Establishing indirectly that a given result will occur from a set of causes by ruling out all other possible results

(C) Providing information that allows for an exception to a rule that is otherwise taken as always true

(D) Making a generalization about every case of a certain sort on the basis of a single atypical case

(E) Asserting confidently that because an outcome is probable it is inevitable in a given case

5. Spokesperson: **We recommend that our clients prepare today for the inevitable consequences of technological development**. The current pace of advancement is such that in less than a decade, most of the technologies currently in use will have been superseded by more efficient, lower cost alternatives. **The cost of replacing outdated technologies need not outweigh the savings these alternatives will allow**, so long as businesses take steps now to streamline their processes so that replacement innovations can be integrated seamlessly into their day-to-day activities.

In the spokesperson's argument above, the two portions in **boldface** play which of the following roles?

(A) The first is evidence offered in support of an opinion that the spokesperson rejects; the second offers information that contradicts that evidence.

(B) The first is a premise that the spokesperson partially accepts; the second offers evidence that explains why that acceptance is not complete.

(C) The first is a position that the spokesperson argues against; the second is the position that the spokesperson defends.

(D) The first is a generalization accepted as accurate and used as a premise in favor of the spokesperson's conclusion; the second is a consideration that further supports the spokesperson's conclusion.

(E) The first is the main conclusion that the spokesperson asserts; the second suggests a potential objection the spokesperson's argument later addresses.

600- to 700-Level Argument Structure Practice Set

1. Last month, The Olde Tyme Creamery introduced a new milkshake flavor, Gravely Choctastic. Within a week, its main competitor, Shakez, announced an almost identical flavor named Ghastly Chocolate. Neither company has accused the other of copying its design, but **the similarity is too close to be coincidental**. Each is equal parts fruit sorbet and Rocky Road, an unorthodox combination. Moreover, **it is absurd to think that two companies working in isolation would simultaneously launch identical products with nearly identical names**.

In the argument above, the two statements in **bold** play which of the following roles?

(A) The first is the argument's main conclusion; the second is a condition sufficient for that conclusion to be true.

(B) The first is a secondary conclusion used to argue in favor of the argument's final conclusion; the second is likewise evidence for the main conclusion.

(C) Both statements are evidence given to support the argument's main conclusion.

(D) Both statements are an explanation that the argument concludes is more likely than one the argument opposes.

(E) Both statements are conclusions; the first is used as evidence demonstrating the truth of the second.

2. The Maillard reaction, first described in the 19th century by a French physician, is the process by which meat turns brown and crispy when cooked. Indeed, applying heat to a food is the key technique to cooking, which means that cooking should be seen as an example of applied physics, rather than as an art. Even though qualities like tastiness of browned meat or the appropriate level of crispiness may be hard to define, this difficulty alone would not relegate cooking to the ranks of the practical arts.

Which of the following is the main conclusion in the argument above?

(A) The Maillard reaction is the process by which meat turns brown and crispy when cooked.
(B) It may be hard to define some qualities that are considered relevant to cooking, like crispiness and tastiness.
(C) Something that is a practical art can never be properly considered an example of an applied science.
(D) Cooking is better classified as an example of applied physics than as an art.
(E) Applying heat to a food is the key technique to cooking.

3. Though there is not yet direct archaeological evidence, it would not come as a surprise to anthropologists to learn that trade routes existed between China and the West millennia ago. Those things that contributed to making the Great Silk Road such an important route during the Middle Ages—its easily traversable mountain passes, desert oases, and level terrain—would also have made it the natural route for emigration to China from Africa and the Middle East, **emigration we know to have occurred as early as 1,000,000 B.C.E.**

The portion in boldface plays which of the following roles in the argument's reasoning?

(A) It is given as conclusive evidence for the argument's main conclusion.
(B) It is an intermediate conclusion about a region made plausible by evidence regarding the region's characteristics.
(C) It is offered as evidence in support of a conclusion that is consistent with facts given elsewhere in the argument.
(D) It is offered as evidence against a claim that the argument's main conclusion opposes.
(E) It is the main conclusion that the argument attempts to establish regarding the region in question.

4. *Le Concorde*, a supersonic transport, was capable of cruising speeds of up to Mach 2.04 (approximately 1,354 mph). Today's airplanes cannot even reach such speeds, much less cruise at them, and thus will never replace *le Concorde*.

    Which of the following most closely parallels the reasoning used in the argument above?

    (A) Peaches may ripen off the tree, but they only become sweeter on the tree. If a fruit can do both while in the supermarket, then it is not a peach.

    (B) Everyday wind waves have a wavelength of about 100 meters (330 feet), but a tsunami has a wavelength of 200 kilometers (120 miles). Therefore, tsunamis are at least two thousand times as damaging as wind waves.

    (C) In the lab, burettes provide a measurement accurate to two decimal points. Graduated cylinders are accurate only to one. For scientific purposes, graduated cylinders will never be able to provide a lab with all necessary measurements.

    (D) The help wanted ads are the part of the newspaper most often read. Thus, if someone reads a newspaper, they likely also read the help wanted ads.

    (E) Fluoride prevents cavities and other forms of tooth decay. If a patient exhibits tooth decay, but was never treated with fluoride, then the patient did not take all necessary precautions.

5. Estragon: Our friend sent word that he would not arrive by train, but by carriage. Almost all of our friends come by train. Our friend who is coming today is like our other friends in most respects. How can he be different in this one? He must no longer be our friend.

    Vladimir: Our friends usually come by train because we usually arrange to meet them at the train station, rather than at our home. Our friend who is coming today knows where we live, so we did not make such arrangements.

    Vladimir responds to Estragon's reasoning by

    (A) offering an alternative explanation for the evidence Estragon cites.
    (B) undermining some of Estragon's evidence while agreeing with his conclusion.
    (C) drawing attention to an inconsistency between two of Estragon's claims.
    (D) pointing out that Estragon's use of the term "friend" is excessively vague.
    (E) presenting evidence that directly contradicts Estragon's evidence.

700- to 800-Level Argument Structure Practice Set

1. **The dividends that shareholders were expecting MegaBiz to pay this quarter were reduced at the last minute,** a sign that many analysts claim does not bode well for MegaBiz's stock price over the short-to-medium term. This analysis is not necessarily correct, however, as **often dividends are reduced in order to conserve capital in preparation for an aggressive expansion**, something only companies otherwise equipped for long-term growth can undertake.

   In the argument above, the two **boldface** portions play which of the following roles?

   (A) The first is evidence for argument's conclusion; the second is that conclusion.

   (B) The first is a phenomenon the argument's conclusion explains; the second is a factor contributing to the likelihood of that explanation being correct.

   (C) The first is a phenomenon the argument's conclusion addresses; the second is an alternate hypothesis the argument rejects.

   (D) The first is a fact that the argument seeks to explain; the second is an alternate explanation the argument proposes.

   (E) The first is a prediction that the argument seeks to explain; the second is the hypothesis the argument presents as the likeliest evidence for that prediction.

2. Insiders within the mayor's party have called for his immediate resignation, hoping to reduce the effect that the negative publicity of the most recent scandal will have on the political future of his deputy mayor. **A swift resignation is unlikely to help the deputy mayor, however.** If the mayor resigns, he will undoubtedly be prosecuted in civil court for his indiscretions, and the deputy mayor will be forced to testify in court. If his testimony were to indicate that he was aware of the indiscretion and did nothing, the deputy mayor's political career would be over. And if he were unaware of such gross violations, voters would rightly think twice about his fitness for future political office. This is precisely why **the mayor ought to remain in office as long as possible and allow the deputy mayor to retain plausible deniability**.

   In the reasoning above, the two **boldface** portions play which of the following roles?

   (A) The first assesses the goal held by certain political insiders; the second presents the goal that the reasoning concludes should be favored instead.

   (B) The first assesses the goal held by certain political insiders; the second presents the strategy the reasoning concludes will be more likely to succeed.

   (C) The first is the main conclusion toward which the reasoning is directed; the second presents a strategy that is counterproductive.

   (D) The first is the conclusion reached about one strategy for a certain goal; the second presents the strategy that the reasoning advocates.

   (E) The first is the main conclusion toward which the reasoning is directed; the second is a consideration raised in order to support that conclusion.

3. Eddie: You won't be able to understand the true themes beneath the surface of the most popular alternative music of the 1990s because you were only a child when it was released. Popular music is always aimed at people in their late teens and early twenties.

Mark: You were not alive during the ancient Roman era, nor were any of us now living, but you trust that professor Bullfinch's interpretations of the *Aeneid* do, in fact, capture that work's deepest meaning. Why should alternative music require what Roman poetry does not?

Mark responds to Eddie's claim by

(A) using an example from classical culture in order to delegitimize contemporary culture.
(B) presenting an analogous situation that suggests Eddie relies on unsupported premises.
(C) contradicting a key piece of evidence that Eddie's argument relies upon.
(D) specifying a definition that Eddie's argument relies upon but leaves implicit.
(E) questioning Eddie's own qualification to make judgments about a similar phenomenon.

4. Physiologists once believed that muscle fatigue was caused by the buildup of lactic acid in muscle tissue. **Excess lactic acid was thought to have a "pickling effect," inhibiting the ability of muscles to contract.** The impact of lactic acid on muscle function is actually mixed. In some cases, it assists muscle function; in others it inhibits. **Other metabolic factors such as the simple lack of energy to fuel contraction are today thought more likely to be the cause of soreness in muscles.**

In the argument above, the portions in **boldface** play which of the following roles?

(A) The first is an assertion that the author opposes; the second is a consideration in support of that assertion.
(B) The first is an assertion that the author contradicts; the second describes a situation that the author posits as contrary to that assertion.
(C) The first is an assertion that the author argues against; the second is evidence presented as contrary to the author's argument.
(D) The first is evidence that the author believes is no longer valid; the second is additional evidence that the author uses to support a different conclusion.
(E) The first is a claim that the author believes to be invalid; the second is a claim the author supports with evidence presented earlier.

5. Minor increases in sea temperature, such as those brought on by human activity, can adversely affect fish and seabird populations, even if the resulting temperature is well within the tolerances of these complex species. Phytoplankton depend upon the vertical mixing of the different strata of sea water in order to obtain nutrients from the lower levels. Without phytoplankton, zooplankton will starve, and zooplankton are critical to the rest of the food chain that ends in seabirds and the fish they eat.

In the argument above, which of the following best describes the role played by the information that without phytoplankton, zooplankton will starve?

(A) It is a hypothesis for which support is offered elsewhere in the argument.

(B) It is an example that illustrates the phenomenon of vertical mixing of sea water.

(C) It is a premise that taken jointly with other premises establishes the argument's validity.

(D) It is offered in support of the conclusion that global warming should be avoided.

(E) It supports the conclusion that temperature change harms all species equally.

Argument Assumption

500- to 600-Level Argument Assumption Practice Set

1. Because of a sharp increase in the number of commercial fishing vessels plying the waters off the coast of Peru in the past decade, the anchovy population there was largely depleted. If the stock of anchovies is ever to recover, the number of fishing vessels must be reduced by at least 50 percent. Since the Peruvian government has recently closed loopholes that allowed foreign fishing vessels to enter its waters without permits, it is likely that the population of anchovies will rise significantly in the coming decade.

Which of the following would it be most useful to establish in evaluating the argument?

(A) Whether high demand for anchovies in Peru or in foreign markets led to the overfishing

(B) Whether the foreign fishing vessels use the same methods and equipment as Peruvian vessels

(C) Whether the Peruvian government was influenced unduly by environmental lobbyists

(D) Whether fishing vessels that previously entered without permits will be able to obtain them in the future

(E) Whether other fish stocks have declined substantially in recent years

2. Some believe that there are a large number of gun-related homicides in the U.S., but they are simply misinformed, as this belief is itself based primarily upon the frequency with which gun-related homicides appear in news reports on television in the U.S. It is precisely because gun-related homicides are such a rare occurrence in the U.S. that they are so frequently the subject of television news.

The argument above is most vulnerable to the objection that

(A) it presupposes that most television news reports are about gun-related homicides.

(B) it presupposes, without warrant, that the television news reports are not biased.

(C) it presupposes the truth of the conclusion that it purports to demonstrate.

(D) it uncritically draws an inference from what is often the case to what will occur in the future.

(E) it uncritically assumes that a characteristic of one member of a group is shared by all members of that group.

3. *News of the Times*, the storied local newspaper, has announced it will cut its price by half, explaining that the unprecedented reduction will allow the paper to better compete with the substantially cheaper tabloid-style newspapers that have stolen much of its market share. The paper's editors reason that since the new price will be only two-thirds that of the least expensive tabloid, many former customers will resume purchasing the paper.

Which of the following statements, if true, provides the best evidence that the editors' reasoning is incorrect?

(A) The tabloid-style newspapers *News of the Times* competes against have kept their prices artificially low by reprinting material from the Internet.

(B) When the tabloid-style newspapers were introduced to the market, their prices were twice *News of the Times'* original price.

(C) Most of those who currently purchase the tabloid-style newspapers never regularly purchased *News of the Times.*

(D) Many of those who currently purchase *News of the Times* have said that they would rather the prices remained higher than risk lowering the paper's quality.

(E) During the average week, tabloid-style newspapers sell nearly five times as many copies per issue than *News of the Times* does.

4. On some cruises, the *Princess Anne*'s entertainment selection includes performances by members of the cast of popular Broadway shows, and on some cruises, their entertainment selection includes "Alternative" bands last popular during the 1990s. Therefore, on some of the *Princess Anne*'s cruises, at least two different types of musical entertainment are available.

The reasoning in the argument is flawed in that the argument

(A) mistakes a condition that sometimes accompanies the presence of one type of musical act with something that necessarily accompanies it.
(B) fails to recognize that one set might overlap with each of the two others even though those two other sets do not overlap with each other.
(C) fails to consider that the fan bases of the two types of musical acts mentioned would rarely overlap.
(D) presupposes the truth of the conclusion that it purports to elsewhere explain.
(E) infers a causal relationship from a situation in which two groups are merely correlated with one another.

5. It would make much more sense for the Jenkins to turn their old vacation home into a bed and breakfast than it would for them to lease it out to a vacationing family for a week at a time. Although there are many potential clients for a leased vacation home, there are also many who would board at a bed and breakfast. However, homes used for vacationing families typically require more expensive maintenance than those used as bed and breakfasts, and there is already a multiweek leasable home in the area owned by the Leroys.

Which one of the following, if true, would most weaken the argument above?

(A) The price a week at a leased vacation home can command is often much greater than the amount paid by a week's worth of bed and breakfast guests.
(B) Due to wear and tear, leased vacation homes tend to be leasable for only a few years, while bed and breakfasts can typically host guests for over a decade.
(C) The taxes on the Jenkins' vacation home would not be substantially higher if it were used as a vacation home than if it were used as a bed and breakfast.
(D) The number of tourists visiting the area in which the Jenkins' vacation home is located has substantially increased in recent years.
(E) There has never been a bed and breakfast in the area in which the Jenkins' vacation home is located.

600- to 700-Level Argument Assumption Practice Set

1. Experts have long been puzzled by how a craftsman of humble origins like Stradivarius could have developed a technique for making such exquisitely perfect violins, but a new hypothesis offers a different explanation. A drought during Stradivarius' lifetime affected the growth of Italian willow and maple trees, resulting in wood with superior acoustic properties, and thus the reputation of these violins owes more to the materials used than the man using them.

   Which of the following is an assumption upon which the hypothesis in the argument above relies?

   (A) No other Italian violin makers produced violins from the same materials as Stradivarius used.
   (B) No violin that is made with different materials could ever match the quality of a Stradivarius.
   (C) A violin made from the wood of trees whose growth was unaffected by drought would be less perfect than a Stradivarius.
   (D) The reputation of Stradivarius violins rests mostly on the name alone and not the qualities of the violin itself.
   (E) The violins made by Stradivarius were not made entirely of wood harvested before he was born.

2. There can be no doubt that Earth is currently experiencing a loss of species diversity. Though it is true that extinction is a natural process and that the rate at which species are going extinct has remained the same since the middle of the last century, it is also true that the rate at which new species emerge to replace those lost cannot be accelerated.

   Which of the following, if true, most strengthens the conclusion that Earth is experiencing a loss of species diversity?

   (A) The media that reports upon the loss of species diversity is not unduly biased in favor of environmentalists.
   (B) The climates and habitats most prone to species loss are also those most conducive to species emergence.
   (C) As no species can survive indefinitely, all species will eventually go extinct.
   (D) By the middle of the last century, fewer species were emerging than were being lost to extinction.
   (E) Scientists have made great advancements in technologies that allow species loss to be recorded.

3. Genetically modified (GMO) crops can be designed so that they are resistant to the effects of a particular herbicide. Consequently, that herbicide can be used to kill harmful weeds without fear of damaging the crop. This advantage comes with too great a price for farmers, however, as the biotech companies that create these crops also render them sterile, requiring seeds for each year's planting to be purchased where before farmers could grow their own seed.

Each of the following, if true, would weaken the conclusion above EXCEPT:

(A) The herbicides used to kill the weeds that threaten genetically modified crops require substantially fewer man-hours to apply than standard alternatives.

(B) When a company is allowed to control the dissemination of its products, it need not increase their price.

(C) The yield realized by farmers growing genetically modified crops is much larger than that of previous nonmodified crops.

(D) The herbicides designed to work with genetically modified crops are sold only by the biotech companies that produce the seeds for those crops.

(E) Crops grown for seed often require a significant investment of time and resources to harvest.

4. Recently, a study of donations to the city's public radio station found that, on average, the dollar value of each pledged donation was higher during the winter drive than during the one held midsummer. The study was funded by the station itself and from it the station's owners concluded that in order to increase the amount of money donated to the station, the winter drive should be extended an extra week.

Which of the following, if true, casts doubt on the station owners' plan?

(A) A study conducted by an independent group found that donations to the station are down 10 percent this year.

(B) Those who pledge donations to the station during the winter often do so in order to obtain an income tax deduction.

(C) People who donate money to public radio typically do so only once per calendar year.

(D) Neither the midsummer drive nor the winter drive are as successful at securing donations as the late fall drive.

(E) Though people may pledge to donate money during a drive, they are under no obligation to actually donate that money.

5. Cornell University's Center for Hospitality Research has conducted many studies of tipping behavior over the past decade. Their research shows that, in general, women receive higher tips than men and that women in their thirties receive better tips than younger or older women. Susan is an attractive single mother in her mid-thirties, so it is reasonable for her to expect to be tipped well.

Which of the following indicates the most serious problem with the reasoning above?

(A) The studies do not provide a basis to expect that an attractive person will receive better tips than an unattractive person.

(B) A general rule is drawn from a series of cases that may be atypical.

(C) No information is given concerning the manner in which the Cornell Center conducted its research.

(D) The studies do not address the question of whether age also affects the tips received by men.

(E) An average trend need not hold true in any particular case.

700- to 800-Level Argument Assumption Practice Set

1. In a typical circus troupe, acrobats perform for one fifth of the show's duration, are involved in one fourth of all performance-related accidents, and account for one third of the cost of insurance premiums paid by the show. In order to remain in business, a circus cannot afford to spend more than one-fourth of its budget on any one type of performer.

Each of the following, if true, would provide support for a ringleader's decision to reduce the performance time of a troupe's acrobats EXCEPT?

(A) The longer a performer performs, the more likely a costly accident will occur.

(B) Insurance premiums for circuses are primarily paid to insure its performers against accidents.

(C) The single biggest cost a circus pays is the cost of insuring its performers against accidents.

(D) Ticket sales for a circus's performances would not decline if acrobats performed less.

(E) The accidents that an acrobat is likely to suffer do not occur primarily at the beginning of a performance.

2. Many businesses hire consultants to formulate plans to manage impending growth, and businesses that hire consultants do subsequently perform better than those that do not. Yet many consultants acknowledge that the advice offered by consultants is not insightful and that in many cases their advice is actually ignored. It is clear then that whatever the reason for these businesses' increased performance, it is not the advice given by the consultants hired.

   Which of the following, if true, would weaken the argument above?

   (A) A consultant can be trusted when he or she provides information about the value of his or her own advice.
   (B) When preparing for the future, the quality of potential strategies considered is less important than the quantity.
   (C) The core leadership at a business should be expected to know more about the businesses' needs than an outsider.
   (D) Businesses that are unable to afford the expense of hiring consultants are unlikely to successfully manage impending growth.
   (E) While no single consultant will be an expert on all types of businesses, consulting firms employ many consultants with different skills.

3. In the famous 1971 Stanford prison experiment, participants were sent to a derelict prison where they were randomly assigned roles as either jailor or prisoner. After a week, the experiment was ended, as in that time those acting as jailors had become so cruel to their "charges" that it was deemed unethical to risk continuing any longer.

   Which of the following is an assumption underlying the decision to end the experiment?

   (A) Whenever people are given unequal amounts of power, those with more power will abuse it.
   (B) Practical considerations are not the only grounds by which to evaluate an experiment.
   (C) If an experiment is damaging to its participants, it must be ended immediately.
   (D) Experimental methods that damage the participants of an experiment unequally are unethical.
   (E) It is possible to determine whether an experiment's results will be unethical after only a week.

4. The most common injury faced by regular swimmers is rotator cuff impingement, which in many cases leads to painful tendonitis in the swimmer's inflamed shoulder. In amateur swimmers, impingement is most often the result of poor stroke technique. The problem plagues even expert swimmers, however, as a properly executed stroke can still damage the cuff when the surrounding muscles are weakened from overtraining. In an effort to keep its expert swimmers from being sidelined by rotator cuff impingement in the crucial lead up to the Olympic Games, the U.S. team has instituted a required program of regular stretching exercises paired with core stability training.

Which of the following, if true, addresses a potential problem with U.S. Olympic swim team's strategy for preventing rotator cuff impingement injuries?

(A) Though some swimmers will resist the new requirement, the Olympic team is unlikely to completely ban a swimmer from competition for failing to complete the required exercises.

(B) The U.S. team adopted the new requirements only after observing that other swim teams who had adopted similar requirements saw a decrease in the number of rotator cuff injuries.

(C) While core stability training does not directly strengthen the muscles near the rotator cuff, those muscles can supplement the function of those muscles that do.

(D) At each of the last three Olympic Games, swimmers on the U.S. team were thought to have failed to perform to their potential after damaging their rotator cuffs during practice.

(E) The doctors and clinicians who advise the U.S. Olympic swim team have been recommending for many years that a new strategy for preventing rotator cuff impingement be instituted by the team.

5. Without a deep, still body of water, the most popular sport fish cannot survive. Such bodies of water inevitably attract substantial beachfront development when those who fish for sport frequent the area. Building a dam on a shallow river is one way to create such a body, but maintaining a dam is economical only if there is also a market for hydroelectric power nearby. Thus, towns with no nearby market for hydroelectric power will tend not to build dams, so they will also be unlikely to have the most popular sport fish in their rivers.

Which of the following most accurately describes a flaw in the reasoning of the argument?

(A) The argument confuses what is necessary for substantial beachfront development with what would guarantee it.

(B) The argument fails to consider that deep, still pools of water might be present even in the absence of a particular condition that would ensure their presence.

(C) The argument confuses what is necessary for the most popular sport fish to survive with what is usually conducive to it.

(D) The argument fails to consider the possibility that hydroelectric power is only one of several advantages of a dam.

(E) The argument bases a claim that there is a causal connection between the presence of deep, still bodies of water and substantial beachfront development on a mere association between them.

Fact-Based Questions

500- to 600-Level Fact-Based Question Practice Set

1. Cement is composed primarily of two ingredients, calcium and silicon, mixed with small amounts of aluminum and iron. Sources of these ingredients are common—shale, limestone, basalt, and even industrial slag may be used—are not expensive, and can easily be substituted with other sources. The price of cement is, however, tightly connected to the price of oil, at least in the modern era, because the process of combining these ingredients into cement requires large amounts of energy.

    If the statements above are true, which of the following is most likely to also be true?

    (A) Oil should be considered one of cement's basic ingredients.
    (B) Oil is the primary source of the energy used in combining ingredients into cement.
    (C) If the price of shale were to increase, the price of cement would rise.
    (D) When the price of oil rises, cement manufacturers lower their overall costs by using cheaper substitutes as ingredients.
    (E) The cement necessary to build a parking garage costs more than the total cost of its basic ingredients.

2. Retail stores often use pleasant scents in order to entice customers to enter the store, a successful technique that usually results in greater sales, though the scent used by a given store need not be the same as that used by another. Indeed, bakeries that use fans to circulate the scent of baking bread to customers see similar increases in sales as clothing retailers that place potpourri strategically through their aisles. However, when a store is the only one in a mall that uses this strategy to increase sales, it generally experiences the opposite.

    Which of the following, if true, most helps to resolve the apparent discrepancy described above?

    (A) If only one store in a mall has a distinguishable scent, customers intuitively suspect the store of manipulation and avoid it.
    (B) When several enticing smells are present in a mall, customers who fail to be enticed by one smell may find another to their liking.
    (C) The presence of an enticing smell emanating from one business can sometimes increase the sales of nearby businesses.
    (D) When there is only one store in a mall that uses a marketing strategy, if it is successful, others will often follow suit.
    (E) If a bakery using this strategy were adjacent to a clothing store also using it, the clash of smells would not be enticing to customers of either.

3. Without the presence of Jupiter in our solar system, Earth would likely not be inhabited. Planets in solar systems with sizeable asteroid belts are subject periodically to meteor strikes that eradicate the biological precursors required for life to develop. The gravitational pull of a large gas giant such as Jupiter protects the other planets in its system from meteor strikes by attracting asteroid debris.

If the statements above are true, which of the following must also be true?

(A) If a solar system does not have a large gas giant such as Jupiter, no planet in it will be inhabited.

(B) If Jupiter were somehow destroyed by meteor strikes, life on Earth would cease to be.

(C) If Jupiter were somehow destroyed by meteor strikes, life would be less likely to develop on currently uninhabited planets in our solar system.

(D) Any planet that is found in a system with an asteroid belt cannot support life unless it is near to a gas giant such as Jupiter.

(E) No planet that is found in a system with more than one asteroid belt can support life.

4. The Bactrian camel (*Camelus ferus*) is likely the ancestor of all domestic two-humped camels. For many years, its chief remaining habitat was used as a nuclear testing site, and though the Bactrian camel is more resistant to radiation than nearly any other animal, its numbers declined. When weapons testing was at last banned in 1992, it was thought that the Bactrian camel would rebound, but, in fact, its population has declined precipitously since 1992, at a much greater rate than prior.

Which of the following, if true, most helps to explain the increased rate of population decline?

(A) Though the Bactrian camel is the ancestor of domestic camels, it is not itself domesticated.

(B) Before the ban, the nation in control of the site had already voluntarily reduced its testing there substantially.

(C) Because of the residual background radiation, the testing site remains hazardous to most animal life.

(D) The greatest single threat to Bactrian camels while the testing site was operational was disease.

(E) Poachers, who hunt the Bactrian camel for its meat, were not able to enter the test site when it was operational.

5. The presence of sugar in the bloodstream directly affects the release of insulin; when more sugar is present, more insulin is released into the body. Yet those who regularly consume large amounts of sugar often have below-average levels of insulin in their blood.

Which of the following, if true, most helps contribute to an explanation of the anomalous phenomenon described above?

(A) The more overweight a person is, the lower the level of insulin in that person's blood.
(B) Though considered healthier diet choices, many fruits contain as much sugar as candy does.
(C) Consuming large amounts of sugar causes the receptors that trigger the release of insulin to become less sensitive to sugar.
(D) Consuming large amounts of processed sugar can be much more dangerous than sugar found naturally in foods.
(E) Insulin does not directly metabolize sugar, but instead triggers the process that metabolizes it.

600- to 700-Level Fact-Based Question Practice Set

1. The years between 1880 and 1905 saw a boom in timber production in Mississippi, which, by 1905, produced as much as one billion board feet of timber per year. Compare that to the rather more meager 300,000 board feet of timber produced annually in 1880. Yet in that same period, the labor force employed by timber mills in Mississippi actually shrank by about 10 percent.

Which of the following, if true, most helps to explain the apparent discrepancy in the timber industry in Mississippi during the period indicated?

(A) The timber industry in Mississippi has never been so productive as it was during the three decades following 1880.
(B) Between 1880 and 1905, the total number of acres of virgin timberland in Mississippi fell substantially.
(C) Since 1905, the majority of lumber produced in Mississippi has relied upon young second-growth timber.
(D) Between 1880 and 1905, timber was such a large part of Mississippi's economy that many new labor saving technologies were implemented by the industry.
(E) Between 1850 and 1950, Mississippi's economy transitioned from primarily agrarian to primarily industrial, due in part to the timber industry's success.

2. Which of the following best completes the argument below?

Moral philosophers contend that it is important for public officials to avoid even the appearance of wrong-doing. However, actions that appear wrong are not always wrong. The main reason that these philosophers give for their contention is that public officials will be unable to maintain public trust if they appear to be doing things that are considered wrong by the general public. Yet no one should be obligated to conform to the moral standards of the general public; therefore, _____.

(A) no public official should be obligated to avoid the appearance of wrong-doing.

(B) all public officials have, to a degree, an interest in maintaining the public's trust.

(C) public officials who have scrupulously avoided even the appearance of wrong-doing will be trusted by the general public.

(D) moral philosophers will never accept that the public might trust a public official who presents the appearance of wrong-doing.

(E) public officials who abuse their power without the public's knowledge are morally wrong for hiding their wrong-doing.

3. Babies who are born deaf and who are raised by deaf parents who communicate with them through sign language begin to "babble" at the same age as those babies born able to hear and who are raised by parents who also can hear and who communicate with them verbally. Only in this first group of babies the babbling takes the form of repetitive hand gestures, while in the second group the babbling manifests as repetitive vocalizations. Scientists believe that these hand gestures are analogous to the vocalizations and that both represent evidence that babbling babies first babble in preparation for subsequent communication with their parents.

The information above provides the most support for scientists to also conclude that

(A) the simplest words in a language are those babies are able to understand early in their development.

(B) if babies are raised by parents who do not communicate with them in any way, they will not babble.

(C) when they first babble, babies are not aware that the sounds or gestures they make could allow them to communicate.

(D) hand gestures made by babies who are able to hear should also be interpreted as precursors to communication.

(E) when their parents are not present, babies who babble with vocalizations will continue to vocalize.

4. Adjuvants are chemicals that farmers apply to plants in order to increase the penetration and adherence of pesticides. Regulators are considering banning the most popular adjuvant because it appears to cause birth defects. There are no substitutes, however, that are as easily applied or as economical to use. If the overall cost of applying pesticide to crops increases, many farmers will go out of business.

Which of the following is most strongly supported by the information above?

(A) If the information about the side-effects of the most popular adjuvant is true, many farmers will go out of business.

(B) If the use of the most popular adjuvant is not banned, the incidence of birth defects will continue to climb.

(C) If the regulators' ban is not enforced, then no farmers will go out of business.

(D) If pesticides become harder to apply or less effective, most farmers will go out of business.

(E) If the regulator's ban is successful, some farmers will go out of business unless they can otherwise reduce their pesticide-related costs.

5. There are 3500 calories in each pound of body fat. It should follow that if a person were to add 3500 calories to their diet beyond their current energy needs, by the end of the year they would be 365 pounds heavier and after 10 years would weigh over 3650 pounds. There are people who have added 3500 extra calories to their daily diets, but the heaviest person ever recorded weighed only 920 pounds.

Which of the following, if true, would best explain why, counter to the expectation, there are no people who weigh more than 920 pounds?

(A) Few people who add 3500 calories to their daily diet will be able to maintain that level of caloric consumption for a decade.

(B) Energy needs vary from person to person and over the course of a single person's life.

(C) Many people who add 3500 calories to their daily diet die from obesity-related health problems before 10 years have passed.

(D) Each extra pound of fat that the body carries increases the energy required for every activity.

(E) No expert would ever recommend that a person consume so much in excess of what their body needs in order to function.

700- to 800-Level Fact-Based Question Practice Set

1. We intuitively know that all acts that are morally wrong should not be done because our intuition senses that these acts violate our basic autonomy as rational human beings. Any violation of our basic autonomy as rational beings ought to be avoided to the same degree as any other violation and punished accordingly. Murder is certainly wrong, whether it be the murder of one elderly criminal or a bus full of innocent children.

    Which of the following judgments follows from the principles stated above?

    (A) If it is noble to risk one's life saving the lives of others, then it is no nobler to risk one's life saving many lives than to risk it saving one life.
    (B) If stealing is morally wrong and adultery is morally wrong, then lying about one's adultery ought to be twice as intuitively obvious as merely lying.
    (C) If murdering is morally wrong, then accidentally causing a person's death is as much a violation of our basic autonomy as murdering that person.
    (D) If lying is morally wrong, then falsely claiming to have murdered someone ought to be punished to the same degree as if the liar had actually committed the murder.
    (E) If asked to choose between killing someone or letting that person kill someone else, there is no choice that is morally correct.

2. The first fishes were jawless, until 400 million years ago one species developed jaws and branched away from its ancestors. These jawed fishes evolved into two distinct lines, those that retained the cartilage-based skeletal structure of their evolutionary ancestors, and those that replaced most of its cartilage with bone. From this latter group, nearly every land-based warm-blooded species evolved, species as different as the field mouse and the elephant.

    If all of the statements in the passage above are true, which of the following must also be true?

    (A) The skeletons of land-based mammals are never composed of cartilage.
    (B) Fish species without jaws became extinct at least 400 million years ago.
    (C) Fish species without jaws did not have skeletons that contained bone 400 million years ago.
    (D) All warm-blooded, land-based species have skeletons composed primarily of bone.
    (E) Field mice and elephants evolved from different species of fish, both of which had jaws.

3. The North Island trade federation is composed of three fully autonomous states: Llassu, Tragda, and Baflazam. Under their trade agreement, each of the members receives a share of the federation's total trade revenues proportional to the state's population as a percentage of the total population of the three states. Though originally Tragda received the greatest share, followed by Baflazam and then Llassu, after the most recent population survey, the federation adjusted the share of trade revenues received by Tragda downward, even though its population grew more than did Llassu's.

If the adjustment to trade revenues that followed the population survey was made in accordance with the trade federation's agreement, which of the following must be true of the three countries in the year surveyed?

(A) The three countries, if arranged from greatest population to least, would be listed Baflazam, Llassu, Tragda.
(B) The three countries, if arranged from greatest population change to least, would be listed Tragda, Baflazam, Llassu.
(C) The three countries, if arranged from greatest population growth to least, would be listed Baflazam, Tragda, Llassu.
(D) The three countries, if arranged from greatest population growth to least, would be listed Tragda, Llassu, Baflazam.
(E) The three countries, if arranged from least population growth to most, would be listed Baflazam, Tragda, Llassu.

4. Studies show that helmets significantly reduce injuries to motorcyclists from accidents. Accordingly, laws have been passed mandating the use of helmets in many states. Yet in states that have passed these laws, substantial numbers of motorcyclists suffering serious injuries of the sort that helmets have been specifically shown to reduce or prevent continue to arrive in the emergency room—nearly as many as before the laws went into effect.

Which of the following, if true, could by itself contribute to an explanation of the apparent persistence of preventable injuries in states that have passed motorcycle helmet laws?

(A) After the passage of laws requiring motorcyclists wear helmets, many more people tend to adopt what comes quickly to be seen as a safe hobby.
(B) Many motorcyclists choose to defy the law, as it is inconsistent with the reasons that made motorcycles attractive to them in the first place.
(C) Helmets cannot adequately protect motorcyclists unless they are regularly worn, and many motorcyclists only wear them occasionally.
(D) Helmets cannot protect motorcyclists against all injuries that might be sustained while riding.
(E) Unless helmets are carefully fitted to their rider, they do not offer the full protection that studies have demonstrated.

5. In the early 1990s, only 10 percent of people in the United States reported that they personally knew someone who was HIV positive. By the end of the decade, that number jumped to 58 percent, even though the number of people suffering from diagnosed cases of HIV in the population of the United States was slightly less in 2000 than it had been in 1990.

Which of the following, if true, could account for the apparent discrepancy in the data above?

(A) Improved therapeutic options allowed many people suffering from HIV to live well beyond initial estimates.

(B) In the decade between 1990 and 2000, several prominent celebrities revealed they had been diagnosed with HIV.

(C) Many of those diagnosed with HIV before 1990 died from complications related to the disease before 2000.

(D) Those with HIV often failed to be diagnosed properly until new techniques were developed in the early 1990s.

(E) The number of treatment options available to people suffering from diagnosed cases of HIV expanded greatly between 1990 and 2000.

Answer Key

ARGUMENT STRUCTURE QUICK REVIEW QUESTIONS

1. **(C)**   2. **(C)**   3. **(A)**   4. **(B)**

ASSUMPTION QUICK REVIEW QUESTIONS

1. **(A)**   2. **(D)**   3. **(C)**   4. **(C)**

ASSUMPTION FAMILY QUICK REVIEW QUESTIONS

1. **(A)**   3. **(C)**   5. **(B)**
2. **(B)**   4. **(E)**

FACT-BASED QUICK REVIEW QUESTIONS

1. **(E)**   3. **(E)**   5. **(D)**
2. **(D)**   4. **(E)**

500- TO 600-LEVEL ARGUMENT STRUCTURE PRACTICE SET

1. **(B)**   3. **(A)**   5. **(E)**
2. **(C)**   4. **(C)**

600- TO 700-LEVEL ARGUMENT STRUCTURE PRACTICE SET

1. **(D)**   3. **(C)**   5. **(A)**
2. **(D)**   4. **(C)**

700- TO 800-LEVEL ARGUMENT STRUCTURE PRACTICE SET

1. **(D)**   3. **(B)**   5. **(C)**
2. **(D)**   4. **(E)**

500- TO 600-LEVEL ARGUMENT ASSUMPTION PRACTICE SET

1. **(D)**   3. **(C)**   5. **(B)**
2. **(C)**   4. **(B)**

600- TO 700-LEVEL ARGUMENT ASSUMPTION PRACTICE SET

1. **(E)**   3. **(D)**   5. **(E)**
2. **(D)**   4. **(C)**

700- TO 800-LEVEL ARGUMENT ASSUMPTION PRACTICE SET

1. **(C)**   3. **(B)**   5. **(B)**
2. **(B)**   4. **(C)**

1. **(E)**   3. **(C)**   5. **(C)**
2. **(A)**   4. **(E)**

600- TO 700-LEVEL FACT-BASED QUESTION PRACTICE SET

1. **(D)**   3. **(B)**   5. **(D)**
2. **(A)**   4. **(E)**

700- TO 800-LEVEL FACT-BASED QUESTION PRACTICE SET

1. **(D)**   3. **(C)**   5. **(C)**
2. **(C)**   4. **(A)**

Explanations

Argument Structure Quick Review Questions

1. **Argument:** The keyword *since* points to evidence for the conclusion *this (having assessors work as salespeople) is a clear conflict of interest.* That evidence is that high diamond prices mean high commissions.

   (C) The statement indicated in the stem is the argument's conclusion, eliminating all answer choices but the correct one, (C).

2. **Argument:** Even though the prompt mentions that continental drift theory was once controversial, we are never given the controversy, only the theory (named in the first bolded statement) and the evidence for it (part of which is in the second bolded statement).

   (C) The answers offer a 2/2/1 split about the first statement's role. Answer Choice (D)'s *phenomenon* is out because the phenomenon is the "single massive continent." Answer Choices (A) and (E)'s *explanations* are also out because the explanation isn't *given* in the first bolded statement, just referenced. Answer Choice (B) can be eliminated because no *test* is found in the prompt, just some reported evidence.

3. **Argument:** There are two arguments here. The professor argues that *the associations people have with words are sometimes unwarranted*, offering the *example of "moist"* as evidence. The student takes issue, providing an **alternate interpretation**, that *some negative associations might "stick" to a word*, but, importantly, the student doesn't contradict the professor's evidence.

   (A) Answer Choices (C) and (D) are out because they don't clearly state that the student's conclusion is *against* or *counter* to the professor's. Answer Choicer (B) is wrong because the student's evidence isn't an *exception* to the rule, and Answer Choice (E) can be dispensed with because the student never specifically indicates that the professor *might* be right.

4. **Argument:** The structure is more important than the content for a Parallel Argument question. Accordingly, this argument's structure is best described as *a conclusion that a practice is bad, supported by the evidence that a necessary part of the practice is, by definition, unable to accomplish the practice's goal.*

   (B) Answer Choices (A), (B), and (C) all get the initial conclusion right, *a practice is bad*, but Answer Choices (D) and (E) do not, so they're out. (A) adds the exception *unless there's no other alternative*, which isn't found in the original, and (C) doesn't present evidence that there's a problem with a part of the plan; rather it states that the plan will later have bad effects.

Assumption Quick Review Questions

1. **Argument:** The conclusion straddles the *therefore*: *The World Bank should shift funds to mosquito nets in order to reduce the rate of malaria*—a **Net Benefit** calculation that cites only one advantage: mosquito nets work. Thus, the argument assumes that *there are no unexplored advantages or disadvantages.*

   (A) The correct answer presents just such an advantage, that malaria exposure is sometimes helpful. Answer Choices (B) and (E) are **Irrelevant Comparisons**, Answer Choice (C) is a false **Extreme**, and Answer Choice (D) is **One Step Removed**, as the argument is not that the effect of the change will be beneficial *overall*, merely to the malaria rate.

2. **Argument:** The conclusion is an absolute **Recommendation**, that there is only *one* method that must be used, the European method. The evidence establishes only that North American and European schools differ with regards to method and performance. Thus, the argument assumes that *all relevant differences have been taken into account* AND that *there are no other ways to accomplish the goal.* This latter assumption shows up in the correct answer choice.

   (D) Answer Choices (A) and (B) are false **Extremes** that go well beyond the scope of the argument, which doesn't claim that every student will be helped, just that students in general will improve. Answer Choice (C) is **Extreme** as well, as the argument doesn't need *most* students to improve, either, just *enough* to reduce the achievement gap. Answer Choice (E) is meant to be close enough to the right answer to fool you, but it is ultimately a **Misplaced Detail**. Note that the argument's conclusion is that the choice of methods is either one or the other, not that the ideology that motivates the methods is important.

3. **Argument:** The argument's conclusion is that *competence* is important to *success*, but the evidence only establishes that there's a relationship between *the number of credits* and *elementary students' reported satisfaction*. Clearly, lots of gaps exist between these four concepts. Because this is an EXCEPT question, four answers will be assumptions, one will not. That one, (C), is **Interesting but Irrelevant**, as the conclusion does not make a **recommendation** of what to do; it merely asserts a connection between two things.

(C) Answer Choice (A) fills the gap between *credits* and *competence*, Answer Choice (B) is a **Defending** assumption against the possibility that elementary students are just bad judges of *competence*, Answer Choice (D) addresses the **Causal** assumption that the correlation isn't just coincidental, and Answer Choice (E) fills the gap between *success* and *satisfaction*.

4. **Argument:** This question features a **Causal** argument (consumer expectations will *probably* cause a recession) that also involves a **Representative** relationship between one sign (durable goods sales) and an economy's overall health. The first assumption appears in the correct answer, **connecting** the cause and effect.

    (C) Answer Choice (A) confuses **Necessity and Sufficiency**—causes are sufficient, but not always necessary. Answer Choice (B) is **Interesting but Irrelevant**, as the conclusion only concerns what happens before a recession, not what happens after, and Answer Choice (D) is the same. Answer Choice (E) is an **Irrelevant Comparison**, since the argument never ranks causes, only asserts that one thing (confidence) is a direct cause.

Assumption Family Quick Review Questions

1. **Argument:** The conclusion is found at the end: once people become aware of the superiority of human cognitive faculties, they will never be able to be happy doing things that don't involve those faculties. The evidence is more modest than the conclusion, establishing only that these faculties exist; thus, the argument assumes *their effect on happiness is inevitable*. The correct answer raises a question directly relevant to this assumption.

    (A) Answer Choice (B) would be **Interesting but Irrelevant**, as the conclusion doesn't concern what happens to people who *aren't* aware of these faculties, and Answer Choice (C) is as well, since the conclusion also doesn't concern whether other animals might be happy or smart. Answer Choice (D) is meant to trap you into **real-world thinking**, and is **one step removed** from relevance to the argument, as we don't know if these people in Answer Choice (D) are aware or not aware of their faculties. Answer Choice (E) follows suit, addressing people the argument doesn't make claims about, those who don't want to be happy.

2. **Argument:** The argument **switches terms** between evidence and conclusion: the evidence is that these *expert people won't be selected* for jury duty because of their *biasing* effect on juries, but the conclusion goes further and says that, thus, jury trials will never be *fair*. Thus, the argument assumes that *experts are required for fairness*. The correct answer gives us reason to suspect the assumption's truth by showing that experts are themselves biased (and thus not fair).

    (B) Answer Choice (A) is **Interesting but Irrelevant**, further fleshing out how often experts are left out, but not addressing whether this affects the *fairness* of the trial. Answer Choice (C) is a **real-world thinking** trap, something probably true, but irrelevant to the argument, which has nothing to do with witnesses who *testify*, only with those who are *excluded*. Answer Choice (D) is similar, as it doesn't matter what happens when jury trials *aren't* used. Answer Choice (E) is also **Interesting but Irrelevant**, as it doesn't matter what happens with the *testifying* experts.

3. **Argument:** While there is some **causal** information in the evidence, the conclusion here is **recommendation** of the **plan** to *add distilled flavonoids to nonalcoholic beverages* in order *reduce the risk of heart disease*. The argument thus has a **feasibility** assumption: *nothing involved in the plan would stop it from working*, namely *removing the flavonoids from their original environment*. Answer Choice (C) strengthens the argument by asserting that the removal won't hurt the flavonoid's efficacy.

   (C) Answer Choice (A) is irrelevant **evidence for the evidence,** providing the explanation of *how* the flavonoids benefit the heart without discussing the *plan*. So, too, is Answer Choice (B), which explains why people don't drink alcohol, **true but irrelevant**. Answer Choice (D) provides an additional benefit to the plan, which would only be relevant if the argument were some sort of **net benefit** calculation, which it isn't. And Answer Choice (E) uses the distraction of *children*, a **misplaced detail**, to provide more **evidence for the evidence** that fat hurts the heart.

4. **Argument:** The editorial's argument is a **recommendation** that a **plan** *not* be enacted, based on evidence whose **connection** to the conclusion isn't established. What does *walking* have to do with *using the pool?* Answer Choice (E) weakens the necessary connection by providing an alternate explanation for why people walk to the pool (not because it's in walking distance, but because they can't drive there).

   (E) Answer Choices (A), (B), and (C) are all **Interesting but Irrelevant**, as none of them touch on the connection between walking and pool use. Answer Choice (D) is also irrelevant, a bit of **real-world thinking** that's reasonable in context. We know money's often the reason why public services get cut, but this argument doesn't concern cost at all.

5. **Argument:** The argument's conclusion, *the CEO must have considered all the risks*, is a bit of a leap from the evidence, which only establishes that *risks are necessary for a company to thrive*. How this necessity demonstrates the CEO's weighing of the risks is left open, and the correct answer points this out.

   (B) (A) is hoping to trick you by bringing up something relevant in the **real world**, but not in the limited world of this argument. We don't need to know *why* she thinks the risk is justified, only that she has considered the risk sufficiently. (C) brings up an **irrelevant comparison** with other companies, (D) and (E) both hint that the flaw is a case of **unexamined alternatives**, but this argument doesn't concern alternatives or multiple options, only whether the CEO has weighed the risk of this *one specific option*.

Fact-Based Quick Review Questions

1. **Facts:** The prompt contains two definite statements that restate the same idea. In a nutshell, insurance is required for happiness; lacking insurance is a guarantee that you will be unhappy. Answer Choice (E) states this through a **double negative** (not lack health insurance = have health insurance).

(E) Answer Choices (A), (B), (C), and (D) each in their own way confuse something necessary with something sufficient and/or vice versa.

2. **Dilemma:** The horns of the **Unrealized Expectation** dilemma: (1) There was a lot of oil-based damage during the war, but (2) the amount of oil-based pollution present after the war was less than before the war's damage. Answer Choice (D) explains away this discrepancy by showing that before the war there were lots of things doing oil-based damage; thus, by comparison, the war was good for pollution counts.

    (D) Answer Choice (A) is **Reasonable but Irrelevant**, as the dilemma doesn't concern health directly, just pollution levels; Answer Choice (B) doesn't resolve the discrepancy, as the rate of dissipation wouldn't have changed between pre- and postwar times; Answer Choice (C) is simply **irrelevant**, as there wasn't any rainfall; and Answer Choice (E) is an **irrelevant comparison**, but clearly meant to distract you by bringing up another expectation, the amount of damage expected to the oil industry (distinct from the amount of pollution caused by the oil-based damage).

3. **Dilemma:** In this **Explain** question, the **dilemma** is a **Rule Violation**. The rule in the first sentence states that lowering the speed limit should result in longer travel times. But the situation on I-511 violates that rule, since speed limits were lowered and rush-hour travel times *decreased*. Answer Choice (D) shows that, in this case, the general rule doesn't apply, because there is an additional factor, *accidents caused by drivers driving over 65 miles per hour*, that was lowering the travel times before the new law went in place and would have been at least partially eliminated by the law.

    (D) Answer Choices (A) and (B) are **irrelevant to the dilemma**, because they don't apply to the specific scenario. It doesn't matter what happened during *off-peak hours* or the *first week*, since the dilemma is specific to *rush hour* and *the first few months*. Answer Choices (C) and (E) **worsen the dilemma** by eliminating possible differences between the period before the reduction and after it took effect that could have possibly accounted for the change.

4. **Facts:** The prompt presents a series of Formal Logic statements. Translated and linked, they reveal

    professor (at state U) $\rightarrow$ 35 or over $\rightarrow$ eligible (by age) to be president
    ineligible to be president $\rightarrow$ under 35 $\rightarrow$ not a professor

    The remaining statements are all "somes." Some intelligent people are professors, some are over 35, and some are under 35. Applying the contrapositive to this under 35 group (which includes no professors), we can infer Answer Choice (E).

    (E) Answer Choice (A) is a clever distraction, since being eligible to be elected president *allows* one to be 35 or over 35. Answer Choice (B) is **too extreme**, moving from our *somes* to *all*. Answer Choices (C) and (D) are both **possible but not definite**, consistent with what we know, but they not 100 percent definitely the case, either.

5. **Dilemma:** The horns of this **flouted trend** dilemma are (1) consumer spending starts high but then dips in a recession, but (2) the inflationary pressure still means that purchases delayed should cost more, AND the consumers have more money when wages rise. Answer Choice (D) provides the extra fact that makes this seemingly contradictory behavior sensible: wages don't rise faster than inflation, so the consumers do actually have less money to spend, regardless of how much they might want to save in the long run by making advance purchases.

(D) Answer Choice (A) **worsens the dilemma** by providing further evidence that early and late parts of a recession are similar; Answer Choice (B) is **reasonable but irrelevant**, since the dilemma takes place after consumer recognition has begun; Answer Choice (C) is also **reasonable but irrelevant**, hoping to prey on your **real-world thinking** (because it's probably true, but doesn't help resolve the dilemma); and Answer Choice (E) **worsens the dilemma** by giving a reason why spending ought to rise rather than fall.

500- to 600-Level Argument Structure Practice Set

1. **Argument:** The first sentence contains the conclusion (also the statement we are asked to find the role of), *increased standards of living contribute the most to global warming by increasing carbon dioxide*, **a causal connection**, supported by the evidence that luxuries require energy, and energy requires carbon dioxide and the evidence that when standards of living fell, the amount of carbon dioxide in the atmosphere fell. The correct role for the statement is thus described by Answer Choice (B).

   (B) The answers split 2/2/1 in the beginning: Answer Choices (A) and (C) label the statement a *phenomenon*, but the phenomenon being explained is global climate change, not the increase in standard of living itself. Answer Choices (D) and (E) label the statement as a sort of evidence, which is likewise incorrect.

2. **Argument:** The argument begins by describing a government plan, its method (paying a snake bounty), and its goal (reducing the number of cobras), and then continues to provide an unexpected negative consequence (snake breeding). With this test case taken to be **representative** of all government interventions, the conclusion is drawn in the last sentence: *governments should not employ market-based solutions*, which is precisely what Answer Choice (C) says.

   (C) Answer Choice (A) confuses the past with the present, as the solution isn't being presented now, it's being described; Answer Choice (B) is the **exact opposite** of the correct method, which goes from case to principle, not principle to case, and the same is true for (D); and Answer Choice (E) is clearly wrong, as there is only one solution in the argument.

3. **Argument:** This argument follows a familiar pattern, it's conclusion *some people say X and they're wrong*, with the people being *atheists* and the X that they don't believe in a higher power. The remainder of the argument is evidence for this claim. Through a bit of **double-negative** trickery, the bolded statement becomes the *and they're wrong (because **this** is right)*, which Answer Choice (A) nails.

(A) Answer Choices (D) and (E) can be eliminated because they are the **exact opposite,** claiming the author opposes the bolded position. Answer Choice (C) brings up the **irrelevant** concept of *cause and effect,* the **right answer to the wrong question,** and Answer Choice (B) gets the explanation backwards; the argument explains the bolded statement.

4. **Argument:** The argument begins with the conclusion that the speaker doesn't need to take the trash to the curb and then proceeds to offer as evidence first how things typically work (which seems to imply the speaker *should* take the garbage out), followed by the evidence that this specific case is different because it is a federal holiday, just as Answer Choice (C) describes.

   (C) Answer Choice (A) is out because of the *irrelevant* dig at the speaker (whose reasoning is relevant); Answer Choice (B) mentions the ruling out of causes that never happens; Answer Choice (D) gets the pattern backward; and Answer Choice (E) mentions a jump from probable to inevitable, a flaw, but not one this speaker made.

5. **Argument:** The conclusion is found in the first bolded statement, which helpfully is labeled as a **recommendation**: clients should prepare today for technological development. This conclusion is supported by an explanation of how development works; then in the second bolded statement, a prediction that might seem counter to the conclusion, but that is shown later to be avoidable if precautions are taken, just as Answer Choice (E) describes.

   (E) The answers split off evidence/conclusion 3/2, allowing Answer Choices (A), (B), and (D) to be eliminated. Answer Choice (C), which understands the first bolded statement's role as a conclusion, is out because it says the conclusion is one the author opposes.

600- to 700-Level Argument Structure Practice Set

1. **Argument:** The argument as presented is partially flawed, as the two bolded statements are just restatements of the same conclusion, that the two companies' certainly influenced each other somehow, as Answer Choice (D) correctly points out.

   (D) The answers split 2/3 over whether the two statements play different roles. Answer Choices (A) and (B) say they are different, and can thus be eliminated. Answer Choice (C) calls the statements evidence, rather than conclusion, and Answer Choice (E) misses that the two are not *different* conclusions; the second one is just a restatement.

2. **Argument:** Rare **Role of a Statement** questions name the role and ask for the part that plays it. Here, the main conclusion is wanted, and that conclusion is *cooking should be seen as an example of applied physics, rather than as an art.* "Should" is always a good sign of a conclusion, as "should" needs support, and conclusions are supported by evidence.

(D) The correct answer is just a slightly reworded version of the conclusion. Answer Choices (A) and (E) are evidence, and Answer Choices (B) and (C) are **misused details**, things the argument never actually said—so there's no way they could be the argument's conclusion!

3. **Argument:** This argument's conclusion is the thing that a certain yet unproven hypothesis wouldn't be surprising to archaeologists, since it fits with evidence they already have. The bolded statement is one of those pieces of evidence, thus Answer Choice (C) is the correct answer.

   (C) The 3/2 evidence/conclusion split allows Answer Choices (B) and (E) to be eliminated immediately. All that's left is to choose the proper description of the evidence. Answer Choice (A) fails because of the word *conclusive*; this evidence is only *consistent* with the hypothesis. And Answer Choice (D) is out because the speaker never *opposes* any arguments.

4. **Argument:** The structure of both the correct answer and the original prompt is as follows: two things are compared, to the detriment of one, and the one that fails is thus said not to be able to replace the one that was the better in the comparison.

   (C) Answer Choice (A) can be eliminated because its conclusion is a **negative bare assertion**, while the argument's conclusion was a **definite negative prediction**. Similarly, Answer Choice (B) has a **comparative** conclusion, Answer Choice (D) is a **qualified positive assertion** and Answer Choice (E) a **definite negative assertion**.

5. **Argument:** Two speakers argue over the best way to take their absent friend's recent behavior. The first says it means he is no longer their friend; the second rebuts that the behavior (which he agrees did occur) doesn't have to mean that and provides an **alternate explanation**, as Answer Choice (A) describes.

   (A) All the remaining answer choices describe the second speaker taking some sort of issue with the *evidence*, not with the *interpretation of the evidence*.

700- to 800-Level Argument Structure Practice Set

1. **Argument:** The argument begins with a phenomenon (the first bolded statement); dividends were reduced at the last minute by MegaBiz. This is followed by an explanation attributed to "analysts" who think it's bad news. The author concludes otherwise, or at least points out another explanation is possible, which is the second bolded statement. Answer Choice (D) nails this relationship of *phenomenon and new interpretation/explanation.*

   (D) Answer Choice (A) is the only answer choice that doesn't get that the first statement is the thing being explained. Of the rest, they split over whether the second is a conclusion/alternate explanation or evidence for that explanation. Answer Choices (B) and (E) wrongly treat the second statement as evidence. Answer Choice (C) can be eliminated because it claims the speaker rejects the conclusion actually supported by the argument.

2. **Argument:** This argument begins with the recommendation of "insiders," immediately rejected by the speaker in the first bolded statement. After providing evidence that explains why the insiders are wrong, the speaker provides an explanation of a better strategy (the opposite of the one the insiders supported), as Answer Choice (D) describes.

(D) The most fruitful split is found in the answers' description of the second statement. The goal of the strategy is *reducing the negative effect on the deputy mayor's political future*, but Answer Choice (A) confuses that with a bolded statement. Answer Choices (B) and (D) correctly describe the second statement, whereas Answer Choice (C) gets it backwards, and Answer Choice (E) gets the relationship between the statements wrong (the second is counter to the first). Answer Choice (B) is wrong in a subtle way. The first bolded statement doesn't *assess the goal* but rather the *strategy* to bring the goal about.

3. **Argument:** In this two-party prompt, Eddie claims that Mark won't be able to understand alternative music because he wasn't born when it was made; Mark counters by using the example of something neither of them were alive to see, but which Eddie thinks he can understand (or that he can understand through the professor's interpretations, at least). Answer Choice (B) calls the example an *analogous situation* (which it is) and describes the way it's used (to weaken Eddie's assumptions, just like a good GMAT test taker would).

(B) Answer Choice (A) **misuses details** from the counterexample, in a way that might be tempting to those who didn't have time to read the original (as this is an argument we hear in the **real world** all the time). Answer Choice (C) is out because Mark doesn't contradict evidence; he merely introduces additional evidence. Answer Choice (D) would be fine if it didn't say *definition*, as Mark's evidence doesn't take the form of a definition, and Answer Choice (E) is another **real-world** trap, since Mark doesn't make personal attacks (even though in this situation a person might be expected to).

4. **Argument:** Here we have a contrast between what people used to believe about something and what they believe now. It's barely an argument, but to the extent that it is, the second bolded statement is the conclusion (the new interpretation is probably right), while the first is the old conclusion (the old interpretation). Answer Choice (E) correctly describes both interpretations as *claims* and gets the relationship between the two correct—the first one's bad, the second one's good.

(E) Answer Choices (A), (B), and (C) all get the first statement's role right, but Answer Choice (A) is wrong because it claims the second agrees with the first, Answer Choice (B) because the second is an explanation or a new hypothesis, not a *situation*, and Answer Choice (C) because it labels the second evidence, rather than conclusion. Answer Choice (D) can be eliminated because the first statement is incorrectly described as evidence, rather than a conclusion.

5. **Argument:** Lots of science jargon is used here to distract you from the fairly straightforward argument structure. The first sentence is a long claim: temperature can hurt birds even if they can stand the heat. The remaining information is evidence to support that claim which establishes a chain of X affects Y affects Z. Answer Choice (C) correctly identifies the statement's role in that chain.

(C) Answer Choice (A) confuses evidence for conclusion; (B) is a **misused detail**, hoping to distract you with something mentioned but not relevant; (D) gets the overall argument's conclusion wrong, hoping for a little tempting **reasonable but irrelevant** action; and (E) likewise gets the conclusion wrong, presenting something **too extreme** in any event, but also never said in the argument.

500- to 600-Level Argument Assumption Practice Set

1. **Argument:** The argument's conclusion comes at the end of the prompt, though there is an **intermediate conclusion** in the middle, the **bare assertion** of a **requirement** for something to come about: If the anchovy population (specifically, the population off the cost of Peru) is ever to recover (and the speaker is not saying its recovery is definite or even possible), then it must be that the number of fishing vessels is reduced by 50 percent (the requirement). This intermediate conclusion is supported by a single piece of evidence, the **explanation** of the current reduction (a **causal connection**): a sharp increase in the *number* of fishing vessels. In a sense, the initial evidence is a miniargument for a **net calculation**: more vessels = more anchovy deaths. The speaker adds another piece of evidence (that recently loopholes allowed foreign fishing vessels to ply Peruvian waters). The speaker's final conclusion is found at the end, a **prediction**: the population of anchovies is going to rebound, thanks to this loophole change.

   (D) Clearly, then, the speaker assumes that all the factors that went into the net calculation before, whatever they were, will continue, whereas no other factors that could change the calculation will emerge. The speaker also must assume that the **plan** will not meet with any hurdles. Answer Choice (D) would be relevant to that assumption, as it raises a possible problem with the plan. If the formerly unlicensed ships could re-enter with fresh licenses, the plan would not block the old factors that caused the decrease in anchovies from reoccurring.

   Answer Choices (A), (B), and (C) are meant to mislead by bringing up things that are often relevant to fishing in the **real world**, but that don't matter in this specific case. Answer Choice (B) is **one step removed** from being relevant, as we don't know what would matter about the specific methods used. Answer Choice (E) is likewise **one step removed**, suggesting an **irrelevant comparison** to other fish species—whatever's happening with them, we don't know that similar things are in play with anchovies.

2. **Argument:** It might have been hard for you to find the conclusion because the speaker essentially says it twice, phrasing it differently each time. Why are people wrong to say that there are lots of gun-related homicides? Because gun-related homicides are a rare occurrence. When an argument's conclusion is the same as its evidence, the argument is said to be **circular**, and Answer Choice (C) is just one way the test maker might phrase that flaw—though it should be noted that most often circular arguments appear as distracting wrong answers on the GMAT.

   (C) Answer Choice (A) is **too extreme** to describe this argument, which merely states that there are *a lot* of TV reports on guns, not that *most* TV reports are on guns. The issue of bias, raised in Answer Choice (B) is a **real-world** distraction, the sort of accusation often thrown around when gun control comes up. There's no prediction about the future, so (D) doesn't apply, nor is there a conclusion made about a group, so Answer Choice (E) is irrelevant as well.

3. **Argument:** This question might be easily mistaken for a **Flaw** question, but notice that the stem adds the qualification *if true*, meaning that the speaker's argument isn't definitely wrong, but that it relies on an assumption that *could* be attacked and thereby the argument **Weakened**. The conclusion of the editors' argument is the **stated effect** (former customers of the paper will return to purchasing it) that a **plan** (reducing the paper's price by half) is predicted to have. As evidence, the editors point to two facts: (1) the current price of the paper is higher than tabloid prices, and (2) tabloids have been selling well. As a **prediction** the argument assumes that nothing relevant to the prediction will change (which doesn't factor into the answer of this question), and as a **plan** it assumes that there is nothing that can block the plan from having its stated effect. Answer Choice (C) points to a potential problem with assuming the latter: if the tabloids didn't steal away customers from the paper in the first place (they somehow got non-paper readers to become tabloid readers), then the plan to steal them back probably won't work.

    (C) Answer Choices (A) and (D) are **real-world** facts brought up as distractions. Answer Choices (B) and (E) are **specific numbers**, things we should know to suspect in the fuzzy-math world of the Verbal. Since we don't know if the tabloids' prices before were lower or higher than the paper's prices before or after the plan, Answer Choice (B) is **one step removed** from the argument here. Answer Choice (E) ends up just being more specific **evidence for the evidence** we already know—the argument tells us that tabloids are popular, so finding out they're five times as popular doesn't really change anything.

4. **Argument:** Any two different majorities drawn from the same group must overlap at least once because you can't fit two majorities into the same whole without some overlap. This argument is structured to look like an inference drawn from overlapping majorities, but it fails because the evidence is built on things true of *some* members of the group, not on *most* members of the group. Answer Choice (B) describes this flaw exactly. (For example, it's possible that the Alternative bands only show up on cruises in June, the Broadway groups in March, and the rest of the year neither is present.)

    (B) Answer Choices (A) and (E) are restatements of the same general problem not found here, confusing **necessity and sufficiency/cause and effect**. Answer Choice (C) is a bit of **real-world** thinking (because you probably *don't* associate Broadway fans with Alternative fans). And Answer Choice (D) describes a **circular argument**, which this speaker doesn't make.

5. **Argument:** The argument's conclusion is found on the first line, a **recommendation** of what would be **most profitable** for the Jenkins to do (in other words, a **net benefit calculation**): the Jenkins should opt for a B&B over a long-term lease. The evidence is that (1) maintenance is expensive for B&Bs, (2) there is some precedence in the area for long-term leases, and (3) there is not much difference in demand for either. Thus, the argument assumes that there are no other factors that could significantly throw off the calculation, and Answer Choice (B) presents just such a potential deal breaker: the

long-term viability of the plan. If the B&B can run for years and years, it might make more money in the long run, even if year-to-year it makes less.

(B) Keep in mind which side is favored in the conclusion. It's long-term over B&B. Information supporting long-term rentals won't **Weaken** the argument, so Answer Choice (A) is out. Answer Choices (C) and (D) wouldn't change the calculation either way, as it applies equally to both options. And Answer Choice (E) is suggestive of a problem with B&B, but is ultimately **one step removed** from the information given. Is the fact that no B&Bs have ever been in the area a sign that they are a bad idea, or an idea whose time has come?

600- to 700-Level Argument Assumption Practice Set

1. **Argument:** The argument's conclusion is that *the reputation of Stradivarius violins is **more** due to the materials they're built from than the person who built them.* In support, the speaker offers evidence about how awesome the materials are and a **hypothesis** about what makes them so. There are two major assumptions here, first that such special wood requires no special artistry to work with, and second, brought out in Answer Choice (E), that *Stradivarius violins are actually made out of this special wood.* (Note that the evidence only says that this wood was *available* in Stradivarius's lifetime, not that he used it.)

    (E) Answer Choice (A) lies somewhere between the two assumptions, but it doesn't quite nail either, as the Opposite Day test would reveal. (Even if other violin makers used the same materials as Stradivarius, it wouldn't mean that Stradivarius used the special wood or that Stradivarius's techniques were *more important* than the materials.) Since the argument is limited only to explaining why Stradivarius violins are impressive, other violins aren't relevant, so Answer Choices (B) and (C) aren't required assumptions. Answer Choice (D) contradicts the conclusion, so couldn't possibly be an assumption in the argument.

2. **Argument:** The conclusion to this argument might have been hard to spot at first, but phrasing the argument's pieces in terms of *[what] because [why]* would help. [The Earth is losing species diversity] because [The extinction rate has been the same for at least 50 years and the rate that species rise to replace can't be sped up] is essentially a **net calculation**: more species are lost than gained; thus, overall species loss is happening. The part left out of this evidence is the *more*—the evidence only establishes that the rates have remained the same, not that one outpaces the other. Thus, Answer Choice (D) strengthens the argument by supporting the assumption that *the rate of loss is greater than the rate of gain.*

    (D) Answer Choice (A) is irrelevant, but it is something that is often said in the **real world**. Answer Choice (B) is likely meant to distract in the same way, offering a possibly familiar but **irrelevant comparison**. Answer Choice (C) is almost certainly true, but it's also irrelevant. Answer Choice (E) might be relevant if there were any hint that the numbers were incorrect at any point or that it established a specific timeframe relevant to the argument (like, say, the last 50 years).

3. **Argument: Weaken EXCEPT** questions require arguments with *lots* of assumptions in order to support four correctly weakening answers. Here, the argument's conclusion is strong, though masked with colloquial phrasing: the use of GMO crops comes with *too great a price*, a **net benefit calculation** based on evidence that (as per usual) only addresses *some* of the factors that go into the calculation and assumes there are no others. Answer Choices (A), (C), and (E) provide possible advantages to GMO crops that aren't addressed in the evidence. Answer Choice (B), on the other hand, eliminates certainty about a possible disadvantage (higher price).

   (D) Answer Choice (D) is a bit of **real-world** distraction that is **one step removed** from the argument given in the prompt. There's not necessarily any disadvantage to the biotech companies selling the seeds. If there were only a small number of these companies, then maybe a monopoly would form—but that maybe and possibly isn't something we know for sure in *this* situation.

4. **Argument:** The argument consists of a **plan** whose **stated goal** is to increase the amount of money donated to the station. The plan is to lengthen the winter pledge drive, which currently receives higher average pledges than does the midsummer drive. Since it features a plan, if the argument is to be true, we must assume that there is nothing that will prevent the plan from being put into effect; additionally, because it is built upon a comparison between two different pledges, we must assume that there's nothing special about one group that would change conclusions drawn about the other. Answer Choice (C) casts doubt on the first assumption. If people only donate once a year, it doesn't matter how long the winter pledge drive is. Those who donate will either have already donated in midsummer or would have already donated during the shorter drive.

   (C) Answer Choice (A) doesn't cast doubt on the plan; it just intensifies the need for the plan. Answer Choice (B) is probably true in the **real world**, but wouldn't really have any effect on the success of a longer winter drive. Answer Choice (D) presents an **irrelevant comparison** that might be mistaken for an **alternate method**; the conclusion of the argument is not, however, that lengthening the winter drive is the *best method* or the *only one* that will succeed, it is just that it will definitely increase the amount of money made by the station. And finally, Answer Choice (E) is also true in the **real world**, but here it is **one step removed** from weakening the argument, since it doesn't tell us that the winter drive is more susceptible to this problem than any other, or that a longer winter drive would be more susceptible to it than a shorter one would.

5. **Argument:** This argument commits the flaw of assuming that something true of one group is true of all members of that group. Indeed, it commits the flaw several times over! Just because women in general get higher tips, doesn't mean any single woman is likely to get higher tips. The same is true for any given woman in her thirties or any given attractive woman. Answer Choice (E) points this out, using the synonym of *trend* for *fact true of a group*.

   (E) Answer Choice (A) actually **contradicts the evidence**, never the right answer on the GMAT. Answer Choice (B) is the **exact opposite** of what we want. Answer Choice (C) seems to suggest some sort of bias in the study, but it never actually presents us with a reason to believe it was biased. Finally, Answer Choice (D) is something you might be interested in knowing, but which isn't relevant to this particular argument either way.

700- to 800-Level Argument Assumption Practice Set

1. **Argument:** This argument presents a **plan** (sneakily presented in the stem, rather than the prompt), reducing the *performance time* of acrobats in a circus, with the **stated goal** of reducing the portion of the circus's *total budget* that is given over to *insurance premiums for the acrobats*. Thus, the argument has two major assumptions: (1) *performance time is in some way related to insurance premium costs* and (2) *insurance premiums are a big part of the budget overall.* Answer Choices (A) and (B) directly support the first assumption. Answer Choice (E) also supports the first, though a bit more obliquely. If accidents to acrobats tended to happen at the beginning of their performance, cutting time from the end wouldn't necessarily reduce the number of accidents. Answer Choice (D) is instead the confirmation of a **defending assumption**, protecting against the **unintended harm** that the budget might suffer from reducing the amount of time that acrobats perform (driving away its paying customers).

   (C) The evidence says only that a single cost cannot rise above one-fourth of the budget. Answer Choice (C) doesn't strengthen the argument because insurance could still be smaller than one-fourth if it was the largest line item in the budget.

2. **Argument:** This argument is the opposite of a **causal connection**: it asserts that the advice given by consultants is *not* the cause of these businesses' increased performance. This conclusion is supported by the evidence that, even though businesses that hire consultants do better, a good bit of advice consultants give is not insightful and is ignored any way. Thus, the argument assumes that there's no way other than *being followed directly* that a consultant's advice might benefit a company. Answer Choice (B) presents this **alternative explanation** of how a consultant's uninsightful and unfollowed advice might be of benefit, by providing a greater *number* of strategies to choose between.

   (B) Answer Choice (A) is the **opposite** of what we want, as it **strengthens** the assumption that the consultants are correct when they say that they are not very helpful. Answer Choice (C) also **strengthens** the argument by making it more likely that something other than the consultants (the business's core leadership) is responsible for the increased performance. Answer Choice (D) is close, but note that it does not attribute the business's success to the consultant's *advice*, rather their *expensiveness* (so ultimately, it, too, **strengthens** the claim that it's not their advice). Answer Choice (E) addresses a **closed issue**, as the evidence already asserts that these consultants are not insightful.

3. **Argument:** The stem of this question warns us to be very careful. The conclusion we're interested in is the *decision to end the experiment*, which we're told was based on the idea that it would be *unethical to risk continuing any longer*. Thus, the argument assumes that an experiment's being *unethical* is a good reason to end it. Answer Choice

(B) says this, though in a roundabout way, substituting *nonpractical considerations* for *ethical considerations*.

(B) Answer Choice (A) is wrong because it doesn't affect the decision to end the experiment but is instead something we'd likely conclude from the behavior of the participants. Answer Choice (C) is **too extreme** for this situation, since the experiment wasn't ended *immediately* as soon as someone was damaged, only when the jailers had become "so cruel" that it was unethical. Answer Choice (D) might seem tempting, but nowhere does the argument state that the participants were damaged unequally—it merely mentions one sort of damage; there could have been other, equal damages elsewhere. And Answer Choice (E) confuses the experiment's *results* with *conducting* or *continuing* the experiment.

4. **Argument:** Keep the scope and **stated goal** of the plan clearly in mind. The U.S. team has instituted these *regular stretching exercises* and this *core stability training* in order to reduce the amount of time that its own swimmers are sidelined by rotator cuff impingement. What does stretching or core stability have to do with rotator cuff impingement? Answer Choice (C) explains: it supplements the function of muscles near the rotator cuff, which the evidence earlier tells us is a problem for expert (read: Olympic) swimmers who are training.

(C) Answer Choice (A) raises a problem rather than addressing one. Answer Choice (B) is irrelevant **corroborating evidence**, **one step removed** from this argument, since we don't know that the U.S. team is like these other teams. Answer Choices (D) and (E) both strengthen the *need* for a plan, but not this particular plan, and so are just **evidence for the evidence**.

5. **Argument:** Treating this argument as a series of connected Formal Logic statements is the surest path to spotting the missing assumption. According to the prompt:

Sport fish → deep, still bodies of water (no dsb of water → no sport fish)
Deep, still bodies of water → beachfront development (no development → no dsb of water)
Dam → deep, still bodies of water (no dsb of water → no dam)
Dam economical → market for hydro power (no market → no economical dam)
Therefore, no market for hydro power → no dam → no sport fish

Notice the gap? From the evidence, we could correctly conclude lots of things, but not that the lack of a dam will guarantee the lack of the deep, still pools of water that sport fish need. A dam is said to be *one way* of ensuring the pools will be there, not the only way: a classic **necessity versus sufficiency** flaw. Answer Choice (B) correctly states this.

(B) Answer Choices (A), (B), (C), and (D) are all different ways of stating **necessity versus sufficiency**, but only Answer Choice (B) concerns the right sufficient thing being mistaken for a necessary one. Answer Choice (E) brings up a flaw not made here, a **causation versus correlation** mistake.

500- to 600-Level Fact-Based Question Practice Set

1. **Facts:** With **Inference** questions, always seek the most definite information in the prompt. Here, there's only one, found in the final sentence: *cement requires large amounts of energy to make.* The correct inference will need to involve this fact.

    (E) Careful with the answer choices. Only Answer Choice (B) directly mentions energy, but it is **too extreme** a claim to infer from what we have. Sentence three tells us that oil is *connected* to the energy requirement, but not that it is the main source of that energy. Answer Choice (A) is **reasonable but unsupported**, since we don't really know what the definition of an ingredient ought or ought not to include. Answer Choice (C) is **directly contradicted** by information about cheap replacements in sentence two. Answer Choice (D) is consistent with the same information about replacements, but we're never given any information about the business practices of cement makers. This leaves only Answer Choice (E), which indirectly connects to the one fact we know. Energy costs are required parts of making cement, so the cost of cement isn't entirely found in the cost of its basic ingredients.

2. **Dilemma: On the one hand**, *the pleasant smell strategy increases sales in general*, **but on the other hand** *the same strategy **reduces sales** if only one store does it*. Answer Choice (A) accounts for the apparent **unrealized expectation** that occurs in this one specific case by providing a reason for the change in outcomes for single stores: they drive away potential customers.

    (A) Remember that the single smelly store doesn't just experience flat sales; its sales actually fall. Answer Choice (B) wouldn't explain the falling sales, only flat sales. Answer Choice (C) might explain why businesses around the smelly store do better, but it does not explain why the store itself does worse. Answer Choice (D) is likewise **irrelevant to the dilemma**, since in our dilemma the strategy isn't working. The same is true for Answer Choice (E), where two stores are using the strategy, but our dilemma only involves a single store.

3. **Facts:** We know from sentence one that *Without Jupiter, the chances of life developing on Earth would have been less.* The second sentence explains why in general this would be true: *something that hurts the chances of life developing (the meteor strikes) happens when there are asteroid belts.* And the third sentence ties this explanation to Jupiter: *without something like Jupiter, there'd be nothing stopping the meteor strikes.* By connecting these facts, we can infer Answer Choice (C): Without Jupiter, the chances of life developing in our solar system would be lowered. Don't be frightened by the absurd situation given in Answer Choice (C). It doesn't matter *why* or *how* Jupiter gets destroyed.

    (C) Answer Choices (A) and (D) are both **too extreme**, as our information only says the chances of developing life are *lowered* without a gas giant, not lowered to zero. Answer Choice (B) is **one step removed** from the information we have, since we don't know what causes life to continue, only what affects its chances of starting. Answer Choice (E) is both **too extreme** and a case of **mixed details** because the prompt never gives information about multiple asteroid belts.

4. **Dilemma:** (1) Before the nuclear testing stopped, the camel population was going down; (2) once one thing that hurt their population was removed, you'd expect things to get better, but they got worse. Ultimately, this **unrealized expectation** is cleared up by Answer Choice (E), which provides information about an **unconsidered factor**: the removed harm (nuclear testing) was itself stopping an even greater harm (poaching) from happening.

   (E) Answer Choice (A) is **interesting but irrelevant** because domestication isn't at issue in the dilemma. Answer Choice (B) **worsens the dilemma** by suggesting that the numbers should have been increasing even before the site was closed. Answer Choices (C) and (D) are, like (A), **interesting but irrelevant**, since neither *other animals* nor *disease* would explain why the lack of nuclear testing would cause the camel population to fall.

5. **Dilemma: On the one hand**, *in general, the more sugar in the blood, the more insulin,* **but on the other hand**, *when there is* **lots** *of sugar in the blood* **regularly**, *insulin levels are below average.* Answer Choice (C) explains what's different about this **specific case**: lots of sugar eaten regularly wears the insulin release system out.

   (C) Answer Choices (A), (B), and (D) all present us with **real-world distractions**. Answer Choice (A) only **worsens the dilemma**, since it shows the weirdness that happens if our specific case happens consistently. Answer Choices (B) and (D) are both **irrelevant to the dilemma** for the same reason, since we don't know that the source of sugar is relevant to insulin. Answer Choice (E) just further explains how insulin works, without tying this explanation to the relevant distinction, the *level of sugar*.

600- to 700-Level Fact-Based Question Practice Set

1. **Dilemma:** The dilemma here is that two things we might assume are connected seem to be unconnected: (1) timber production went up during the period but (2) labor employed by timber mills went down. Answer Choice (D) presents the **unconsidered factor** that reconciles the two trends: labor-saving technologies were introduced during the period in question.

   (D) Answer Choices (A) and (C) are both **irrelevant to the dilemma** because they concern different time periods than the one we're interested in. Answer Choices (B) and (E) give us extra facts about the time period, but neither would account directly for a difference between production and labor.

2. **Facts:** The *therefore* in front of the blank flags this question as close cousin to the **Inference** question, since the only thing we are allowed to put in that blank is something inferable from the definite information in the prompt. Here, the correct answer, (A), is inferable by applying the definite piece of formal logic rule right before the semicolon (*no one should be obligated to conform to the moral standards of the public*) to the specific case of *public officials*. As part of "anyone," public officials, too, should not be obligated.

   (A) Answer Choice (B) could be inferred if only we knew that the moral philosophers are definitely right (and the speaker doesn't seem to think they are, anyway). Answer

Choice (C) confuses **necessity and sufficiency**. Answer Choice (D) seems reasonable (if you agree with the speaker), but it is unsupported here, as we know only what moral philosophers have said before, not what they will always and forever say. And Answer Choice (E), while a laudable sentiment in the real world, is not specifically addressed here.

3. **Facts:** If we agree with the scientists' final conclusion that *babies first babble in preparation for communication with their parents*, then babies who aren't preparing for communication won't start babbling. Thus, Answer Choice (B) must be true.

   (B) Answer Choice (A) is **one step removed** from our information, which doesn't allow us to say anything for certain about *simple words*. Answer Choice (C) is explicitly **contradicted** by the scientists' conclusion. Answer Choices (D) and (E) might seem reasonable, but the scientists' evidence never provides any information about children who don't fit into the two groups in the prompt or about what happens with babies when no one's around.

4. **Facts:** Build out from the most definite piece of information to find the credited inference. Here, that piece comes at the very end: *if the overall cost of applying adjuvants goes up, many farmers will go out of business*. Add to that the second definite fact, found in the middle of the prompt: *there are no substitutes as easy to apply or as economical to use as the most popular adjuvant*, the one that will be banned if the proposals go through. Thus, if the ban goes through, one of the costs of pesticide use—the adjuvants—will go up. Answer Choice (E) says this directly while adding the helpful loophole closer caveat that this will only be true so long as these farmers don't find some other way to reduce their costs.

   (E) Answer Choices (A) and (D) both forget the loophole that Answer Choice (E) covers. Answer Choice (B) forgets a different loophole—that it might be possible to reduce birth defects some other way than banning this one adjuvant. Answer Choice (C) confuses **necessity and sufficiency**—the ban will be sufficient to drive farmers out of business, but it's not the only possible way their businesses might fail.

5. **Dilemma:** This dilemma may not have felt very dilemma-like, since we all know that people don't continue to gain weight indefinitely, no matter how much they eat. Nevertheless, that's the dilemma: **on the one hand**, people eat enough to grow indefinitely, yet **on the other hand**, they top out at a particular weight. This must be an **unconsidered factor**, right? Answer Choice (D) presents that factor: as weight increases, energy requirements increase, so eventually the body will hit a point where what was once an "extra 3500 calories" is not required.

   (D) Answer Choices (A) and (C) are not **relevant to the dilemma**, which doesn't involve *all possible people*, just those who have already eaten that much for a decade and lived that long; the existence of *many people* who are exceptions just doesn't matter. Answer Choice (B) hints at what (D) says explicitly, but it never ties the energy needs to the increase in weight. Finally, Answer Choice (E) is **reasonable but unsupported** by the information we have, which never mentions what an expert might or might not recommend.

1. **Facts:** The first two sentences of this prompt consist of two Formal Logic statements that can be connected: morally wrong → violates autonomy → should be avoided and punished the same. The prompt also tells us that murder is morally wrong. Each of the answer choices provide an if, but the only if that will "trigger" the chain of logic will be "If <something> is morally wrong." Answer Choice (D) begins just this way and correctly concludes that if lying and murder are both morally wrong, then they should be punished equally.

   (D) Answer Choice (A) is out because the prompt provides no rules to judge whether something is *noble* or not, and the same is true for Answer Choice (E) because there are no rules about what is morally *correct*. Answer Choice (B) concludes that something is *twice as obvious*, but all the information in the prompt is about things being *equally wrong*. Answer Choice (C) would be right if we knew that accidentally causing a person's death were morally wrong, but neither the answer nor the prompt contain this information.

2. **Facts:** This **Inference** question follows the pattern of **so and so** and **such and such**—lots of placeholder words are used to add information about groups previously mentioned. Answer Choice (C) is correctly inferable because the jawed fish split into two groups: the first group *retains* the cartilage-based skeletons of their ancestors, their ancestors being all fish that lived before jaws.

   (C) Answer Choice (A) is wrong because the only thing we know about land-based mammals is that most of them evolved from the bone-having fish. It's possible they lost their bone-skeletons after they diverged from the fish. Answer Choice (B) brings up *extinction*, a totally new concept we know nothing about. Answer Choice (D) is just (A) rephrased. And Answer Choice (E) is a **misused detail**, combining the last sentence with earlier pieces of information that we have no way to know with certainty can be combined.

3. **Facts:** Beneath this question lies one of the GMAT's favorite facts, the difference between **percentages and numbers**. According to the prompt, the trade federation's members split revenues proportional to the size of their populations. Originally, the sizes were Tragda > Baflazam > Llassu. After the census, Tragda lost revenue, which means that, as a percentage, its population was no longer as large as it had been. We're also told that Llassu's population grew *less* than Tragda's, meaning that the reason for Tragda's decrease can't be Llassu's population increase. Therefore, it must be Baflazam's increase that reduced Tragda's share. And if Baflazam grew more than Tragda, it must also have grown more than Llassu. Thus, Answer Choice (C) is inferable, the order of population *growth* (not absolute population number) must be Baflazam, Tragda, Llassu.

   (C) Answer Choice (A) concerns total population, not rate of population growth. Answer Choices (B) and (D) get the nations out of order, and Answer Choice (E) pulls a **but for one word** trick by changing the list to *least to most* instead of *most to least*.

4. **Facts:** The dilemma itself is relatively straightforward: **on the one hand**, studies show *in general* helmets reduce injuries to motorcyclists, but **on the other hand**, *in states that mandate helmets for motorcyclists*, the number of injuries (specifically those injuries that studies say helmets prevent) is going up. The dilemma is a classic **percent versus number** pattern, since the risk of injury is a probability, and a probability is a percentage. The number of injuries is going up, even though the percentage of injuries should be going down. Thus, somehow, the overall number of people who could possibly be injured must be going up. Answer Choice (A) provides a way this can occur, increasing the number of motorcycle riders in states where the helmets are mandated.

(A) The key to this question is the innocuous phrase found in the question stem, *by itself.* Unlike a normal Explain question, the fact that resolves the dilemma has to do so absolutely, without any other information. For Answer Choice (B) or (C) to resolve the dilemma, we'd need to know how many motorcyclists, as a percentage, are defying the law, and whether this results in more or less helmet-wearing motorcyclists. The same goes for Answer Choice (E), except in that case we'd need to know instead how often the helmets aren't properly fitted. Answer Choice (D) is, on the other hand, a **closed issue**, since the evidence limits the dilemma specifically to the *injuries that helmets have been shown to prevent*, not all possible injuries.

5. **Facts:** This is such a depressing topic! It is also another version of the old **percent versus number** problem. This time, the dilemma is that from 1990–2000 (1) the absolute number of people with HIV has gone down, even as the overall population has gone up, but (2) the percentage of people who say they personally knew someone who is *suffering* from HIV has gone way up. How can fewer people be suffering, yet more people say they *knew* someone suffering? The obvious answer is that the cases of suffering have been better publicized—but this doesn't show up as an answer choice. Instead, Answer Choice (C) explains how the number of sufferers could go down while the number of *known sufferers* could go up: if lots of known sufferers are now dead, they are not *currently suffering*.

(C) Answer Choice (A) is **one step removed** from the dilemma because it is not limited to the right timeframe. Answer Choice (B) is meant to seem like the obvious answer, but note that it is about *celebrities*, not necessarily people that Americans *personally know*. Answer Choice (D) **worsens the dilemma**, because it should increase the number of people suffering from *diagnosed* cases. Answer Choice (E) likewise **worsens the dilemma** because increased treatment should be slowing down the death rate, causing there to be more, rather than fewer, diagnosed sufferers for Americans to learn about.

Sentence Correction 14

INTRODUCTION

The main challenge the Sentence Correction questions present is not grammar but *timing*. By design, the sentences that make up these questions are repetitively and confusingly worded, meant to cause you to doubt yourself, double back, and reread answer choices again and again, leaving you less time than you need to tackle the longer Reading Comprehension passages and the more intricate Critical Reasoning questions.

Sentence Corrections are scattered throughout the Verbal section as potential momentum killers, and so your approach to them must be disciplined and efficient.

What the GMAT *Says* Sentence Correction Tests

According to the GMAC, Sentence Correction questions are meant to test three general areas of English language proficiency: "correct expression, effective expression, and proper diction."

If those terms seem somewhat subjective and hard to define, it's because they are!

Much of the time, the quickest path to the credited answer will lie in selecting the answer choice that matches the GMAT house style or that "sounds like the GMAT"—which is rarely the same as the choice that "sounds right" in your head. Indeed, the GMAT loves throwing weird but grammatically correct things into the correct answer choice precisely because the weirdness will "sound wrong" and send the unwary test taker on a wild goose chase for a better answer choice that simply does not exist.

What Sentence Correction Actually Tests . . . and What It Doesn't

Don't get tripped up on the word "best" in the instructions for the sentence correction questions. That's because "best" has a very specific meaning on the GMAT. The "best" answer to a Sentence Correction question is the one that manages to *avoid* making one of a handful of easily testable errors. The "best" sentence still might not pass muster in any real-world publication.

You are not being asked to select the sentence that you would personally write to best convey the information in the question. The credited answer to a Sentence Correction often sounds awkward and convoluted. But the important thing is that the credited answer avoids

TIP

If no answer seems clearly right, eliminate ones that have definable errors.

making easily singled out errors, while the incorrect answers all contain specific document-able mistakes. Often it helps to think about it as selecting the answer that is the *least wrong*.

Grammar can be touchy subject. Tell people that the GMAT will test their grammar, and they're likely to worry about exactly the wrong sorts of things, like:

- "Is it wrong to split infinitives, or can I use 'to boldly go'?"
- "And are you allowed to start a sentence with a conjunction?"
- "What about ending sentences with a preposition?"
- "Do I need to use a comma before the 'and' in a list?"
- "It is always wrong to use the passive?"

If any of these questions have been worrying you, put your mind at ease.

All those pet peeves that people love to argue about could never be on the test, because *people argue about them*. The GMAC has to be able to defend GMAT questions against unhappy test takers who might want to dispute their scores. In practice, any grammatical issue about which there is reasonable disagreement among experts cannot serve as the only reason an answer choice is incorrect.

Whether you prefer to use the Oxford comma or to omit it will, thankfully, not be part of what gets you into business school—at least not as far as the GMAT is concerned.

GMAT GRAMMAR 101

The rest of this chapter will go more smoothly if we take a few pages first to refresh your memory of the most basic grammatical terms. We promise that no unnecessarily compli-cated jargon lies ahead, only the bare bones necessary for us all to be on the same page as you learn the best ways to dominate GMAT Sentence Correction questions.

> ### !!!WARNING!!!
>
> The classification system we use in the following chapter should NOT be considered an attempt to recreate or represent any actual system—used either by real academic grammarians or by amateur self-appointed guardians of the English tongue. This section is called "*GMAT* Grammar 101" for a reason: things will only be classified or named as would be helpful in getting to the credited answer of a Sentence Correction question **on the GMAT**.

The Parts of Speech

Words can be classified many different ways; when you classify a word according to its **function** in communication, you assign it to one of the categories together called the **parts of speech**. For the GMAT, it is necessary to be able to recognize only a few: **nouns**, **verbs**, **pronouns**, **prepositions**, **adjectives**, **adverbs**, and **conjunctions**.

NOUNS

As you probably heard back in first grade, a noun is "the name of a person, place, or thing." *Dog, cat, mom, Albuquerque, sandwich, kettle, CD, elevator, Abraham Lincoln*—all are nouns.

So, too, ideas such as *love, marriage, correctness, number, sluggishness, justice,* and *symmetry.*

> **Noun.** A word indicating the name of a person, place, thing, or idea.

VERBS

Verbs are a bit trickier than nouns. We usually define them as either "an action" or "a state of being." Actions include *walk, run, sing, sit, bark,* and *love.* States of being are instead things like *is, was, will, does, shall, could, might.*

The reason we say verbs are trickier than nouns is that they can appear in a variety of different forms depending on what sort of action they're describing. The noun *dog* appears in sentences as just that: *dog* (with the occasional *s* tacked on to make it plural or apostrophe *s* to make it possessive). But *bark* appears in all kinds of different forms: *to bark, barks, barking, is barking, barked, has barked, will have been barking, were to have been barking.* The most common way a verb changes is in relation to what is called its **tense**, forms that allow us to keep track of the different times an action occurs.

The simple tenses include **present**, **past**, **and future**: *I walk today, I walked yesterday, I will walk tomorrow,* and so on. But tenses can get complicated quickly. Special ones exist for actions that are ongoing (the continuous: *I am walking now*), that occurred in the past but continue into the present (the present perfect: *I have walked for some time*), that occurred frequently in the past (the past habitual: *I used to walk*), and even that occurred in the past but that we worry might be doubted (the emphatic: *I did walk*).

> **Verb.** A word indicating an action that is being performed or a state of being and that takes on special forms to indicate such things as the time when the action or state occurred.

Fluent English speakers usually have little trouble navigating the distinctions between tenses and person. It's only when called upon to provide the tense's exact name or when the tense is one that is rarely used in speech that they get flummoxed. Luckily, those exact names aren't *ever* essential to getting the right answer in GMAT Sentence Correction, nor are most of the really weird tenses. If you can recognize these tenses

Example	had walked	has walked	walked	walk	will walk
Tense	past perfect	present perfect	past	present	future

then you're where you need to be.

PRONOUNS

While not as complicated as verbs, nouns do have one special added consideration: **pronouns**. A pronoun is a word that is allowed to "stand in for" or "replace" another noun. The noun that's being swapped for the pronoun also has a special name that we should add to our vocabulary for convenience's sake. We call these referenced nouns the **antecedents** of the pronoun.

> **Pronoun.** A word that stands in for another noun.
> **Pronoun Antecedent.** The noun that a pronoun is standing in for.

Notice that pronouns change their form depending on the sort of noun they're replacing: people get pronouns like *he* and *us, objects use it* and *its; singular nouns get his* and *it, plural their* and *those*, and so on. That's because in order to be clear about a pronoun's antecedent we give the pronoun characteristics to match it.

Take comfort in knowing that on the GMAT pronouns are directly tested in just two ways: (1) whether a pronoun agrees with its antecedent and (2) whether its antecedent is clear enough or left ambiguous.

PREPOSITIONS

Prepositions come in many different varieties, depending on the way that they describe the noun or verb they've been attached to:

Time and duration: *at, on, in, during, until, after*

> The noisy dogs bark *throughout* the night.

Movement: *to, toward, through, across, over, into, onto, after*

> The noisy dogs accompany the hunter *after* the fox.

Agency: *by, with*

> The noisy dogs were chased *by* the enormous cat.

Manner or instrument: *with, by*

> The noisy dogs were silenced *with* muzzles.

Location: *above, below, in*

> The noisy dogs accompany the hunter *in* the woods.

> **Preposition.** A connecting word that clarifies the relationship between two words, including manner, instrument, time, location, and direction.
> **Prepositional Phrase.** A phrase that has a preposition as its head word, composed of the preposition and its **object**, connected in a sentence to an **antecedent** word or phrase.

Notice that we slipped a word from our description of pronouns into the definition of preposition: **antecedent**. For the purposes of GMAT grammar, we will call the word or phrase that the preposition describes "the preposition's **antecedent**." In the examples above, the antecedent changes from sentence to sentence. Here they are again, with the antecedents in **bold**:

The noisy dogs bark *throughout the night.*
(*Throughout* describes the length of time the dogs **bark**.)

The noisy dogs accompany the hunter *after the fox.*
(*Across* describes the dogs' **movement** as they accompany the hunter.)

The noisy dogs were chased *by the enormous cat.*
(*By* describes the **agent** who chased the dogs.)

The noisy dogs were silenced *with muzzles.*
(*With* describes the **manner** in which the dogs were silenced.)

> **Prepositional Antecedent.** The original thing that the preposition refers to or describes.

When the *Official Guide* claims that a preposition "refers illogically" to something or that it is "stranded" or "unattached," it is describing ways that a preposition's relationship to its antecedent might be unclear.

There was one more new term in the definition: **object**. An **object** is the third fundamental unit (like subject and predicate) that sentences in English are built out of. Within a prepositional phrase, the object is the word or phrase that follows the preposition and that contains the descriptive bit that the preposition links to the antecedent.

> Real grammar books rarely use the word **antecedent** or **object** when discussing prepositions. As far as we're concerned, **antecedent** will do as a general term for anything that a word refers to or is meant to describe; **object** will cover anything to which a word does something or the descriptive content a word is meant to apply to its antecedent.

> **Prepositional Object.** The word or phrase that follows a preposition and contains the descriptive information the pronoun introduces.

To put it another way, we could say that a prepositional object "provides" the description that the preposition "delivers" to the antecedent.

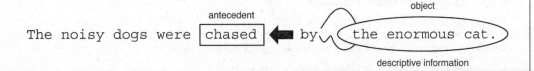

ADJECTIVE

Some words can describe another word directly, without needing a word like a preposition to help them. These **modifiers** come in two different varieties, classified by the things that they are able to modify. The easiest and most limited of the two are called **adjectives**, words that can directly describe nouns. In the sample sentence, *noisy* was an adjective. *Small, weird, tight, gigantic, outstanding,* and *squeaky* are all adjectives.

> **Adjective.** A word that describes or modifies a noun (or pronoun).

ADVERBS

Adverbs are much more flexible than adjectives. While adjectives can only be used to describe nouns and pronouns, adverbs can be used to modify verbs, adjectives, and even other adverbs. For example:

The dogs bark loudly.
(*loudly* describes the verb *bark*)

The dogs have a very loud bark.
(*very* describes the adjective *loud*)

The dogs bark very loudly.
(*very* describes the adverb *loudly*)

> **Adverb.** A word that describes or modifies a verb, an adjective, or another adverb.

For the purposes of GMAT grammar, we're also going to call the things that adverbs and adjectives are meant to describe their **antecedents**.

> **Modifier's Antecedent.** The thing the modifier—whether adjective, adverb, or otherwise—is meant to modify.

CONJUNCTIONS

TIP

In a way, a preposition is a limited kind of subordinating conjunction (one used to connect a noun with a description about its time, manner, place, etc.).

Conjunctions are the grammatical "glue" that allows us to move beyond words to the larger combinations called **phrases**, **clauses**, and **sentences**. Depending on the type of words being connected and on the type of connection made, we can further classify them.

Cats and dogs hate baths.
(*And* coordinates the two subjects in the sentence.)

Both cats and dogs make good pets.
(*Both … and* are used to correlate cats and dogs.)

Although dogs hate baths, they are easier to bathe than cats.
(*Although* subordinates the first clause to the second.)

Conjunction. A word that connects two words, phrases, or clauses together structurally.

Coordinating Conjunction. These connect words, phrases, or clauses that are independent or equal.

Correlative Conjunction. These also connect words, phrases, or clauses that are independent or equal, but come in pairs like *both ... and*.

Subordinating Conjunction. These connect clauses of unequal status in a sentence.

Words, Phrases, Clauses, and Sentences

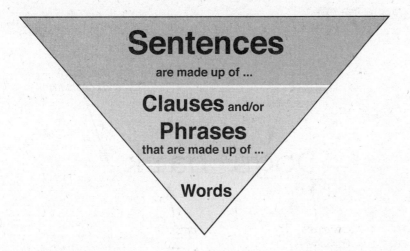

THE PARTS OF THE SENTENCE

Take a noun (or pronoun) and a verb, put them together, make sure they agree, capitalize the first word, add appropriate end punctuation, and voila—you've got yourself a sentence. Like so:

Dogs bark.

Mom said.

She did?

I ache.

He left.

That's weird!

In a sentence the verb is used to indicate what kind of action is taking place and the noun is used to indicate who's engaged in that action.

Sentence. A collection of words describing an action and its actor.

SUBJECTS AND PREDICATES

As it turns out, you can't just use any old noun or verb you'd like when making a sentence. *Dogs to bark* is nonsense because *to bark*, the infinitive form of the verb, can't anchor a sentence. The noun also has to be of the type that can describe an action doer when linked to an action-describing verb. Grammarians helpfully gave these "sentence type of nouns" and "verb type of nouns" names: **subject** and **predicate**. We'll borrow them for our GMAT Grammar vocabulary list.

> **Subject.** The actor described in a sentence. The person, place, thing, or idea that is engaged in the action or state of being described by the sentence's predicate.
>
> **Predicate.** The action or state of being attributed to the subject of a sentence.

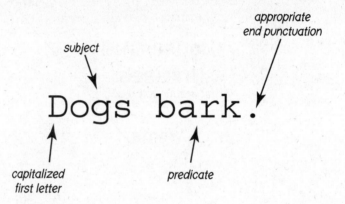

Notice one last thing about our simple sentence. Lacking other options, it's clear that the subject of the sentence must be dogs and bark must be its predicate. When sentences get more complicated, it can be hard to remember what the subject and predicate were supposed to be. This is why English demands that the subject and predicate (noun and verb) of a sentence must "agree."

Alas, the GMAT never gives us sentences of only two words to correct. However, lots of questions on the GMAT are as simple as making sure subjects and predicates agree; on the GMAT, such questions are just camouflaged so that they don't *look* so simple to the untrained test taker.

How do they pull off that subterfuge? The answer lies in the sentence's less complicated parent concepts, **phrases and clauses**.

PHRASES

A **sentence** is a special type of arrangement of nouns and verbs, one we often say "expresses a complete thought." A **phrase** is just an arrangement of words that makes sense; completeness is optional. In addition to all the sentences we've used thus far, all these count as **phrases**, too:

> the noisy dogs
> a faintly speckled toad
> the long and winding road
> without so much as a word
> who always before drove down this road
> eating all the porridge before it got cold
> his cell phone provider's persistent network instability problem

> **Phrase.** A sequence of related words that act as a single unit.

NOUN AND VERB PHRASES

The most important thing about phrases is that any part of a sentence that can be occupied by a word can be occupied instead by a multiword phrase with that word as its head.

So far, we only know two parts of a sentence, **subject** and **predicate**. Swap out our single words for phrases and you can build a more respectable looking sentence like *The noisy dogs are always barking*. Subjects can thus be nouns *or* noun phrases; predicates can be verbs *or* verb phrases.

Phrases are the secret to how the test maker can build a question around the simple concept while pretending that something more complicated is happening. All the GMAT has to do is pile a cartload of complicated phrases on top of *dogs bark* and sit back confident that you'll not notice when they tried to slip *dogs barks* past you instead. Like so:

1. The violent, noisome, obnoxious dogs that typically accompany the hunter in the woods after the fox <u>barks constantly until their prey, desperate with fear, has been run to exhaustion</u>, much more efficiently concluding the hunt than did previous even more brutal methods.

    (A) barks constantly until their prey, desperate with fear, has been run to exhaustion
    (B) are barking constantly until to exhaustion their prey desperate and fearing is run
    (C) bark constantly until their prey is desperately with fear run to exhaustion
    Etc.

The test maker expands *dogs*, the subject, into the longer **noun phrase** *the violent, noisome, obnoxious dogs*. The verb is similarly expanded from *barks* to *barks constantly*. Yet no matter how much is piled onto the dogs or their barking, the core of the sentence remains the same: a subject and a predicate. Everything else is just some form of **modifier** or **modification**.

noun phrases

> The violent, noisome, obnoxious **dogs**
>
> previous even more brutal **methods**

verb phrases

> **bark** constantly
>
> **has been run** to exhaustion
>
> typically **accompany** the hunter
>
> **concluding** the hunt

MODIFYING PHRASES

English has many different types of modifiers, but the GMAT is most interested in testing your ability to handle modifying phrases, phrases that—like our noun and verb phrases—are built on a single head word and used in the sentence in some way to further describe or characterize the subject and predicate. We've already discussed one type of modifying phrase, the **prepositional phrase**:

prepositional phrases

> **after** the fox
>
> **in** the woods

Just like nouns, verbs, and prepositions, adjectives and adverbs can be used as a phrase's head word to create adjective phrases and adverb phrases.

adverb phrases

> much more **efficiently**

adjective phrases

> **desperate** with fear
>
> **previous** even more brutal

Such phrases can be used in a sentence any way that the head adjective or adverb could when alone.

Thus, it would be equally grammatically correct to say:

> The dogs bark until their *desperate* prey has been run to exhaustion *efficiently*.

and

> The dogs bark until their prey, *desperate with fear*, has been run to exhaustion *much more efficiently*.

You may have noticed that in the second sentence the adjective phrase is set off from the thing it modifies by commas, whereas the adjective in the first is attached directly to and in front of the noun.

If the sentence were instead

> The dogs bark until desperate with fear their prey has been ....

TIP

"The desperate with fear prey..." is unidiomatic.

it would be hard to tell whether the dogs are barking until **the dogs** are desperate with fear or whether they chase their prey until **their prey** is desperate with fear. In this revised sentence, **desperate with fear** is stranded between the dogs and their prey, rendering the thing that the modifier is meant to modify unclear.

Since "the thing the modifier is meant to modify" is a bit long, we can use that term from our discussion of prepositional phrases, **antecedent**, to indicate it.

> **Modifying Phrase.** A collection of words that jointly describe another word in a sentence.
>
> **Modifier's Antecedent.** The thing the modifier—whether adjective, adverb, or phrase—is meant to modify.
>
> **Dangling Modifiers.** Modifying phrases that don't clearly describe any one thing in a sentence.

Because English is a language that relies heavily on word order for its meaning, the general rule for modifiers is that their antecedent should be placed closest to them in the sentence.

Consider the difference between these:

> Only I love you.
> I only love you.
> I love you only.

Only is a special sort of word that is used sometimes as an **adjective** and sometimes as an **adverb**, so in the sentences above it would be allowed to modify the pronoun *I*, the verb *love* and its object, the noun *you*. Tell a person special to you "only I love you" and you're saying that people in general hate him or her; "I love only you" and there's nobody else for you. Order matters.

In fact, order matters a lot on the GMAT. Take the sentence: "Coming out of the wall, I saw termites." On the GMAT, that sentence would be considered incorrect. The initial modifying phrase *coming out of the wall* is said to have been misplaced or left "dangling" because it rightfully refers to termites, not "I."

DIRECT AND INDIRECT OBJECTS

Just as prepositions have a bit that follows them, which we say "receives" the effect the preposition provides, a sentence's predicate can have a bit that "receives" the action described by the predicate's verb. The **direct object** gets acted upon, usually in a way that completes that idea of the verb's action. Some verbs almost require objects in order to make sense. We don't often say *the dog bit* without adding what or who was bitten, or *I saw* without saying what was seen. The thing bitten or seen would be the verb's **direct object**.

Other verbs can get by perfectly well without direct objects but can take them if need be. *We danced* and *the police left* could stay as they are, or we could add that *we danced **a waltz*** and *the police left **the building***. Either works.

The **indirect objects** are rarer creatures and require that there already be a direct object in the sentence before they can appear at all. The **indirect object** is typically the recipient not of the verb but of the direct object. Usually a preposition is involved.

TIP

Indirect objects can sometimes be found without prepositions. *Bob threw Peter the ball* would mean the same as *Bob threw the ball to Peter.* No preposition is needed.

Take the simple sentence *Bob threw the ball.* Bob is the subject of the sentence and what the predicate says, he does. So he's the guy who throws the direct object, the ball. If we want to add an indirect object, it'll be the person who receives the ball. *Bob threw the ball to Peter.*

> **Direct Object.** The thing directly affected by the action of the sentence's predicate verb.
>
> **Indirect Object.** The thing that indirectly is affected by the action of the sentence's predicate verb; usually the recipient of the verb's action and usually connected to the verb by a preposition such as *to.*

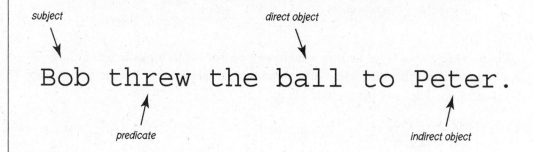

CLAUSES

Phrases that have subjects and verbs are called **clauses**. As we already know, to be a complete sentence, a sentence must have both a **subject** and a **predicate**. Taken together, we call this **subject-predicate** pair an **independent clause**. It can "stand on its own" or "express a complete thought."

> The dog is very tall.
> They built the boat quickly.

Some clauses can't stand on their own; they aren't in and of themselves complete sentences. We call such clauses **dependent clauses**. What makes a clause dependent? Primarily, a clause is "demoted" to dependent status through the use of a **subordinating conjunction** (such as *unless, after, where, when, since, though, as,* and *if*). Thus, these clauses do not count as sentences on their own:

> before they built the boat
> because the dog is very tall
> unless you do as I say

For a dependent clause to become a sentence, it has to be attached to an independent clause with a conjunction and a comma. Without the independent clause, the dependent all by its lonesome gets labeled a **sentence fragment**.

TIP

Occasionally, you'll need to pick a preposition that makes sense to link the indirect object and the verb.

> **Clause.** A level of grammatical organization between sentence and phrase, a clause is composed of a subject and a predicate and may be **dependent** or **independent**.
>
> **Dependent Clause.** A clause in a compound sentence that cannot stand on its own as a sentence due to the presence of a subordinating word.
>
> **Independent Clause.** A clause in a compound sentence that could serve as a sentence on its own without any of its subordinate clauses; it contains both a subject and a predicate.

It's also possible to have too much of a good thing. If a sentence has more than one independent clause, we call that sentence a **run-on**.

> **Sentence Fragment.** A dependent clause without an accompanying independent clause.
>
> **Run-On Sentence.** A sentence that has too many independent clauses or whose independent clauses are not connected properly.

If two or more independent clauses are to appear in a sentence, use a semicolon to link them. For example,

She ran; she tripped.

NOT: *She ran, she tripped.*

THE ESSENTIAL GMAT GRAMMAR VOCABULARY LIST

noun	subject	preposition
verb	predicate	conjunction
tense	prepositional object	subordination
phrase	direct object	coordination
sentence	indirect object	pronoun
dependent clause	antecedent	adjective
independent clause		adverb

THE FOUR-STEP METHOD FOR SENTENCE CORRECTION QUESTIONS

Step 1: Read the Original Sentence

The task is the same in every Sentence Correction question. Eliminate answer choices that contain obvious grammatical errors until you are left with one. Start by reading the sentence looking for an error. There's usually more than one error in a question, so if you spot multiple errors, just focus on the one that you know the most about. That's the error you're going to carry forward into the next step.

If nothing sticks out, that's fine, too. Answer Choice (A) is there for cases when the sentence is fine as originally written. But at this point, you shouldn't just select (A) and move to the next question. There are undoubtedly some errors that don't seem obviously wrong on the first pass. In order to make sure there aren't any lurking in this potentially correct question, you'll still want to eliminate down to (A).

Here's the sentence as originally written:

> As a vocalist and, just as importantly, as a songwriter, <u>Dolly Parton is one of the most successful cross-over artists of all time who inspired many of the singer-songwriters who today routinely top</u> the country and rock and roll charts simultaneously.

Step 2: Scan the Answers

In Sentence Correction questions, the most important information to process is found in those **Decision Points**, the places where the answer choices clump together in groups of two and three that all share the same feature. These are the possible errors we must vet in order to find the credited answer choice. So Step 2 of the Sentence Correction method is to pick one **Decision Point** and compare your options.

We've already directed your attention to one possible **Decision Point**. There's a long descriptive phrase, *who inspired many of the singer-songwriters who today …*, that's clearly meant to describe Dolly Parton, the subject of the sentence. Three answer choices keep Dolly on the other side of the long **Distractor** *is one of the most successful …*, and two of them move her. Pause to consider whether there is a grammatical reason to favor one way over the other.

Step 3: Eliminate

As it turns out, there's not really a grammatical reason why Dolly needs to be at the front of the sentence. Answer Choices (D) and (E) probably feel clunkier than the others, but grammatically speaking, they're in the clear on this issue. The first **Decision Point** was a dud, but that's not a problem. Not every difference between the answer choices is something you need to settle. We just move on to the next step.

Step 4: Repeat

When you've done all you can with one **Decision Point**, go back up to Step 2 and scan for another one.

Here's one you probably would have noticed while you were processing the front versus middle question:

(A) Dolly Parton [...] **who inspired** many of [...]
(B) Dolly Parton [...], **inspired** the singer-songwriters [...]
(C) Dolly Parton [...], **inspiring** many of the [...]
(D) [...] Dolly Parton **who inspired** many [...]
(E) [...] Dolly Parton, **routinely inspired** many [...]

Two of the answers stick *who* between *inspired* and the rest of the sentence. Does the *who* matter? Absolutely. One of the most frequently tested errors in the Sentence Correction section concerns **phrases and clauses** and how they are **connected**.

In Answer Choices (A) and (D), the *who* does not have a comma separating it from the words in front of it, and that creates a problem. The *inspiration* becomes a description of the group of artists Dolly Parton is one of—in effect, there's a group of artists, who inspire people, and Dolly is the most successful one of them. It makes much more sense if the inspiration is an *effect* of her success. She was so successful that she inspired others.

That leaves us with three answer choices, (B), (C), and (E). We need another **Decision Point**! We don't need to look far. The three answer choices that lacked the *who* have a split of their own. Answer Choices (B) and (E) use *inspired*; (C) uses *inspiring*.

    (B) [...] of all time, **inspired** many of [...]

    (C) [...] of all time, **inspiring** many of the [...]

    (E) [...] of all time, **routinely inspired** many [...]

The answer lies again in the relationship between three big phrases in the sentence. Start with the nonunderlined section. *As a vocalist, etc.* This is an introductory descriptive phrase that describes the way in which *Dolly is successful*. Her success is further described in the second big chunk of the sentence (where we learn she was a cross-over artist). So then how do we attach the third thought (that she inspired other artists) to the first two?

Using the *comma-inspired* found in (B) and (E) would create a list of two things that are each described by the first phrase, *As a vocalist, etc.* In effect, Dolly did two things as a vocalist. She was successful as a vocalist and she inspired some singer-songwriters as a vocalist. That doesn't sound right at all. As we've already said, the inspiration seems like it ought to be an effect of her *success*, not of her simply *being a vocalist*.

Can Answer Choice (C) work? It's the only one left, so it has to. If you're nearing the minute mark on time spent on this question, then it'd be best to just pick (C) and move on. You don't have to prove that a sentence is correct. You only need to prove that the other four aren't.

But, since you might be wondering, (C) does work. Changing the verb *interested* to its -ing form *interesting* makes it clearly a description of the stuff immediately on the other side of the comma. So now it's Dolly's *success as a cross-over artist* that inspired today's singer-songwriters, the ones who are themselves cross-over artists who can have number one hits on two different charts at the same time.

TAKE-HOME POINTS

- To succeed on the GMAT's Sentence Correction questions, you must train yourself to recognize the "GMAT House Style."
- Sentence Correction questions often are still clunky, awkward, and unsatisfying when all the errors are corrected.
- The grammatical pet peeves that people argue about might appear in a question, but never as the single deciding issue that makes one answer right and another wrong.
- In general, look for the sentence that's the least wrong, the one that avoids the errors commonly tested on GMAT.
- Beware of **distractors**: descriptive or qualifying phrases that serve only to obscure the grammatical issues being tested.
- Look for **decision points**. Scan the answer choices up and down to find places where words differ systematically. Use these to quickly eliminate answers.

Sentence Correction Diagnostic Quiz

During the Sentence Correction diagnostic quiz, you should attempt to mirror "test-like" conditions as closely as you can. On the real computer-based GMAT, you must complete each question in the order presented. You may not skip ahead or return to previous questions, so limit yourself similarly here. Mark your answer to each question before proceeding to the next. If you do not know the answer, then select your best guess or, barring that, select an answer at random. Do not give in to the temptation to change an answer once you have moved on from a question. There will be 15 questions in all, and you should spend no more than 20 minutes on the entire quiz.

Instructions for Sentence Correction questions will contain the following (in slightly different, GMAT language):

> **DIRECTIONS:** In the sentences that follow, we have underlined either part of the sentence or the entire sentence. Below that sentence, five different possible phrasings of the underlined portion will be listed. The first option will always repeat the original phrasing; the other four will alter it, each in a different way. If you believe the sentence is grammatically correct as originally written, select answer A; otherwise, select the answer choice you believe best corrects the original.
>
> These questions are meant to test both the correctness of the grammar used and the overall effectiveness of the expressions within the sentence. When making your decisions, keep the rules and requirements standard to formal written English in mind. Grammar, word choice, and sentence construction should factor into your decision. The answer you choose should produce the most effective possible sentence given the five options presented. The credited answer will be grammatically correct, clear, and precise, lacking ambiguity, awkwardness, and redundancy.
>
> You may only select one of the five answers for each question. Answer each to the best of your ability.

1. The oldest fossil organisms presently known <u>has been dated to be 3.4 billion years old and thus is</u> taken as evidence that life evolved soon after a planetary bombardment 3.8 billion years ago that would have sterilized Earth of any incipient life.

   (A) has been dated to be 3.4 billion years old and thus is
   (B) has been dated at 3.4 billion years old and thus
   (C) has been dated to be 3.4 billion years old and thus are
   (D) have been dated at 3.4 billion years old and thus are
   (E) have been dated as being 3.4 billion years old and thus

2. In many recent cases, incumbent politicians, including such once popular politicians as Charlie Crist, Florida's two-term governor, has elected early retirement rather than facing primary challenges from within their own parties.

   (A) has elected early retirement rather than facing
   (B) has elected early retirement instead of facing
   (C) have elected retiring early instead of facing
   (D) have elected to retire early rather than to face
   (E) have elected to retire early rather than face

3. The essential difference between a discrete and a continuous annuity is that one thinks of the former's payments as being made continuously over the year instead of discreet points in time.

   (A) instead of
   (B) as opposed to
   (C) in contrast with
   (D) rather than at
   (E) as against being at

4. Recovering addicts agree that it is often more difficult to overcome the social humiliation as well as the stigma associated with the use of drugs.

   (A) the social humiliation as well as the stigma associated with the use of drugs
   (B) the social humiliating as well as stigma associated with the use of drugs
   (C) the social humiliation and stigma associated with the use of drugs
   (D) socially both the humiliation and stigma associating with drug use
   (E) socially the humiliating and stigma associated in drug use

5. Because its military is larger by far than its allies in Western Europe, the United States accounts for over a third of NATO's deployable ground and air forces.

   (A) its military is larger by far than its allies in Western Europe
   (B) their military is larger by far than their allies in Western Europe
   (C) their military is larger by far than that of its allies in Western Europe
   (D) its military is larger by far than those of its allies in Western Europe
   (E) its military has been larger by far than those of their allies in Western Europe

6. They are not as famous for their waves than for their importance to the early history of the sport, East Coast beaches nevertheless remain home to a vibrant community of professional surfers who compete internationally.

   (A) They are not as famous for their waves than for
   (B) Even though they are not as famous as for their waves as compared to
   (C) They have not been famous for their waves as they are for
   (D) While not as famous for their waves as they are for
   (E) Since they are not as famous for their waves as they are for

7. At the Battle of Salamis, the Greek general Themistocles, recognizing that although the Persians outnumbered his fleet, the cramped conditions of the Straits prevented the larger force from being able to maneuver and coordinate its attacks, and pressed them back into the fray.

   (A) Themistocles, recognizing that although the Persians outnumbered his fleet, the cramped conditions of the Straits prevented
   (B) Themistocles, recognizing that although his fleet was outnumbered by the Persians, the cramped conditions of the Straits preventing
   (C) Themistocles recognized that, although outnumbering his fleet, the cramped conditions of the Straits prevented the Persians,
   (D) Themistocles recognized that, although his fleet was outnumbered by the Persians, the cramped conditions of the Straits preventing
   (E) Themistocles recognized that, although the Persians outnumbered his fleet, the cramped conditions of the Straits prevented

8. If healthcare costs continue to sharply rise, the search for new ways to contain health benefit exposures has become the primary focus of most businesses.

   (A) If healthcare costs continue to sharply rise,
   (B) As healthcare costs are continuing their sharp rise,
   (C) As healthcare costs continue their sharp rise,
   (D) The continuation of sharply rising healthcare costs mean
   (E) Healthcare costs' sharp rise continuing means that

9. On their trek from the border into the interior of the United States, immigrants face terrain that is hostile at best and often deadly, where little available water or landmarks exist.

   (A) little available water or landmarks exist
   (B) there are few landmarks and little available water
   (C) there is little water or landmarks available
   (D) little available water or landmarks exists
   (E) few landmarks and little available water exists

10. England was ruled by the francophone Norman nobility for a century, with the exception of the formal environment of the court the French language was seldom if ever spoken.

    (A) with the exception of
    (B) excepting for
    (C) but excepting for
    (D) except in
    (E) but except in

11. Many more lives will be saved in the coming century because of the development of new techniques for avoiding rejecting of synthetic and transplanted organs.

 (A) development of new techniques for avoiding rejecting of synthetic and transplanted organs
 (B) development of new rejection avoidance techniques for transplanting and synthetic organs
 (C) new development of synthetic and transplanted organ rejection and avoiding techniques
 (D) development of the rejection avoidance of techniques for new synthetic and transplanted organs
 (E) development of new techniques to avoid the rejection of synthetic and transplanted organs

12. Though the term "Web 3.0" may suggest a new version of HTML code or new configurations of servers, they simply describe the introduction of devices that range from smartphones to cars to household appliances.

 (A) suggest a new version of HTML code or new configurations of servers, they simply describe the introduction of devices that range
 (B) suggest a new version of HTML code or new configurations of servers, it simply describes the introduction of devices ranging
 (C) suggests new configurations of servers or versions of HTML code, it has simply described the introducing of devices ranging
 (D) has suggested a new version of the HTML code or new server configurations, it has simply described the ranges of newly introduced devices
 (E) has suggested configuring servers or HTML code in new versions, they simply describe the range of newly introduced devices

13. As the former president of the state board of regents for over two decades and a member of the board for over three, Jason Lowbrook oversaw the development of nearly three thousand different curriculum guidelines.

 (A) As the former
 (B) As he was
 (C) As the
 (D) The former
 (E) Former

14. Unlike Ernest Hemingway's bluster and blatant competitiveness, the reticent F. Scott Fitzgerald had much less of a penchant for venting his negative evaluations of his competitors' accomplishments in public.

(A) Unlike Ernest Hemingway's bluster and blatant competitiveness, the reticent F. Scott Fitzgerald had much less of a penchant for venting

(B) Unlike the blustery and competitive Ernest Hemingway, the reticent F. Scott Fitzgerald had much less of a penchant for venting

(C) Unlike Ernest Hemingway's bluster and blatant competitiveness, the reticent F. Scott Fitzgerald had much less of a penchant to vent

(D) Unlike the blustery and competitive Ernest Hemingway, F. Scott Fitzgerald was reticent to have much less of a penchant for venting

(E) Unlike the blustery and competitive Ernest Hemingway, the reticence of F. Scott Fitzgerald had much less of a penchant to vent

15. Each of the 16 recent cases in which excessive force complaints were lodged against a police officer was reviewed by the county attorney's office, and the majority were dismissed.

(A) Each of the 16 recent cases in which excessive force complaints were lodged against a police officer was reviewed

(B) The cases in which an excessive force complaint was lodged against police officers, each of them was reviewed

(C) Each of the 16 recent cases in which excessive force complaints were lodged against police officers was reviewed

(D) The cases where an excessive force complaint was lodged against police officers, each of them were reviewed

(E) Every one of the 16 recent cases in which complaints of excessive force was lodged against police officers were reviewed

Your Sentence Correction Diagnosis

Now's the time to take an honest look at your current strengths and weaknesses—so don't shy away from your mistakes, and don't cut yourself any breaks. There's no room for "I kind of knew that …" or "Oh, yeah … now I get it" in the issue spotter. Either you recognized the issue or you didn't, knew what to do or didn't.

ISSUE SPOTTER

DIRECTIONS: For each question, several key concepts have been listed and briefly explained. Near each you'll find two boxes, one marked **Recognized**, the other **Corrected**.

If you were aware that some grammatical concept was being employed in the question, give yourself a check in the box marked **Recognized**—regardless of whether you ultimately selected the correct answer.

Similarly, if your selected answer to the question correctly meets the requirements of the grammatical rule being tested, give yourself a check for **Corrected**—even if your answer was incorrect for some other reason, and even if you did not really recognize that you were being tested on that concept.

At the end of the diagnosis, count up your checkmarks for each category and write the value in the **Totals** box. A brief analysis of your overall performance and the path that lies ahead will follow.

1. (D) <u>Recognize:</u> (1) the **idiomatic construction** *dated at*; (2) **subject-predicate agreement** required for the plural subject *organisms* and both verbs *have been dated* and *are taken*.

<u>Correct:</u> (1) Only Answer Choices (B) and (D) contain the correct form *dated at*; (2) only the credited Answer Choice (D) manages to get the agreement correct for *both* verbs.

Recognized	Corrected	Issue
☐	☐	**idiomatic construction**
☐	☐	**subject-predicate agreement**

2. (E) <u>Recognize:</u> (1) the **idiomatic construction** *have [done] X rather than Y*; (2) **subject-predicate agreement** required for plural *incumbent politicians* and the verb *have elected*; (3) parallelism—the requirement that both the X and the Y in the idiomatic construction be expressed as the same part of speech

Correct: (1) Answer Choices (A), (D), and (E) all correctly use *X rather than Y.* (2) The plural *have* been appears in Answer Choices (C), (D), and (E); (3) the correct parallelism is subtle, however, and only appears in the credited Answer Choice (E), since the *rather than* is used to indicate that the politicians are doing one thing (electing to retire) rather than another (facing primary challenges).

Recognized	Corrected	Issue
☐	☐	**idiomatic construction**
☐	☐	**subject-predicate agreement**
☐	☐	**parallelism**

3. (D) Recognize: (1) the **idiomatic construction** *rather than*, used here to create a (2) **parallel comparison**

Correct: (1) Once again, only the credited Answer Choice (D) uses the correct idiom to create the contrast; (2) both Answer Choices (D) and (E) include the preposition *at* needed to make the parallelism work, creating a contrast between two descriptions of how we think of the payments being made (*continuously* versus *at discreet points in time*)

Recognized	Corrected	Issue
☐	☐	**idiomatic construction**
☐	☐	**parallelism (comparisons)**

4. (A) Recognize: (1) **parallelism** (*X and Y*); (2) the **idiomatic construction** *associated with*

Correct: (1) Both Answer Choices (A) and (C) create parallel items for the coordinated list of things that are difficult to overcome (*humiliation* and *stigma*)—even though (C) uses an unacceptable idiom to connect the two things; (2) only Answer Choice (D) gets the idiom *associated with* wrong, so credit for (A), (B), (C), and (E) alike.

Recognized	Corrected	Issue
☐	☐	**parallelism**
☐	☐	**idiomatic construction**

5. (D) Recognize: (1) a **comparison** that needs to be between **parallel** things (here *logically parallel*); (2) the correct singular **pronoun** to **reference** the singular noun *the United States*

Correct: (1) Answer Choices (A) and (D) catch both instances of the singular pronoun *its* that stands in for the singular noun *the United States*—(B) and (C) miss the obvious *their* at the start of the line, while (D) gets the first *its* and misses the second; (2) items compared must be logically parallel, and in this question only (C) and (D)'s comparisons between *the US's military* and the *military of its allies* work—comparing a *military* with *an ally* won't do.

Recognized	Corrected	Issue
☐	☐	**parallelism (comparisons)**
☐	☐	**pronoun reference**

6. (D) <u>Recognize:</u> This sentence features two **clauses and connectors** errors: (1) **connecting clauses**: when a sentence has two clauses, it should only have one truly independent clause (unless fancy punctuation is used); 2) **connecting words**: the words used to connect those clauses must be in the right form and make logical sense; (3) comparisons must be formed with the right **idiomatic construction**, here *as famous for X as for Y.*

<u>Correct:</u> (1) Answer Choices (B), (D), and (E) all contain at least one and only one independent clause because they all use a **subordinating conjunction** (*even though, while,* and *since*) to turn the sentence's first clause into a **dependent clause**. (2) Of those three subordinating conjunctions, only Answer Choices (B) and (D)'s *even though* and *while* create the proper contrasting relationship between the two facts expressed in the sentence's two clauses. (3) The correct form of the idiomatic phrase *as famous for X as for Y* is found in (C), (D), and (E).

Recognized	Corrected	Issue
☐	☐	**clauses and connectors (the clause issue)**
☐	☐	**clauses and connectors (the connecting words)**
☐	☐	**idiomatic construction**

7. (E) <u>Recognize:</u> (1) **clauses and connectors**: as above, at least one and only one independent clause; (2) **modification**: modifying phrases like *recognizing that ...* need to refer clearly and unambiguously to the correct word in the sentence (who's recognizing what?)

<u>Correct:</u> (1) Most of the answer choices are a mess of **dependent clauses** all jammed together, and only Answer Choices (D) and (E) manage to have something that can properly qualify as an **independent clause**; (2) the various descriptive phrases are also a mess here, so messy that only the credited Answer Choice (E) manages to keep everything lined up.

Recognized	Corrected	Issue
☐	☐	**clauses and connectors**
☐	☐	**modification**

8. (C) <u>Recognize:</u> (1) **clauses and connectors** (making the first clause **dependent**); (2) **subject-predicate agreement** (which word is the subject and which the predicate changes between the answer choices, however); (3) the **sequence of tenses** for the verbs describing the *rise* of the costs and the *becoming* later needs to make chronological sense.

<u>Correct:</u> (1) The *as* in Answer Choices (B) and (C) is needed to make the initial phrase a dependent clause (and Answer Choice (A)'s *if* is nonsensical). (2) Answer Choices (A), (B), (C), and (E) all contain correctly matched subject-predicate pairs—only (D)'s *continuation means* fails. (3) Since the healthcare costs are continuing their rise at the same time as the search for new ways is becoming the focus of the industry, the tenses for the verbs in the sentence need to be able to sustain simultaneous actions, a requirement only Answer Choices (A) and (C) manage.

Recognized	Corrected	Issue
☐	☐	**clauses and connectors**
☐	☐	**subject-predicate agreement**
☐	☐	**less-frequently tested errors (sequence of tenses)**

9. (B) <u>Recognize</u>: (1) **idiomatic constructions** (the proper use of *little* versus *few*); (2) **subject-predicate agreement** (primarily the plural verb required by **compound subjects**)

<u>Correct</u>: (1) *Little* is a quantity word that describes things that cannot be counted (like *water*), whereas *few* is used for countable things (like *landmarks*), and here Answer Choices (B) and (E) mind that distinction. (2) Only the use of the word *and* creates a **compound subject**, which requires a plural predicate (while *or* creates a list of subjects, the predicate agreeing only with the final member of the list), and only Answer Choices (A), (B), and (C) correctly handle the intricacies of that error.

Recognized	Corrected	Issue
☐	☐	**idiomatic constructions**
☐	☐	**subject-predicate agreement**

10. (A) <u>Recognize</u>: (1) **connecting words** (the choice between *but, but except*, etc.)

<u>Correct</u>: (1) Since only one error is tested, only the credited Answer Choice (A) gets this slightly obscure connection correct (if you read the sentence without the phrase *except in the formal environment of the court* the structure is clearer).

Recognized	Corrected	Issue
☐	☐	**clauses and connectors**

11. (E) <u>Recognize</u>: (1) **modification** (the correct relationship between all those prepositional descriptions of *development*); (2) **parallelism** (for the elements connected with *and* at the end of the sentence).

<u>Correct</u>: The modification error is so tightly entwined with the parallelism error, it's almost impossible to treat them singly, so instead award yourself two checks, one for each, if you saw that only in Answer Choice (E) is the coordinated object of the preposition *of* correctly parallel (*synthetic* and *transplanted* are both adjectives for *organs*), and likewise only in Answer Choice (E) are the modifying prepositional phrases *of new techniques, to avoid*, and *of synthetic* ... correctly arranged so that everything makes clear, logical sense.

Recognized	Corrected	Issue
☐	☐	**modification**
☐	☐	**parallelism**

12. (B) <u>Recognize</u>: (1) **subject-predicate agreement** (*the term ... may suggest*); (2) **pronoun reference** (*it* versus *they* for *term*)

<u>Correct</u>: (1) Note that the main verb of the sentence is not *suggest*, but rather *may suggest*, the singular form found only in Answer Choices (A) and (B) is correct. (2) Answer Choices (B), (C), and (D) all correctly fix the problem with the original sentence's plural pronoun *they* used to replace the singular *term*.

Recognized	Corrected	Issue
☐	☐	**subject-predicate agreement**
☐	☐	**pronoun reference**

13. (E) <u>Recognize:</u> (1) **modification** (for the relationship between the first and second clause)

<u>Correct:</u> (1) If the sentence's first clause is introduced by *as*, it becomes a description of what Jason *oversaw*—but since he didn't oversee things *as a former director*, but rather while he was a director, the *as* can't stand. If the *the* is used, the first clause becomes independent, resulting in two independent clauses linked only by a comma, a **run-on sentence**, meaning only Answer Choice (E) is correct.

Recognized	Corrected	Issue
☐	☐	**modification**

14. (B) <u>Recognize:</u> (1) **idiomatic construction** (*less of a penchant for Xing*); (2) **comparisons** (logically parallel)

<u>Correct:</u> (1) The more obscure *less of a penchant for* is correctly formed in Answer Choices (A), (B), and (D). (2) The comparison introduced by *unlike* must be between logically similar things—Answer Choices (B) and (D) compare *Hemingway* and *Fitzgerald*, two authors, whereas the other answers compare an author with competitiveness and an author with reticence.

Recognized	Corrected	Issue
☐	☐	**idiomatic construction**
☐	☐	**parallelism (comparisons)**

15. (B) <u>Recognize:</u> (1) **subject-predicate agreement** (*each … was, complaints … were*), (2) **clauses and connectors** (the connecting words *in which* versus *where*)

<u>Correct:</u> (1) The subject of the sentence, the singular *each*, is correctly paired with a singular verb in Answer Choices (A) and (C). (2) On the GMAT, *where* is reserved for places, not descriptions of things like cases, requiring the *in which* that appears in Answer Choices (A), (B), and (E).

Recognized	Corrected	Issue
☐	☐	**subject-predicate agreement**
☐	☐	**clauses and connectors**

ISSUE SPOTTER TOTALS

clauses and connectors

recognized	_____ of 6	_____%
corrected	_____ of 6	_____%
total points	_____ of 12	_____%

modification

recognized	_____ of 3	_____%
corrected	_____ of 3	_____%
total points	_____ of 6	_____%

subject-predicate agreement

recognized	____ of 6	____ %
corrected	____ of 6	____ %
total points	____ of 12	____ %

pronoun reference

recognized	____ of 2	____ %
corrected	____ of 2	____ %
total points	____ of 4	____ %

parallelism

recognized	____ of 6	____ %
corrected	____ of 6	____ %
total points	____ of 12	____ %

idiomatic construction

recognized	____ of 7	____ %
corrected	____ of 7	____ %
total points	____ of 14	____ %

less-frequently tested errors

recognized	____ of 1	____ %
corrected	____ of 1	____ %
total points	____ of 2	____ %

Congratulations! On the day of the test, you'll face about 15 Sentence Correction questions—as many as you have just now completed. The difficulties and the exact mix of topics will vary from test taker to test taker and test sitting to test sitting, of course, but just doing 15 questions in roughly 20 minutes is good practice for the challenges you'll wrestle with on test day.

But more important for our current purposes, you should now have a better idea both of the kinds of grammar issues that will appear on the GMAT and the areas where you are strongest and weakest. Take a look at the totals you've calculated above and compare your percentages against the following:

SUBJECT AREAS ...

... with great recognition AND correctness (each over 75 percent)
Good news! You'll still want to study these concepts, but you're starting off ahead of the game. You will want to pay more attention to the higher-difficulty complications at the end of the section covering these errors. And when you take the GMAT, these issues will probably become your fallbacks, the parts of the sentence you go to first when deciding how to set up your personal Process of Elimination.

... with great recognition (over 75 percent) and not-so-great correctness (less than 50 percent)
As a certain children's TV show famously put it, "Knowing is half the battle!" At least you know when something is up, even if you don't know quite what to do about it. Look carefully at the kinds of errors you made when trying to correct an issue.

Did you get distracted by other issues and forget about what you knew was at stake with these? Do you actually not know the right version of the rule? In the chapter ahead, make sure that you understand the basic version of the rule thoroughly before worrying about exceptions and complications. Until you master the basics, these will likely not be a first or even second place you'll go to for process of elimination on the day of the test.

... great correctness (over 75 percent) but terrible recognition (less than 50 percent)

You're a savant! You know some rules intuitively, even if you would be hard pressed to state them or explain them to someone else. These are the areas where you can usually "trust your ear" during your first pass over the question and its answers. Be careful not to categorically eliminate answers that feel "off," though, as (until you begin to recognize the underlying rules) you don't really have a concrete, specific reason to pick one answer choice over the other. Lean harder on the places where you *do* know the specific rule so that you don't have to over-extend your ear.

... terrible recognition AND not much correctness (both less than 50 percent)

These are the grammar rules you'll want to hit the hardest in your study, both as you read the coming chapter and as you do practice work with our targeted question banks and in the *Official Guides.* The review component of your practice problems will be critical here. You need to gather more data on your performance to figure out how the test maker is slipping these issues under your grammatical radar and how the wrong answers are conning you into thinking that they're right.

THE BIG 6: ERRORS MOST COMMONLY TESTED

As we mentioned back in the *Verbal Introduction,* the number of errors that have shown up on the GMAT is actually quite small—approximately 30 in the many decades during which the test has included some sort of grammar question. And of those 30 or so errors, only about a dozen appear with any regularity, so that the lion's share of Sentence Correction questions involve one or more of a group of just six errors. Ninety-five percent involve one of the six; about 60 percent test two or more. They are:

SUBJECT/PREDICATE AGREEMENT—The subject of the sentence (a noun) must match the predicate (the verb); singular subjects get singular predicates, and plural subjects get plural predicates.

PRONOUN REFERENCE—Pronouns must refer unambiguously to a single noun, and they must also match the noun they replace in number, gender, and case.

PARALLELISM—Parts of a sentence that play the same role must be put into matching forms. This includes words in lists, in comparisons, and in other multipart constructions.

CLAUSES AND CONNECTORS—Clauses can be either independent or dependent. Linking them incorrectly can result in a run-on sentence or a sentence fragment.

MODIFICATION—Modifying elements, such as adjectives, adverbs, and prepositional phrases, must be placed so that it's clear what they're supposed to modify and so that the modification makes logical sense.

IDIOMATIC CONSTRUCTION—Certain words are paired with other words in English not because of any logical rule, but because that's just the way they're expected to be. Usually, this involves preposition choice (i.e., you sleep *in* a bed, not *at* a bed).

In this book, we are going to call these most-frequently appearing errors "The Big 6."

The bulk of your study time should be devoted to mastering The Big 6. They will pay off more often than any other type of error, and even when other errors form the basis of a question, The Big 6 will still eliminate a couple of answer choices.

If you hit a question and have no idea where to start, always fall back on The Big 6. Use these errors as a quick-and-dirty checklist to help you find your first **decision point**.

For an even quicker quick-and-dirty checklist of The Big 6, think verbs, pronouns, modifiers, parallelism, clauses, idioms—in that order.

Any time you find yourself going back and forth on what seems like an obscure grammar point (is it "throw the ball to him" or "throw him the ball"?). Odds are, either (1) you don't know the obscure rule, or (2) there isn't actually a rule (and you're trying to create one). Either way, stop grasping at straws. Start grasping The Big 6.

Agreement Errors

The first three of The Big 6 errors—verbs, pronouns, and parallelism—all involve selecting the right *form* for a word so that it matches up with some other word.

BIG ERROR #1: SUBJECT/PREDICATE AGREEMENT

The **subject** of the sentence (a noun) must **match** its **predicate** (the verb); singular subjects get singular predicates, and plural subjects get plural predicates.

> Teacher: Would you kindly give me a sentence starting with the word "I"?
>
> Student: I is...
>
> Teacher: No, no! Always say, "I am."
>
> Student: All right ... I am the ninth letter of the alphabet.

As we all know, Dogs *bark*, but a dog *barks*. Bees *fly*, but a bee *flies*. Yes, we *have* no bananas; we don't *has* no bananas. Making verbs agree with their subjects is rarely a challenge for a fluent speaker of English.

The verbs featured in GMAT Sentence Correction questions aren't difficult to conjugate, usually following the standard pattern (*I walk, you walk, he/she/it walks, we walk, you (plural) walk, they walk*).

Never will you be asked to determine whether the verb goes *fling, flang, flung*, or *fling, flung, flung*, or *fling, flung, flinged*. (Instead, verbs follow the standard *walk, walked, has/have/had walked*.)

Moreover, questions like whether you use *fly out* or *flew out* for a baseball player and a fly ball aren't part of the GMAT's arsenal of trickery.

So how can they test subject-verb agreement in so many different Sentence Correction questions? They hide the subject or the verb—or both.

Subject-Predicate Variation #1: The Separated Subject-Predicate Pair

It is easy to disguise the subject of the sentence by either burying it under modifiers or separating it from its predicate with the same. For instance, on your Diagnostic Quiz:

TIP

When in doubt, follow *The Rule of S*. Singular nouns don't end in *S*, but singular verbs usually do (in the present tense). One *S* per sentence!

| distractor | **subject** | distractor | **predicate** |

The oldest fossil **organisms** presently known **has been dated** [...]

| **subject** | distractor |

[...] **incumbent politicians,** including such once popular politicians
as Charlie Crist, Florida's two-term governor, **has elected** [...]

predicate

In the first sentence, the plural *organisms* requires the plural form *have been dated*, but if you mistook the first distractor, *fossil*, for the subject, you would have gone with the singular *has been dated*.

In the second sentence, the subject *incumbent politicians*, again plural, is separated from its predicate by 12 words and two lines! Notice how the nouns closest to the predicate—*Charlie Crist, Florida, governor*—are all singular? The predicate *has elected* agrees with these singular distractors; *have elected* agrees with the plural *incumbent politicians*.

No matter what the test makers try to put between them, do not be fooled. In English, however far apart they may be, the subject and predicate must agree.

Subject-Predicate Variation #2: The "Placeholder" or "Dummy" Subject

The phrases *there are*, *there is*, and *it is* can be used to delay the subject in a sentence. Even though the word *there* or *it* starts the sentence, the sentence's real subject follows the predicate verb. Suppose the test maker hit you with

> There are, without a doubt, a wealth of good reasons to invest
> early in one's own retirement.

you'd look after the verb (and after another distractor) to find the real subject of the sentence, the singular *a wealth*—and not the plural *reasons*. *Are* must change to *is*.

> There is, without a doubt, a wealth of good reasons
> to invest

In a sense, *there* and *it* are just "dummy" subjects that are holding the spot for the subject of the sentence that will be introduced later.

A related sort of place-holding occurs with words like *everybody, each, anybody, someone, no one,* and *nobody*. They're called **indefinite pronouns**, and most indefinite pronouns are treated as **singular**. Earlier, you saw

> Each of the 16 recent cases in which excessive force complaints
> were lodged against police officers was reviewed [...]

Look past the **distractors** to see the subject of the sentence is the indefinite pronoun *each*, which is here correctly paired with the singular verb *was reviewed*. *Were reviewed* would be incorrect, though it might "feel right" considering three plural nouns come between the singular subject and predicate: *complaints, cases,* and *officers*.

There are three big exceptions to the indefinite pronoun rule that we mention here for completeness's sake, not because they're tested very frequently on the GMAT.

TIP

In everyday speech, we usually make our predicates agree with whatever noun we said most recently, which is why "sounds right" can be so misleading.

Exception 1: A small number of indefinite pronouns are singular or plural depending on whether the noun they're replacing is countable or not. These include *all* and *some*. (More on this under *Error #6: Idioms*.)

> **Some** of the hovercrafts **are** full of eels. (You can count hovercrafts, so they are plural.)
>
> **All** of the milk **was drunk** yesterday. (You can't count milk, so it is singular.)

Exception 2: A small number of indefinite pronouns are always plural. They're easy to remember, since they all clearly describe multiple things: *both, few, others,* and *several*.

Exception 3: The word *none* switches between singular and plural depending on whether the *none* is being used by the writer to mean *not any* or *not one*. Since you can't read the test maker's mind, it doesn't really matter which one you use; either is correct. Hooray!

> She looked in the cupboard for lights, but there **were none**.
> (How many lights? *Not any*.)
> He looked in the cupboard for a flashlight, but there **was none**.
> (How many flashlights? *Not one*.)

TIP

See also: *Error #5: Clauses and Connectors,* because *and* is a connector and *Error #3: Parallelism,* because *and* creates coordination, which requires parallelism.

Subject-Predicate Variation #3: Compound Subjects

The word *and* has a special quirk in English. When you link two subject nouns with the word *and*, you create what is known as a "compound subject," and **compound subjects are always treated as plural**, no matter whether the individual items linked by the *and* are plural or singular.

Question 9 on your Diagnostic Quiz had an answer choice that ended

> few landmarks and little available water exists

Subject-predicate pairs that appear in dependent clauses must agree, just as the pairs that appear in independent clauses, so here the *and* in this dependent clause means that the plural verb *exist* is needed instead of the singular *exists*—even though the singular word *water* is closer to the verb.

You can also expect the compound subject rule to be tested in the negative, too. That is, only the word *and* can create a compound subject. The word *or* does not. When *or* is used to link two subjects, the predicate agrees with whichever subject is ***closest***, so it is usually the second item in an *either... or* or *neither... nor* list. This issue was also tested in Question 9, where Answer Choice (D) read

> little available water or landmarks exists

Since the *plural* landmarks is closest to the verb *exists*, the plural *exist* is needed instead, because *or* does not create a compound subject. But had the answer choice instead read

> little landmarks or available water exist

it would ***still*** be wrong because now the closest word to *exist* is the singular *water,* demanding the singular *exists*.

Drilling Down to the Subject and Predicate

GMAT Sentence Correction sentences are crammed full of dependent clauses, prepositional phrases, and long parenthetical interruptions in order to keep you from recognizing the subject and predicate. The key to finding them is learning to identify and block out all that noise. We call this **Drilling Down** to the sentence's core structure.

Take, for example, the longest Sentence Correction question from your Diagnostic Quiz.

> At the Battle of Salamis, the Greek general Themistocles recognized that, although the Persians outnumbered his fleet, the cramped conditions of the Straits prevented the larger force from being able to maneuver and coordinate its attacks, and pressed them back into the fray.

Who is the subject and what is the subject doing? Peel away the layers. The main subject of a sentence can never be found inside a prepositional phrase. So let's delete those.

> The Greek general Themistocles recognized that, although the Persians outnumbered his fleet, the cramped conditions prevented the larger force, and pressed them back.

At, of, from, to, and *into* and everything attached to them just provide extra description. We're looking for the sentence's heart. It's a good bit more manageable now, but there's still more we could cut.

When a sentence includes a part set off from the rest by commas, it's probably another sort of optional description like an appositive or parenthetical phrase. Snip. Snip.

> The Greek general Themistocles recognized that the cramped conditions prevented the larger force, and pressed them back.

Just like prepositions, relative pronouns like *that, who,* and *which* subordinate anything that follows them, so they cannot hold the main subject and predicate, either.

> The Greek general Themistocles recognized and pressed them back.

It's probably obvious by now: the subject of the sentence is general *Themistocles*; the predicate is compound, two actions that Themistocles does: first he *recognized* (all that military strategy stuff) and later he *pressed* (his troops).

If you train yourself to read past the extra information, Sentence Correction becomes a snap:

> **Each** of the 16 recent cases in which excessive force complaints were lodged against a police officer **was reviewed** by the county attorney's office, **and** the **majority were dismissed**.
>
> (A) **Each** of the 16 recent cases in which excessive force complaints were lodged against a police officer **was reviewed**
>
> (B) The cases in which an excessive force complaint was lodged against police officers, **each** of them **was reviewed**
>
> (C) **Each** of the 16 recent cases in which excessive force complaints were lodged against police officers **was reviewed**
>
> (D) The cases where an excessive force complaint was lodged against police officers, **each** of them **were reviewed**
>
> (E) **Every one** of the 16 recent cases in which complaints of excessive force was lodged against police officers **were reviewed**

To find the subject and predicate and the sentence's basic structure:

1. Read past the **prepositional phrases**.
2. Ignore the **parenthetical phrases**.
3. Cut out **relative clauses** (and other **subordinate** descriptions).
4. If needed, drop out any adjectives, adverbs, and articles.

Drilling Down Quick Practice Drill

DIRECTIONS: *Drill down to the core subject and predicate pair in the following sentences.*

1. The acid spilled in the laboratory caused a delay in the unrelated investigation into the possibility that the laboratory director had misspent grant-generated funds.

2. Regardless of what their original name might have been, in the retelling, the name of the butler in a popular story, as if by some sort of law of narrative momentum, will inevitably become "Jeeves."

3. The effect on the economy of irrational agents acting in unpredictable fashions is one of the many aspects of currency markets that had not been incorporated into the complicated computer models used by so-called experts to predict future price fluctuations.

4. His baggage now ready, the chancellor, after kissing his mother and sisters on the cheek and once more embracing his adored girlfriend Gretchen who, dressed in simple white muslin that contrasted starkly with her rich brown hair, departed for the train that waited on the tracks.

DRILL KEY

1. Acid caused.
2. Name will become.
3. Effect is.
4. Chancellor departed.

BIG ERROR #2: PRONOUN REFERENCE

> Teacher: Beavis, name two pronouns!
> Beavis: Uh ... who, me?

> Pronouns must (1) refer unambiguously to a single noun, and they must also (2) **match the noun they replace (or refer to) in number, person, gender, and case.**

Pronouns are words that stand in for nouns. We call the word that the pronoun stands in for its **antecedent**. Pronouns must agree with their antecedents, just as subjects must agree with predicates.

As far as agreement is concerned, subjects and predicates get off easy. They merely have to agree in number (singular versus plural), but there is a whole host of ways that pronouns and antecedents must agree.

Pronoun Variation #1: Basic Pronoun Agreement

Agreement by Number

Simply put, singular pronouns must replace singular nouns, plural pronouns plural nouns, regardless of what type of pronoun is involved.

> Anyone who uses this miter saw must put it back where they got it from.

Anyone is singular, but *they* is plural. Thus, the credited answer to the question above might be:

> (B) All who use this miter saw must put it back where they got it from.

Notice that in the sentence above the verb had to change (*uses* versus *use*) to accommodate the new plural pronoun. Verb and pronoun errors are often tested in the same question on the test, so if you decide a pronoun must be changed from plural to singular, be sure that all the verbs in the sentence still match—particularly, any verbs hiding in the nonunderlined part of the sentence.

It's also important to note that on the GMAT, number agreement is really the bread and butter agreement error. Scour questions for stray *it*s and *they*s. Their appearance almost always means a pronoun error is going to be among the errors tested.

Because they involve such distinctive little words, pronoun agreement by number errors make for great **decision points**.

Agreement by Person and Gender

In grammar, "person" refers to the relationship between a subject and its verb. First-person (*I, me, we*) is used for those talking or speaking about themselves; second, for direct address (*you*); third, for speaking about an absent party (*him, her, he, they, it*).

Agreement by person is rare but does occasionally get tested, usually as a misplaced *you*. If we found both gender and person in a question, it might look like this:

INCORRECT
2nd person **you**

As Dorothy Parker observed, if a woman wants to succeed in this world, you have to play the game better than a man.

CORRECT
3rd person feminine **she**

she has to play the game better than a man

Agreement by Case

Of all the pronoun agreement error flavors, agreement by case is the one most likely to worry test takers, even though it appears much less frequently than agreement by number—probably because nobody quite remembers what "case" means anymore. Let us curse you with this rare knowledge:

> **Case.** The grammatical role that a noun or pronoun plays in a sentence.

Nouns in English look the same in most cases.

If *Rusty* is the subject of the sentence, you use the **subjective case** *Rusty*.

> *Rusty* is the subject of this sentence.

If *the flag* is the object of a sentence's predicate verb, you use the **objective case** *the flag*.

> We raised *the flag* to half-mast.

Only in the **plural** and the **possessive** do we change the form of a noun, and most of the time all we do then is add an *-s*, an *-es*, or a *-'s* (*apostrophe + s*).

> The *record player's* needle is broken, and who stocks *needles* for *record players* anymore?

Pronouns retain a few more case distinctions. **She** *went to the store*, but *Yoshiko went with* **her**.

The GMAT expects you to be familiar with these distinctions, but only passingly so:

If the subject of the sentence is replaced by a pronoun, you use the *subjective case*.

> *Rusty* is the subject of this sentence, and what the predicate says *he* does.

If the object of the sentence is replaced by a pronoun, you use the *objective case*.

> Throw the ball to *Regina*? Of course I'm going to throw it to *her*!

If a noun that's possessive is replaced by a pronoun, you use the *possessive case*.

> Which of the record players is *Xian's*? That one over there is *her* record player.

If both the owner and the owned noun are replaced by a pronoun, you use the *absolute possessive case*.

> Which of these is *Xian's record player*? That one over there is *hers*.

There is only one version of the case error that shows up very often, when the verb *to be* is the main verb of a sentence and a pronoun follows it. Which of these two answer choices "sounds right" in your head?

> (A) The right people to blame for the failure of the conference are you and he.
>
> (B) The right people to blame for the failure of the conference are you and him.

While you'd almost never hear someone say a sentence like Answer Choice (A) aloud, it is nevertheless correct, and Answer Choice (B) is incorrect. Cut out the descriptive phrase *to blame for the failure of the conference* and it might—but only *might*—sound different:

> (A) The right people [...] are you and he.
>
> (B) The right people [...] are you and him.

The reason that (A) is correct is that the verb *to be* doesn't take a direct object, so the objective case *him* is incorrect. Instead, *to be* acts as kind of an "equals sign" grammatically. The noun on the left is being equated with the nouns on the right, so both sets of nouns need to be in the same case, the subjective.

TIP

"It is I, Arthur, King of the Britons" not "It is me, Arthur, King of the Britons."

Pronoun Variation #2: Lots and Lots of Pronouns

This variation is less a grammar rule and more a matter of bookkeeping. The GMAT often gives test takers a question with a long underlined section that contains multiple pronouns, several of which agree correctly, save one that the test makers hope is overlooked.

If a GMAT question contained this sentence:

> Every **one** of the great chef's recipes were catalogued and filed according to **their** country of origin, **its** required ingredients, and **their** reception by the critics.

the correct and credited answer would be

> Every **one** of the great chef's recipes was catalogued and filed according to **its** country of origin, **its** required ingredients, and **its** reception by the critics.

because the antecedent *one* is singular, demanding a possessive singular *its* for each of the three items in the list that follows.

The more places to hide a pronoun, the more vigilant we must be.

Pronoun Variation #3: Ambiguous Pronoun Reference

Just as the test makers like to quiz you on pronoun agreement, they also like to give you sentences in which there are too many possible antecedents for the pronoun. In these cases, the trick is to replace the pronoun with a more specific word or phrase.

Faced with

> The government launched an attack on the rogue nation after **it** violated UN airspace.

we would select

> after **that nation** violated UN airspace.

Often people preparing for the GMAT cry foul on hearing this trick. It is obvious by context, they insist, that it was the rogue nation that violated the UN's airspace. Why else would the government attack them?

As always, structure is king on the GMAT. The *it* is a singular third-person subject pronoun, and there are two possible singular third-person antecedents in the sentence, the *government* and the *rogue nation*. The solution to the ambiguity is to remove the offending pronoun entirely, replacing it with a demonstrative pronoun and a repeat of the original word: *that nation*.

The unspecified antecedent is one of the test makers' favorite ways to test pronouns, so you are almost certain to see it in some form, either on an official practice test or on the actual test, so be prepared.

You'll even see the ambiguous pronoun slipped into a single answer choice in a question that doesn't otherwise concern pronouns, most often when the answer choices are long and involve a lot of reorganizing of clauses and phrases. If you're having trouble finding a grammatical reason to choose between two answer choices, do a quick scan for a stray *they* or *it*.

BIG ERROR #3: PARALLELISM

> Parts of a sentence that play the same role must be put into matching forms. This includes words in lists, in comparisons, and in other multipart constructions.

There are two main relationships that elements in a sentence may have to each other. Take our simple sentence we used back in "GMAT Grammar 101" again: *Dogs bark*.

Suppose we wanted to add a second barker to the sentence, to have two subjects but only one predicate. Easy: *Dogs* **and** *seals bark*.

When two elements both play the same role in a sentence, we say that they are **coordinated**. Any part of a sentence can be expanded by coordinating two words or phrases.

Coordinated Subjects

> **The dogs and the three seals** barked at the waves.

Coordinated Predicates

> The dogs **barked and growled** at the mailman.

Coordinated Objects

> The dogs barked **at the mailman and his partner.**

> The dogs bit the **one mailman but not the other one.**

> **Coordination.** When two words or phrases are linked so that they form a compound sentence part.

TIP

Coordination is found in about 60 percent of GMAT Sentence Correction questions.

COORDINATING CONJUNCTIONS

For

And

Not

But

Or

Yet

So

The words that connect the two coordinated things are technically called **coordinating conjunctions**. There are only seven of them in English, and they can be arranged so that their first letters spell out FANBOYS.

English also has one hard and fast rule about coordination that the GMAT seems to want to test in every other Sentence Correction question. When you coordinate two words or phrases, you have to use the same part of speech for both. You can coordinate *nouns with nouns* and *noun phrases with noun phrases*, but never *nouns and verbs*. The elements coordinated must be **parallel**.

> **Parallelism.** The requirement that coordinated items must share the same part of speech.

This doesn't mean that we can't ever connect dissimilar words in a sentence—but when we do, we have to use a different kind of connection and a different kind of connecting word. That other way of connecting is called **subordination**, and we'll talk about it in a moment, when we discuss *Big Error #5: Clauses and Connectors*.

Elements in a list or a series, elements in a comparison, or elements in any other multipart construction must be parallel in this way. They must share the same part of speech and the same relationship to any "accompanying words," including prepositions (such as *by, for,* and *of*), conjunctions (*and* and *or*), and articles (*a, the,* and *an*).

Parallelism Variation #1: Basic Lists and Other Compound Sentence Parts

Parallelism is most easily demonstrated with a simple sentence that would never appear on the GMAT:

I like to hop, skip, and jump.

Here we have a simple list of things that *I like to (do)*. Each of the elements—in this case, the actions *hop, skip,* and *jump*—is a verb in the **infinitive** form, and they all share the same relationship to that little accompanying word *to*.

When a sentence is properly parallel, you could separate it into multiple sentences with the same form that all make sense:

I like to hop, skip, and jump → I like to hop. I like to skip. I like to jump.

We're not allowed to mix and match our parts of speech in a coordinated list. So this sentence isn't parallel:

I like to hop, skipping, and to jump.

Infinitive, noun, infinitive isn't allowed.

We are, however, allowed to change the part of speech of members of a list, so long as we change each element. So it would still be correct for a sentence to say

I like hopping, skipping, and jumping.

Now the list is composed of three different nouns that *I like*: (1) *hopping,* (2) *skipping,* and (3) *jumping.*

And even if we were to return to our infinitive verb list, we could still change the list a different way and be in the clear—the *to* can be attached to each infinitive if we so desire. Thus:

I like to hop, to skip, and to jump.

Now we have a list of things that I like: (1) *to hop,* (2) *to skip,* and (3) *to jump.*

English grammar lacks a consistent bit of jargon for what words like *to* should be called when lumped together with words like *the* and *a,* like *these* and *those,* or like *did* and *could.* In this book we'll use the term of convenience "accompanying words."

TIP

Little helping verbs like "do" are often omitted in English, and it is perfectly correct to do so, both on the GMAT and in your own writing.

> **Accompanying Words.** The small words like *to*, *a*, *the*, *did*, and *could* that contribute to parallelism.

The requirement for parallel accompanying words is often confusing for GMATers who struggle with grammar and for those for whom English is a not a native tongue. The best way to clear up the confusion is to think about the relationship between the parallel items and their accompanying words as a matter of balance.

Consider the list of infinitives that *I like* and that list of verbs that *I like to*. I can "hang" each of the elements in the list on the beginning of the sentence and each element has the same available accompanying words as any other.

I like:	to hop,		I like to:	hop,
	to skip,			skip,
and	to jump.		and	jump.

For purposes of "balance," ignore the word *and*. It's not part of the list's items, it's part of the list's structure.

Change the sentence to *I like to hop, skip, and to jump.* and the result is unbalanced. It is neither a list of things *I like* nor a list of things *I like to*.

I like:	to hop,		I like to:	hop,
	skip,			skip,
and	to jump.		and	to jump.

Either we're omitting the *to* that should go with *skip* in a list of things *I like* or we're saying that *I like to to jump*. Consider how the sentences would look split apart:

I like to hop. I like skip. I like to jump.

Or

I like to hop. I like to skip. I like to jump.

OK, enough with the hopping and skipping. How will the GMAT ***actually*** test the requirement that lists be parallel? In a basic question, like so:

> In preparation for a rigorous MBA program, all business students should familiarize themselves with <u>word processing programs, how to keep accounts, and to maintain their computer</u>.

Here we have a list of things that business students *should familiarize themselves with*. Is it balanced?

familiarize themselves with:	word processing programs,	(a noun phrase)
	how to keep accounts,	(a conjunction followed by an infinitive)
and	to maintain their computer.	(an infinitive with its modifiers)

Three different parts of speech in a three-item list is about as unbalanced as you can get! If the sentence is to be parallel, we need to see three noun phrases:

> **word processing programs, accounting, and computer maintenance**

or three conjunctions followed by infinitives:

> **how to use word processing programs, how to keep accounts, and how to maintain their computers**

or three infinitives with their modifiers (delete "with" from the sentence):

> **to use word processing programs, to keep accounts, and to maintain their computers**

When scanning answer choices for parallelism, it's important not to "fall in love" with any one part of speech. If the question had originally been written

> **In preparation for a rigorous MBA program, a business student should become familiar with word processing programs, accounting, and to properly maintain their computers.**

the fact that *word processing programs* and *accounting* are a noun and a noun phrase, respectively, tends to bias test takers toward answer choices that change the third list item to a noun phrase.

> **word processing programs, accounting, and the proper maintenance of their computers**

Though it does have a parallel three-noun list, this answer choice also has the plural pronoun *their* used to stand in for the singular noun phrase *a business student*. The more obvious parallelism can be used to hide other errors.

The correct answer may well change the first two list-elements to match the third. That's fine, so long as that answer also gets rid of the *their*.

Parallelism Variation #2: Multipart Constructions

All of the coordinating conjunctions (FANBOYS) require parallelism between the things they coordinate:

> **Apples *and* peaches will sell well.**
> [noun] *and* [noun]

> **The treasure was hidden under Henderson's mattress *or* beneath the big X.**
> [prepositional phrase] *or* [prepositional phrase]

> **What he promised *and* what he delivered were markedly different.**
> [dependent clause] *and* [dependent clause]

> **Tomas ate all the Ramen, *so* Harry kicked him out of the apartment.**
> [independent clause], *so*   [independent clause]

Notice that the demands of parallelism are not so strict that the coordinated elements must be *exactly* the same. It doesn't matter that *under Henderson's mattress* has one fewer word than *beneath the big X*. Both are prepositional phrases, and that's enough.

Naturally, the coordinating conjunctions aren't the only words we use in English to connect two equal items. We also use correlating conjunctions and certain idiomatic expressions. The following is a small sample of the possibilities:

either X or Y	neither X nor Y	both X and Y
not only X but also Y	sacrifice X for Y	just as X, so too Y
X as much/little/etc. as Y	not so much X as Y	

Any time you see a sentence built around one of these multipart constructions, make sure that whatever's in the X position is expressed in the same part of speech as whatever's in the Y.

Incorrect: Destiny was *not so much* a **genius** *as* **she worked hard.**

not so much [noun phrase] *as* [independent clause]

Correct: Destiny was *not so much* a genius *as* **a hard worker.**

not so much [noun phrase] *as* [noun phrase]

Parallelism Variation #3: Comparisons

Comparisons are a special type of multipart construction that requires parallelism on two different levels. The first level you're already familiar with: compared items must be expressed as the same part of speech. Thus, regardless of what you may have heard elsewhere, it's perfectly acceptable (on the GMAT and in real life) to compare apples and oranges. Just make sure that you phrase both parts of the comparison as the same part of speech.

Apples are denser than oranges and are more fun to throw.

Oranges grow better in the winter than apples do.

I like oranges just as much as apples.

But on top of being grammatically parallel, items in comparisons must also be **logically parallel**.

Because apples and oranges are both fruits, they pass the logical parallelism requirement easily. Trouble arises when you do something like this, instead:

I like **apples** more than I like **the taste of oranges.**

Apples' skin is thinner than **an orange.**

The farmer grew more apples than in the nearby farmer's fields.

In the first sentence, a kind of fruit (apples) is compared with a particular quality (taste) that another fruit has. In the second, part of a fruit (the skin of an apple) is compared with the whole of different fruit. In the last sentence, many things might be the subject of the comparison, it's so completely muddled.

You encountered this variation several times during your Diagnostic Quiz. Question 5 contained a comparison between two things: *X is larger by far than Y.*

> Because **its military** *is larger by far than* **its allies in Western Europe**, the United States accounts for over a third of NATO's deployable ground and air forces.

> X: **its military** ← a noun phrase and a military

> Y: **its allies in Western Europe** ← a noun phrase and several countries

In the original sentence, the comparison was incorrectly made between *the US military* and *its allies*, when the intending meaning was a comparison between two militaries, the United State's military and its allies' military. The correct answer rewrote the sentence thus:

> Because **its military** is larger by far than **those of its allies in Western Europe**, the United States accounts for over a third of NATO's deployable ground and air forces.

> X: **its military** ← a noun phrase and a military

> Y: **those of its allies in Western Europe** ← a pronoun phrase and several militaries

TIP

Avoid overcorrection. Plurals may correctly be compared with singulars and nouns with pronouns.

Parallelism Variation #4: I'm Sorry, You're Not on the List

Sometimes, the test maker will try to trip you up by putting something in a parallel list that actually doesn't make sense there:

> In order to improve his golf game, Mr. Morton began a regimen of stretching exercises, added weight training to his daily workout, and seeing a consequent substantial change within weeks.

There are three actions in this sentence, which might suggest that you need to create a parallel three-item list:

X	began a regimen [...]	→	began a regimen [...]
Y	added weight training [...]	→	added weight training [...]
Z	seeing a substantial change	→	saw a substantial change.

Now look back at that modifying phrase in the first nonunderlined section, *in order to improve his golf game.* Would it make sense to say "In order to improve his golf game, Mr. Morton saw a substantial change within weeks?" Of course not. The change Mr. Morton saw is not part of the plan to improve but rather the improvement that followed the plan. Instead, the credited answer contains a two-item list and makes it clear that the last part of the sentence is a separate thought.

> began a regimen of stretching exercises and added weight training to his daily workout, and consequently he saw a

PARALLELISM DRILL: I GO BOTH WAYS

As we said before, don't fall in love with a particular version of a parallel list. Even though you might think the sentence would sound better with three noun phrases, the test maker might only give you that list in an answer choice that has other errors, trusting you'll ignore the correct version that changes the sentence into a list of three verbs.

Thus, below you'll be given a list of items that are not parallel. Rewrite the list as directed.

1. Today I will tidy up the bedroom, the living room, and dust the wallpaper.

    Create a list of three noun phrases:

    Today I will tidy up _____, _____, and _____.

    Now change it to a list of three verb phrases:

    Today I will _____, _____, and _____.

2. The company's annual meeting consists almost entirely of reviewing the minutes of the previous annual meeting, a vote for the location of next year's meeting, and closing remarks from the CEO.

    Create a list of noun phrases to follow *entirely of* but do not use *-ing* words like *reviewing*:

    The company's annual meeting consists almost entirely of _____, _____, and _____.

    Now change it to a list of *-ing* phrases to follow *entirely of*:

    The company's annual meeting consists almost entirely of _____, _____, and _____.

3. The new edition of the DIY guide describes how to build a tree house and painting it.

    Create a list of *how to* phrases to follow *describes:*

    The new edition of the DIY guide describes _____ and _____.

    Now change it to a list of phrases to follow *how to*:

    The new edition of the DIY guide describes how to _____ and _____.

4. Let your doctor know if your child is unable to identify shapes and colors, speaking or putting together phrases and sentences, or maintain balance while walking.

    Create a list of verb phrases to follow *unable:*

    Let your doctor know if your child is unable _____, _____, or _____.

    Now change it to a list of compliments to follow the verb *is*:

    Let your doctor know if your child is _____, _____, or _____.

DRILL REVIEW

These are possible ways you could have rephrased the sentences.

1. Today I will tidy up the bedroom, the living room, and the wallpaper.

   Today I will tidy up the bedroom, tidy up the living room, and dust the wallpaper.

2. The company's annual meeting consists almost entirely of a review of the minutes of the previous annual meeting, a vote for the location of next year's meeting, and final remarks from the CEO.

   The company's annual meeting consists almost entirely of reviewing the minutes of the previous annual meeting, voting for the location of next year's meeting, and listening to the concluding remarks from the CEO.

3. The new edition of the DIY guide describes how to build a tree house and how to paint it.

   The new edition of the DIY guide describes how to build a tree house and paint it.

4. Let your doctor know if your child is unable to identify shapes and colors, to speak or put together phrases and sentences, or to maintain balance while walking.

   Let your doctor know if your child is unable to identify shapes and colors, unable to speak or put together phrases and sentences, or unable to maintain balance while walking.

TAKE-HOME POINTS ABOUT AGREEMENT ERRORS

- Don't be fooled by **distractors**! The test maker loves to disguise the subject of a sentence.
- Indefinite pronouns are almost always taken as singular—except for *none*, *all*, and *some*, which go both ways.
- Compound subjects are treated as plural, but only *and* creates a compound subject.
- Be on the lookout for stray *it*, *its*, *they*, *them*, and *their* in the middle of underlined sections.
- Structure is king on the GMAT, while meaning takes a back seat. Don't let an answer choice off the hook by assuming a context for the sentence.
- Parallelism is required by many different things: lists, comparisons, and many multipart constructions.
- It's not enough for a comparison to be grammatically parallel; it must be logically parallel, too.

Agreement Errors Quick Review Quiz

> **DIRECTIONS:** Try to complete the following five questions in less than 5 minutes to test your understanding of the most commonly tested errors relating to agreement.

1. The recent surge in military activity in the country's more mountainous regions <u>were intended to reduce the presence overall of the insurgent militia</u>; however, their numbers have continued to grow steadily.

   (A) were intended to reduce the presence overall of the insurgent militia
   (B) were intended overall to reduce the presence of the insurgent militia
   (C) was to have intended to reduce the insurgent militia's presence overall
   (D) was intended to reduce the presence of the insurgent militia overall
   (E) overall was intending reducing the presence of the insurgent militia

2. Although not the first animals to evolve eyes, trilobites were <u>as likely among the first species as</u> the animal kingdom to develop a sophisticated visual system.

   (A) as likely among the first species as
   (B) as likely to have been among the first species as
   (C) as likely in the first species among
   (D) among the first likely species with
   (E) likely among the first species in

3. <u>Western restaurants in Korea are often either devoted to burgers or feature burgers</u> as a prominent part of a larger menu.

   (A) Western restaurants in Korea are often either devoted to burgers or feature burgers
   (B) In Korea, Western restaurants often either are devoted to burgers or feature burgers
   (C) Those Western restaurants that are in Korea often either are devoted to burgers or to the feature of a burger
   (D) Western restaurants in Korea are often either devoting burgers or featuring a burger
   (E) In Korea, the Western restaurants that are often either devoted to burgers or feature burgers

4. Iowa, Georgia, and North Carolina produce swine <u>that are worth almost as much as</u> <u>that of the forty-seven states that remain</u>.

   (A) that are worth almost as much as that of the forty-seven states that remain.
   (B) of a worth that is almost as much as the forty-seven states that remain.
   (C) worth almost as much as those of the remaining forty-seven states.
   (D) almost as much in worth as those of the remaining forty-seven states.
   (E) almost as much in worth as that of the remaining forty-seven states.

5. When testing new methods of compressing the data contained in files, researchers found that redundancy <u>among different file types is, on average, far greater as that</u> <u>among files from</u> the same file type, and can thus be ignored.

   (A) among different file types is, on average, far greater as that among files from
   (B) among different file types is, on average, far greater than that among files from
   (C) among different file types is, on average, far greater than that among files of
   (D) between different file types is, on average, far more than that between files of
   (E) between different file types is, on average, greater by far than is that between files from

Answers and Explanations for these questions can be found at the end of the chapter.

SENTENCE ORGANIZATION ERRORS

While *agreement errors* involved the forms of individual **words**, *sentence organization* errors are built on **phrases** and **clauses**.

The larger the portion of the sentence that's underlined, the more likely it is that large chunks of the sentence (its phrases and clauses) will get moved around and reorganized in the answer choices. If the entire sentence is underlined, it's pretty much a foregone conclusion: at least one of the next two of our Big 6 will be the key to the credited answer.

BIG ERROR #4: MODIFICATION

> The other day, I shot an elephant in my pajamas. How he got in my pajamas, I'll never know.
>
> —Groucho Marx

> A dangling modifier walks into a bar. After finishing a drink, the bartender asks it to leave.
>
> —Unknown

Modifiers must be placed in the sentence so that (1) it is **clear** what they are supposed to modify and so that 2) the modification makes **logical** sense.

Everything that isn't the subject or predicate of a sentence is, in some way, a **modifier**: it adds descriptive information to either the subject or the predicate (or to some *other* modifier). Consider the corrected version of the sentence from the first question on your Diagnostic Quiz:

> The oldest fossil organisms presently known have been dated at 3.4 billion years old and thus are taken as evidence that life evolved soon after a planetary bombardment 3.8 billion years ago that would have sterilized Earth of any incipient life.

When you **drilled down** to the core of the sentence, you realized that it had a simple subject (*organisms*) and a compound predicate (*have been dated* and *are taken*):

> The oldest fossil **organisms** presently known **have been dated** at 3.4 billion years old **and** thus **are taken** as evidence that life evolved soon after a planetary bombardment 3.8 billion years ago that would have sterilized Earth of any incipient life.

Organisms have been dated and are taken. The remaining 34 words all provide some sort of description of what kind of *organisms* we are talking about (the subject):

> **The oldest fossil** organisms
> organisms **presently known**

or of how they *have been dated* and what they *have been taken* to be (the compound predicate):

> have been dated **at 3.4 billion years old**
> are taken **as evidence**

or of one of the previous modifiers:

> evidence **that life evolved**
> evolved **soon after a planetary bombardment**
> evolved **3.8 billion years ago**
> bombardment **that would have sterilized Earth**
> sterilized **of any incipient life**

There are so many modifiers! And so many varieties! Adjectives, adverbs, participial phrases, verbal adjuncts, direct objects, etc.

However many modifiers appear in a GMAT sentence and whatever kind of modifier you're dealing with, the key is to make sure that the modifying element clearly and unambiguously modifies only one possible thing in the sentence (AKA **the modifier's antecedent**) and to make sure that the modifying element modifies (AKA **whatever it modifies**) in a logical way.

In other words, when organizing the sentence, make sure that the modifiers all make sense in their new contexts.

Incorrect:	Dangled over the precipice, the climber's hands nearly slipped.
	*It's **not clear** who's dangling over the precipice and **illogical** to think it's the climber's hands.*
Correct:	While the climber dangled over the precipice, his hands nearly slipped.
	Ah, it was clearly the climber dangling and not his hands.

Modification errors appear on the GMAT most commonly in the following ways:

Variation #1: The Misplaced Comma-Phrase

The most common way that the GMAT springs modification errors on you is with a sentence that has an initial modifying phrase set off from the rest of the sentence by a comma:

> Singing the opening aria "E lucevan le Stelle," <u>the tenor's eyes filled with tears that he did not try to hide.</u>

When you see an initial modifying phrase like *Singing the opening aria "E lucevan le Stelle,"* ask yourself who or what the detail is meant to apply to. In other words, who's singing the aria?

In GMAT English, modifying phrases with commas always modify the **closest available word** on the other side of the comma. So technically, in this sentence, it's the tenor's *eyes* that are singing, not the tenor! Your job will be to rearrange the words and/or change their forms until the appropriate word is closer to the comma than any other.

Thus, the GMAT would have you pick this answer;

> the tenor did not try to hide the tears filling his eyes

Sometimes, the test maker will instead underline the initial phrase itself.

> <u>Singing the opening aria "E lucevan le Stelle,"</u> the tenor's eyes filled with tears that he did not try to hide.

In this case, you can't rearrange the words used for the thing described, so you must instead change the initial phrase so that it either (1) works as a description of whatever is on the other side of the comma or (2) is no longer a modifying phrase. The second option is by far the more common. Like so:

> As he sang the opening aria "E lucevan le Stelle,"

What was once a modifying phrase is now a dependent clause, thanks to the addition of the word *he* (forming the subject) and the change from *singing* to *sang* (forming the predicate). Dependent clauses play by different rules than modifying phrases, so it doesn't matter what's on the other side of their comma.

Variation #2: The "Dangling" Comma-Phrase

When a modifying phrase doesn't seem to apply to *anything* in the sentence, we call it a "dangling modifier."

> <u>Thoroughly inspecting its hoses and wires, the engine was deemed to be fully functional.</u>

Who thoroughly inspected the hoses and wires? Certainly not the engine, but then there's not anyone left in the sentence who could plausibly conduct the inspection. Sometimes, the GMAT will solve this problem by changing the phrase into a description of something else:

> After a thorough inspection of its hoses and wires,

Now the modifying phrase is anchored to the word *after*, here used as a preposition to describe the *time* a *verb* happened. The **closest available word** is the verb *was deemed*.

Alternately, the test maker could change the modifying phrase into a different sort of modifier, one that would logically apply to the first available word after the comma.

> Its hoses and wires thoroughly inspected,

Now the phrase is written so that it doesn't describe the actor doing the inspection (the missing mechanic), but rather the state of the thing that has been inspected (the engine).

Other times, the GMAT will solve this error by introducing a proper antecedent for the modifying phrase. You'll more often see this in cases where more than just the initial modifying phrase has been underlined. Thus, if the sentence had instead been underlined like so

> <u>Thoroughly inspecting its hoses and wires, the engine was deemed to be fully functional.</u>

The correct answer could have been instead

> Thoroughly inspecting its hoses and wires, **the mechanic deemed the engine** to be fully functional.

Some test takers cry foul when they see the GMAT pulling this trick. "Where'd this mechanic come from?" they worry, or they protest, "But wait, doesn't that change the meaning of the sentence!?" The mechanic is new and the mechanic's appearance does change the meaning of the sentence, true, but neither is a reason to eliminate an answer choice on the GMAT—no matter what you may have heard elsewhere.

On the GMAT, meaning takes a back seat to structure. Don't toss out structurally sound answers because you feel like they "change the original meaning of the sentence."

TIP

Often, the key to fixing a clause error is to turn the clause into a modifying phrase, and vice versa.

TIP

The preposition can't describe the noun *the engine*, so the modification "skips over" that word in favor of the verb.

Nor should you select answers because they make sense if you ignore structure and just go for what the speaker probably meant. For example, on the GMAT

> **The guy <u>with the hat named Dave waved</u>.**

will always be considered incorrect, even though it's clear from context—that is, from everything we know about guys, Daves, and hats in the real world—that Dave is the guy who owns the hat, not the name *of* the hat. They want

> **whose name was Dave and who was wearing a hat waved.**

Always begin by eliminating the things that are nonsensical purely because of their structure. Once those are gone, only then can you consider things that are structurally sound but that make no sense in context.

Variation #3: Follow the Bouncing Modifier

In "GMAT Grammar 101," we described adverbs as being more flexible than adjectives, because they can be used to describe a much wider variety of words. Adjectives only describe nouns, while adverbs can describe verbs, adjectives, and other adverbs.

This flexibility means that you have to be more careful with the placement of an adverb in a sentence. Modifiers modify the closest available candidate, and adverbs have a lot more candidates.

Thus, when you spot an adverb in the underlined part of a sentence, sweep your eyes over the answers to see if the adverb is moving around.

Suppose you were given this sentence on the GMAT:

> **The countess was strangely, very frugal, even though she was quite wealthy.**

The *strangely very* (two adverbs in a row) would be a hint to search for a split based around *strangely*. So let's look at five answer choices that might have accompanied that sentence, ignoring everything but the adverbs:

> (A) The countess was strangely, very frugal [...]
> (B) The countess was very strangely frugal, [...]
> (C) The countess was, strangely, very frugal, [...]
> (D) Strangely, the countess was very frugal, [...]
> (E) The strangely countess was very frugal, [...]

Technically, we don't have a split, as each answer choice places the word *strangely* in a different place. But if this were your **decision point**, what could you eliminate?

In Answer Choice (A), the word *strangely* is separated by a comma from *very*. When you stack modifiers on something and use a comma to separate them, it creates a kind of **coordinated list** of modifiers. It's only allowable when the modifiers could each *independently* appear in the sentence. So, here, the countess was *very frugal*, and she was *strangely frugal*. *Very frugal* is fine, but what would it mean to be *strangely frugal*? Only buying items at Addams Family yard sales?

In Answer Choice (B), there's no comma, but moving the word *strangely* to after the *very* means that it can now modify only *frugal*, which is just as nonsensical as in Answer Choice (A).

In Answer Choice (C), the commas set the word *strangely* apart from the rest of the words in the sentence, making it into what we call a **sentence adverb**. As a sentence adverb, *strangely* describes *the entire situation*, which makes sense here. It's strange how frugal this countess is because she has lots of money and doesn't need to pinch her pennies.

In Answer Choice (D), we find another way of using a **sentence adverb**—the most common way, actually, putting it at the front of the sentence. Again, this makes sense in context.

In Answer Choice (E), however, the word *strangely* has been moved in front of the countess, creating something that's just plain incorrect. *Countess* is a noun, so she has to be described by adjectives like *strange* and not adverbs like *strangely*.

At the end of our first **decision** point, we'd be down to only Answer Choices (C) and (D) and would have to look to what's behind the […]'s to make our final choice.

Variation #4: Use the Appropriate Modifier

Answer Choice (E) from the last example provides us an example of our last common modification error variation. Sometimes, the test maker will try to switch an adjective for an adverb or an adverb for an adjective and hope you don't notice.

Remember, adjectives modify nouns. Adverbs modify everything else.

> **Incorrect:** The **strangely** countess was very frugal,
>
> **Correct:** The **strange** countess was very frugal,

BIG ERROR #5: CLAUSES AND CONNECTORS

> Q: What does a grammar teacher call Santa's helpers?
> A: Subordinate Clauses.

> Sentences must contain one **independent clause**; they can contain any number of **dependent clauses** (also known as **subordinate clauses**) as long as the proper connecting words are used to join them to the rest of the sentence.

Errors of parallelism crops up whenever two parts of a sentence are **coordinated**, that is, whenever two parts of a sentence play the same role. **Clause and connector** errors, instead involve cases where one part of the sentence is attached to or made dependent on another—not coordinated, but **subordinated**.

There are three levels of organization within a sentence:

Sentences are made of clauses. Clauses are made of phrases. And phrases are made of words.

Think of these levels as a hierarchy. Subordinate one word to another word and you get a phrase. In "GMAT Grammar 101," we called the main word in a phrase its "head word." Phrases can be "stacked" so that one phrase is itself subordinate to another head word.

head word + other words = phrase
Ex: *the + Secretary*   *of + the Interior*
noun phrase   prepositional phrase

phrase + phrase = bigger phrase
Ex: *the Secretary of the Interior*
noun phrase

TIP

Other sentence adverbs: hopefully, truly, thankfully, first, second, third, finally.

Phrases act as a unit and can occupy any role in a sentence that the head word of the phrase could occupy, but none of the subordinate words can occupy any role in the sentence individually. They only act as a unit.

A phrase is "promoted" to clause status when it acquires a subject-predicate pair.

noun phrase + verb phrase = clause

Ex: *the Secretary of the Interior* + *complained about his plantar wart*

noun phrase   +   verb phrase

Clauses and Connectors Variation #1: Run-ons and Fragments

Some clauses can stand on their own as sentences, and some cannot—**independent clauses** and **dependent clauses**, respectively. A dependent clause is merely an independent clause with a **subordinating word** attached to it.

subordinating word + independent clause = dependent clause

Ex: *because the Secretary of the Interior complained about his plantar wart*

subordinating   independent clause
word

As long as there are enough **subordinating words** (and appropriate punctuation to go with them), then you can add as many dependent clauses to a sentence as you'd like. Forget one and the sentence will have two independent clauses, which results in a grammar error called the **run-on sentence**.

> *The Secretary went to the gym, he did not wear flip-flops in the shower* is a **run-on sentence**.
>
> *When the Secretary went to the gym, he did not wear flip-flops in the shower* is OK, because the word "when" is a **subordinating conjunction**.

TIP

The fancy name for this kind of run-on is a "comma splice."

You saw this error in Question 6 on your Diagnostic Quiz:

> They are not as famous for their waves than for their importance to the early history of the sport, East Coast beaches nevertheless remain home to a vibrant community of professional surfers who compete internationally.

Here, two full independent clauses are connected only by a comma. The error was fixed by adding the subordinating conjunction *while* to make the first clause dependent.

EXAMPLES OF SUBORDINATING CONJUNCTIONS			
after	as	where	because
although	until	wherever	though
if	when	since	
unless	whenever	while	

The only acceptable way for a sentence to have two fully **independent** clauses (without any **subordinating words**) is through special punctuation: the semicolon.

> The Secretary went to the gym; there he picked up a plantar wart.

On the other hand, if a sentence doesn't have a fully independent clause, just a string of dependent clauses, it's considered a **sentence fragment**, also grammatically incorrect.

Fragments don't have to be short—though the name might suggest otherwise. In fact, the primary way that the GMAT tries to pass fragments off on you as full sentences is by piling up dependent clauses and modifying phrases, resulting in very long fragments indeed. One of the incorrect answers to Question 7 on your Diagnostic Quiz did just that:

> At the Battle of Salamis, the Greek general Themistocles, recognizing that although his fleet was outnumbered by the Persians, the cramped conditions of the straits preventing the larger force from being able to maneuver and coordinate its attacks, and pressed them back into the fray.

Look clause by clause, and you'll see there's nothing that can stand on its own as a sentence. The only full clause, *his fleet was outnumbered by the Persians,* is made dependent with the subordinating conjunction *that.*

Clauses and Connectors Variation #2: Relative Clauses

One special type of dependent clause tends to give GMAT test takers fits is the **relative clause**, formed by using a **relative pronoun** (like *who, that, which,* etc.), a kind of word that serves both as the subject of the dependent clause and as the subordinating word that connects the clause to the rest of the sentence. You can think of the relative clause as a way of connecting two sentences with identical parts.

Two sentences:	This box contains heavy **books. The books** were written by my aunt.
Combined:	This box contains heavy books **that** were written by my aunt.
Two sentences:	**Major Major Major** is a character in *Catch-22*. **Major Major Major** has a purposely silly name.
Combined:	Major Major Major is a character in *Catch-22* **who** has a purposely silly name.

There are two types of relative clause, called **restrictive** and **nonrestrictive. Restrictive clauses** add information that is necessary for the sentence to make sense. **Nonrestrictive clauses** contain information that isn't essential and could be removed. The relative pronouns *who, whom, whose,* and *which* are used for nonrestrictive clauses, *that* for restrictive ones.

Many GMAT books devote a lot of time to the distinction between these two types of clauses, and that's unfortunate because the correct answer in a Sentence Correction question almost never comes down to deciding which of the two ought to be used. And how could it? It's hard to tell from a single context-free sentence whether a piece of information is essential.

Instead, the GMAT tests restrictive clauses by using them to create sentence fragments or run-ons and nonrestrictive clauses as matters of modification. For the first, it comes down to the use of a comma. Put a comma in front of *that* and the clause is no longer relative; it's a sentence with the word *that* as its subject, and without a subordinating word in front of the *that,* the result is a **run-on**.

> **Incorrect:** The police officers quickly ate the box of donuts, that was in the squad room.
>
> **Correct:** The police officers quickly ate the box of donuts that was in the squad room.

As for nonrestrictive clauses, you'll usually see one that uses a comma and the pronoun *which* used in a way that makes it unclear what is being described by the information in the clause.

> The plan relied on information gathered from defectors, <u>which was unlikely to be current</u>.

By the rules of modification, the *which was unlikely to be current* describes whatever is closest to the comma. So is it the information that's not current or the defectors who aren't current? The GMAT would prefer to see either

> <u>who were unlikely to be current</u>

or

> <u>and that information was unlikely to be current</u>

Clauses and Connectors Variation #3: "Illogical" Connecting Words

The subordinating word used to connect an independent and dependent clause isn't just a hollow placeholder. It usually contains some information about the relationship between the two clauses. Sometimes, the GMAT will build a question that turns on the use of the proper connecting word to match the most logical relationship.

Fortunately, the relationships tested don't go beyond whether the two clauses agree with one another or contrast with one another. In Question 6 on your Diagnostic Quiz, you had the choice between two answer choices, one beginning with *while* and the other with *since*.

> (D) <u>While not as famous for their waves as they are for</u>
> (E) <u>Since they are not as famous for their waves as they are for</u>

The path to the credited answer (D) lay in deciding whether not being famous for their waves was meant to agree with what followed or contrast with it. Since the sentence's second clause described a way in which the beaches were notable, contrast was intended and *while* was needed.

Clauses and Connectors Variation #4: Too Many Connectors

As a matter of course, you should always check the words just after the underlined section, but when clause errors are being tested, it becomes doubly important. The test maker has a habit of adding an extra conjunction there. Some answer choices, in light of the extra word, would thus have too many connecting words.

> Because the price of oil is subject to seasonal swings, <u>so the cost of cement can vary greatly</u> depending on the time of year.

The *because* at the beginning of the sentence makes the first clause dependent; thus, the second clause can't also have a connecting word. The credited answer deletes the *so*.

> <u>the cost of cement can vary greatly</u>

TIP

Contrast Conjunctions: *although, even though, unless, whereas, while, rather than*

Agreement Conjunctions: *as, when, because, now that, since*

TAKE-HOME POINTS ABOUT MODIFICATION ERRORS

- It doesn't matter if the modifier is a single word adjective or a long participial phrase, it still must be placed so that the modification is **clear and logical.**
- Watch out for sentences that begin with phrases set off by commas. Often the modification error will prove the quickest **decision point.**
- Sometimes the best way to avoid a modification error is to change the modifier into some other kind of phrase, like a subordinate clause.
- Don't over-correct! There are multiple correct places some modifiers may be found in a sentence.
- Prepositional phrases usually aren't themselves part of a modification error being tested; instead, they are used to **distract** attention away from the error.

Sentence Organization Errors Quick Review Quiz

DIRECTIONS: Try to complete the following five questions in less than 5 minutes in order to check your understanding of the most frequently tested errors relating to overall sentence construction.

1. <u>A swashbuckling adventurer, Layton Kor's claims to fame include</u> the discovery of four of the six most popular technical routes up the storied Diamond of Longs Peak.

   (A) A swashbuckling adventurer, Layton Kor's claims to fame include
   (B) The claims to fame of Layton Kor, a swashbuckling adventurer, include
   (C) Layton Kor was a swashbuckling adventurer including in his claims to fame
   (D) Included in the swashbuckling adventurer Layton Kor's claims to fame are
   (E) The swashbuckling adventurer's claims to fame of Layton Kor include

2. Distracted by the initial bustle and tumult of the eager crowd, <u>Seamus was asked by one audience member to repeat his poem's prologue.</u>

   (A) Seamus was asked by one audience member to repeat his poem's prologue
   (B) one audience member asked Seamus to repeat the prologue to his poem
   (C) Seamus was asked to repeat his prologue to the poem by one audience member
   (D) one audience member asked Seamus to repeat the poem's prologue
   (E) one audience member then asked the speaker for a repeat of the poem's prologue

3. The National Lung Screening Trial, a research study sponsored by the National Cancer Institute, relied upon results derived from a somewhat atypical sample of <u>smokers, ranging from 56 to 78 years old, which had smoked</u> more than a pack a day for no fewer than thirty years.

   (A) smokers, ranging from 56 to 78 years old, which had smoked
   (B) smokers ranged from 56 to 78 years old, and that had smoked
   (C) smokers, ranging from 56 to 78 years old, that smoked
   (D) smokers, which ranged from 56 to 78 years old, and who had smoked
   (E) smokers who ranged from 56 to 78 years old and who had smoked

4. Though the theory that filter-feeding whales evolved from land animals that swam with open mouths was once regarded as "Darwin's Folly," fossils of amphibious mammals discovered in Pakistan <u>provide the most compelling evidence yet unearthed of the surprisingly close evolutionary relationship between whales and bears.</u>

   (A) provide the most compelling evidence yet unearthed of the surprisingly close evolutionary relationship between whales and bears

   (B) provide evidence more compelling than what has yet been unearthed of the surprising close evolutionary relationship between whales and bears

   (C) provides more compelling surprising evidence of the close evolutionary relationship than any yet unearthed between whales and bears

   (D) has provided the most surprisingly compelling evidence of the close evolutionary relationship between whales and bears that have yet been unearthed

   (E) have provided more compelling evidence than any that has yet been surprisingly unearthed of the close evolutionary relationship between whales and bears

5. <u>Over 100 missing votes from a single precinct and hundreds of wrongly rejected ballots have been cited by the state canvassing board for the 2008 Senate election in Minnesota, which were reasons that they delayed the final decision to award the election to former comedian Al Franken.</u>

   (A) Over 100 missing votes from a single precinct and hundreds of wrongly rejected ballots have been cited by the state canvassing board for the 2008 Senate election in Minnesota, which were reasons that they delayed the final decision to award the election to former comedian Al Franken.

   (B) Citing over 100 missing votes from a single precinct and hundreds of wrongly rejected ballots, the state canvassing board for the 2008 Senate election in Minnesota were reasons that delayed the final decision to award the election to former comedian Al Franken.

   (C) Citing over 100 missing votes from a single precinct and hundreds of wrongly rejected ballots, were reasons that the final decision to award the election to former comedian Al Franken in the 2008 Senate election in Minnesota, the state canvassing board delayed.

   (D) The state canvassing board has cited over 100 missing votes from a single precinct and hundreds of wrongly rejected ballots as reasons for the delaying of the final decision to award the election to former comedian Al Franken in the 2008 Senate election in Minnesota.

   (E) The state canvassing board for the 2008 Senate election in Minnesota, citing over 100 missing votes from a single precinct and hundreds of wrongly rejected ballots as reasons, delayed the final decision to award the election to former comedian Al Franken.

Answers and Explanations for these questions can be found at the end of the chapter.

BIG ERROR #6: IDIOMS

> The bit about applying the glaze to the shapely jug—that's where I tend to stumble.
>
> In English, it's easy enough—"I put this on that"—but in French, such things have a way of [coming back to bite you]. I might have to say, "Do you like the glaze the shapely jug accepted from me?" or "Do you like the shapely jug in the glaze of which I earlier applied?"
>
> —David Sedaris, *When You Are Engulfed in Flames*

id·i·om ('i-dē-əm) n. 1. An ordering of words that relies on custom rather than grammar or logic for its meaning and correctness. 2. A colloquial expression in a language that cannot be understood from the individual meanings of its elements, as in *keep tabs on* or *raining cats and dogs*.

The final member of The Big 6 is in a class all by itself: errors of **idiomatic construction**.

As anyone trying to learn a new language for the first time quickly discovers, languages are *weird*. English is no exception.

You sleep *in* a bed, not *at* a bed, but why exactly is that? Things happen *at* a party, not *in* a party, but why is it that you're *in* the Army, not *at* the Army? You *get up* from your bed in the morning, but you don't *get down* when you fall asleep. We call these and other expected word combinations **idiomatic constructions** or simply **idioms**.

Logic goes out the window with idioms. There's no reason for most other than "because that's how we say it." This can be particularly galling for GMAT test takers whose first language is something other than English. But even for those who've spoken English all their lives, it can seem like there's always going to be one more idiom you've never heard of in the next Sentence Correction question that pops up on the CAT screen.

Some students react to this worry by trying to cram as many idioms into their brains as possible, which does sometimes work, but is also a lot of effort for very little reward. You've probably seen lists of 100, 200, even 1000 "Essential" GMAT Idioms floating around on the Internet. If you haven't, don't bother tracking them down, and if you have, know that there are many better ways to spend your Sentence Correction prep time.

The most important thing about idioms is that the test maker rarely makes a question whose credited answer turns *solely* on a correct idiom. Most often, incorrect idioms appear in answer choices that are wrong for some other reason, too.

Think of idioms as shortcuts. Don't make your first cut on an idiomatic issue, but when you spot something you think doesn't work idiomatically, use that feeling as a cue to look for an error elsewhere in the sentence.

IDIOM VARIATION #1: PREPOSITIONAL CHOICE IDIOMS

Lots of idioms come down to choosing the preposition that the context demands. Questions testing these sorts of idioms on the GMAT are generally easy to spot. Either the underlined section is extremely short, or the beginning or ending of the underlined section bears a flip-flopping preposition, and it's probably an idiom that forms the core of the question:

(A) in danger of
(B) in the danger to
(C) as a danger for
(D) of danger to
(E) in danger

IDIOM VARIATION #2: IDIOMS IN COMPARISONS

A lot of questions on the GMAT come down to the difference between *as* and *than*. There are many ways to form comparisons in English, and many of them use either *as* or *than*. For whatever reason, the question writers employed by GMAC love flip-flopping the two in incorrect answer choices.

Over the last few years, the rate the economy has grown were at least twice as slow **as** economists have predicted.

(A) were at least twice as slow **as** economists have predicted
(B) was at least twice as slow **as** economists have predicted
(C) was at least twice as slow **as** economists had predicted
(D) was at least twice more slow **than** economists have predicted
(E) were at least twice slower **than** economists had predicted

Use your skills at **drilling down** to isolate the comparison: *as slow as* is the proper idiom, therefore *as slow than* can be eliminated.

IDIOM VARIATION #3: NUMBERS AND AMOUNTS

This variation tends to be tested in many of the same questions as the last. English makes a distinction between quantities that can easily be counted—like *teeth, puppies, cities, grains of sand, children, grammar errors*, and *colors*—and things that cannot—like *water, blood, luck, sand, smoke*, and *courage*.

We call the countables **count nouns** and the uncountables **mass nouns**. Certain expressions in English change depending on whether you're dealing with a count noun or a mass noun. For example:

Count Nouns	Mass Nouns
many puppies	much barking
a number of errors	an amount of whiskey
few zebras	little water

The two to watch out for in particular are *a number* and *an amount*, as they often appear in comparisons.

Instead of memorizing lists of count and mass nouns, you can generally rely on a couple of quick-and-dirty tests to determine whether you're dealing with a count noun or a mass noun.

Can you think of its plural form? Count nouns have plurals (children, roosters, robots, etc.), but mass nouns do not (no *courages, moneys,* or *bloods*).

Can you use the word "a" or "an" in front of it? A pound, a bagel, an octopus—these work, but there's no such thing as *a gravel, an advice, a money.*

Note that some words can be both count and mass nouns, depending on what you're talking about.

> I spilled a lot of **beer**.
>
> There are many **beers** available at the gourmet liquor store.

IDIOM VARIATION #4: GMAT SUPERSTITIONS

We said at the beginning of this chapter that most of the "gotcha" rules that strict grammarians like to toss around aren't tested on the GMAT, and that's true . . . mostly. Passive voice, ending sentences with prepositions, splitting infinitives—none of these will be the difference between a right and wrong answer on the GMAT. There are a few exceptions, however, things that aren't really hard-and-fast grammatical rules but that the GMAT treats as though they are.

Use *like* for comparisons, *such as* for examples.

For some reason, GMAT question writers tend to dislike the word *like*. Thus:

> Avoid: I want a salty snack **like** pretzels.
>
> Prefer: I want a salty snack **such as** pretzels.
>
> Prefer: **Like** his cousin, Tom was very tall.

Limit *where* and *when* to actual places and times.

The GMAT is also a bit picky about the words *where* and *when* if they're used as **relative pronouns**. In general, the test will swap them out for *in which*.

> Avoid: Baseball is a sport **where** players often have long careers.
>
> Prefer: Baseball is a sport **in which** players often have long careers.
>
> Avoid: In situations **when** prices are rising, purchases should be delayed.
>
> Prefer: In situations **in which** prices are rising, purchases should be delayed.

Use *whether* for options, *if* for hypothetical situations, and avoid *whether or not*.

In everyday speech, we use *whether* and *if* interchangeably, but on the GMAT, use *whether* for cases when two different options are being presented (or are assumed). *If*, on the other hand, is reserved for conditional statements. And whatever you do, do not select an answer choice that uses *whether or not*—the GMAT considers that redundant.

Avoid:	I cannot tell **if** Sudesh wants to play basketball or go fishing.
Prefer:	I cannot tell **whether** Sudesh wants to play basketball or go fishing.
Prefer:	**If** Lark comes home early, she is going to be mad.
Avoid:	**Whether or not** Lark comes home tonight, she will eventually find out.

Use *between* when comparing two things, *among* when comparing three.

If someone said to you, "I can't decide among going to see *Aliens, Predator,* or *Aliens vs. Predator,*" it'd strike you as odd. You'd expect them to say *between.* Not so on the GMAT. Whenever there's more than two options, *among* is the way to go. If there's only two, choose *between.*

In the end, it should be noted that the GMAT has reduced the number of questions that turn on these errors of late. Maybe they even count as "American-centric" idioms. Nearly always, if one of these little GMAT superstitions appears in a question, it will not be the *sole* deciding issue. When in doubt, look about for one of the other major errors somewhere else in the underlined section. Use these as rules of thumb.

Idiomatic Errors Quick Review Quiz

DIRECTIONS: Try to complete the following five questions in less than 5 minutes in order to check your understanding of idiomatic constructions and how they're tested on the GMAT.

1. Twelve years after the trial ended, the verdict was overturned on the grounds of the improper admission by the trial judge of hearsay statements and left out a pertinent jury instruction.

   (A) of the improper admission by the trial judge of
   (B) of the trial judge's improperly admitting
   (C) that the trial judge had improperly admitted
   (D) that the trial judge was admitting improper
   (E) that improperly admitted by the judge the

2. Unlike his student Aristotle, Plato believed in two levels of reality, the natural and supernatural, and claimed that mortals may have contact with it only indirectly, through the contemplation of transcendent ideal forms.

   (A) contact with it only indirectly, through
   (B) only indirect contact with them by way of
   (C) contact only with the latter through indirectly
   (D) only indirect contact with the latter by means of
   (E) only contact indirectly with the supernatural level due to

3. According to the California Driving Code, no vehicle shall at any time be driven to the left side of the roadway where the driver's view is obstructed within such a distance as to create a hazard in the event another vehicle might <u>approach toward the opposite direction</u>.

(A) approach toward the opposite direction
(B) approach toward the opposite directions
(C) approach from the opposite direction
(D) be approached from the opposite directions
(E) be approaching from opposite directions

4. Because the chef mistook an unlabeled canister of sugar <u>as one containing unrefined salt</u>, the soufflé, while quite sweet, failed to please his dinner guests.

(A) as one containing unrefined salt
(B) as the one containing unrefined salt
(C) as a container for unrefined salt
(D) for one containing unrefined salt
(E) for that of one containing unrefined salt

5. After many years of distrust and unhealthy competition, the doctor may now just as often be found <u>besides the lawyer, each working with the other</u> against the health insurance companies that, in the name of lowered costs, would do a patient harm.

(A) besides the lawyer, each working with the other
(B) besides the lawyer, working with each other
(C) beside the lawyer, working with one another
(D) beside the lawyer, each working with him
(E) beside the lawyer, working with each other

Answers and Explanations for these questions can be found at the end of the chapter.

500- to 600-Level Sentence Correction Practice Set

1. Tokyo, though visited by many millions of tourists each year, remains inwardly focused, largely <u>because of having</u> such strict expectations of its residents' public behavior.

   (A) because of having
   (B) because it has
   (C) because they have
   (D) on account of having
   (E) on account of their having

2. Although powerful enough <u>to bring down power lines, leave</u> substantial portions of the city without power, last night's thunderstorm did relatively little lasting damage.

   (A) to bring down power lines, leave
   (B) that it brought down power lines, leave
   (C) that power lines were brought down, leave
   (D) that power lines were brought down and leaves
   (E) to bring down power lines and leave

3. When attacked, slugs contract their bodies, making <u>themselves harder and more compact</u>.

   (A) themselves harder and more compact
   (B) themselves hard and the more compact
   (C) their selves harder and more compact
   (D) itself harder and more compact
   (E) it become harder and the more compact

4. Unlike the rules governing professional athletes, which require total abstention from performance enhancing substances, <u>the military actively encourages soldiers to extend</u> their capabilities artificially.

   (A) the military actively encourages soldiers to extend
   (B) with active encouragement of the military soldiers extend
   (C) the military's rules actively encourage soldiers to extend
   (D) the military does actively encourage the soldiers' extending
   (E) the military's active encouragement is for the soldiers to extend

5. <u>Without the adequate amounts of supervision, children in</u> daycare facilities can come to resemble nineteenth-century mad houses.

   (A) Without the adequate amounts of supervision, children in
   (B) Without an adequate amount of supervision, children's
   (C) If children do not get adequate amounts of supervision they need, children's
   (D) If children do not get the adequate amount of supervision, they have
   (E) If they do not have an adequate amount of supervision, children at

6. Laws requiring every able-bodied man registering with the Selective Service constitute a disservice by not requiring the same of women.

    (A) Laws requiring every able-bodied man registering
    (B) Laws that require every man that is able bodied should register
    (C) Laws that require that every able-bodied man ought to register
    (D) Laws requiring every able-bodied man be registered
    (E) Laws requiring every man of able body that they register

7. Except for being adamantly against Chicago, not one of our mutual friends have an opinion on whether I ought to move to a big city or a small one.

    (A) have an opinion on whether I ought to
    (B) have opinions on whether I should
    (C) have no opinions about if I ought to
    (D) has an opinion on if I should be
    (E) has an opinion on whether I ought to

8. Never before the advent of the firearm has a single person had the power to do such substantial harm.

    (A) Never before the advent of the firearm has a single person had
    (B) The advent of the firearm has never before had a single person
    (C) Before the advent of the firearm a single person has not had ever
    (D) Before the advent of the firearm, never did a single person have had
    (E) Never before has one person had since the advent of the firearm

9. Minorities in this country—even after adjusting for differences in affluence or education—is not sentenced in numbers proportionate to those of the majority population.

    (A) is not sentenced in numbers proportionate to
    (B) is not being proportionate in their sentencing numbers with
    (C) have not made their sentencing numbers proportionate with
    (D) are not being sentenced in numbers proportionate to
    (E) are not being proportionate in their sentencing to

10. Whether or not the proposed limitations on trout fishing are instituted, fishermen have been and will continue to have been flouting any regulation seen as unduly restrictive.

    (A) have been and will continue to have been flouting
    (B) have and will continue to flout
    (C) will continue to flout
    (D) will continue to flout, as they have already been,
    (E) will continue flouting, as they already have been,

Answers and Explanations for these questions can be found at the end of the chapter.

600- to 700-Level Sentence Correction Practice Set

1. On average 15 Americans die each year due to violence related to terrorism—less by far than are killed by falling television sets in their own homes.

    (A) terrorism—less by far than are
    (B) terrorism—fewer by far than are
    (C) terrorism, which is by far less than those
    (D) terrorism, a number lower by far than the people
    (E) terrorism, by far fewer than the ones

2. This new idea of the female's ovum as actively taking part in the acquisition of fertilizing material, rather than a mere inert recipient, have emerged from the careful examination of the two *in vivo* throughout the process, including immediately post coitus.

    (A) a mere inert recipient, have emerged from the careful examination of the two *in vivo* throughout the process, including
    (B) as a mere inert recipient, have emerged from extensively examining the two *in vivo*, which includes
    (C) as merely inert recipients, has emerged from extensively examining the two *in vivo* that includes
    (D) merely inertly receiving, has emerged from the extensive examination of the two *in vivo*, which includes
    (E) as merely inertly receiving, has emerged from the extensive examination of the two *in vivo*, including

3. In spite of centuries of critical inattention, Aphra Behn's long-form prose *Oroonoko* had been recently come to being regarded as an important precursor to the novel for many, a milestone of early feminist literature.

    (A) had been recently come to being regarded as an important precursor to the novel
    (B) had recently come to be regarded as an important precursor to the novel that
    (C) has recently come to be regarded as an important precursor to the novel, and
    (D) has been recently regarded as coming as an important precursor to the novel
    (E) has recently come to be regarded an important precursor to the novel, and,

4. Presently just over 7 billion, the world has a population rising at a rate of 1.1 percent with each passing year.

    (A) the world has a population rising at a rate of
    (B) world population is rising at a rate of
    (C) the world's population is rising up at the increasing rate of
    (D) the rise in the rate of the world's population is
    (E) world population has been being increased by a rate of

5. A much anticipated addition to the "extreme" candy scene is the world's largest gummy worm that is 128 times more massive than its smaller brethren, measuring 36 inches long and weighing in at approximately 3 pounds.

(A) A much anticipated addition to the "extreme" candy scene is the world's largest gummy worm that is

(B) As much-anticipated addition to the "extreme" candy scene, the world's largest gummy worm that is

(C) A much-anticipated addition to the "extreme" candy scene, the world's largest gummy worm is

(D) As much anticipated as an addition to the "extreme" candy scene, the world's largest gummy worm is

(E) Much-anticipated as an addition to the scene of "extreme" candy, is the world's largest gummy worm

6. The final cake layer at last baking in the oven, the caterers could safely shift their attention to the long-neglected *hors d'oeuvres*.

(A) The final cake layer at last baking in the oven,

(B) With the final cake layer baking in the oven, so

(C) Because the final layer of the cake was in the oven baking

(D) The final cake layer baking in the oven, and

(E) The cake's final layer was in the oven baking,

7. Big product launches and their coincident costs are one thread at this year's industrial fastener convention, however supply chain considerations and materials sourcing still occupy its core.

(A) however supply chain considerations and

(B) however, supply chain considerations along with

(C) as supply chain considerations and their

(D) but as supply chain considerations or

(E) but supply chain considerations and

8. The artist secretly recorded passengers in his taxi and created an audio collage that he played looped over loudspeakers at the museum installation.

(A) secretly recorded passengers in his taxi and created

(B) having secretly recorded passengers in his taxi and created

(C) secretly recording passengers in his taxi, creating

(D) and his secret recordings of his taxi's passengers created

(E) with his secret recording passengers in his taxi created

9. If the regular season was any indication, the coming championship series will be full of uncertainty.

   (A) If the regular season was any indication, the coming championship series will be full of uncertainty.
   (B) Were the regular season any indication, the coming championship series will be full of uncertainty.
   (C) The coming championship series, if the regular season has been indicating anything, would have to be filled by uncertainty.
   (D) Were the regular season to be any indication, then the coming championship series should be full of uncertainty.
   (E) Whether the regular season should be any indication or not, then the coming championship series will be fully uncertain.

10. The election of the new dean focus scrutiny on her role to secure funding at the university's foundation for the new science center, which is still woefully behind schedule.

   (A) focus scrutiny on her role to secure funding at the university's foundation for
   (B) focuses scrutiny to her role in securing funding for the university's foundation by
   (C) focusing scrutiny on her role at the university's foundation which secures funding of
   (D) is focusing scrutiny on her role at the university's foundation securing funding for
   (E) is focusing scrutiny at her role with the university's foundation and securing the funding

Answers and Explanations for these questions can be found at the end of the chapter.

700- to 800-Level Sentence Correction Practice Set

1. Much of the recent musical's regard among critics are due to its topical subject matter—a feature typical of musicals of the 2000s and that will hinder subsequent revival.

   (A) are due to its topical subject matter—a feature typical of musicals of the 2000s and that
   (B) are due to its topical subject matter—a feature that is typical of musicals of the 2000s and they
   (C) is due to its topical subject matter—a feature typical of musicals of the 2000s, and
   (D) is due to its topical subject matter—a feature that is typical of musicals of the 2000s and that
   (E) is due to its topical subject matter—a feature typical of musicals of the 2000s and they

2. Ironically, successful candidates for a party's presidential nomination have found victory in the subsequent general election all but impossible <u>if there is an absence of support from those who directly opposed them during</u> the primary.

    (A) if there is an absence of support from those who directly opposed them during
    (B) if there is an absence of support from the direct opposition to them during
    (C) with an absence of direct support of those who were their opponents from
    (D) without the support of the direct opposition during
    (E) without the support of those who opposed them directly during

3. <u>In contrast to its strict previous monetary policy, freer use of the yuan in Shenzen was recently approved.</u>

    (A) In contrast to its strict previous monetary policy, freer use of the yuan in Shenzen was recently approved.
    (B) Contrasted with its previously strict monetary policy, the free use of the yuan has recently been approved in Shenzen.
    (C) In contrast to their previous strict monetary policy, their free use of the yuan in Shenzen has been approved recently.
    (D) In contrast to the strictness of previous monetary policy, the freer use of the yuan in Shenzen was recently approved.
    (E) In contrast with Shenzen's freer use of the yuan, its previous strict monetary policy has been disapproved.

4. Once smart-phones were considered luxury items, limited to no more than an 8 percent share of the market, but today <u>the percentage is nearly seven times higher</u>.

    (A) the percentage is nearly seven times higher
    (B) their share is nearly seven times higher
    (C) their share is nearly seven times higher than that
    (D) their numbers are nearly seven times greater
    (E) the percentage is nearly seven times as great as that

5. <u>Between 2002 and 2007 the national debt expanded more than it had during the 226 years from the founding of the nation</u> to 2002.

    (A) Between 2002 and 2007 the national debt expanded more than it had during the 226 years from the founding of the nation
    (B) Between 2002 and 2007 the expansion of the national debt was more than that during 226 years, from when the nation was founded
    (C) The expansion of the national debt between 2002 and 2007 exceeds that which had been for 226 years from the founding of the nation
    (D) The expansion of the national debt between 2002 and 2007 exceeds what it has been for 226 years, from when the nation was founded
    (E) The expansion of the national debt between 2002 and 2007 exceeded what it did for the 226 years from the founding of the nation

6. Although Congress's proposed ban on the use of anabolic steroids by Major League Baseball players is currently the subject of much discussion in the popular press, <u>significant revision is to be expected before it is to be passed by either chamber.</u>

(A) significant revision is to be expected before it is to be passed by either chamber

(B) either chamber does not expect to pass it without significantly revising it

(C) either chamber expects significant revision to pass it

(D) it is not expected to be passed by either chamber without it being revised significantly

(E) it is not expected to pass in either chamber without significant revision

7. <u>There are no governing bodies, as there are for French and Russian, to determine if loanwords are acceptable for formal English use, a situation that contributes to their swift incorporation into the language.</u>

(A) There are no governing bodies, as there are for French and Russian, to determine if loanwords are acceptable for formal English use, a situation that contributes to their swift incorporation into the language.

(B) There are no governing bodies to determine if loanwords are acceptable for formal English use, unlike French and Russian, a situation that contributes to incorporating them swiftly into its language.

(C) There are governing bodies to determine if a loanword is acceptable for formal French and Russian use, but not for English, which contributes to their swift incorporation into the language.

(D) Unlike French and Russian, there is no governing body to determine if a loanword is acceptable for formal English use, which swiftly contributes to it being incorporated into the language.

(E) Unlike the French and Russian languages, there are no governing bodies to determine if a loanword is acceptable for formal English use, contributing to their swift incorporation.

8. <u>As the male's venom is nonlethal, merely incapacitating its target briefly, this results in the surprising tendency of platypuses using</u> it during courtship.

(A) As the male's venom is nonlethal, merely incapacitating its target briefly, this results in the surprising tendency of platypuses using

(B) As the nonlethal venom of the male merely incapacitates its target briefly, with the surprising tendency of platypuses use

(C) The male's venom, nonlethal and merely incapacitating its target briefly, results in the surprising fact that platypuses tend toward using

(D) The nonlethal venom of the male merely incapacitates its target briefly, and results in the platypus's surprising tendency to use

(E) The male's venom is nonlethal and merely incapacitates its target briefly, with the surprising result that platypuses tend to use

9. His position is rather like <u>the statement, because having a haircut reduces your total hair, and because bald people</u> have no hair, haircuts cause baldness.

(A) the statement, because having a haircut reduces your total hair, and because bald people

(B) the statement that having a haircut reduces your total hair, and because bald people

(C) saying that because having a haircut reduces your total hair and because bald people

(D) saying having a haircut reduces your hair and that because bald people

(E) the statement that having a haircut reduces your hair because bald people

10. A majority of paleontologists contend <u>nearly all of the thousands of extinct driven species at the beginning of the Triassic were driven</u> by one single extinction event, rather than by a series of minor catastrophes.

(A) nearly all of the thousands of extinct driven species at the beginning of the Triassic were driven

(B) the thousands of species all nearly driven extinct had been so at the beginning of the Triassic

(C) at the beginning of the Triassic that thousands of species were nearly all driven so extinct and

(D) that nearly all of the thousands of species driven extinct at the beginning of the Triassic were so driven

(E) the extinction that nearly all of the thousand species at the beginning of the Triassic were driven was

Answers and Explanations for these questions can be found at the end of the chapter.

ANSWER KEYS

Agreement Errors Quick Review Quiz

1. **(D)**   3. **(B)**   5. **(C)**
2. **(E)**   4. **(C)**

Sentence Organization Errors Quick Review Quiz

1. **(B)**   3. **(E)**   5. **(E)**
2. **(D)**   4. **(A)**

Idiomatic Errors Quick Review Quiz

1. **(C)**   3. **(C)**   5. **(C)**
2. **(D)**   4. **(D)**

500- to 600-Level Sentence Correction Practice Set

1. **(B)**   4. **(C)**   7. **(E)**   10. **(C)**
2. **(E)**   5. **(B)**   8. **(A)**
3. **(A)**   6. **(D)**   9. **(D)**

600- to 700-Level Sentence Correction Practice Set

1. **(B)**   4. **(B)**   7. **(E)**   10. **(D)**
2. **(E)**   5. **(C)**   8. **(A)**
3. **(C)**   6. **(A)**   9. **(A)**

700- to 800-Level Sentence Correction Practice Set

1. **(D)**   4. **(A)**   7. **(A)**   10. **(D)**
2. **(E)**   5. **(A)**   8. **(E)**
3. **(D)**   6. **(E)**   9. **(C)**

Explanations

Diagnostic Quiz

Explanations for the Diagnostic Quiz are presented in the text of the chapter.

Agreement Errors Quick Review Quiz

1. **Issues: subject-predicate agreement** (*the surge … was*), **idiomatic constructions** (*intended to*), **modification** (placement of *overall*)

   (D) The verb at the beginning of the underlined section is your cue to check for a **subject-predicate** agreement error. Here, the subject is the singular *surge*, so strike the plural *were*s in Answer Choices (A) and (B). Answer Choices (C) and (E) can be tossed for incorrect versions of the idiomatic construction *intended* + <*infinitive verb*, leaving only Answer Choice (D).

2. **Issues: comparisons** (idiom and parallelism requirement), **modification** (placement of *likely*), **idiomatic construction** (*with* versus *in*)

   (E) This sentence presents a completely garbled comparison, *trilobites* (a species) were *as likely as the animal kingdom* (the bigger group of species to which trilobites belong). Answer Choices (B) and (C) do no better, meaning the comparison must be eliminated from the sentence. Of Answer Choices (D) and (E), only (E) makes any sense.

3. **Issues: modification** (as a distraction), **parallelism** (either X or Y)

   (B) Two of the answer choices, (B) and (E), move "in Korea" around, but the move is not necessary and not useful as a **decision point**. *Either … or* is, instead, the most fruitful place to start, a two-part construction that requires parallelism. Placing the *either* after the main verb *are* creates a list of things that the restaurants *are*: they *are devoted to* is fine, but *are feature* makes no sense, so Answer Choices (A) and (E) are out. Likewise, Answer Choice (C)'s *are devoted* and *are to the feature* are out. Answer Choice (D) creates parallel *are devoting* and *are featuring*, but *devoting burgers* makes no sense. Answer Choice (B) works by moving the *either*, so that a different set of parallel items is created, parallel verbs: the restaurants either (1) ***are*** *devoted to* or (2) ***feature***.

4. **Issues: idiomatic construction** (*almost as much as*), **pronoun reference** (*that/those*), **modification** (*remain* versus *remaining*), **comparison** (X *is worth almost as much as* Y)

   (C) Comparisons are always useful places to begin, and since *swine* is in the non-underlined part of the sentence, the underlined part of the comparison will need to be a *noun* and the same sort of thing as a *swine*, logically speaking. Answer Choice (B) compares *swine* to *states*, illogical and thus out. Answer Choice (A)'s *that* is parallel but doesn't agree in number with its antecedent, the *plural* states Answer Choices (C), (D), and (E) all feature the correctly parallel and correctly agreeing with *those*, but (D) and (E) botch the idiom used to make the comparison with a stray *in*—*swine* aren't *almost as much in worth*.

5. **Issues: agreement/idiomatic construction** (*among* versus *between* and *greater* versus *more* and *of* versus *from*), **pronoun reference** (*that*)

(C) The most obvious splits in this question are at either end of the underlined section. The GMAT is a stickler for the *among/between* distinction: among is used to compare more than two entities, *between* is saved only for a comparison between two (a slippery *agreement* issue, as the idiom used must match the number used in the sentence). Here, there's no telling how many file types there are, meaning *among* is needed, eliminating Answer Choices (D) and (E). Answer Choices (A), (B), and (E) can all be thrown for the idiomatically incorrect *from*, leaving only (C).

Sentence Organization Errors Quick Review Quiz

1. **Issues: modification, subject-predicate agreement, idiomatic construction**

   (B) The initial descriptive phrase set off by a comma is a common sign of a GMAT modification error. As written, it's describing Layton Kor's *claims* (and not the man himself), so out it goes. The remaining answer choices offer different ways of rephrasing that are prone to different errors. Answer Choice (C) uses the idiomatically unacceptable *including in*, Answer Choice (D) makes the subject of the sentence the singular *discovery* but uses the plural *are*, and Answer Choice (E) changes the subject to plural *claims*, which no longer matches the singular *include*.

2. **Issues: modification, pronoun reference** (*his*), **passive voice** (a distraction)

   (D) The introductory descriptive phrase in this sentence is not underlined, meaning that whatever follows the comma needs to be something that could sensibly be described as being *distracted by the noisy crowd*. The poet Seamus wasn't the one who was distracted, so Answer Choices (A) and (C) are out in favor of moving the *one audience member* up to the comma. The question then becomes an issue of **pronouns**, as the singular *his* could apply to either *Seamus* or to the *audience member* (either or both of whom could be male, as far as we know). Only Answer Choice (D) avoids the ambiguous *his*.

   Notice also that, although the wrong answer choices were in the *passive voice*, they were not wrong **because** of the passive. Most often on the GMAT, passive versus active voice is just a distraction.

3. **Issues: modification, parallelism**

   (E) The original sentence has two descriptive details that are meant to describe the smokers in the study, the range of their ages and the length of time that they smoked. The original sentence uses a *comma-which* for the second detail, and on the GMAT comma-which always describes the word immediately on the other side of the comma, in this case *years*, not smokers, so Answer Choice (A) is out. Answer Choicers (B) and (C) opt to connect this detail with a *that*, a better option, but the *and* in Answer Choice (B) demands parallelism that's absent. Answer Choice (C)'s fine as far as the second detail is concerned, but the first detail, the age range, set off with commas, shouldn't interrupt the phrase *smokers that smoked*. Answer Choice (D) has a *comma-which* for the first detail—here fine, since it is the smokers who ranged—but the *and* that follows again demands parallelism that this answer choice lacks. That leaves only Answer Choice (E), which has the *and*, but also the correct detail on either side, both details put into *who* clauses.

4. <u>Issues:</u> **subject-predicate agreement** (fossils *provide* or *have provided*), **modification** (placement of *surprising* and choice versus *surprisingly*)

(A) The initial verbs help to narrow the choices down initially. Drill down to discover the sentence's plural subject, *fossils*, which eliminates (B)'s *provide* and (D)'s *has provided*. (Technically speaking, there's nothing wrong with Answer Choices (D) and (E)'s switch to the present perfect *has/have provided*.) Of the answer choices remaining, the easiest decision point is probably the placement of the word *surprising/surprisingly*. Only (Answer Choice A) makes sense—it's the *closeness* of the relationship that's surprising, not the *evidence* itself as in Answer Choice (C) or (E)'s *unearthing*.

5. <u>Issues:</u> **sentence organization, idiomatic construction, subject-predicate agreement**

(E) Long sentences that are entirely underlined usually present a problem of overall organization: multiple descriptive phrases and clauses must be ordered so that it's clear what's being described by what and so that no run-ons or fragments are created. They also usually lack a clear single-word **decision point**, so it's generally best to pick a single detail/bit of description and track how it is used from answer to answer.

This question presents a 1/2/2 split with the initial phrase. Answer Choice (A) takes two long noun phrases connected by an *and* and follows them with a *comma-which*; since *Minnesota* is not a reason that the decision was delayed (nor is the *election*, or the *canvassing board*, nor any of the nouns close to the comma), *comma-which* won't do. Answer Choices (B) and (C) each turn the two noun phrases into part of one long descriptive phrase headed by the word *citing*, and thus whatever follows the comma after *ballots* must be the person or thing that's *citing*. Answer Choice (C)'s *were* is clearly wrong because a verb is where a noun would be needed.

Answer Choice (B) has the proper party doing the citing, *the state canvassing board*, but it garbles the rest of the sentence: *the state canvassing board … were reasons* links the wrong subject to the sentence's verb (the board aren't reasons; they *cite* reasons) and lacks subject-predicate agreement to boot!

Answer Choices (D) and (E) each move the two noun phrases further into the sentence, making the canvassing board the sentence's subject, and both correctly link up the board with a reasonable verb (*has cited* and *delayed*, respectively). Answer Choice (D) would be fine if not for the unidiomatic *reasons for the delaying of*. When a gerund is used as the object of a preposition like *for* (here: *delaying*), written English demands the use of the possessive pronoun, so *their* would be needed instead of *the*.

Idiomatic Errors Quick Review Quiz

1. <u>Issues:</u> **idiomatic construction** (*on the grounds that*), **sequence of tenses** (*was overturned … had admitted*)

(C) This question's tested idiom might not be familiar, but court decisions are made on the *grounds that* not the *grounds of*, eliminating Answer Choices (A) and (B) right off the bat. Ultimately, though, the idiom isn't needed to answer the question (nor does it help eliminate the remaining three answer choices), because a simpler issue splits 1/1/1/1/1, the proper way to phrase the sentence's second verb, *to admit*. Since the overturning happens because of something the judge did *earlier*, the second verb needs to be chronologically prior to the sentence's original past tense *was overturned*. Only Answer Choice (C)'s *had admitted*, the past perfect, qualifies.

2. **Issues: idiomatic construction**, **pronoun reference** (*the latter* versus *it* versus *them*), **modification** (placement of *only*)

(D) The answer choices here all offer different ways to connect the *contemplation* with the *mortals* who are trying to *have contact* with the *supernatural*. Answer Choices (A) and (C) use *through*, which is acceptable, as is Answer Choice (D)'s *by means of* and even Answer Choice (B)'s *by way of* (though the latter isn't something the GMAT tends to stick into the right answer, usually appearing in choices wrong for other reasons). Answer Choice (E)'s *due to* doesn't make sense in context, though, since *the contemplation* isn't the cause of the indirect contact, it's a *way* to have indirect contact.

The **pronoun** issue proves a more fruitful **decision point**. Since there are two things in this sentence that might or might not be contacted—the *supernatural* and the *natural*—the singular *it* in Answer Choice (A) is ambiguous (it could reference either). The plural *them* in Answer Choice (B) doesn't have a logical antecedent, since the only plural noun earlier in the sentence is the *mortals* (who aren't contacting themselves and, if they were, would still need *themselves* to do it grammatically).

Answer Choices (C), (D), and (E) all utilize a successful strategy for dealing with the ambiguity. Answer Choices (C) and (D) go for *the latter*, always referring to the second element in a *X and Y* list, and Answer Choice (E) eliminates the pronoun entirely. This leaves only the question of *only* and *indirect/indirectly* and where each ought to reside in the sentence. Answer Choicer (C)'s *indirectly* doesn't match up with *the contemplation* that follows, leaving us with only Answer Choice (D).

3. **Issues: idiomatic construction** (*approach from*), **verb form**, **modification** (*direction* versus *directions*)

(C) The first word of the answer choices offers a 3/2 split between *approach* and *be approaching*, but either would work in context (though, as always, here the question sticks *be* + *<-ing verb>* in answers that are wrong for other reasons). The words following *approach* are another matter. Since the other vehicle's approach is from the *opposite direction*, *toward* doesn't make sense, eliminating Answer Choices (A) and (B) outright. The remaining answer choices split 1/2/2 over the question of singular *direction* or plural *directions*. Since there is only one vehicle doing the approaching, it'd be impossible for the vehicle to be coming from multiple directions simultaneously, eliminating Answer Choices (D) and (E).

Incidentally, this is how the actual California Driving Code is written, so if you're studying for your California driver's license, consider this question a bit of bonus test prep, on the house. (Aren't we generous?)

4. **Issues: idiomatic construction** (*mistook X for Y*), **modification**

(D) You don't need to know that soufflés, even sweet ones, need salt in order to turn out right to be able to answer this question. The idiom *mistook/mistake X for Y* is all messed up in Answer Choices (A), (B), and (C). Answer Choice (E) gets the idiom right but fails the parallelism requirement that it creates for the X and Y on either side of the *for—an* *unlabeled canister of sugar* doesn't match up with *that of one containing* because of the extra *that of.*

5. Issues: idiomatic construction, pronoun reference

(C) Take out the little distracting description *just as often* and the idiom is clearer: *X may be found/is found **beside** Y.* Answer Choices (A) and (B) use *besides,* a word indicating contrast and not to be confused with *beside.* When two parties are doing an action to each other (*working with*), the reciprocal pronoun is demanded, so the choice between the remaining answers comes down to the proper use of *one another,* found only in Answer Choice (C).

500- to 600-Level Sentence Correction Practice Set

1. Issues: idiomatic construction (*because*), **pronoun choice** (*it*), **connecting clauses** (*remains inwardly focused, because it*)

(B) Both *because of having* in Answer Choice (A) and *on account of having* in Answer Choices (D) and (E) fall short of the correct *because,* doubly required here because *because* is both the correct **idiom** and is needed as a **subordinating conjunction** to render the second half of the sentence a **dependent clause** to the **independent** *Tokyo … remains inwardly focused.* The only difference between Answer Choices (B) and (C) is the pronoun whose antecedent is the singular *Tokyo;* Answer Choice (B)'s *it* is singular; Answer Choice (C)'s *they* is incorrectly plural.

2. Issues: coordination (*powerful enough to X and Y*), **idiomatic construction** (*powerful enough + infinitive verb*)

(E) The sentence as originally written suggests a parallel list of things the storm was: it was powerful, it left the city without power, and it didn't do much lasting damage. But since the underlined parts of the sentence do not contain the adjective phrase (*powerful enough …*) and the independent clause (*last night's thunderstorm did …*), they can't be part of such a list. The only correct option is to use **coordination** to create a compound object for the adverb phrase tacked onto the adjective *powerful.* It was powerful enough to (bring) … and (leave). The entire phrase is itself made **subordinate** by the word *although,* leaving a sentence with a dependent clause linked by a comma and a conjunction to an independent one. Only Answer Choice (E) lines up all those parts correctly.

3. Issues: pronoun choice (reflexive pronoun *themselves*), **coordination** (the comparative adjectives *harder* and *more compact*)

(A) A compound object for the verb *making* is found in the sentence as originally written. Slugs make themselves harder and more compact. Answer Choice (B) ruins the neat **coordinated compound** with an extra *the,* as does Answer Choice (E). Answer Choices (C) and (D) introduce a pronoun error. *Themselves* already properly refers to the plural antecedent slugs, and it is in the proper case (objective) to boot. *Their selves* in Answer Choice (C) isn't a real pronoun, though it might be mistaken for one, and *itself* in Answer Choice (D) is singular. The already eliminated Answer Choice (E) also contains a singular, so it's doubly wrong.

4. <u>Issues:</u> **comparisons** (*Unlike the rules … the military's [rules]*)

(C) *Unlike* at the beginning of a sentence signals a comparison, and comparisons must be parallel. The first half of the comparison can't be changed, *the rules*, so the second half in the underlined section must also be a noun (or able to stand in for one). Comparisons must also be logically parallel, so it must be a noun of the same sort as "the rules." Answer Choices (A) and (D) compare *the military* to the rules, Answer Choices (B) and (E) compare it instead to the *military's encouragement*. Neither works, leaving only Answer Choice (C).

5. <u>Issues:</u> **comparisons** (*daycare facilities resemble mad houses*)**, modification** (the adverb phrase *without … supervision* describes *facilities*), **pronoun choice** (the answers introduce ambiguous *they*)

(B) Whether the children require plural amounts or a singular amount of supervision is a distractor; both are acceptable. In fact, the question of the initial modifying phrase's antecedent doesn't work as a decision point, as we could describe both the children and the daycare as lacking enough supervision. The comparison begun at the end of the line is the key; the end of the two-part comparison (*mad houses*) is not up for grabs, so the beginning must be changed to match it. Answer Choices (A) and (E) compare the *mad houses* to *children*, Answer Choice (D) to an unspecified *they*. The choice between (B) and (C) is easy: Answer Choice (C)'s *adequate amounts of supervision they need* doesn't work as the object of the verb that precedes it, *get*. It's also redundant.

6. <u>Issues:</u> **subjunctives** (*requiring every … be registered*)

(D) Words of command and demand like *require* take verbs in the **subjunctive** form as their objects. Both (D)'s *be registered* and (B)'s *register* will work. (*Laws requiring* and *laws that require* are both correct.) Answer Choice (B) includes an extra *should* between *require* and *register*—a no-no with the **subjunctive**, which has a "built in" sense of *should* and *ought*, rendering those words redundant.

7. <u>Issues:</u> **idiomatic construction** (*has an opinion on*), **subject-predicate agreement** (*not one … has*), **word choice** (*whether,* not *if* for options)

(E) The idiom *has an opinion on* eliminates Answer Choice (C) and its *opinions about if*. The choice between ***whether*** and ***if*** eliminates (D) [and (C) *again*!]; on the GMAT, *whether* is used to describe options (*whether I do this or that*), and *if* is for conditional statements (*if I were the king of the forest*). The **subject-predicate agreement** is the most useful decision point, eliminating Answer Choices (A), (B), and (C) (one more time); all contain the plural verb *have* instead of the singular *has* that would agree with the subject pronoun *one*. One is clearly singular. *Friends* is part of a prepositional phrase that modifies *one* and thus can't be the subject. (But it makes a good distractor.)

8. <u>Issues:</u> **idiomatic construction** (*never before X has Y + verb*), **subject-predicate agreement** (*has a single person had*),

(A) Reverse the word order and the idiom makes more sense: *A single person has never had the kind of power …* (that they have today, now that firearms are available)—weird, but acceptable. On the easier end of the difficulty spectrum, you will still see the occasional odd, infrequently used idiom like this one, but not paired with very attractive alternative answers. Here, the others answers are just shy of gibberish.

Answer Choice (B) swaps the subject and object creating nonsense (the advent can't have a person); the *ever* in Answer Choice (C)'s *has not had ever [the power]*, a stranded modifier, is also nonsensical; Answer Choice (D)'s *did ... have had* is nonsense as a verb (and fails the **subject-predicate agreement test**, too); and Answer Choice (E) strands *since the advent of the firearm* in the middle of a clause and *never before* at the beginning, each where they have no clear antecedent.

9. **Issues: modification** (the placement of *proportionate*), **idiomatic construction** (*proportionate to*, not *with*), **subject-predicate agreement** (*Minorities ... are*)

(D) The long interjected phrase between the two dashes is meant as a distractor to cover a **subject-predicate agreement** error. Plural *minorities* takes plural *have* or *are*, not *is*, as found in Answer Choice (A) and (B). Answer Choice (C) gets the agreement right but introduces an ambiguous pronoun and confuses the subject and object of the original sentence, resulting in *minorities* who seem to be sentencing themselves. Answer Choice (E) could be eliminated by either the modification error—numbers are proportionate, not minorities—or the expected idiom—*proportionate **to***, not *proportionate **in***. Answer Choices (A) and (B) both make versions of the same modification error, and Answer Choices (B) and (C) have the incorrect idiomatic construction *proportionate with*.

10. **Issues: verb choice** (whether *have been* and *will* are separate), **style** (the redundancy of *have and will*)

(C) Question 10 is a one of the rare single-error Sentence Correction questions. Just follow the verbs.

Answer Choice (A) has an impossible to follow verb construction: *will continue to have been flouting*. Answer Choice (B) looks like it has a compound verb, but the two parts can't be made parallel no matter how you parse them. The fishermen can't *have* without an object (what do they have?), nor can the fishermen *have continue to flout* or *have to flout*. Answer Choice (D) sees the fishermen trying to *have already been to flout* or *have already been continue to flout*, also incorrect, and Answer Choice (E) tries the same, *already have been continue flouting* or *already have been flouting*.

Style is rarely tested on its own on the GMAT, meaning unstylish or awkward answer choices usually also contain a separate grammatical error. But as a rule of thumb, it'd be OK to pick Answer Choice (B) because all the other choices are redundant.

600- to 700-Level Sentence Correction Practice Set

1. **Issues: comparisons** (*15 Americans die due to ... fewer than are killed by*), **modification** (the choice of a dash or comma), **quantities and counts** (*fewer/less*)

(B) The alternating *less* and *fewer* in the answer choices signals that a **quantities and counts** rule is being tested, and, as usual, tested alongside a comparison rule. Comparisons are usually easier to check than other errors and reward us with more eliminated answers. As always, items compared must be parallel: *15 die* in the unchangeable part of the sentence, so the second half of the comparison must also be verb like *die*. Answer

Choice (E) compares the noun *ones,* so it's out, and Answer Choice (D) changes the comparison to one between *number* and *people,* both nouns, but not logically parallel. Answer Choices (A) and (B) both have *are,* acceptable verbs, leaving the **quantities and counts** question as the tie-breaker. Fifteen Americans can be counted, so they must be compared with *fewer,* not *less.* (Of the other answers, only the already eliminated Answer Choice (E) gets this second issue correct.)

2. Issues: **parallelism** (*as X rather than as Y*), **subject-predicate agreement** (*this new idea … has emerged*), **modifiers** (*extensive/extensively*), **word-phrase-clause problems** (the choice of form for the final phrase *including immediately …*)

   (E) *Rather than* signals another comparison. The parts of the two part idiom as *X rather than as Y* must be parallel. The static half of the sentence establishes the first part as *actively taking part …* a verb phrase with lots of modifiers. Even if not so heavily modified, the second part must also be a verb (or verb phrase). Answer Choices (A), (B), and (C) all would compare nouns, *recipient* or *recipients,* and can be eliminated. Though it might not sound as graceful as we'd like, *merely inertly receiving* will still do for a verb.

   Answer Choice (D) is eliminated by both of the other issues present. The idiom must be completed with a second *as,* but Answer Choice (D) omits it [as (A) and (D) also do]. And the phrase ending in *immediately post coitus* can work as a descriptive modifying phrase with Answer Choicer (E)'s *including,* but not with Answer Choicer (D)'s *which* preceded by a comma. "*Comma*" *which* attaches the description that follows the *which* to whatever is on the other side of the comma, and here that would be ambiguous, with us left uncertain as to whether its antecedent is *two, vivo,* or *examination.*

3. Issues: **verb tense** (had/has), **idiomatic construction** (*X is regarded as Y*), **word-phrase-clause problems** (the choice in comma placement and conjunction after *novel*)

   (C) This question contains the idiom *X is regarded as Y,* which Answer Choices (B), (C), and (D) use correctly. The verb at the beginning of the underlined section must agree with the subject. While it might not be clear what *Oroonoko* is meant to be at first, but the rest of the sentence clues us in to the fact that it's a book, and thus singular. *Has* is demanded, and *have* eliminates Answer Choices (A) and (B). The choice between Answer Choices (C) and (D) comes down to the end of the underlined section, whose form will determine whether the remainder of the sentence forms a compound object of *regarded as,* as it would in Answer Choice (D), or an **appositive phrase,** a rarer form of coordination that starts showing up on the test's more difficult questions.

   Appositives link the phrases on either side of the comma, treating the comma like an equals sign, sort of. Like in comparisons, the phrases on either side of the comma need to be the same part of speech as the other and make logical sense. Logic kills Answer Choice (E). The placement of the comma would indicate that coming to be regarded by lots of people as a precursor to the novel counts as a milestone of early feminist literature. The **coordination** in Answer Choice (C) is preferable: the book has come to be regarded as two things, a feminist milestone and a precursor to the novel. The *for many* set off by commas is used here as—surprise, surprise—a distractor, meant to make it harder to see the coordination it's interrupting.

4. <u>Issues</u>: **modification** (the arrangement of *world, population, rising*), **idiomatic construction** (*is rising at a rate of*), **numbers and amounts** (sorting out the *rate, rise,* and *percentage*)

(B) The non-underlined introductory modifying phrase modifies whatever sits on the other side of the comma. As written originally, the *world* is the thing being counted as over 7 billion. Clearly, it's the population we're counting, and Answer Choice (B), (C), and (E) do just that, while Answer Choice (D) has the *rise* as being over 7 billion. To arrive at Answer Choice (B), we can look to the number question. If the population is at 7 billion, what is rising? The percentage is rising. How is it rising? At a rate of 1.1 percent. Answer Choice (C) gets the idiom wrong, inserting an extra *up*. Answer Choice (E) changes the *at* to a *by*, which, when combined with the switch to the passive voice, would mean that the rate is the thing that's making the population number go up. The *rate* should be the amount the population is going up by, not the cause of its increase.

5. <u>Issues</u>: **modification** (choosing an antecedent for *A much anticipated …*), **connecting clauses** (**coordinating** the first two clauses)

(C) The switch between *that is* and *is* across the end of the answer choices would be an easy decision point to start with. *That* would serve as a conjunction, making one long phrase out of the two *is* phrases, resulting in the circular statement that this giant gummy worm is the largest worm that is 128 times as big as a normal worm, or, in other words, the largest worm that is the size that it is. Out go Answer Choices (A) and (B). The remaining answer choices turn the last clause in the sentence into some sort of modifying phrase.

6. <u>Issues</u>: **connecting clauses** (choosing description over a dependent or independent clause)

(A) Four wrong ways to connect sentence classes are found in this question, attempts to lure you away from the sentence as originally written. Answer Choice (B)'s *with* and *so* create two dependent clauses, resulting in a sentence fragment. Answer Choice (C) would be perfect if there were a comma after baking; as written it's a run-on. Answer Choice (D) has a dependent clause linked with *and*, instead of *a*, the subordinating conjunction needed. Answer Choice (E) has no conjunctions, resulting in two independent clauses linked by a comma, another run-on.

7. <u>Issues</u>: **idiomatic construction** (punctuating *however*), **connecting clauses** (**coordination** with two layers of *and*s and *but*s), **subject-predicate agreement** (*supply chains and materials sourcing occupy*)

(E) *However* can be used in two ways: at the beginning of a sentence followed by a comma or separating two clauses, with a semicolon before and a comma after. Neither is found in Answer Choice (A) or (B), so *however* must be removed. *But* wins as a replacement option over *as* because the two clauses are establishing a contrast—"these new things are one thread, but these others are still there,"—eliminating Answer Choice (C). Finally, the plural verb *occupies* means that the subject of the clause following *but* must be compound, linked with an *and* instead of an *or*, eliminating Answer Choice (D).

8. **Issues: connecting clauses** (**coordination:** *recorded* and *created*), **modification** (avoiding unclear modifiers)

(A) The artist did two things, *recorded* and *created*, the two verbs linked by an *and* must be parallel, as they are in Answer Choice (A) but not in (B). Answer Choice (C)'s *recording* and *creating* would count as parallel, but they're not linked by an *and*, the comma instead turning them into the verbs of two dependent clauses, resulting in a sentence fragment. Answer Choice (D) and (E) introduce another error, trying to turn *recorded* into a noun and linking that noun to *the artist*. Answer Choice (D) uses *and* to create a compound subject, resulting in the nonsensical statement that the (presumably inanimate) *recordings created* the *collage*. Answer Choice (E) does the same thing, its *with* making the *secret recordings* into equal partners with the *artist*, rather than things the artist used to make the collage out of.

9. **Issues: word choice** (*if* for conditionals), **subjunctive** (avoiding incorrect versions), **sequence of tenses** (*was, will be*)

(D) Answer Choices (A) and (B) flirt with the **subjunctive**, which would be correct if *Were ... would* were in an answer choice. *Were ... should* in Answer Choice (A) and *Were ... will* in Answer Choice (B) are both incorrect versions. The regular season's indication comes at an earlier point in time than the coming championship series, so clearly the first clause needs a verb that is in an earlier tense than the second. Answer Choice (C)'s tortured clauses pass this requirement: *has been indicating* and *would have* but doesn't make any sense as a whole. The choice between Answer Choices (D) and (E) comes down to the *if/whether* distinction. On the GMAT, *whether* is for options, and *if* is for hypothetical and conditional statements. The sentence's meaning works best in the conditional, rendering Answer Choice (E) incorrect.

10. **Issues: modification** (organizing modifiers without commas), **idiomatic construction** (the obscure *is focusing scrutiny on*), **subject-predicate agreement** (*the election focuses/ is focusing*)

(D) On an easier question, we'd expect the GMAT to use commas to separate several of the modifying phrases in the original sentence, but in this more advanced one the organization is instead accomplished by placement and proximity. Keep the elements straight: the scrutiny is focused on the dean's *role*, which took place *at the university's foundation*, and the role was *securing funding for the science center.* Answer Choice (B) incorrectly uses *by*, which would make the science center something the dean used (or something near the dean). Answer Choice (C) incorrectly uses *of*, and it also uses *which* incorrectly; a comma or a preposition would be needed. Answer Choices (A) and (D) get the descriptions into a sensible order, but (A) falls to a much simpler error, matching the singular *election* with the plural *focus.*

Don't let the compound verb tense *is focusing* scare you away from Answer Choices (D) and (E). Both *is focusing scrutiny on* and *focuses scrutiny on* are correct idiomatic constructions, but the *at* in Answer Choice (E) breaks the idiom [as does the *to* in Answer Choice (B)].

700- to 800-Level Sentence Correction Practice Set

1. Issues: subject-predicate agreement (*much … is*), **connecting clauses** (constructing a descriptive phrase after the dash)

(D) The tricky subject *much* is singular, demanding *is*, instead of the *are* found in Answer Choices (A) and (B).

Additionally, the tail end of the underlined section is mislinked with what follows it in all but Answer Choice (D). The correct answer coordinates two descriptions of the *feature*. It is one *that is typical … and that will hinder*. Answer Choice (A) drops the first *that*, and (B) turns the second into a *they*. Answer Choice (C) turns the second half of the coordinated description into a verb phrase, which doesn't match the adjective phrase *typical …*, and Answer Choice (E) turns the second one into an independent clause, incorrectly linked to what precedes it with an *and*, instead of the *and* and a comma that would be needed.

2. Issues: idiomatic construction (*X is all but impossible without Y2*), **modifiers** (the migrating *direct* and *during*), **word-phrase-clause errors** (*if* versus *with* or *without*)

(E) A slightly more obscure idiom than on easier questions, (*X is all but impossible without Y*) eliminates the *if*'s in Answer Choices (A) and (B) as well as the *with* in Answer Choice (C). The words *during* and *direct* move around a great deal from answer choice to answer choice, and the movement results in various nonsensical meanings for the incorrect choices. Answer Choice (A)'s arrangement is perfectly acceptable, but Answer Choice (B) is ambiguous (it's not clear whether the opposition happened during the primary or whether the victory is impossible during the primary). Answer Choice (C) tries to avoid the error with *from*, but the resulting phrase *were their opponents from the primary* is itself idiomatically incorrect. Answer Choice (D)'s *during* is as ambiguous as Answer Choice (B)'s. (How can the opposition support the nominee *during* the primary, the time when they are the opposition?).

3. Issues: comparisons (In contrast to X, Y), **pronoun choice** (*its* is ambiguous)

(D) The GMAT is hypersensitive to ambiguity. *Its* could refer to either the *yuan* or to *Shenzen*, so must be removed or made unambiguous. Answer Choices (A), (B), and (E) have the ambiguous *its*, while Answer Choice (C) swaps it for *their*, which has no clear antecedent (as there are no plural nouns around that it could refer to).

The correct comparison must use the correct form of the comparative phrase *In contrast to X, Y* and the two parts of the comparison must be parallel. Answer Choice (B)'s comparative phrase *contrasted with* is unidiomatic in context.

4. Issues: numbers and amounts (*percentage/share is higher/greater*), **comparisons** (the *percentage* now is seven times higher *than 8 percent*), **idiomatic constructions** (*X is higher than Y* [*was*])

(A) A complicated comparison between two percentages presents itself. Since a *percentage* can be counted, it is *higher* rather than the *greater* found in Answer Choices (D) and (E). The comparison must be made between like things. The *share* can't be compared with a *percentage of the share*, thus eliminating Answer Choices (B) and (C). Answer Choice (D)'s *numbers* is trickier, but still wrong, as the specific number of cell phones shouldn't be compared with the earlier percentage. Answer Choices (C) and (E) introduce a *that* at the end of the underlined section, ruining the comparing idiom *X is higher than Y.*

5. **Issues: comparisons** (*the debt expanded more than it had [expanded]*), **idiomatic constructions** (the obscure *the years from X to Y*)

(A) Comparisons are found with increasing ubiquity as the questions climb in difficulty. Here, the correct Answer Choice (A) compares a verb and a verb (*expanded* and *had expanded*), made harder to spot as correct by the omission of the second *expanded*—a form of **elision** that is acceptable. Answer Choice (B) compares *expansion* to *that*, a noun/noun comparison that would also work. Answer Choices (C), (D), and (E) try to avoid the comparison by changing the verb to *exceeds*, but the result is nonsensical.

Additionally, the idiom *the years from X to Y* is found in the correct answer but is used there because of its rarity as an attempt to scare test takers away from an otherwise obviously correct answer choice.

6. **Issues: word-phrase-clause problems** (deciding what type of clauses make sense together), **idiomatic constructions** (*pass in a chamber*)

(E) Another obscure idiom appears, as they tend to do in the upper reaches of GMAT difficulty: bills *pass in Congress* (and other legislative bodies), rather than being *passed by.*

The major challenge of the sentence is organizing the subjects and predicates of the clauses so that they make sense. The bill should be the one passing or not, and the chambers aren't the ones expecting the passage.

7. **Issues: wholesale reorganization** (an entirely underlined clause, multiple **coordinations** and subordinations)**, comparisons** (*there are no X for Y as there are for Z*), **pronoun choice** (avoiding overcorrecting *them* for ambiguity)

(A) Fully underlined sentences usually involve organizing all the sentence's clauses into a sensible order, and this question is no different. Tracking the comparison proves the key to that sensible organization. Answer Choices (B), (D), and (E) compare languages *French and Russian* to *English use.* Answer Choice (C) does the opposite, comparing *French and Russian use* to the language *English.*

8. **Issues: word-phrase-clause problems** (deciding what should modify what), **modifiers** (placement of *merely, briefly*), **idiomatic construction** (*with the result that*)

(E) The challenge of this question is making sure that each modifying phrase is modifying something that makes sense and that the subject and predicate pairs are likewise sensible. The venom can't *result* in anything, as it does in Answer Choices (C) and (D). Answer Choice (A)'s *this* is ambiguous and the final *tendency of platypuses using it* is awkward to boot. The *as* and *with* in Answer Choice (B) result in two dependent clauses, turning the whole sentence into a fragment.

9. **Issues: comparisons** (*his position is like saying*), **connecting clauses** (**coordinating** *because ...* and *because ...*)

(C) The choice between *the statement* and *saying* is irrelevant as far as the comparison is concerned, but the two things said in the saying/statement must still be properly coordinated in the sentence: either *that X* and *that Y* or *that X and Y* would do. Answer Choice (C)'s *saying that because X ... and because Y* is the only good option. Answer Choice (A)'s *because ... because* result in two dangling dependent clauses. Answer Choice (B) does the same, though with only one *because*. Answer Choice (D)'s *having* and *that because* creates a run-on instead, while Answer Choice (E)'s placement of the *because* spoils the sentence's meaning. (Bald people having no hair isn't a cause of the statement or of the reduction in hair from the haircut.)

10. **Issues: idiomatic construction** (two: *contend that* and *so driven by*), **modification** (placement of *so*)

(D) Two idiomatic constructions combine to form a thorny mess. The easiest idiom to track would be *contend that*. Answer Choices (A), (B), and (E) have no *that*. The organization of modifiers in Answer Choice (C), which has a *that*, suggests that the contention happened at the beginning of the Triassic, instead of the extinction.

So driven is used in the correct answer to drive the unwary away from the otherwise clearly correct Answer Choice (D), and moving the *so* around in the other answer choices only results in awkward or nonsensical phrasings. (In particular, the *so* doesn't work as an intensifier for *extinct*; nothing can be driven *so extinct*, as extinction is an all-or-nothing kind of thing.)

Reading Comprehension

15

→ **SUBJECTS COVERED**

→ **ADAPTIVE DIFFICULTY IN READING COMPREHENSION**

→ **PASSIVE VERSUS ACTIVE READING**

→ **KEYS TO READING COMPREHENSION**

→ **THE SIX-STEP METHOD FOR TACKLING QUESTIONS**

→ **READING COMPREHENSION QUESTION TIPS**

→ **GLOBAL QUESTIONS**

→ **FUNCTION**

→ **RECALL QUESTIONS**

→ **INFERENCE**

Reading Comprehension questions will make up about a third of the 41 Verbal questions you'll see on the day of your GMAT—about 14 in all, mixed in among the rest. Unlike Sentence Correction or Critical Reasoning questions, Reading Comprehension questions are grouped in sets of three to four that draw on the same 200- to 400-word passage.

The screen splits into two columns when Reading Comprehension questions appear, with the passage on the left and questions on the right, so it's unlikely you'll mistake them for any other type of question.

TIP

Official GMAC documents claim that the passages max out at 350 words, but slightly longer passages may appear.

SUBJECTS COVERED

GMAT Reading Comprehension passages are drawn from three major subject areas in about equal proportions:

1. **SOCIAL SCIENCE**—History, philosophy, economics, sociology, linguistics, etc.—the "soft sciences" built on statistical analysis and studies, surveys, and other experiments involving people.

2. **PHYSICAL SCIENCE**—Biology, physics, astronomy, chemistry, etc.—the "hard sciences" where data and experiments built on physical phenomena (gravity, plate tectonics, recombinant DNA, and so on) are king.

3. **BUSINESS**—Marketing, strategic planning, sales techniques, taxation, profit margins— all the things you'd expect from a test related to the MBA.

To make the test feel more inclusive (and, for lack of a better term, "politically correct"), the test maker tends to focus on topics in the Social Science passages that relate to traditionally underrepresented minorities.

What the GMAT *Says* Reading Comprehension Tests

According to the MBA.com, Reading Comprehension questions break into three categories, "interpretive, applied, and inferential"—whatever those mean! How do you apply or infer without interpreting? Yeah, we don't know either.

On the other hand, the *Official Guide* uses a slightly different classification with twice as many categories: main idea, supporting idea(s), logical structure, inference, evaluation, application. But when you read the explanations that accompany the questions in the *Official Guide,* it's clear that the choice between "supporting ideas" and "logical structure" is almost random. (How could it be otherwise? Unless you understand the passage's logical structure, how could you understand how an idea supports the main idea?)

What's the reason for all the categories and jargon? It's all smoke and mirrors meant to disguise the very simple tasks being called for and the rigorous limitations the questions must operate under.

Truth is, the reason most people do poorly on Reading Comprehension is that they give the test maker too much credit. Test takers overthink the questions, avoiding the simpler answers because, surely, a test of comprehension requires a lot of subtle upper-level thinking. If only that were true!

What Reading Comprehension *Really* Tests . . .

The key to answering Reading Comprehension questions is understanding the limitations that the test maker operates under, the most important being that every question must be answerable on the basis of what is DIRECTLY STATED IN THE PASSAGE. No outside knowledge is allowed because the test maker doesn't want to give an advantage to test takers who happen to know about a given subject area. EVERYTHING necessary is on the screen—you just have to train yourself to find it.

In actual practice then, Reading Comprehension ought to be called Information Organization. You have 350ish words worth of information that you need to organize so that you can deal with three or four questions based on it. The 350ish words is a lot less than you usually digest in one sitting, even a 5- to 10-minute sitting (the amount of time you'll be spending on a single passage and question set).

The range of questions is limited, too, by the requirement that every correct answer be linked to something specific in those 350ish words. There really are only four basic things that the test maker can ask:

1. What was the main point the author was driving at in the 350ish words you just read?
2. What role did this small part of those 350ish words play in the overall point the author was trying to make?
3. Which of the following answer choices can be found written out somewhere in the 350ish words you just read?
4. Which of the following answer choices is directly implied (in that Critical Reasoning sense of the word) by something written explicitly in the 350ish words you just read?

Or, as you'll learn to call them soon, you can be asked to answer one of four categories of question: **Main Point, Function, Detail, and Inference.**

. . . and What It Doesn't

There are lots of things you do when you read a 350ish-word chunk of text in your day-to-day life that won't help you here.

1. **GMAT READING COMPREHENSION READING ISN'T LIKE ACADEMIC READING.** In college you no doubt learned to read with a critical eye, questioning the motives of the author,

making connections to things you've read elsewhere. On the GMAT, that sort of thing will only slow you down and leave you less able to navigate the answer choices. How you feel about the text is irrelevant. Whether the text is right or wrong doesn't matter in the slightest.

2. **GMAT READING COMPREHENSION READING ISN'T LIKE PROFESSIONAL READING.** If you're out in the working world, you've probably been given assignments that involve summarizing and presenting vast quantities of written material, material you have to pore over, anticipating your boss's questions, memorizing the more salient details so you can rattle them off under pressure. Even though the GMAT will put the pressure on you, the important details will always remain on the screen for you to refer back to. Thankfully, the only questions you need to anticipate are those in that list of four from a couple of paragraphs back.

3. **GMAT READING COMPREHENSION READING ISN'T LIKE PLEASURE READING.** There is, unfortunately, a timer tick-tocking as you read on the GMAT. You'll find no leisurely beach reading here. Even more unfortunately, GMAT Reading Comprehension passages tend to be bone dry, snooze-inducing boredom bullets. Part of the challenge that's "baked into" Reading Comprehension is focusing on material that you wouldn't care to read under any other circumstance.

TIP

The main thing that Reading Comprehension *doesn't test* is this: *most of the passage.*

There are only three or four questions attached to each passage, and the test maker in no way attempts to make those four questions cover the entire passage or somehow split the content equally among them. Only a very small portion of those 350ish words will actually be relevant to the questions.

In the pages that follow, you'll learn how to identify and isolate the important bits and quickly pass over the rest.

ADAPTIVE DIFFICULTY IN READING COMPREHENSION

It's not been clearly established whether the GMAT algorithm continues "adapting" during each three-to four-question Reading Comprehension passage and question set. It's likely that the test maker has a smaller subpool of questions available for each passage, so that if you were to get the first two questions attached to a passage correct, the final question would be statistically harder than the previous two. It's also possible that the test maker assigns difficulty to the entire passage plus question set—so that missing the first two of three questions wouldn't noticeably reduce the difficulty on the third.

It's hard to tell which of these two models the test maker uses because part of what makes a question hard or easy is the passage it's attached to, and that can't change once you start a set. So, it's probably best to just not think about it. Do each question as it comes, and don't worry about whether one "feels" harder or easier.

PASSIVE VERSUS ACTIVE READING

To succeed at GMAT Reading Comprehension, you have to force yourself to read a new way, to **read actively, rather than passively**. This means that you need to read with an eye toward the specific tasks that the test maker can ask you to do.

Thus, as you read, you **interrogate the author**, taking in each piece of information one at a time. As each bit of information comes in, ask yourself, "What does this have to do with

TIP

You might want to go back and reread "Reading the GMAT Way" from the Verbal Introduction before diving into this next section.

what the author already said?" and "Why is the author talking about this now?" and "Is this something new or just the continuation of a previous thought?"

Start slowly. The first sentence of a passage is not necessarily the most important. It might be a relatively meaningless bit of contextual flavor meant to throw you off the scent of the real purpose of the passage. Or it might be the author's main point, laid out as clear as day. Whichever it is, you're not going to know immediately because you have no context to put that first sentence into. The context will grow as you read each new sentence, and with that growing context, you'll be able to pick up speed.

Don't be afraid to circle back and reread a sentence or even a paragraph if something you read doesn't make sense. If you find yourself saying, "Wait, I thought this was about otters and how they clean their food, so why is the author talking about whales?" then go back and reread the otter bit. The relationship will always be spelled out somewhere.

This doesn't mean you have to understand each new bit of information completely. It's far more important to **understand the *relationship* to the author's overall point** and to the information you've already read. Your understanding of that relationship will only need to be specific enough to answer the sorts of questions that the test maker asks. (We'll discuss this more momentarily.)

Don't rush on to the next paragraph until you know what to make of the first. The second paragraph will usually go faster, and the third (if there is one) will go faster still. Build momentum by being an active reader!

When you're done reading, you won't have every answer to every possible question committed to memory or summarized in your notes, but you will know the general "shape" of the passage and the locations of the various kinds of details, and, most importantly, you will have a grasp on what the different parts of the passage contribute to the author's overall agenda.

KEYS TO READING COMPREHENSION

1. Read quickly, but don't rush.

2. Know the four basic questions and what they ask.

3. Take notes to help you answer the four basic questions.

4. Learn to predict and spot the wrong-answer traps.

5. Ignore your real-world knowledge about the passage content.

Taking Notes

Your noteboard is your best friend during Reading Comprehension passage sets, so long as you know what is helpful to write and what isn't. You don't have to summarize the passage in any detail as you read. In fact, writing out summaries of paragraphs tends to take longer than just rereading a paragraph would. Instead, let your noteboard keep track of

- the passage's basic **structure** (the role each paragraph plays, the relationship between paragraphs) and
- the author's **argument** and how it's developed (where does the author take a side, how does the author develop the argument?),

and use your notes to create

- a rough guide to help you recall where certain kinds of details are found (examples, definitions, exceptions).

Reading for Structure

Knowing the structure of a passage is much more important than knowing all the nitty-gritty details of its content. Being able to say, "in the first paragraph, the author introduced this one guy's theory, and in the second, he attacked it by giving counterexamples" will get you a lot further than trying to commit each detail of the first theory and each detail of the second to memory because **the details will stay on the screen**. If you're faced with a **Detail** question that asks

> **According to the passage, the first theoretical model of tectonic plate movement relied on the analogy that**

you can always just go back to the paragraph that talks about the first theoretical model and confirm the answer—provided your notes helped you divide up the passage into its component parts. Now, how do we find those parts?

Structural Keywords

Just as with the Critical Reasoning questions, structural keywords will help you immensely as you answer Reading Comprehension questions if you know what to do when you see them. The most important of these keywords you can think of as the "road signs" that will help you navigate the passage, telling you either "Caution: things get tricky ahead, slow down," or "Nothing to see here, move along." These are the keywords that indicate **continuation** or **contrast.**

Continuation Keywords

These words let you know that the author is continuing the same line of thought. There's no contradiction, no change in direction, no additional considerations. Some examples include:

moreover	as well as	in addition
likewise	further	by the same token
additionally	not only	along the same lines
also	thus	

However you are taking notes on the passage, continuation keywords tell you that the same note will cover what you've already read and what you're about to read. You don't need to slow down to make sure you've got a handle on a subtle distinction because *there won't be any.* Not here, at least.

Contrast Keywords

On the other hand, **contrast keywords** are signals that the author of the passage either just has or soon will make a distinction, so *slow down and be careful until you understand it.* Some examples:

however	but	except
nevertheless	rather	unless
despite	in spite of	on the other hand
yet	notwithstanding	
although	while	

Keywords and phrases aren't the only way the test maker can make a structural distinction in the passage. Some are more subtle. For example, if the author introduces something as *the usual view* or *as many believe*, that's a good sign that not too far down the screen you'll be introduced to something we might call "the unusual view" or "what a few (including the author) believe." If there's an old, established way of doing something that is specifically called something like the **original method** or **the widespread practice**, nine times out of ten you'll see a new method or a minority practice further down the screen.

To borrow a cliché, we can refer to this as "waiting for the other shoe to drop." Your upstairs neighbor takes off one shoe and drops it to the floor, so you expect to hear a second drop. The test maker tells you **some critics believe**, and you expect to be told **what others believe**. See **on the one hand**, and you expect an **on the other hand**. Indeed, any time the author starts dividing up concepts, that's a sign to slow down your reading and figure out what the division is.

Boil down the points, but don't exaggerate them for clarity. The author isn't going to say that X is the worst thing ever, just that it is really rather bad.

Using the keywords to guide us, we could see that this technical passage (that you first saw in the Verbal Introduction), for all its jargon, has a rather simple structure:

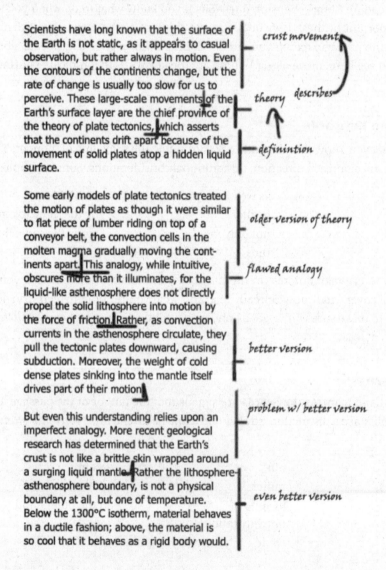

Essentially, the author introduces a natural phenomenon, the movement of the Earth's crust, then defines a theory that describes how it works. Then the author goes back in time to talk about an earlier version of the theory and why it was bad. A better version of the same theory is presented, but it, too, has a problem. Finally, the theory is revised one more time, and the passage is over.

Notice how little content we've included in these notes—that's because the content stays on the screen. Instead, the notes keep track of our understanding of the relationship between the pieces of information in the passage, things we can't easily spot without reading the entire passage again.

It'd be great if you actually could draw those division lines and labels right on the screen. Instead, you'll have to settle for reproducing them somehow on your noteboard. For example, you could label each paragraph or fall back on a standard outline.

Reading for Argument

When you break a passage down into its component parts, when you understand its basic structure, then the argument is easy to understand. Here, the author isn't really arguing directly with anyone. The "drama" of the passage lies in the small tweaks to the theory of plate tectonics that the author says are necessary and important. As a whole, the author seems to agree that the theory is correct, so long as the tweaks are considered.

We probably would need to add very little to our notes in order to capture this author's argument. The words "better" and "even better" already indicate where the author's sympathies lie.

Don't Look for Topic Sentences

Back in high school, you probably learned the three-part thesis statement/five-paragraph model for writing essays; consequently, you might expect that reading comprehension passages will follow something similar. Strike that thought from your mind!

The main point of a Reading Comprehension passage can be found at any point in the passage—first sentence, last sentence, thirteenth sentence, fourth-from-last-sentence, etc. There's no secret place to look, no place where the author always says, as you were once taught to do, "in this essay, I will prove that A is true, for X, Y, and Z reasons." There are, sadly, many superstitions about where to look to find the passage's topic, and if you've come across any in some other GMAT book, it's time to let it go.

In fact, the test maker *exploits* the fact that many people believe there's a "topic sentence" by often putting concise, easy-to-understand sentences that are only tangential to the main topic in those spots. The test maker is always one step ahead of the bone-headed test taker (which is why we try hard not to be one).The topic may well be expressed in the first or last sentence. It's just not always there.

Reading for Recall

Even though the structure of this passage is fairly straightforward, there are many little details in it. Does that mean we should include a summary of each paragraph and try to note the location of as many details as possible? No, not really.

Remember, specific details will remain on the screen. Certain questions will direct us to look for specific details and, using our notes, we can go back and find them.

We should, however, notice that there's a logic to the layout of all these details. Throughout the passage, facts can be split into two categories: those about (1) the solid, plate-like crust pieces and (2) the liquid, molten mantle beneath.

The GMAT is full of passages in which there are multiple points of view, parties, theories, explanations, etc., because it's an easy way to create wrong answers to questions that "sound familiar"—just take a correct detail about one group and attribute it to the other.

The best way to avoid that easy wrong answer trap is to use your notes to sort those details. If we had paper tests and highlighters, we could just highlight parts of the text corresponding to one party and underline parts corresponding to the other, but unfortunately, the GMAT is a computer-based test. Everything we do, we have to take down to the wet erase noteboard.

For keeping multiple parties straight, the best tactic is to create a jot list inventory of facts that apply to each group. Don't summarize the information. Write just enough to jog your memory should you see a question on a given fact. Like so:

Solid	Liquid
~top	~hidden
~lumber	~conveyor, convection
~cold, dense, sinks	~asthenosphere
~not brittle	~subduction
~above isotherm	~above isotherm, ductile

Truthfully, the above is a bit more writing than you'd end up doing, since you could freely abbreviate, as long as you don't abbreviate so much that you no longer remember what you meant by your notes. Remember, the only person who needs to understand your notes is you!

The test maker knows that lots of people taking the GMAT are put off by specialized jargon, particularly scientific terminology. This passage has its fair share of off-putting terminology.

As long as you can distinguish the terms within a passage from each other, you really don't need to spend time making sure you can pronounce them in your head or even that you understand what they mean.

THE SIX-STEP METHOD FOR TACKLING QUESTIONS

Step 1: Read and Take Notes on the Passage

What do you know? That's exactly what we've been doing these past few pages. But there's still one final thing to do before you head into the questions.

Step 2: Restate the Author's Agenda to Yourself

Most Reading Comprehension questions demand that you be able to take a step back from the passage's details and understand the author's overall agenda. So, before attempting any of the questions, take a moment and ask yourself "What was the author trying to do here?"

If you've been reading for structure and argument and taking notes accordingly, this should be a snap. First, think about the author's **overall tone**. Broadly speaking, all passages are either positive, negative, or neutral in tone.

Positive authors have something that they want to convince you of. Sometimes, there's a mysterious phenomenon that needs an explanation, and the author will present one or more explanations and then take a side, saying one is clearly the best. Other times, there's a problem, and the author likes one particular solution for it. No matter how many sides there may be, the author is on one.

Negative authors also have something they want to convince you of: that someone else is wrong about something. Again, there's a phenomenon that needs explaining, but these authors find there are problems with a presented explanation. There's a problem that *won't* be solved if one plan is used.

Neutral authors don't take sides. Sometimes they're purely descriptive: here's how something works. Other times, they present competing theories or explanations but never tell you which one is right and which one wrong.

Sometimes authors will straddle the line between these emotional charges. They're mostly negative, but at the end they cautiously present a theory they like but don't spend much time on it. Or they're neutral as they describe something, but they seem dismissive of one of the things they describe. Don't worry if you feel the author's being wishy-washy. Just make that part of your statement of the author's agenda.

In the passage we've been working with about tectonic plates, the author probably falls into the neutral to slightly positive range. Most of the passage is descriptive, but there is a growing sense as the passage goes on that there's a "best" understanding of how plate tectonics work, and a couple of not-so-good ones.

To nail our author down in a few phrases, we might put the agenda thus:

> The author describes the theory of plate tectonics and some
> of the earlier, less-successful versions of it, before ending by
> presenting the most current, best version.

Step 3: Identify the Question (Based on the Stem)

Just like Critical Reasoning questions, Reading Comprehension questions have a stem and five answer choices. You'll learn (in the coming chapter) to recognize the tell-tale words and phrases the test maker uses to delineate each.

Let's tackle the question we've been flirting with this whole chapter:

> According to the passage, the first theoretical model of
> tectonic plate movement relied on the analogy that
>
> (A) the solid plates that compose the Earth's crust are similar
>   to the contours of the continents.
> (B) the brittle skin of the crust is wrapped around a surging
>   molten layer.
> (C) the materials that compose the crust and mantle are not
>   physically separate.
> (D) the liquid mantle is like a conveyor carrying the solid
>   crust by friction.
> (E) the crust is like a solid, dense plate that sinks into the
>   liquid core beneath.

In this question, the phrase "According to the passage" followed by the word "relied" indicates that the test maker wants us to find a specific **detail** somewhere in the passage that corresponds to one of the five answer choices, a question you'll soon learn to call a **Detail** question.

Step 4: Research the Relevant Text

Never be afraid to reread the passage before looking at the answer choices. Remember, the answers are *designed* to make you uncertain about what you've read. Most of the wrong answer traps rely on your not quite remembering and jumping at an answer that seems familiar but is ultimately wrong.

Don't avoid rereading the passage; just avoid aimlessly rereading. The notes you take while reading the passage will be your guide as to where to look. Our notes tell us that there was an "earlier version" of the theory described in the first part of the second paragraph, so that is what we should reread. When we do, we'd see:

> ...Some early models of plate tectonics treated the motion of plates as though it were similar to a flat piece of lumber riding on top of a conveyor belt, the convection cells in the molten magma gradually moving the continents apart. This analogy...

Step 5: Prephrase or Predict an Answer

The best way to avoid the various wrong answer traps that the test maker has laid is to know what you're looking for in the answer choices before you go looking. Based on what we just read, we'd say something like "the solid bits were like planks, and the liquid bit was like a conveyor belt."

Step 6: Evaluate the Answer Choices

Take the answer choices one at a time, keeping in mind that the correct answer usually doesn't use the exact same words as the passage originally did.

> (A) the solid plates that compose the Earth's crust are similar to the contours of the continents.

Answer Choice (A) might seem familiar from a misreading of the first paragraph, where the "contours of the continents" phrase appears. This doesn't match our prediction, and it's a bit of nonsense. The plates aren't *similar* to the contours of the continents. They're what causes the contours to change. We'll later learn to call this a **distortion**—when the test maker purposely garbles something from the passage but uses familiar phrasing to make it seem tempting.

> (B) the brittle skin of the crust is wrapped around a surging molten layer.

Here is something else that should be familiar: a near direct restatement of an analogy in the passage, but not one attributed to the earlier version of the theory. It's found in the third paragraph and seems to be referring to the second version of the explanation, not the first. You'll soon come to recognize this as a **wrong party** trap—a true fact, but one that belongs to someone or something the current question isn't asking you about.

      (C) the materials that compose the crust and mantle are not physically separate.

Here is yet another distortion, taking pieces from the very end of the passage and repeating them incorrectly. Since the discussion of the separation of the mantle and core on either side of the isotherm came at the very end of the passage, it might trip up those test takers who didn't bother to do a little targeted rereading of the passage before looking at the answer choices.

      (D) the liquid mantle is like a conveyor carrying the solid crust by friction.

Jackpot! Even though it starts with the conveyor belt and doesn't mention the planks on the belt, this is still the analogy we predicted.

If you find an answer choice that matches your prediction so closely, you might be able to click and confirm without even reading the rest. For completion's sake, what's wrong with Answer Choice (E)?

      (E) the crust is like a solid, dense plate that sinks into the liquid core beneath.

It's another **wrong party** trap, taking details from the second explanation in the passage, the one that's used to correct the original interpretation.

Reading Comprehension Diagnostic Quiz

As always, try your best to simulate testlike conditions while working through the following 14 Reading Comprehension questions. If you are working at a testlike pace, you should spend no more than 35 minutes on the entire set. On the day of the test, your Reading Comprehension instructions will look something like this:

> **DIRECTIONS:** The following questions are based on the content of the passage that immediately precedes them. Upon reading the passage, choose the best answer to each question. Only information that is stated in or implied by the passage may be used to answer the questions.

Questions 1–3 are based on the following passage.

The Chartist movement takes its name from its stated goal, the enactment of the *People's Charter*. Published in England in 1838, the Charter stipulated six main aims: the establishment of annual parliaments, a vote for every man (save invalids
Line and criminals), a secret ballot, strictly proportional representation, and payment for
(5) all who served in the parliament. This last, it was hoped, would ensure that honest tradesmen and other working men be able to afford time away from their businesses to serve.

Many regard the Chartist's as history's first mass worker's movement, and in some ways it was. It drew its numbers primarily from the working class, those who
(10) were disenfranchised under the system the *People's Charter* would reform. Yet while many of the supporters of Chartism displayed the beginnings of a working class consciousness and while the six stated goals align to a substantial degree with the tenets of democratic-socialism, it would be an error to regard the Chartists as a new type of movement or as a true mass workers movement *per se*. It was certainly
(15) not the first radical movement to demand a widening of the right to vote; in fact, it drew its membership from the remnants of several such movements, including the Friends of the People Society and the Tolpuddle Martyrs. Moreover, these multiple parties were drawn together not by a leader drawn from the working class itself, but rather by prominent "gentlemen leaders," members of the propertied class, Feargus
(20) O'Connor, the radical Irish aristocrat perhaps the most prominent. In light of this, Chartism is more plausibly described as a popular movement in which the elements of a worker's movement were developing, the first sparks of the flame that would later alight in subsequent political organizations composed of and led by England's working class.

1. Which of the following best states the author's main agenda?

   (A) To critique the common fallacies of a field of study
   (B) To argue against a common interpretation of a historical movement
   (C) To describe an anomalous historical phenomenon
   (D) To support the findings of a recent study
   (E) To chronicle the development of a social innovation

2. The passage lists each of the following as characteristics of a workers' mass movement EXCEPT:

   (A) demanding that the right to vote be extended to propertied classes.
   (B) the possession of a working class consciousness.
   (C) leaders being drawn from the working class itself, rather than the aristocracy.
   (D) possessing goals in agreement with those of democratic-socialists.
   (E) being composed primarily of the lower, disenfranchised classes.

3. The author mentions the Tolpuddle Martyrs (line 17) primarily in order to

   (A) emphasize the extent to which the Chartists drew its membership from previous movements.
   (B) argue that the Chartists were more reliant on prominent "gentlemen leaders" than previous data suggested.
   (C) provide evidence that the Chartist movement was not so novel a phenomenon as many have maintained.
   (D) contradict the interpretation of data gathered by previous researchers.
   (E) support the contention that the workers' mass movements are more common than once believed.

Questions 4–7 are based on the following passage.

There has long been a consensus in the medical and scientific communities that saturated fat is bad for the heart. In particular, this form of fat—found in substantial quantities in such foods as dairy products, meat, eggs, and palm oil—has been found
Line to raise blood cholesterol levels, which contributes directly to cardiopulmonary dis-
(5) ease by promoting the growth of plaques on the arterial walls. Yet many Northern European countries have a relatively low incidence of coronary heart disease (CHD) despite having a diet that is relatively rich in saturated fat, an epidemiological observation that is frequently called "the French paradox."

In 2002, the average French person consumed 108 grams per day of fat from
(10) animal sources, while the average American consumed only 72 grams. According to data from the American Heart Association for the same year, however, the rates of death from CHD among males 35–74 years old was 115 per 100,000 people in the U.S. but only 83 per 100,000 in France. And the other known major risk factors for CHD, including low physical activity, high blood pressure, and advanced age, are no
(15) greater in the U.S. than in France. Many pointed to the higher consumption of alcohol in France, particularly of red wine, in order to explain the difference in deaths from CHD. Certain compounds in red wine, including resveratrol, have been shown in clinical trials to interfere with the formation of arterial plaque.

Some proponents of the connection between CHD and dietary saturated fat con-
(20) tend that the "paradox" is an illusion. For example, Malcolm Law and Nicholas Wald
attributed approximately 20 percent of the difference in the observed rates of CHD
to undercertification caused by differences in the way that French authorities collect
health statistics. To account for the rest, Law and Wald presented a time-lag hypothesis. The consumption of animal fat and other high-cholesterol foods had increased
(25) only recently in France but had done so decades before in Britain and the United
States. Just as there is a recognized time lag between smoking and lung cancer, they
argued, the current rates of mortality from CHD ought to be correlated with the
dietary fat levels of thirty years prior. The low mortality from CHD reflects the earlier
low levels of saturated fat consumption, for which wine is simply an indirect marker
(30) or confounding factor. Moreover, data collected over the last decade appears to bear
the theory out: the incidence of deaths related to CHD has tracked steadily upward,
nearly mirroring the advance of saturated fat into the Northern European diet.

4. Which of the following best characterizes the overall organization of the passage?

   (A) A medical procedure is detailed, some risks associated with the procedure are
       discussed, and a solution to mitigate those risks is described.
   (B) A medical phenomenon is explored, a consequence of that phenomenon is given,
       and an explanation that allows the consequence to be avoided is advocated.
   (C) An explanation for a medical phenomenon is introduced, support for that
       explanation is given, and an alternate explanation is presented and rebutted.
   (D) A medical phenomenon is described, competing explanations for that
       phenomenon are advanced, and data is given to reconcile those two explanations.
   (E) A medical phenomenon is introduced, an explanation for that phenomenon is
       presented, and an alternate explanation is presented.

5. The primary function of the death rate statistics presented in the second paragraph
   is to

   (A) explain the relationship between CHD and risk factors such as high blood
       pressure.
   (B) trace the role that resveratrol has in reducing the risk of heart disease.
   (C) summarize the differences between French and American health care practices.
   (D) present the counterintuitive health findings for which explanations will be later
       presented.
   (E) suggest that the "French paradox" is a misrepresentation caused by differences in
       data collection.

6. According to the passage, which of the following is most likely true of the French health care system?

(A) It spends less per patient treating the negative health effects of CHD than do other Northern European nations.

(B) Its employees are less likely than those in the American system to study high blood pressure.

(C) It would not always classify some deaths as CHD-related that would be so classified as such in the American system.

(D) In general, it is better prepared to combat the dangers associated with smoking than with a high-cholesterol diet.

(E) Data collected at French hospitals regarding heart disease is often less accurate than that collected in American hospitals.

7. According to the passage, the "French paradox" is defined as

(A) the tendency of French health care officials to undercertify deaths related to CHD.

(B) the relatively long time lag between smoking and the subsequent development of cancer.

(C) the inverse relationship between saturated fat consumption and levels of heart disease.

(D) the comparatively low rate of heart disease in a culture that has a high-fat diet.

(E) the ineffectiveness of compounds such as resveratol in treating heart disease among the French.

Questions 8–11 are based on the following passage.

Over the past 160 years, life expectancy in the industrialized world has increased at the steady rate of a quarter year every year. At first, the change was driven by the spread of things today often taken for granted: clean water, sewage and waste
Line disposal, better nutrition, vaccines, and antibiotics. By the late 1970s, these innova-
(5) tions had reached the point of diminishing returns, yet at almost the same time, new technologies began to produce real gains in the fight against the most deadly remaining threats: cancer, heart disease, and strokes. Even counting the least-developed countries, the average person worldwide can expect to live to nearly 70, up from the mid-30s at the turn of the twentieth century. While the past decade has
(10) seen these later developments likewise begin to lose their efficacy, a second wave of information-fueled advances promises to push back the present limitations on human lifespan still further.

Though the future is certainly impossible to predict, many forward-looking think-ers have begun to broach the possibility that at some point in the next twenty years a
(15) child will be born who will live to the now unimaginable age of one hundred forty; his or her children may, in turn, look forward to a world in which there exists no "natu-ral" limit on the age to which one might expect to live. Barring random accident or deliberate homicide, men and women separated from us by only two generations might live indefinitely. In principle, all that is required is for technology to continue
(20) advancing faster than one ages. Increase the current rate by a factor of four and life expectancy will advance one year for every year a person ages.

Such optimism must, however, be tempered with an awareness of life's social and physical limitations. Today's developing technologies will no doubt be expensive and increasingly so at the upper ends of the age spectrum, further increasing the

(25) gap between rich and poor. As lifespan increases, previously rare maladies will loom ever larger. Alzheimer's, a growing threat to today's elderly, was almost unknown before the 1950s, primarily because, statistically speaking, most people died before symptoms developed.

8. According to the passage, which of the following is true of lifespan-increasing technologies?

(A) Some once revolutionary technologies have reached the limit of their effectiveness.

(B) All will one day reach the point of limiting returns in their ability to extend the average lifespan.

(C) Previously underestimated technological developments are today the most promising.

(D) Within two generations they will bring about an average indefinite lifespan.

(E) Historically their effect on the poorest and least-developed countries has been slight.

9. Which of the following best states the main idea of the passage?

(A) Promising new technologies to extend human lifespan will likely never overcome social and physical limitations.

(B) Optimism regarding new lifespan-extending technologies should be rejected in favor of a more realistic, less philosophical approach.

(C) The potential for technological developments to remove previous limitations on the average human lifespan has been overstated.

(D) It seems likely that technological development will increase the average human lifespan, but indefinite increases may be limited by other factors.

(E) It is impossible to predict the effect that lifespan-enhancing technological developments may have on human society.

10. Which of the following, if true, would indicate the most serious flaw with the reasoning behind the predictions made by those "forward-looking thinkers" discussed in the passage's second paragraph?

(A) As the population of the Earth increases, armed conflict and other sources of violence are likely to increase as well.

(B) Due to the inherent role that chance plays in life, accidental death can never truly be eliminated.

(C) During some decades of the previous century, the rate of technological advancement was much swifter than the average.

(D) Certain previously rare diseases of old age may prove more difficult to cure than those that currently plague the elderly.

(E) The challenges to extended lifespan overcome during the past century are far more amenable to technological solution than those ahead.

11. The author most likely believes that which of the following will be true of treatments to extend lifespan in the next century?

(A) They will be fundamentally unlike the technologies that extended lifespan significantly prior to 1970.

(B) They will be more fueled by advances in information technology than by physical and social developments.

(C) Some will need to be designed to combat diseases whose symptoms are rarely if ever seen in patients today.

(D) Most will be too expensive to implement widely and will thus be limited to the use of a select few.

(E) They will be unable to extend lifespan indefinitely, though they will certainly extend the average beyond one hundred forty years.

Questions 12–14 are based on the following passage.

As social media outlets such as Facebook and Twitter become as insuperable a part of day-to-day life for the average American worker as the water cooler or company cafeteria once were, employers are stepping up their attempts to control
Line employer behavior online, both during working hours and during an employee's
(5) off-the-clock time outside the workplace. Few can deny that a business has a vested interest in minimizing the amount of productive work time lost to personal activity during the work day; however, employers have become bolder in their demands related to their employees' online habits. Do not discuss company matters publicly, a company's social media policy might say, nor disparage managers, coworkers, or
(10) the company itself. Violations, naturally, are punishable and may even result in an employee's termination.

Recently, labor regulators have begun pushing back, issuing a series of rulings and advisories that declare many such blanket restrictions to be illegal, pointing to the longstanding principle that workers ought to have the right to discuss working
(15) conditions without fear of reprisal from their employers. It should matter not, they contend, whether the discussion takes place at the office or on Twitter. Bans on "disrespectful" comments about one's supervisors or that criticize company policies are illegal, according to the National Labor Relations Board, if those policies dis-courage the free exercise of a worker's right to communicate and organize in order
(20) to improve wages and working conditions. A company would be on shaky ground to terminate an employee who made offensive comments in an online forum. Even "simply venting" can be construed as a commentary on one's working environment and would thus be protected. A lone worker, however, might not be protected, if that worker's online comments fail to constitute "concerted activity"—if, for instance,
(25) the expected audience of the comments did not include any coworkers.

12. The primary purpose of the passage is to

    (A) explain the need for further regulations on an activity.

    (B) recommend a course of action to combat a problem.

    (C) suggest a novel approach alternative to one currently utilized.

    (D) reconcile differing interpretations of a recent ruling.

    (E) present factors that might be relevant when considering a policy.

13. According to the passage, which of the following is the basis of the rulings prohibiting employers from demanding their employees not disparage their company online?

    (A) The established policy of the National Labor Relations Board to advocate for the rights of all workers against management

    (B) The belief that disrespectful and offensive comments are a necessary component of the freedom of speech

    (C) The fear that, without such rulings, it would be impossible for workers to ever successfully lobby against their employers

    (D) The precedent that fear of retribution ought not interfere with worker discussions of the conditions of their employment

    (E) The vested interest of businesses in minimizing the amount of the workday spent online

14. According to the standards given in the third paragraph, which of the following types of online behavior would most likely not be protected by labor law?

    (A) Negative comments written on an online bulletin board by internal critics of the National Labor Relations Board

    (B) A series of disrespectful status updates posted by an executive assistant on a social networking site after a workplace altercation

    (C) Emails containing personal and sensitive information about management forwarded en masse to all employees at a company

    (D) Posts from a fisherman in Nova Scotia who vents to international players of an online game about recent weather's effect on his catch

    (E) Pictures of cats humorously captioned to indicate that one's immediate supervisor shares with them many negative traits

Your Reading Comprehension Diagnosis

This Diagnostic Quiz was meant to help you evaluate three major skills that are part of Reading Comprehension success:

1. note taking,
2. question identification, and
3. accuracy.

Answer Key and Answer Explanations can be found at the end of the chapter.

Complete explanations for the questions are found at the end of the section. The discussion below is meant to help you focus your attention on your initial weaknesses in skills relevant to the Reading Comprehension questions as you proceed through the remainder of the chapter.

Diagnosing Your Notes

You should have taken some notes as you read these passages and then tried to use those notes to help answer the questions.

Alas, it's harder to translate your note taking into a series of tick marks and checkboxes, so you will have to evaluate how useful your notes were in a more qualitative way.

Of course, the only one who can judge whether your notes were useful or not is you. There is no single set of annotations that you simply had to use in order to get these questions right. So instead of pretending like there are, let's talk instead about how to evaluate your own notes.

If you took notes on a noteboard, grab a wet erase marker of a different color than the one you used to take your notes. If you took your notes on paper, grab a highlighter. Now, begin with the first question. Take note of the right answer. Read the explanation of the answers found at the end of this section. Now, look back at your notes. Did anything you wrote correspond directly to the right answer? Were there any marks or symbols that could have helped you find the right answer or eliminate the wrong answer?

Even if you didn't actually use the note—could it have helped you? If so, go over the note in highlighter (or underline it with a different colored marker). If not, leave it be. Proceed to the next question, and the next, and so on, until you've reviewed all the questions from the passage. When you're all done, take stock of how many of your original notes are covered in highlighter.

If there's highlighter all over the place, then congratulations! You're taking notes that translate directly into right answers.

If, on the other hand, **you see huge swaths of bare pencil** (or wet erase marker), you're doing a lot of work that isn't translating into points. So, what are you writing notes about? Did you fall into the trap of summarizing the passage's contents? Are you making the sorts of connections that the test maker doesn't build questions around? Unhighlighted notes aren't definitely useless, but they're guilty until proven innocent.

Finally, if **you see neither pencil nor highlighter**—you're not taking very many notes at all. That's OK, of course. Not everyone will fill their noteboard come test day. But ask yourself as you review the answers and explanations, how often did you have to go back and reskim the passage when you were answering the questions? How easy was it to juggle all those facts in your head? If your accuracy was high and you didn't feel tired out, then you're one of those lucky people who doesn't need the notes.

Diagnosing Your Question Identification and Accuracy

Here, we can be a little more clinical. Either you recognized the question type or you didn't. Granted, your skill here is likely not what you'd hope it to be at the end of your studies. You've only barely been introduced to the different question types after all.

The main thing at this point is being able to see the two big tasks in the questions. Specific classification can wait until you've had more experience.

TIP

This is step one of the Reading Comprehension method!

Remember that the two major types of question are (1) **Global** questions, the ones that ask you **why** the authors say what they say and for their overall agenda, and (2) **Recall** questions, the ones that just ask you to find a fact buried somewhere in those 350ish words of text.

Questions 1, 3–5, 9, and 12 were **Global** questions.

Questions 2, 6–8, 10–11, and 13–14 were **Recall** questions.

As you read through the remainder of the chapter, pay special attention to those areas that you had difficulty with.

READING COMPREHENSION QUESTION TYPES

The nice thing about GMAT Reading Comprehension questions (and Reading Comprehension questions on any standardized test, for that matter), is the limited question selection. Even though the questions might be dressed up in distracting language, at heart they boil down to two questions: (1) **what** does the author say? and (2) **why** did the author say it? Or, to use our fancy lingo: **Recall** questions and **Global** questions. Let's handle them one at a time, starting with the trickier of the two, **Global** questions.

GLOBAL QUESTIONS

Main Point

Almost every passage you see on the GMAT will have one **Global** question in which the test maker asks about the main point of the passage as a whole. Accordingly, we'll call these **Main Point** questions.

You'll recognize them easily, because their stems will usually be phrased like this:

- The **primary purpose** of the passage is to
- Which of the following best states the **main idea** of the passage as a whole?
- The author's **overall goal** can best be described as

TIP

The only passages that don't tend to ask about the author's primary purpose are almost purely descriptive. Such passages are rare on the test.

Note the clues: some synonym for the word **primary** and another for the word **purpose** combined with some hint that you should be thinking about the **entire passage**, not just a part.

You saw several **Main Point** questions during your Diagnostic Quiz at the beginning of this chapter:

1. Which of the following best states the author's main agenda?
9. The main idea of the passage is that
12. The primary purpose of the passage is to

As you'll recall, we recommend that the last thing you do when you read a passage is to pause and ask yourself, "What was the author's main goal here?" The reason you ask yourself this is twofold. First, if you aren't able to give yourself an answer, then odds are you didn't understand what you just read. (Time to reread!)

Second, you ask yourself to sum up the main idea to **prepare yourself for this question**, which you will almost always (90 percent of the time) see as one of the three or four questions accompanying the passage. When it appears on the screen, smile confidently and search for the answer that you already know to be correct!

The test maker tends to phrase the answers to **Main Point** questions in two different ways and to use only one of the ways in a single question. Think back to the first passage (questions 1–3) from the Diagnostic Quiz, the Chartist passage. In that passage, the author didn't get around to explaining the passage's main point until the third sentence of the second paragraph: "it would be an error to regard the Chartists ... as a true mass workers movement *per se.*" Now look back at the right answer to question 1:

> **(B)** To argue against a common interpretation of a historical
>   movement

That is a roundabout way of saying "the Chartists weren't a mass worker's movement" isn't it? The word Chartist isn't even used!

So one way the test maker likes to phrase the answers to a Global question is obliquely. Instead of naming the movement, the GMAT says *a movement*. Instead of saying what the wrong interpretation is, they just call it a common interpretation. When you see answer choices phrased like this, you'll have to do a bit of mental juggling to line your prediction up with the convoluted descriptions in the answer choices.

Answer Choice Language	=	**Prediction**
to argue against…	=	some people were wrong to see…
…of a historical movement	=	…the Chartists…
…a common interpretation…	=	…as the first mass workers movement

This is similar to Structure Family Critical Reasoning questions, no?

If you're having difficulty choosing between two answer choices to a Main Point question like this, try lining the pieces up. The wrong choice might work with some of the pieces, but not all of them. For example, consider incorrect Answer Choice (A):

> **(A)** to critique the common fallacies of a field of study

Answer Choice Language	≠	**Prediction**
to critique…	=	some people were wrong to see…
…of a field of study	≠	…the Chartists… ← **Not a field!**
…the common fallacies…	≠	…as the first mass workers movement ← **kind of a stretch…**

The Vertical Scan

When you spot a set of answer choices phrased in this more abstract way, generally the first word of each answer choice will be a verb. Use this to your advantage!

Verbs are action words that carry with them a certain tone. Recall that one of the first things you ask yourself when trying to determine the author's overall goal is "What's the author's tone? Is it positive, negative, or neutral?" The Chartist author had a negative tone. Somebody was wrong. Thus, the only answer choices that are likely to be correct are those that start with a verb that can handle that negative tone.

Thus, when the answer choices start with a verb, you might not need to read every answer carefully. On your first pass, just scan your eyes vertically over the first few words of each.

1. The author's main agenda was
   (A) to critique...
   (B) to argue against...
   (C) to describe...
   (D) to support...
   (E) to chronicle...

Of all the answers, only Answer Choices (A) and (B) have a sufficiently negative charge. Answer Choice (D)'s "support" is way too positive, and (E)'s "chronicle" is way too neutral, too purely descriptive. The author of the Chartist passage had an agenda: disprove something that many people believe.

Of course, you should read the rest of the answer before committing to either Answer Choice (A) or (B). For one, you do have to pick one over the other. And the test maker can be sneaky sometimes. The words that follow the verb might change the tone. Answer Choice (C) might well continue on to say "to describe ... the way that critics are wrong about the Chartists' "—but it is best to check the answers that match the tone first.

If you don't find the answer, you've lost nothing; just read on. If you do find the answer, then you can get out of reading three whole answer choices!

About half of the **Main Point** questions on the GMAT will be phrased in this indirect, descriptive way. The remaining half will put the descriptive meat on this skeletal description. If the Chartist question had answers phrased this way, you would have seen something like:

1. Which of the following best states the author's main
   agenda?
   (B) To argue against classifying the Chartist movement as
       the first true workers' movement

You saw one of these questions in the third passage on your Diagnostic Quiz, question 9.

9. The main idea of the passage is that

   (C) technology to prolong the human lifespan indefinitely, while
       promising, must contend with certain nontechnological
       factors

These answers aren't quite so coy: they come out directly and include the specific content of the passage. Consequently, many test takers find this answer choice pattern easier to handle—but don't limit yourself! Indeed, you'll improve your Reading Comprehension performance a great deal if, during review, you consider how the correct answer would have been written if the answer choices were of the other type. Mental flexibility is a key GMAT Reading Comprehension skill. With a little work, you'll likely see no difference between

   (C) to suggest an additional set of considerations required
       before a prediction can be accepted

and

   (C) technology to prolong human lifespan indefinitely, while
       promising, must contend with certain nontechnological
       factors

Lining up the pieces, you can see that it's the same answer written two different ways:

Abstract	=	Concrete
...an additional set of considerations required...	=	...must contend with... certain nontechnological factors
...a prediction	=	technology to prolong human lifespan indefinitely...

Rarer Main Point Variations

Naturally, the test maker does have a few more tricks up the GMAT sleeve for **Main Point** questions. Consider these variations on a theme. The underlying principle is still the same. Take the author's agenda you predicted at the end of reading the passage and look for it in the answer choices.

By and large, you'll see ten **primary purpose** or **main idea** questions for every one of these three variations—although they do become more common as you answer questions correctly and breeze through the difficulty levels.

Passage Structure/Organization. These questions ask for answer choices that are one step more abstract. If our Chartists had one of these questions attached, the stem and correct answer would have instead looked like this:

> 1. Which of the following best describes the organization of the passage?
> (B) An interpretation of a historical event is presented, and evidence is introduced to argue against that interpretation in favor of another.

The notes you take while reading the passage the first time will be your biggest help with these questions. Write down the role of each major chunk of the passage as you go, and you'll find you breeze right through **Passage Structure** questions.

Author's Tone/Attitude. These questions tend to have one- to two-word answers and ask for a very general summation of the passage as a whole. Again, with the Chartists, we might have seen:

> 1. The author's attitude toward the view that Chartists should be considered the first true workers' movement can best be described as
> (B) opposition.

With Author's Tone or Author's Attitude questions, the positive/negative/neutral charge you predict as part of summing up the passage will be your guide. Pick the clearest, most defendable version of the charge you predicted.

By "most defendable," we mean than you should not pick an answer choice that is more nuanced than you can defend by pointing to something the author said explicitly. Suppose the Chartists passage had two-word answer choices instead. Which of these two would you pick?

> 1. The author's attitude toward the view that Chartists should be considered the first true workers' movement can best be described as
> (B) complete rejection.
> (C) reluctant rejection.

TIP

The stem to a tone question has to be long so that its answers can be so short.

Many test takers are tempted to select Answer Choice (C) because the extra layer of nuance sounds appealing, and for good reason. In school and on the job we're rarely rewarded for stripping away subtlety and generally applauded for recognizing it. But "reluctance" is a very specific emotion. For us to select Answer Choice (C), we'd need to be able to point to somewhere where the author said. "As much as I'd like to agree with this view…" or "It pains me to have to reject so popular an idea…." No pain, no hesitation, no reluctance!

Title the Passage. Of all the Main Point variations, this one is probably the rarest and the most dreaded because none of the titles offered in the answer choices would make the cut at a newspaper or a magazine. No editor in his or her right mind would clear something like this:

> (B) "The Chartists: A Movement of Workers? Yes. A Worker's Movement? No."

The whole story is right there in the title. Why read the article? Exactly. Remember, the test maker can't be clever or subtle in the traditional way. The right answer must be 100 percent defendable based solely on what's written in the text of the passage. So, once again, the correct answer to these questions proves to be rephrasing that predicted purpose you made when you finished reading the passage.

Wrong Answers to Main Point Questions

The tricks the test maker will try to pull on you with Reading Comprehension questions are largely similar to those found in Critical Reasoning questions. Your old friends the **exact opposite**, the **half-right/half-wrong**, **but for one word**, **irrelevant comparisons**, and the **reasonable but wrong** all will make an appearance here. As well, be on the lookout for

1. **PART NOT THE WHOLE**—The correct answer to a Main Point question must be able to cover the content of the entire passage; many wrong answers will correctly describe something the author actually said in the passage, but maybe just in one paragraph out of three, or in a few lines before taking a turn to the passage's real point.

2. **TOO EXTREME**—Many of the passages on the GMAT "seem to be going somewhere" but never get there. The wrong answer choices often will act as though they did. An author might criticize a policy but stop short of calling for its reversal. A passage might list many benefits of an activity but never recommend it be adopted. Remember also that the authorial voice of a Reading Comprehension passage is measured and cautious: things are rarely the most important cause, merely among the more important causes.

3. **RIGHT IDEA, WRONG PARTY**—Many GMAT passages involve multiple points of view. Be careful to keep track of which of these the author sides with (if any). Many wrong answers to Main Point questions correctly note something the passage said—only it was the position of the critics the author opposed, not that of the author.

FUNCTION

Function questions ask you why the author includes a particular fact or part of the passage. Why bring up the Duchess of York there in the second paragraph? Why call the critics "small-minded nitwits"? To answer Function questions, you must understand the passage's underlying logic and how the author develops the passage's main argument.

TIP

Do Function questions remind you of Bolded Statement questions from the Critical Reasoning section? They should!

In some way, then, Function questions involve "why?"—though they don't all use the word "why." For example:

- The author refers to the Declaration of Independence primarily **in order to**
- Which of the following best describes the **relationship of the third paragraph** to the rest of the passage?

There were a couple of **Function** questions scattered through your Diagnostic Quiz:

3. The author **mentions** the Tolpuddle Martyrs (line 17) primarily **in order to**
5. Which of the following best describes the **function** of the information presented in the second paragraph?

Before you head into the answer choices to a Function question, stop, refer to your notes, and, if necessary, reread the relevant portions of text. The key to the right answer is to keep the author's overall purpose in mind—so the final step of the Reading Comprehension method proves critical here as well as in **Main Point** questions. If you don't recall the author's overall agenda, it's impossible to say what part a certain bit of the passage plays in that agenda.

Beware the "Helpful" Highlighter

If the stem refers to a specific line or name from the passage, the computer will generally highlight the reference in yellow for the duration of the question. Be careful! The correct answer is generally not found in the highlighted text itself or in the few words on either side. Whenever you reread the passage in order to answer a Function question, be sure to read at least the sentence before and the sentence after.

Wrong Answers to Function Questions

Function questions share wrong answer traps with **Main Point** questions (**too extreme**, the **exact opposite**, etc.), but they also have one unique pitfall to avoid: the **what not why**.

> **what not why**—These answer choices merely restate a fact from the passage instead of explaining the fact's connection to the author's overall goal.

The test maker knows that many test takers will mistake a **Function** question for a **Recall** question, and rather than looking for the answer that explains *why* the author included a specific piece of information, they'll settle for a restatement of *what* the author said. Consider question 3 from your Diagnostic Quiz. It featured two **what not why** traps:

3. The author mentions the Tolpuddle Martyrs (line 17) primarily in order to
   (A) emphasize the extent to which the Chartists drew its membership from previous movements
   (B) argue that the Chartists were more reliant on prominent "gentlemen leaders" than previous data suggested.

Answer Choice (A) is essentially a restatement of the first part of the sentence in which the Martyrs appear, whereas Answer Choice (B) is a garbled version of the part that follows.

TIP

In pencil-and-paper exams and practice questions, instead of highlighting text, these questions instead make line references.

> ...in fact, it drew its membership from the remnants of several
> such movements, including the Friends of the People Society
> and the Tolpuddle Martyrs. Moreover, these multiple parties
> were drawn together not by a leader drawn from the working
> class itself, but rather by prominent "gentlemen leaders,"...

Neither answer choice explains *why* the author included the Martyrs; they only restate what the author said about them. For the why, we need to look back before those two continuation keywords (in fact and moreover), to find out what thought is being continued. And lo and behold:

> ...it would be an error to regard the Chartists as a new type
> of movement or as a mass workers movement *per se*. It was
> certainly not the first radical movement to demand a widening
> of the right to vote; in fact...

The Tolpuddle Martyrs are just examples used in service of the author's main point, that it would be wrong to call the Chartists "the first mass workers movement." Thus, the correct answer:

> (C) provide evidence that the Chartist movement was not so
> novel a phenomenon as many have maintained.

Global Questions Quick Review Quiz

DIRECTIONS: Try to complete the following two passage sets in **less than 13 minutes** total (3–4 minutes per passage, 45–75 seconds per question). NOTE: These passages do not have a full complement of question types; instead, they will either be **Main Point** or **Function** questions. (No **Detail** or **Inference** questions until the next quick review quiz!)

Questions 1–4 are based on the following passage.

Biologists have long recognized that deception is a fundamental part of communications between different species of animals. Communication within a species, however, has usually been thought to be reliable and honest and bluffing among
Line animals of a single species rare or even impossible. Yet research recently published
(5) in the *Journal of Theoretical Biology* suggests that deception between members of the species is not only possible, but evolutionarily beneficial.

The researchers studied confrontations between mantis shrimp, two-inch, crayfish-like crustaceans that compete with one another over control of small naturally occurring cavities in the warm waters in which they live. When confrontation looms,
(10) the two potential adversaries must decide whether to fight or flee. When choosing to fight, a shrimp will invoke a threat display, holding its limbs out to the side and lifting its head aggressively. If the opponent responds in kind, the two will scrabble, using their rock-hard limbs to strike each other. Though the shrimp are small in size, the force of their strikes is considerable: they regularly prey upon crabs and other much
(15) larger armored sea creatures by cracking open their shells to consume the soft flesh beneath.

If the shrimp were always honest when making threats, only the strongest shrimp engage in this aggressive display, those with the ability to back up their threat with deadly shell-cracking force. However, the researchers observed both strong and
(20) weak shrimp standing their ground and threatening other shrimp that came near to their chosen cavities. Indeed, the shrimp seemed to rely most on threats when they were at their weakest, immediately after molting, when their appendages are too soft to deliver the advertised blows. These threats were certainly not reliable; in fact, shrimp in such a state would be easily killed were a fight to occur. The researchers
(25) concluded that this bluffing behavior was similar to that found in a game of poker in which players are aware of the strength of their own hand but not that of their opponent's. A player with a weak hand may raise the stakes, hedging on the possibility that the opponent's hand is weak as well.

1. The primary purpose of the passage is

    (A) to describe the findings of a recent series of experiments.
    (B) to propose a new explanation for a biological phenomenon.
    (C) to present the conclusions of a research group.
    (D) to argue against a previous interpretation of experimental data.
    (E) to question the accuracy of a research team's analysis.

2. The author mentions the diet of mantis shrimps (lines 14–15) primarily in order to

    (A) highlight the diversity of the shrimp's food sources, which include prey much larger than it.
    (B) demonstrate the negative consequences that would follow from a weaker shrimp's failed bluff.
    (C) emphasize the power of the shrimp's strike as being disproportional to its size.
    (D) provide a biological motive for the evolution of the shrimp's deadly strength.
    (E) explain why intraspecific competition is necessary to individual shrimps' success.

3. Which of the following best states the main idea of the passage as a whole?

    (A) As the case of the mantis shrimp demonstrates, intraspecies deception may be evolutionarily beneficial.
    (B) A recent study has made unanticipated conclusions about the mantis shrimp (and, by extension, intraspecies competition).
    (C) The mantis shrimp is one of very few species that participates in intraspecies competition.
    (D) Intraspecies deception, in the case of the mantis shrimp, has evolutionary benefits.
    (E) The hunting strategies and territorial nature of the mantis shrimp necessitate its unusual intraspecies deception.

4. The primary purpose of the first paragraph is to

  (A) alert the reader to a long-held scientific misconception that has recently been disproven.

  (B) put forward a hypothesis that the remainder of the passage works to contradict.

  (C) explain to readers the biological significance of deception in mantis shrimp.

  (D) present a conclusion that the remainder of the passage is used to support.

  (E) resolve a discrepancy between a long-held scientific belief and the findings of a new study.

Questions 5–7 are based on the following passage.

Freud believed that jokes have only two purposes: aggression and exposure. The laughter brought by the joke, he maintained, can best be understood as marking the pleasurable release of built-up energy in the psyche. Repressed aggression is
Line released, according to this view, by the hostile joke, which, though not necessarily
(5) violent, springs from the repressed urge to overcome or dominate another. "By making our enemy small, inferior, or comic," Freud wrote, "we achieve in a roundabout way the enjoyment of overcoming him." Dirty jokes, on the other hand, allow the teller to gain pleasure from exposing or displaying that which society usually suppresses or forbids, a means of avoiding the censor and giving acceptable expression
(10) to otherwise inhibited emotions. In both cases, the joke performs its psychological function, in part, by allowing both the teller and the audience to, however fleetingly, cease expending the energy needed to keep these unlicensed emotions in check.

Freud's theories do not, however, work as well for humorous nonsense and absurd humor as they do for humorous aggression and sexuality. Consider the fol-
(15) lowing: A man at the dinner table dipped his hands in the mayonnaise and then ran them through his hair. When his neighbor looked astonished, the man apologized: "I'm so sorry. I thought it was spinach." If we laugh at this, it is surely not because of our forbidden sexual attraction to mayonnaise or because of a feeling of superiority over the foolish diner who would make such a mistake.

5. The primary concern of the passage's author is

  (A) summarizing the distinctions Freud made when linking jokes to their psychological origins.

  (B) presenting a theory and a valid objection to it.

  (C) pointing out a flaw that conclusively invalidates a theorist's original reasoning.

  (D) using an example to apply the author's reasoning to new situations.

  (E) describing a theory and a supporting example.

6. Which of the following best describes the role played in the passage by the mayonnaise anecdote (lines 15–17)?

(A) Scenario to which the theory presented in the first paragraph has been successfully extended

(B) Allegory that serves to relay an important interpersonal consideration

(C) Counterexample that problematizes the view presented in the first paragraph

(D) Hypothetical that showcases an extreme case to which the theory at hand could be applied

(E) Example that serves to validate a theory that has come under questioning

7. The first paragraph serves primarily to

(A) present a view that is conclusively refuted by evidence presented in the second paragraph.

(B) describe the distinctions a theorist made in classifying types of humor.

(C) explain the theory that is shown to be incomplete later in the passage.

(D) present a counterargument to the information relayed in the second paragraph.

(E) introduce the work that led to a controversial theory.

RECALL QUESTIONS

The remaining two types of GMAT questions are "little picture" tasks. Instead of focusing on the author's overall point, these questions just ask about something small that the author said explicitly at some point in the passage. The trick is finding that specific point and matching it up to the corresponding answer choice.

Detail Questions

Most **Recall** questions begin with the magic phrase "According to the passage/author...." You'll be able to distinguish a **Detail** question from its close cousin the **Inference** question by paying attention to the verb used in the part of the stem that comes after that "According to...." For example:

- The author **mentions** which one of the following as reasons why the experiment described in the first paragraph was unsuccessful?
- According to the passage, which of the following is true of the mating habits of the flying squirrel?
- The passage **states** that the humble bumblebee is

You saw several **Detail** questions during your Diagnostic Quiz, including:

2. The passage **lists** each of the following as characteristics of a workers' mass movement EXCEPT:

7. According to the passage, the "French paradox" **is defined as**

8. According to the passage, which of the following **is true** of lifespan-increasing technologies?

To use one of those fancy grammatical terms that we assured you in the Sentence Correction section you'd never need to know, **Detail** questions have verbs in the "indicative" mood. To put it more directly, these questions ask about what the passage *says/said, does/did, states/*

stated, *is/was true*—not what the passage suggests, *implies*, or what *might be true*. There's nothing hypothetical here.

The nice thing about Detail questions is that the correct answer to them is written somewhere in the passage. You can literally put one finger on the left-hand passage side of your monitor and one finger on the correct answer choice and you'll be pointing at the same fact with both.

Detail Question Word Games

Of course, the devious minds behind the GMAT don't want the right answer to be obvious, so they will almost never phrase it using the exact same language that appeared in the passage. Instead, they employ the ancient ninja art of … using a thesaurus.

To a certain extent, improving your performance on Detail questions becomes a matter of learning to spot a GMAT synonym, being able to see "factors that led to" in the answer and realize that in GMAT-speak that counts as the same thing as the "causes" mentioned in the passage.

Drill: Spot the Synonyms!

Each of the following synonym and faux synonym pairs are taken from actual GMAT questions. Can you spot which ones the GMAT considers the same thing and which aren't?

1. a consciousness receptive to his message
   an ideal constituency for someone with his message
2. participate in the traditional ethos of individual success
   fulfill ideals of personal attainment
3. affirm the importance of
   validate the significance of
4. promoting pay equity between X and Y
   encouraging equitable pay for X and Y
5. did not mention
   does not refer to
6. X for a given period can be deduced from Y
   the degree of X can be determined by analyzing Y
7. the more X, the more slowly Y
   the speed of Y varies with X
8. speed up the creation of a solution to the problem
   move rapidly to engender a plausible solution
9. synthesize isolated bits of data and practice into an integrated picture
   bring together disparate facts
10. comparing the probable effects of different solutions to a problem
    estimating the likelihood of success

Drill Analysis

Correct pairs: 1, 2, 3, 4, 5, 6, 7, 8, 9, 10
That's right. All of them.

All the pairs above are taken from credited answer choices and the passage they draw upon.

Take from this that the test maker is actually fairly liberal when it comes to paraphrasing passage content.

If you find yourself splitting hairs on the test, wondering if *being vulnerable to attack* is really the same thing as having been left unprotected, stop! Answer choices are usually made or broken by small words like every, only, always, never, no, and except. The nouns, adjectives, and verbs are fairly forgiving.

Beware of Directly Repeated Language

As a corollary to the GMAT-synonym smokescreen, when you see part of an answer choice that is close to word-for-word something said in the passage, be careful. The GMAT knows that "Yeah, I think I remember something about that…" or "That sounds right…" are powerful impulses, so they use direct quotations to lure you into picking the wrong answer.

This doesn't mean that the right answer *never* quotes the original passage directly. Think of this warning as a rule of thumb, not an ironclad guarantee. Still, if both passage and answer choice use the phrase "consequences of oligarchical privilege," that similarity is a sign to slow down and make doubly sure that the answer choice says what you think it says in the parts that aren't quoted directly.

Wrong Answer Choices in Detail Questions

Detail questions have their share of **too extreme**, the **exact opposite**, **half-right/half-wrong**, **irrelevant comparisons**, etc. that you've come to expect from most Reading Comprehension questions. But the main two sources of wrong answers fall into two categories, which we'll call the **misused detail** and the **distortion**.

MISUSED DETAIL—You can think of these answers as "the right answer, but to the wrong question." When you read an answer choice that corresponds directly to something you know the passage said, a little "Aha!" should go off in your head. But remember, the task of a **Detail** question isn't just to select a true answer from the five given—the answer has to be relevant to the question being asked, too!

DISTORTION—These answer choices take something from the passage and tweak it so that it's not quite what the passage said. Still, the answer choice will contain language familiar to you and talk about concepts and facts presented in the passage. It may even twist the answer choice so that it corresponds more directly to something that you know to be true from your **real-world experience** but which the author never explicitly said.

Finally, there's one sort of answer choice trap that is closely related to these two and common enough in Detail questions to warrant its own fancy name, the **wrong party** trap.

WRONG PARTY—Many GMAT Reading Comprehension passages contain multiple sources of information. There might be two to three theories discussed, or explanations given, or competing groups described. Whenever a passage features multiple parties, expect that many of the wrong answers to **Detail** questions will attribute a correct, directly stated fact to the wrong party.

INFERENCE

The second type of **Recall** question and the final GMAT Reading Comprehension question type will seem familiar if you've already read the Critical Reasoning chapter: **Inference** questions. Just like their Critical Reasoning brethren, Reading Comprehension **Inference** questions ask you to select an answer choice that is directly deducible from information given in the passage but never said explicitly.

Inference questions are thus similar to **Detail** questions in that they both require you to stick religiously to the actual text of the passage; inference just asks you to go that one extra step further, to take two facts and add them together or to turn a double negative into a positive.

Both **Inference** and **Detail** questions tend to use the phrase "According to the passage/the author"; however, rather than speaking in the *is/was/says/did* voice of **Detail** questions, **Inference** questions deal in *likelihoods* and *possibilities*, things that the *author would most likely agree with*, things that are *inferred*, *suggested*, or *implied*. For example:

- The passage provides support for which of the following statements?
- Which of the following can be inferred from the passage about the study participants?
- The passage implies that which of the following steps must first be taken in order to achieve Olympic-level competitiveness?

Inference questions make up the majority of Reading Comprehension questions, so you saw several on your Diagnostic Quiz, including:

6. According to the passage, which of the following is most likely true of the French health care system?

11. The author most likely believes that which of the following will be true of treatments to extend lifespan in the next century?

14. According to the standards given in the third paragraph, which of the following types of online behavior would most likely not be protected by labor law?

Learning to Spot Inferences-in-Waiting

The secret to getting **Inference** questions right is to see them coming as you read the passage. Not every inference can be predicted ahead of time, but the more experience you have with the GMAT test makers, the more you'll begin to see the ways that they lay the groundwork for Inference questions in the text of the passage.

Hit 'Em Where They Ain't—The Shadow Subject Your Critical Reasoning practice will be invaluable to you here. The Critical Reasoning Inference Patterns appear in Reading Comprehension as well (though inferences based on Formal Logic and other absolute statements tend to be much rarer).

If you see a **double negative** in the passage (it is not impossible that…), or a **requirement** (as a preliminary step, one must…) or some fancy **placeholder words** (such theories, the latter subject, etc.) jot its location down in your notes for future reference.

One trick the test maker likes to play over and over again is to ask you to make an inference about a group, time period, or concept that the passage has, until that question, had relatively little to say about. This "shadow subject" is mentioned in passing if at all, with the majority of the passage's time spent talking about a different group.

If the passage as a whole centers on vertebrates, you may well see an Inference question about *invertebrates*. If most of the passage concerns married men, you may be asked to draw an inference about *bachelors* or *widowers*. If the subject was *post-World War I Impressionist painters*, the correct inference might involve *pre-World War I painters* or *painters post-World War I* that *weren't Impressionists*.

To prepare yourself for these sneaky "shadow" **Inference** questions, get in the habit of looking for starts and stops, causes and effects, limitations and changes.

See: "Female dinosaurs were chosen for the experiment because of their relative docility."

Think: "Oh, so male dinosaurs must not have been as docile as the females."

See: "While ETS administered its first standardized test in 1901, the SAT was first given in 1926."

Think: "There must have been at least one standardized test by ETS that wasn't the SAT."

See: "*The Doors* were the first band to top the R&B charts without a drummer."

Think: "*The Association* (#1 the week before "Light My Fire") must have had a drummer."

See: "As a result of overharvesting, the diversity of fish stocks has declined sharply since 1900."

Think: "Before 1900, fish stocks were much more diverse."

Variations on the Inference Question

Though Inference questions can be phrased in a variety of ways, the phrasing is, for the most part, simply ornamental. It still boils down to looking for something that is 100 percent supported by a specific piece of text in the passage.

There is one case, however, that deserves special attention, the **Application** question. With these Inference questions, the test maker asks you to apply your understanding of the passage to make an evaluation of a new situation. For example, recall this oddball question from your Diagnostic Quiz:

14. According to the standards given in the third paragraph, which of the following types of online behavior would most likely not be protected by labor law?

What distinguishes this question from the "vanilla" **Inference** question is the answer choices. Each will contain a situation that is completely new, not found in the text of the passage anywhere. Your job is to take your understanding of the passage and apply it to these new situations.

In effect, the passage gives you a rule. Applying that rule to something new counts as an inference in the test maker's book. Thus, the correct answer choice will line up exactly with the rule as stated. On question 14, the relevant rules were found in the passage's final paragraph. There, you learned that if a worker's actions didn't meet the standard for "concerted" effort (if the audience was so limited that it was unlikely to include any coworkers), then it might not be protected.

Thus, Answer Choice (D) was correct, even though it brought up the activity of fishermen in Nova Scotia, a group that you might have felt were completely out of left field. Whether you've heard of the group or idea in the answer choice is beside the point on an *Application Inference* question.

Indeed, be wary of answer choices that mention, as Answer Choice (A) did, groups that do appear in the passage. These we refer to as **same subject traps**—laid for students who don't understand the boundaries of the question and think that any new concept automatically disqualifies an answer choice.

Wrong Answers in Inference Questions

There's really not much difference between the typical wrong answers to a Reading Comprehension Inference question and those from the Critical Reasoning section. The key thing to keep in mind when sorting through answer choices is the GMAT's definition of an inference, something that 100 percent must be true, if the passage is taken as true.

Anything that's merely **reasonable**, **possible**, or **interesting** won't do—and boy, does the test maker provide you with ample answer choice selections that are just that, but not **definite** or **necessary**.

Other Critical Reasoning Questions in Reading Comprehension

There is one final type of question that appears in Reading Comprehension that isn't really a new question type at all: the Critical Reasoning question. Any of the question types that appear in the Critical Reasoning section can appear in Reading Comprehension section, although, in general, you'll only see Weaken, Strengthen, and Evaluate questions, with the occasional Assumption question tossed in for good measure. You saw only one of these on your Diagnostic Quiz:

> 10. Which of the following, if true, would indicate the most serious flaw with the reasoning behind the predictions made by those "forward-looking thinkers" discussed in the passage's second paragraph?

In general, Critical Reasoning questions that make their way over to Reading Comprehension use the same language as you'd expect. (Weaken questions will ask you to weaken or undermine a question, etc.)

The only real difference between Critical Reasoning and Reading Comprehension questions of this type is that there's more text to sort through in Reading Comprehension. Critical Reasoning prompts are nicely contained. You're asked about the argument given in the prompt. In Reading Comprehension questions, you're given a reference ("the argument made by the panelist described in line 27," for instance), but it's up to you to, in a sense, find the Critical Reasoning prompt hidden in the Reading Comprehension passage, to decide where the argument begins and ends.

Otherwise, you can treat these exactly the same as you would if you encountered them attached to a short Critical Reasoning prompt.

Recall Questions Review Quiz

DIRECTIONS: Try to complete the following two passage sets in **less than 13 minutes** total. NOTE: These passages do not have a full complement of question types; instead, they will either be **Inference** or **Detail** questions. (There are no Global questions here—neither **Function** nor **Main Point**.)

Questions 1–4 are based on the following passage.

With a price tag nearing $350 billion (more than $600 million per plane), the F-35 Joint Strike Fighter program exemplifies both the technological lead and military supremacy of the United States military. But this family of radar-deflecting stealth
Line aircraft also demonstrates the pitfalls of a procurement system designed to be
(5) "platform-centric," the result of military focused on building complex, increasingly costly ships, tanks, and planes with built-in systems intended to combat specific threats. "Luxury-car" platforms such as the F-35 are the legacy of the last days of the Cold War, and few have been able to adapt to present-day military objectives, their sophisticated weaponry meant to combat sophisticated foes who, by and large,
(10) have never materialized. Instead, the military's typical missions since the turn of the millennium have been decidedly less glamorous—small-scale antipiracy raids, coastal patrols, and support operations for counterinsurgency and counterterrorist campaigns—operations that demand greater flexibility than sophistication.

The modern military requires "payload-centric" vehicles: highly adaptable plat-
(15) forms with the power and space to carry weapons and sensors that can be swapped on the fly depending on the dictates of the mission. Because of its sheer size, massive onboard electrical generators, and relatively small array of integral systems, the most adaptable ship in the U.S. fleet remains the 50-year-old *USS Enterprise*. Unlike modern, densely packed designs, this veteran carrier has both the storage and power-
(20) generating capacity to carry aircraft and munitions that were not even dreamt of when it was first put into service. The same is true of the B-52 bomber, which first took flight shortly after World War II. Though conceived of as a strategic bomber to combat Soviet missile technology, the B-52 has been recast many times and today stands as the most cost-effective, dependable platform for precision GPS-guided
(25) bombs. Given the investment required in building a new platform, from drafting table to production line, the wise military will seek to implement more "trucks": long-lasting, easily maintained, and built for capacity over sophistication.

1. Which of the following would be an example of a "platform-centric" weapon, as defined by the passage?

   (A) An older, very adaptable ship, like the *USS Enterprise*
   (B) A spacious, highly dependable plane, like the B-52
   (C) A sophisticated, expensive aircraft, like the F-35
   (D) A simple, easily maintained vehicle, like the military trucks
   (E) A densely packed, highly adaptable plane like those that the United States seeks to implement in the future

2. Which of the following can most justifiably be inferred from the passage?

   (A) The U.S. military intends to build a line of terrestrial trucks that will prioritize durability over sophistication.
   (B) Modernity often sacrifices reliability, as in the case of the *USS Enterprise.*
   (C) The B-52 never fulfilled its original purpose as a counter to Soviet missile technology.
   (D) The *USS Enterprise* is not densely packed.
   (E) Counterinsurgency campaigns would benefit from platform-centric vehicles.

3. Each of the following is a role at least some "payload-centric" vehicles are suited to EXCEPT:

   (A) Radar-deflecting stealth
   (B) Carrying sufficient weapons to "improvise" during missions
   (C) Fulfilling the military objectives of the modern world
   (D) Precision GPS-guided bombing
   (E) Carrying munitions via the waters

4. Which of the following can be said to be true of the B-52?

   (A) It is payload-centric.
   (B) It is platform-centric.
   (C) It was utilized solely to defend the United States against the Soviets.
   (D) It is not highly adaptable but remains sophisticated to this day.
   (E) Though dependable, it is more expensive than most platform-centric weapons.

Questions 5–7 are based on the following passage.

Eminent domain refers to the government's power to take private property for public use, either for the government's direct use, by delegation to third parties who will devote it to similar purpose, or, in some rare cases, simply for economic devel-
Line opment. Most commonly, eminent domain is the means by which the state seizes
(5) land used to build government buildings and other facilities, as well as utilities, highways, and railroads. It may even be used in order to take control of property for reasons of public safety, as in the case of Centralia, Pennsylvania, where residents' property was condemned and the former owners relocated in the wake of an underground mine fire that began burning beneath the city and could not be extinguished.

(10)   Following the 2007 financial crisis, many cities around the United States considered using eminent domain in a novel manner, to take control of troubled mortgages in their city. Since eminent domain generally requires some public purpose for the taking of an asset, municipal governments have argued that property tax revenues can be boosted by preventing mass foreclosure sales. Studies conducted by the
(15) National Association of Realtors show a strong correlation between increases in foreclosure sales and lower housing values in nearby neighborhoods. It was ironic, then, that the most vocal opponents to the cities' proposals were local realtors and real estate agents. These groups argued that when weighed against the chilling effects the plans would have on mortgage lending more broadly, the benefit to troubled mort-
(20) gage holders would be dwarfed by the negative impact on those who subsequently did obtain new mortgages. In the face of a government willing to take direct action that would threaten their bottom line, lenders would have no choice but to raise mortgage rates for everyone in the area on subsequent loans.

5. According to the passage, which of the following is necessary for a government seizure of property to fall under "eminent domain"?
   (A) Sufficiently low mortgage rates in a given area
   (B) A risk of danger to individuals currently holding the property in question
   (C) The consent of city realtors and other real estate agents
   (D) A public purpose for seizure of that property
   (E) The need for utilities, highways, and railroads in a specific area

6. According to the definition presented in the passage, which of the following would NOT be considered a use of a government's power of eminent domain?

   (A) Governmental allocation of existing public property to a new purpose
   (B) Seizure of private property from residents who are in the midst of a natural catastrophe
   (C) Use of previously private property to create much-needed public roads
   (D) Governmental allocation of private property to an approved organization with a public service purpose
   (E) Distribution of private property to agents capable of using it to promote a country's economic health

7. What sort of city would be LEAST likely to be affected by the negative consequences cited by the opposition to the plan discussed in the passage?

   (A) A city with very few incoming citizens wishing to hold new mortgages
   (B) A town primarily composed of novel mortgage holders
   (C) A city in which many citizens intend to continue financing their housing through regular mortgage payments
   (D) A city with as many emigrants as new, incoming mortgage holders
   (E) A town in which a portion of mortgage holders port their mortgages

Now What?

Once you're done with the lessons in this book, the practice sets, and the practice tests, what else can you do to increase your GMAT Reading Comprehension performance?

A Sample Study Plan

Studying Reading Comprehension is similar to studying Critical Reasoning, so follow the same basic three-phase study plan discussed in the Critical Reasoning chapter. The main difference is that the time you allow yourself to complete practice Reading Comprehension sets will vary based on the number of questions. As a rule of thumb, try for 3–4 minutes to read and map the passage and 45–75 seconds for each question.

When reading the Answers and Explanations, even those prepared by GMAC, remember to take the passage summaries and sample sets of notes with a grain of salt. Your notes only have to be useful to you. They don't have to replicate these best-case-scenario notes written by people who have had hours of hindsight to help.

Use the Official GMAT Guide and the Official Verbal Guide

Unfortunately, you can't easily target a specific question type (Main Point, Inference, etc.) by using the official practice materials because every Reading Comprehension passage set will include questions of at least three different types. You can, however, target passages that lean heavily toward the type of question you're aiming to improve.

Add a Few High-Brow Magazine Subscriptions to Your Reading Diet

Four out of five GMAT prep coaches agree, the single best non-GMAT source of GMAT-sounding reading material is *The Economist* magazine. It's got that special blend of ten-dollar words and qualified, measured, scholarly prose. The more science-y and economics-heavy *The New York Times Sunday Magazine* pieces also come close to replicating the GMAT-author experience. For online reading material that best exemplifies that signature GMAT style, consider:

- *The Scientific American*—*http://www.scientificamerican.com/* (great for hard science practice)
- "Investigations" at *The University of Chicago Magazine*—*http://magazine.uchicago. edu/0910/investigations/* (in particular, the pre-2010 articles)
- The "Research" articles at *The Harvard Magazine*—*http://harvardmagazine.com/topic/ research/*

And for a crash course in topics that are likely to show up in future GMAT Reading Comprehension pieces, check out *Freakanomics* (available in book, audiobook, radio, podcast, and blog forms). The blog (*http://www.freakanomics.com/*) can be a little chatty (i.e., written in not very GMAT-like prose), but the topics covered by the two *Freakanomics* authors Steven Levitt and Stephen J. Dubner are exactly the sorts of things that the people who write test questions love. See also: Malcom Gladwell's books (*Blink, The Tipping Point, Outliers*).

In a Pinch, Practice with LSAT Materials

Just as with Critical Reasoning materials, LSAT prep materials can be used for extra Reading Comprehension work. There's just a couple of differences to be mindful of:

- LSAT Reading Comprehension passages come out in sets of four with each test, with one law passage, one social science, one natural science, and one humanities. Even though the humanities passage will be good practice with the Reading Comprehension concepts, the content isn't likely to show up on the GMAT. Pure business passages are pretty rare on the LSAT (as you might expect).
- The LSAT passages are generally longer than those on the GMAT, and there's no good LSAT analogue for the shortest (150–250 words) GMAT passages. The LSAT does have two short passages per test, but they always appear in sets of two on the same topic. This sort of comparative reading doesn't happen on the GMAT.
- LSAT Reading Comprehension is in general much more complicated. Some LSAT preppers start out with GMAT questions as "training wheels."
- The LSAT is a pencil-and-paper test, so you'll be tempted to take notes directly onto your passage. Don't! Always use some sort of practice noteboard (or a separate piece of paper at the very least).

Otherwise, the ground rules for each test's Reading Comprehension sections are the same—just as with Logical Reasoning/Critical Reasoning.

Reading Comprehension Practice Set

Questions 1–3 are based on the following passage.

Josephus, the first-century Romano-Jewish historian notes that when the Romans destroyed Jerusalem in 70 C.E., there were so many slaves on the market that they could not be sold, even at fire-sale prices. But why not buy a slave at no cost? There
(Line) was certainly no ethical compunction involved; slavery was then and would remain a
(5) long-standing and popular facet of Roman life. The law of supply and demand would suggest that even as the available stock of human chattel rose, the market would find the appropriate lower (but still positive) price point. The answer, presumably, is that potential buyers owned so many slaves already that any addition to their workforce would be so marginal as to fall short of the cost of the slave's upkeep. In other words,
(10) the variable cost of maintaining the slave would have exceeded his or her output. Josephus notes in the same chapter that nearly eleven thousand men and women died from want of food, and that even the lowest forms of wheat (barley and rye, likely) used to feed the poor and servile classes were in short supply. The true price of slave ownership had, in effect, become negative and would remain there until new
(15) fields could be cleared for tillage and mills constructed to be worked. The large, sudden influx of available workers could not be matched in the near term by the meager rate of expansion of agriculture and industry.

1. What of the following best describes the main point of the passage?

   (A) To argue against slavery, given the conditions imposed upon its victims

   (B) To examine the reason for the unusually low price at which slaves were sold

   (C) To review Josephus' analysis of the slave trade in Jerusalem in 70 C.E.

   (D) To explore the applications of economics to a common problem in ancient morality

   (E) To examine the reasons for which slaves were introduced to Jerusalem

2. According to the passage, what is a reason for the low prices at which slaves were sold?

   (A) Otherwise usual food was scarce.

   (B) Ancient Romans were averse to the idea of owning slaves.

   (C) Not even the poor and servile classes could be fed.

   (D) Jerusalem's citizens were viewed as unworthy of being sold at higher prices.

   (E) Most slaves were of a working quality insufficient to merit higher sale prices.

3. The author mentions that "there was certainly no ethical compunction involved" (lines 3–4) primarily in order to

   (A) lend a historical background to the discussion at hand.

   (B) tug at the reader's ethical heartstrings.

   (C) eliminate an alternative, reasonable explanation for a phenomenon.

   (D) criticize the Romans for the cruelty inherent to their slave trade.

   (E) introduce a claim that the second paragraph will support.

Questions 4–7 are based on the following passage.

For the past ten years, the world has been experiencing a commodity price boom. From coffee to coal and platinum to pork, the general rule has been that if you took the trouble to mine it from the ground or grow it on a farm, you would likely make
Line money selling it, with one glaring exception: lobster. In 2005, Maine lobster sold for
(5) just under six dollars a pound wholesale, yet by 2013 lobster off the boat was selling for as little as two dollars a pound, less than the price of ground chuck in the supermarket. Huge lobster harvests, believed by many to be a consequence of global climate change, have glutted the market, flooding supermarkets with so much lobster that many Maine lobstermen must wonder how they can possibly remain afloat.
(10) Paradoxically, even as the wholesale price of lobster has collapsed, the price for lobster tails in high-end restaurants has remained stable and, in many cases, increased over the same span of time. Even the less glamorous lobster roll sold at roadside stands throughout the Northeast has resisted the downward pricing trend. While restaurateurs are generally slow to reduce prices even as the cost of ingre-
(15) dients falls, such a substantial and extended decline in commodity prices almost invariably results in lower priced dishes. One possible explanation is that over the past fifty years, lobster has become more a luxury good than a commodity. During previous decades in which overharvesting depleted lobster supplies, it came to be associated chiefly with the wealthy, the only ones who could continue to afford it.

(20)   Moreover, restaurants rightly worry about the message that price cuts send. Studies from as far back as the 1940s strongly suggest that people wrongly assume a correlation between a product's price and quality, particularly when they cannot objectively evaluate the product before they buy it. Since few consumers follow the commodity market closely enough to know what's been happening to the wholesale

(25)   price of lobster, cheaper lobster tails could convince customers that your lobster is inferior to that at the expensive white tablecloth establishment down the street.

4. The primary purpose of the passage is

   (A)   to discuss the state of the lobster industry and the consequences for those involved.
   (B)   to compare the commercial success of lobster and pork in the last decade.
   (C)   to examine the consequences of the collapsing wholesale price of lobster for restaurateurs.
   (D)   to argue against over-harvesting and other scarce marine life in Maine.
   (E)   to argue that prices have declined not solely in Maine but throughout the Northeast.

5. The author mentions "ground chuck" primarily in order to

   (A)   mention another good that has steadily been declining in price.
   (B)   emphasize just how low the price of lobster is, given its value.
   (C)   provide readers with another way of approximating the price of lobster.
   (D)   showcase that lobster prices remain elevated in comparison to the prices of some other goods.
   (E)   contrast lobster with a good whose price has steadily been climbing.

6. According to the passage, what sort of product might retain its price even when wholesale prices are declining?

   (A)   Products that proceed through a middleman business (e.g., a distributor of fish who sells lobsters to restaurants)
   (B)   Goods that were previously regarded as luxurious
   (C)   An everyday necessity consumed by a large quantity of people (e.g., coffee)
   (D)   Food crafted and sold at high-end establishments
   (E)   Lobster caught and sold in small, independent markets

7. According to the passage, what can be inferred about "luxury goods" (line 17)?

   (A)   Lobster is not the only luxury good whose price may have rapidly fallen in one scenario while remaining relatively elevated in another.
   (B)   They include all of the previously described goods: pork, coffee, and lobster, specifically.
   (C)   They experience declines in price according to the regions in which they are sold.
   (D)   There is an inconsistent demand for them even among those who can afford them.
   (E)   Their prices are inflated for no foreseeable reason.

ANSWER KEYS

DIAGNOSTIC QUIZ

1. **(B)**	5. **(D)**	9. **(D)**	13. **(D)**
2. **(C)**	6. **(C)**	10. **(E)**	14. **(D)**
3. **(C)**	7. **(D)**	11. **(C)**	
4. **(E)**	8. **(A)**	12. **(E)**	

GLOBAL QUESTIONS QUICK REVIEW QUIZ

1. **(C)**	3. **(A)**	5. **(B)**	7. **(C)**
2. **(B)**	4. **(D)**	6. **(C)**	

RECALL QUESTIONS QUICK REVIEW QUIZ

1. **(C)**	3. **(A)**	5. **(D)**	7. **(A)**
2. **(D)**	4. **(A)**	6. **(A)**	

READING COMPREHENSION TARGETED REVIEW

1. **(B)**	3. **(C)**	5. **(B)**	7. **(A)**
2. **(A)**	4. **(A)**	6. **(D)**	

DIAGNOSTIC QUIZ

1. The *author's main agenda* signals a **Main Point** question. The correct answer must line up with the content of the passage as a whole. Here, the correct answer (B) fits the passage best, the *common interpretation* being the belief the author opposes, that the Chartists (the *historical movement*) are properly called a *mass workers movement*.

(B) A **vertical scan** of verbs can eliminate Answer Choices (C), (D), and (E), as they lack the negative thrust of the author's agenda. Answer Choice (A) can be eliminated because the author does not critique an entire *field of study* (like *history* or *sociology*) but rather just a single topic within a broad field.

2. As a **Detail EXCEPT** question, four of these answers will correspond directly to information in the passage, while only one "odd man out" won't be supported—or, as in the case of Answer Choice (A), outright **contradicted** by the passage. According to information found in the middle of the second paragraph, one thing that disqualifies the Chartists from being considered a workers' mass movement is that its leadership was drawn from the aristocracy.

(C) Answer Choice (A) corresponds to information in the middle of the second paragraph, Answer Choices (B) and (D) are found at the beginning of the same paragraph, and Answer Choice (E) comes from the last sentence.

3. The use of "in order to" signals a **Function** question. As such, the correct answer must be an explanation of how the author utilizes the Tolpuddle Martyrs to advance some point within the passage. In this case, mention of the Tolpuddle Martyrs follows the author's claim that the Chartists were "certainly not the first radical movement to demand a right to vote" as an example of a preceding, similar movement; this corresponds directly to Answer Choice (C).

(C) Answer Choice (A) is an overstatement that does not align with the main goal of the text; Answer Choice (B) is mentioned in a different place within the passage; there is no concrete mention of the kind of data and research that Answer Choice (D) suggests in the passage. Answer Choice (E) is also not to the point—we were not ever discussing whether these movements are common: we are trying to chronologically order the Chartists.

4. "Overall" suggests that a **Global** question is presenting itself; we are then asked for the "organization of the passage," which makes this question of the **Passage Structure/ Organization** type. Looking at our first paragraph, we see that it explains a surprising finding in the medical world—that saturated fat intake doesn't coincide with incidence of heart disease. This is our introduction to a "medical phenomenon." We are then given statistics concerning the relationship between CHD and dietary saturated fat in France and the U.S., and are presented with a potential explanation for the French paradox— our first "explanation for that phenomenon" is presented. Another explanation is then presented in the last paragraph. This all aligns perfectly with Answer Choice (E).

(E) Answer Choice (A) speaks of a "medical procedure"; the passage does not mention one; Answer Choice (B) suggests that there is some consequence of the phenomenon we're exploring, but nothing in the passage mentioned any consequences of the discrepancy between CHD and dietary saturated fat. Answer Choice (C) suggests that some conclusion has been made, but we are told only that "the last decade *appears*" to bear out a theory. Finally, no data is given to reconcile the two explanations in the passage— our discussion of the second one ends the passage, so Answer Choice (D) is incorrect.

5. We are asked *why* the author mentions death rate statistics, making this a Function question. It is clear from question 4 that the function of the second paragraph—within which these statistics appear—is to generally *explain* the French paradox, which is a set of "counterintuitive health findings." So, we align nicely with Answer Choice (D).

(D) Statistics speak only to death rates from CHD, not risk factors, so Answer Choice (A) is wrong; Answer Choice (B) suggests that death rate statistics could be used to explain the role of a compound, which is obviously false. Death rate statistics are, presumably, related to CHD and possibly dietary saturated fat; nowhere is there mention of health care practices, which makes Answer Choice (C) incorrect. Finally, the death rate statistics are given to illustrate the French paradox, not dispose of it, so they wouldn't be suggesting that it is a "misrepresentation"—this strikes out Answer Choice (E).

6. "Most likely" tells us that this isn't a **Detail** question—we can't quite be sure of what the passage is telling us, but we can find the *most likely* truth via an **Inference**. We are told in the third sentence of the third paragraph that differences in the observed rates of CHD may be due to "undercertification caused by differences in the way that French authorities collect health statistics"—that's directly Answer Choice (C).

(C) Answer Choices (A), (B), and (D) are not at all mentioned; whereas Answer Choice (E) may be derived from Answer Choice (C), it is an overstatement.

7. We are asked what's true "according to the passage"; this signals a **Detail** question. Returning to the passage, we see that Answer Choice (D) is the best explanation for what's going on—relatively low CHD, relatively high saturated fat intake (this is directly stated in lines 5–8 of the first paragraph).

(D) Answer Choice (A) may contribute to what appears to be a paradox, but the paradox itself is the unexpectedly low CHD given high saturated fat, not the tendency of French officials. Answer Choice (B) can be eliminated relatively quickly, as we know from a general reading of the passage that the paradox at least in some way concerns CHD and saturated fat. Answer Choice (C) suggests an inverse relationship—one in which levels of heart disease decrease as saturated fat intake increases; this is a drastic overstatement and was never suggested. Answer Choice (E) again refers to resveratrol; no drug-related paradox exists in the passage.

8. We are again told to provide a **Detail** straight from the passage; we are directly told that Answer Choice (A) is true in lines 2–3 and 9–10 of the first paragraph—first, "change was driven by the spread of things today often taken for granted," but that "reached the point of diminishing returns" (line 5); now, "the past decade has seen these later developments likewise begin to lose their efficacy."

(A) Answer Choice (B) does not work well with the end of the passage, which seems to refer to potential consequences for ever-increasing lifespans. Answer Choice (C) goes against the part of the passage that tells us that all previous technology is somewhat outdated, but that we're hoping for new advances. Answer Choice (D) directly violates the author's statement that "the future is certainly impossible to predict," and Answer Choice (E) contradicts the passage's assertion that "even counting the least developed countries," we see significant improvement.

9. We're asked for what "best states the main idea," so this is evidently a **Main Point** question. Recall that the main idea is that which should appear throughout the passage, not just in small instances. We are told in the first paragraph that lifespans are getting longer; the second one tells us they may get even longer. However, somewhere within the second paragraph, we are also told that "men and women ... might live indefinitely" *barring* random accident or deliberate homicide—this coincides very well with the "other factors" that limit "indefinite increases." Answer Choice (D), therefore, is our answer.

(D) Answer Choice (E) does not function with the last part of the passage, which does, in fact, seek to predict the effect that lifespan enhancements will have on human society. Answer Choice (C) is unlikely again in the face of the last two paragraphs, given that the author explores the idea of a future with longer lifespans. Answer Choice (B) is not stated anywhere in the passage—there is no distinction between philosophy and reality made anywhere inside it, either. Finally, although Answer Choice (A) may be true and advocated by some components of the passage (e.g., the author's allusions to Alzheimer's), it is only mentioned to question the role of lifespan-extending technologies in society; the purpose of the whole passage is, rather, to explore whether or not they are possible.

10. A weakening question means that we're temporarily reverting to Critical Reasoning. Remember that you should find the claim of the subject in question, and then try your best to flip it right around. The "forward-looking thinkers" in the passage are so optimistic as to think that there will eventually be no natural limit, barring incidents, to the length of a human life. How do we flip this? Provide evidence that it will be *more* difficult to continue extending lifespans in the future than it already was—this invalidates the forward-looking thinkers' arguments, which are based on past technological advancements. We can best do this with Answer Choice (E).

(E) Answer Choices (A) and (B) argue that chance will always kill; this doesn't invalidate the forward-looking thinkers' arguments, as they are referring to no natural limit on the length of a human life. Answer Choice (C), again, does not generate a problem for these arguments, as this increased rate of technological advancement may well be the reason for their claims. Answer Choice (D) doesn't quite make sense—if these diseases were "previously rare," they are now common, so they are the diseases that currently plague the elderly.

11. "Most likely" hints that we have an **Inference** question. Given passage information, what might the author think? He has already noted in his last paragraph that Alzheimer's—incredibly evident now—was not so common fifty years ago merely because people did not live long enough to see it affect them: this resonates well with Answer Choice (C); "some" is a nice, moderate term that coincides well with the author's uncertainty about the future.

(C) The author explicitly notes that we cannot accurately predict the future, so he is unlikely to make such decisive claims as "they will be unable to extend lifespan indefinitely" in Answer Choice (E). Though the author mentions in the last paragraph that technology will be expensive, he does not claim that this will necessarily restrict usage to a small group of people—it will merely widen the gap between rich and poor, so Answer Choice (D) is an overstatement. Answer Choice (B) is entirely unknown, as we haven't discussed distinctions in the types of technologies to be used; no concrete information is given to suggest Answer Choice (A).

12. We are told right away that we should find the "primary purpose" of the passage, so this is a **Main Point**. The passage starts by relaying a past state, and then discussing a new, proposed one. That coincides best with Answer Choice (C).

(C) Answer Choice (A) goes directly against the point of Paragraph Two, which stresses decreased regulations. Answer Choice (B) is too forceful—the author is merely presenting the ways in which "labor regulators have begun pushing back"—he is not necessarily advocating this. The passage ends without a conclusion or reconciliation—we're just comparing two different views, so Answer Choice (D) fails; Answer Choice (E) does not describe any sort of factors but rather speaks to how another group entirely (the laborers) is handling the regulations imposed by those in Paragraph One.

13. We are again asked to search "according to the passage"—this means that we should be looking for a fragment that's directly stated. Answer Choice (D) is directly paraphrased in the second and third lines of our second paragraph.

(D) Answer Choice (E) is coming from the employers, not the employees, and would thus most probably not be a basis for an employee-centric ruling. Answer Choice (C) does not make any sense—the ruling is carried out purely so that future, similar rulings may be carried out? Answer Choice (B) overstates—the workers' ruling is not made in defense of *necessarily* disrespectful or offensive comments, but of any and all commentary on one's working environment. Answer Choice (A) mixes up the policies that the National Labor Relations Board reviews with the idea that it follows a specifically stated mandate.

14. "Most likely" again signals an **Inference**. We're speaking, in this paragraph, of employee-employer relationships; that necessitates that both an employer and an employee exist. A fisherman certainly has a job but is not employed by the weather; if he complains about it, he is not in any way commenting on his workplace. This makes Answer Choice (D) an easy answer.

(D) Answer Choices (A), (B), (C), and (E) all involve employers, and are thus more likely than Answer Choice (D) to be protected by labor law.

GLOBAL QUESTIONS QUICK REVIEW QUIZ

1. "Primary purpose" signals a **Main Point** question. At the beginning of this passage, we are told that a specific piece of research recently published in the *Journal of Theoretical Biology* is responsible for a certain development in biology; in the second paragraph, we are introduced to the confrontations that researchers studied; in the final paragraph, we are told what researchers observed. Cumulatively, then, it would seem that our purpose is Answer Choice (C)—to present the conclusions of a research group.

(C) Answer Choice (A) suggests more than one experiment; we don't know how many were conducted. Answer Choice (B) is far too dramatic a statement—a single study cannot independently be grounds for revising biological truth. Furthermore, this isn't just a *new explanation* for a biological phenomenon: this is a new biological phenomenon altogether. There are no counterarguments in this passage, so Answer Choice (D) fails, and the author does not appear to be critically analyzing the work of the team, so Answer Choice (E) fails.

2. "In order to" suggests a **Function** question. We are asked to explain why the author cites the diet of mantis shrimps. When answering functional questions, try to think about the relevance of the piece of information to the entirety of the author's point. We're trying to prove that it's good to bluff. Why? Because if we're weak, it isn't good to fight. Why? Because strong shrimps have very strong limbs, as is *evidenced* by the fact that they regularly prey upon crabs and other larger armored sea creatures, as in Answer Choice (B).

(B) Answer Choice (A) is irrelevant; Answer Choice (C) is a minute detail. Feeding is plausible as a biological motive for strong appendages, certainly, but it is not the motive in question, so we eliminate Answer Choice (D). Answer Choice (E) is far too difficult to piece through—an overly complex choice.

3. "As a whole" leads us to **Main Point**! Answer Choice (A) nicely summarizes precisely what's going on: we're using evidence about the mantis shrimp to make a general point. Make sure to get the big picture with Main Point questions.

(A) Answer Choice (B) suggests that the main point of the whole passage is the fact that a recent study has made unanticipated conclusions, which doesn't make sense. No one said intraspecific deception was rare—just unstudied; this disposes of Answer Choice (C). Answer Choice (D) seems to suggest that intraspecies deception only has benefits in the case of the shrimp, which is not necessarily true. Answer Choice (E), while it may be true, is definitely not the focus of the entirety of the passage—we're looking at effects (the actual act of bluffing) here, not causes (the motivations for it).

4. Another "primary purpose" question, this time about the first paragraph. The first paragraph clearly suggests a thesis: "research … suggests that deception between members of the species is not only possible, but evolutionarily beneficial." We then support this with the researchers' findings in the remainder of the passage. Answer Choice (D) holds.

(D) Answer Choice (A) suggests that we've conclusively disproven something; this is not true. Answer Choice (B) does not reflect the structure of the passage—there are no contradictions within it. Answer Choice (C) suggests that the first paragraph is providing the "how" and "why" of deception; that's not true, either. Finally, discrepancies between older views and this new study are never resolved, and especially not in the first paragraph, so Answer Choice (E) fails.

5. "Primary concern" means **Main Point**! Answer Choice (B) is the simplest possible way of saying what is going on—the author starts with a summary of the situations to which Freud's work is applicable and then presents an example that epitomizes an objection to Freud's theory.

(B) Answer Choice (A) is certainly a function of the first paragraph, but not the second; Answer Choice (C) suggests that the author's argument invalidates all of Freud's reasoning, which is not true. Answer Choice (D) suggests that the example in the second paragraph *successfully* applies Freud's theory, which is also false; Answer Choice (E) states, again, that our second-paragraph example supports Freud—again untrue.

6. A **Function** question—why include the mayo? If we know that the second paragraph serves to highlight an issue in Freud, then we can expect this scenario to serve as a counterexample (C).

(C) Answer Choices (A), (E), and (D) seem to claim that this example, again, validates Freud; Answer Choice (B) speaks to interpersonal concerns, which don't appear in the passage.

7. What does the first paragraph do? As we've said numerous times, it describes a theory. However, make sure you take it in the context of the whole passage—always do that with Main Point questions. Maintaining context, we see that this paragraph explains a theory *which we will show to be incomplete* (C).

(C) Answer Choice (A) suggests that all of Freud is refuted in the next paragraph, which is not true. Answer Choice (B) is far too specific; Answer Choice (D) doesn't structurally make sense. Answer Choice (E) suggests that Freud's work led to another theory that is controversial; this is slightly off, as it is, in fact, Freud's own theory that is controversial.

RECALL QUESTIONS QUICK REVIEW QUIZ

1. "Would be" suggests that we won't explicitly be told; hence, it is an inference question. Combine what you know from the passage to get at the correct answer. Platform-centric weapons tend to be "complex, increasingly costly" systems to combat "specific threats." We see "sophisticated" and "expensive" in Answer Choice (C), and upon looking for "F-35" in the passage, we see it used as a platform-centric example.

(C) Platform-centric weapons are usually not too adaptable [Answer Choice (A) is gone] and may not be particularly spacious [Answer Choice (B) is also gone because the B-52 is also an example of a payload-centric vehicle]. Answer Choice (D) suggests that there are actual military trucks; within the passage, "truck" was just used as a cover term for a certain type of vehicle. Answer Choice (E) is far too wordy and contradicts definitions of "platform-centric"—we also don't know what the United States will seek to implement later in the future.

2. We have the word "inferred" right in our prompt! Gauge, on the basis of the passage, what is most likely. This time, in fact, we are near-explicitly told our answer: (D). Within the passage, we are told that, "unlike modern, *densely packed designs*," the *USS Enterprise* has different qualities.

(D) Answer Choice (A) again makes the figurative trucks real; Answer Choice (B) suggests that reliability was sacrificed in the *USS Enterprise*, which is not true. Answer Choice (C) is not suggested anywhere in the passage, and Answer Choice (E) is directly opposite to what is stated in the passage.

3. "Is" suggests that we know for sure what is and what isn't—this is not an inference question. We're looking for details. It turns out that we are explicitly told in the first paragraph of our passage that the F-35 is a radar-deflecting stealth craft—it is platform-centric and functional, given that it demonstrates the "technological lead" of the United States, so it is at least somewhat effective in its own capacity. See Answer Choice (A).

(A) Answer Choices (B), (C), (D), and (E) are explicitly stated characteristics of payload-centric crafts; although Answer Choice (E) could, one would think, be applied to platform-centric ones as well, we have no mention of platform-centric ships here and a definite mention of a payload-centric one that's working well.

4. Explicit detail. The B-52 is discussed as being highly adaptable, having been "recast" in an assortment of capacities; it is even included in the paragraph that discusses payload-centric craft. See Answer Choice (A).

(A) Answer Choice (B) directly contradicts the passage's description of the B-52, as do Answer Choices (C) and (D); Answer Choice (E) is never directly stated.

5. Again, we're looking at a **Detail** question, given that we're told to find information "according to the passage." A recurring point in the passage is that there is need for eminent domain to occur only in the fact of public purpose; that's your easiest answer. When in doubt, gravitate toward a main point—here Answer Choice (D).

(D) Answer Choice (A) does not make any sense. Answer Choices (B) and (E), while potential situations under which eminent domain would be called, are not conditions upon which it is contingent. Answer Choice (C) is derived from an irrelevant detail in the passage and has nothing to do with the situation at hand.

6. Work off of details (a definition) to process new information (make an inference). This is also an exercise in careful reading! Eminent domain, we're told right away, involves *private* property being turned to public use. Repurposing existing public property wouldn't, therefore, count as eminent domain. (A) is the answer. Make sure to also be mindful of the "NOT"—small words of its kind can be killers on the GMAT.

(A) Answer Choices (B), (C), (D), and (E) are all passage-described notions of eminent domain.

7. This is another inference question. Given some information, gauge a likely new scenario. To answer this question, we should rely on information found toward the end of the last paragraph of the passage: we are told in the last four or so lines that old mortgage holders would benefit somewhat but that new mortgage holders would suffer immensely. Thus, it makes sense that a city with few new mortgage holders would be least negatively affected. Again, watch for that "LEAST."

(A) Answer Choice (B) would be most affected; Answer Choices (C), (D), and (E) are not directly relevant to the passage.

READING COMPREHENSION TARGETED REVIEW

1. "The main point" signals that, not surprisingly, we are looking at a **Main Point** question. This passage proceeds by introducing a Romano-Jewish historian (Josephus) who observed that Romans were unable to sell slaves on the market for high prices. It then discusses assorted possible reasons for the extremely low prices, and culminates by hypothesizing that food was insufficient to support slaves. Cumulatively, then, the passage "examines the reason for the unusually low price at which slaves were sold"—Answer Choice (B).

(B) Answer Choice (A) is not clearly done anywhere within the passage—the other, quite contrastingly, seems to just acknowledge slavery as a normal facet of Roman life. Answer Choice (C) suggests that Josephus affected an analysis that this passage is geared at critiquing, which isn't true. The main point of the passage is to explain a specific situation, too, not to explore economics [Answer Choice (D), therefore, fails]. Answer Choice (E) is not mentioned anywhere in the passage.

2. "According to the passage" points us to a **Detail** question. Reading over the passage, it is constantly emphasized that there was a food shortage—the answer to the question of low slave selling prices "presumably, is that potential buyers [would] fall short of the slave's upkeep," and we are told right after that about the thousands of men and women of even the servile classes dying without food and of agriculture's being stagnant. All this points to the idea that a food shortage would be responsible and leaves us with Answer Choice (A).

(A) We are told that Romans did not object to owning slaves, so Answer Choice (B) is invalidated. Even though Answer Choice (C) is true, this is a Critical Reasoning-esque logic trap—to say that slaves were sold for low prices *exactly because* not even the poor and servile classes could be fed is false. Both circumstances arise from a food shortage, but one does not cause the other. Answer Choices (D) and (E) aren't ever mentioned.

3. "In order to" signals a **Function** question! Look at the placement of this line inside the passage. It occurs just after we're asked why slave selling prices were so low. As such, it's highly likely that we're trying Answer Choice (C): to eliminate an alternative, reasonable explanation (moral concerns) for a phenomenon (the inability to sell slaves).

(C) Answer Choices (B), (D), and (A) are likely, reasonable answers, but they are not in any way supported by the passage. Answer Choice (E) is not true.

4. This is another **Main Point** question. Look over all of the paragraphs to arrive at the largest sense of what we're discussing: lobster, its decline (and, in some places, continued success), and the consequences of this decline. See Answer Choice (A)!

(A) Answer Choice (B) is far too specific—although both lobster and pork are mentioned, they are never compared. Answer Choice (C) is also too specific—even though we do briefly mention that restaurateurs will suffer, this is not elaborate enough to be our main point. Answer Choices (D) and (E) are completely irrelevant.

5. Here is another "in order to," another Function question. Look, again, at the part of the passage in which you find "ground chuck" (which, by the way, is a form of beef). Just after saying how glaringly lobster prices have fallen, the author mentions that lobster can cost less than ground chuck—there's an "even less" hanging in the air there. This allows us to infer that we would typically see lobster costing more than ground chuck, and that Answer Choice (B) is a good choice.

(B) Answer Choices (A) and (E) are not mentioned, and Answer Choice (C) is useless, given that we are told a precise amount. Answer Choice (D) is untrue, as ground chuck presumably costs less than lobster.

6. "Might" signals an **Inference** question. Search the passage for details that help you make a generalization. We're told in the passage that, sure, even though wholesale prices are dropping, the lobster being sold at high-end establishments is still comparatively expensive. There's our Answer Choice (D).

(D) Answer Choices (A), (B), (C), and (E) cannot be supported on the basis of passage assertions.

7. We're directly told that this one is an **Inference** question. Look, again, for "luxury goods" inside the passage. We're told that the paradoxical state of lobster prices might be

explained by the fact that lobster is a luxury good toward the end of Paragraph Two. It's not unreasonable, therefore, to think that we know this because other "luxury goods" have experienced similar patterns in pricing. See Answer Choice (A).

(A) Answer Choices (B) and (C) are never stated; while region is mentioned in the passage, it is not used to prove what Answer Choice (D) claims. Answer Choice (E) is definitely not true, as the whole passage is dedicated to finding a reason for the changes in price.

Sample
Tests

Sample
Tests

Sample Test 1 with Answers and Analysis

→ TEST
→ ANSWERS
→ ANALYSIS
→ EVALUATING YOUR SCORE

INTEGRATED REASONING SECTION

1. i. Ⓐ Ⓑ Ⓒ Ⓓ
   ii. Ⓐ Ⓑ Ⓒ Ⓓ

2.
Could Be Classified	Could Not Be Classified	Animal
◯	◯	Penguin
◯	◯	Flamingo
◯	◯	Flying Squirrel
◯	◯	Pterodactyl
◯	◯	Eagle

3.
Yes	No
◯	◯
◯	◯
◯	◯

4.
Yes	No
◯	◯
◯	◯
◯	◯
◯	◯

5. Ⓐ Ⓑ Ⓒ Ⓓ Ⓔ

6.
Either Day	Neither Day	Speaker
◯	◯	Branson, male, U.K.
◯	◯	Robinson, female, U.K.
◯	◯	D'Agostino, female, Brazil
◯	◯	Miller, female, Canada
◯	◯	Soares, male, India

7. i. Ⓐ Ⓑ Ⓒ Ⓓ
   ii. Ⓐ Ⓑ Ⓒ Ⓓ

8. Ⓐ Ⓑ Ⓒ Ⓓ Ⓔ

9.
True	False
◯	◯
◯	◯
◯	◯

10. i. Ⓐ Ⓑ Ⓒ Ⓓ
   ii. Ⓐ Ⓑ Ⓒ Ⓓ

11.
True	False
◯	◯
◯	◯
◯	◯

12.
Would Help Explain	Would Not Help Explain
◯	◯
◯	◯
◯	◯

ANSWER SHEET
Sample Test 1

QUANTITATIVE SECTION

1. Ⓐ Ⓑ Ⓒ Ⓓ Ⓔ   11. Ⓐ Ⓑ Ⓒ Ⓓ Ⓔ   21. Ⓐ Ⓑ Ⓒ Ⓓ Ⓔ   31. Ⓐ Ⓑ Ⓒ Ⓓ Ⓔ
2. Ⓐ Ⓑ Ⓒ Ⓓ Ⓔ   12. Ⓐ Ⓑ Ⓒ Ⓓ Ⓔ   22. Ⓐ Ⓑ Ⓒ Ⓓ Ⓔ   32. Ⓐ Ⓑ Ⓒ Ⓓ Ⓔ
3. Ⓐ Ⓑ Ⓒ Ⓓ Ⓔ   13. Ⓐ Ⓑ Ⓒ Ⓓ Ⓔ   23. Ⓐ Ⓑ Ⓒ Ⓓ Ⓔ   33. Ⓐ Ⓑ Ⓒ Ⓓ Ⓔ
4. Ⓐ Ⓑ Ⓒ Ⓓ Ⓔ   14. Ⓐ Ⓑ Ⓒ Ⓓ Ⓔ   24. Ⓐ Ⓑ Ⓒ Ⓓ Ⓔ   34. Ⓐ Ⓑ Ⓒ Ⓓ Ⓔ
5. Ⓐ Ⓑ Ⓒ Ⓓ Ⓔ   15. Ⓐ Ⓑ Ⓒ Ⓓ Ⓔ   25. Ⓐ Ⓑ Ⓒ Ⓓ Ⓔ   35. Ⓐ Ⓑ Ⓒ Ⓓ Ⓔ
6. Ⓐ Ⓑ Ⓒ Ⓓ Ⓔ   16. Ⓐ Ⓑ Ⓒ Ⓓ Ⓔ   26. Ⓐ Ⓑ Ⓒ Ⓓ Ⓔ   36. Ⓐ Ⓑ Ⓒ Ⓓ Ⓔ
7. Ⓐ Ⓑ Ⓒ Ⓓ Ⓔ   17. Ⓐ Ⓑ Ⓒ Ⓓ Ⓔ   27. Ⓐ Ⓑ Ⓒ Ⓓ Ⓔ   37. Ⓐ Ⓑ Ⓒ Ⓓ Ⓔ
8. Ⓐ Ⓑ Ⓒ Ⓓ Ⓔ   18. Ⓐ Ⓑ Ⓒ Ⓓ Ⓔ   28. Ⓐ Ⓑ Ⓒ Ⓓ Ⓔ
9. Ⓐ Ⓑ Ⓒ Ⓓ Ⓔ   19. Ⓐ Ⓑ Ⓒ Ⓓ Ⓔ   29. Ⓐ Ⓑ Ⓒ Ⓓ Ⓔ
10. Ⓐ Ⓑ Ⓒ Ⓓ Ⓔ   20. Ⓐ Ⓑ Ⓒ Ⓓ Ⓔ   30. Ⓐ Ⓑ Ⓒ Ⓓ Ⓔ

VERBAL SECTION

1. Ⓐ Ⓑ Ⓒ Ⓓ Ⓔ   12. Ⓐ Ⓑ Ⓒ Ⓓ Ⓔ   23. Ⓐ Ⓑ Ⓒ Ⓓ Ⓔ   34. Ⓐ Ⓑ Ⓒ Ⓓ Ⓔ
2. Ⓐ Ⓑ Ⓒ Ⓓ Ⓔ   13. Ⓐ Ⓑ Ⓒ Ⓓ Ⓔ   24. Ⓐ Ⓑ Ⓒ Ⓓ Ⓔ   35. Ⓐ Ⓑ Ⓒ Ⓓ Ⓔ
3. Ⓐ Ⓑ Ⓒ Ⓓ Ⓔ   14. Ⓐ Ⓑ Ⓒ Ⓓ Ⓔ   25. Ⓐ Ⓑ Ⓒ Ⓓ Ⓔ   36. Ⓐ Ⓑ Ⓒ Ⓓ Ⓔ
4. Ⓐ Ⓑ Ⓒ Ⓓ Ⓔ   15. Ⓐ Ⓑ Ⓒ Ⓓ Ⓔ   26. Ⓐ Ⓑ Ⓒ Ⓓ Ⓔ   37. Ⓐ Ⓑ Ⓒ Ⓓ Ⓔ
5. Ⓐ Ⓑ Ⓒ Ⓓ Ⓔ   16. Ⓐ Ⓑ Ⓒ Ⓓ Ⓔ   27. Ⓐ Ⓑ Ⓒ Ⓓ Ⓔ   38. Ⓐ Ⓑ Ⓒ Ⓓ Ⓔ
6. Ⓐ Ⓑ Ⓒ Ⓓ Ⓔ   17. Ⓐ Ⓑ Ⓒ Ⓓ Ⓔ   28. Ⓐ Ⓑ Ⓒ Ⓓ Ⓔ   39. Ⓐ Ⓑ Ⓒ Ⓓ Ⓔ
7. Ⓐ Ⓑ Ⓒ Ⓓ Ⓔ   18. Ⓐ Ⓑ Ⓒ Ⓓ Ⓔ   29. Ⓐ Ⓑ Ⓒ Ⓓ Ⓔ   40. Ⓐ Ⓑ Ⓒ Ⓓ Ⓔ
8. Ⓐ Ⓑ Ⓒ Ⓓ Ⓔ   19. Ⓐ Ⓑ Ⓒ Ⓓ Ⓔ   30. Ⓐ Ⓑ Ⓒ Ⓓ Ⓔ   41. Ⓐ Ⓑ Ⓒ Ⓓ Ⓔ
9. Ⓐ Ⓑ Ⓒ Ⓓ Ⓔ   20. Ⓐ Ⓑ Ⓒ Ⓓ Ⓔ   31. Ⓐ Ⓑ Ⓒ Ⓓ Ⓔ
10. Ⓐ Ⓑ Ⓒ Ⓓ Ⓔ   21. Ⓐ Ⓑ Ⓒ Ⓓ Ⓔ   32. Ⓐ Ⓑ Ⓒ Ⓓ Ⓔ
11. Ⓐ Ⓑ Ⓒ Ⓓ Ⓔ   22. Ⓐ Ⓑ Ⓒ Ⓓ Ⓔ   33. Ⓐ Ⓑ Ⓒ Ⓓ Ⓔ

Analytical Writing Analysis

Time: 30 minutes

> **DIRECTIONS:** In this section, you will be asked to write a critique of the argument presented. You are NOT being asked to present your own views on the subject.
>
> **WRITING YOUR RESPONSE:** Take a few minutes to evaluate the argument and plan a response before you begin writing. Be sure to organize your ideas and develop them fully, but leave time to reread your response and make any revisions that you think are necessary.
>
> **EVALUATION OF YOUR RESPONSE:** College and university faculty members from various subject matter areas, including management education, will evaluate the overall quality of your thinking and writing. They will consider how well you: organize, develop, and express your ideas about the argument presented; provide relevant supporting reasons and examples; and control the elements of standard written English.

Question: The following appeared in the editorial section of a local daily newspaper:

> "Although forecasts of elections based on opinion polls measure current voter preference, many voters keep changing their minds about whom they prefer until the last few days before the balloting. Some do not even make a final decision until they enter the voting booth. Forecasts based on opinion polls are therefore little better at predicting election outcomes than a random guess would be."

Discuss how well reasoned you find this argument. In your discussion be sure to analyze the line of reasoning and the use of evidence in the argument. For example, you may need to consider what questionable assumptions underlie the thinking and what alternative explanations or counterexamples might weaken the conclusion. You can also discuss what sort of evidence would strengthen or refute the argument, what changes in the argument would make it more logically sound, and what, if anything, would help you better evaluate its conclusion.

STOP

ON THE ACTUAL GMAT,
AFTER YOU HAVE CONFIRMED YOUR ANSWER,
YOU CANNOT RETURN TO IT.

INTEGRATED REASONING SECTION

Time: 30 minutes

12 questions

This section consists of four types of questions: Graphics Interpretation, Table Analysis, Two-part Analysis, and Multi-Source Reasoning.

> **DIRECTIONS:** The new Integrated Reasoning section consists of four question types. Some require the use of both quantitative and verbal skills. Others involve the use of graphics, tables, or text material. The questions also use various response formats.
>
> For each question, review the text, graphic, or text material provided and respond to the task that is presented. *Note: An onscreen calculator is available in this section on the actual test.*

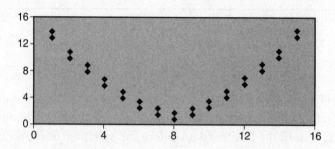

1. The scatter plot above shows the relationship between two variables.

    Complete each statement according to the information presented in the diagram.

    i. Which of the following statements is the only one that can be said to be true based on the chart?

    (A) The slope is positive.
    (B) The relationship is strong.
    (C) The slope is negative.
    (D) The slope is linear.

    ii. If you plotted the absolute difference between the two variables at each point in the chart, what slope would the graph have?

    (A) a positive slope
    (B) a slope of zero
    (C) a negative slope
    (D) a parabolic slope

2. Birds are a class of vertebrate animals. Birds (class Aves) are a more homogeneous group than many other vertebrate classes, such as mammals. Birds possess very distinct characteristics. The top two are as follows:

(i) **The beak or bill** is a bony, toothless structure that extends from the jawbone. It is used primarily for eating, grooming, and feeding young.

(ii) **The wings**, which are a pair of forelimbs, are uniquely adapted for flying.

Based on the information above and ignoring all other characteristics of birds, which of the following could be classified as a "Bird" and which could not?

Could Be Classified	Could Not Be Classified	Animal
◯	◯	Penguin
◯	◯	Flamingo
◯	◯	Flying squirrel
◯	◯	Pterodactyl
◯	◯	Eagle

3. The table below displays data concerning UltraMart stores in Canada.

Store Number	City	Province	# of Employees	Grocery Section
3145	Concord	Ontario	27	N
3004	Brandon	Manitoba	28	N
3149	Mascouche	Quebec	31	N
3122	Belleville	Ontario	36	N
3065	Orleans	Ontario	38	N
3148	Levis	Quebec	42	N
3007	Brossard	Quebec	44	N
3134	Kanata	Ontario	44	N
3063	North Bay	Ontario	48	N
3097	Sudbury	Ontario	48	N
3140	Saint Bruno	Quebec	49	N
3000	Agincourt	Ontario	50	N
3080	Rosemere	Quebec	53	N
3642	St. Constant	Quebec	55	N
3046	La Salle	Quebec	59	N
3090	St. Jean	Quebec	59	Y
3161	Oshawa	Ontario	60	Y
3039	Joliette	Quebec	61	Y
3044	Kirkland	Quebec	64	Y
3189	Laval	Quebec	65	Y
3047	Laval	Quebec	66	N
3146	St. Foy	Quebec	66	Y
3053	Markham	Ontario	68	Y
3084	Saskatoon	Saskatchewan	68	Y
3135	Brampton	Ontario	70	N
3195	Richmond Hill	Ontario	70	Y
3130	Brampton	Ontario	72	Y
3186	Pickering	Ontario	72	Y
3054	Meadowvale	Ontario	77	Y
3159	Scarborough	Ontario	79	Y
3125	Gatineau	Quebec	80	Y
3131	Ottawa	Ontario	82	Y
3111	Scarborough	Ontario	83	N
3051	London	Ontario	84	N
3029	Edmonton	Alberta	86	Y
3656	Montreal	Quebec	86	Y
3635	Scarborough	Ontario	87	Y
3043	Kingston	Ontario	88	Y
3012	Calgary	Alberta	98	N
3074	Quebec City	Quebec	98	Y
3050	London	Ontario	99	Y
3119	Winnipeg	Manitoba	102	Y
3654	Mississauga	Ontario	103	N
3055	Mississauga	Ontario	107	Y
3009	Calgary	Alberta	112	Y
3106	Toronto	Ontario	119	Y
3165	Montreal	Quebec	121	Y
3105	Toronto	Ontario	128	N
3740	Toronto	Ontario	131	Y
3031	Etobicoke	Ontario	142	Y

For each of the following statements, select *Yes* if the statement can be shown to be true based on the information in the table. Otherwise, select *No*.

Yes	No	
○	○	The median number of employees in a store in Quebec is higher than the median number of employees in a store in Ontario.
○	○	If a store has less than 60 employees, it does not have enough resources to support a grocery section.
○	○	More than seven cities have at least two stores.

Questions 4 and 5 refer to the following articles.

Article 1: From an environmental journal

February 28—Given the global increase of deforestation, some experts predict that in 50 years, Earth may lose over 20% of wildlife species to extinction. In addition, the destruction of forests provokes further global warming. CO_2 levels are predicted to rise by 100% in the same time period, which could have disastrous effects. Lastly, the loss of trees in an area also decreases the amount of water within that region, thus affecting the world's water supply. Governments and industry have failed to put sufficient restrictions and regulations in place. Although recycling programs have made a significant dent in reducing paper use, there is still much more work to be done. However, one of the challenges is that many citizens vote down proposals for recycling program expansion or regulations on industry.

Article 2: Interview with a well-known scientist

March 6—Dr. James Finnegan, special advisor to the New York City Mayor's Program on Environment Sustainability, has been most critical of the forest industry, which continually hires and utilizes aggressive lobbyists to ensure that expanded recycling program proposals are defeated. He advises that without a significant increase in recycling programs, the rate of global warming could soon quadruple in the next generation.

"It's true that most voters keep rejecting costly measures to reduce paper and lumber usage, such as more aggressive 'reduce, reuse, and recycle' programs. Worse yet, CEOs are unsurprisingly going to avoid taking huge risks for unpopular policies among their key stockholders. However, if something isn't done soon, by 2060, a bottle of water may become so expensive that only the rich can afford it as a luxury item."

Article 3: From a forestry magazine

April 2—The price of bottled water over the last two decades has increased by 200% as a decrease in supply has met with an increased demand. Despite an increase in recycled paper products available to the public, most paper companies charge a premium for them. This has encouraged some companies to exploit many large natural water resources around the world. This has also motivated many companies to continue using nonrecycled paper products. Several American environmental groups have expressed concern that certain pulp and paper companies choose the economics of extraction and manufacturing over the well-being of the ecosystem. Some North American scientists have called for an increase in regulations to protect deforestation and water sources. However, companies from both industries caution that this may dramatically increase the cost of both recycled paper and fresh water.

4. Consider each of the following statements. Does the information in the three articles support the inferences as stated?

Yes	No	
◯	◯	Deforestation is the most significant cause of increasing CO_2 levels in the atmosphere.
◯	◯	Citizens tend to vote down environmentally friendly proposals due to the strong lobbying of the forestry industry.
◯	◯	Dr. James Finnegan would prefer to pass legislation to regulate the forestry industry than legislation to regulate the bottled-water industry.
◯	◯	Business leaders in environmentally affected industries may not always agree with science experts on environmental sustainability.

5. Each of the following is true based on the passage EXCEPT:

(A) at least 15% of Earth's wildlife species may become extinct within 50 years.
(B) a bottle of water will cost the same as a bottle of premium vodka by the year 2060.
(C) bottled water has doubled in price over the past 20 years.
(D) for most consumers, recycled paper can cost more to purchase than nonrecycled paper.
(E) CO_2 levels are expected to double before the end of the 21st century.

An organization of technology leaders is arranging a two-day business conference in California that will bring together the top minds in leadership and development from around the world. The conference organizers want to get a diverse range of speakers for the event. Each day will have six speakers. To reflect the global diversity, one day will feature a majority of international speakers (i.e., not from North America) and the other day will feature a majority of female speakers. Neither day should have more than 2 speakers from the same country unless they are from the United States. So far, 10 speakers have already booked. The list of speakers for each day, including the speaker's country of origin, is as follows:

Day 1 (Majority International)	Day 2 (Majority Female)
Smith, female, U.K.	Fiorina, female, U.S.A.
Dalton, female, U.K.	Godin, male, U.S.A.
Xiang, male, China	Rodrigues, male, Brazil
Sharma, male, Spain	Hayek, female, Mexico
Robbins, male, U.S.A.	Valentino, female, Brazil

6. Select a speaker who could be added to the schedule for either day. Then select a speaker who could not be added to either day. Make only two selections, one in each column.

Either Day	Neither Day	Speaker
◯	◯	Branson, male, U.K.
◯	◯	Robinson, female, U.K.
◯	◯	D'Agostino, female, Brazil
◯	◯	Miller, female, Canada
◯	◯	Soares, male, India

Question 7 refers to the following graphs and information.

Graph 1

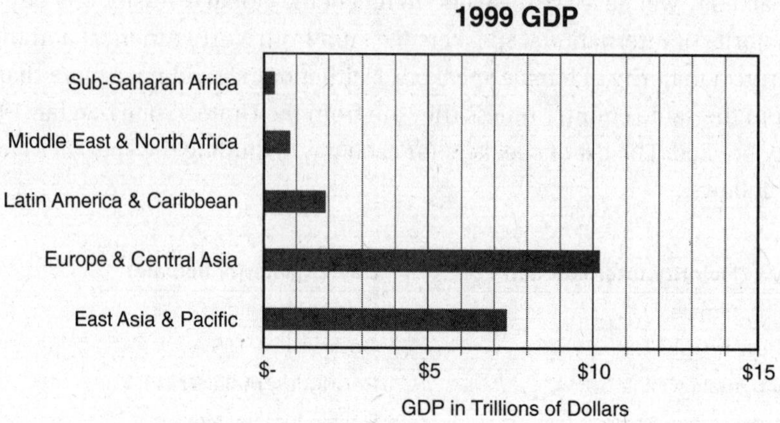

1999 GDP

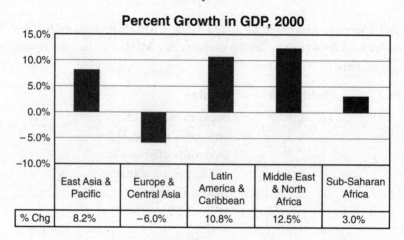

Graph 2

Percent Growth in GDP, 2000

	East Asia & Pacific	Europe & Central Asia	Latin America & Caribbean	Middle East & North Africa	Sub-Saharan Africa
% Chg	8.2%	−6.0%	10.8%	12.5%	3.0%

7. Complete each statement according to the information presented in the graphs.

i. What is the approximate dollar amount by which Europe and Central Asia's GDP increased from 1999 to 2000?

(A) −$610 billion
(B) −$439 billion
(C) −$6 billion
(D) $610 billion

ii. Which is closest to the combined growth in GDP in 2000 for all five regions?

(A) −3%
(B) 0%
(C) 4%
(D) 8%

Questions 8 and 9 refer to the following information and tables.

Sally is the head of the party planning committee for Dinder Mufflin. She takes her job very seriously. She loves to plan each office party and personalize it for the specific employee. Sally buys her party supplies from the Big Blast Boxstore.

Sally makes her purchases monthly to take advantage of Big Blast Boxstore's end-of-the-month clearance sales. Depending on the number of birthdays and the birthday person's party preferences, Sally plans accordingly.

Big Blast Boxstore Price List

Party Supply	Packaging	Cost
Ribbon	8 feet rolls, 6 per package	$8.00
Streamers	10 feet rolls, 10 per package	$6.00
Balloons	20 balloons per bag	$4.00
Goodie bags	24 bags per package	$12.00

Big Blast Boxstore Monthly Clearance Sale Discounts

Amount Spent	Ribbon	Streamers	Balloons	Goodie Bags
$30–$50	$15.00	$10.00	$5.00	None
Over $50	$25.00	$20.00	$10.00	$10.00

8. Which of the following options would result in the lowest cost?

   (A) August has 3 birthdays. Sally needs 180 feet of ribbon, 300 feet of streamers, 50 balloons, and 100 goodie bags.
   (B) February has 3 birthdays. Sally needs 300 feet of ribbon, 200 feet of streamers, 30 balloons, and 60 goodie bags.
   (C) September has 4 birthdays. Sally needs 300 feet of ribbon, 300 feet of streamers, 150 balloons, and 120 goodie bags.
   (D) December has 5 birthdays. Sally needs 360 feet of ribbon, 400 feet of streamers, 100 balloons, and 30 goodie bags.
   (E) April has 6 birthdays. Sally needs 336 feet of ribbon, 900 feet of streamers, 260 balloons, and 120 goodie bags.

9. Answer the following True or False statements.

   True   False

   ○   ○   If Sally was able to put leftover party supplies in storage, it would be cheaper to purchase 9 packages of streamers and 7 packages of ribbon instead of 8 packages of streamers and 6 packages of ribbon.

   ○   ○   It is cheaper for Sally to purchase 300 feet of ribbon and 900 feet of streamers than to purchase 144 goodie bags and 24 balloons.

   ○   ○   In order to get the maximum discount possible from purchasing all four products, Sally needs to spend at least $222.00.

The scatter plot below charts the test scores for an English exam and a math exam for 22 students in Mrs. Rosenblatt's class.

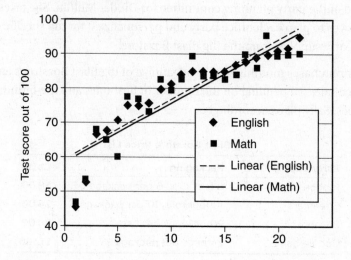

10. Complete each statement according to the information given by the graph.

i. How does the slope of the regression line for the English exam compare with the slope of the regression line for the math exam?

(A) The slope of the regression line for the English exam is greater than the regression line for the math exam.

(B) The slope of the regression line for the English exam is less than the regression line for the math exam.

(C) The slope of the regression line for the English exam is equal to the regression line for the math exam.

(D) The slope of the regression line for the English exam is undefined and cannot be compared with the slope of the regression line for the math exam.

ii. How do Mrs. Rosenblatt's students tend to score in math as compared with English?

(A) They tend to score better in math than in English.

(B) They tend to score worse in math than in English.

(C) They tend to score the same in math and English.

(D) Since each student is an individual, the scores of the entire class cannot be compared with each other.

Questions 11 and 12 refer to the following table.

The table below shows data for the major types of sliced deli cheeses.

Type of Sliced Deli Cheese	Share of Market (lb.)	Change in Sales vs. Last Year (lb.)	Change in % Volume (lb.)	Share of Market ($)	Sales vs. Last Year ($)	Change in % Volume ($)
King Light Swiss	0	–17,489	–100	0	–168,120	–100
King Light Havarti	0	–17,893	–100	0	–172,403	–100
King Havarti	0	–22,860	–100	0	–218,829	–100
King Swiss	0	–27,648	–100	0	–265,065	–100
Kruger Mozzarella	16.2	8,547	4.2	14.7	124,537	7.6
King Swiss w/Zipper	11.5	64,852	74	11.9	641,205	81
Kruger Swiss	7.4	–10,292	–9.5	8.5	–58,444	–5.4
King Swiss Light w/Zipper	6.8	38,301	73.1	7.9	428,774	81.3
Aggio Jarlsberg	4.5	1,345	2.3	6.3	55,857	7.9
King Mozzarella w/Zipper	4.1	25,302	85.3	3.8	224,430	94.3
Davinci Swiss w/Zipper	3.4	44,729	NA	4.0	485,913	NA
Kruger Cheddar Mild	2.9	27,184	247.3	1.6	136,576	258
Davinci Havarti	2.7	26,911	290.2	3.2	292,398	320
Davinci Part Skim Mozzarella	2.6	7,797	29.2	2.4	92,119	45.4
Davinci Provolone	2.3	13,019	73.7	2.5	146,653	98.3
Norway Jarlsberg	2.1	361	1.3	1.8	7,186	3.5
Norway Jarlsberg Light	2.0	7,584	40.6	2.8	107,464	45.8
Kruger Part Skim Mozzarella	1.9	–14,941	–37.3	1.7	–121,058	–36.7
King Provolone w/Zipper	1.6	13,236	176	1.8	143,205	188
King Havarti w/Zipper	1.6	10,326	90.7	1.7	103,554	103
King Raclette w/Zipper	1.3	4,205	33.3	1.7	55,905	37.2

11. Consider each of the following statements. For each statement, indicate whether the statement is true or false based on the information provided in the table.

True	False	
○	○	Cheddar and mozzarella cheese slices have a higher in-store price point than Swiss or Havarti cheese slices.
○	○	Swiss cheese slices accounted for more dollar sales than any other type of cheese slice.
○	○	King's cheese slices have had the largest overall absolute growth per pound since last year.

12. For each of the following statements, select *Would help explain* if it would, if true, help explain some of the information in the table. Otherwise select *Would not help explain*.

Would Help Explain	Would Not Help Explain	
○	○	Consumers tend to prefer cheese slice packages with zippers versus packages with no zipper.
○	○	King discontinued some of their SKUs (stock keeping units) and replaced them with products that were packaged with zippers.
○	○	Light cheese slices are more expensive to manufacture than regular cheese slices.

STOP

ON THE ACTUAL GMAT,
AFTER YOU HAVE CONFIRMED YOUR ANSWER,
YOU CANNOT RETURN TO IT.

QUANTITATIVE SECTION

Time: 75 minutes

37 questions

This section consists of two types of questions: Problem Solving and Data Sufficiency.

Problem Solving

DIRECTIONS: Solve each of the following problems; then indicate the correct answer.

NOTE: A figure that appears with a problem is drawn as accurately as possible so as to provide information that may help in answering the question.

Numbers in this test are real numbers.

Data Sufficiency

DIRECTIONS: Each of the following problems has a question and two statements that are labeled (1) and (2). Use the data given in (1) and (2) together with other available information (such as the number of hours in a day, the definition of *clockwise*, mathematical facts, etc.) to decide whether the statements are *sufficient* to answer the question. Then fill in space

(A) If you can get the answer from **(1) ALONE** but not from (2) alone

(B) If you can get the answer from **(2) ALONE** but not from (1) alone

(C) If you can get the answer from **BOTH (1)** and **(2) TOGETHER** but not from (1) alone or (2) alone

(D) If **EITHER** statement **(1) ALONE OR** statement **(2) ALONE** suffices

(E) If you **CANNOT** get the answer from statements (1) and (2) **TOGETHER** but need even more data

All numbers used in this section are real numbers.

A figure given for a problem is intended to provide information consistent with that in the question, but not necessarily with the additional information contained in the statements.

All figures lie in the plane unless you are told otherwise.

Figures are drawn as accurately as possible; straight lines may not appear straight on the screen.

1. What is the remainder when 320 is divided by 400?

    (A) 0
    (B) 0.8
    (C) 80
    (D) 320
    (E) 400

2. Which of the following is a factor of both 21 and 24 but not of 50?

    (A) 2
    (B) 3
    (C) 4
    (D) 5
    (E) 7

3. Which of the following must be odd?

    (A) The sum of an odd and an even number
    (B) The sum of a positive and negative number
    (C) The difference between two even numbers
    (D) The quotient of two even numbers
    (E) The product of an odd and an even number

4. A store owner marked an item for $50. When he sold the item at a 10% discount, he made a 20% profit. What was the original cost of the item?

    (A) $36.00
    (B) $37.50
    (C) $39.00
    (D) $40.00
    (E) $40.09

5. If $1000 is placed into account X, yielding 10% interest compounded annually and $1000 is placed into account Y using 10% simple annual interest, how much more will be in account X than in account Y at the end of 5 years?

    (A) $0
    (B) $100
    (C) $110.51
    (D) $133.31
    (E) $146.41

6. May and June both work for April, who owns a used-car dealership. May sold 18 cars in August, and June sold 12 cars in July. Of the cars that May sold, the range of the selling price was $16,000 and the lowest selling price was $5500. Of the cars that June sold, the range of the selling price was $17,500, and the lowest selling price was $7200. What was the range of the selling prices of the 30 cars sold by May and June for April?

    (A) $16,200
    (B) $18,700
    (C) $19,200
    (D) $21,500
    (E) $22,700

7. If $st + u = u$, and s does not equal 0, which of the following must be true?

    (A) $|s - t| = 0$
    (B) $t = 0$
    (C) $s > t$
    (D) $st = 1$
    (E) $s + t = 0$

8. What is the ratio of the number of teaspoons of baking soda to the number of cups of chocolate chips required in a certain brownie recipe?

    (1) The number of cups of chocolate chips required in the recipe is 350% of the number of teaspoons of baking soda required in the recipe.

    (2) $2\frac{1}{2}$ more cups of chocolate chips than teaspoons of baking soda are required in the recipe.

9. A certain list consists of many different integers. Is the product of all the integers in that list positive?

    (1) When you multiply the smallest and the largest integers in the list, you get a positive number.

    (2) There are an even number of integers in the list.

10. If T is a line in the xy-plane, what is the slope of T?

    (1) The y-intercept of T is 4.
    (2) The x-intercept of T is 5.

11. Is positive integer y divisible by 3?

    (1) $\dfrac{144}{y^2}$ is an integer

    (2) $\dfrac{y^2}{36}$ is an integer

12. How many more worker compensation insurance claims were filed in month V than in month Z?

    (1) For months W, X, Y, Z, the average number of first-time insurance claims filed was 272,000.

    (2) For months V, W, X, Y, the average number of first-time insurance claims filed was 277,250.

13. Machine A produces 1000 widgets in 5 hours. Machine B produces 450 widgets in 3 hours. While working together at their respective rates, how long will it take the machines to produce 2000 widgets?

    (A) $4\dfrac{4}{9}$ hours

    (B) 5 hours

    (C) $5\dfrac{9}{20}$ hours

    (D) $5\dfrac{5}{7}$ hours

    (E) 6 hours

14. Leonardo da Vinci was invited to exhibit 3 new paintings, 4 new sculptures, and 2 new inventions at the local museum. If Leonardo has 5 new paintings, 5 new sculptures, and 3 new inventions from which he must choose, how many different combinations of paintings, sculptures, and inventions are available to him?

    (A) 24

    (B) 150

    (C) 300

    (D) 450

    (E) 1050

15. If T is a set of six positive, distinct integers with an average (arithmetic mean) of 12 and a median of 8, what is the smallest possible value of the largest number in the set?

    (A) 19
    (B) 20
    (C) 21
    (D) 22
    (E) 23

16. A certain granola mix is made up of raisins, bran flakes, and pecans. The mixture contains 30% bran flakes by weight and 40% pecans by weight. The bran flakes cost twice as much as the raisins per pound, and the pecans costs $2\frac{1}{2}$ times as much as the bran flakes per pound. Approximately what percent of the cost of the granola mix do the bran flakes contribute?

    (A) 18%
    (B) 20.7%
    (C) 22.5%
    (D) 24%
    (E) 25%

17. In a rectangular coordinate system, what is the x-intercept of a line passing through (4, 3) and (6, 9)?

    (A) (–3, 0)
    (B) (0, 3)
    (C) (–3, –3)
    (D) (1, 0)
    (E) (3, 0)

18. At what speed must a runner return from the gymnasium to home, a distance of 30 km, if the trip there took 2.5 hours and she wishes to average 15 km/h for the entire trip?

    (A) 12 km/h
    (B) 15 km/h
    (C) 18 km/h
    (D) 20 km/h
    (E) 24 km/h

19. If Jonathan is 12 years younger than Sebastian, how old is Sebastian today?

    (1) In three years from now, the combined ages of Sebastian and Jonathan will be 11 times the current age of Jonathan.
    (2) Four years from today, Jonathan will be one-third the age of Sebastian.

20. The upscale restaurant Sassafras adds an 18% gratuity to all bills with groups of 6 or more but adds no gratuity for groups with fewer than 6 people. If a group of friends ate at this restaurant, what was their total bill, not including any gratuity?

    (1) There were 6 people in the group of friends.
    (2) The total gratuity for the meal was $16.30.

21. A square lawn is reduced in size by removing 3 feet from one dimension and 5 feet from the other. By what percentage did these changes reduce the area of the original lawn?

    (1) The area of the lawn was 35 square feet after the changes.
    (2) After the changes, the longer dimension was three-tenths shorter than before the changes.

22. Is x an integer?

    (1) $4x$ is an integer.
    (2) $x - 1$ is not an integer.

23. For any triangle Q in the xy-coordinate plane, the center of Q is defined to be the point whose y-coordinate is the average of the y-coordinates of the vertices of Q and whose x-coordinate is the average of the x-coordinates of the vertices of Q. If a certain triangle has vertices on the points (0, 0) and (10, 0) and center at the point (5, 4), what are the coordinates of the remaining vertex?

    (A) (5, 12)
    (B) (5, 8)
    (C) (10, 5)
    (D) (7.5, 6)
    (E) (6, 10)

Province	Amount of Organic Waste Collected Normally	Amount of Organic Waste Extracted from Regular Garbage
New Brunswick	21,400	4100
Nova Scotia	49,100	8900
Prince Edward Island	17,200	3400
Quebec	112,600	17,800
Ontario	62,500	14,100

24. The table above shows the amount of organic waste, in metric tons, collected by five provinces in Canada and the amount of organic waste extracted from regular garbage in a certain year. Which province has the highest ratio of normal organic waste collected to extracted organic waste collected?

(A) New Brunswick
(B) Nova Scotia
(C) Prince Edward Island
(D) Ontario
(E) Quebec

25. The equilateral triangle above has sides of length x, and the square has sides of length y. If the two regions have the same area, what is the ratio of $x : y$?

(A) $\dfrac{2}{3}$

(B) $\dfrac{4}{3}$

(C) $\dfrac{2}{\sqrt{3}}$

(D) $\dfrac{2}{\sqrt[4]{3}}$

(E) $\dfrac{4}{\sqrt[4]{3}}$

(A) If you can get the answer from **(1) ALONE** but not from (2) alone

(B) If you can get the answer from **(2) ALONE** but not from (1) alone

(C) If you can get the answer from **BOTH (1)** and **(2) TOGETHER** but not from (1) alone or (2) alone

(D) If **EITHER** statement **(1) ALONE OR** statement **(2) ALONE** suffices

(E) If you **CANNOT** get the answer from statements (1) and (2) **TOGETHER** but need even more data

26. The marketing team at Alpha Company decides to go to lunch to celebrate Jim's birthday. The lunch costs a total of L dollars, and there are C members on the marketing team, not including Jim. If F of the team members forget their wallets, which of the following represents the extra amount, in dollars, that each of the remaining team members would have to pay?

   (A) $\dfrac{FL}{(C(C-F))}$

   (B) $\dfrac{L(C-F)}{C}$

   (C) $\dfrac{L}{(C-F)}$

   (D) $\dfrac{FL}{(C-F)}$

   (E) $\dfrac{L}{C}$

27. Is $\dfrac{1}{x} > \dfrac{y}{(y^2+2)}$?

   (1) $y > 0$
   (2) $x = y$

28. The operation Ω is defined for all positive integers a and b by $a\,\Omega\,b = \dfrac{2^a}{2^b}$.

   What does $(4\,\Omega\,2)\,\Omega\,5$ equal?

   (A) 0
   (B) 2^{-2}
   (C) 2^{-1}
   (D) 4
   (E) 2^5

29.   What is the greatest prime factor of $4^{23} - 2^{40}$?

(A) 3

(B) 5

(C) 7

(D) 11

(E) 13

30.   If $z + y < 0$, is $z - x > 0$?

(1) $x < y < z$

(2) $x + y = 0$

31.   A teacher creates a test with x statements, each of which is true or false. What is the smallest value for x where the probability is less than $\frac{1}{1000}$ that a person who randomly guesses every question could get them all right?

(A) 10

(B) 20

(C) 25

(D) 50

(E) 100

32.   Machines A, B, and C can each print the required number of magazines in 12, 15, and 18 hours, respectively. What is the ratio of the time it takes machines C and B working together to print the required magazines to the time it takes all three machines working together to print them?

(A) $\frac{11}{90} : \frac{7}{30}$

(B) $\frac{11}{60} : \frac{9}{30}$

(C) $\frac{1}{11} : \frac{2}{37}$

(D) $\frac{90}{7} : \frac{30}{9}$

(E) $\frac{60}{14} : \frac{90}{22}$

33. There are 500 delegates at a leadership conference. During the day, breakout sessions are offered. Participants can attend workshops on networking, social media, or business plans. 80% of the delegates attend the workshops. 310 delegates attend the networking session. 250 delegates attend the business plan session. At least 45 delegates that attend at least one session do not attend either the networking or the business plan sessions. The number of delegates that attend both the networking and business plan workshops must be between:

(A) 160 and 205

(B) 205 and 250

(C) 160 and 250

(D) 205 and 310

(E) 250 and 310

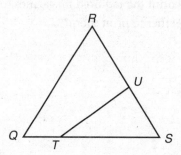

34. Equilateral triangle *QRS* has sides of length 6. The line *UT* is perpendicular to *RS*. If the length of *UR* is 4, what is the area of the quadrilateral *QRUT*?

(A) $\dfrac{7}{3}$

(B) $\dfrac{7}{\sqrt{3}}$

(C) $7\sqrt{3}$

(D) $9\sqrt{3}$

(E) $7 - 2\sqrt{3}$

35. Sheriff Roscoe travels from Hazzard County to Beaufort County by car in 35 minutes with a 5-minute bathroom stop on the way. He wants to shave his driving time on the way back by half. What average rate does Sheriff Roscoe need to reach on his way back?

   (1) Sheriff Roscoe's average speed traveling from Hazzard County to Beaufort County was 40 miles per hour.

   (2) The distance between Hazzard County and Jethro County, where Sheriff Roscoe made his bathroom stop, is 10 miles.

36. If sets x and y each have the same number of terms, is the standard deviation of set x greater than that of set y?

   (1) The first two terms and the last two terms of sets x and y are identical.

   (2) The range of set y is greater than the range of set x.

37. A jar contains g green marbles, r red marbles, and w white marbles. If one marble is chosen at random from the jar, is the probability that white will be chosen greater than the probability that red will be chosen?

   (1) $\dfrac{w}{(g+r)} > \dfrac{r}{(g+w)}$

   (2) $g - r > w$

STOP

ON THE ACTUAL GMAT,
AFTER YOU HAVE CONFIRMED YOUR ANSWER,
YOU CANNOT RETURN TO IT.

VERBAL SECTION

Time: 75 minutes

41 questions

Reading Comprehension

DIRECTIONS: This section contains three reading passages. You are to read each one carefully. When answering the questions, you *will* be allowed to refer back to the passages. The questions are based on what is *stated* or *implied* in each passage.

Critical Reasoning

DIRECTIONS: For each question in this section, choose the best answer from among the listed alternatives.

Sentence Correction

DIRECTIONS: This part of the section consists of a number of sentences, in each of which some part or the whole is underlined. Each sentence is followed by five alternative versions of the underlined portion. Select the alternative you consider both most correct and most effective according to the requirements of standard written English. Answer (A) is the same as the original version; if you think the original version is best, select answer (A).

In considering the answer choices, be attentive to matters of grammar, diction, and syntax, as well as clarity, precision, and fluency. Do not select an answer that alters the meaning of the original sentence.

Questions 1–3 are based on the following passage.

Though the modern recycling movement did not percolate up into the public consciousness until the mid-1970s, recycling itself has been a feature of human society as long as there have been human societies. Indeed, before the industrial
Line age made a variety of goods available quickly and cheaply, virtually every consumer
(5) product was recycled after it was no longer fit for its original purpose. Long before large-scale recycling programs became the norm, thrifty households used clothing too frayed and threadbare to itself be salvaged to patch and repair clothing not quite so worn. Even sweaters so moth-eaten that they could neither be darned themselves nor serve as darning for other clothing were put to use, first to sop up
(10) spills of precious oils in the kitchen and garage, thereafter as kindling or fire starters in cooking and heating fires.

The need in recent decades for large-scale recycling programs can be traced to the otherwise beneficial advances in mass production brought about by industry. When a tablecloth can be produced and purchased for less than the cost of the food
(15) served upon it, it makes economic sense to simply throw it away when it becomes soiled or ripped. What once might have been pressed into service as, if nothing else, a cheap source of household cleaning rags, is consigned instead to a landfill, along with cleaning rags purchased new *as* cleaning rags—an innovation no eighteenth- or nineteenth-century maid would ever have predicted. Why ever would one be so
(20) foolish as to spend good money on something that one could easily make at home for free?

1. The passage is primarily concerned with

   (A) describing the beneficial effects of the industrial age upon consumer products.
   (B) explaining the need for programs to increase the amount of consumer goods recycled.
   (C) discussing how some practices considered modern are in fact much older.
   (D) explaining how harmful the unintentional side effects of mass production have been.
   (E) describing one manner in which technological progress has changed economic behavior.

2. Each of the following is given in the passage as an example of a premodern recycling program EXCEPT:

   (A) repairing damaged clothing with clothing too damaged to be repaired.
   (B) consigning household cleaning rags to a landfill only after using them repeatedly.
   (C) using the side products of food preparation to prepare other foods.
   (D) employing an item originally purchased as a household furnishing to maintain other furnishings.
   (E) extending the lifespan of personal accoutrements by patching or darning them.

3. The function of the rhetorical question given in the last line of the passage is primarily to

(A) explain why many eighteenth- and nineteenth-century households were so frugal.

(B) contrast modern large-scale recycling efforts with earlier smaller-scale ones.

(C) suggest that what is now considered valuable was once considered useless.

(D) illustrate one way in which a modern problem has been created by technological change.

(E) emphasize the difference between impoverished and affluent households.

4. Employee morale is of tantamount importance to a business, as anything that reduces morale reduces the business's profitability. Thus, while it might seem like a prudent policy to reward exceptional employees with raises, parking spaces, and other perks, in practice this policy will backfire when those who do not receive such perks become aware of their existence.

Which of the following, if true, most strengthens the argument?

(A) Employee morale is generally reduced when compensation is unequal, even when performance is unequal.

(B) Of the things that reduce a business's profitability, damage to employee morale is the hardest to reverse.

(C) Businesses that reward performance with perks that do not include stock options are less profitable overall.

(D) Eliminating perks for employees is itself a way to increase the profitability of a company.

(E) When exceptional employees are rewarded with perks, their productivity and morale are both increased.

5. Only those with memberships at the Simon Island Country Club are allowed to use its golf course. Richard recently was admitted to membership at the Simon Island Country Club, so he will surely begin using the golf course.

The reasoning in the argument above is questionable because it

(A) confuses a policy that is regularly enforced with one that sometimes has exceptions.

(B) proceeds as though a fact that is required for the conclusion to be valid is also sufficient for it to be valid.

(C) asserts that in a given case only one of two options is possible, without eliminating other possible options.

(D) presupposes that a group of people who are alike in one respect must necessarily be alike in others.

(E) draws a conclusion that the premises of the argument, when taken to be true, explicitly contradict.

6. The Black Death (also known as the Bubonic Plague) <u>resulting in the death of about 75 million people, nearly one-third</u> of whom died in Europe alone.

   (A) resulting in the death of about 75 million people, nearly one-third
   (B) resulting in the death of nearly 75 million people, one-third nearly
   (C) resulted in the death of nearly 75 million people, nearing one-third
   (D) resulted in 75 million people having died, one nearly a third
   (E) resulted in the death of about 75 million people, nearly one-third

7. New research has enabled "bulk" silicon <u>to be able to emit broad-spectrum visible light and opening the possibility</u> of using the element in devices with both photonic and electronic components.

   (A) to be able to emit broad-spectrum visible light and opening the possibility
   (B) to emit broad-spectrum visible light and opening the possibility
   (C) to emit broad-spectrum visible light, opening the possibility
   (D) emit visible light and a broad-spectrum and open the possibility
   (E) be able to emit visible light in a broad-spectrum and to open the possibility

8. During the era of Jim Crow <u>many still were African-Americans treated like second-class citizens, even though they were freed</u> by the Emancipation Proclamation decades before.

   (A) many still were African-Americans treated like second-class citizens, even though they were freed
   (B) many African-Americans still were treated as second-class citizens, even though they had been free
   (C) many African-Americans were still treated as second-class citizens, despite having been freed
   (D) many African-Americans still were being treated as second-class citizens, even they had been freed
   (E) many second-class citizens still were treated, like African-Americans, even though they were freed

9. When Bogota's traffic problem grew too great to ignore, the mayor took an unorthodox step, firing many of the city's traffic officers and replacing them with mimes. These mimes followed traffic law violators and mimicked their behavior silently. In months, traffic had ceased to be a problem. This proves that sometimes the answer to a problem of compliance with the law is to shame law breakers rather than punishing them.

Each of the following is an assumption required by the argument above EXCEPT:

(A) the act of shaming someone for breaking a law should not be considered a form of punishment.

(B) the mimes who followed traffic violators did not single out a few habitual breakers of the law to mimic.

(C) the law breakers who were followed by mimes in Bogota afterward stopped breaking those laws.

(D) the traffic officers who were not fired did not markedly increase the rate at which they punished people for breaking traffic laws.

(E) noncompliance with traffic laws in some way contributed to the traffic problem in Bogota.

10. In order to both reduce their overall insurance costs and provide extra compensation to their employees, many companies now offer to match funds that employees pay into flexible healthcare spending accounts. After a three-year analysis of this practice in the tech industry, researchers concluded that the benefits to the companies went well beyond these expectations. In that industry, companies matching employee contributions to flexible healthcare spending accounts could, on average, expect their employee absentee rate to be 20% lower than among companies who did not.

Which of the following would most weaken the conclusion of the three-year study?

(A) Those technology companies able to afford to match employee contributions to health accounts are usually so successful that they are able to be very selective about those they hire.

(B) At companies that offer flexible healthcare spending accounts, employees may use them to pay for eye and dental care not covered by the normal health plan.

(C) Starting a flexible healthcare spending account requires substantial effort for the employees who desire one.

(D) In other industries where companies match employee contributions to flexible healthcare accounts, similar improvements in absentee rate have been seen.

(E) In the technology companies that match employee contributions to flexible healthcare accounts, average worker productivity is also higher.

Neuroscientists have for many years characterized sleep as a "whole brain phenomenon," a fully encompassing mental and biochemical state that is entirely distinct from those under which the brain operates when awake or even when
Line extremely fatigued. New research suggests, however, that the divide between
(5) wakefulness and sleep may not be so clear-cut as it once appeared.

Recently, a team led by Dr. Guilio Tononi conducted a series of experiments on sleeping rats in order to measure changes in activity in the brain as it slips from consciousness to unconsciousness and back again. Using a combination of scalp-mounted E.E.G. (or electroencephalography) and microwave arrays implanted
(10) directly in the frontal and parietal cortexes of the test subjects, the scientists were able to analyze both the sleeping and waking brain with a level of precision that had heretofore been unavailable. As expected, after falling asleep, the E.E.G. showed delta wave activity within the rats' brains, strong slow waves of electrical activity that are typical of deep, dreamless "slow wave sleep." The electrodes in the brain,
(15) however, told a different story. Although they recorded delta waves most of the time, they also revealed that there were episodes lasting from a few seconds to up to two minutes in which the motor cortex suddenly went into "waking mode." Delta waves disappeared and were replaced with fast, unpredictable activity.

Alternately, by recording the activity of many small populations of neurons while
(20) the rats had been kept awake artificially for a prolonged period, Tononi's team was also able to detect extremely brief, highly localized incidences of slow delta wave activity, the very hallmark of a brain in "sleeping mode." While the research remains in the early stages of completion, neuroscientists are cautiously optimistic that Tononi's research into the now increasingly nebulous border between these two
(25) modes of neural operation may help science arrive at a better understanding of the function of sleep itself.

11. Which of the following best describes the relationship between the experimental findings described in the second paragraph and those described in the third?

(A) The findings described in the second paragraph are revealed by the author to be anomalous when contrasted with those in the third.

(B) The findings described in the third paragraph are revealed by the author to be anomalous when contrasted with those in the second.

(C) Both sets of findings when taken together reveal that the experimental methodology of the researchers described in the passage is suspect.

(D) The findings described in the third paragraph each independently support the contention described by the author in the first paragraph.

(E) Neither set of findings independently support the researcher's original contention, but taken jointly suggest a new hypothesis worthy of further research.

12. Which of the following does the author indicate was true of the series of experiments performed by Tononi's lab?

(A) The researchers utilized technology that no rival lab could have fashioned with equal precision.

(B) The researchers utilized at least two sets of devices to obtain their experimental data.

(C) The highly localized incidence of slow delta wave activity detected could only be detected in test subjects that had been kept awake artificially.

(D) The delta waves detected by the first experiment interfered with the detection of other types of brain activity.

(E) Other labs lacking the unique combination of monitoring equipment used in the experiment will be unable to duplicate the experimental results.

13. Based on the passage, it can be inferred that prior to the work carried out by Tononi's research team, neuroscientists would have been surprised to detect

(A) slow wave delta activity in the brain of an unconscious test subject.

(B) microwave arrays implanted directly in the frontal and parietal cortexes of a waking test subject.

(C) two distinct biochemical states exhibited by a test subject before and after being awoken.

(D) fast, unpredictable activity within the motor cortex of a test subject whose brain is in "sleeping mode."

(E) a lack of activity other than delta waves in a sleeping test subject.

14. The primary purpose of the passage is to

(A) review research demonstrating the benefits of a new experimental technique and suggest future hurdles that it may bring about.

(B) present the findings of a group of researchers and the practical therapies their work will soon allow.

(C) describe the results of a recent set of experiments that challenge a significant assumption of a field of study.

(D) critique the callousness with which a provocative researcher conducts his clinical trials.

(E) lament the lack of practical applications for a series of experiments that were once thought to be promising.

_____

15. By signing the Kyoto Protocol a nation <u>is required to reduce their greenhouse gas emissions and to research an increase</u> in technology to increase the absorption of these gases already present in the atmosphere.

(A) is required to reduce their greenhouse gas emissions and to research an increase

(B) is required to reduce its greenhouse gas emissions and to increase research

(C) is required to reduce their greenhouse gas emissions and to researching an increase

(D) requires to reduce their emitting of greenhouse gas and to increasing research

(E) required to reduce its greenhouse gas emissions and to research increasing

16. Traders <u>who predicted a continuing of the loss in value of the commodity</u> were surprised Wednesday when pig futures posted a strong rally.

(A) who predicted a continuing of the loss in value of the commodity
(B) who predicted continuing losses in the commodity's value
(C) who had predicted the continuation of losses of the commodity's value
(D) who had predicted continuing losses in value for the commodity
(E) who had predicted a continuing loss for the value in the commodity

17. Researchers at the famous Copenhagen Institute <u>is working on developing new transgenic treatments and investigating the role played by tRNA in the spread of</u> cancer cells between tumorous sites within an individual.

(A) is working on developing new transgenic treatments and investigating the role played by tRNA in the spread of
(B) is working to develop new transgenic treatments and investigating the role played by tRNA in the spreading of
(C) are working to develop new transgenic treatments and investigating the role played by tRNA in the spread of
(D) are working on development of new transgenic treatments and the investigation of the role tRNA plays for the spread of
(E) are working on developing new transgenic treatments and investigating the role played by tRNA in the spread of

18. To combat gun violence, restrictions on private handgun ownership are often proposed, the idea being that the fewer guns available, the fewer guns will be used in violent crimes. The problem with such proposals is not, as is often said, that **when guns are outlawed, only outlaws have guns**, but rather that not all guns have the same likelihood of being used in a violent crime. Unless gun legislation is tailored so that it primarily reduces the number of these more dangerous guns—ones currently in the hands of criminals, or those which criminals might easily obtain—**such legislation will fail to reduce the amount of gun violence in a society**.

In the argument above, the two portions in **boldface** play which of the following roles?

(A) The first is an observation that the author uses to support a particular position; the second is that position.
(B) The first is a position the author takes as inadequate to explain a phenomenon; the second is the author's conclusion about certain plans that would address the phenomenon.
(C) The first is a prediction that the author argues will not hold in a specific case; the second is the prediction the author argues is more likely.
(D) The first is a prediction that the author believes to be untrue; the second is a restatement of that prediction treated as though it were an independent conclusion.
(E) The first is a direct relationship that the author asserts will not hold in this case; the second offers evidence in support of the author's assertion.

A collaborative artwork produced by Donatello and Michelozzo, the tomb monument of Antipope John XXIII is almost unanimously regarded among art historians as one of the earliest masterpieces produced during the Florentine
Line Renaissance of the Fifteenth Century. Precisely which master is responsible for which
(5) piece is a subject on which there is far less agreement. Nearly every element of the tomb, from the gilded bronze recumbent effigy that adorns the papal sarcophagus to intricately designed marble reliefs of the personified Virtues in niches beneath, has been attributed to both Donatello and Michelozzo by different art historians at one time or another. In making such attributions, a critic or commentator often indicates
(10) more about what he or she finds to be valuable. Those things prized will inevitably be seen as the work of the master Donatello. Aspects attributed to Michelozzo will almost always be supported by the observation that they are "less well executed." In the end then, the many varied and extensive discussions of the iconography and design of the monument tomb are most valuable to historiographers, art historians
(15) who study the history of art history itself, and are far less useful for those seeking to understand the development of the techniques used by either artist.

19. The author's primary purpose is to

   (A) refute the idea that particular features of the tomb of Antipope John XXIII can reliably be attributed.
   (B) describe the characteristics of an early masterpiece of Renaissance art.
   (C) argue that critical evaluations of a widely praised work of art are inevitably biased.
   (D) assert that certain works of art history reveal more about the historian than about the art.
   (E) rebut previous art historians who have incorrectly attributed the work of Donatello to Michelozzo.

20. If an art historian were to declare that one of the marble reliefs of personified Virtues found on the tomb of John XXIII required much more artistic skill to produce than the other two, the author would most likely take the assertion as evidence that

   (A) the relief in question was most likely the work of Donatello, rather than Michelozzo.
   (B) the more-skilled relief is equally likely to have been the work of either Donatello or Michelozzo.
   (C) the exact artist responsible for all three of the reliefs will never be reliably determined.
   (D) at least two of the reliefs should be considered to be the work of the same unknown artist.
   (E) the relief in question will provide insight into the qualities valued by the appraiser.

21. Which of the following can be inferred from the passage?

(A) The observations about a work of art's execution that are the most valuable are those that do not attempt to determine that work's original artist.

(B) Those works of art that cannot be reliably attributed to one artist are most likely to have been created by a collaboration between artists.

(C) Some works of art history that are unable to provide valuable information on their stated subject may provide other valuable information.

(D) Some works of history that are seen as more valuable by certain historians who study history are worthless to the general public.

(E) Many of those features of the monument tomb that are currently attributed to Donatello were probably the work of someone else.

---

22. A researcher studying the habits of highly effective CEOs found that there was a positive correlation between those who described themselves as having "goal-oriented" personalities and those who were rated as most effective by annual surveys of their employees. The researcher concluded that people with "goal-oriented" personalities are more likely, on average, than those without to seek a job as a CEO.

Each of the following, if true, would weaken the argument above EXCEPT:

(A) CEOs and other top executives are unlikely to be able to describe their own personality accurately.

(B) The annual surveys of employees are usually conducted immediately after the employees have been paid their annual bonuses.

(C) The term "goal-oriented" is so vague as to be able to apply to nearly any set of personal characteristics.

(D) CEOS who do not describe themselves as "goal-oriented" rarely remain CEOs for long.

(E) The researcher made no effort to control for other variables that might have influenced the finding.

23. Analyst: Offshoot Records has weathered changes in the music marketplace for over sixty-four years. However, as customers become accustomed to purchasing music via downloadable file, rather than via physical media such as CDs and LPs, it will become increasingly difficult for locally owned music stores like Offshoot to remain profitable. Expect Offshoot to close its doors within the next year.

   Which of the following, if true, makes the analyst's prediction about the future viability of Offshoot Records more likely to be correct?

   (A) There are no other locally owned music stores that have successfully adapted to the challenge of digitally distributed music.
   (B) The only way that a music store can remain profitable is if its customers remain loyal and eschew general trends.
   (C) Sales at Offshoot Records have not been increasing over the past few months.
   (D) CDs and LPs make up the vast majority of the stock on sale at a locally owned music store like Offshoot Records.
   (E) The past sixty-four years have presented Offshoot with challenges largely dissimilar to the present shift toward digital distribution.

24. The U.S. Supreme Court recently ruled that the military commissions enacted as part of the response to global terrorism are not constitutional; as they are violating the separation of powers.

   (A) constitutional; as they are violating
   (B) constitutional; a violation of
   (C) constitutional, but rather they violate
   (D) constitutional; but rather that they violate
   (E) constitutional, but rather it violates

25. The newly elected board of regents must consider whether to recommend that the disgraced head of the football program be released from his contract.

   (A) whether to recommend that the disgraced head of the football program be released
   (B) whether to recommend that the disgraced head of the football program should be released
   (C) whether it should recommend that the disgraced head of the football program be released or not
   (D) if it should make the recommendation that the disgraced head of the football program should be released
   (E) if to recommend that the disgraced head of the football program should be released

26. After a decade that saw steep increases in the average price of cars aimed at the middle of the market, overall sales of cars in this category have finally begun to suffer. In an attempt to stem the loss of sales, one major Detroit automaker has reduced the price of its middle-tier cars by 12%. However, since few other automakers are likely to follow suit, the average price of a middle-tier car is unlikely to fall significantly.

Which of the following indicates the main conclusion of the argument above?

(A) The average price of cars aimed at the middle of the market has increased steeply over the past decade.

(B) One major Detroit automaker has reduced the price of its middle-tier cars by 12%.

(C) Few automakers are likely to adopt the price reduction that one automaker has recently announced.

(D) The sales of middle-tier cars have suffered significantly over the past decade.

(E) The actions of one automaker are not likely to affect the average price of cars aimed at the middle of the market.

27. You may know Martha Rose Shulman as a food critic, but in her kitchen she leads a double life as a ghost-writer of pastry cookbooks.

(A) You may know Martha Rose Shulman as a food critic, but

(B) You might know Martha Rose Shulman to be a food critic,

(C) Although you may know of Martha Rose Shulman as a food critic, still

(D) While you may know that Martha Rose Shulman is a food critic, although

(E) You might know Martha Rose Shulman as a food critic,

28. The Battle of Bull Run—or Manassas, as it was known in the South—was the first major ground engagement of the American Civil War resulting in over 2,000 dead and nearly half again that number were wounded.

(A) resulting in over 2,000 dead and nearly half again that number were wounded

(B) and resulting in over 2,000 dead and nearly that number and half wounded

(C) resulted in over 2,000 dead and nearly that number plus half of the wounded

(D) and resulted in over 2,000 dead and nearly half again that number wounded

(E) and resulted in over 2,000 and nearly half again that number that were wounded

The principles of economics, Guido Calabresi argues in his Cost of Accidents, suggest that we ought to reject the idea that the central aim of tort law should be the minimization of the harm caused by accidents themselves, but rather the
Line minimization of the costs associated with accidents, including the costs that accrue
(5) from minimizing the risks of harm that accidents cause. Since any economically fruitful endeavor will increase the risk of some accident, he contends, any risk reduction will reduce in turn some economically fruitful activity, which would itself entail a cost. If a society wishes to minimize the overall cost of accidents and apportion those costs fairly, it must consider the amount expended reducing
(10) risk. After all, no one would ever seriously argue for a 5 mph speed limit on all motorways; the lost time and productivity would be unfathomably costly, no matter the lives saved.

Paradoxically, in order to make the case that the constraints faced by real-world actors necessitate the adoption of a legal analogue of the Neoclassical rational
(15) choice model of human agency—his chief and most influential contention— Calabresi resorts to the same idealized hypotheticals that he initially decries in previous critics when advocating this real-world turn toward economically driven legal analysis, a rhetorical weakness that is often noted. Nowhere is the tension between Calabresi's means and ends more evident than in the chapter concerning
(20) his insurance-incentive thesis, presented through hypothetical drivers Taney and Marshall and their carefully idealized decision whether to install a new kind of brake. The cost of installation is set by Calabresi's fiat at a flat $50, the cost of the accidents Taney would cause without it $25, Marshall $200.

As these intentionally oversimplified numbers nevertheless illustrate, a tort
(25) system that motivates Marshall to install the brake while allowing Taney to forgo it is clearly to be preferred, even though such a system would allow Taney to engage in risky behavior traditionally punished in civil courts. The proper venue for ensuring the desired outcome, Calabresi concludes, is the economic incentives inherent in the insurance system. If viewed as rational agents motivated by their own self-
(30) interest, as economists suggest, private insurers will set their premiums relative to the harm that drivers can be expected to cause, as the insurers will bear the cost of those accidents that occur. Since Marshall is far more costly without the brake than Taney, the insurers will increase his insurance premium commensurately. Similarly, Marshall will, if rational, certainly choose to pay the lower cost of installing the brake.

(35) The problem in Calabresi's use of hypotheticals in making his tidy case for the necessity of considering economic incentives when evaluating a legal system is, however, not simply a rhetorical one, for with them he avoids the central question he purports to answer: how to best determine the cost of accidents. In the real world governed by economic principles in which Taneys, Marshalls, and insurance
(40) companies must operate, who possesses the Calabresian insight to determine with such precision that one driver will cause $200 of damage in accidents per year, another $25, and to take action accordingly?

29. Which of the following titles most accurately expresses the main point of the passage?

(A) "Calabresi's Cost of Accidents: More Relevant Today Than Ever Before"
(B) "Calabresi's Insight as Oversight: Implications of His Hypotheticals"
(C) "Calabresi's Folly Revisited: The Underappreciated Genius"
(D) "When Marshall Met Taney: Real-World Data Confirms Calabresi"
(E) "Guido Calabresi Reconsidered: The Influence of an Economic Titan"

30. If the author's appraisal of Calabresi's work is accurate, which of the following must he also believe?

(A) When there arises a conflict between rational self-interest and the behavior traditionally punished by courts, economic considerations must be put aside.
(B) A legal theory's use of economic calculations that are too simple to correspond closely to the real world is not alone cause to reject all the claims made by that theory.
(C) Rhetorical weaknesses are usually the least serious defects that a theoretical framework is vulnerable to.
(D) Whether an activity is economically fruitful is less important a consideration in its continuation than whether that activity causes substantial harm.
(E) Only those theories that reconcile the competing self-interests of multiple rational agents will be able to accurately guide public policy concerning the cost of accidents.

31. Based on the passage's description of Calabresi's argument, each of the following would contradict at least one of Calabresi's theoretical commitments EXCEPT:

(A) there are some real-world costs associated with the harm caused by attempts to minimize larger harms that we ought to ignore for the purposes of devising a legal theory.
(B) in cases where a risk can be mitigated without government intervention, it is unlikely that there is any harm associated with that risk.
(C) an agent acting in accord with the dictates of rational self-interest will often elect to ignore the costs that another party's behavior will later cause that agent.
(D) the value of a human life is so great that attempts to create an economic theory robust enough to guide our behavior in most cases will always fail in those cases where many lives will inevitably be lost.
(E) should an economic theory seem to imply that we engage in behavior that is currently considered improper, that is grounds enough to reject that theory's application.

32. With which of the following evaluations of Calabresi's theories is the author of the passage most likely to agree:

(A) Because of the tension between his theories' ends and means, it is unlikely to be accepted widely in society.

(B) Because his own theories insist upon the necessity of taking economic considerations into account when evaluating a legal theory, they display little insight into economic affairs more broadly.

(C) Because his theories share assumptions and methodologies with Neoclassical economic theory, they are less useful to lawyers than the theory of accident cost that they replaced.

(D) Even though his theories fail to provide a manner in which the exact costs associated with accidents may be determined, they are still correct in asserting that accident cost ought to include the costs of risk aversion.

(E) Even though his theories sometimes appear to advocate outcomes that are at odds with current jurisprudence, they should be rejected only if they also fail to explain the economic component of those outcomes.

33. Unlike older televisions that used cathode ray tubes, which required heavy lead shielding to protect viewers, no shielding is needed by LED or LCD televisions, allowing them to be much lighter than their predecessors.

(A) to protect viewers, no shielding is needed by LED or LCD televisions, allowing them to be much lighter than their predecessors

(B) to protect viewers, LED or LCD televisions need no shielding that allows them to be much lighter than their predecessors were

(C) protecting viewers, LED or LCD televisions are allowed to be much lighter without shielding than their predecessors

(D) for viewers' protection, no shielding is needed by LED or LCD televisions to allow them to be much lighter than their predecessors

(E) for viewers' protection, LED or LCD televisions need no shielding, allowing them to be much lighter than their predecessors

34. Foreign aid is said to be "tied" when it is given with the stipulation that it may only be used to purchase items from the nation lending the aid. This practice has fallen out of favor in the international community, as it always results in economies more dependent on foreign money than before the aid. Even the relatively successful tied aid given by China to Singapore to rebuild in the wake of a devastating earthquake would today be frowned upon.

Which of the following can most reasonably be inferred from the passage?

(A) Even when ethical considerations outweigh a nation's self-interest, tied aid will not produce an ethical outcome.

(B) Countries that give tied aid most often do so out of a desire to benefit domestic businesses and industries.

(C) Even when tied aid is motivated by purely ethical concerns, it will exacerbate at least one economic problem in the receiving nation.

(D) China's actions would be more frowned upon if there had not been a recent earthquake in Singapore.

(E) Tied aid has caused more damage to the economies of the nations receiving it than most other economic factors.

35. When we read the histories written centuries ago, we must remember that many, if not most, works of history ever written have been lost, for histories must be transmitted in books, yet books are fragile things prone to much abuse even in one lifetime, unlikely to survive more than a handful of centuries. To combat this constant reduction of existing copies across the millennia, a history must be recopied, and no book will be recopied if it does not manage to speak across the centuries to those who would do that recopying. Thus, no matter how valueless an ancient history might seem to our modern sensibilities, its very existence is testament to its value.

Which of the following, if true, most strengthens the conclusion above?

(A) No work of ancient history would have been copied in sufficient quantities to allow a small fraction of its copies to remain without being recopied.

(B) No work of ancient history will be able to speak across the centuries unless it appeals equally to those living in each century.

(C) No work of ancient history that has failed to survive to the modern day would have appealed to modern sensibilities if it had survived.

(D) All works of ancient history that are valuable were recopied.

(E) All works of ancient history that speak across centuries are recopied in sufficient quantities to allow their survival.

36. Noble gases are inert because <u>the completion of their outer electron orbital makes these elements more stable and less reactive when</u> in the presence of other atoms and molecules.

(A) the completion of their outer electron orbital makes these elements more stable and less reactive when

(B) the completing of its outer electron orbital makes these elements more stable and less reactive when it is

(C) the completion of its outer electron orbitals making them more stable and less reactive within

(D) of completing their outer electron orbitals, which makes these elements more stable and less reactive if

(E) the completion of their outer electron orbital makes these elements more stable and less reactive if

37. Though the press releases and other official statements of oil companies take great pains to emphasize that the scientific community is not unanimous in the belief that global warming can be tied to the burning of fossil fuels and other human activities, oil companies clearly do not believe this to be the case. If there were actually credible, respected scientists who rejected human-caused climate change, these companies would surely spend more money to support the research done by these dissenting voices, for they have a vested interest in making sure debate on the issue continues indefinitely.

Which of the following best explains the apparent discrepancy described above?

(A) Oil companies have only recently begun investing in scientific research that addresses climate change.

(B) Unless a researcher can credibly claim independence from those whom their research might benefit, they will not be as successful as those who can.

(C) Oil companies typically earmark money spent on research for technologies that would directly benefit their profits.

(D) Oil companies spend substantial amounts circulating their press releases and publicizing their other official statements.

(E) If a company spends money to support one side of a contentious issue, such support will be taken as a sign that the issue is already decided.

38. Fertilizer runoff caused by industrial-scale farm practices <u>overwhelm streams and rivers with excess nitrogen and fertilizes blooms of algae, depleting oxygen and leaving</u> vast "dead zones" in their wake.

(A) overwhelm streams and rivers with excess nitrogen and fertilizes blooms of algae, depleting oxygen and leaving

(B) overwhelm streams and rivers, with excess nitrogen that fertilizes blooms of algae, depleting oxygen and leaving

(C) overwhelms streams and rivers with excess nitrogen, fertilizing blooms of algae that deplete oxygen and leave

(D) overwhelms streams and rivers with excess nitrogen that fertilize blooms of algae and deplete oxygen, leaving

(E) has overwhelmed streams and rivers with excess nitrogen and have fertilized blooms of algae, depleting oxygen and leaving

39. Consolidated Foodstuffs recently changed the ingredients of its infant formula recipe, replacing high-fructose corn syrup (HFC) with cane sugar, even though **the greater expense of the latter means that the company will make less profit**. Because cane sugar is much better for the developing infant than HFC, doctors have praised the move, saying that **Consolidated Foodstuffs has demonstrated that it places more value on the health of its customers than on purely financial considerations**, as well it should. Unfortunately, there is a more likely explanation for the change. Pending regulation will likely remove the subsidy that currently ensures that the price of HFC remains artificially low.

The two **boldfaced** portions play which of the following roles?

(A) The first supports the argument's conclusion; the second calls into question that conclusion.

(B) The first supports the doctors' conclusion; the second states that conclusion.

(C) The first states the conclusion of the argument; the second supports that conclusion.

(D) The first states the doctors' conclusion; the second provides evidence used to support that conclusion.

(E) Both statements support the primary conclusion of the argument, but the second does so indirectly.

40. Though crocodiles and alligators both possess rows of sharp teeth, <u>before their food reaches the stomach the gizzard has stones swallowed earlier which further grind it.</u>

 (A) before their food reaches the stomach the gizzard has stones swallowed earlier which further grind it

 (B) before it reaches the stomach, the gizzard in which stones they have swallowed earlier is used to further grind their food

 (C) before it reaches the stomach, the gizzard in which stones swallowed earlier further grinds their food

 (D) their food is further ground into pieces in their gizzards by stones swallowed earlier before it reaches their stomach

 (E) before reaching the stomach in their gizzards, in which stones they swallow earlier further grind their food into pieces

41. <u>Purring, though often thought to be a sign of a cat's good mood, is actually an involuntary response caused by the stimulation of certain nerves.</u>

 (A) Purring, though often thought to be a sign of a cat's good mood, is actually an involuntary response caused by the stimulation of certain nerves.

 (B) Though often it is thought that cats purr because of its good mood, it is actually involuntary and responds to the cause of nerve stimulation.

 (C) Though often thought that cats purr because they are in a good mood, it is actually an involuntary response caused by the stimulation of certain nerves.

 (D) A cat's purring, though often thought to signify a good mood, is actually involuntarily a response caused by the stimulation of certain nerves.

 (E) The purring of a cat, thought often as though a sign of a good mood, is actually caused by the involuntary stimulation of certain nerves.

STOP

ON THE ACTUAL GMAT,
AFTER YOU HAVE CONFIRMED YOUR ANSWER,
YOU CANNOT RETURN TO IT.

INTEGRATED REASONING SECTION

1. i. B

  ii. B

2.

Could Be Classified	Could Not Be Classified	Animal
○	●	Penguin
●	○	Flamingo
○	●	Flying Squirrel
●	○	Pterodactyl
●	○	Eagle

3.

Yes	No
○	●
○	●
●	○

4.

Yes	No
○	●
○	●
○	●
●	○

5. B

6.

Either Day	Neither Day	Speaker
○	●	Branson, male, U.K.
○	○	Robinson, female, U.K.
○	○	D'Agostino, female, Brazil
●	○	Miller, female, Canada
○	○	Soares, male, India

7. i. A

  ii. B

8. B

9.

True	False
●	○
●	○
○	●

10. i. A

  ii. B

11.

True	False
○	●
●	○
○	●

12.

Would Help Explain	Would Not Help Explain
●	○
●	○
○	●

ANSWER KEY
Sample Test 1

QUANTITATIVE SECTION

1.	D	11.	B	21.	D	31.	A
2.	B	12.	C	22.	B	32.	C
3.	A	13.	D	23.	A	33.	B
4.	B	14.	B	24.	E	34.	C
5.	C	15.	E	25.	D	35.	A
6.	C	16.	B	26.	A	36.	E
7.	B	17.	E	27.	C	37.	A
8.	A	18.	D	28.	C		
9.	C	19.	D	29.	C		
10.	C	20.	B	30.	A		

VERBAL SECTION

1.	E	12.	B	23.	E	34.	C
2.	B	13.	D	24.	C	35.	A
3.	D	14.	C	25.	A	36.	A
4.	A	15.	B	26.	E	37.	E
5.	B	16.	D	27.	A	38.	C
6.	E	17.	E	28.	D	39.	B
7.	C	18.	B	29.	B	40.	D
8.	C	19.	D	30.	B	41.	A
9.	B	20.	E	31.	A		
10.	A	21.	C	32.	D		
11.	E	22.	B	33.	E		

SELF-SCORING GUIDE
Analytical Writing

Evaluate your essay (or have a friend or teacher evaluate it for you) on the following basis. Read your essay completely, paying special attention to its logical organization and use of examples and facts to buttress its claims or position. Assign a holistic score between 0 and 6, using the scale below.

6 OUTSTANDING

Cogent, well-articulated analysis of the issue or critique of the argument. Develops a position with insightful reasons and persuasive examples. Well organized. Superior command of language and variety of syntax. Only minor flaws in grammar, usage, and mechanics.

5 STRONG

Well-developed analysis or critique. Develops a position with well-chosen examples or reasons. Generally well organized. Clear control of language and variety of syntax. Minor flaws in grammar, usage, and mechanics.

4 ADEQUATE

Competent analysis or critique. Develops a position with relevant reasons or examples. Adequately organized. Adequate control of language, but may lack syntactic variety. May have some flaws in grammar, usage, and mechanics.

3 LIMITED

Competent but clearly flawed analysis or critique. Vague or limited in developing a position. Poorly organized. Weak in using relevant examples or reasons. Language used imprecisely or lacking in sentence variety. Contains major errors or frequent minor errors in grammar, usage, and mechanics.

2 SERIOUSLY FLAWED

Serious weaknesses in analysis and organization. Unclear or seriously limited in presenting or developing a position. Disorganized. Few relevant examples or reasons. Frequent serious problems in language and sentence structure. Numerous errors in grammar, usage, or mechanics that interfere with meaning.

1 FUNDAMENTALLY DEFICIENT

Little evidence of ability to organize and develop a coherent response to issue or argument. Severe and persistent errors in language and sentence structure. Pervasive pattern of errors in grammar, usage, and mechanics that severely interfere with meaning.

0 UNSCORABLE

Illegible or not written on the assigned topic.

ANSWERS EXPLAINED
Integrated Reasoning Section

1. **i. (B)** If you look at the scatter plot, you can see a distinct relationship between the two curved lines. Assuming that one variable is always a little bit more than the other variable at each point on the graph, the relationship is very strong. Even if you assume that one variable is larger than the other at some of the points and vice versa for the rest, the relationship is still strong given that the distance apart appears small and constant. Therefore, the correct answer is **B**.

   ii. (B) The absolute difference between the variables at each point in the chart is constant. Therefore, the graph would be plotted along the same number across, resulting in a straight line. Since the question doesn't say which variable is plotted on the x-axis and which is plotted on the y-axis, the only possible answer of the choices given is zero. Note that if "an undefined slope" was one of the choices instead of "a slope of zero," an undefined slope would be correct. Therefore, the answer is **B**.

2. **(Could Not Be Classified, Could Be Classified, Could Not Be Classified, Could Be Classified, Could Be Classified)**
   (i) Although the penguin has the appropriate beak, its forelimbs are not adapted for flying as described in the second criterion. Therefore a penguin **could not be classified** as a bird.
   (ii) The flamingo matches both criteria given: having a beak or bill and having wings adapted for flying. Therefore a flamingo **could be classified** as a bird.
   (iii) The flying squirrel's forelimbs could technically be said to have been adapted for flying. However, the flying squirrel clearly does not have a beak as defined in the first criterion. Therefore a flying squirrel **could not be classified** as a bird.
   (iv) The pterodactyl matches both criteria given: having a beak or bill and having wings adapted for flying. Therefore a pterodactyl **could be classified** as a bird.
   (v) The eagle matches both criteria given: having a beak or bill and having wings adapted for flying. Therefore an eagle **could be classified** as a bird.

3. **(No, No, Yes)**
   (i) First you need to determine the median number of employees per stores in Quebec. If you sort the chart by province, you can see that Quebec has 16 stores. Then if you sort by number of employees, you can see that the 8th and 9th largest numbers are 61 and 64, respectively. Therefore the median is 62.5. If you look quickly at the Ontario stores, you can count 27 of them. Just by going down the chart, which is already sorted by number of employees, you can quickly estimate that the median is within a group of Ontario stores with numbers of employees in the 70s. More specifically, the median is the 14th number, which is 77. Therefore the answer is **No**.
   (ii) If you sort by number of employees, you can see that the St. Jean store has 59 employees and also has a grocery section. Therefore the answer is **No**.
   (iii) If you sort by city, you will find more than 7 cities that have either two or three locations. Therefore the answer is **Yes**.

4. (No, No, No, Yes)

(i) Article 1 does mention that deforestation affects CO_2 emissions. However, no direct link is given in any article suggesting that deforestation is the only or the major cause of increasing CO_2 levels. Therefore the answer is **No**.

(ii) Both articles 1 and 2 cite that citizens vote down some environmental proposals. There is also mention of aggressive lobbying by the forestry industry. However, no direct link between the lobbying and voters striking down environment proposals is provided. Lobbying may be a strong cause but is not necessarily the main reason. Therefore the answer is **No**.

(iii) Dr. Finnegan mentions both the forestry industry and bottled-water industry in article 2. However, there is no mention of where his focus is or whether he would support one type of legislation over another. Therefore the answer is **No**.

(iv) Both articles 2 and 3 imply that scientists, one of whom is Dr. Finnegan, have opinions that differ from those of leaders of both industries. So you can say that the two parties may not always agree. Therefore the answer is **Yes**.

5. (B)

This question is a bit tougher because you are looking for support in the articles for four of the answer choices. Only one answer is not supported by the articles. Answer choice A is fine because article 1 mentions 20% of wildlife may become extinct. Answer choice C is supported because article 3 mentions that the price has actually tripled over the past two decades. Answer choice D is supported in article 3. Answer choice E is supported by article 1 since levels are expected to double in 50 years, which is still within the 21st century. Only answer choice B is not supported since there is no mention of vodka. Article 2 does mention that bottled water may have a premium price as a luxury item, but no specifics are given in the passage. Therefore the answer choice is **B**.

6. (Branson, Miller)

This problem has 3 constraints.

- Four or more international speakers are needed on Day 1.
- Four or more female speakers are needed on Day 2.
- No more than two speakers from the same country can appear on either day.

Day 1 already has four international speakers, but two are from the U.K. Therefore the only constraint that applies is that you cannot add speakers from the U.K. on Day 1. This constraint eliminates Branson and Robinson from Day 1.

Day 2 already has three female speakers. In addition, two speakers are from the U.S.A. and two are from Brazil. Therefore, you cannot add any speakers who are male, from the U.S.A., or from Brazil. These constraints eliminate Branson, D'Agostino, and Soares.

Therefore Branson can attend on neither day and Miller can attend on either day.

7. i. (A)

Graph 1 shows that Europe and Central Asia's GDP in 1999 was approximately $10 trillion. Graph 2 shows that Europe and Central Asia's growth in 2000 was −6.0%. The increase in GDP is approximately:

$$\$10 \text{ trillion} \times -0.06 = -\$0.6 \text{ trillion}$$

This amount, which converts to –$600 billion, is close to –$610 billion. Therefore the answer is **A**.

ii. (B) You already know from question 7. i. that Europe and Central Asia's GDP decreased by approximately $600 billion. Graph 1 shows that East Asia and Pacific have the only other significant GDP, approximately $7.5 trillion. Use the information from graph 2 and the calculator to determine the increase in GDP in 2000 for East Asia and Pacific:

$$\$7.5 \text{ trillion} \times 0.082 = \$0.62 \text{ trillion}$$

This GDP increase for East Asia and Pacific almost matches the GDP decrease for Europe and Central Asia, so they cancel out each other. You can estimate Latin America GDP growth to be approximately $0.2 trillion. Similarly, Middle East and North Africa have an approximate GDP growth of $0.1 trillion. The increase in GDP for Sub-Saharan Africa is insignificant. This total increase of approximately $0.3 trillion in GDP for all five regions, which is a little over $20 trillion, works out to approximately 1.5% growth. Therefore the closest answer is **B**.

8. **(B)** First notice how the answer choices vary. Then determine which products have a greater effect on the total cost. Goodie bags are far more expensive and have the smallest discounts, so answer choices C and E are likely to be quite high, especially since the ribbon and streamer amounts are also quite high. Next notice how many feet of ribbon and streamers are in each package. The ribbon package yields 48 feet of ribbon, while the streamer package yields 100 feet of streamers. Calculate the costs for the other answer choices:

A: ($8 × 4) + ($6 × 3) + ($4 × 3) + ($12 × 5) = $122 subtotal
$122 – ($15 ribbon discount + $10 goodie bag discount) = $97 total

B: ($8 × 7) + ($6 × 2) + ($4 × 2) + ($12 × 3) = $112 subtotal
$112 – $25 ribbon discount = $87 total

D: ($8 × 8) + ($6 × 4) + ($4 × 5) + ($12 × 2) = $132 subtotal
$132 – $25 ribbon discount = $107 total

Therefore the answer is **B**.

9. **(True, True, False)**

(i) At first glance, this problem doesn't seem to make sense. However, the trick is to consider the discounts given for large-scale spending. Since 9 packages of streamers cost $54, a $20 discount is given. This results in a total cost of only $34. In contrast, 8 packages of streamers cost $48 before the $10 discount is applied. The total cost for 8 packages of streamers is $38. Similarly, 7 packages of ribbons cost $56 minus the $25 discount, resulting in a total cost of only $31. In contrast, 6 packages of ribbons cost $48 before the $10 discount is applied. The total cost for 6 packages of ribbons is $38. Add the amounts:

9 streamers plus 7 ribbons: $34 + $31 = $65
8 streamers plus 6 ribbons: $38 + $33 = $71

Therefore the answer is **True**.

(ii) Calculate the cost of buying 300 feet of ribbon plus 900 feet of streamers and the cost of purchasing 144 goodie bags plus 24 balloons.

300 feet of ribbon: 7 packages × $8 = $56 subtotal

$56 – $25 discount = $31 total

900 feet of streamers: 9 packages × $6 = $54 subtotal

$54 – $20 discount = $34 total

300 feet of ribbon plus 900 feet of streamers: $31 + $34 = $65

144 goodie bags: 6 packages × $12 = 72 subtotal

$72 – $10 discount = $62 total

At this point, you can stop since you know a package of balloons will cost $4 and take the price of goodie bags and balloons above the price of the ribbons and streamers. Therefore the answer is **True**.

(iii) To get the maximum discount from all four products, Sally needs to spend more than $50 for each product. She would need:

- 7 packages of ribbons totaling $56
- 9 packages of streamers totaling $54
- 13 packages of balloons totaling $52
- 5 packages of goodie bags totaling $60

The total cost looks like it would be $222. Wait! Do not forget to include the discounts. When the discounts kick in, the total amount that Sally has to spend is reduced by $25 + $20 + $10 + $10 = $65. Therefore the total amount Sally spends is $157 and the answer is **False**.

10. i. (A) The regression lines for both math and English scores are very close to each other. However, you can see from the scatter plot that the dotted regression line (English) has a steeper slope than the solid regression line (math). Therefore the slope for the English score regression line is greater than the slope for the Math score regression line. The answer is **A**.

ii. (B) The easiest way to solve this is by looking at the scatter plot and counting how often a square (math) is above a diamond (English). Excluding the points where the square and diamond are too close to tell, you can find at least 13 diamonds that are higher than squares. This represents more than half of the 22 students. Therefore the students tend to score worse in math than in English. The answer is **B**.

11. (False, True, False)

(i) It's important to learn how to use the data given. In order to determine the in-store price points, look at the share of market in pounds (lb.) and the share of market in dollars ($). Calculate the average price per pound ($/lb.) just by dividing share in dollars by share in pounds. Determine the price per pound of the four cheeses:

Kruger Cheddar Mild: $\frac{\$1.60}{2.9 \text{ lb.}} = \$0.55/\text{lb.}$ Kruger Swiss: $\frac{\$8.50}{7.4 \text{ lb.}} = \$1.15/\text{lb.}$

Kruger Mozzarella: $\frac{\$14.70}{16.2 \text{ lb.}} = \$0.91/\text{lb.}$ Davinci Havarti: $\frac{\$3.20}{2.7 \text{ lb.}} = \$1.86/\text{lb.}$

Both cheddar and mozzarella give values of less than $1/lb. Both Swiss and Havarti give values higher than $1/lb. Looking at the other examples of these cheeses would show the same relationship. Therefore the cheddar and mozzarella are not higher priced than the Swiss and Havarti. The answer is **False**.

(ii) The best way to figure this out is by sorting by the share of market ($). You can use the calculator to add up all the shares by dollar for Swiss cheese products:

$$11.9 + 8.5 + 7.9 + 4.0 = 32.3$$

The only other competitor would be mozzarella. Add up the shares by dollar for mozzarella:

$$14.7 + 5.9 + 3.8 + 2.4 + 1.7 = 28.5$$

Therefore the answer is **True**.

(iii) The easiest way to determine King's cheese slices growth per pound is to sort by product. Then look at the change in sales vs. last year (lb.). Instead of using the calculator for a long list of numbers, just estimate. Try matching up the negative and positive values for King brand products. You should be able to estimate a little less than 70,000 lb. Now do the same for Davinci products. You will get a ballpark figure of around 90,000 lb. for Davinci. This should be enough information for you to answer the question with confidence. The answer is **False**.

12. **(Would Help Explain, Would Help Explain, Would Not Help Explain)**

(i) If you sort by change in % volume ($), you will see that most of the zippered packages are at the top of the list. This suggests a trend where consumers favor packages with zippers and would help to explain the statement. Therefore the answer is **Would Help Explain** the statement.

(ii) If you sort by change in % volume (lb.) or by change in % volume ($), you will notice four King products that have decreased by 100%. This would imply that they were discontinued. You may also notice that the same flavors were replaced by packages with zippers. Therefore the table **Would Help Explain** the statement.

(iii) The table does show that the price per pound of light cheese (e.g., King Swiss Light w/ Zipper) is higher than the price per pound of regular cheese (e.g., King Swiss w/ Zipper). However, no information is given regarding the manufacturing costs of any of the sliced cheeses. Therefore the table **Would Not Help Explain** the statement.

Quantitative Section

1. What is the remainder when 320 is divided by 400?

   (A) 0
   (B) 0.8
   (C) 80
   (D) 320
   (E) 400

   (D) In arithmetic, a remainder is what's left after dividing a divisor into a dividend. In this case, the divisor is 400 and the dividend is 320. When we divide through we get a quotient of 0 and a remainder of 320.

2. Which of the following is a factor of both 21 and 24 but not of 50?

   (A) 2
   (B) 3
   (C) 4
   (D) 5
   (E) 7

   (B) The best way to do this problem is to break down the prime factors. We get

   $$21 = 3 \cdot 7$$
   $$24 = 2 \cdot 2 \cdot 2 \cdot 3$$
   $$50 = 2 \cdot 5 \cdot 5$$

   Both 21 and 24 have the factor 3, but 50 does not.

3. Which of the following must be odd?
   (A) The sum of an odd and an even number
   (B) The sum of a positive and negative number
   (C) The difference between two even numbers
   (D) The quotient of two even numbers
   (E) The product of an odd and an even number

   (A) This is a property of numbers question. The two main ways to do this are to use your understanding of the properties of numbers or just to pick numbers and prove the answer. By definition, when you add an odd and an even number together, you always get an odd number. For example, $3 + 4 = 7$.

4. A store owner marked an item for $50. When he sold the item at a 10% discount, he made a 20% profit. What was the original cost of the item?
   (A) $36.00
   (B) $37.50
   (C) $39.00
   (D) $40.00
   (E) $40.09

   (B) Let the original cost of the item be x. At a 10% discount, the market item is now $45. In order to yield a 20% profit, we get

   $$1.2x = 45$$
   $$x = \$37.50$$

5. If $1000 is placed into account X, yielding 10% interest compounded annually and $1000 is placed into account Y using 10% simple annual interest, how much more will be in account X than in account Y at the end of 5 years?

(A) $0
(B) $100
(C) $110.51
(D) $133.31
(E) $146.41

(C) A good way to handle this question is to use a chart and calculate the amounts for each subsequent year using the percent increases given in the question:

Year	Account X	Account Y
0	$1000	$1000
1	$1100	$1100
2	$1210	$1200
3	$1331	$1300
4	$1464.10	$1400
5	$1610.51	$1500

The difference between the year 5 amounts is $110.51.

6. May and June both work for April, who owns a used-car dealership. May sold 18 cars in August, and June sold 12 cars in July. Of the cars that May sold, the range of the selling price was $16,000 and the lowest selling price was $5500. Of the cars that June sold, the range of the selling price was $17,500, and the lowest selling price was $7200. What was the range of the selling prices of the 30 cars sold by May and June for April?

(A) $16,200
(B) $18,700
(C) $19,200
(D) $21,500
(E) $22,700

(C) First look at the cars that May sold. If the lowest selling price was $5500 and the range was $16,000, then the highest selling price was 5500 + 16,000 = $21,500. Similarly for June, her highest selling price was 7200 + 17,500 = $24,700. Therefore, the range of all the car prices was $24,700 − $5500 = $19,200.

7. If $st + u = u$, and s does not equal 0, which of the following must be true?

(A) $|s - t| = 0$
(B) $t = 0$
(C) $s > t$
(D) $st = 1$
(E) $s + t = 0$

(B) If we subtract the u from both sides, we get $st = 0$. We know that either s or t must be zero. However, the question tells us that s cannot be zero. Therefore, t must be zero.

8. What is the ratio of the number of teaspoons of baking soda to the number of cups of chocolate chips required in a certain brownie recipe?

(1) The number of cups of chocolate chips required in the recipe is 350% of the number of teaspoons of baking soda required in the recipe.

(2) $2\frac{1}{2}$ more cups of chocolate chips than teaspoons of baking soda are required in the recipe.

(A) We're looking for the ratio of teaspoons of baking soda to cups of chocolate chips. Statement 1 gives us exactly that, saying that if we had 1 teaspoon of baking soda, there would be 3.5 cups of chocolate chips. *Sufficient*

Statement 2 gives us the difference between the numbers of cups of chocolate chips and the number of teaspoons of baking soda. This is not enough to give us a ratio because we don't know exactly how much of each ingredient there is. *Insufficient*

9. A certain list consists of many different integers. Is the product of all the integers in that list positive?

(1) When you multiply the smallest and the largest integers in the list, you get a positive number.

(2) There are an even number of integers in the list.

(C) Statement 1 tells us that there are either two positive numbers or two negative numbers, but we still don't know anything about the other numbers in the set. *Insufficient*

Statement 2 doesn't tell anything about what those numbers are, either positive or negative. *Insufficient*

When we combine both statements, we have two possibilities. If both numbers from statement 1 are positive, then all numbers in between are positive. Similarly, if both numbers are negative, then all the numbers in between are negative. Either way, with an even number of integers we will always have a positive product.

10. If T is a line in the xy-plane, what is the slope of T?

(1) The y-intercept of T is 4.

(2) The x-intercept of T is 5.

(C) This is a coordinate geometry question. Each statement by itself only gives us one point of line T and no idea what the slope is. When we combine the statements, we have two points on the graph, which is all we need to calculate the slope.

11. Is positive integer y divisible by 3?

    (1) $\dfrac{144}{y^2}$ is an integer

    (2) $\dfrac{y^2}{36}$ is an integer

(B) The best way to handle this question is to break it down into prime factors.

In statement 1, the number 144 breaks down into $12 \cdot 12 = 2 \cdot 2 \cdot 3 \cdot 2 \cdot 2 \cdot 3$. Since dividing by y is an integer, it's possible that y could be a multiple of 3 or a multiple of 2. *Insufficient*

In statement 2, the number 36 breaks down into $2 \cdot 3 \cdot 2 \cdot 3$. Since y is now a multiplier of 36, y must have all of the prime factors that 36 has. Therefore, y is at least a multiple of 6 and y is divisible by 3. *Sufficient*

12. How many more worker compensation insurance claims were filed in month V than in month Z?

    (1) For months W, X, Y, Z, the average number of first-time insurance claims filed was 272,000.

    (2) For months V, W, X, Y, the average number first-time insurance claims filed was 277,250.

(C) Each statement by itself is insufficient because statement 1 mentions only month Z and not month V, while statement 2 does the reverse. When we put both statements together, we can see conceptually that there are more insurance claims in month V because the average went up.

13. Machine A produces 1000 widgets in 5 hours. Machine B produces 450 widgets in 3 hours. While working together at their respective rates, how long will it take the machines to produce 2000 widgets?

    (A) $4\dfrac{4}{9}$ hours

    (B) 5 hours

    (C) $5\dfrac{9}{20}$ hours

    (D) $5\dfrac{5}{7}$ hours

    (E) 6 hours

(D) The best approach to solving any work rate problem is to create a unit rate. In this case

Machine A:
    1000 widgets/5 hours = 200 widgets/hour

Machine B:
    450 widgets/3 hours = 150 widgets/hour

We find the combined rate by just adding these 2 rates together = 350 widgets/hour.

To produce 2000 widgets, we get

$$\dfrac{2000}{350} = \dfrac{40}{7} = 5\dfrac{5}{7} \text{ hours.}$$

14. Leonardo da Vinci was invited to exhibit 3 new paintings, 4 new sculptures, and 2 new inventions at the local museum. If Leonardo has 5 new paintings, 5 new sculptures, and 3 new inventions from which he must choose, how many different combinations of paintings, sculptures, and inventions are available to him?

(A) 24
(B) 150
(C) 300
(D) 450
(E) 1050

(B) This is a combinations problem because the order doesn't matter. For each subgroup—paintings, sculptures, and inventions—we first calculate the separate combinations. Then we multiply them all together. We are given 5 paintings, 5 sculptures, and 3 inventions from which to choose 3 paintings, 4 sculptures, and 2 inventions. Using standard notation we get:

$_NC_K$(paintings) • $_NC_K$(sculptures) • $_NC_K$(inventions)
$= _5C_3 • _5C_4 • _3C_2 = (5 • 4) • 5 • 3 = 150$ possible combinations.

---

15. If T is a set of six positive, distinct integers with an average (arithmetic mean) of 12 and a median of 8, what is the smallest possible value of the largest number in the set?

(A) 19
(B) 20
(C) 21
(D) 22
(E) 23

(E) The key to this question is the word "distinct" and the fact that there are an even number of integers in the set. If the average is 12 and there are 6 integers, then the sum of the terms must be 72. If the median is 8, then the two middle numbers are 7 and 9. We want to minimize the numbers on the right-hand side, so we should maximize numbers on the left-hand side. This gives us the integers 5 and 6. At this point, we have:

$$(5, 6, 7, 9, ?, ?)$$

The sum of the first four terms is 27. To get to 72, the next two terms must add up to 45. To create the smallest possible value of the largest number in the set the numbers should be 22 and 23.

---

16. A certain granola mix is made up of raisins, bran flakes, and pecans. The mixture contains 30% bran flakes by weight and 40% pecans by weight. The bran flakes cost twice as much as the raisins per pound, and the pecans costs $2\frac{1}{2}$ times as much as the bran flakes per pound. Approximately what percent of the cost of the granola mix do the bran flakes contribute?

(A) 18%
(B) 20.7%
(C) 22.5%
(D) 24%
(E) 25%

(B) When a question contains too much information to easily manage, consider using a chart. We can set up the following:

Ingredient	Weight (%)	Cost/lb.	Weighted Cost
Raisins	30	x	$0.3x$
Bran Flakes	30	$2x$	$0.6x$
Pecans	40	$5x$	$2.0x$

We can see that the relative weighted cost of the bran flakes is $0.6x$ and the total cost is $2.9x$. The percent of the cost would be $\frac{6}{29} = 20.7\%$.

17. In a rectangular coordinate system, what is the *x*-intercept of a line passing through (4, 3) and (6, 9)?

(A) (–3, 0)
(B) (0, 3)
(C) (–3, –3)
(D) (1, 0)
(E) (3, 0)

(E) By using 2 points on a coordinate plane, we can calculate the slope, which is

$$\frac{(9-3)}{(6-4)} = \frac{6}{2} = 3$$

This means that every time the *y*-coordinate decreases by 3, the *x*-coordinate decreases by 1. So if we look at (4, 3), the *x*-intercept will be where *y* = 0, which will be at (3, 0).

---

18. At what speed must a runner return from the gymnasium to home, a distance of 30 km, if the trip there took 2.5 hours and she wishes to average 15 km/h for the entire trip?

(A) 12 km/h
(B) 15 km/h
(C) 18 km/h
(D) 20 km/h
(E) 24 km/h

(D) The best way to do distance-rate-time (DRT) problems is with a chart. We can input the information we are given as well as the information that is implied (in bold type).

	Trip to Gym	Trip to Home	Total
D	30 km	**30 km**	60 km
R			15 km/hr.
T	2.5 hrs.	**1.5 hrs.**	4 hrs.

Since we know the total distance and the average rate required for both of the trips combined, we get 4 hours total. This means that the time to go home takes 1.5 hours. Finally, we can calculate the rate for the trip home, which is $\frac{30}{1.5}$ = 20 km/hr.

---

19. If Jonathan is 12 years younger than Sebastian, how old is Sebastian today?

(1) In three years from now, the combined ages of Sebastian and Jonathan will be 11 times the current age of Jonathan.

(2) Four years from today, Jonathan will be one-third the age of Sebastian.

(D) We know that $J = S - 12$. We need to solve for S. To do this, you will likely need another distinct equation with J and S.

Statement 1 gives you a relationship between J and S. Note that we don't need to create the distinct algebraic equation because you already know conceptually that we have one. *Sufficient*

In case you're curious, the equation would be

$$J + 3 + S + 3 = 11J$$

$10J = S + 6$, combining with the original equation $J = S - 12$, we can then subtract the equations to get $9J = 18$, $J = 2$. Therefore $S = 14$.

Note that in data sufficiency problems, we do not have to solve for the equation. We just have to know that we can. Two distinct equations and two unknowns is enough to know that this statement is sufficient to solve the problem.

Statement 2 also gives you a relationship between J and S. *Sufficient*.

The equation here would be $J + 4 = \left(\frac{1}{3}\right)(S + 4)$.

20. The upscale restaurant Sassafras adds an 18% gratuity to all bills with groups of 6 or more but adds no gratuity for groups with fewer than 6 people. If a group of friends ate at this restaurant, what was their total bill, not including any gratuity?

(1) There were 6 people in the group of friends.

(2) The total gratuity for the meal was $16.30.

(B) Statement 1 tells us the number of people in the group but says nothing about the bill. *Insufficient*

Statement 2 gives us the total gratuity, from which you can use the 18% to calculate the total bill. The trick here is that it doesn't matter how many friends there are as a gratuity value is all we need. *Sufficient*

---

21. A square lawn is reduced in size by removing 3 feet from one dimension and 5 feet from the other. By what percentage did these changes reduce the area of the original lawn?

(1) The area of the lawn was 35 square feet after the changes.

(2) After the changes, the longer dimension was three-tenths shorter than before the changes.

(D) A good way to proceed is to draw the square.

A square of side s has an area of s^2. With the changes, the area becomes $(s-3) \cdot (s-5)$.

Statement 1 tells us $(s-3) \cdot (s-5) = 35$. If you pick numbers, you can see that if $s = 10$, then the equation becomes $7 \cdot 5 = 35$. Thus we can determine that $s = 10$. *Sufficient*

Statement 2 tells us that $s-3 = \left(\dfrac{7}{10}\right) \cdot s$. We can solve this equation to get

$$s - \left(\dfrac{7}{10}\right) \cdot s = 3$$

$\left(\dfrac{3}{10}\right) \cdot s = 3$, which gives us $s = 10$. *Sufficient*

---

22. Is x an integer?

(1) $4x$ is an integer.

(2) $x - 1$ is not an integer.

(B) Statement 1 tells us that x could be an integer such as 1 or 2 or a noninteger such as $\dfrac{1}{2}$ or $\dfrac{1}{4}$. *Insufficient*

Statement 2 tells us that x could only be a noninteger. Therefore, the answer to the macro data sufficiency question is no. *Sufficient*

23. For any triangle Q in the xy-coordinate plane, the center of Q is defined to be the point whose y-coordinate is the average of the y-coordinates of the vertices of Q and whose x-coordinate is the average of the x-coordinates of the vertices of Q. If a certain triangle has vertices on the points (0, 0) and (10, 0) and center at the point (5, 4), what are the coordinates of the remaining vertex?

(A) (5, 12)

(B) (5, 8)

(C) (10, 5)

(D) (7.5, 6)

(E) (6, 10)

(A) A lot of information is provided in this question. The key is that the triangle's center point is the average of the other 3 points on the triangle. So we would get (0, 0), (10, 0), (x, y), which averages out to (5, 4).

If we isolate the x- and y-values we get

$$0 + 10 + x = 3 \bullet 5, \text{ therefore } x = 5.$$

$$0 + 0 + y = 4 \bullet 3, \text{ therefore } y = 12.$$

Province	Amount of Organic Waste Collected Normally	Amount of Organic Waste Extracted from Regular Garbage
New Brunswick	21,400	4100
Nova Scotia	49,100	8900
Prince Edward Island	17,200	3400
Quebec	112,600	17,800
Ontario	62,500	14,100

24. The table above shows the amount of organic waste, in metric tons, collected by five provinces in Canada and the amount of organic waste extracted from regular garbage in a certain year. Which province has the highest ratio of normal organic waste collected to extracted organic waste collected?

(A) New Brunswick

(B) Nova Scotia

(C) Prince Edward Island

(D) Ontario

(E) Quebec

(E) Whenever we see a table in problem solving, we can usually approximate the top few possibilities. Alternatively, we can just estimate the ratios to isolate our best choices quickly. If we look at answer choices A, B, and E, their ratios are approximately 5:1. Looking more closely at our two finalists shows us that Quebec's ratio is little over 6:1 and Prince Edward Island's ratio is closer to 5:1. Be careful here not to be tricked by the shuffling of the answer choices!

25. The equilateral triangle above has sides of length x, and the square has sides of length y. If the two regions have the same area, what is the ratio of $x : y$?

(A) $\dfrac{2}{3}$

(B) $\dfrac{4}{3}$

(C) $\dfrac{2}{\sqrt{3}}$

(D) $\dfrac{2}{\sqrt[4]{3}}$

(E) $\dfrac{4}{\sqrt[4]{3}}$

(D) The area of the equilateral triangle is $\dfrac{(x^2\sqrt{3})}{4}$ and the area of the square is y^2.

If we set them equal to each other, we get

$$\frac{(x^2\sqrt{3})}{4} = y^2$$

$\dfrac{x^2}{y^2} = \dfrac{4}{\sqrt{3}}$. If we take the square root of both sides, we get

$$\frac{x}{y} = \frac{2}{\sqrt[4]{3}}$$

---

26. The marketing team at Alpha Company decides to go to lunch to celebrate Jim's birthday. The lunch costs a total of L dollars, and there are C members on the marketing team, not including Jim. If F of the team members forget their wallets, which of the following represents the extra amount, in dollars, that each of the remaining team members would have to pay?

(A) $\dfrac{FL}{(C(C-F))}$

(B) $\dfrac{L(C-F)}{C}$

(C) $\dfrac{L}{(C-F)}$

(D) $\dfrac{FL}{(C-F)}$

(E) $\dfrac{L}{C}$

(A) Determining the correct answer to this question involves algebra, so it's particularly important to keep track of what each variable means. We can break this down into 2 parts.

The cost per team member $= \dfrac{L}{C}$

The cost for each remaining member when F people can't pay $= \dfrac{L}{(C-F)}$

The additional cost for those members who can pay is $\dfrac{L}{(C-F)} - \dfrac{L}{C}$

When we manipulate this equation to have a common denominator, we get

$$\frac{(L \cdot C - L \cdot (C-F))}{C(C-F)} = \frac{FL}{(C(C-F))}.$$

27. Is $\dfrac{1}{x} > \dfrac{y}{(y^2+2)}$?

(1) $y > 0$

(2) $x = y$

(C) Statement 1 doesn't tell us anything about x. *Insufficient*

Statement 2 looks sufficient, but the original equation is an inequality with variables. Whenever that happens, we must ask ourselves, "Are we multiplying or dividing by a negative number?" Since we don't know for sure, we cannot answer the question. *Insufficient*

When we put both statements together, we know that y is positive. So we can manipulate the equation to reach a solution. *Sufficient*

---

28. The operation Ω is defined for all positive integers a and b by $a \, \Omega \, b = \dfrac{2^a}{2^b}$. What does $(4 \, \Omega \, 2) \, \Omega \, 5$ equal?

(A) 0

(B) 2^{-2}

(C) 2^{-1}

(D) 4

(E) 2^5

(C) Many people find operation or symbol questions difficult. The key is to understand the function given and simply replace the values given for a and b. We proceed in two steps.

$$4 \, \Omega \, 2 = \dfrac{2^4}{2^2} = 4$$

$$4 \, \Omega \, 5 = \dfrac{2^4}{2^5} = 2^{-1}$$

---

29. What is the greatest prime factor of $4^{23} - 2^{40}$?

(A) 3

(B) 5

(C) 7

(D) 11

(E) 13

(C) This question appears intimidating because the calculations would be very time consuming. We need a shortcut. Whenever exponents are being added or subtracted, look for common factors to take out of each term.

You should also work with the same prime factor base, in this case 2.

$$4^{23} - 2^{40} = 2^{46} - 2^{40} = 2^{40}(2^6 - 2^0) = 2^{40}(64 - 1)$$
$$= 2^{40}(63) = 2^{40}(3 \bullet 3 \bullet 7).$$

The highest prime factor here is 7.

---

30. If $z + y < 0$, is $z - x > 0$?

(1) $x < y < z$

(2) $x + y = 0$

(A) Whenever you see variables and inequalities in data sufficiency problems, consider using properties of numbers, algebraic manipulation, and picking numbers as strategies.

Let's jump ahead to statement 2, which has no mention of z. *Insufficient*

By examining the information provided in statement 1, we see that the question is really asking if $z > x$. Statement 1 tells us exactly that. *Sufficient*

31. A teacher creates a test with x statements, each of which is true or false. What is the smallest value for x where the probability is less than $\frac{1}{1000}$ that a person who randomly guesses every question could get them all right?

(A) 10
(B) 20
(C) 25
(D) 50
(E) 100

(A) Suppose we have a true or false test with only one question. The probability that we will get the right answer is $\frac{1}{2}$. If the test had 2 questions, the probability of getting all questions right would be $\frac{1}{4}$. So using this construct, we should be able to see a pattern.

$$P(3 \text{ questions right}) = \frac{1}{8} \text{ or } \frac{1}{2^3}$$

$$P(4 \text{ questions right}) = \frac{1}{16} \text{ or } \frac{1}{2^4}$$

So the real question is what powers of 2 are greater than 1000? The answer is $2^{10} = 1024$.

---

32. Machines A, B, and C can each print the required number of magazines in 12, 15, and 18 hours, respectively. What is the ratio of the time it takes machines C and B working together to print the required magazines to the time it takes all three machines working together to print them?

(A) $\frac{11}{90} : \frac{7}{30}$

(B) $\frac{11}{60} : \frac{9}{30}$

(C) $\frac{1}{11} : \frac{2}{37}$

(D) $\frac{90}{7} : \frac{30}{9}$

(E) $\frac{60}{14} : \frac{90}{22}$

(C) By looking at the answer choices, we can see that this problem has complicated values. We need to break it down into 2 sections. First, let's calculate the rates that this question requires.

$$R_B = \frac{1}{15} \text{ job/hr.}$$

$$R_C = \frac{1}{18} \text{ job/hr.}$$

$$R_{B\&C} = \frac{1}{15} + \frac{1}{18} = \frac{(6+5)}{90} = \frac{11}{90} \text{ job/hr.}$$

This means that the time it takes machines B and C working together is $\frac{90}{11}$ hours.

Similarly, calculate the rate of all 3 machines working together.

$$\frac{11}{90} + \frac{1}{12} = \frac{(22+15)}{180} = \frac{37}{180} \text{ job/hr.}$$

So the time it takes all 3 machines to complete the job is $\frac{180}{37}$ hours. The ratio would reduce to $\frac{1}{11} : \frac{2}{37}$.

33. There are 500 delegates at a leadership conference. During the day, breakout sessions are offered. Participants can attend workshops on networking, social media, or business plans. 80% of the delegates attend the workshops. 310 delegates attend the networking session. 250 delegates attend the business plan session. At least 45 delegates that attend at least one session do not attend either the networking or the business plan sessions. The number of delegates that attend both the networking and business plan workshops must be between:

(A) 160 and 205
(B) 205 and 250
(C) 160 and 250
(D) 205 and 310
(E) 250 and 310

(B) This is a Venn diagram problem. Draw it out, and input the information that you know.
Total: 400

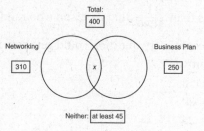

When we use the standard formula for Venn diagrams, we get

Total = Networking + Business Plan + Neither – Both

$$400 = 310 + 250 + \text{at least } 45 - x$$

$$x = \text{at least } 205$$

We can't have more than 250 people taking the business plan workshop since that is the total amount possible from our Venn diagram.

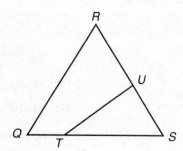

34. Equilateral triangle QRS has sides of length 6. The line UT is perpendicular to RS. If the length of UR is 4, what is the area of the quadrilateral $QRUT$?

(A) $\dfrac{7}{3}$

(B) $\dfrac{7}{\sqrt{3}}$

(C) $7\sqrt{3}$

(D) $9\sqrt{3}$

(E) $7 - 2\sqrt{3}$

(C) Equilateral triangles have angles of 60° and UT is perpendicular to RS. Thus angle UTS is 30° and triangle UTS is a 30-60-90 triangle. Using 30-60-90 ratios, which are $1:\sqrt{3}:2$, we can calculate that $UT = 2\sqrt{3}$. Now we can calculate the area of both triangles.

Area of equilateral triangle $= \dfrac{S^2\sqrt{3}}{4} = \dfrac{(6^2\sqrt{3})}{4} = 9\sqrt{3}$

Area of smaller triangle $= \dfrac{1}{2}\, b \bullet h$

$$= \dfrac{1}{2} \bullet 2 \bullet 2\sqrt{3} = 2\sqrt{3}$$

Therefore the area of quadrilateral $QRUT$ is

$$9\sqrt{3} - 2\sqrt{3} = 7\sqrt{3}\ .$$

35. Sheriff Roscoe travels from Hazzard County to Beaufort County by car in 35 minutes with a 5-minute bathroom stop on the way. He wants to shave his driving time on the way back by half. What average rate does Sheriff Roscoe need to reach on his way back?

(1) Sheriff Roscoe's average speed traveling from Hazzard County to Beaufort County was 40 miles per hour.

(2) The distance between Hazzard County and Jethro County, where Sheriff Roscoe made his bathroom stop, is 10 miles.

(A) The best way to solve DRT problems is with a chart. With data sufficiency questions, it's always good to sort out what we know, both direct and implied. Note that the bathroom break shouldn't matter because the question says driving time. If we fill in the chart, using hours instead of minutes for the time, we get the following. Given information is in bold type.

	Hazzard to Beaufort	Beaufort to Hazzard	Total
D			
R	**R = 40 miles/hr**		
T	0.5 hours	want 0.25 hours	

We want the time back to be 15 minutes. We need more information on the distance and rate that Sheriff Roscoe traveled on his trip from Hazzard County to Beaufort County.

Statement 1 gives us the average rate from Hazzard to Beaufort. From this, we can calculate the distance from Hazzard to Beaufort because $D = rt = (0.5) \cdot 40 = 20$ miles. We can then calculate the required rate to get back in half the time using 20 miles = $(R_{back}) \cdot (0.25$ hours$)$. This will give us that the rate would be 80 mph.

A simpler way to do this is to realize that once we know the original rate is 40 mph, then we just need to double the rate in order to half the time going back. *Sufficient*

Statement 2 gives us the rate from Hazzard to Jethro. There is no way to determine how far Jethro is from Beaufort. Be careful that you don't assume it is halfway there. Statement 1 may have told you the distance was 20 miles, but you can't take information from one statement and apply it to another statement. You need to look at each statement independently. *Insufficient*

36. If sets x and y each have the same number of terms, is the standard deviation of set x greater than that of set y?
 (1) The first two terms and the last two terms of sets x and y are identical.
 (2) The range of set y is greater than the range of set x.

(E) Statement 1 gives us no information about the middle elements in the set, so we have no idea how many elements are in sets x and y. *Insufficient*

Even though statement 2 tells us that the range of set y is greater than the range of set x, we still do not know all of the actual elements. The average of the elements may vary greatly. Standard deviation is a measurement of the spread of numbers around the mean. *Insufficient*

When we put both statements together, it appears that we have quite enough information for sufficiency. We know the first two terms and the last two terms are equal, and we know the range of y is greater than the range of x. However, depending on the number of elements in the set, the mean could vary significantly. Therefore, we cannot determine which set has the higher standard deviation. *Insufficient*

37. A jar contains g green marbles, r red marbles, and w white marbles. If one marble is chosen at random from the jar, is the probability that white will be chosen greater than the probability that red will be chosen?
 (1) $\dfrac{w}{(g+r)} > \dfrac{r}{(g+w)}$
 (2) $g - r > w$

(A) To solve this, what we really need to know is if there are more white marbles than red marbles in the jar, or if $w > r$. What does statement 1 tell us? Well, we may assume that if g is the same on both sides of the denominator (say $g = 1$), then the equation implies that $w > r$. This would allow us to answer the question. Is it possible, though, that r, g, and w are negative? No, because you cannot have a negative number of marbles. Be careful about the assumptions you make in the question. Thus, we can answer the question. *Sufficient*

For statement 2, we can rearrange the equation to get $g > r + w$.

This tells us only that the jar has more green marbles than any other types of marbles. We don't know whether $r > w$ or $w > r$. Therefore, we are unable to answer the question. *Insufficient*

Verbal Section

The passage for questions 1–3 appears on page 579.

1. The passage is primarily concerned with
   (A) describing the beneficial effects of the industrial age upon consumer products.
   (B) explaining the need for programs to increase the amount of consumer goods recycled.
   (C) discussing how some practices considered modern are in fact much older.
   (D) explaining how harmful the unintentional side effects of mass production have been.
   (E) describing one manner in which technological progress has changed economic behavior.

Question: Main Point questions are often made easier with a firm understanding of the author's tone, but not in this case, as all the answer choices are neutral in tone. Luckily, the content of this passage is not hard to ascertain. Answer Choice (E) works, as long as we realize that the *one manner* is the use of disposable products (and the subsequent need for recycling) and the *technological progress* is the changes to consumer goods mentioned as following the Industrial Revolution.

(E) The incorrect answers to this question are mostly of the "hoping to catch you sleeping" variety. Answer Choices (A) and (C) are mentioned, but they aren't the main idea (**part not the whole**), and Answer Choices (B) and (D) are both **real-world ideas** the test maker hopes you let bleed into your understanding of the passage.

2. Each of the following is given in the passage as an example of a premodern recycling program EXCEPT:
   (A) repairing damaged clothing with clothing too damaged to be repaired.
   (B) consigning household cleaning rags to a landfill only after using them repeatedly.
   (C) using the side products of food preparation to prepare other foods.
   (D) employing an item originally purchased as a household furnishing to maintain other furnishings.
   (E) extending the lifespan of personal accoutrements by patching or darning them.

Question: Whenever a passage contains a list of examples or a list of features of some phenomenon, a Detail EXCEPT question is always a good bet to expect. Usually, three of the details are found right next to each other, while one requires a bit of hunting (and is disguised through the clever use of synonyms). Here, there's no hidden answer; instead, one example is stated in two different ways (another way to get four wrong answers from a list of three examples). The incorrect answer is usually a **distortion** or a **misused detail**, and Answer Choice (B) is both. Landfills are mentioned, though using them repeatedly is something said to have happened when there weren't any landfills.

(B) Answer Choices (A) and (E) are both a restatement of the example of *clothing too frayed and threadbare to itself be salvaged [used] to patch and repair clothing not quite so worn.* Answer Choice (C) is an oblique way of saying that the rags used for sopping up spills of precious oils are later used as fire starters in cooking fires (the end of the first paragraph). And, finally, Answer Choice (D) is the example of the tablecloth from later in the passage, a furnishing later cut up to be used as cleaning rags.

---

3. The function of the rhetorical question given in the last line of the passage is primarily to

(A) explain why many eighteenth- and nineteenth-century households were so frugal.

(B) contrast modern large-scale recycling efforts with earlier smaller-scale ones.

(C) suggest that what is now considered valuable was once considered useless.

(D) illustrate one way in which a modern problem has been created by technological change.

(E) emphasize the difference between impoverished and affluent households.

Question: While finding the function of an example usually requires reading a few lines up, there might as well have been a colon following the immediately previous sentence, since the rhetorical question is just an example of *an innovation no eighteenth- or nineteenth-century maid would ever have predicted.* Recognize that since the maids wouldn't have understood the problem, it must be a modern one, and Answer Choice (D) becomes the clear choice.

(D) Beware of Answer Choice (A), a **distortion** placed earlier in the answer choice list in hopes of your not reading all the answers or reading the answers all the way through. The maids are here, but the question doesn't explain *why* they were frugal. Answer Choice (B) is an **irrelevant comparison** never made though suggested by the first line of the passage. Speaking of suggestions, our author never makes them, eliminating Answer Choice (C), which is probably also a **distortion**, since in this passage it's actually the things now considered useless (torn tablecloths) that were once considered valuable. Answer Choice (D) is actually almost the **opposite** of the passage's content, though reasonable if seen through modern prejudices. In this passage, something today seen as frugal (reusing every scrap) was just what you did, affluent and impoverished households alike, because there weren't any disposables available to anyone.

4. Employee morale is of tantamount importance to a business, as anything that reduces morale reduces the business's profitability. Thus, while it might seem like a prudent policy to reward exceptional employees with raises, parking spaces, and other perks, in practice this policy will backfire when those who do not receive such perks become aware of their existence.

Which of the following, if true, most strengthens the argument?
(A) Employee morale is generally reduced when compensation is unequal, even when performance is unequal.
(B) Of the things that reduce a business's profitability, damage to employee morale is the hardest to reverse.
(C) Businesses that reward performance with perks that do not include stock options are less profitable overall.
(D) Eliminating perks for employees is itself a way to increase the profitability of a company.
(E) When exceptional employees are rewarded with perks, their productivity and morale are both increased.

Argument: The conclusion is the **prediction** given at the end: *this practice (giving rewards to the best employees) will backfire when the other employees find out*, supported by a single piece of evidence (that's stated twice) that anything that reduces morale reduces profits. Thus, the argument must assume that *the policy will affect the morale of some employees negatively*. Strengthening the argument means supporting this assumption, which Answer Choice (A) does directly.

(A) Answer Choices (B) and (C) are **irrelevant comparisons** that do not concern the argument's assumptions; Answer Choice (D) is meant to seem reasonable, though it's **one step removed** from relevant and the **opposite** of what we want (as if it were true, *and* we knew that the increases were huge, it would weaken the argument). Answer Choice (E) is just additional **evidence for the evidence**, further explaining the positive effect the bonuses have on the employees who get raises; it's the ones that don't that really matter to us.

5. Only those with memberships at the Simon Island Country Club are allowed to use its golf course. Richard recently was admitted to membership at the Simon Island Country Club, so he will surely begin using the golf course.

The reasoning in the argument above is questionable because it
(A) confuses a policy that is regularly enforced with one that sometimes has exceptions.
(B) proceeds as though a fact that is required for the conclusion to be valid is also sufficient for it to be valid.
(C) asserts that in a given case only one of two options is possible, without eliminating other possible options.
(D) presupposes that a group of people who are alike in one respect must necessarily be alike in others.
(E) draws a conclusion that the premises of the argument, when taken to be true, explicitly contradict.

Argument: The conclusion is the **definite prediction** that *Richard will surely begin using the golf course*, supported by two pieces of evidence: (1) Richard is a member of the club and (2) membership is required in order to use the course. The evidence would make for a good **applied rule** argument, but the speaker instead **confuses necessity and sufficiency** as Answer Choice (B) indicates by taking the fact that the meeting is a *requirement* (having a membership) is itself a *guarantee*.

(B) The answers would mostly be flaws if they had been done, but our speaker never did them. We have no evidence that there are any *exceptions* as in Answer Choice (A), no *multiple options* as in Answer Choice (C), no *group/whole confusions* as in Answer Choice (D), and no *contradiction* as in Answer Choice (E).

---

6. The Black Death (also known as the Bubonic Plague) <u>resulting in the death of about 75 million people, nearly one-third</u> of whom died in Europe alone.
    (A) resulting in the death of about 75 million people, nearly one-third
    (B) resulting in the death of nearly 75 million people, one-third nearly
    (C) resulted in the death of nearly 75 million people, nearing one-third
    (D) resulted in 75 million people having died, one nearly a third
    (E) resulted in the death of about 75 million people, nearly one-third

    Issues: subject/predicate agreement (*The Black Death... resulted*), **modification** (the correct form of *nearly one-third*)

    (E) Though separated by the distracting parenthetical phrase, the subject *The Black Death* is *singular* and needs a verb in the **predicate form**, eliminating Answer Choices (A) and (B)'s *resulting*. The descriptive phrase after the *people,* needs the proper form to maintain the meaning that the *nearly one-third* is a subdivision of the *75 million*. Answer Choice (B)'s placement of *nearly* is wrong, Answer Choice (C)'s switch to *nearing* makes the *of whom* nonsensical, and Answer Choice (D)'s *one nearly a third* is a random **word salad**.

---

7. New research has enabled "bulk" silicon <u>to be able to emit broad-spectrum visible light and opening the possibility</u> of using the element in devices with both photonic and electronic components.
    (A) to be able to emit broad-spectrum visible light and opening the possibility
    (B) to emit broad-spectrum visible light and opening the possibility
    (C) to emit broad-spectrum visible light, opening the possibility
    (D) emit visible light and a broad-spectrum and open the possibility
    (E) be able to emit visible light in a broad-spectrum and to open the possibility

    Issues: idiom: redundant constructions (*enabled... to be able*), **connecting clauses** (avoiding parallel but nonsensical constructions by eliminating the *and*), and **idiomatic construction** (of *enabled + infinitive*)

    (C) Because *enabled* already means *to be able*, the *able*s in Answer Choices (A) and (E) are redundant. The *and* in Answer Choices (A), (B), (D), and (E) sets up a two-part coordination of things that the research enabled silicon to do, which is nonsensical, as silicon can't open a possibility. Idiomatically, the word *enable* takes the infinitive *to emit* rather than Answer Choice (D)'s *emit* or (E)'s *be able to emit*.

8. During the era of Jim Crow <u>many still were African-Americans treated like</u>
<u>second-class citizens, even though they were freed</u> by the Emancipation Proclamation
decades before.

(A) many still were African-Americans treated like second-class citizens, even though
they were freed

(B) many African-Americans still were treated as second-class citizens, even though
they had been free

(C) many African-Americans were still treated as second-class citizens, despite having
been freed

(D) many African-Americans still were being treated as second-class citizens, even
they had been freed

(E) many second-class citizens still were treated, like African-Americans, even though
they were freed

Issues: sequence of tenses (*were treated... had been freed*), **passive voice** (the *by the*
Emancipation Proclamation demands a verb in the passive), **connecting clauses**
(making sensible the relationship between the clauses in the sentence)

(C) As written, the sentence is a confused mess. The *African-Americans* were *treated*
as *second-class citizens*, not the other way around, as in Answer Choices (A) and (E).
The *Emancipation Proclamation* in the non-underlined sentence is treated as the
instrument by which the freeing was conducted, meaning that the final verb in the
underlined section needs to be in the passive voice (X was verbed by Y); Answer Choice
(B)'s *free by* makes no sense as an alternative. The relationship between the last clause
and the rest of the sentence could work with either *even though* or *despite*, but Answer
Choice (D)'s *even they had* won't work.

9. When Bogota's traffic problem grew too great to ignore, the mayor took an unorthodox
step, firing many of the city's traffic officers and replacing them with mimes. These
mimes followed traffic law violators and mimicked their behavior silently. In months,
traffic had ceased to be a problem. This proves that sometimes the answer to a
problem of compliance with the law is to shame law breakers rather than punishing
them.

Each of the following is an assumption required by the argument above EXCEPT:

(A) the act of shaming someone for breaking a law should not be considered a form of
punishment.

(B) the mimes who followed traffic violators did not single out a few habitual breakers
of the law to mimic.

(C) the law breakers who were followed by mimes in Bogota afterward stopped
breaking those laws.

(D) the traffic officers who were not fired did not markedly increase the rate at which
they punished people for breaking traffic laws.

(E) noncompliance with traffic laws in some way contributed to the traffic problem in
Bogota.

Argument: Since this is an EXCEPT question, we can expect an argument with *lots* of assumptions. The argument's conclusion is an **explanation** of what happened in a situation, or how a **plan** was successful. The situation was a city with a high traffic problem where mimes replaced traffic cops and the problem went down. The explanation has multiple parts, each of which requires an assumption: (1) the traffic problem was a problem of *compliance with the law* (and thus, we must assume *not something else*), (2) it was shame rather than punishment (so we assume that *mimes are shaming and not punishing*), (3) the mimes caused the reduction (requiring everything a **causal connection** must assume), and (4) the specific things the mimes did were relevant (assuming it was the *following and mimicking, not something else*). Answer Choice (B) has nothing to do with any of these assumptions; it is meant to appear as though it is addressing a **representativeness** assumption, which this argument does not require.

(B) Answer Choice (A) addresses the assumption in part 2; Answer Choice (C) is required for the **causal connection**; Answer Choice (D) eliminates an **alternate explanation** (again part of the causal connection); and Answer Choice (E) addresses part 1.

---

10. In order to both reduce their overall insurance costs and provide extra compensation to their employees, many companies now offer to match funds that employees pay into flexible healthcare spending accounts. After a three-year analysis of this practice in the tech industry, researchers concluded that the benefits to the companies went well beyond these expectations. In that industry, companies matching employee contributions to flexible healthcare spending accounts could, on average, expect their employee absentee rate to be 20% lower than among companies who did not.

    Which of the following would most weaken the conclusion of the three-year study?
    (A) Those technology companies able to afford to match employee contributions to health accounts are usually so successful that they are able to be very selective about those they hire.
    (B) At companies that offer flexible healthcare spending accounts, employees may use them to pay for eye and dental care not covered by the normal health plan.
    (C) Starting a flexible healthcare spending account requires substantial effort for the employees who desire one.
    (D) In other industries where companies match employee contributions to flexible healthcare accounts, similar improvements in absentee rate have been seen.
    (E) In the technology companies that match employee contributions to flexible healthcare accounts, average worker productivity is also higher.

Argument: The stem points us to the argument's conclusion (the study's explanation): *the benefits (of matching funds paid to flexible healthcare accounts) did more than just what was expected (reduced insurance costs and extra compensation).* The evidence is mostly **setup information** that explains what happened in this situation: (1) the analysis took three years; (2) it concerned the tech industry only; (3) on average, studied companies that used the matching funds had a lower absentee rate than those that didn't. The correct answer weakens the argument by attacking the necessary assumption that the participants in the study were **representative**—or, in other words, there was nothing special about them, like what Answer Choice (A) describes. (Selective companies might be able to hire employees who are so good that they have a low absentee rate anyway.)

(A) Answer Choices (B) and (E) are the **exact opposite** of the answer, as they actually **strengthen** the argument, adding additional benefits to the practice said to be beneficial in other ways. Answer Choice (C) is **reasonable but irrelevant**, since however difficult it is for employees to take advantage of the program, that difficulty would be the case throughout the study's participants. Answer Choice (D) is an **irrelevant comparison** to other industries (also a **closed issue**, as the **setup** limits the study only to tech companies).

The passage for questions 11–14 appears on page 583.

---

11. Which of the following best describes the relationship between the experimental findings described in the second paragraph and those described in the third?
(A) The findings described in the second paragraph are revealed by the author to be anomalous when contrasted with those in the third.
(B) The findings described in the third paragraph are revealed by the author to be anomalous when contrasted with those in the second.
(C) Both sets of findings when taken together reveal that the experimental methodology of the researchers described in the passage is suspect.
(D) The findings described in the third paragraph each independently support the contention described by the author in the first paragraph.
(E) Neither set of findings independently support the researcher's original contention, but taken jointly suggest a new hypothesis worthy of further research.

Question: Because it asks us to relate two different facts in the passage, which goes beyond merely confirming a correct detail, this is a Function question. The function will accord with the author's overall goal, which, as indicated in Question 1 above, was to describe how two experiments suggest a new direction for research, which is almost exactly what Answer Choice (E) says.

(E) Answer Choice (A) is out because there are no anomalous findings in the passage. Answer Choice (B) is the same as Answer Choice (A,) merely rearranging the order of the two experiments, but there are still no anomalous findings. The author never censures or otherwise casts doubt on the researchers, so Answer Choice (C) is a no-go. And Answer Choice (D) doesn't work because the author merely enthusiastically describes the experiments; no argument is made that says they're correct or that they prove anything.

12. Which of the following does the author indicate was true of the series of experiments performed by Tononi's lab?

(A) The researchers utilized technology that no rival lab could have fashioned with equal precision.

(B) The researchers utilized at least two sets of devices to obtain their experimental data.

(C) The highly localized incidence of slow delta wave activity detected could only be detected in test subjects that had been kept awake artificially.

(D) The delta waves detected by the first experiment interfered with the detection of other types of brain activity.

(E) Other labs lacking the unique combination of monitoring equipment used in the experiment will be unable to duplicate the experimental results.

<u>Question:</u> When the question asks what was true according to the author or passage, it is a Detail question. The correct answer (B) corresponds to information contained in lines 8–9.

(B) Although the author does suggest that the researcher's equipment was more precise than previously available, the author does not state that the researchers were uniquely able to create it, so Answer Choice (A) is out. Answer Choice (C) is a **distortion**, a garbled account of the experiments, as is Answer Choice (D). Answer Choice (E) is meant to be **reasonable but unmentioned**, as the gear does come off as new and shiny, but there is no suggestion that the findings could not have been obtained without it.

13. Based on the passage, it can be inferred that prior to the work carried out by Tononi's research team, neuroscientists would have been surprised to detect

(A) slow wave delta activity in the brain of an unconscious test subject.

(B) microwave arrays implanted directly in the frontal and parietal cortexes of a waking test subject.

(C) two distinct biochemical states exhibited by a test subject before and after being awoken.

(D) fast, unpredictable activity within the motor cortex of a test subject whose brain is in "sleeping mode."

(E) a lack of activity other than delta waves in a sleeping test subject.

<u>Question:</u> Answering this inference question requires keeping track of the details that are assigned to the brain in "waking mode" and "sleeping mode" as well as understanding that because Tononi's research is cited as a revolutionary discovery in the field of neuroscience, anything first detected in his team's research would qualify as surprising to neuroscientists working prior to his team's effort. This allows Answer Choice (D) to be inferred.

(D) Answer Choice (A) would not be surprising because delta wave activity (lines 21–22) is the hallmark of a brain in sleeping mode (or unconscious as the question phrases it), so neuroscientists before Tononi would surely expect this. Answer Choice (B) is a **misused detail**, as the implantation of electrodes in the rats' brains is a technique employed by Tononi, not a discovery. Answer Choice (C) could never have been surprising, as we are told in lines 3–5 that neuroscientists have long thought this very thing. Answer Choice (E) is **too extreme** an inference from the information given; we know from the passage that delta wave activity is characteristic of the sleeping brain, but we do not know that it is the ONLY activity that could be detected.

---

14. The primary purpose of the passage is to
  (A) review research demonstrating the benefits of a new experimental technique and suggest future hurdles that it may bring about.
  (B) present the findings of a group of researchers and the practical therapies their work will soon allow.
  (C) describe the results of a recent set of experiments that challenge a significant assumption of a field of study.
  (D) critique the callousness with which a provocative researcher conducts his clinical trials.
  (E) lament the lack of practical applications for a series of experiments that were once thought to be promising.

Question: In the first paragraph, the author introduces a supposition held by neuroscientists who study sleep, namely that sleep is a "whole brain phenomenon," that being awake and being asleep are entirely different mental states. The author then presents the work of a scientist, Tononi, whose research challenges that supposition. He details the researchers' technique in the second and third paragraphs and concludes by suggesting that the work may one day have a highly sought after effect, increasing scientists' understanding of sleep itself. Overall, the author is mostly descriptive, though there is no hint of censure or disapproval of the research he describes, and thus Answer Choice (C) is the best match.

(C) Answer Choice (A) is **half-right/half-wrong** because nowhere does the author point to future hurdles or any other possible negative consequence to the research. Answer Choice (B) is another **half-right/half-wrong** because there are no practical therapies discussed in the passage. Answer Choice (D) has the **wrong tone**, as the author has no words of critique for anyone and remains neutral to positive on everything discussed in the passage. Likewise, Answer Choice (E) has the **wrong tone** because *lamenting* suggests disapproval, but the author never speaks in disapproving terms in the passage (additionally, practical applications and lost promise are not discussed in the passage).

---

15. By signing the Kyoto Protocol a nation is <u>required to reduce their greenhouse gas emissions and to research an increase</u> in technology to increase the absorption of these gases already present in the atmosphere.
  (A) is required to reduce their greenhouse gas emissions and to research an increase
  (B) is required to reduce their greenhouse gas emissions and to increase research
  (C) is required to reduce their greenhouse gas emissions and to researching an increase
  (D) requires to reduce their emitting of greenhouse gas and to increasing research
  (E) required to reduce its greenhouse gas emissions and to research increasing

Issues: **pronoun agreement** (*a nation... its*), **coordination** (creating a correctly coordinated list of things the nation *is required to [do]*), and **idiomatic construction** (picking a relationship between *research* and *increasing* that is both grammatically correct and that makes sense in context)

(B) Because *a nation* is a singular noun phrase, *its* is required, eliminating the *their*s in Answer Choices (A), (C), and (D). Whether it is the nation that requires or the Kyoto Protocol (though the latter makes more sense), the requirement is compound because of the later *and*, meaning **parallel** forms are needed for both the reducing of greenhouse gas emissions and the researching—Answer Choices (C) and (D) fail by having the first as a verb in the infinitive (*to reduce*) and the second as a prepositional followed by a gerund (*to increasing* or *to researching*). Answer Choice (E) fails to construct a correct idiom to connect the non-underlined *in technology* with its *research increasing in technology.*

16. Traders <u>who predicted a continuing of the loss in value of the commodity</u> were surprised Wednesday when pig futures posted a strong rally.
    (A) who predicted a continuing of the loss in value of the commodity
    (B) who predicted continuing losses in the commodity's value
    (C) who had predicted the continuation of losses of the commodity's value
    (D) who had predicted continuing losses in value for the commodity
    (E) who had predicted a continuing loss for the value in the commodity

    Issues: **sequence of tenses** (*had predicted... were surprised*), **idiomatic construction** (*predicted for, losses in value*), **modification** (a sensible form for and placement of *continuing*)

    (D) Because the prediction happened at an earlier point in time than the rally, the **past perfect** *had predicted* is needed, the only tense prior to the non-underlined **past tense** *posted*, eliminating Answer Choices (A) and (B). Answer Choice (C)'s version of the *continuing losses* question is the only one that is absolutely wrong, and Answer Choice (E) has an unacceptable version of the idiom used to connect value and loss.

17. Researchers at the famous Copenhagen Institute <u>is working on developing new transgenic treatments and investigating the role played by tRNA in the spread of</u> cancer cells between tumorous sites within an individual.
    (A) is working on developing new transgenic treatments and investigating the role played by tRNA in the spread of
    (B) is working to develop new transgenic treatments and investigating the role played by tRNA in the spreading of
    (C) are working to develop new transgenic treatments and investigating the role played by tRNA in the spread of
    (D) are working on development of new transgenic treatments and the investigation of the role tRNA plays for the spread of
    (E) are working on developing new transgenic treatments and investigating the role played by tRNA in the spread of

Issues: parallelism (the coordinated list of things the researchers *are working on* doing), **subject/predicate agreement** (*is/are working*), **idiomatic construction** (*working on* versus *working to*)

(E) The subject of the sentence, *researchers*, is plural, requiring *are* and eliminating Answer Choices (A) and (B)'s *is*. The *and* creates a compound object for what the researchers are working on or working to do, and each element must be the same form and have the same complement of small words attached. Thus, Answer Choices (B) and (C)'s *to develop… investigating* are out, as is Answer Choice (D)'s *development… the investigation*.

Both *working on* and *working to* are correct idioms, but *working on* has to be followed by a noun like *development* (or a verb in the noun form called a **gerund** like *developing*), while the *to* in *working to* is generally part of an infinitive verb (*to develop*). You can't mix and match, as Answer Choice (C) tries to do.

---

18. To combat gun violence, restrictions on private handgun ownership are often proposed, the idea being that the fewer guns available, the fewer guns will be used in violent crimes. The problem with such proposals is not, as is often said, that **when guns are outlawed, only outlaws have guns**, but rather that not all guns have the same likelihood of being used in a violent crime. Unless gun legislation is tailored so that it primarily reduces the number of these more dangerous guns—ones currently in the hands of criminals, or those which criminals might easily obtain—**such legislation will fail to reduce the amount of gun violence in a society**.

In the argument above, the two portions in **boldface** play which of the following roles?

(A) The first is an observation that the author uses to support a particular position; the second is that position.

(B) The first is a position the author takes as inadequate to explain a phenomenon; the second is the author's conclusion about certain plans that would address the phenomenon.

(C) The first is a prediction that the author argues will not hold in a specific case; the second is the prediction the author argues is more likely.

(D) The first is a prediction that the author believes to be untrue; the second is a restatement of that prediction treated as though it were an independent conclusion.

(E) The first is a direct relationship that the author asserts will not hold in this case; the second offers evidence in support of the author's assertion.

Argument: The subject of the argument is probably familiar, so it is important not to let **real-world thinking** intrude. The argument's structure should also be familiar; **somebody says X (and they're wrong)**: somebody says the first bolded statement (that when guns are outlawed, only outlaws will have guns) is the best way to understand why gun legislation fails, and the speaker in the argument thinks this is wrong, preferring instead the explanation given in the unbolded section that follows. The prompt concludes by restating the thing that the two competing explanations are trying to explain, given in bold, which is why gun legislation will fail. Thus, Answer Choice (B) is the correct description of the roles of the statements, though it is tricky for one reason. The second statement is described as "a conclusion about certain plans"—which is not the same as saying the author's *overall conclusion*, but is a plausible way to describe what the author says.

(B) If you realized that neither statement is *evidence* for a position (either the author's or the **somebody** who **says X**), Answer Choices (A) and (E) could be eliminated quickly. Answer Choices (C) and (D) both call the first statement a **prediction**, which it isn't— it's an **explanation** used as evidence to support a prediction (that gun legislation won't work).

The passage for questions 19–21 appears on page 586.

19. The author's primary purpose is to
- (A) refute the idea that particular features of the tomb of Antipope John XXIII can reliably be attributed.
- (B) describe the characteristics of an early masterpiece of Renaissance art.
- (C) argue that critical evaluations of a widely praised work of art are inevitably biased.
- (D) assert that certain works of art history reveal more about the historian than about the art.
- (E) rebut previous art historians who have incorrectly attributed the work of Donatello to Michelozzo.

Question: With short dense passages like this one, it can often be difficult to spot the author's main idea. In such cases, you can fall back on your Critical Reasoning skills, knowing that Reading Comprehension passages are almost always an argument of some sort. Here, the author's conclusion comes at the very end of the passage (helpfully pointed out by the conclusory keywords "in the end"); thus, Answer Choice (D) is the correct answer.

(D) Because the answer choices all begin with verbs, a **vertical scan** can assist your process of elimination on the first pass. Answer Choices (A) and (E) both have the **wrong tone**, since the author isn't directly attacking someone else's conclusion. Answer Choice (B) arguably has the wrong tone as well, but should be checked, since neutral verbs (like *describe*) can be used to mask positive tones—though that doesn't happen here, where it instead introduces a **part not the whole** (since characteristics of the tomb are in fact given in the passage). Choosing between Answer Choices (D) and (C) is the final task, and the *inevitably biased* is **too extreme** to describe our passage, so Answer Choice (C) is out.

20. If an art historian were to declare that one of the marble reliefs of personified Virtues found on the tomb of John XXIII required much more artistic skill to produce than the other two, the author would most likely take the assertion as evidence that
- (A) the relief in question was most likely the work of Donatello, rather than Michelozzo.
- (B) the more-skilled relief is equally likely to have been the work of either Donatello or Michelozzo.
- (C) the exact artist responsible for all three of the reliefs will never be reliably determined.
- (D) at least two of the reliefs should be considered to be the work of the same unknown artist.
- (E) the relief in question will provide insight into the qualities valued by the appraiser.

Question: The complicated stem hides a simple and familiar **Inference** task. **Apply** the author's conclusion, which is a sort of **rule**, to a **specific case**. The author's rule says that when an art historian praises a feature as being objectively better, that usually reveals more about their personal values than about the artwork itself. Thus, Answer Choice (E) is the correct inference resulting from applying that rule to this particular case in which one of the three virtues is singled out as being better than the other two.

(E) Answer Choices (A) and (B) exist to trick those who only skimmed the passage, ultimately the **exact opposite** of what our author believes, which is that historians' appraisals don't actually correspond to which artist likely made a particular piece of the tomb. Answer Choice (C) is, however, **too extreme**—though the author is skeptical of such evaluations, the passage doesn't go so far as to say these evaluations are *always* wrong. (D) brings up something possible in the real world, but for which there is no information here.

---

21. Which of the following can be inferred from the passage?
- (A) The observations about a work of art's execution that are the most valuable are those that do not attempt to determine that work's original artist.
- (B) Those works of art that cannot be reliably attributed to one artist are most likely to have been created by a collaboration between artists.
- (C) Some works of art history that are unable to provide valuable information on their stated subject may provide other valuable information.
- (D) Some works of history that are seen as more valuable by certain historians who study history are worthless to the general public.
- (E) Many of those features of the monument tomb that are currently attributed to Donatello were probably the work of someone else.

Question: More difficult passages often ask multiple **Inference** questions, so the later a passage comes in your test, the more you should be on the lookout as you read the passage for the common **Inference** clues. Here, you might have noticed that the only really definite information is the author's conclusion, and Answer Choice (C) is a **but that's too obvious!** restatement of that conclusion. The art historians' attributions aren't valuable for information about the work, but they are valuable to people studying art historians.

(C) Answer Choice (A) is an **irrelevant comparison** that's ultimately unsupported by the passage's definite information. Answer Choices (B) and (E) are **reasonable but unsupported**, things we might conclude if we heard someone making this argument in real life but that will never be the correct answer to a GMAT Inference question. Answer Choice (D) goes **too extreme** to the claim that there is *no worth* to these art historians' evaluations of the tomb.

22. A researcher studying the habits of highly effective CEOs found that there was a positive correlation between those who described themselves as having "goal-oriented" personalities and those who were rated as most effective by annual surveys of their employees. The researcher concluded that people with "goal-oriented" personalities are more likely, on average, than those without to seek a job as a CEO.

    Each of the following, if true, would weaken the argument above EXCEPT:
    (A) CEOs and other top executives are unlikely to be able to describe their own personality accurately.
    (B) The annual surveys of employees are usually conducted immediately after the employees have been paid their annual bonuses.
    (C) The term "goal-oriented" is so vague as to be able to apply to nearly any set of personal characteristics.
    (D) CEOS who do not describe themselves as "goal-oriented" rarely remain CEOs for long.
    (E) The researcher made no effort to control for other variables that might have influenced the finding.

    Argument: Weaken EXCEPT sets up an argument with many assumptions or a single assumption with lots of ways to attack it. Here, it's sort of both at the same time, as the speaker concludes that *"goal-oriented" personalities* **cause** *people to become CEO's*, based on evidence of a **correlation** between the two found in a **study**. Answer Choices (A) and (C) attack the **feasibility assumptions** this study relies upon, that CEOs actually know what their own personalities are and could possibly describe them. Answer Choice (D) attacks the **causal connection** somewhat subtly, by showing the correlation might be coincidental (since the appearance of one of the two parts of the correlation is unpredictable and changes a lot), and Answer Choice (E) attacks another **feasibility assumption** that goes with **studies**, probably the most common assumption, which is that studies must be **representative**.

    (B) Answer Choice (B) fails to weaken the argument because though it suggest a sort of bias to the study, it's a bias that we would require more information to verify was in fact a bias. How do we know that bonuses change the evaluations of employees in one consistent way that would bias the results? Thus, the answer is **one step removed** from the assumption of **representativeness** of the **study**.

23. Analyst: Offshoot Records has weathered changes in the music marketplace for over sixty-four years. However, as customers become accustomed to purchasing music via downloadable file, rather than via physical media such as CDs and LPs, it will become increasingly difficult for locally owned music stores like Offshoot to remain profitable. Expect Offshoot to close its doors within the next year.

Which of the following, if true, makes the analyst's prediction about the future viability of Offshoot Records more likely to be correct?
(A) There are no other locally owned music stores that have successfully adapted to the challenge of digitally distributed music.
(B) The only way that a music store can remain profitable is if its customers remain loyal and eschew general trends.
(C) Sales at Offshoot Records have not been increasing over the past few months.
(D) CDs and LPs make up the vast majority of the stock on sale at a locally owned music store like Offshoot Records.
(E) The past sixty-four years have presented Offshoot with challenges largely dissimilar to the present shift toward digital distribution.

Argument: The argument concludes that Offshoot will close within the next year, a very specific **prediction**, based on the evidence that there is **one problem** (one disadvantage) that Offshoot faces and information about the past. To strengthen this argument, we must support one of its assumptions; here, Answer Choice (E) supports the assumption that *the past will be representative of the future* (an assumption always implicit with **predictions**).

(E) Answer Choice (A) is **too extreme** and **irrelevant corroboration**. Answer Choice (B) relies on confusing this argument for one involving **formal logic**. Answer Choice (C) is meant to be tempting as it is something we might reasonably expect, but which doesn't actually strengthen the argument (and it might even **weaken** the prediction). Answer Choice (D) is **one step removed** from the argument's assumptions, since the argument never tells us that the reason Offshoot will fail has anything to do with how it makes *the majority* of its money (instead relying on the less extreme evidence that *part* of Offshoot's revenue stream will be endangered).

24. The U.S. Supreme Court recently ruled that the military commissions enacted as part of the response to global terrorism are not <u>constitutional; as they are violating</u> the separation of powers.
(A) constitutional; as they are violating
(B) constitutional; a violation of
(C) constitutional, but rather they violate
(D) constitutional; but rather that they violate
(E) constitutional, but rather it violates

Issues: connecting clauses (semicolons and linking independent clauses with conjunctions), **pronoun reference** (*commissions... they*)

(C) The semicolons in Answer Choices (A), (B), and (D) would require what followed to be an independent clause, but Answer Choices (A)'s *as* and (D)'s *that* both render the clauses attached **dependent**. Answer Choice (B)'s *a violation of* lacks a verb, so is essentially an unacceptable stray fragment. That leaves only Answer Choices (C) and (E), which both share the less often used compound conjunction *but rather* (used correctly with a comma to link two independent clauses) whose unfamiliarity is used to steer you away from the correct answer. Both Answer Choices (C) and (E) also introduce pronouns, but Answer Choice (E)'s singular *it* does not match the antecedent *commissions*, which is plural.

25. The newly elected board of regents must consider <u>whether to recommend that the disgraced head of the football program be released</u> from his contract.
    (A) whether to recommend that the disgraced head of the football program be released
    (B) whether to recommend that the disgraced head of the football program should be released
    (C) whether it should recommend that the disgraced head of the football program be released or not
    (D) if it should make the recommendation that the disgraced head of the football program should be released
    (E) if to recommend that the disgraced head of the football program should be released

Issues: idiomatic construction (*if* versus *whether*), **the subjunctive** (of command, for *recommend* AND *consider*)

(A) On the GMAT, *if* is always used for hypotheticals (*if it rains, we will get wet*), *whether* for choices or options, so Answer Choices (D) and (E) are out. The verbs *consider* and *recommend* require that a version of the subjunctive be used, the subjunctive of command, which requires either *consider/recommend + infinitive* or *consider/recommend + be + past participle*. Because they are command/demand verbs, *consider* and *recommend* also should not be followed by *should*, which eliminates Answer Choices (B), (C), (D), and (E) all in one fell swoop. Additionally, the *or not* is considered redundant by the GMAT when paired with *whether*, as in Answer Choice (C).

26. After a decade that saw steep increases in the average price of cars aimed at the middle of the market, overall sales of cars in this category have finally begun to suffer. In an attempt to stem the loss of sales, one major Detroit automaker has reduced the price of its middle-tier cars by 12%. However, since few other automakers are likely to follow suit, the average price of a middle-tier car is unlikely to fall significantly.

Which of the following indicates the main conclusion of the argument above?
(A) The average price of cars aimed at the middle of the market has increased steeply over the past decade.
(B) One major Detroit automaker has reduced the price of its middle-tier cars by 12%.
(C) Few automakers are likely to adopt the price reduction that one automaker has recently announced.
(D) The sales of middle-tier cars have suffered significantly over the past decade.
(E) The actions of one automaker are not likely to affect the average price of cars aimed at the middle of the market.

Argument: Be careful! Even though there is a **plan** given, the conclusion is a **prediction** about something that will (fail to) follow in the wake of the plan, not that the plan itself will or won't work. The prediction is that the average price of middle-tier cars won't fall significantly, based on the evidence that only the one major automaker will be reducing its prices. Answer Choice (E) states the conclusion directly, although it masks the conclusion through synonyms and the reordering of words.

(E) Answer Choices (A), (B), and (D) are all pieces of **setup information** describing the little world in which the argument takes place. Answer Choice (C) is a piece of **evidence** used to support the conclusion.

---

27. You may know Martha Rose Shulman as a food critic, but in her kitchen she leads a double life as a ghost-writer of pastry cookbooks.
(A) You may know Martha Rose Shulman as a food critic, but
(B) You might know Martha Rose Shulman to be a food critic,
(C) Although you may know of Martha Rose Shulman as a food critic, still
(D) While you may know that Martha Rose Shulman is a food critic, although
(E) You might know Martha Rose Shulman as a food critic,

Issues: connecting clauses (one dependent, one independent), **idiomatic construction** (here a distraction)

(A) The sentence is correct as written. Later answer choices either add too many subordinating words, turning the sentence into two dependent clauses linked by a comma—as Answer Choices (C) and (D) do—or delete the *but* and turn the sentence into two independent clauses linked by a comma—Answer Choices (E) and (B). The former is a sentence fragment, the later a run-on, and both are incorrect. The choice between *may* and *might* and the various changes to *as a, to be,* etc. are simply distractions and there is no grammatical reason to rule any of them out.

28. The Battle of Bull Run—or Manassas, as it was known in the South—was the first major ground engagement of the American Civil War <u>resulting in over 2,000 dead and nearly half again that number were wounded.</u>

   (A) resulting in over 2,000 dead and nearly half again that number were wounded

   (B) and resulting in over 2,000 dead and nearly that number and half wounded

   (C) resulted in over 2,000 dead and nearly that number plus half of the wounded

   (D) and resulted in over 2,000 dead and nearly half again that number wounded

   (E) and resulted in over 2,000 and nearly half again that number that were wounded

Issues: idiomatic construction (the rare idiom *twice again that number*), **connecting clauses**

   (D) Though a bit obscure, *<some number> and nearly half again that number* is a correct English construction. The stray *that* in the middle of the idiom in Answer Choice (E), however, is not. The *were* in Answer Choice (A) does not ruin the idiom, but it does turn the sentence into a run-on, two independent clauses connected by a conjunction without a comma (*The battle was… and nearly half… were wounded*). Answer Choices (B) and (C) botch the idiom and make the sentence nonsensical.

The passage for questions 29–32 appears on page 590.

---

29. Which of the following titles most accurately expresses the main point of the passage?

   (A) "Calabresi's Cost of Accidents: More Relevant Today Than Ever Before"

   (B) "Calabresi's Insight as Oversight: Implications of His Hypotheticals"

   (C) "Calabresi's Folly Revisited: The Underappreciated Genius"

   (D) "When Marshall Met Taney: Real-World Data Confirms Calabresi"

   (E) "Guido Calabresi Reconsidered: The Influence of an Economic Titan"

Question: Asking for a title to a passage is a way of asking about the passage as a whole, a less common variant on the standard Global question. The best title for a passage will be one reflecting the author's overall purpose. In the end, Answer Choice (B) proves the best title, concocting a clever play on words out of two things the author explicitly says in the passage that comprise his main point: (1) Calabresi's theories are insightful, and (2) his insufficient attention to the implications of his own hypothetical commitments is an oversight.

   Because the implication of specific words in a title may not always be immediately clear, it is often best to start these questions with a process of elimination.

   (B) Answer Choice (A) is wrong because there is no indication that the relevance of Calabresi's work has changed over time; Answer Choice (C) is wrong because this title would be appropriate for something like the opposite of this passage. Our author takes a respected theory and shows it has a big hole (that doesn't completely invalidate its worth); the passage this title suits would take a theory thought to have a hole in it and show it should be respected; Answer Choice (D) can be eliminated because there is neither real-world data in the passage nor a confirmation of Calabresi's work; Answer Choice (E) is meant to be tempting, but it does not go far enough (the passage does represent a reconsideration of Calabresi; however, the point is not to prove his influence but to critique him).

30. If the author's appraisal of Calabresi's work is accurate, which of the following must he also believe?

(A) When there arises a conflict between rational self-interest and the behavior traditionally punished by courts, economic considerations must be put aside.

(B) A legal theory's use of economic calculations that are too simple to correspond closely to the real world is not alone cause to reject all the claims made by that theory.

(C) Rhetorical weaknesses are usually the least serious defects that a theoretical framework is vulnerable to.

(D) Whether an activity is economically fruitful is less important a consideration in its continuation than whether that activity causes substantial harm.

(E) Only those theories that reconcile the competing self-interests of multiple rational agents will be able to accurately guide public policy concerning the cost of accidents.

Question: Asking what the author must believe, but did not "say" or "state" is asking us to make an Inference. The information necessary to eliminate the wrong answers is scattered across the passage, but the correct answer may be derived from the author's description of Calabresi's hypotheticals in line 25 and from his overall attitudes toward Calabresi's theories (that they have serious problems, but nevertheless provide valuable insights). Since the author both believes that Calabresi oversimplifies things in his analysis and that his theories should not be rejected outright, our author must believe Answer Choice (B).

(B) Answer Choice (A) is wrong because although both rational self-interest and behavior traditionally punished by courts are mentioned, they are not given as a reason to avoid economic considerations. Answer Choice (C) is built on a true fact that the author does seem dismissive of people who worry over rhetorical weaknesses, but they are never said to be the least important problems. There may be a great many problems that the author would be even more dismissive of. Answer Choice (D) is a confused and incorrect version of Calabresi's main argument. Answer Choice (E) should seem like a probable extension of Calabresi's work, and we do know that the author feels Calabresi's work is incomplete, but we do not know that the author would extend Calabresi in precisely this way, nor do we know that the author believes that only theories like Calabresi's will work.

31. Based on the passage's description of Calabresi's argument, each of the following would contradict at least one of Calabresi's theoretical commitments EXCEPT:

(A) there are some real-world costs associated with the harm caused by attempts to minimize larger harms that we ought to ignore for the purposes of devising a legal theory.

(B) in cases where a risk can be mitigated without government intervention, it is unlikely that there is any harm associated with that risk.

(C) an agent acting in accord with the dictates of rational self-interest will often elect to ignore the costs that another party's behavior will later cause that agent.

(D) the value of a human life is so great that attempts to create an economic theory robust enough to guide our behavior in most cases will always fail in those cases where many lives will inevitably be lost.

(E) should an economic theory seem to imply that we engage in behavior that is currently considered improper, that is grounds enough to reject that theory's application.

Question: Because it asks us to make a determination based on Calabresi's argument, the question demands a correctly drawn Inference. And because it is an EXCEPT question, four of the answers correspond directly to information presented in the passage. The question is further complicated by asking us for four contradictions to that information. The correct answer thus requires an exception to a contradiction, which could be either something that is necessarily true on the basis of something Calabresi said or something that we lack information about. To put it another way, if the passage lacks information on a subject, then we cannot say that subject is contradicted by the passage.

The correct answer (A) is a bit subtle. We do know from the author's description of Calabresi's theory in the first paragraph that Calabresi's legal theory involves weighing the costs of avoiding risks. The passage does not go so far as to say that Calabresi demands that every possible real world cost or real world harm should be included in our legal theories. Since it remains possible that there are some harms Calabresi allows to be excluded, this answer choice does not contradict Calabresi's theories.

(A) (B) is wrong because it contradicts lines 4–5 which clearly state that any mitigation of risk inevitably involves a harm of some sort under Calabresi's view. (C) is out because lines 30–33 indicate that according to Calabresi's theories, insurance companies will not ignore the costs associated with Marshall's behavior if they follow the dictates of rational self-interest. This answer says this should never happen. (D) won't work because we know from the author's explanation of Calabresi's theory in the first paragraph that it explains why we would not accept a 5 mph speed limit in exchange for the many human lives that would be saved; thus, Calabresi doesn't believe theories that take the value of human life into account must fail, rather the opposite. (E) is the **exact opposite** of what we want: we are told Calabresi's theory insists society should incentivize behavior that is currently punished (thus, improper).

32. With which of the following evaluations of Calabresi's theories is the author of the passage most likely to agree:

(A) Because of the tension between his theories' ends and means, it is unlikely to be accepted widely in society.

(B) Because his own theories insist upon the necessity of taking economic considerations into account when evaluating a legal theory, they display little insight into economic affairs more broadly.

(C) Because his theories share assumptions and methodologies with Neoclassical economic theory, they are less useful to lawyers than the theory of accident cost that they replaced.

(D) Even though his theories fail to provide a manner in which the exact costs associated with accidents may be determined, they are still correct in asserting that accident cost ought to include the costs of risk aversion.

(E) Even though his theories sometimes appear to advocate outcomes that are at odds with current jurisprudence, they should be rejected only if they also fail to explain the economic component of those outcomes.

Question: When a question asks about what an author would agree with, rather than what is stated directly in the passage, we are dealing with an Inference question. The correct answer is (D). The author's approval of the general idea of using risk aversion costs in order to calculate accident costs can be found at the end of the first paragraph. That Calabresi's theories do not exactly explain how to determine these costs is the author's chief criticism of them. Nevertheless, this criticism does not mean that we ought to reject the general theory, just refine it somehow.

(D) Answer Choice (A) takes something the author says in passing, that there is a certain ends/means tension in Calabresi's view, and incorrectly concludes the author expects the theory to meet with popular disapproval, a **misused detail**. If anything, the author seems to take it as a given that Calabresi's theories have been widely accepted, even though they remain open for critique. Answer Choice (B) concerns what the author thinks about economic affairs broadly, which is not information included in this passage, so we may make no certain inferences about it. Answer Choice (C) is another **misused detail**, a **distortion**, as we know Calabresi's theory supplanted previous views and that he uses Neoclassical economic theory, but these two thoughts are not connected in any meaningful way by the author. Answer Choice (E) is out because even though Calabresi's theories do advocate outcomes that are counter to the current behavior of courts (their jurisprudence), the author does not connect this idea to a rule that demands we reject Calabresi's theories.

33. Unlike older televisions that used cathode ray tubes, which required heavy lead shielding to protect viewers, no shielding is needed by LED or LCD televisions, allowing them to be much lighter than their predecessors.

(A) to protect viewers, no shielding is needed by LED or LCD televisions, allowing them to be much lighter than their predecessors

(B) to protect viewers, LED or LCD televisions need no shielding that allows them to be much lighter than their predecessors were

(C) protecting viewers, LED or LCD televisions are allowed to be much lighter without shielding than their predecessors

(D) for viewers' protection, no shielding is needed by LED or LCD televisions to allow them to be much lighter than their predecessors

(E) for viewers' protection, LED or LCD televisions need no shielding, allowing them to be much lighter than their predecessors

Issues: comparisons, modification

(E) When a word such as *unlike* begins a sentence, it's a clear key to look for a comparison error. Entities compared must be parallel, both grammatically and logically. In Answer Choices (A) and (D), *older televisions* are compared with *shielding* (a property of TVs), which is incorrect. Answer Choices (B) and (C) add or change words that create peculiar nonsense—shielding doesn't allow something to be lighter, as (B) would have it, nor is there a person or entity that allows televisions to be a certain weight, as in (C).

34. Foreign aid is said to be "tied" when it is given with the stipulation that it may only be used to purchase items from the nation lending the aid. This practice has fallen out of favor in the international community, as it always results in economies more dependent on foreign money than before the aid. Even the relatively successful tied aid given by China to Singapore to rebuild in the wake of a devastating earthquake would today be frowned upon.

Which of the following can most reasonably be inferred from the passage?

(A) Even when ethical considerations outweigh a nation's self-interest, tied aid will not produce an ethical outcome.

(B) Countries that give tied aid most often do so out of a desire to benefit domestic businesses and industries.

(C) Even when tied aid is motivated by purely ethical concerns, it will exacerbate at least one economic problem in the receiving nation.

(D) China's actions would be more frowned upon if there had not been a recent earthquake in Singapore.

(E) Tied aid has caused more damage to the economies of the nations receiving it than most other economic factors.

Facts: Because this is an **Inference** prompt, you should read it on the lookout for **definite information** or other common **Inference** keys. The correct answer is a very safe inference (note the "at least one" language) based on the rule in the middle of the prompt: *it (tied aid) inevitably results in economies more dependent on foreign money* (the answer's "one economic problem" that is exacerbated). The first half of the answer is meant to distract you away from this simple **rule application** inference, as it is true that nowhere does the argument tell us that anyone is motivated "purely by ethical concerns," but the rule applies to any case in which tied aid is used (and thus even those cases not explicitly described in the passage).

(C) Answer Choice (A) is out because we have no rules by which to infer whether an outcome is *ethical* (just its economic effects); Answer Choice (B) is **reasonable but unsupported**, since the motives for aid aren't given to us in the prompt. Answer Choice (D) is an **irrelevant comparison**, as we have no rules explaining the *degree* to which anything will be frowned upon, and Answer Choice (E) is as well, since *other economic factors* are beyond the information given.

---

35. When we read the histories written centuries ago, we must remember that many, if not most, works of history ever written have been lost, for histories must be transmitted in books, yet books are fragile things prone to much abuse even in one lifetime, unlikely to survive more than a handful of centuries. To combat this constant reduction of existing copies across the millennia, a history must be recopied, and no book will be recopied if it does not manage to speak across the centuries to those who would do that recopying. Thus, no matter how valueless an ancient history might seem to our modern sensibilities, its very existence is testament to its value.

Which of the following, if true, most strengthens the conclusion above?
(A) No work of ancient history would have been copied in sufficient quantities to allow a small fraction of its copies to remain without being recopied.
(B) No work of ancient history will be able to speak across the centuries unless it is appeals equally to those living in each century.
(C) No work of ancient history that has failed to survive to the modern day would have appealed to modern sensibilities if it had survived.
(D) All works of ancient history that are valuable were recopied.
(E) All works of ancient history that speak across centuries are recopied in sufficient quantities to allow their survival.

Argument: The argument's conclusion is found in the confusingly worded final sentence, which we could rephrase as *ancient histories that survive must still be valuable even if we can't see the value.* This conclusion is supported by a chain of **formal logic** that might not apply to all situations. A book's being recopied is a guarantee that it spoke to people. But the argument still assumes that all histories that currently survive have been recopied, and Answer Choice (A) strengthens the argument by eliminating an **alternate explanation** for how a book could survive (that lots of copies were made in the book's "original print run," allowing for it to survive attrition without ever being recopied).

(A) All the wrong answers are bits of formal logic that are either **irrelevant** to the relationship between conclusion and evidence or that are the **exact opposite** of what we'd need to assume.

36. Noble gases are inert because <u>the completion of their outer electron orbital makes these elements more stable and less reactive when</u> in the presence of other atoms and molecules.

(A) the completion of their outer electron orbital makes these elements more stable and less reactive when

(B) the completing of its outer electron orbital makes these elements more stable and less reactive when it is

(C) the completion of its outer electron orbitals making them more stable and less reactive within

(D) of completing their outer electron orbitals, which makes these elements more stable and less reactive if

(E) the completion of their outer electron orbital makes these elements more stable and less reactive if

Issues: pronoun (both agreement and avoiding ambiguous *them*), **idiomatic construction** (*if* versus *when*)

(A) The sentence is correct as written. Answer Choices (B) and (C) change the *their* to *it*, making the pronoun no longer agree with the plural *gasses*. Answer Choice (C) also introduces a stray *within* that would be ungrammatical preceding *in the presence*. Answer Choices (D) and (E) change the *when* to *if*, which makes the meaning of the sentence ambiguous (does the completion of the outer orbital only make them less reactive if there are other atoms around or less reactive if brought into contact with other atoms?). Answer Choice (D)'s switch to *comma-which* is not problematic, but also not necessary. And finally, Answer Choice (D)'s *because of completing* is almost never deemed acceptable by the GMAT.

---

37. Though the press releases and other official statements of oil companies take great pains to emphasize that the scientific community is not unanimous in the belief that global warming can be tied to the burning of fossil fuels and other human activities, oil companies clearly do not believe this to be the case. If there were actually credible, respected scientists who rejected human-caused climate change, these companies would surely spend more money to support the research done by these dissenting voices, for they have a vested interest in making sure debate on the issue continues indefinitely.

Which of the following best explains the apparent discrepancy described above?

(A) Oil companies have only recently begun investing in scientific research that addresses climate change.

(B) Unless a researcher can credibly claim independence from those whom their research might benefit, they will not be as successful as those who can.

(C) Oil companies typically earmark money spent on research for technologies that would directly benefit their profits.

(D) Oil companies spend substantial amounts circulating their press releases and publicizing their other official statements.

(E) If a company spends money to support one side of a contentious issue, such support will be taken as a sign that the issue is already decided.

Dilemma: The apparent discrepancy is a sort of **violated expectation.** Since (1) oil companies have an interest in making sure the debate over climate change keeps going, we would expect that they would fund any research that might be taken as credible (and thus extend the debate), but (2) they don't. Answer Choice (E) resolves the discrepancy by providing information that shows that the apparent violation is itself a demonstration of the expectation. If the oil companies want the debate to continue, they can't fund this research because people will decide the issue is no longer debatable.

(E) Primarily, the question is designed as one long **reasonable but irrelevant** trap, as it is based on a situation often discussed these days and that most test takers will have an opinion on. Beware of your **real-world thinking**! Answer Choices (A) and (C) actually **worsen the dilemma**, giving further support to the claim that oil companies don't spend money in this way. Answer Choice (B) brings up the **one step removed** topic of whether a researcher is *successful*, whereas Answer Choice (D) does the same by addressing *press releases*.

---

38. Fertilizer runoff caused by industrial-scale farm practices <u>overwhelm streams and rivers with excess nitrogen and fertilizes blooms of algae, depleting oxygen and leaving</u> vast "dead zones" in their wake.
(A) overwhelm streams and rivers with excess nitrogen and fertilizes blooms of algae, depleting oxygen and leaving
(B) overwhelm streams and rivers, with excess nitrogen that fertilizes blooms of algae, depleting oxygen and leaving
(C) overwhelms streams and rivers with excess nitrogen, fertilizing blooms of algae that deplete oxygen and leave
(D) overwhelms streams and rivers with excess nitrogen that fertilize blooms of algae and deplete oxygen, leaving
(E) has overwhelmed streams and rivers with excess nitrogen and have fertilized blooms of algae, depleting oxygen and leaving

Issues: subject/predicate agreement (*runoff… overwhelms*), **coordination and subordination** (at multiple points), **parallelism** (required between coordinated elements)

(C) The easiest decision point to exploit is the agreement required for *overwhelms* (whose subject *runoff* is separated from it by the distractor phrase *caused by industrial-scale runoff*), which eliminates Answer Choices (A) and (B). Answer Choice (E) also fails the agreement test because the *and* before *have fertilizes* creates a compound predicate (so *has fertilized* or just *fertilized* would be needed). Answer Choice (D) fails a different agreement problem, the *that* connects *fertilize* and *deplete* with the singular *nitrogen* which requires *fertilizes* and *depletes*.

39. Consolidated Foodstuffs recently changed the ingredients of its infant formula recipe, replacing high-fructose corn syrup (HFC) with cane sugar, even though **the greater expense of the latter means that the company will make less profit**. Because cane sugar is much better for the developing infant than HFC, doctors have praised the move, saying that **Consolidated Foodstuffs has demonstrated that it places more value on the health of its customers than on purely financial considerations**, as well it should. Unfortunately, there is a more likely explanation for the change. Pending regulation will likely remove the subsidy that currently ensures that the price of HFC remains artificially low.

The two **boldfaced** portions play which of the following roles?

(A) The first supports the argument's conclusion; the second calls into question that conclusion.

(B) The first supports the doctors' conclusion; the second states that conclusion.

(C) The first states the conclusion of the argument; the second supports that conclusion.

(D) The first states the doctors' conclusion; the second provides evidence used to support that conclusion.

(E) Both statements support the primary conclusion of the argument, but the second does so indirectly.

Argument: Like in many bolded statement questions, the prompt here is a **somebody says X (and they're wrong)**. The second bolded statement is the X, the conclusion being countered by the speaker's argument whereas the first is **setup information** that serves as **evidence** for the conclusion the speaker is arguing against, as Answer Choice (B) describes perfectly.

(B) The answer choices split 3/2 over the first statement. Answer Choices (A), (B), and (E) all correctly peg the first statement as evidence, whereas Answer Choices (D) and (C) get it wrong. Answer Choice (E) can be eliminated because it treats both statements as evidence, and Answer Choice (A) describes the speaker's conclusion, not the conclusion of the **somebody** (here the doctors).

---

40. Though crocodiles and alligators both possess rows of sharp teeth, <u>before their food reaches the stomach the gizzard has stones swallowed earlier which further grind it</u>.

(A) before their food reaches the stomach the gizzard has stones swallowed earlier which further grind it

(B) before it reaches the stomach, the gizzard in which stones they have swallowed earlier is used to further grind their food

(C) before it reaches the stomach, the gizzard in which stones swallowed earlier further grinds their food

(D) their food is further ground into pieces in their gizzards by stones swallowed earlier before it reaches their stomach

(E) before reaching the stomach in their gizzards, in which stones they swallow earlier further grind their food into pieces

Issues: pronoun reference (ensuring only one plural antecedent for the *their*s and one singular antecedent for the *it*s), **modification** (making sense of all the prepositional phrases without creating dangling modifiers), **connecting clauses** (avoiding creating a run-on or a fragment)

(D) Targeting individual small errors is probably the best way to handle these messy options, rather than trying to sort out the modification from the very beginning. Answer Choice (A) uses a *which* without a comma, and Answer Choice (E) uses a comma with *in which*, errors of connecting clauses. Answer Choices (A), (B), (C), and (E) all fail to correctly sort out their pronoun references, as well. The *it* in Answer Choices (A), (B), and (C) could refer to at least two singulars (*gizzard, stomach, food*), and Answer Choice (E)'s *they* could refer to multiple plurals (*gizzards, alligators and crocodiles*). Most of the incorrect answer choices also create illogical descriptions of one sort or another [for example, Answer Choice (E) puts the stomach inside the gizzards].

---

41. Purring, though often thought to be a sign of a cat's good mood, is actually an involuntary response caused by the stimulation of certain nerves.
    (A) Purring, though often thought to be a sign of a cat's good mood, is actually an involuntary response caused by the stimulation of certain nerves.
    (B) Though often it is thought that cats purr because of its good mood, it is actually involuntary and responds to the cause of nerve stimulation.
    (C) Though often thought that cats purr because they are in a good mood, it is actually an involuntary response caused by the stimulation of certain nerves.
    (D) A cat's purring, though often thought to signify a good mood, is actually involuntarily a response caused by the stimulation of certain nerves.
    (E) The purring of a cat, thought often as though a sign of a good mood, is actually caused by the involuntary stimulation of certain nerves.

Issues: clause organization (actually a distracting issue here, as the various reorganizations are all correct in their own way), **modification** (the sensible placement and form of *actually* and *involuntary*), **pronoun** (avoiding **ambiguity** for *it*, but also **agreement** between the pronoun and its antecedent)

(A) The sentence, though a little halting, is grammatically correct as written. Pronoun problems creep up in some answer choices: Answer Choices (B) and (C) have no clear antecedent for the *it* that starts the phrase *it is actually*, whereas Answer Choice (D) introduces a stray *they*. *Actually* and *involuntary* get confused in Answer Choice (D) by the switch to *involuntarily*. In Answer Choice (E) moving *involuntary* to describe the stimulation changes the meaning of the sentence [though a bigger problem with Answer Choice (E) is the **unidiomatic** *thought often as though a sign*].

EVALUATING YOUR SCORE

Tabulate your score for the Quantitative and Verbal sections of the Sample Test by giving yourself one point for every correct answer, and record the results in the Self-Scoring Table below. Then find your approximate rating for each score on the Self-Scoring Scale and record it in the appropriate blank.

SELF-SCORING TABLE		
Section	**Score**	**Rating**
Quantitative		
Verbal		

SELF-SCORING SCALE—RATING				
Section	**Poor**	**Fair**	**Good**	**Excellent**
Quantitative	0–12	13–20	21–29	30–37
Verbal	0–15	15–25	26–30	31–41

Study again the Review sections covering material in Sample Test 1 for which you had a rating of FAIR or POOR. Then go on to Sample Test 2.

*Important note: Up-to-date scoring guidelines for all sections of the GMAT can be found at *mba.com*.

Sample Test 2 with Answers and Analysis

→ TEST
→ ANSWERS
→ ANALYSIS
→ EVALUATING YOUR SCORE

ANSWER SHEET
Sample Test 2

INTEGRATED REASONING SECTION

1. i. Ⓐ Ⓑ Ⓒ Ⓓ

ii. Ⓐ Ⓑ Ⓒ Ⓓ

2.

Amount Needed to Spend on New Hires	Amount Each Student Expects to Make	Amount in $
◯	◯	0
◯	◯	720
◯	◯	1,080
◯	◯	1,920
◯	◯	2,560
◯	◯	3,840

3.

Would Help Explain	Would Not Help Explain
◯	◯
◯	◯
◯	◯

4. Ⓐ Ⓑ Ⓒ Ⓓ Ⓔ

5.

True	False
◯	◯
◯	◯
◯	◯

6.

Yes	No
◯	◯
◯	◯
◯	◯

7.

Would Definitely be Part of the Optimite Program	Would Definitely NOT be Part of the Optimite Program
◯	◯
◯	◯
◯	◯
◯	◯
◯	◯

8. Ⓐ Ⓑ Ⓒ Ⓓ Ⓔ

9. i. Ⓐ Ⓑ Ⓒ Ⓓ Ⓔ

ii. Ⓐ Ⓑ Ⓒ Ⓓ Ⓔ

10. i. Ⓐ Ⓑ Ⓒ Ⓓ

ii. Ⓐ Ⓑ Ⓒ Ⓓ

11.

True	False
◯	◯
◯	◯
◯	◯

12. Ⓐ Ⓑ Ⓒ Ⓓ Ⓔ

ANSWER SHEET
Sample Test 2

QUANTITATIVE SECTION

1. Ⓐ Ⓑ Ⓒ Ⓓ Ⓔ   11. Ⓐ Ⓑ Ⓒ Ⓓ Ⓔ   21. Ⓐ Ⓑ Ⓒ Ⓓ Ⓔ   31. Ⓐ Ⓑ Ⓒ Ⓓ Ⓔ
2. Ⓐ Ⓑ Ⓒ Ⓓ Ⓔ   12. Ⓐ Ⓑ Ⓒ Ⓓ Ⓔ   22. Ⓐ Ⓑ Ⓒ Ⓓ Ⓔ   32. Ⓐ Ⓑ Ⓒ Ⓓ Ⓔ
3. Ⓐ Ⓑ Ⓒ Ⓓ Ⓔ   13. Ⓐ Ⓑ Ⓒ Ⓓ Ⓔ   23. Ⓐ Ⓑ Ⓒ Ⓓ Ⓔ   33. Ⓐ Ⓑ Ⓒ Ⓓ Ⓔ
4. Ⓐ Ⓑ Ⓒ Ⓓ Ⓔ   14. Ⓐ Ⓑ Ⓒ Ⓓ Ⓔ   24. Ⓐ Ⓑ Ⓒ Ⓓ Ⓔ   34. Ⓐ Ⓑ Ⓒ Ⓓ Ⓔ
5. Ⓐ Ⓑ Ⓒ Ⓓ Ⓔ   15. Ⓐ Ⓑ Ⓒ Ⓓ Ⓔ   25. Ⓐ Ⓑ Ⓒ Ⓓ Ⓔ   35. Ⓐ Ⓑ Ⓒ Ⓓ Ⓔ
6. Ⓐ Ⓑ Ⓒ Ⓓ Ⓔ   16. Ⓐ Ⓑ Ⓒ Ⓓ Ⓔ   26. Ⓐ Ⓑ Ⓒ Ⓓ Ⓔ   36. Ⓐ Ⓑ Ⓒ Ⓓ Ⓔ
7. Ⓐ Ⓑ Ⓒ Ⓓ Ⓔ   17. Ⓐ Ⓑ Ⓒ Ⓓ Ⓔ   27. Ⓐ Ⓑ Ⓒ Ⓓ Ⓔ   37. Ⓐ Ⓑ Ⓒ Ⓓ Ⓔ
8. Ⓐ Ⓑ Ⓒ Ⓓ Ⓔ   18. Ⓐ Ⓑ Ⓒ Ⓓ Ⓔ   28. Ⓐ Ⓑ Ⓒ Ⓓ Ⓔ
9. Ⓐ Ⓑ Ⓒ Ⓓ Ⓔ   19. Ⓐ Ⓑ Ⓒ Ⓓ Ⓔ   29. Ⓐ Ⓑ Ⓒ Ⓓ Ⓔ
10. Ⓐ Ⓑ Ⓒ Ⓓ Ⓔ   20. Ⓐ Ⓑ Ⓒ Ⓓ Ⓔ   30. Ⓐ Ⓑ Ⓒ Ⓓ Ⓔ

VERBAL SECTION

1. Ⓐ Ⓑ Ⓒ Ⓓ Ⓔ   12. Ⓐ Ⓑ Ⓒ Ⓓ Ⓔ   23. Ⓐ Ⓑ Ⓒ Ⓓ Ⓔ   34. Ⓐ Ⓑ Ⓒ Ⓓ Ⓔ
2. Ⓐ Ⓑ Ⓒ Ⓓ Ⓔ   13. Ⓐ Ⓑ Ⓒ Ⓓ Ⓔ   24. Ⓐ Ⓑ Ⓒ Ⓓ Ⓔ   35. Ⓐ Ⓑ Ⓒ Ⓓ Ⓔ
3. Ⓐ Ⓑ Ⓒ Ⓓ Ⓔ   14. Ⓐ Ⓑ Ⓒ Ⓓ Ⓔ   25. Ⓐ Ⓑ Ⓒ Ⓓ Ⓔ   36. Ⓐ Ⓑ Ⓒ Ⓓ Ⓔ
4. Ⓐ Ⓑ Ⓒ Ⓓ Ⓔ   15. Ⓐ Ⓑ Ⓒ Ⓓ Ⓔ   26. Ⓐ Ⓑ Ⓒ Ⓓ Ⓔ   37. Ⓐ Ⓑ Ⓒ Ⓓ Ⓔ
5. Ⓐ Ⓑ Ⓒ Ⓓ Ⓔ   16. Ⓐ Ⓑ Ⓒ Ⓓ Ⓔ   27. Ⓐ Ⓑ Ⓒ Ⓓ Ⓔ   38. Ⓐ Ⓑ Ⓒ Ⓓ Ⓔ
6. Ⓐ Ⓑ Ⓒ Ⓓ Ⓔ   17. Ⓐ Ⓑ Ⓒ Ⓓ Ⓔ   28. Ⓐ Ⓑ Ⓒ Ⓓ Ⓔ   39. Ⓐ Ⓑ Ⓒ Ⓓ Ⓔ
7. Ⓐ Ⓑ Ⓒ Ⓓ Ⓔ   18. Ⓐ Ⓑ Ⓒ Ⓓ Ⓔ   29. Ⓐ Ⓑ Ⓒ Ⓓ Ⓔ   40. Ⓐ Ⓑ Ⓒ Ⓓ Ⓔ
8. Ⓐ Ⓑ Ⓒ Ⓓ Ⓔ   19. Ⓐ Ⓑ Ⓒ Ⓓ Ⓔ   30. Ⓐ Ⓑ Ⓒ Ⓓ Ⓔ   41. Ⓐ Ⓑ Ⓒ Ⓓ Ⓔ
9. Ⓐ Ⓑ Ⓒ Ⓓ Ⓔ   20. Ⓐ Ⓑ Ⓒ Ⓓ Ⓔ   31. Ⓐ Ⓑ Ⓒ Ⓓ Ⓔ
10. Ⓐ Ⓑ Ⓒ Ⓓ Ⓔ   21. Ⓐ Ⓑ Ⓒ Ⓓ Ⓔ   32. Ⓐ Ⓑ Ⓒ Ⓓ Ⓔ
11. Ⓐ Ⓑ Ⓒ Ⓓ Ⓔ   22. Ⓐ Ⓑ Ⓒ Ⓓ Ⓔ   33. Ⓐ Ⓑ Ⓒ Ⓓ Ⓔ

Analytical Writing Analysis

Time: 30 minutes

> **DIRECTIONS:** In this section, you will be asked to write a critique of the argument presented. You are NOT being asked to present your own views on the subject.
>
> **WRITING YOUR RESPONSE:** Take a few minutes to evaluate the argument and plan a response before you begin writing. Be sure to organize your ideas and develop them fully, but leave time to reread your response and make any revisions that you think are necessary.
>
> **EVALUATION OF YOUR RESPONSE:** College and university faculty members from various subject matter areas, including management education, will evaluate the overall quality of your thinking and writing. They will consider how well you: organize, develop, and express your ideas about the argument presented; provide relevant supporting reasons and examples; and control the elements of standard written English.

Question: The following appeared as part of the business plan of By Jove, a venture capital firm:

> "In the Cleveland Heights district, the Theatre d'Arte, Purple People Pizza, and the Extra-Select Gym have all had business increases over the past two years. By Jove should therefore invest in the Playhouse Theater, the Pizza X-'Plosion, and the Curvy Gym, three new businesses across town in the Saints Row district. As a condition, we should require them to participate in a special loyalty program: Any customer who patronizes two of the businesses will receive a substantial discount at the third. By motivating customers to patronize all three, we will thus contribute to the profitability of each and maximize our return.

Discuss how well reasoned you find this argument. In your discussion be sure to analyze the line of reasoning and the use of evidence in the argument. For example, you may need to consider what questionable assumptions underlie the thinking and what alternative explanations or counterexamples might weaken the conclusion. You can also discuss what sort of evidence would strengthen or refute the argument, what changes in the argument would make it more logically sound, and what, if anything, would help you better evaluate its conclusion.

STOP

ON THE ACTUAL GMAT, AFTER YOU HAVE CONFIRMED YOUR ANSWER, YOU CANNOT RETURN TO IT.

INTEGRATED REASONING SECTION

Time: 30 minutes

12 questions

This section consists of four types of questions: Graphics Interpretation, Table Analysis, Two-part Analysis, and Multi-Source Reasoning.

> **DIRECTIONS:** The new Integrated Reasoning section consists of four question types. Some require the use of both quantitative and verbal skills. Others involve the use of graphics, tables, or text material. The questions also use various response formats.
>
> For each question, review the text, graphic, or text material provided and respond to the task that is presented. *Note: An onscreen calculator is available in this section on the actual test.*

Question 1 refers to the following information and graph.

1. The graph below charts the cumulative frequency of height (in inches) of college basketball players at USC in 2002.

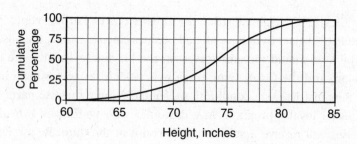

Answer each question according to the information presented in the diagram.

i. What is the range of heights within the third quartile?

(A) 3 inches

(B) 4 inches

(C) 5 inches

(D) Cannot be determined

ii. Approximately what percentage of players is within 6 inches of the median height?

(A) 66.7%

(B) 75%

(C) 83.3%

(D) 90%

2. The painting company Youth Pro Painters has just hired ten students this year for the 12-week summer season. Their target is to paint 1,200 houses over the summer. On average, ten students can paint four houses in 16 hours. Each student painter makes $8 per hour and is expected to work 40 hours per week.

In the table below, identify how much money the company needs to spend on additional hires in order to meet its objective. Also identify the amount of money each student can expect to make in half the summer. Choose only one option in each column.

Amount Needed to Spend on New Hires	Amount Each Student Expects to Make	Amount in $
○	○	0
○	○	720
○	○	1,080
○	○	1,920
○	○	2,560
○	○	3,840

3. The table below shows data for the percentage of the eligible population subgroups attending school.

Country	Kindergarten	Primary School	Secondary School	Post-Secondary
Argentina	71	95	90	54
Bolivia	59	91	79	38
Chile	56	88	88	22
Columbia	62	98	95	60
Paraguay	67	86	77	45
Peru	32	81	68	19
Ecuador	45	93	65	21

For each of the following statements, select *Would Help Explain* if it would, if true, help explain some of the information in the table. Otherwise select *Would Not Help Explain*.

Would Help Explain	Would Not Help Explain	
○	○	In South America, kindergartens are not as available as are primary schools.
○	○	Peru has a larger rural and agricultural population than the other countries, and most of the farms are maintained by the families that live on them.
○	○	Parents in Argentina value education more than parents in the other South American countries shown in the chart.

Questions 4–6 refer to the following documents.

Document 1:

Curlypro, a hair product manufacturing company based in Chicago, is evaluating expansion options for its product line. The company has two plants that are currently operating at full capacity. Management has finalized its top three production plant options.

Nanning, the capital of Guangxi Province in Southern China
This 30,000-square-foot plant has the capacity to produce and deliver 1,500 crates per month. The plant manager has asked for a three-year commitment and a minimum order of 1,000 crates per month. Curlypro has some concerns about shipping costs and time, but this would be an issue only if shipping the minimum amount for all three years.

Chennai, India
This 20,000-square-foot plant features a large capacity of 2,500 crates per month. The plant manager requires a three-year commitment and a minimum order of 1,000 crates per month. Similar to the Nanning plant, this plant may have prohibitive shipping costs and timing. The primary concern is that the region's reputation for underage factory workers might instigate a consumer backlash. The plant manager assures us that they do not hire anyone under the age of 18.

Sandusky, Ohio
This 18,000-square-foot plant has a capacity of 1,200 crates per month. Both Curlypro and the Sandusky plant are eager to have American workers supply the company as this will have great marketing appeal. They can also take advantage of some government assistance that will allow the Sandusky plant to require only a one-year contract and no minimum order size.

Document 2:

Curlypro produces two main products—Curlypro shampoo and Curlypro conditioner. Sales have grown substantially in the past two years. Curlypro estimates sales for the current year will reach 400 crates per month for each product line.

The current forecast for sales in the next three years is approximately a 25% to 50% increase each year for both lines. Although all the plants have significant capacity, Curlypro management wants to make the right investment for the long term. They are leaning toward the Sandusky plant due to its flexibility and the chance to keep production within the country.

Document 3:

Market research has suggested that Curlypro should launch two new lines of hair products—a Curlypro 2-in-1 shampoo/conditioner and a Curlypro dandruff control shampoo. Management is very eager to take advantage of the current success and rising brand awareness. Forecasts for the sales of each new product line are 200 crates per month, with a growth rate of 100% in year two and 50% in year three.

4. What is the difference in three-year sales forecasts for Curlypro between the most optimistic and most pessimistic forecasts, including launching either both new product lines or neither?

(A) 1,137.5 crates per month

(B) 2,025 crates per month

(C) 2,337.5 crates per month

(D) 2,800 crates per month

(E) 3,137.5 crates per month

---

5. Answer the following true or false statements.

True **False**

○ ○ If each crate sold generates $1,000 in profit, if Curlypro decides to work with the Chinese plant, if the shipping costs increase by $100,000 total, and if Curlypro's sales equal the most pessimistic forecast, net monthly profits will be over $1 million in year 1.

○ ○ Curlypro would sell more units overall in the first year if it launched both new products, even with the most pessimistic forecast of its current product lines, than if it continued to produce only two products and sold them at the most optimistic forecast.

○ ○ If Curlypro chose the Chennai plant and the subsequent negative public perception caused the sales increase to be 25% lower than the most optimistic sales forecast, launching one new product line would not entirely offset this loss over three years.

---

6. For each of the following scenarios, determine if the selected plant will have enough capacity to manage the production demands of Curlypro. Select *Yes* if the plant will have sufficient capacity. Otherwise, select *No*.

Yes **No**

○ ○ Nanning plant, year 2: Assuming Curlypro's most pessimistic forecast and the introduction of the 2-in-1 shampoo/conditioner in the second year

○ ○ Sandusky plant, year 2: Assuming Curlypro's most optimistic forecast and no new product launches

○ ○ Chennai plant, year 1: Assuming Curlypro's most optimistic forecast and the launch of both new product lines in year 1

Questions 7 and 8 refer to the following excerpt from a fictitious education report about a fictitious new school program called Optimite.

The new Optimite program has found considerable success in eastern Europe over the past two years. Two school boards on the North Shore have now called for its experimental introduction in North Chicago. The program is complex, requiring a classroom size of 60 students in grade 11. Within an Optimite class would be three teachers working simultaneously. The Optimite objective is to have collaborative learning on site via case studies and matches, physical and mental challenges, and high-level discussions. Students are encouraged to research and discuss social, political, and economic topics and to use advanced technology tools in the classroom. Optimite also requires a diverse student body of cultural and socioeconomic backgrounds, with no majority of any distinct group. Students will be evaluated before participating and again after a two-semester trial. They will be tested on skills such as leadership, innovation, quantitative analysis, verbal reasoning, and communication.

7. Based on the description in the excerpt, which of the following activities would definitely be part of the fictitious Optimite program? Which of the following activities would definitely not be part of the program? Make only two selections, one in each column.

Would Definitely Be Part of the Optimite Program	Would Definitely Not Be Part of the Optimite Program	
○	○	Capoeira martial arts
○	○	Delivering a presentation on business ethics
○	○	A case competition
○	○	A field trip to a museum of marine biology
○	○	Moderated debate on local politics

8. Which of the following issues would not be a concern to the school board in order to launch the Optimite program?

(A) Classroom size and technology resources
(B) Transportation of students to the location
(C) Finding enough students to meet the diversity requirements
(D) Maintaining a teacher-student ratio below the state standard of 24 students per teacher
(E) Finding enough qualified instructors to teach the program

Question 9 refers to the following Venn diagram and information.

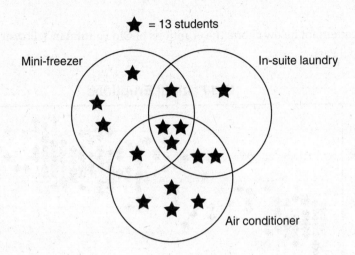

9. Refer to the Venn diagram above. Each ★ represents 13 student residents living in New College dormitories. The student dormitories have mini-freezers, in-suite laundry, air conditioners, or a combination. Complete each statement according to the information presented in the diagram.

    i. If one student resident is selected at random from the New College dormitories, what is the probability that the student will have in-suite laundry?

    (A) 2 out of 5
    (B) 7 out of 15
    (C) 3 out of 5
    (D) 2 out of 3
    (E) 7 out of 10

    ii. If a student resident has air conditioning in the dormitory, what is the probability that the student will also have a mini-freezer?

    (A) 1 out of 10
    (B) 1 out of 3
    (C) 3 out of 10
    (D) 2 out of 5
    (E) 1 out of 2

Question 10 refers to the following scatter plot and information.

The scatter plot below charts the eruptions of Old Faithful in Yellowstone National Park.

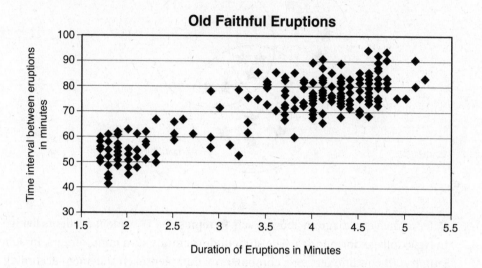

10. Complete each statement according to the information given by the graph.

i. Approximately how much time occurs between eruptions of Old Faithful?

(A) It's not possible to predict
(B) Every 55 minutes
(C) Every 80 minutes
(D) Either every 55 minutes or every 80 minutes

ii. Which of the following is closest to the length of the average duration of Old Faithful eruptions?

(A) 2 minutes
(B) 2.5 minutes
(C) 3.5 minutes
(D) 4.5 minutes

Questions 11 and 12 refer to the following table.

The table below shows data for revenues and profits of the top 13 companies globally in 2010.

Company	Revenues ($ billions)	Revenue Rank	% Change in Revenue Since 2009	Profits ($ billions)	% Change in Profits Since 2009
Wal-Mart Stores, Inc.	421.8	1	3.3	16.4	14.3
Exxon Mobil	354.7	2	24.6	30.5	58.0
Chevron	196.3	3	20.1	19.0	81.5
ConocoPhillips	185.0	4	32.6	11.4	133.8
Fannie Mae	153.8	5	429.2	-14.0	n/a*
General Electric	151.6	6	-3.3	11.6	5.6
Berkshire Hathaway	136.2	7	21.1	13.0	61.0
General Motors	135.6	8	29.6	6.2	n/a*
Bank of America Corp.	134.2	9	-10.8	-2.2	-135.7
Ford Motor	129.0	10	9.0	6.6	141.5
Hewlett-Packard	126.0	11	10.0	8.8	14.4
AT&T	124.6	12	1.3	19.9	58.5
J.P. Morgan Chase & Co.	115.5	13	-0.1	17.4	48.1

*n/a means that the actual number could not be calculated due to a negative profit change value in 2008

11. Consider each of the following statements. For each statement, indicate whether the statement is true or false based on the information provided in the table.

True False

○   ○   The amount of revenue growth of the top five ranked companies combined is greater than that of the rest of the companies in the list.

○   ○   The median profit amount is larger than the difference between the average of the top six profitable companies and the bottom six profitable companies.

○   ○   If Fannie Mae's percentage change in revenue dropped by 95% in 2010 and assuming operation costs remain constant, Fannie Mae should become profitable by 2010.

12. If stock market value was based on only the average rank of three values—percentage change in revenue, total profit amount, and percentage change in profit—which company would be the best one to invest in?

(A) Wal-Mart Stores, Inc.
(B) Berkshire Hathaway
(C) Fannie Mae
(D) Exxon Mobil
(E) ConocoPhillips

STOP

ON THE ACTUAL GMAT,
AFTER YOU HAVE CONFIRMED YOUR ANSWER,
YOU CANNOT RETURN TO IT.

QUANTITATIVE SECTION

Time: 75 minutes

37 questions

This section consists of two types of questions: Problem Solving and Data Sufficiency. According to the GMAC, the directions for these question types are as follows.

Problem Solving

DIRECTIONS: Solve each of the following problems; then indicate the correct answer.

NOTE: A figure that appears with a problem is drawn as accurately as possible so as to provide information that may help in answering the question.

Numbers in this test are real numbers.

Data Sufficiency

DIRECTIONS: Each of the following problems has a question and two statements that are labeled (1) and (2). Use the data given in (1) and (2) together with other available information (such as the number of hours in a day, the definition of *clockwise*, mathematical facts, etc.) to decide whether the statements are *sufficient* to answer the question. Then fill in space

(A) If you can get the answer from **(1) ALONE** but not from (2) alone

(B) If you can get the answer from **(2) ALONE** but not from (1) alone

(C) If you can get the answer from **BOTH (1)** and **(2) TOGETHER** but not from (1) alone or (2) alone

(D) If **EITHER** statement **(1) ALONE OR** statement **(2) ALONE** suffices

(E) If you **CANNOT** get the answer from statements (1) and (2) **TOGETHER** but need even more data

All numbers used in this section are real numbers.

A figure given for a problem is intended to provide information consistent with that in the question, but not necessarily with the additional information contained in the statements.

All figures lie in the plane unless you are told otherwise.

Figures are drawn as accurately as possible; straight lines may not appear straight on the screen.

1. Set T consists of 3 numbers with only one mode. Does the range equal the mode?

   (1) The largest number is twice the value of the smallest number.
   (2) The median equals the range.

2. A coin is tossed three times. What is the probability that there will be at least one head?

   (A) $\dfrac{1}{16}$

   (B) $\dfrac{3}{8}$

   (C) $\dfrac{1}{2}$

   (D) $\dfrac{5}{8}$

   (E) $\dfrac{7}{8}$

3. What is x?

   (1) $3x - 2y = 5$

   (2) $y = -\dfrac{5}{2} + \left(\dfrac{3}{2}\right)x$

4. What is the x-intercept of the equation $y = 6x^2 - 13x - 5$?

   (1) $x < 1$
   (2) $3x$ is an odd integer.

5. If $2^{x-7} \cdot 3^{2x-3} = 27^{(3x-10)/3}$, what is x?

   (A) -1
   (B) 0
   (C) 3
   (D) 7
   (E) 9

SAMPLE TEST 2

6. Is *x* a positive integer?

    (1) $xy = 210$

    (2) *x* and *y* are prime numbers

7. Of the 3,200 people living in town *A*, 25% live downtown. Of these people, 60% live in a high-rise, 40% rent, and 25% both live in a high-rise and rent. If one person is selected randomly from the 3,200 people, what is the probability that the one selected will live downtown in a high-rise but not rent?

    (A) $\dfrac{1}{10}$

    (B) $\dfrac{7}{80}$

    (C) $\dfrac{3}{20}$

    (D) $\dfrac{24}{320}$

    (E) $\dfrac{48}{320}$

8. *A*, *B*, and *C* are positive integers, such that *A* is a factor of *B* and *B* is a factor of *C*. Is *C* an even number?

    (1) *AB* is an even number.

    (2) *B* is even.

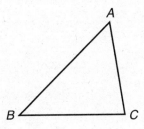

9. In triangle *ABC*, what is the height from the base *AB*?

    (1) The perimeter of *ABC* is 12.

    (2) The triangle is isosceles with one angle measuring 60°.

10. If *r*, *s*, and *t* are integers greater than 1, what is the value of $r + s + t$?

    (1) $\dfrac{100r}{st} = 70$

    (2) $2rst = 462$

11. Marisa's new car gets 37 miles per gallon. She drove her new car 410 miles on a tank of gas at an average speed of 41 mph. Which of the following can be determined from the given information?

   I. Approximate capacity of the gas tank
  II. Number of days traveled
 III. Cost per gallon of gas

(A) I only

(B) II only

(C) III only

(D) Both I and III

(E) None of the above

12. 1,000 tickets numbered from 1 to 1,000, inclusive, were sold in a lottery. What is the probability of selecting a ticket with a 6 as either the hundreds digit or the tens digit?

(A) $\dfrac{1}{10}$

(B) $\dfrac{12}{100}$

(C) $\dfrac{3}{20}$

(D) $\dfrac{19}{100}$

(E) $\dfrac{1}{5}$

13. Is x a prime number?

  (1) xyz has only 8 distinct factors.

  (2) xy is even when y is a prime number.

14. A set contains a parallelogram, 2 isosceles trapezoids, 3 squares, a rectangle, and 2 rhombuses that are not squares. A figure is chosen at random. What is the probability that the figure's diagonals will be of equal length?

(A) $\dfrac{3}{9}$

(B) $\dfrac{5}{9}$

(C) $\dfrac{2}{3}$

(D) $\dfrac{8}{9}$

(E) 1

15. How much older than Paul is Mary?

(1) Peter is 10 years older than Paul.

(2) Mary in 2 years will be twice as old as Paul.

16. Nancy's family is out visiting the grandparents when Grandpa Joe decides everyone should go out for ice cream. The family takes two cars, Nancy's and Grandpa's. The ice cream shop is 10 km away, and Nancy drives at an average speed of 80 km/hr. Nancy gets pulled over for speeding, and the police officer who writes her ticket delays her by 5 minutes. Nancy and Grandpa arrive at the ice cream shop at the exact same time. What was Grandpa's average speed?

(A) 36 km/hr
(B) 40 km/hr
(C) 48 km/hr
(D) 56 km/hr
(E) 60 km/hr

17. At a candy store, the ratio of the number of jellybeans to the number of gumdrops is 9 to 5, and the ratio of the number of chocolate bars to jellybeans is 2 to 5. If the ratio of the number of licorice sticks to the number of gumdrops is 4 to 3, what is the ratio of the number of chocolate bars to the number of licorice sticks?

(A) 27 to 100
(B) 27 to 75
(C) 27 to 50
(D) 54 to 75
(E) 20 to 27

18. Machines X and Y, while working simultaneously at their respective constant rates, produce 1,200 widgets in Z days. While working alone at its constant rate, machine Y produces 1,200 widgets in W days. How many days does it take machine X, while working at its constant rate, to produce 1,200 widgets in terms of W and Z?

    (A) $\dfrac{W}{(W+Z)}$

    (B) $\dfrac{Z}{(W+Z)}$

    (C) $\dfrac{WZ}{(W+Z)}$

    (D) $\dfrac{WZ}{(W-Z)}$

    (E) $\dfrac{WZ}{(Z-W)}$

19. For all positive integers x, y and z, $x \circledR y^{z+1}$ means that y^{z+1} and y^z are divisors of x. If $162 \circledR 3^{z+1}$, then what does z equal?

    (A) $-3 < z < -1$

    (B) $-1 < z < 4$

    (C) $-2 < z < 5$

    (D) $0 < z < 6$

    (E) $1 < z < 4$

20. In a class graduating from medical school, the male students took an average of 9.7 years to obtain their degrees and the female students took an average of 9.0 years. What was the ratio of the number of female graduates to the number of male graduates?

    (1) The average number of years for the current graduating class as a whole to graduate from medical school was 9.5 years.

    (2) There were 47 female graduates.

21. In city A, 72% of the employed population are blue-collar workers and the rest are white-collar workers. If 75% of the white-collar workers are male and $\dfrac{5}{12}$ of the blue-collar workers are female, what percent of the employed population of city A are female?

(A) 37%
(B) 40%
(C) 43%
(D) 47%
(E) 53%

22. Is $s > -r$?

(1) $s - 4r > 0$
(2) $3r - s > 0$

23. At a fraternity keg party, Ogre mixes three drinks that are 3%, 8% and 12% alcohol by volume. If x pints of 3% alcohol, y pints of 8% alcohol, and z pints of 12% alcohol mixed give $x + y + z$ pints of a 9% alcohol drink, what is x in terms of y and z?

(A) $\dfrac{3}{(3y+z+6)}$

(B) $\dfrac{(3z-y)}{6}$

(C) $\dfrac{(3z+y)}{6}$

(D) $\dfrac{(21z+17y)}{12}$

(E) $\dfrac{3}{(3z-y)}$

24. For all positive numbers x and y, for which of the following functions is $f(x - y) = f(x) - f(y)$?

(A) $f(t) = -2t$
(B) $f(t) = t^2 + 1$
(C) $f(t) = t - 1$
(D) $f(t) = \sqrt{(t+3)}$
(E) $f(t) = \dfrac{3}{t}$

25. If $a^4 < b^2 < c$, which of the following statements could be true?

   I. $a > b > c$
   II. $a < b < c$
   III. $c > a > b$

   (A) I only
   (B) I and II only
   (C) I and III only
   (D) II and III only
   (E) All of the above

26. Mary needs to sort her toys. She has several identical items, including three dolls, three cars, three teddy bears, three tennis balls, and three trains. In how many ways can she arrange them?

   (A) $\dfrac{(3!)^5}{15}$

   (B) $\dfrac{15!}{(5 \cdot 3!)}$

   (C) $\dfrac{15!}{(5!3!)}$

   (D) $\dfrac{15!}{(3!)^5}$

   (E) $\dfrac{3^{15}}{15!}$

27. Charles put an amount of money into each of two investments, X and Y, which pay simple annual interest. If the annual interest rate of X is 40% more than that of investment Y, what amount did Charles put into investment Y?

   (1) The amount that Charles put into investment X is three times the amount that he put into investment Y.
   (2) The interest for one year is $100 for investment X and $200 for investment Y.

28. When a bacterial culture was created, the medium consisted of 7.2×10^{20} molecules and the amount decreased every hour by a constant amount. At the end of the 7th hour, the number of molecules was $\frac{1}{8}$ less than it was at the end of the 5th hour. How many molecules did the culture medium lose each hour?

    (A) 8.8×10^{17}
    (B) 3.6×10^{18}
    (C) 9.0×10^{18}
    (D) 3.6×10^{19}
    (E) 7.2×10^{19}

29. Is $x \geq y$?

    (1) $-x \leq -y$
    (2) $x^2 - y^2 = 0$

30. What is the surface area of a cube?

    (1) The length of $\frac{1}{4}$ of the diagonal is $\sqrt{2}$.

    (2) The maximum distance between one vertex on the cube to another is $4\sqrt{3}$.

31. Sam plans to travel across the country by hitchhiking. He immediately gets picked up by a large transport rig that takes him k miles at an average speed of r miles per hour. He then waits 10 hours before being picked up by a van of students who are on their way to San Francisco. They agree to drive him the rest of the way. They drive at a speed of s miles per hour and finish the trip. If the total cross-country trip is D miles, how long did it take Sam to complete his trip?

    (A) $\dfrac{60k}{r} + \dfrac{(D-k)}{60s}$

    (B) $\dfrac{k}{r} + (D-k)s + 10$

    (C) $\dfrac{(k+10)}{r} + (D-k)s$

    (D) $\dfrac{k}{r} + \dfrac{(D-k)}{60s} + 60$

    (E) $\dfrac{k}{r} + \dfrac{(D-k)}{s} + 10$

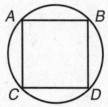

32. In the figure above, what is the largest rectangle that can be inscribed in the circle?

    (1) The arc *AB* is equal to 4.
    (2) The rectangle is a square.

33. While in detention, Oliver is given the task of calculating the volume of 1,000 hot dogs, where each hot dog is 6 inches in length from end to end and each end of the hot dog is shaped as a half sphere with a radius *r*. The volume of a sphere is $V = \left(\dfrac{4}{3}\right)\pi r^3$. What is the volume of 1,000 hot dogs?

    (A) $\dfrac{(6\pi r^2 - \left(\frac{10}{3}\right)\pi r^3)}{1,000}$

    (B) $5\pi r^2 - \left(\dfrac{2}{3}\right)\pi r^3$

    (C) $6,000\pi r^2 + \left(\dfrac{4}{3}\right)\pi r^3$

    (D) $1,000(6\pi r^2 - \left(\dfrac{2}{3}\right)\pi r^3)$

    (E) $500(5\pi r^2 + \left(\dfrac{4}{3}\right)\pi r^3)$

34. A box contains red marbles, green marbles, and yellow marbles. If a marble is randomly selected from the box, what is the probability that the marble selected will be either green or yellow?

(1) $P(\text{yellow marble}) = \dfrac{1}{3}$

(2) $P(\text{red marble}) = \dfrac{1}{4}$

35. Each gardener employed by company ABC Estates receives the following pay: x dollars per hour for each of the first z hours in a week and $x + y$ dollars per hour for each hour over z hours per week, where $x > y$. How much less pay will an ABC Estates gardener who works $z + y$ hours earn than one who works $z + x$ hours?

(A) $x^2 - y^2$
(B) $(y - x)(x + y + z)$
(C) $yz + xz - yx$
(D) $y - x$
(E) $z(y - x)$

36. There are at least 200 students at a cooking school studying French cuisine. The only other cuisine available for study is Indian cuisine. If 8% of the students at this school who study Indian cuisine also study French cuisine, do more students study Indian cuisine than French cuisine?

(1) 32 students at the school study both Indian and French cuisine.
(2) 20% of the students who study French cuisine also study Indian cuisine.

37. A sequence is defined by $A_n = (A_{n-1})^2 - 2(A_{n-1})(A_{n-2}) + (A_{n-2})^2$, where $n > 2$. If $A_3 = 2$ and $A_5 = 1$, what is A_6?

(A) 1
(B) 4
(C) 6
(D) 9
(E) 25

VERBAL SECTION

Time: 75 minutes

41 questions

Reading Comprehension

DIRECTIONS: This section contains three reading passages. You are to read each one carefully. When answering the questions, you *will* be allowed to refer back to the passages. The questions are based on what is *stated* or *implied* in each passage.

Critical Reasoning

DIRECTIONS: For each question in this section, choose the best answer from among the listed alternatives.

Sentence Correction

DIRECTIONS: This part of the section consists of a number of sentences, in each of which some part or the whole is underlined. Each sentence is followed by five alternative versions of the underlined portion. Select the alternative you consider both most correct and most effective according to the requirements of standard written English. Answer (A) is the same as the original version; if you think the original version is best, select answer (A).

In considering the answer choices, be attentive to matters of grammar, diction, and syntax, as well as clarity, precision, and fluency. Do not select an answer that alters the meaning of the original sentence.

SAMPLE TEST 2

Questions 1–4 are based on the following passage.

Seeking to distinguish themselves from nearby competitors, some small businesses that primarily sell their services locally—for example, nonchain restaurants, florists, and fitness studios—have begun to advertise their services through "group coupons"
Line offered at nationally known deal-of-the-day websites. Such coupons typically offer
(5) a limited number of the site's visitors (usually between 100 and 1,000) access to the business's services for a limited time (typically a month to three months) at a deep discount off the company's standard prices (sometimes reaching as much as 75 percent) if paid in advance. These group coupon arrangements have the potential to measurably increase local customers' awareness of a business's presence in the
(10) market due to the large reach of the coupon website's online presence and also due, at least in part, to the novelty currently enjoyed by these sites, many of which have been featured prominently in media outlets in the past year as the latest revolutionary trend in marketing to emerge from the much fêted realm of social media. Since customers pay before they have received the service or even spoken
(15) with the local provider, their purchases result in a large immediate influx of cash for the business.

Use of these group coupon websites is not without its risks, however, and most small businesses would do well to carefully consider their capacity for expansion and the composition of their current client base before jumping onto this "next big
(20) thing." Ironically, part of the danger of offering a group coupon through a deal-of-the-day website lies in the very thing that is most valuable about them: their reach. The number of customers who regularly check deal-of-the-day sites and who will purchase the services advertised there sight unseen is usually many times the size of a local service provider's normal client base. While a significant percentage never
(25) redeem the coupons purchased, those who do can flood the service provider with demands for service that far outstrip the business's available resources. Long-term customers may consequently feel slighted when they are unable to obtain services from these local businesses with the speed or frequency that they were once accustomed. While the business is occupied meeting the sudden demand the group
(30) coupon generated, these customers may quietly take their business elsewhere. Moreover, the new customers who discovered the business through the group coupon seldom remain loyal to the business once the discounted service has been provided, instead moving on to some other promotion advertised by the deal-of-the-day sites.

1. The primary purpose of the passage as a whole is to

    (A) account for the popularity of a practice.
    (B) explain the reasons for pursuing a strategy.
    (C) demonstrate how to institute a practice.
    (D) advocate the use of one strategy over another.
    (E) evaluate the utility of a practice.

2. Which of the following is cited in the passage as a goal of some local services providing businesses for using group coupons?

(A) To diversify the business's normal client base
(B) To obtain a large immediate influx of cash for the business
(C) To differentiate the business from others offering the same services
(D) To associate the business with the latest marketing trends
(E) To test the business's ability to meet demands for expanded service

3. Which of the following may be inferred from the passage?

(A) The service providers most likely to benefit by offering a group coupon are those who offer discounts lower than 75 percent off their usual prices.
(B) The service providers least likely to benefit with a group coupon are those that operate in markets with few competitors.
(C) If a business that offers services also sells physical goods, it will be better able to survive the loss of long-term customers caused by offering a group coupon.
(D) If a business has excess capacity that is being underutilized, it will stand to benefit substantially from offering a group coupon.
(E) If a business typically provides services that customers use infrequently for only a few days, it is likely to avoid the risk of offering a group coupon.

4. Which of the following hypothetical situations best exemplifies the potential problem the passage identifies for businesses offering a group coupon?

(A) A tattoo parlor is unable to obtain permission to open a new location after their reputation spreads throughout the community.
(B) A lawyer is forced to alter the composition of his print ads in order to avoid alienating new customers.
(C) A business consultant's reputation for excellent service with new clients creates an expectation of continued performance she cannot satisfy long term.
(D) A culinary school finds that its classes have declined in popularity as tastes in the community change.
(E) A flower arranger cannot meet all the orders pending at his shop because his usual supplier cannot provide roses in sufficient quantities.

5. Environmentalist: Genetically engineered (GE) rice would, if introduced on a large scale, exacerbate the very problem it was designed to solve: diseases caused by malnutrition in parts of the world where rice is the primary staple crop. Use of GE rice altered so that it contains, for example, Vitamin A, further encourages a diet based on one staple food rather than the reintroduction of many vitamin-rich foods that were once cheap and available.

The environmentalist's reasoning depends on assuming which of the following?

(A) Whenever a genetically engineered food is introduced on a large scale, it encourages a diet that is unhealthy in at least one respect.
(B) In areas of the world where rice is a staple crop, sufficient quantities of naturally occurring vitamin-rich foods cannot be grown without genetic modification.
(C) The companies that typically produce genetically modified crops do so out of a desire to maximize profits.
(D) There is no way to genetically modify grain in such a way that it will contain all of the necessary vitamins previously provided by other foods.
(E) If the reintroduction of vitamin-rich foods is discouraged, some necessary vitamins will inevitably be absent from the diets of those vulnerable to malnutrition.

6. Karl Rove, the former senior adviser and deputy chief of staff for President George W. Bush, never graduated college. So, all other things being equal, a college degree is not required for career success.

Which of the following would be most useful to know in evaluating the argument above?

(A) Would Karl Rove have been named senior adviser if he had obtained a college degree?
(B) Does a person's success in a given field relate to the jobs that person has held in that field?
(C) Did other college dropouts find places in President Bush's administration?
(D) Is it possible for two candidates for the same job to be equally qualified?
(E) Would Karl Rove describe himself as successful in his chosen field?

7. Unlike previous centuries, the greatest challenges of the present era were caused by technological advancement and will likely not be solved by it.

(A) previous centuries, the greatest challenges of the present era
(B) previous centuries, the present era's greatest challenges
(C) that of previous centuries, the present era's greatest challenge
(D) those of previous centuries, the greatest challenges of the present era
(E) the previous centuries, the greatest challenge of the present era

8. The earliest clocks relied on shadows cast by the sun, forcing primitive societies to rely on the stars alone to track the passage of time during the night, and this remained the case until at least the third century B.C.E., the earliest point <u>when it is known that early clockmakers did perfect</u> the water-powered escapement mechanism.

   (A) when it is known that early clockmakers did perfect
   (B) that early clockmakers are known to be perfecting
   (C) of early clockmakers who were known to perfect
   (D) at which it is known that early clockmakers had perfected
   (E) at which early clockmakers are known to have perfected

9. Ironically, in recent years countries such as Switzerland and <u>Denmark have been stronger advocates of the "American dream" than America,</u> a set of ideals in which freedom includes the opportunity for success.

   (A) Denmark have been stronger advocates of the "American dream" than America,
   (B) Denmark have been stronger for advocating the "American dream" than has been America,
   (C) Denmark have been stronger advocates than America for the "American dream,"
   (D) Denmark has advocated more strongly the "American dream" than America has
   (E) Denmark, stronger than America as advocates of the "American dream,"

10. Regrettably, it has become increasingly common to find the remains of once majestic blue whales <u>with their fatal injuries from being struck when they slept</u> in busy shipping lanes.

   (A) with their fatal injuries from being struck when they slept
   (B) with fatal injuries from their sleeping and their being struck
   (C) with fatal injuries from their having been struck while sleeping
   (D) with fatal injuries from having been struck when they have slept
   (E) with fatal injuries from having been struck as they are sleeping

11. TerraBite CFO: Recently, the popular television show *Omega Factor* ran two stories on our company that many of our staff considered unfair, one attacking the lavishness of our product launch parties, the other our generous executive bonuses. In the week since the show's airing, several of our most important sources of venture capital have all but dried up, and our available capital on hand is insufficient to meet our prior financial obligations. Obviously, the *Omega Factor*'s biased coverage is to blame for the dire fiscal straits our company now faces.

Which of the following issues would it be most important to resolve in evaluating the CFO's explanation of TerraBite's financial situation?

(A) Whether the *Omega Factor* typically runs stories that are considered biased

(B) Whether the executive bonuses paid by TerraBite are commensurate with bonuses offered by other companies

(C) Whether the venture capitalists were aware of the damaging content of the stories prior to their decision to withdraw funding

(D) What specific allegations were made in the *Omega Factor* story about TerraBite

(E) Whether the funding withdrawn by the venture capitalists would have been sufficient to meet reasonable financial obligations

Questions 12–14 are based on the following passage.

Once TED was merely a weeklong conference organized by the celebrated "information architect" Richard Saul Wurman, the letters of its name drawn from the conference's intended focus on "technology, entertainment, and design." In 2002,
Line Wurman sold the conference to a nonprofit foundation, under whose guidance TED
(5) has grown from a disorganized brainstorming session (and vacation opportunity) for a boys club of Silicon Valley millionaires to a giant global brand.

As a nonprofit, TED is able to bring in a tremendous amount of money from members and corporate sponsorships, and, to be sure, much that is laudable is done with the infusion of resources. TED's multiple worldwide events can boast of an
(10) impressive and informative speakers list that would cost a fortune to assemble if the speakers had not agreed to donate their time for free. Much of the money brought in by these events is used to award grants to "TED-certified" lifetime achievers and up-and-coming innovators. However, to even attend a live TED conference in its present form, a donation of between $7,500 and $125,000 is required, and this in
(15) addition to a thoroughly opaque admissions process whose only stated requirement is that the applicant be "TED material." Everyone else must be content to watch the conference online.

Ironically, becoming a nonprofit has allowed what would otherwise be only a slightly interesting video podcast (the sort useful mostly as a source of factoids to
(20) wow friends at cocktail parties) to become a massive, money-soaked bacchanalia of puffed-up futurism and baseless prognostication. Today's TED is still as unclear as when Wurman first organized it, only now with its outsized delusions of grandeur masked by the thinnest veneer of public good.

12. Which of the following can be inferred from the passage?

(A) If it were not a nonprofit, TED would be unable to afford to assemble a quality speaker's list.

(B) If the requirements for being considered "TED material" were less obscure, more people would apply for the honor.

(C) If the TED conference organizers did not award grants, fewer speakers would be willing to donate their time for free.

(D) If a speaker is unwilling to donate at least $7,500, then they will not be allowed to attend a subsequent live TED conference.

(E) If the TED conferences were still organized by Richard Wurman, they would be less successful, though just as disorganized, as they are today.

13. The author indicates that which of the following was part of the original conception of TED?

(A) A slate of speakers whose presentations were not limited to a single topic

(B) A requirement that all conferences concern innovation in some form

(C) The hope that the conference would grow into something other than a Silicon Valley boys club

(D) A thoroughly opaque admissions process without clear requirements beyond the financial

(E) A desire to work for the public good

14. Which of the following, if true, would weaken the conclusion given in the first sentence of the third paragraph?

(A) Much of the good that TED currently does would not be possible if the conference were still a for-profit enterprise.

(B) Millionaires whose fortunes are built upon technology often waste their money supporting baseless ventures.

(C) In its original form, a TED conference hosted many talks that, while disorganized, formed the basis for many successful innovations.

(D) The standards by which an applicant is determined to be "TED material," while confusing to outsiders, are nevertheless fair.

(E) Richard Saul Wurman made comparatively little money on the sale of the TED conference rights.

15. City Auditor: In the city of Boudreaux, municipal law demands that new adult residents moving into the city register their home and mobile telephone numbers at City Hall within two weeks of arrival. Residents moving out of the city must notify City Hall to cancel their registrations within an equivalent period of time. In the ten years since the law was put into place, registrations of new phone numbers have outpaced notifications of cancellation by at least three to one in every single year. Therefore, we can conclude with near certainty from the telephone registration data alone that the population of Boudreaux has grown substantially over the past decade.

Which one of the following, if true, most calls into question the City Auditor's claim that the population of Boudreaux has grown substantially over the past decade?

(A) In the ten years since the law was put into place, many of the people who moved out of Boudreaux later returned.

(B) Many of the people who moved into Boudreaux in the past decade did not own or have access to a telephone and were thus exempt from the requirements of the law.

(C) Many of the people who moved into Boudreaux in the past decade were young professionals who registered a work phone number in addition to their home and mobile numbers.

(D) There are stiff penalties for failing to register a number and for failing to cancel a registration, but those penalties are difficult to enforce outside the city's immediate domain.

(E) Several towns in the same county as Boudreaux with similar laws have reported their populations have increased substantially over the past decade.

16. Consultant: The goals that you have provided me are hopelessly vague. Any concrete goal a business has must either be related to the desire to maximize profits or be something the business admits is counter to its bottom line. Your business has done many things lately that are counter to your bottom line—your ill-conceived new product line and your excessive executive bonuses among them. This, therefore, is why you ought not hire any more consultants.

The consultant's reasoning is vulnerable to which of the following criticisms?

(A) It generalizes from an unrepresentative listing of the company's activities to all of its activities.

(B) It makes the unsupported claim that the company's goals are hopelessly vague.

(C) It ignores the fact that some businesses find consultants to be of great practical use.

(D) It fails to show any specific link between hiring practices and the vagueness of the company's goals.

(E) It is presented by someone who has a conflict of interests with regards to the hiring of consultants.

17. According to four out of five dentists surveyed, flossing regularly is nearly six times more likely <u>as any other method used for improving the majority of their patients' gum health.</u>

(A) as any other method used for improving the majority of their patients' gum health

(B) to improve gum health for the majority of their patients than any other method

(C) than any other method to improve gum health for the majority of their patients

(D) that the majority of their patients will improve their gum health by using any other method

(E) for the use of any other method than improving gum health for the majority of their patients

18. <u>Crawford Long did not initially publicize his experiments with anesthesia, but when he learned, in 1849, of William T. G. Morton's public demonstration of its use in surgery,</u> he quickly came forward.

(A) Crawford Long did not initially publicize his experiments with anesthesia, but when he learned, in 1849, of William T. G. Morton's public demonstration of its use in surgery,

(B) Crawford Long had not initially publicized his experiments with anesthesia, but when he learned of William T. G. Morton demonstrating its use in surgery publically in 1849,

(C) Crawford Long, even though he had not initially publicized his experiments with anesthesia, on learning, in 1849, that William T. G. Morton had publically demonstrated its use in surgery,

(D) Even though Crawford Long did not initially publicize his experiments with anesthesia, on learning when William T. G. Morton had a public demonstration, in 1849, of using it in surgery

(E) Crawford Long did not initially publicize his experiments with anesthesia, but on learning, in 1849, that William T. G. Morton had been demonstrating its use in surgery in public,

19. Which of the following best completes the argument given below?

A recent study has shed new light on the relationship between time spent playing violent video games and aggression in children. Aggressive behavior was noted among children who played violent games often and those who played only rarely. Differences in aggression seemed to correspond more to differences in parenting philosophy. Absent, career-focused parents with hectic schedules whose children rarely played violent games had more aggressive children than did parents with balanced schedules, even when those schedules allowed for long periods spent playing violent games. In light of this study, it is safe to conclude that

(A) even small amounts of time spent playing violent video games can be dangerous.

(B) the amount of time spent playing violent video games has no effect on the behavior of children.

(C) if career-focused parents would make time, their children would be less aggressive.

(D) prolonged sessions spent playing violent video games are dangerous only when parents are absent.

(E) time spent playing violent video games is not on its own enough to predict a child's behavior.

20. Unlike the Aztec and Maya, who did not have pack animals and relied on slaves for difficult physical labor, the llama was first domesticated by the Inca shortly after arriving on the South American continent.

(A) the Aztec and Maya, who did not have pack animals and relied on slaves for difficult physical labor, the llama was first domesticated by the Inca

(B) the Aztec and Maya, who relied on slaves for difficult physical labor because they did not have pack animals, the llama had been domesticated first by the Inca

(C) the Aztec and Maya, whose lack of pack animals made them rely on slaves for difficult physical labor, the Inca's first domestication of the llama

(D) not having pack animals, the Aztec and Maya relied on slaves for difficult physical labor, while the Inca first domesticated the llama

(E) the Aztec and Maya, who did not have pack animals and relied on slaves for difficult physical labor, the Incans first domesticated the llama

21. Which of the following most logically completes the argument?

Patent law exists to protect the rights of inventors to profit from their innovations, and copyright laws to protect those of artists from their art. While a chef who creates a new recipe might seem a similar case, a recipe is not a work of art, nor is it an innovation, so neither law protects the rights of a chef to profit from an original recipe. Thus, chefs' rights to profit from new recipes will never be protected by the law, since

(A) chefs lack the social capital and economic clout to convince judges to throw these laws out.
(B) there are no other laws outside the copyright and patent law systems that currently protect chefs' rights.
(C) most recipes are modifications of a previous chef's work.
(D) copyright and patent laws are considered to be so comprehensive by legislators that they will never address the gap.
(E) it is impossible to patent basic processes like mixing or baking and copyright does not protect facts.

22. The newly revised *Diagnostic and Statistical Manual of Mental Disorders* has only further complicated the controversy about whether Asperger syndrome should be classified as a unique condition or if it is one of the autism spectrum disorders.

(A) about whether Asperger syndrome should be classified as a unique condition or if it is
(B) about Asperger syndrome and if it should be classified as a unique condition or it is
(C) concerning whether Asperger syndrome should be classified as a unique condition or
(D) with respect to Asperger syndrome being classified as a unique condition or if it is more
(E) whether or not Asperger syndrome should be classified as a unique condition or it is

23. The recent spike in the cost of heating oil to heat homes this winter is due to a dramatic decrease in the supply of heating oil relative to demand. However, the total amount of heating oil available is greater now than it was last winter.

If the statements above are true, which of the following must also be true?

(A) The efficiency of oil-burning furnaces has not increased since the past winter.
(B) The number of homes that use oil for heating has decreased since the past winter.
(C) The demand for heating oil has increased since the past winter.
(D) The cost of transporting heating oil from refineries has increased since the past winter.
(E) The percentage of homes using oil for heating has increased since the past winter.

In the United States, credit reports are maintained by three major credit reporting agencies: Experian, Equifax, and TransUnion. Files are only opened and information tracked once an application for some form of credit has been submitted to a creditor, Line but as modern society inches closer to a truly cashless economy, nearly every adult (5) has a file with at least one of the three, if not all of them.

Before consumers apply for their first credit card or make an appointment with the loan officer at their local bank, it is important that they check with each of the credit reporting agencies to make sure there is not a false credit report open in their name. More than 20,000 children and teenagers were victims of identity theft in (10) 2008, so it is possible that someone has already used their name and stolen Social Security number to apply for credit. Moreover, all borrowers, not just first-timers, are encouraged to obtain a credit report at least once a year and to scan it for any errors or illegitimate lines of credit.

24. The author of the passage would most likely agree with which of the following statements?

(A) Cash-based societies are less prone to identity theft than cashless ones.
(B) Consumers who do not check their credit reports frequently are more likely to be poor managers of their money.
(C) It is less likely that those with a long-established credit history will have errors on their credit report.
(D) If someone has never applied for a line of credit, there would be no reason for one of the credit agencies to have a file on them.
(E) Even when a consumer has applied for a line of credit, it is possible for one of the credit agencies to fail to open a file.

25. If the information contained in the passage is accurate, which of the following groups would be most likely to not have a file at one of the three credit reporting agencies?

(A) Consumers who have never opened a legitimate line of credit
(B) Consumers who have not applied for a form of credit for at least seven years
(C) Consumers who have either been victims of identity theft or who have applied for credit themselves
(D) Consumers who have never been the victim of identity theft nor applied for a form of credit
(E) Consumers who have avoided opening lines of credit except when such credit was necessary

26. Which of the following best describes the organization of the passage as a whole?

(A) A financial practice is described; exceptions to the practice are presented; and recommendations to replace the practice are listed, but none are supported.

(B) A financial practice is criticized; an explanation of the criticism is given; and the conclusion is advanced that the practice is, nevertheless, inevitable.

(C) A financial practice is recommended; some considerations against the practice are given; and a rebuttal to those considerations is presented.

(D) A financial practice is described; a consequence of that practice is given; and further explanation of that consequence is presented.

(E) A financial practice is described; recommendations against that practice are given; and further details of that recommendation are provided as support.

Questions 27–30 are based on the following passage.

Civil law, as opposed to criminal law, deals with private disputes where one party accuses the other of injury—whether physical, psychological, emotional, or financial—and sues for damages. However, the price of sustained legal action often
Line exceeds several hundred thousand dollars, which prevents most investors from
(5) using a civil lawsuit to recoup damages from investment fraud. It was for this reason that lawyers and judges first developed the class action lawsuit. Such suits allow multiple parties to sue over the same legal grounds, although a single representative or lead plaintiff is the only one whose name appears on the case.

When evidence of massive accounting fraud brought down the Enron Corporation
(10) in the late 1990s, its collapse took with it nearly $65 million from the stockholders' balance sheets. In the class action suit that ultimately won damages of $8 billion for these investors, the University of California was chosen as the lead plaintiff, even though it was in many senses not representative of the other plaintiffs in the class, having lost much more than any one single investor, but far less than the investment
(15) groups that were party to the suit.

As a single entity, the university was deemed better able to coordinate the litigation, and due to the size of its losses—over $150 million lost from its pension and endowment funds—it was also seen as more likely to remain party to a suit that might stretch on for several years. Such practical considerations are not, however,
(20) counter to the justifications used by the jurists who pioneered this civil litigation device. Indeed, many initial objections to the use of the class action lawsuit were successfully answered by appeal to the principle that a system of law which could only be used by the powerful would never be used, since the powerful have and always will have other means to protect themselves from damages.

27. The passage implies which of the following things about representative plaintiffs in class action lawsuits?

   (A) It is preferable that they share at least one quality with each member of the class, though not strictly required.

   (B) It is both preferable and required that they share at least one quality with each member of the class.

   (C) If they do not share any qualities with a substantial majority of the members of the class, the suit will be unsuccessful.

   (D) Their similarity to other members of the class will have little to no effect on the ultimate success of the suit.

   (E) The likelihood that they will be eventually proved unable or unwilling to continue the suit is a factor in their selection.

28. With which of the following evaluations of the civil law system would the author most likely agree?

   (A) Although imperfect, the class action lawsuit is preferable to any other previously proposed solution to the problem of a selectively useable system of justice.

   (B) Only in those cases where a criminal judgment is impossible should a class action lawsuit be used.

   (C) Objections against a practice in civil law can sometimes be answered by appeal to concerns beyond the letter of the law.

   (D) When one party accuses the other of injury, physical and financial damages should be rewarded before psychological or emotional ones are considered.

   (E) If the financial barriers to entry in the system were relaxed, then the class action lawsuit would not be necessary.

29. According to the passage, one reason that the University of California was chosen as lead plaintiff was that

   (A) its losses from its pension fund were at least as great as those from its endowment fund.

   (B) the award for damages would have been much less than $8 billion without its participation.

   (C) the expected duration of the suit would have been unduly burdensome upon other plaintiffs.

   (D) it was more likely to see the suit through to its final conclusion than some other plaintiffs

   (E) it was deemed to be the most similar to the largest percentage of parties to the suit.

30. The primary purpose of the passage is to

(A) explain the factors that contribute to a plaintiff being selected to lead a class action suit.

(B) compare strategies used in civil courts to those used in criminal courts.

(C) illustrate the considerations involved in the development of a device used in civil courts.

(D) describe the manner in which litigants in the Enron stock collapse were able to achieve success.

(E) rebut the assertion that practical considerations should never be used to evaluate a legal practice.

---

31. Added to the tax bill that they already pay to fund their local fire departments, home owners in some cash-strapped municipalities are now being charged a hefty "accident tax."

(A) Added to the tax bill that they already pay to fund their local fire departments, home owners in some cash-strapped municipalities are now being charged a hefty "accident tax."

(B) Added to the property taxes that they already pay to fund their local fire departments, some cash-strapped municipalities are now charging home owners a hefty "accident tax."

(C) Some cash-strapped municipalities are now charging home owners a hefty "accident tax" to be added to fund their local fire departments with the property taxes that they pay already.

(D) In addition to the property taxes that they already pay to fund their local fire departments, some cash-strapped municipalities are now charging home owners a hefty "accident tax."

(E) In addition to the property taxes they already pay to fund their local fire departments, home owners in some cash-strapped municipalities are now being charged a hefty "accident tax."

32. Fire prevention experts agree that inebriated and intoxicated people are more likely to cause fires—both accidentally and deliberately—than they are when sober. The damage done by such fires is exacerbated by the fact that the chemically impaired are also less capable at extinguishing fires they have started. Nevertheless, the damage from fires started by the sober far exceeds that done by fires started by intoxicated and inebriated people combined.

Which of the following, if true, best explains the discrepancy above?

(A) It can be difficult to determine who started a fire and in what condition they were in when it was started.

(B) Naturally occurring fires or those caused by accidents do more damage than those set deliberately.

(C) Most people who become inebriated or intoxicated do so for only a few hours each week.

(D) Many people prone to starting fires abstain completely from alcohol or other intoxicating chemicals.

(E) The sight of a burning fire often is sufficient to allow a person to temporarily overcome the impairment caused by intoxication.

33. The Tennessee Valley Authority brought electricity to rural Americans, <u>who had long been isolated due to its lack, and consequently no longer able to</u> operate at a complete remove from the national government.

   (A) who had long been isolated due to its lack, and consequently no longer able to

   (B) whose lack had long isolated them, due to their no longer being able to consequently

   (C) who due to its lack had long been isolated, and was consequently no longer able to

   (D) who had long been isolated due to its lack; consequently, they were no longer able to

   (E) which had long been isolated due to their lacking it; consequently, they were no longer able to

34. Because it has outgrown its current space and because that space cannot be expanded, the county animal shelter must be moved to a larger facility. Vacant buildings of sufficient size that are located near the current shelter are far more expensive than those found near the county line. Since the cost of rent is the biggest single cost associated with running the shelter, it would be cheaper to move the shelter to the county line.

   Which of the following is an assumption made by the argument above?

   (A) It is not possible to build an entirely new facility for the animal shelter.

   (B) The animals that are currently housed in the shelter will be able to be moved to a new shelter.

   (C) Volunteers who currently work at the shelter will not be dissuaded from continuing if the shelter moves.

   (D) The possible sites for the shelter near its location do not require substantially less energy to heat and cool.

   (E) City codes do not prevent the shelter from being placed in any of the buildings near its current location.

35. The biotech companies that sell genetically modified foods have always claimed that their products are no more dangerous to eat than unmodified foods. In support of this, they have widely touted the results of research published by an independent study group, the Sunbelt Foundation. But it has recently come to light that the Sunbelt Foundation's chief scientist falsified data, likely because his family was heavily invested in biotech stocks. Clearly, there is good reason to worry that these purportedly safe foods are actually harmful.

The reasoning in the argument above is suspect because

(A) the failure to prove a claim is taken as equivalent as proof that the claim has been disproven.

(B) generalizes from a single case of wrongdoing to an insupportably broad conclusion

(C) fails to consider the possibility that financial interest alone is not sufficient to discredit a party

(D) takes the behavior of an individual as representative of a group to which the individual does not belong

(E) assumes without justification that independent research is sufficient to establish safety

36. Economist #1: Rises and falls in the global economy correlate almost exactly with the amount of volatility in the currency market. Clearly, regardless of what politicians may think, the global economy's health is strictly a function of currency market volatility.

Economist #2: Absurd. Any true economist would know that in a system as complicated as the global economy, no single variable could account for its overall performance.

The second economist's rejection of the first economist's position employs which of the following argumentative strategies?

(A) Establishing by counterexample that a proposed rule is false as stated

(B) Supporting a conclusion about a specific case by appeal to a general rule

(C) Showing that an apparent correlation is actually the result of direct causation

(D) Rejecting a purely theoretical conclusion on the grounds that it has no practical value

(E) Suggesting that the argument against a conclusion is based on personal animus rather than logic

37. The tyrannical conduct of Tarquinius Superbus led to the abolition of the Roman monarchy, which ruled for nearly three centuries and had claimed to trace their royal authority to Romulus, legendary founder of Rome.

   (A) which ruled for nearly three centuries and had claimed to trace their royal authority
   (B) by which it was ruled for nearly three centuries and claimed to trace its royal authority
   (C) ruled for nearly three centuries and which they claimed that royal authority traced
   (D) which ruled for nearly three centuries and claimed to trace its royal authority
   (E) who ruled for nearly three centuries and claiming to trace its royal authority

38. If asked in 1600 to predict which nation would come to dominate North America, a reasonable person likely would guess Spain, England, or France and be absolutely wrong.

   (A) guess Spain, England, or France and be
   (B) guess Spain, England, or France and it would have been
   (C) have guessed Spain, England, or France and been
   (D) have guessed that it would have been Spain, England, or France and
   (E) have guessed Spain, England, or France and would be

39. Six out of every seven long-practicing doctors agree about one thing, the *Washington Post* health editor reports: the nation's insurance system, as currently constituted, cannot long endure.

   (A) Six out of every seven long-practicing doctors agree about one thing, the *Washington Post* health editor reports
   (B) Out of every seven, six doctors of long-standing practice agree about one thing, the *Washington Post*'s health reports
   (C) One thing is agreed upon by six out of every seven long-practicing doctors, the *Washington Post*'s health editor reports
   (D) Six out of every seven long-practicing doctors agree upon one thing, the *Washington Post*'s health editor has reported
   (E) Out of every seven doctors who have practiced for long, six agree about one thing, the *Washington Post* health editor has reported

40. The manuscript tradition of Julian of Norwich's *Revelations* is fraught by ambiguity with no surviving autograph, only one of the extant manuscripts being medieval, and we do not even know if the work was ever disseminated in the medieval period at all.

(A) by ambiguity with no surviving autograph, only one of the extant manuscripts being medieval, and we do not even know if

(B) by ambiguity: with no autograph surviving, only one of the extant manuscripts is medieval and we do not know even if

(C) with ambiguity; no autograph survives, only one of the extant manuscripts is medieval, and we do not even know whether

(D) with ambiguity; without an autograph that survives, only one of the extant manuscripts is medieval; and we do not even know whether

(E) ambiguously with no autograph surviving, only one of the extant manuscripts being medieval, and us not knowing whether or not

41. Ranked first among the emotions that Aristotle thought an orator must learn to manipulate are moral indignation, used both to incite citizens against injustice and for punishing those who would rise above their station.

(A) are moral indignation, used both to incite citizens against injustice and for punishing those who would rise

(B) are moral indignation to use inciting citizens against injustice and, for punishing, those who would be raised

(C) is moral indignation, used both to incite citizens against injustice and punish those who would rise above their station

(D) is moral indignation for both inciting citizens against injustice and used to punish those who might rise

(E) are moral indignation, which was used both to incite citizens against injustice and punishment of those who would have rose

STOP

ON THE ACTUAL GMAT,
AFTER YOU HAVE CONFIRMED YOUR ANSWER,
YOU CANNOT RETURN TO IT.

ANSWER KEY
Sample Test 2

INTEGRATED REASONING SECTION

1. **i.** A

    ii. B

2.

Amount Needed to Spend on New Hires	Amount Each Student Expects to Make	Amount in $
●	○	0
○	○	720
○	○	1,080
○	●	1,920
○	○	2,560
○	○	3,840

3.

Would Help Explain	Would Not Help Explain
●	○
●	○
○	●

4. C

5.

True	False
○	●
●	○
●	○

6.

Yes	No
●	○
○	●
●	○

7.

Would Definitely be Part of the Optimite Program	Would Definitely NOT be Part of the Optimite Program
○	○
○	○
●	○
○	●
○	○

8. D

9. **i.** B

    ii. D

10. **i.** D

    ii. C

11.

True	False
●	○
○	●
●	○

12. D

ANSWER KEY
Sample Test 2

QUANTITATIVE SECTION

1.	B	11.	A	21.	A	31.	E
2.	E	12.	D	22.	C	32.	A
3.	E	13.	A	23.	B	33.	D
4.	D	14.	C	24.	A	34.	B
5.	D	15.	E	25.	E	35.	A
6.	B	16.	C	26.	D	36.	B
7.	B	17.	C	27.	E	37.	B
8.	D	18.	D	28.	D		
9.	C	19.	B	29.	A		
10.	B	20.	A	30.	D		

VERBAL SECTION

1.	E	12.	D	23.	C	34.	D
2.	C	13.	A	24.	E	35.	A
3.	E	14.	B	25.	D	36.	B
4.	E	15.	D	26.	D	37.	D
5.	E	16.	D	27.	E	38.	C
6.	B	17.	B	28.	C	39.	A
7.	D	18.	A	29.	D	40.	C
8.	E	19.	E	30.	C	41.	C
9.	C	20.	E	31.	E		
10.	C	21.	D	32.	C		
11.	C	22.	C	33.	D		

> ## SELF-SCORING GUIDE
> ## Analytical Writing
>
> Evaluate your essay (or have a friend or teacher evaluate it for you) on the following basis. Read your essay completely, paying special attention to its logical organization and use of examples and facts to buttress its claims or position. Assign a holistic score between 0 and 6, using the scale below.
>
> ### 6 OUTSTANDING
>
> Cogent, well-articulated analysis of the issue or critique of the argument. Develops a position with insightful reasons and persuasive examples. Well organized. Superior command of language and variety of syntax. Only minor flaws in grammar, usage, and mechanics.
>
> ### 5 STRONG
>
> Well-developed analysis or critique. Develops a position with well-chosen examples or reasons. Generally well organized. Clear control of language and variety of syntax. Minor flaws in grammar, usage, and mechanics.
>
> ### 4 ADEQUATE
>
> Competent analysis or critique. Develops a position with relevant reasons or examples. Adequately organized. Adequate control of language, but may lack syntactic variety. May have some flaws in grammar, usage, and mechanics.
>
> ### 3 LIMITED
>
> Competent but clearly flawed analysis or critique. Vague or limited in developing a position. Poorly organized. Weak in using relevant examples or reasons. Language used imprecisely or lacking in sentence variety. Contains major errors or frequent minor errors in grammar, usage, and mechanics.
>
> ### 2 SERIOUSLY FLAWED
>
> Serious weaknesses in analysis and organization. Unclear or seriously limited in presenting or developing a position. Disorganized. Few relevant examples or reasons. Frequent serious problems in language and sentence structure. Numerous errors in grammar, usage, or mechanics that interfere with meaning.
>
> ### 1 FUNDAMENTALLY DEFICIENT
>
> Little evidence of ability to organize and develop a coherent response to an issue or argument. Severe and persistent errors in language and sentence structure. Pervasive pattern of errors in grammar, usage, and mechanics that severely interfere with meaning.
>
> ### 0 UNSCORABLE
>
> Illegible or not written on the assigned topic.

ANSWERS EXPLAINED
Integrated Reasoning Section

1. i. (A) The third quartile of the graph is the area between 50% and 75%. If you look at the graph, you can see where the line crosses the *x*-axis at 50% and at 75%. At 50%, the *x*-axis is at 74 inches. At 75%, the *x*-axis is at 77 inches. This gives you the range of heights:

$$77 - 74 = 3$$

Therefore, the answer is **A**.

ii. (B) From question 1, you know that the median height, or 50% of all the players, is 74 inches. Since you need to look at all players within 6 inches of that height, you should look at the graph between 68 inches and 80 inches. At 68 inches, the line is approximately halfway between 0% and 25%. At 80 inches, the line is approximately halfway between 75% and 100%. This represents about 75% of all the players. Therefore, the answer is **B**.

2. ($0, $1,920)

(i) This is a three-tiered rate problem that tracks the number of painters, houses, and hours. Since the question asks for how many new people you need to hire, let's first calculate how many hours are required to paint 1,200 houses.

10 students paint 4 houses in 16 hours = 10 students paint 1,200 houses in 4,800 hours

From this you know that Youth Pro Painters needs 4,800 student painter hours to complete 1,200 houses. Since there are 12 weeks in the summer and 40 working hours in a week, you can calculate how many students are needed.

$$4,800 \text{ hours} \div 40 \text{ hours/week} \div 12 \text{ weeks} = 10 \text{ students}$$

The company has just enough students to paint 1,200 houses, so the total amount needed to spend on additional hires is **$0**.

(ii) To calculate the amount of money each student can make in half the summer, first calculate the amount each student will earn during the summer.

$$40 \text{ hr/week} \times 12 \text{ weeks} \times \$8.00/\text{hr} = \$3,840$$

To determine how much each student makes in half the summer, divide by 2. The answer is **$1,920**.

3. (Would Help Explain, Would Help Explain, Would Not Help Explain)

(i) This can be easily found by sorting through either the primary school column or kindergarten column. The kindergarten column ranges from 71 to 32 while the primary school column ranges from 98 to 81. This chart would help explain that kindergartens are not offered as much as are primary schools. The answer is **Would Help Explain**.

(ii) If you look at the data from the table for Peru, you can see a much lower percentage for both kindergarten and post-secondary education compared with primary and secondary. If you sort the primary and secondary school numbers, you can also see that Peru ranks among the bottom. This could suggest that farming families are keeping children away from school. Therefore, the answer is **Would Help Explain**.

(iii) You could associate the data in the chart with where education is more valued by its country's citizens. However, when you check on Argentina and how it ranks, it is the highest in the kindergarten column and is second in the other three columns. Columbia ranks first in the other three columns. Thus the table could not help you infer anything about Argentinean parents. Therefore, the answer is **Would Not Help Explain**.

4. (C) The best way to sort out all the information here is with a chart. In fact, if you look at the question first, you might decide to set up a chart with all the detailed information while reading the documents. Then you can reference the chart when answering the question.

| | Two Current Product Lines (crates per month) | | New Product Lines (crates per month) | |
	Pessimistic	Optimistic	2-in-1	Dandruff
Year 0	800	800	0	0
Year 1	1,000	1,200	200	200
Year 2	1,250	1,800	400	400
Year 3	1,562.5	2,700	600	600

Most pessimistic forecast without new product launches: 1,562.5

Most optimistic forecast with new product launches: $2,700 + 1,200 = 3,900$

Find the difference: $3,900 - 1,562.5 = 2,337.5$

Therefore, the answer is **C**.

5. (False, True, True)

(i) Since you are looking at only year 1 and just the existing product line, you can calculate this using the information you already organized in the chart from question 5. Sales are 1,000 units × $1,000 per crate, giving you $1 million monthly. Since the shipping costs are $100,000, this brings our overall profit down to $900,000 monthly. Therefore, the answer is **false**.

(ii) Since you are looking at only year 1, you can break down this question into each scenario. Again, using a chart would help you organize the data.

Scenario 1: Pessimistic, 25% growth, 2 new product launches:

$$800 \times 1.25 + 200 + 200 = 1,400 \text{ crates}$$

Scenario 2: Optimistic, 50% growth, no new product launches:

$$800 \times 1.5 = 1,200 \text{ crates}$$

Scenario 1 does sell more units than scenario 2. Therefore, the answer is **true**.

(iii) In this case, the question is much easier if you use a chart. You also need to understand that the 25% decrease due to the negative perception affects just the sales increase, not the total sales.

	Two Current Product Lines (crates per month)		One New Product Line
	Total Optimistic Sales	With 25% Decrease	
Year 0	800	n/a	0
Year 1	1,200	1,100	200
Year 2	1,650	1,512.5*	400
Year 3	2,079.7	600	

*At this point, you may notice that the cumulative percentage increase is 37.5% per year for the current product lines. So you can easily calculate year 3.

As you can see, the total sales of the one new product line over three years are 1,200 crates. The total growth of the current lines over three years is 2,080 − 800 = 1,280. Therefore, launching one new product will not "entirely" offset the launch (even though it's pretty close). The answer is **true**.

6. (Yes, No, Yes)

(i) From the chart you created for question 5, you can extract the second-year pessimistic forecast and the new product launch of just one product in one year.

$$1,250 + 200 = 1,450$$

Nanning's capacity is 1,500 crates per month. Therefore, the answer is **yes**.

(ii) Similar to part (i), you can extract the second-year optimistic forecast from the chart you created for question 5, which is 1,800 crates per month. Sandusky's capacity is 1,200 crates per month. Therefore, the answer is **no**.

(iii) Again, you can use the chart you created for question 5 to extract the optimistic forecast for year 1 and two new product launches for the first year.

$$1,200 + 200 + 200 = 1,600$$

Chennai's capacity is 2,500 crates per month. Therefore, the answer is **yes**.

7. (A case competition, A field trip to a museum of marine biology)

This challenging question gives us a considerable amount of multilayered information. Some of it is useful, and some of it is not. You need to know the difference. The question is trying to get you to focus on the key support that is necessary to make the conclusion.

At first glance, many of the answers seem possible, but the key here is to find what must be true based on the passage. Capoeira martial arts, delivering a presentation on business ethics, and moderated debate on local politics are all quite possible given the scope of the Optimite program. However, they are all too specific. It's equally possible that the program would have alternative physical challenges, presentations, or debates. Having a case competition, generally speaking, is the only activity that must be part of the program since the passage says "case studies and matches." Therefore, **a case competition** would definitely be part of the program.

A field trip to a museum of marine biology would not be part of the program for two reasons. The first is that the Optimite program focuses on learning "on site." The second is that the description does not mention science. Therefore, **a field trip to a museum of marine biology** would definitely **not** be part of the program.

8. (D) In this question, four of the answer choices would be issues of concern to the school board.

Choice A is a concern since the program has a class size of 60 and requires advanced technology tools in the classroom.

Choice B is a concern because of the diversity of the eligible students and the preexisting concern of getting all the students to school.

Choice C is a concern because it may be difficult to find 60 diverse and talented students.

Choice E is a concern for two reasons. First, like any new program, Optimite will require teachers to learn the new curriculum. Second, the format is different than that in traditional classrooms. Optimite uses a "team" teaching structure. It's possible that some teachers may not want to get involved.

Since the Optimite program requires three teachers for 60 students, it thus has a ratio of 20 students per teacher. This is already under the standard of 24 students per teacher. The correct answer is **D**.

9. i. (B) This is a hard Venn diagram because it consists of three circles. The process to review and analyze the chart is the same as if it consisted of two, though. Determine the total number of residents with laundry and the total number of residents. There are 7 stars in the laundry circle and the total number of stars in the Venn diagram is 15. The probability is 7 out of 15. Therefore, the answer is **B**.

ii. (D) For this question, you need to consider only those residents with air conditioning. The circle for air conditioning contains 10 stars. The number of stars with air conditioning that also have mini-freezers is $3 + 1 = 4$. This gives us a probability of 4 out of 10 or 2 out of 5. Therefore, the answer is **D**.

10. i. (D) This is among the more tricky scatter plot distributions because it is bimodal, which means that the data suggest two distinct areas or patterns of Old Faithful's eruptions. The first significant section is on the bottom left, and the second significant section is on the top right. Since the answer choices are looking at eruption intervals, you can approximately determine two separate ones: 55 minutes and 80 minutes. Therefore, the answer is **D**.

ii. (C) This question is also challenging because you need to use weighted averages to determine the duration of the average eruption. You certainly don't need to count all the plot points, but you can see that more are in the top right section than in other sections. Therefore, the average will be closer to the right side of the x-axis. If the average of the plots at the bottom left section is approximately 2 minutes and at the top right section is between 4 and 4.5 minutes, the weighted average should be more than 3 or 3.25 minutes. The only answer that fits these criteria is 3.5 minutes. Therefore, the answer is **C**.

11. (True, False, True)

(i) This question requires you to extrapolate new information—revenue growth. Rather than using the calculator to create an entirely new column, you should try to estimate whenever possible. If you look at the top two companies, Wal-Mart and Exxon Mobil, they have much higher revenues than the rest. In addition, Exxon

Mobil's growth is substantial. In addition, Fannie Mae is in the top five. Since its revenue grew 429.2%, that would mean a revenue growth of over 80% of the total revenue, or over $120 billion. This would far outweigh the rest of the companies, two of which had negative growth. Therefore, the answer is **true**.

(ii) First, you need to sort the profit column. The median number is General Electric at $11.6 billion. Again, it is quicker to use ballpark numbers. The top half's average would be approximately $20 billion. The bottom half's average would be quite low because of the combined –$16.2 billion of Fannie Mae and Bank of America. This will bring the average profit of the bottom half to approximately $2 to $5 billion. The difference between the top half and the bottom half will be much greater than $11.6 billion. Therefore, the answer is **false**.

(iii) This question requires you extrapolate from the table. Fannie Mae's revenue change was about 430%. (Remember you don't need to use specific numbers here.) A 95% drop would give you a little over a 20% revenue increase for 2010/2011. Since Fannie Mae's profit loss was $14 billion and its operating costs are the same, you can calculate how much new revenue it will earn. Since 20% of $150 billion is $30 billion, Fannie Mae would have to earn profits. Therefore, the answer is **true**.

12. **(D)** The definition given here of a good value stock is based on only the first three columns containing numbers. So you need to sort through each column quickly and find the best company in which to invest. When you sort the column "% Change in Revenue Since 2009," you see that Fannie Mae comes out on top. However, you can eliminate it since the other two columns will decrease Fannie Mae's value significantly. Of the other four answer choices, Exxon Mobil, ConocoPhillips, and Berkshire Hathaway rank in the top five.

At this point, a quick way to solve this problem is to create a chart to track the ranks. The more complicated a question is and the more information you are dealing with, the more important it is that you add structure to the problem. Charts are a great way to do this.

Company	% Change in Revenue	Profit	% Change in Profit	Average Rank
Exxon Mobil	4	1	6	11/3
ConocoPhillips	2	8	2	12/3
Berkshire Hathaway	5	6	STOP!	

Once you get to the percent change in profit for Berkshire Hathaway, you can stop filling in the chart. This is because even if Berkshire Hathaway ranks number one in percentage change in profit (it does not), its average rank would still be greater than that of Exxon Mobil. You could have also quickly added Wal-Mart if you had thought to chart this whole question out at the beginning of this section. However, it would not have ranked high. Therefore, the answer is **D**.

Quantitative Section

1. Set *T* consists of 3 numbers with only one mode. Does the range equal the mode?
   (1) The largest number is twice the value of the smallest number.
   (2) The median equals the range.

(B) Let set *T* be {*x*, *y*, *z*}. If there is only one mode, then at least 2 of the 3 numbers must be the same.

Statement 1 tells us that the set looks like this: {*x*, *y*, 2*x*}. Since there is only one mode, *y* = *x* or *y* = 2*x*. If we pick numbers this could be {2, 2, 4} or {0, 0, 0} or {2, 4, 4}. In the first 2 cases, the range, 4 − 2 = 2 or 0 − 0 = 0, equals the mode. However in the 3rd case, the range does not equal the mode. *Insufficient*

Statement 2 tells us that the middle number of the set equals the range. Some of the possibilities for set *T* are {2, 2, 4} or {0, 0, 0} or {0, 4, 4}. In all three cases, the range equals the mode. Note that we cannot use the set {2, 4, 4} because this would violate the median equaling the range. In all cases where there is one mode in a set of 3 numbers and the median equals the range, then the range does indeed equal the mode. *Sufficient*

---

2. A coin is tossed three times. What is the probability that there will be at least one head?
   (A) $\frac{1}{16}$
   (B) $\frac{3}{8}$
   (C) $\frac{1}{2}$
   (D) $\frac{5}{8}$
   (E) $\frac{7}{8}$

(E) This is a classic Mirror Rule probability problem. So we should get
$$P(\text{at least one head}) = 1 - P(\text{no heads})$$
$$= 1 - P(T, T, T)$$
$$= 1 - \frac{1}{2} \cdot \frac{1}{2} \cdot \frac{1}{2} = 1 - \frac{1}{8} = \frac{7}{8}.$$

---

3. What is *x*?
   (1) $3x - 2y = 5$
   (2) $y = -\frac{5}{2} + \left(\frac{3}{2}\right)x$

(E) We know from the statements that to solve for *x*, we need 2 distinct equations and 2 unknowns. Selecting C here seems a bit too easy, so let's check and make sure that we have not missed something. If we look more closely, we see that statement 1 and statement 2 are the same equation that just manipulated algebraically. Thus, each statement is telling us the same thing. Since "no news is good news," the answer will be either D or E. Each statement by itself does not help us solve for *x* as we have 2 unknowns and only one distinct equation. Thus, even when combining the statements, no solution is possible. *Insufficient*

4. What is the x-intercept of the equation $y = 6x^2 - 13x - 5$?

(1) $x < 1$

(2) $3x$ is an odd integer.

(D) When we factor the equation, we determine that $y = (3x + 1)(2x - 5)$, which tells us that the x-intercepts could be $-\frac{1}{3}$ and $\frac{5}{2}$.

In statement 1, if $x < 1$, then there is only one x-intercept: $-\frac{1}{3}$. *Sufficient*

Statement 2 tells us that $3x$ is an odd integer. Again only $x = -\frac{1}{3}$ would work as the x-intercept and give us an odd integer when multiplied by 3. *Sufficient.*

---

5. If $2^{x-7} \cdot 3^{2x-3} = 27^{(3x-10)/3}$, what is x?

(A) -1

(B) 0

(C) 3

(D) 7

(E) 9

(D) Since there is no multiple of 2 on the right-hand side of the equation, we can assume that the right-hand side has 2^0 (which is really just 1) in it. Thus, using the base of 2, we can calculate that $2^{x-7} = 2^0$. Therefore, $x - 7 = 0 \rightarrow x = 7$

If you want to be sure of your answer, you can plug it into the expression with base 3, rather than calculating it all out.

$$3^{2x-3} = 3^{3(3x-10)/3} \rightarrow 2(7) - 3 = 3(7) - 10$$
$$\rightarrow 11 = 11$$

---

6. Is x a positive integer?

(1) $xy = 210$

(2) x and y are prime numbers

(B) Statement 1 tells us that x and y could be either both positive or both negative. *Insufficient.*

Statement 2 confirms that x is positive since prime numbers cannot be negative. *Sufficient*

---

7. Of the 3,200 people living in town A, 25% live downtown. Of these people, 60% live in a high-rise, 40% rent, and 25% both live in a high-rise and rent. If one person is selected randomly from the 3,200 people, what is the probability that the one selected will live downtown in a high-rise but not rent?

(A) $\frac{1}{10}$

(B) $\frac{7}{80}$

(C) $\frac{3}{20}$

(D) $\frac{24}{320}$

(E) $\frac{48}{320}$

(B) Since we have the percentages, we can calculate the number of people in each group. Using fractions make the calculations much easier. There are:

$3200 \cdot \frac{1}{4} = 800$ people who live downtown

$800 \cdot \frac{3}{5} = 480$ people who live downtown in a high-rise

$800 \cdot \frac{2}{5} = 320$ people who rent downtown

$800 \cdot \frac{1}{4} = 200$ people who both live downtown in a high-rise and rent

$480 - 200 = 280$ people who live downtown in a high-rise but do not rent

Therefore, the probability of selecting someone in a high-rise and not a rental is $\frac{280}{3200} = \frac{7}{80}$.

8. *A*, *B*, and *C* are positive integers, such that *A* is a factor of *B* and *B* is a factor of *C*. Is *C* an even number?

   (1) *AB* is an even number.

   (2) *B* is even.

(D) Let's first jump ahead to statement 2 because it looks easier to resolve.

In statement 2, if *B* is even, then *C* must be even because *C* is a multiple of *B*. If you are not sure of this concept, it is the same idea where 6 is a multiple of 2. Any multiple of an even number will also be even. *Sufficient*

Going back to statement 1, if *AB* is even, then either *A* or *B* is even, or both are even. If *B* is a multiple of *A* (because "*A* is a factor of *B*"), then *B* must be even, whether *A* is odd or even. For example, *A* = 2, *B* = 6 works because *AB* = 12, an even number. When *A* = 3 and *B* = 6, *AB* = 18, which also works. However, if *B* = 9, *A* cannot equal 3 because *AB* must be even. Since *B* must be even, then *C* must also be even. *Sufficient*

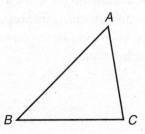

9. In triangle *ABC*, what is the height from the base *AB*?

   (1) The perimeter of *ABC* is 12.

   (2) The triangle is isosceles with one angle measuring 60°.

(C) We know we have triangle *ABC*. What we want is the height. What we need is the area and the length of the sides.

Statement 1 gives us only the perimeter. We have no idea about the lengths of any side. *Insufficient*

Statement 2 tells us we have an equilateral triangle. Because if one angle is 60° and the triangles is isosceles, then the other 2 equal angles must total 120°. Thus all the angles are 60°. However, we still don't have any values for the lengths of the sides, so we cannot calculate the area or the height. *Insufficient*

By putting the statements together, we know we have an equilateral triangle of sides 4. We can use the equilateral triangle formula $A = \frac{(s^2\sqrt{3})}{4}$ to calculate the height. *Sufficient*

$$A = \frac{4^2\sqrt{3}}{4} = 4\sqrt{3} \rightarrow A = \frac{1}{2} \cdot base \cdot height$$

$$\rightarrow 4\sqrt{3} = \frac{1}{2}(4)h = 2h \rightarrow h = 2\sqrt{3}$$

10. If r, s, and t are integers greater than 1, what is the value of $r + s + t$?

(1) $\dfrac{100r}{st} = 70$

(2) $2rst = 462$

(B) Statement 1 gives us the equation $100r = 70st$, which reduces to $10r = 7st$. This does not give us any unique values for r, s, and t; therefore, we cannot solve for $r + s + t$. *Insufficient*

Statement 2 gives us the equation $rst = 231$. If we break down 231 into prime factors, we get $3 \times 7 \times 11 = 231$. Since r, s, and t are integers greater than 1, they must all be prime numbers. Thus we can determine that $r + s + t = 21$. *Sufficient*

---

11. Marisa's new car gets 37 miles per gallon. She drove her new car 410 miles on a tank of gas at an average speed of 41 mph. Which of the following can be determined from the given information?

   I. Approximate capacity of the gas tank
  II. Number of days traveled
 III. Cost per gallon of gas

(A) I only
(B) II only
(C) III only
(D) Both I and III
(E) None of the above

(A) Given the question, we can determine the capacity of the gas tank by dividing 410 by 37. We cannot find the cost per gallon as there is no price given for the gasoline used. Finally, we cannot determine the number of days as we do not know whether she drove continuously in one day or over two days. We also do not know if she stopped several times and drove her cars over several days or even weeks. Therefore, we can determine only statement I with certainty.

---

12. 1,000 tickets numbered from 1 to 1,000, inclusive, were sold in a lottery. What is the probability of selecting a ticket with a 6 as either the hundreds digit or the tens digit?

(A) $\dfrac{1}{10}$

(B) $\dfrac{12}{100}$

(C) $\dfrac{3}{20}$

(D) $\dfrac{19}{100}$

(E) $\dfrac{1}{5}$

(D) We need to count all the tickets with a 6 in the tens digit or the hundreds digit. Out of all the tickets sold, there are 100 tickets from 600 to 699. There also 10 tickets each from 60 to 69, 160 to 169, all the way to 960 to 969. This occurs 10 times. The total number of tickets is now at 200. Don't forget that we need to subtract tickets that have the number 66x in them because we have already double counted them. There are 10 of them. The final total is now 190. The probability will be $\dfrac{190}{1000}$ or $\dfrac{19}{100}$.

13. Is x a prime number?

    (1) xyz has only 8 distinct factors.

    (2) xy is even when y is a prime number.

(A) In statement 1, if xyz has only 8 distinct factors, then each of x, y, and z are prime numbers. For example $2 \cdot 3 \cdot 5 = 30$, which has 1, 2, 3, 5, 6, 10, 15, and 30 as factors. Therefore x is a prime number. *Sufficient*

    In statement 2, if xy is even and y is a prime number, then all we know about x is that it is an even number if y is odd. However, x is either odd or even when $y = 2$, the only even prime number. *Insufficient*

---

14. A set contains a parallelogram, 2 isosceles trapezoids, 3 squares, a rectangle, and 2 rhombuses that are not squares. A figure is chosen at random. What is the probability that the figure's diagonals will be of equal length?

    (A) $\dfrac{3}{9}$

    (B) $\dfrac{5}{9}$

    (C) $\dfrac{2}{3}$

    (D) $\dfrac{8}{9}$

    (E) 1

(C) Only an isosceles trapezoid, a square, and a rectangle will have diagonals that are equal. For example,

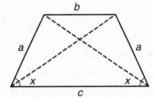

Thus, there are 6 possibilities out of 9, which simplifies to $\dfrac{2}{3}$.

---

15. How much older than Paul is Mary?

    (1) Peter is 10 years older than Paul.

    (2) Mary in 2 years will be twice as old as Paul.

(E) Statement 1 does not work because we have no information about Mary. Insufficient

    Statement 2 gives us the equation

$$M + 2 = 2(P + 2) \ \rightarrow \ M = 2P + 2.$$

However, when we solve this, we have 1 equation and 2 unknowns, which we cannot solve. *Insufficient*

    Combining the statements gives us 2 equations and 3 unknowns, which we cannot solve. *Insufficient*

16. Nancy's family is out visiting the grandparents when Grandpa Joe decides everyone should go out for ice cream. The family takes two cars, Nancy's and Grandpa's. The ice cream shop is 10 km away, and Nancy drives at an average speed of 80 km/hr. Nancy gets pulled over for speeding, and the police officer who writes her ticket delays her by 5 minutes. Nancy and Grandpa arrive at the ice cream shop at the exact same time. What was Grandpa's average speed?

(A) 36 km/hr
(B) 40 km/hr
(C) 48 km/hr
(D) 56 km/hr
(E) 60 km/hr

(C) We need to use $D = RT$ to solve this problem. If Nancy had driven straight to the shop, she would have taken $\frac{1}{8}$ of an hour, or 7.5 minutes. Since she was delayed by 5 minutes, then Grandpa took $5 + 7.5 = 12.5$ minutes to get there. Therefore, Grandpa drove at an average speed of 10 km/12.5 min $\times$ 60 min/1 hr = 48 km/hr.

---

17. At a candy store, the ratio of the number of jellybeans to the number of gumdrops is 9 to 5, and the ratio of the number of chocolate bars to jellybeans is 2 to 5. If the ratio of the number of licorice sticks to the number of gumdrops is 4 to 3, what is the ratio of the number of chocolate bars to the number of licorice sticks?

(A) 27 to 100
(B) 27 to 75
(C) 27 to 50
(D) 54 to 75
(E) 20 to 27

(C) The key to solving this problem is to combine the ratios by finding a common multiple. A chart is a nice way to keep track of information. Let's focus on linking the 2 gumdrop ratios first and then link that to the chocolate ratio. Let L be licorice, G be gumdrop, and C be chocolate bars.

① → $\underline{L : G}$ $\underline{G : J}$ ② → $\underline{L : G : J}$ $\underline{J : C}$
　　4 : 3　　5 : 9　　　　20 : 15 : 27　　5 : 2
　　*5　　　*3　　　　　　*5　　　　　　*27
　　20 : 15　15 : 27　　100 : 75 : 135　135 : 54

③ → $\underline{L : G : J : C}$
　　100 : 75 : 135 : 54

Thus, the ratio of the number of chocolate bars to the number of licorice is $\frac{54}{100} = \frac{27}{50}$.

18. Machines X and Y, while working simultaneously at their respective constant rates, produce 1,200 widgets in Z days. While working alone at its constant rate, machine Y produces 1,200 widgets in W days. How many days does it take machine X, while working at its constant rate, to produce 1,200 widgets in terms of W and Z?

(A) $\dfrac{W}{(W+Z)}$

(B) $\dfrac{Z}{(W+Z)}$

(C) $\dfrac{WZ}{(W+Z)}$

(D) $\dfrac{WZ}{(W-Z)}$

(E) $\dfrac{WZ}{(Z-W)}$

(D) The "job" itself is 1200 widgets and is constant throughout the question. Therefore, we can use the standard work rate formula.

$$\frac{1}{X} + \frac{1}{Y} = \frac{1}{Both}$$

→ where X, Y, and both are the time it takes machine X, machine Y, and both machines to finish a job, respectively. This gives us

$$\frac{1}{X} + \frac{1}{W} = \frac{1}{Z}$$

→ We have to solve for X

$$\frac{1}{X} = \frac{1}{Z} - \frac{1}{W}$$

→ $\dfrac{1}{X} = \dfrac{(W-Z)}{WZ}$

→ $X = \dfrac{WZ}{(W-Z)}$

---

19. For all positive integers x, y and z, $x \circledP y^{z+1}$ means that y^{z+1} and y^z are divisors of x. If $162 \circledP 3^{z+1}$, then what does z equal?

(A) $-3 < z < -1$

(B) $-1 < z < 4$

(C) $-2 < z < 5$

(D) $0 < z < 6$

(E) $1 < z < 4$

(B) This is a symbol question that defines a unique relationship among the variables x, y, and z. Using the example given, we know that 162 is a multiple of 3. Let's break it down into prime factors first.

$$162 = 81 \cdot 2 = 9*9*2 = 3 \cdot 3 \cdot 3 \cdot 3 \cdot 2 \rightarrow$$
$$3^{z+1} \text{ and } 3^z \text{ are both divisors.}$$

To be a divisor of 162, the exponent of the base 3 can be anything from 0 to 4. Remember that $3^0 = 1$ is also a divisor! Note that the answer choices give us a range of numbers, which is a clue that z can have more than one value. The definition states that both 3^{z+1} and 3^z are divisors. If $z = 4$ then 3^z works but 3^{z+1} doesn't work. If $z = -1$, then, 3^{z+1} works but 3^z doesn't work. Therefore, z must be 0, 1, 2, or 3.

20. In a class graduating from medical school, the male students took an average of 9.7 years to obtain their degrees and the female students took an average of 9.0 years. What was the ratio of the number of female graduates to the number of male graduates?

(1) The average number of years for the current graduating class as a whole to graduate from medical school was 9.5 years.

(2) There were 47 female graduates.

(A) This is a good example of using the jump ahead tactic, as statement 2 is less complicated. Clearly it is not sufficient to answer the problem because we have information only about the number of females and none about the number of males. *Insufficient*

Statement 1 gives us the overall average. Using a line graph, we can leverage our understanding of weighted average to determine how far away the males and females are from the overall average.

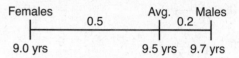

This relationship is the inverse of the overall ratio of males to female students, which means the ratio of male students to female students is 5 : 2. *Sufficient*

---

21. In city A, 72% of the employed population are blue-collar workers and the rest are white-collar workers. If 75% of the white-collar workers are male and $\frac{5}{12}$ of the blue-collar workers are female, what percent of the employed population of city A are female?

(A) 37%
(B) 40%
(C) 43%
(D) 47%
(E) 53%

(A) This is a matrix box question because we have a group broken into two subgroups of two each with no overlap. By using the matrix box table, we get:

Employed population of City A	Blue Collar	White Collar	Total
Males		$\frac{3}{4} \bullet 28\% =$ **21%**	
Females	$\frac{5}{12} \bullet 72\% =$ **30%**		x
Total	72%	28%	100%

Note that we calculated the white-collar males by taking 75% or $\frac{3}{4}$ of the total white-collar workers. Similarly, we calculated the blue-collar females by taking $\frac{5}{12}$ of 75%. Now that we have these numbers, we can easily fill in the rest of the chart. What we want, though, is x. The number of white-collar female workers is 28% − 21% = 7%. So the total percent of employed females is 30% + 7% = 37%.

22. Is $s > -r$?

    (1) $s - 4r > 0$

    (2) $3r - s > 0$

(C) One of the best ways to deal with inequalities and variables in data sufficiency questions is to try picking numbers. Another strategy to keep in mind is to try to determine sufficiency by proving insufficiency. This can be done by finding two possibilities, one that gives you a yes answer and another that gives you a no answer.

Statement 1 tells us that $s > 4r$. If $s = 5$ and $r = 1$, then the expression $s > -r$ becomes $5 > -1$, which works. But if $s = -12$ and $r = -4$, then the expression $s > -r$ becomes $-12 > 4$, which does not work. *Insufficient*

Statement 2 tells us that $s < 3r$. Again we can pick numbers to try to prove insufficiency. If $s = 2$ and $r = 1$, then the expression $s > -r$ becomes $2 > -1$, which works. If $s = -5$ and $r = 4$, then the expression $s > -r$ becomes $-5 > -4$, which does not work. *Insufficient*

When we combine both statements, we know that $s < 3r$ and $s > 4r$. We could pick numbers to determine sufficiency, but let's solve instead. Unlike most data sufficiency questions with algebraic equations, we actually have to solve the two inequalities to determine sufficiency because it's still possible to get values for r and s that are not necessarily sufficient.

$$
\begin{array}{ccc}
s - 4r > 0 & \text{multiply by 3} \rightarrow & 3s - 12r > 0 \\
\underline{+\; -s + 3r > 0} & \text{multiply by 4} \rightarrow & \underline{+\; -4s + 12r > 0} \\
-r > 0 & & -s > 0 \\
\rightarrow r < 0 & & \rightarrow s < 0
\end{array}
$$

Since both r and s are negative, then any value of s would not be greater than $-r$. *Sufficient.*

23. At a fraternity keg party, Ogre mixes three drinks that are 3%, 8% and 12% alcohol by volume. If x pints of 3% alcohol, y pints of 8% alcohol, and z pints of 12% alcohol mixed give $x + y + z$ pints of a 9% alcohol drink, what is x in terms of y and z?

(A) $\dfrac{3}{(3y+z+6)}$

(B) $\dfrac{(3z-y)}{6}$

(C) $\dfrac{(3z+y)}{6}$

(D) $\dfrac{(21z+17y)}{12}$

(E) $\dfrac{3}{(3z-y)}$

(B) This is a mixture problem combined with algebra. When we express this situation algebraically, we get:

The 3 different drinks	The final mixed drink
$0.03x + 0.08y + 0.12z$	$= 0.09(x + y + z)$

→ expanding this out and solving for x we get

$$0.03x + 0.08y + 0.12z = 0.09x + 0.09y + 0.09z$$
$$\to \quad 0.09x - 0.03x = 0.08y - 0.09y + 0.12z - 0.09z$$
$$0.06x = 0.03z - 0.01y \to 6x = 3z - y$$
$$\to \quad x = \frac{(3z-y)}{6}$$

---

24. For all positive numbers x and y, for which of the following functions is $f(x - y) = f(x) - f(y)$?
(A) $f(t) = -2t$
(B) $f(t) = t^2 + 1$
(C) $f(t) = t - 1$
(D) $f(t) = \sqrt{(t+3)}$
(E) $f(t) = \dfrac{3}{t}$

(A) There is a lot of information at play in this question. Using a chart is a great way to organize it all. First we will let $x = 1$ and $y = 2$. Then we can see what the functions in this scenario would work out to be.

Let $x = 1$ and $y = 2$ thus $x - y = -1$	$f(x) = f(1)$ What is $f(1)$?	$f(y) = f(2)$ What is $f(2)$?	$f(x) - f(y)$ What is $f(1) - f(2)$?	$f(x - y) =$ $f(1 - 2) = f(-1)$ What is $f(-1)$?	Do they equal? Is $f(x - y) =$ $f(x) - f(y)$?
$f(t) = -2t$	-2	-4	**2**	**2**	**YES**
$f(t) = t^2 + 1$	2	5	-3	2	No
$f(t) = t - 1$	0	1	-1	-2	No
$f(t) = \sqrt{(t+3)}$	2	$\sqrt{5}$	$2 - \sqrt{5}$	$\sqrt{2}$	No
$f(t) = \dfrac{3}{t}$	3	$\dfrac{3}{2}$	$\dfrac{3}{2}$	-3	No

25. If $a^4 < b^2 < c$, which of the following statements could be true?

   I. $a > b > c$
   II. $a < b < c$
   III. $c > a > b$

(A) I only
(B) I and II only
(C) I and III only
(D) II and III only
(E) All of the above

(E) Let's pick numbers to determine which of the statements could be true.

I: If $a = \dfrac{3}{4}$, $b = \dfrac{1}{2}$, $c = \dfrac{1}{3}$ then $a > b > c$
   AND $a^4 < b^2 < c$ could be true.

II: If $a = \dfrac{1}{3}$, $b = \dfrac{1}{2}$, $c = 1$ then $a < b < c$
   AND $a^4 < b^2 < c$ could be true.

III: If $a = \dfrac{1}{3}$, $b = -\dfrac{1}{3}$, $c = 2$ then $c > a > b$
   AND $a^4 < b^2 < c$ could be true.

All three statements could be true.

---

26. Mary needs to sort her toys. She has several identical items, including 3 dolls, 3 cars, 3 teddy bears, 3 tennis balls, and 3 trains. In how many ways can she arrange them?

(A) $\dfrac{(3!)^5}{15}$

(B) $\dfrac{15!}{(5 \cdot 3!)}$

(C) $\dfrac{15!}{(5!3!)}$

(D) $\dfrac{15!}{(3!)^5}$

(E) $\dfrac{3^{15}}{15!}$

(D) This is a permutation problem because the order of the elements matters. This is also a special case scenario where we have repeated elements.

$$\text{Number of arrangements} = \frac{N!}{(A! B! \ldots)}$$

where N is the total number of elements at play in the questions and A, B, ... are the number of repeated elements. In this question, $N = 15$ toys. We have 5 different elements, or toys, that repeat 3 times each. This gives us

$$\frac{N!}{A!B!C!D!E!} \rightarrow \frac{15!}{(3!3!3!3!3!)} = \frac{15!}{(3!)^5}$$

27. Charles put an amount of money into each of two investments, X and Y, which pay simple annual interest. If the annual interest rate of X is 40% more than that of investment Y, what amount did Charles put into investment Y?

(1) The amount that Charles put into investment X is three times the amount that he put into investment Y.

(2) The interest for one year is $100 for investment X and $200 for investment Y.

(E) All we know is that there are two investments, X and Y, and that $r_X = 1.4r_Y$, where r_X and r_Y are the interest rates of investments X and Y, respectively.

Statement 1 tells us that $P_X = 3P_Y$, where P_X is the principal paid in investment X and P_Y is the principal paid in investment Y. However, we have no way to solve for an actual amount. *Insufficient*

Statement 2 gives us actual amounts of the interest paid on the principal. Without exact interest rates or principal amounts, though, we cannot solve. *Insufficient*

At this point we have 4 different variables at play in the question. When we combine both statements, we have $r_X = 1.4r_Y$ and $P_X = 3P_Y$. We also have $100 = P_X \cdot r_X$ and $200 = P_Y \cdot r_Y$. We still cannot solve because the principal amounts invested could still vary in magnitude, just as interest rates could. For example, you could have $1000 invested at 10% yielding $100, or you could have $1,000,000 invested at 0.01%, yielding the same $100. *Insufficient*

---

28. When a bacterial culture was created, the medium consisted of 7.2×10^{20} molecules and the amount decreased every hour by a constant amount. At the end of the 7th hour, the number of molecules was $\frac{1}{8}$ less than it was at the end of the 5th hour. How many molecules did the culture medium lose each hour?

(A) 8.8×10^{17}
(B) 3.6×10^{18}
(C) 9.0×10^{18}
(D) 3.6×10^{19}
(E) 7.2×10^{19}

(D) The key to this problem is that the decrease is constant. We can map out the timeline and let the change be y.

Hours	1	2	3	4	5	6	7
	7.2×10^{20}	y	y	y	y	y	y

The number of molecules at the 7th hour is $7.2 \times 10^{20} - 6y$.

The number of molecules at the 5th hour is $7.2 \times 10^{20} - 4y$. The 7th hour was $\frac{1}{8}$ less than the 5th hour, so that gives us

$$7.2 \times 10^{20} - 6y = \frac{7}{8}(7.2 \times 10^{20} - 4y)$$

$$\rightarrow 8 \cdot (7.2 \times 10^{20}) - 8 \cdot 6y = 7 \cdot (7.2 \times 10^{20}) - 7 \cdot 4y$$

$$57.6 \times 10^{20} - 48y = 50.4 \times 10^{20} - 28y$$

$$\rightarrow 7.2 \times 10^{20} = 20y \rightarrow y = \frac{7.2}{20} \times 10^{20}$$

$$\frac{7.2}{20} \cdot \frac{5}{5} = \frac{36}{100}$$

$$\rightarrow y = 0.36 \times 10^{20} = 3.6 \times 10^{19}$$

29. Is $x \geq y$?

(1) $-x \leq -y$

(2) $x^2 - y^2 = 0$

(A) Statement 1 can be manipulated to give us $x \geq y$, which is exactly what we are looking for. *Sufficient.*

Statement 2 factors out to give us $(x - y)(x + y) = 0$, which means that either $x = y$ or $x = -y$. Knowing that $x = y$ answers the question, but what about $x = -y$? Well, you can just pick numbers to see.

If $x = 0$, $y = 0$. If $x = 1$, $y = -1$. However, if $x = -1$, $y = 1$, which doesn't work. *Insufficient*

---

30. What is the surface area of a cube?

(1) The length of $\frac{1}{4}$ of the diagonal is $\sqrt{2}$.

(2) The maximum distance between one vertex on the cube to another is $4\sqrt{3}$.

(D) To find the surface area of a cube, we need to find the length of any side.

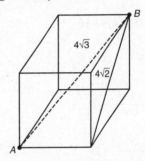

Statement 1 gives us the length of the diagonal, which is $4 \cdot \sqrt{2} = 4\sqrt{2}$. The length of a diagonal will give us the length of the side through the 45-45-90 triangle identity. The ratios of 45-45-90 triangles are $1 : 1 : \sqrt{2}$; therefore the triangle sides would be $4 : 4 : 4\sqrt{2}$. Thus the side of this cube would be 4.

Surface area (SA) of a cube is $6s^2$.

$$\rightarrow 6 \cdot 16 = 96 \text{ Sufficient}$$

Statement 2 gives us the longest distance from vertex to vertex. This will also give us the length of a side through the formula for longest length in a cube, which is $\sqrt{(3s^2)}$.

$$4\sqrt{3} = \sqrt{(3s^2)} \rightarrow 48 = 3s^2 \rightarrow s^2 = \frac{48}{3}$$

$$\rightarrow s^2 = 16 \rightarrow s = 4$$

$$\text{SA} = 6s^2 \rightarrow 6(16) = 96 \text{ Sufficient}$$

31. Sam plans to travel across the country by hitchhiking. He immediately gets picked up by a large transport rig that takes him k miles at an average speed of r miles per hour. He then waits 10 hours before being picked up by a van of students who are on their way to San Francisco. They agree to drive him the rest of the way. They drive at a speed of s miles per hour and finish the trip. If the total cross-country trip is D miles, how long did it take Sam to complete his trip?

(A) $\dfrac{60k}{r}+\dfrac{(D-k)}{60s}$

(B) $\dfrac{k}{r}+(D-k)s+10$

(C) $\dfrac{(k+10)}{r}+(D-k)s$

(D) $\dfrac{k}{r}+\dfrac{(D-k)}{60s}+60$

(E) $\dfrac{k}{r}+\dfrac{(D-k)}{s}+10$

(E) The best way to solve this problem is to break it down into parts.

Part 1 is the time Sam spent in the transport rig. Using $D = RT$, the total time taken is $\dfrac{k}{r}$.

The second part is the wait, which was 10 hrs.

The third part is the time spent in the van. Since the total distance is D, then the distance for the last leg was $D - k$. Therefore, the time taken was $\dfrac{(D-k)}{s}$. Therefore, the total time taken to cross the country was $\dfrac{k}{r}+\dfrac{(D-k)}{s}+10$.

You could also have used the DiRTy chart, but you would need to account for the wait of 10 hours.

	Part 1	Part 2	Part 3	Total
D	k	0	$D-k$	D
R	r	0	s	Average rate
T	$\dfrac{k}{r}$	10	$\dfrac{(D-k)}{s}$	

Using the chart you can now sum up the total time to get the same answer as above.

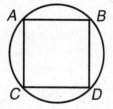

32. In the figure above, what is the largest rectangle that can be inscribed in the circle?
(1) The arc AB is equal to 4.
(2) The rectangle is a square.

(A) If we know the radius of the circle, we can find the diagonal of the rectangle, which in order to have the largest area, the rectangle must be a square.

In statement 1, the arc AB gives us the radius through the circumference formula, as we know the central angle to the arc is 90° or $\dfrac{1}{4}$ the total circumference of the circle. This gives us the radius through the circumference formula.

$$C=2\pi r=4\cdot 4=16 \;\rightarrow\; r=\dfrac{8}{\pi} \;\rightarrow\; \text{diameter}=\dfrac{16}{\pi}$$

Now we can apply the 45-45-90 triangle identity to find the side of the square and then calculate its area. It's a messy calculation. The good news with data sufficiency is that you don't have to do calculations to solve; you just have to know that you can solve. *Sufficient*

The largest rectangle inscribed in a circle has to be a square, so statement 2 is redundant information. *Insufficient*

33. While in detention, Oliver is given the task of calculating the volume of 1,000 hot dogs, where each hot dog is 6 inches in length from end to end and each end of the hot dog is shaped as a half sphere with a radius r. The volume of a sphere is $V = \left(\dfrac{4}{3}\right)\pi r^3$. What is the volume of 1,000 hot dogs?

(A) $\dfrac{\left(6\pi r^2 - \left(\dfrac{10}{3}\right)\pi r^3\right)}{1,000}$

(B) $5\pi r^2 - \left(\dfrac{2}{3}\right)\pi r^3$

(C) $6,000\pi r^2 + \left(\dfrac{4}{3}\right)\pi r^3$

(D) $1,000\left(6\pi r^2 - \left(\dfrac{2}{3}\right)\pi r^3\right)$

(E) $500\left(5\pi r^2 + \left(\dfrac{4}{3}\right)\pi r^3\right)$

(D) Since no diagram is given, let's make sure we draw properly and understand clearly what we are calculating.

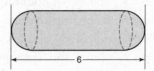

If we break this down into sections we have a half-sphere, a cylinder, and another half-sphere. The 2 half-spheres are equivalent to one full sphere, with volume $\left(\dfrac{4}{3}\right)\pi r^3$. The cylinder has a radius of r and a length of $6 - r - r = 6 - 2r$. This gives us

Volume of cylinder =
$$\pi r^2 h = \pi r^2(6 - 2r) = 6\pi r^2 - 2\pi r^3$$

Total volume $= V_{\text{cylinder}} + V_{\text{sphere}}$
$$= 6\pi r^2 - 2\pi r^3 + \left(\dfrac{4}{3}\right)\pi r^3 = 6\pi r^2 - \left(\dfrac{2}{3}\right)\pi r^3$$

Since there are 1000 hotdogs, the volume is $1000\left(6\pi r^2 - \left(\dfrac{2}{3}\right)\pi r^3\right)$.

---

34. A box contains red marbles, green marbles, and yellow marbles. If a marble is randomly selected from the box, what is the probability that the marble selected will be either green or yellow?

(1) $P(\text{yellow marble}) = \dfrac{1}{3}$

(2) $P(\text{red marble}) = \dfrac{1}{4}$

(B) Statement 1 tells us only about the yellow marbles. We don't know anything about the probability of selecting a green marble. *Insufficient* Statement 2 tells us one thing but actually implies another. If we select one marble from the box, the probabilities are

$$P(\text{red marble}) + P(\text{yellow marble})$$
$$+ P(\text{green marble}) = 1$$

The probabilities of selecting one marble must add up to 1. Since statement 2 gives the probability of selecting a red marble, then the probability of picking a green or yellow marble would be $\dfrac{3}{4}$. *Sufficient.*

35. Each gardener employed by company ABC Estates receives the following pay: x dollars per hour for each of the first z hours in a week and $x + y$ dollars per hour for each hour over z hours per week, where $x > y$. How much less pay will an ABC Estates gardener who works $z + y$ hours earn than one who works $z + x$ hours?

(A) $x^2 - y^2$

(B) $(y - x)(x + y + z)$

(C) $yz + xz - yx$

(D) $y - x$

(E) $z(y - x)$

(A) This question can get quite confusing because several numbers are at play in the question and they are all given as algebraic variables. You can either chart this out or at least sort the information in a clear way.

Pay rate for 1st z hours	Pay rate for hours > z hours
$\$x$/hr	$\$(x + y)$/hr

Gardener 1 works $z + y$ hours, so he makes $zx + y(x + y)$ dollars

Gardener 2 works $z + x$ hours, so she makes $zx + x(x + y)$ dollars

The difference in pay is

$$zx + x(x + y) - zx - y(x + y) = x^2 + xy - xy - y^2 = x^2 - y^2$$

---

36. There are at least 200 students at a cooking school studying French cuisine. The only other cuisine available for study is Indian cuisine. If 8% of the students at this school who study Indian cuisine also study French cuisine, do more students study Indian cuisine than French cuisine?

(1) 32 students at the school study both Indian and French cuisine.

(2) 20% of the students who study French cuisine also study Indian cuisine.

(B) With a Venn diagram, we can compare the French cuisine students to the Indian cuisine students.

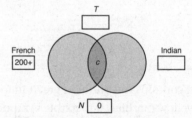

In statement 1, we have only the number for those who study both Indian and French, or the middle number. From that, we can calculate the total number of students and the approximate number of students who study Indian cuisine.

$$32 = 8\% \text{ of total or } \frac{32}{\text{total}} = \frac{8}{100}$$

$$\text{Total} = 400$$

Using the Venn formula, we get $T = A + B - c + N$

$$400 = (200+) + I - 32 + 0$$

I represents the number who study Indian cuisine and $N = 0$ because students study either French or Indian cuisine.

We cannot determine sufficiency because the number of French cuisine students is "at least" 200. If it was 200, then $I = 232$. If it was 240, then $I = 192$. Hence, the number of students studying French cuisine could be greater or less than the number of students studying Indian cuisine. *Insufficient*

In statement 2, we are told that 20% of the French cuisine students study Indian cuisine as well. This means that the 8% who study both French and Indian cuisine represent 20% of the total number who study French cuisine.

$$8\% = 0.2F \rightarrow F = 0.4T$$

Since 40% study French cuisine, the number of students studying only Indian cuisine must be 60% and thus greater. This means that a total of 60% + 8% = 68% of the students are studying Indian cuisine. *Sufficient*

---

37. A sequence is defined by
$A_n = (A_{n-1})^2 - 2(A_{n-1})(A_{n-2}) + (A_{n-2})^2$,
where $n > 2$. If $A_3 = 2$ and $A_5 = 1$, what is A_6?

(A) 1
(B) 4
(C) 6
(D) 9
(E) 25

(B) First let's make sure we understand the definition. We can actually simplify the sequence definition by factoring it out because it is one of the algebraic equation identities

$$(a - b)^2 = a^2 - 2ab + b^2$$
$$(A_{n-1})^2 - 2(A_{n-1})(A_{n-2}) + (A_{n-2})^2 = (A_{n-1} - A_{n-2})^2$$

Next, let's list the terms, leaving gaps for the ones we don't know.

$$A_3 = 2 \qquad A_4 = ? \qquad A_5 = 1 \qquad A_6 = ?$$

In order to find A_6, we first need to determine A_4. The only link we have is the sequence definition for A_5. According to the definition,

$$A_5 = (A_4 - A_3)^2 \rightarrow 1 = (A_4 - 2)^2 \rightarrow A_4 = 1 \text{ or } 3$$

Since we have two values for A_4, we have to try each value out.

If $A_4 = 1$ $A_6 = (A_5 - A_4)^2 \rightarrow (1 - 1)^2 = 0$
If $A_4 = 3$ $A_6 = (A_5 - A_4)^2 \rightarrow (1 - 3)^2 = 4$

Since there is no answer choice with 0 and there is an answer with 4, then $A_6 = 4$.

ANSWERS EXPLAINED

Verbal Section

The passage for questions 1–4 appears on page 675.

---

1. The primary purpose of the passage as a whole is to
- (A) account for the popularity of a practice.
- (B) explain the reasons for pursuing a strategy.
- (C) demonstrate how to institute a practice.
- (D) advocate the use of one strategy over another.
- (E) evaluate the utility of a practice.

<u>**Question:**</u> Because it asks about the passage as a whole and inquires about the author's overall purpose, this is a Main Idea question. In this question, the short answer choices mean the correct answer will describe the author's purpose obliquely, rather than summarizing the author's central claim. Answer Choice (E) does this, as it is true that the author evaluates the utility of using group coupons (and finds the practice to be a mixed bag).

(E) Answer Choices (A) and (B) are both **part**(s) **only** because the author is not primarily accounting for the group coupon's popularity, though reasons for its popularity and why a business might pursue the strategy are mentioned in passing. Answer Choices (C) and (D) describe things that **never happened**, as the practice is described, but never demonstrated, and there is only one strategy described (and never advocated).

---

2. Which of the following is cited in the passage as a goal of some local services providing businesses for using group coupons?
- (A) To diversify the business's normal client base
- (B) To obtain a large immediate influx of cash for the business
- (C) To differentiate the business from others offering the same services
- (D) To associate the business with the latest marketing trends
- (E) To test the business's ability to meet demands for expanded service

<u>**Question:**</u> *Is cited* is another way of saying "is written explicitly in the text," making this a **Detail** question. The correct answer, (C), corresponds to information given in the very first line of the passage.

(C) Answer Choice (A) is **reasonable but not said**, as this might be an expected result of the practice but is never given as a *goal* of businesses. Answer Choices (B) and (C) are **misused details**; Answer Choice (B) is mentioned, but never said to be a goal, and Answer Choice (D) is said to be trendy, but also not said to be a goal. Answer Choice (E) is very nearly the **exact opposite** of the answer: group coupons test businesses (and often find them wanting), but businesses aren't described as using group coupons as tests.

3. Which of the following may be inferred from the passage?
  - (A) The service providers most likely to benefit by offering a group coupon are those who offer discounts lower than 75 percent off their usual prices.
  - (B) The service providers least likely to benefit with a group coupon are those that operate in markets with few competitors.
  - (C) If a business that offers services also sells physical goods, it will be better able to survive the loss of long-term customers caused by offering a group coupon.
  - (D) If a business has excess capacity that is being underutilized, it will stand to benefit substantially from offering a group coupon.
  - (E) If a business typically provides services that customers use infrequently for only a few days, it is likely to avoid the risk of offering a group coupon.

Question: *May be inferred* is the simplest way of indicating an **Inference** question is to follow. The question stem provides no guidance as to where to look for the information that will produce the inference, but it may be found via information toward the end of the second paragraph, although it's a touch tricky. It requires us to first understand that the one risk the answer choice corresponds to is the problem of a company driving away existing long-term customers and not replacing them with new ones from the group coupon pool. If the business only needed short-term nonrepeating customers, it would not be subject to the described risk.

(E) Answer Choices (A) and (B) cannot be inferred because the author does not give us a hierarchy or a rule that any particular type of business is the most likely or least likely to do anything. Answer Choice (C) is **reasonable but unsupported**, made attractive through the red herring of "physical goods." Though the businesses in the passage are service providers, and it is their services that will be strained by the group coupons, we're never told it would be better for them if they sold physical goods, too. Answer Choice (D) is a **distorted fact**. We know that businesses should examine their capacity for expansion, but not that they should have excess, underutilized capacity, nor are we told that such a thing would equate to a substantial benefit.

---

4. Which of the following hypothetical situations best exemplifies the potential problem the passage identifies for businesses offering a group coupon?
  - (A) A tattoo parlor is unable to obtain permission to open a new location after their reputation spreads throughout the community.
  - (B) A lawyer is forced to alter the composition of his print ads in order to avoid alienating new customers.
  - (C) A business consultant's reputation for excellent service with new clients creates an expectation of continued performance she cannot satisfy long term.
  - (D) A culinary school finds that its classes have declined in popularity as tastes in the community change.
  - (E) A flower arranger cannot meet all the orders pending at his shop because his usual supplier cannot provide roses in sufficient quantities.

Question: *Hypothetical situations* is the tipoff: since it asks us to consider something not presented in the passage, this can only be an Inference question. The information needed to evaluate these extra-passage scenarios is found throughout the passage; the correct answer, (E), is derived from information found in two places in the passage. The author mentions that (1) businesses need to carefully consider their capacity for expansion or (2) risk not being able to provide customers the service they have come to expect. This florist has overshot his capacity and thus cannot meet the demand for an arrangement that his long-term customers expect him to provide.

(E) While gaining a bad reputation is part of the risk outlined by the passage, Answer Choice (A) does not link that reputation to anything that would have come from the use of a group coupon. Alienating new customers is surely something to avoid, but this isn't the problem cited by the author, so Answer Choice (B) is **reasonable but unsupported**. The concern is alienating existing customers. The business consultant in Answer Choice (C) is surely getting in over her head because she will one day disappoint new customers, not because she will drive away existing customers. Answer Choice (E) is **reasonable but unsupported**, as changing tastes is an issue not raised by the passage at all.

---

5. Environmentalist: Genetically engineered (GE) rice would, if introduced on a large scale, exacerbate the very problem it was designed to solve: diseases caused by malnutrition in parts of the world where rice is the primary staple crop. Use of GE rice altered so that it contains, for example, Vitamin A, further encourages a diet based on one staple food rather than the reintroduction of many vitamin-rich foods that were once cheap and available.

The environmentalist's reasoning depends on assuming which of the following?
(A) Whenever a genetically engineered food is introduced on a large scale, it encourages a diet that is unhealthy in at least one respect.
(B) In areas of the world where rice is a staple crop, sufficient quantities of naturally occurring vitamin rich foods cannot be grown without genetic modification.
(C) The companies that typically produce genetically modified crops do so out of a desire to maximize profits.
(D) There is no way to genetically modify grain in such a way that it will contain all of the necessary vitamins previously provided by other foods.
(E) If the reintroduction of vitamin rich foods is discouraged, some necessary vitamins will inevitably be absent from the diets of those vulnerable to malnutrition.

Argument: The environmentalist's conclusion is a **prediction** about the **net harm** a **plan** will cause (a lot of common patterns combined), namely that the GE rice plan will *exacerbate the problem (diseases caused by malnutrition in places where rice is the staple crop)*. The evidence supporting this bold conclusion is rather meager, only that one benefit (Vitamin A) results in one harm that the plan will encourage a diet based on one staple food rather than a different option, reintroducing vitamin rich foods. Thus, the argument must assume that not doing the other option (or making it less likely) will harm people more than the benefit they'll get from the Vitamin A. Since the argument's benefit is strictly phrased in terms of missing vitamins (malnutrition), Answer Choice (E) is part of the speaker's assumption that the benefit will not be realized.

(E) Answer Choice (A) is a **closed issue** because the argument's conclusion is specifically limited to areas *where rice is the staple crop*, not *all areas*. Answer Choice (B) is the opposite of what we want, as it would **weaken** the argument's assumptions. Answer Choice (C) is reasonable but irrelevant, as *profit* is not part of this benefit/harm calculation. And Answer Choice (D) is tricky **but for one word**, though meant to appear as though it is a **defending assumption** against the possibility of an **alternate explanation**. The word that eliminates Answer Choice (D) is *grain*—if the answer said *rice*, we would have been in business.

---

6. Karl Rove, the former senior adviser and deputy chief of staff for President George W. Bush, never graduated college. So, all other things being equal, a college degree is not required for career success.

Which of the following would be most useful to know in evaluating the argument above?
(A) Would Karl Rove have been named senior adviser if he had obtained a college degree?
(B) Does a person's success in a given field relate to the jobs that person has held in that field?
(C) Did other college dropouts find places in President Bush's administration?
(D) Is it possible for two candidates for the same job to be equally qualified?
(E) Would Karl Rove describe himself as successful in his chosen field?

Argument: The conclusion is the **general rule** presented at the end of the argument: *college degrees are not required for success.* It is supported by evidence of a **single case**: Karl Rove. **Representativeness** likely leapt to mind as an assumption required here, and it is, but in a slightly less direct way than usual and is better described by a **term switch**. The evidence establishes that Karl Rove had various impressive jobs, but the conclusion is that he was *successful*; thus the argument assumes that *success* can be equated with these *impressive jobs*. **Evaluate** questions interrogate an argument's assumptions, and Answer Choice (B) pretty much does this directly.

(B) Answer Choice (A) confuses the conclusion that college degrees aren't **required** with some sort of **guarantee**. Answer Choice (C) asks for corroborating evidence, which is almost always irrelevant, **one step removed** from the argument's assumptions because it requires the additional assumption that the parties used to corroborate (other dropouts) are similar to the case (Rove) in the evidence. Answer Choice (D) is an **irrelevant comparison** (and probably also **too extreme**), as various levels of qualification are irrelevant so long as the applicant (Rove) lacks the college degree, and Answer Choice (E) is a trap hinting at **biased evidence**, another thing the GMAT is almost never interested in.

---

7. Unlike previous centuries, the greatest challenges of the present era were caused by technological advancement and will likely not be solved by it.
(A) previous centuries, the greatest challenges of the present era
(B) previous centuries, the present era's greatest challenges
(C) that of previous centuries, the present era's greatest challenge
(D) those of previous centuries, the greatest challenges of the present era
(E) the previous centuries, the greatest challenge of the present era

Issues: comparisons (which must be **parallel**), **subject/predicate agreement** (with the plural *were*)

(D) This question is built on two related issues, keeping the two parties in the comparison introduced by *Unlike...* **parallel** both logically and grammatically. As written in Answer Choice (A), *previous centuries* are compared with the *challenges* faced by the present era, two entities that are not logically similar; either *challenges to challenges* or *centuries to the present era* (time periods) would be correct. Answer Choices (B) and (E) likewise compares centuries to challenges, though they rephrase one or the other. Answer Choices (C) and (D) correct the comparison (by using a **placeholder pronoun** to make the previous centuries a **descriptive prepositional phrase**) but introduce a new problem. The verb *were* that follows the underlined section is plural and must be linked to a plural subject. Answer Choice (C) changes the subject challenge to singular. The already eliminated Answer Choice (E) does as well, but we already have enough to know that Answer Choice (D) is the only correct option left.

---

8. The earliest clocks relied on shadows cast by the sun, forcing primitive societies to rely on the stars alone to track the passage of time during the night, and this remained the case until at least the third century B.C.E, the earliest point <u>when it is known that early clockmakers did perfect</u> the water-powered escapement mechanism.
   - (A) when it is known that early clockmakers did perfect
   - (B) that early clockmakers are known to be perfecting
   - (C) of early clockmakers who were known to perfect
   - (D) at which it is known that early clockmakers had perfected
   - (E) at which early clockmakers are known to have perfected

Issues: modification (using the **idiomatically** and logically correct connector), **sequence of tenses** (*relied, remained, is known*)

(E) The split found at the beginning of the answer choices could eliminate only one answer, (C), as the *of* makes for modification nonsense. *When* is usually reserved for specific times on the GMAT (*when you called yesterday*), but it is probably OK here.

The verb sequence error ultimately proves deciding. Since the clockmakers' perfection/perfecting happens after the *relied* and *remained*, a tense that can occur after the past tense is required for that perfecting; Answer Choice (B) tries to avoid the error but creates nonsense with *be perfecting*; Answer Choice (D)'s *had perfected* (**past perfect**) occurs *earlier* in the sequence than *relied*'s **past**. (The already eliminated Answer Choice (C) does pass this requirement, however.)

Answer Choice (A)'s *did perfect* meets that requirement but is itself ruled out by a second sequence issue, the sequence between when the perfecting happened and when the knowing happened. The latter came second, so it, too, must be chronologically later than the verb for the former, and *did perfect* and *is known* are both present tense. This leaves only Answer Choice (E), that passes both sequence requirements with the sequence *are known* (**present**), *have perfected* (**present perfect**), and *relied* (**simple past**).

9. Ironically, in recent years countries such as Switzerland and <u>Denmark have been stronger advocates of the "American dream" than America,</u> a set of ideals in which freedom includes the opportunity for success.

   (A) Denmark have been stronger advocates of the "American dream" than America,
   (B) Denmark have been stronger for advocating the "American dream" than has been America,
   (C) Denmark have been stronger advocates than America for the "American dream,"
   (D) Denmark has advocated more strongly the "American dream" than America has
   (E) Denmark, stronger than America as advocates of the "American dream,"

   Issues: comparisons (logically **parallel**), **modification** (the correct object for the appositive phrase *a set of ideals…*), **subject/predicate agreement** (the compound *Switzerland and Denmark* is treated as plural), **sentence structure** (avoiding fragments)

   (C) This underlined section could have been tackled from either end. On the front end, a comparison error has been set up by the *stronger… than*. Answer Choices (A) and (C) pass this error, as **elliptical constructions** are allowed on the GMAT (the verb is left assumed, so the comparison becomes *have been stronger … than America [has]*). Answer Choice (B) fails (*stronger for advocating … than America has been*). Answer Choices (D) and (E) both *technically* pass, though the forms wouldn't be preferred by the GMAT.

   The more fruitful decision point thus becomes the modification error. In the non-underlined section of the sentence the **appositive phrase** *a set of ideals…* appears. Appositives must be placed next to the noun that they describe, separated only by a comma. So who or what is *a set of ideals*? Surely, *the "American dream,"* eliminating Answer Choices (A), (B), and (D) all in one fell swoop.

   That leaves only Answer Choice (E) to deal with, and it creates a fragment by deleting the verb attached to Denmark and Switzerland, creating a **sentence fragment**.

10. Regrettably, it has become increasingly common to find the remains of once majestic blue whales <u>with their fatal injuries from being struck when they slept</u> in busy shipping lanes.

    (A) with their fatal injuries from being struck when they slept
    (B) with fatal injuries from their sleeping and their being struck
    (C) with fatal injuries from their having been struck while sleeping
    (D) with fatal injuries from having been struck when they have slept
    (E) with fatal injuries from having been struck as they are sleeping

    Issues: modification (which must be **idiomatically correct**), **sequence of tenses** (*has become… have been struck*)

    (C) The **sequence** requirement for the two events (finding the whales that were *earlier* struck) eliminates Answer Choices (D) and (E). The other answer choices avoid the error by turning the second half of the sentence into the object of the prepositional phrase with *from* as its head word, used to describe the source of the *injuries*, but in doing so other errors are introduced. Answer Choice (A)'s *when* is idiomatically incorrect, as the GMAT typically reserves *when* for specific times (*when we were at your house last Saturday*), not for general descriptions of time. Answer Choice (B) creates nonsense by using *and*, so now the whales get injuries from two different things, *sleeping* and *being struck*.

The underlined section itself is part of a modifying phrase describing *whales*, and thus must make sense logically and use idiomatically correct words to connect the description. Answer Choice (A)'s introduction of an ambiguous *there* is a pronoun error and also an illogical way to connect the description to boot!

---

11. TerraBite CFO: Recently, the popular television show *Omega Factor* ran two stories on our company that many of our staff considered unfair, one attacking the lavishness of our product launch parties, the other our generous executive bonuses. In the week since the show's airing, several of our most important sources of venture capital have all but dried up, and our available capital on hand is insufficient to meet our prior financial obligations. Obviously, the *Omega Factor*'s biased coverage is to blame for the dire fiscal straits our company now faces.

Which of the following issues would it be most important to resolve in evaluating the CFO's explanation of TerraBite's financial situation?
(A) Whether the *Omega Factor* typically runs stories that are considered biased
(B) Whether the executive bonuses paid by TerraBite are commensurate with bonuses offered by other companies
(C) Whether the venture capitalists were aware of the damaging content of the stories prior to their decision to withdraw funding
(D) What specific allegations were made in the *Omega Factor* story about TerraBite
(E) Whether the funding withdrawn by the venture capitalists would have been sufficient to meet reasonable financial obligations

Argument: This argument is a basic **causal connection** hidden under a few layers of distraction. The conclusion is the CFO's explanation that it was the stories that the *Omega Factor* ran that caused the company's money woes. There is precious little direct evidence given for this claim, mostly just the **setup information** that the stories were run and that the company is facing problems. To **Evaluate** an argument, the required information will help us understand an assumption the argument relies upon, and with a **causal** argument, that assumption can be stated as *there's nothing that would stop the stated cause from producing the stated effect*. Answer Choice (C) is directly relevant to that assumption, as if the venture capitalists were unaware of the story prior to pulling the funding. It would have been unlikely that the stories caused the pull, and vice versa.

(C) Answer Choices (A) and (B) rely on **real-world thinking** to distract you with some **irrelevant comparisons**, as it doesn't matter what the stories are *generally* like, only whether these two stories caused the venture capitalists to pull their money, or whether TerraBite is like *other companies*. Answer Choice (D) is more real-world thinking that would only provide **more evidence for the evidence**, which never strengthens or weakens a GMAT argument. Answer Choice (E) is the trickiest of the bunch, right **but for one word**, the word *reasonable*. It'd be reasonable to think that *reasonable* financial burdens are relevant, but we don't know if TerraBite's obligations were reasonable or not, so we don't know if this is relevant or not.

The passage for questions 12–14 appears on page 679.

12. Which of the following can be inferred from the passage?

(A) If it were not a nonprofit, TED would be unable to afford to assemble a quality speaker's list.

(B) If the requirements for being considered "TED material" were less obscure, more people would apply for the honor.

(C) If the TED conference organizers did not award grants, fewer speakers would be willing to donate their time for free.

(D) If a speaker is unwilling to donate at least $7,500, then they will not be allowed to attend a subsequent live TED conference.

(E) If the TED conferences were still organized by Richard Wurman, they would be less successful, though just as disorganized, as they are today.

Question: If you spotted the **Inference** key while reading this passage, this question would've been a snap. A definite requirement is presented at the end of the second paragraph. Between $7,500 and $125,000 is required in order to *attend* a live conference. This rule applies to everyone, including Answer Choice (D)'s *speakers*—at the conferences *subsequent* to their speaking, at least.

(D) Answer Choice (A) is a **too extreme** trap built on a potential misreading of another Inference key, the earlier statement that, *without the nonprofit status, the speakers list would cost a fortune*—which is not the same thing as being too expensive to put together. Maybe TED's original backers (millionaires) could have ponied up the money. Who knows? Answer Choices (B), (C), and (E) are all **reasonable but unsupported**, requiring information not present in the passage to infer.

13. The author indicates that which of the following was part of the original conception of TED?

(A) A slate of speakers whose presentations were not limited to a single topic

(B) A requirement that all conferences concern innovation in some form

(C) The hope that the conference would grow into something other than a Silicon Valley boys club

(D) A thoroughly opaque admissions process without clear requirements beyond the financial

(E) A desire to work for the public good

Question: Finding the right answer to a **Detail** question is a matter of locating information through the haze of synonyms and indirect phrasing the test maker uses to disguise it. The correct detail is found near the beginning of the passage, which lists three topics originally considered acceptable for the TED conference. Thus, Answer Choice (A) is mentioned (three means not just one, right?).

(A) Answer Choice (B) is a **misused detail**, as we know innovation is important, but not that it was considered necessary for every conference. Answer Choices (C) and (E) are both **reasonable but never said**, never the answer to a Detail question. Answer Choice (E) even throws in a bit of **heartstring-tugging** to make it extra appealing but no less wrong. Answer Choice (D) is another **misused detail**, something said in almost

ANSWERS EXPLAINED

those exact words, but that is never linked to the conference's original conception (and seems to be a new development).

---

14. Which of the following, if true, would weaken the conclusion given in the first sentence of the third paragraph?
(A) Much of the good that TED currently does would not be possible if the conference were still a for-profit enterprise.
(B) Millionaires whose fortunes are built upon technology often waste their money supporting baseless ventures.
(C) In its original form, a TED conference hosted many talks that, while disorganized, formed the basis for many successful innovations.
(D) The standards by which an applicant is determined to be "TED material," while confusing to outsiders, are nevertheless fair.
(E) Richard Saul Wurman made comparatively little money on the sale of the TED conference rights.

Question: Remember that sometimes the GMAT cheats a little and throws a Critical Reasoning question at you in Reading Comprehension. Treat these according to whatever strategy is appropriate in Critical Reasoning. Here, the *Weaken* requires us to find the conclusion and think about the assumptions. The correct answer attacks the assumptions. Also, remember that when a Critical Reasoning question appears in Reading Comprehension, the weakeners and strengtheners are often indistinguishable from contradictions and restatements of evidence, respectively.

Argument: The conclusion referenced in the stem is a **causal connection**: the nonprofit status caused the conference to become something it otherwise couldn't have become, a money-fueled such-and-such. To weaken the argument, all we need to do is find an **alternate cause** that could have resulted in the stated effect. Answer Choice (B) provides this, showing us the money (that we ought to have remembered from the original description of the conference as a millionaire boys club for technology magnates).

(B) Answer Choice (A) is irrelevant to the conclusion—a bit of wishful thinking. In fact, so are Answer Choices (C) and (E)—reasonable things to believe, but not directly relevant to the stated conclusion. Answer Choice (D) is also irrelevant, a **misused detail** referencing the memorable disdain that the author had for the TED application process.

15. City Auditor: In the city of Boudreaux, municipal law demands that new adult residents moving into the city register their home and mobile telephone numbers at City Hall within two weeks of arrival. Residents moving out of the city must notify City Hall to cancel their registration within an equivalent period of time. In the ten years since the law was put into place, registrations of new phone numbers have outpaced notifications of cancellation by at least three to one in every single year. Therefore, we can conclude with near certainty from the telephone registration data alone that the population of Boudreaux has grown substantially over the past decade.

Which one of the following, if true, most calls into question the City Auditor's claim that the population of Boudreaux has grown substantially over the past decade?

(A) In the ten years since the law was put into place, many of the people who moved out of Boudreaux later returned.

(B) Many of the people who moved into Boudreaux in the past decade did not own or have access to a telephone and were thus exempt from the requirements of the law.

(C) Many of the people who moved into Boudreaux in the past decade were young professionals who registered a work phone number in addition to their home and mobile numbers.

(D) There are stiff penalties for failing to register a number and for failing to cancel a registration, but those penalties are difficult to enforce outside the city's immediate domain.

(E) Several towns in the same county as Boudreaux with similar laws have reported their populations have increased substantially over the past decade.

Argument: The City Auditor's conclusion is helpfully given to us in the question stem: *the population of Boudreaux has grown substantially over the past decade* and is supported by two explicit pieces of information (1) that there is a law that forces people who come to the city to register their phones and forces those who leave to cancel that registration and (2) that the number of people doing the first has gone up much faster—three times as fast—as those doing the second.

Essentially, the Auditor's conclusion is an **explanation** of the difference between those numbers: the only reasonable thing to believe is that many more people are immigrating than emigrating. The correct answer weakens the argument by suggesting an **alternate explanation**. If the law can only effectively punish you within the city, as Answer Choice (D) proposes, it is very possible that the number of people leaving the city is greater than the number of people canceling phone subscriptions.

(D) The *many*s in Answer Choices (A), (B), and (C) all render these answer choices irrelevant, as we don't know if the *many* is *many enough* to affect the calculation the Auditor is making. Answer Choice (E) is irrelevant corroboration, a form of **evidence for the evidence** that the GMAT doesn't worry much about.

16. Consultant: The goals that you have provided me are hopelessly vague. Any concrete goal a business has must either be related to the desire to maximize profits or be something the business admits is counter to its bottom line. Your business has done many things lately that are counter to your bottom line—your ill-conceived new product line and your excessive executive bonuses among them. This, therefore, is why you ought not hire any more consultants.

The consultant's reasoning is vulnerable to which of the following criticisms?
(A) It generalizes from an unrepresentative listing of the company's activities to all of its activities.
(B) It makes the unsupported claim that the company's goals are hopelessly vague.
(C) It ignores the fact that some businesses find consultants to be of great practical use.
(D) It fails to show any specific link between hiring practices and the vagueness of the company's goals.
(E) It is presented by someone who has a conflict of interests with regards to the hiring of consultants.

Argument: **Flaw** questions direct our attention to an assumption and declare that assumption unwarranted. Here, the argument's conclusion (that the company shouldn't hire any more consultants) is supported by the evidence that the business does a lot of dumb things and provides vague goals to its consultants, requiring the assumption that *doing dumb things and having vague goals is a good reason not to hire any more consultants.* Answer Choice (D) calls the speaker out for never making that **linking assumption** explicit.

(D) Answer Choice (A) is a great flaw, an unwarranted **representativeness** assumption that *this speaker* doesn't assume; Answer Choice (B) is directly contradicted by the prompt, which does offer support for the claim. Answer Choice (C) is something that the speaker ignores, surely, but it's **one step removed** from the specific case at hand, and Answer Choice (E) is the old trap of **implying bias** to the speaker. We don't attack the motives of the speaker on the GMAT, only the connections between the speaker's evidence and conclusion.

---

17. According to four out of five dentists surveyed, flossing regularly is nearly six times more likely as any other method used for improving the majority of their patients' gum health.
(A) as any other method used for improving the majority of their patients' gum health
(B) to improve gum health for the majority of their patients than any other method
(C) than any other method to improve gum health for the majority of their patients
(D) that the majority of their patients will improve their gum health by using any other method
(E) for the use of any other method than improving gum health for the majority of their patients

Issues: **comparisons** (which must be **idiomatically correct** and **logically parallel**), **modification**

(B) With a sentence this messy, the best place to start is with the most obvious decision point. The first part of the underlined section splits completely on the words used to set up the comparison, an issue of the correct **idiom** to use. Answer Choice (A)'s *more likely as* doesn't work, nor does Answer Choice (E)'s *more likely for*, but Answer Choice (C)'s *more likely than* is OK, as is Answer Choice (B)'s *more likely... than* (the intervening words don't change the idiom). Answer Choice (D)'s *more likely that* is both wrong and nonsensical. Answer Choice (C) introduces a new **modification** error, by rearranging the words following *likely to...* so that the sentence seems to indicate that flossing is *to be used*, not *to improve* the health of patients.

---

18. Crawford Long did not initially publicize his experiments with anesthesia, but when he learned, in 1849, of William T. G. Morton's public demonstration of its use in surgery, he quickly came forward.

   (A) Crawford Long did not initially publicize his experiments with anesthesia, but when he learned, in 1849, of William T. G. Morton's public demonstration of its use in surgery,

   (B) Crawford Long had not initially publicized his experiments with anesthesia, but when he learned of William T. G. Morton demonstrating its use in surgery publically in 1849,

   (C) Crawford Long, even though he had not initially publicized his experiments with anesthesia, on learning, in 1849, that William T. G. Morton had publically demonstrated its use in surgery,

   (D) Even though Crawford Long did not initially publicize his experiments with anesthesia, on learning when William T. G. Morton had a public demonstration, in 1849, of using it in surgery

   (E) Crawford Long did not initially publicize his experiments with anesthesia, but on learning, in 1849, that William T. G. Morton had been demonstrating its use in surgery in public,

Issues: modification, sentence structure

(A) The sentence is correct as written; the various rearrangements offered in the other answers all fail in some way to make sense of the modification or of the sentence structure.

   Also, Answer Choices (D) and (C) change *did not* to *had not*, as if the **sequence of tenses** were incorrect in the original (it's not).

19. Which of the following best completes the argument given below?

A recent study has shed new light on the relationship between time spent playing violent video games and aggression in children. Aggressive behavior was noted among children who played violent games often and those who played only rarely. Differences in aggression seemed to correspond more to differences in parenting philosophy. Absent, career-focused parents with hectic schedules whose children rarely played violent games had more aggressive children than did parents with balanced schedules, even when those schedules allowed for long periods spent playing violent games. In light of this study, it is safe to conclude that

(A) even small amounts of time spent playing violent video games can be dangerous.

(B) the amount of time spent playing violent video games has no effect on the behavior of children.

(C) if career-focused parents would make time, their children would be less aggressive.

(D) prolonged sessions spent playing violent video games are dangerous only when parents are absent.

(E) time spent playing violent video games is not on its own enough to predict a child's behavior.

Facts: Complete (Conclusion) questions are just Inference questions with a fancy blank at the end. The correct conclusion must be *inferable* directly from the other evidence in the prompt. Here, the evidence takes the form of a study that is very **qualified**. *Some* children who were parented in one way showed less violent behavior than some other children parented in a different way. The only inference permissible in situations like this, where everything's qualified and nothing's definite will be of the **but that's too obvious!** variety, as in Answer Choice (E), which is definitely consistent with the information. On its own, time in front of the X-Station doesn't directly correlate with violent behavior, it's influenced by other factors.

(E) Answer Choice (A) is the **exact opposite** of what the evidence supports; Answer Choices (B), (C), and (D) are all **too extreme** given the qualified evidence.

---

20. Unlike the Aztec and Maya, who did not have pack animals and relied on slaves for difficult physical labor, the llama was first domesticated by the Inca shortly after arriving on the South American continent.

(A) the Aztec and Maya, who did not have pack animals and relied on slaves for difficult physical labor, the llama was first domesticated by the Inca

(B) the Aztec and Maya, who relied on slaves for difficult physical labor because they did not have pack animals, the llama had been domesticated first by the Inca

(C) the Aztec and Maya, whose lack of pack animals made them rely on slaves for difficult physical labor, the Inca's first domestication of the llama

(D) not having pack animals, the Aztec and Maya relied on slaves for difficult physical labor, while the Inca first domesticated the llama

(E) the Aztec and Maya, who did not have pack animals and relied on slaves for difficult physical labor, the Incans first domesticated the llama

__Issues: comparisons__ (which must be __logically similar__), __modification__ (placement of _first_), __sentence structure__ (maintaining logical connections between ideas)

(E) The easiest place to start when a sentence has a comparison is by checking to see that logically similar items are compared. Answer Choices (A) and (B) compare _the Aztec and Maya_ (peoples) with _the llama_ (an animal used by people, which is illogical and insulting to boot). Answer Choice (C) branches out and compares _the Aztec and Maya_ with _domestication_ (an activity), whereas Answer Choice (D) goes even further into the realm of the nonsensical by comparing the state of _not having pack animals_ with _the Aztec and Maya_ peoples.

---

21. Which of the following most logically completes the argument?

Patent law exists to protect the rights of inventors to profit from their innovations, and copyright laws to protect those of artists from their art. While a chef who creates a new recipe might seem a similar case, a recipe is not a work of art, nor is it an innovation, so neither law protects the rights of a chef to profit from an original recipe. Thus, chefs' rights to profit from new recipes will never be protected by the law, since

(A) chefs lack the social capital and economic clout to convince judges to throw these laws out.

(B) there are no other laws outside the copyright and patent law systems that currently protect chefs' rights.

(C) most recipes are modifications of a previous chef's work.

(D) copyright and patent laws are considered to be so comprehensive by legislators that they will never address the gap.

(E) it is impossible to patent basic processes like mixing or baking and copyright does not protect facts.

__Argument:__ In general, __Complete (Evidence)__ questions can be treated just like "pure" __Assumption__ questions. The best thing to add to a blank in an argument is always evidence that confirms one of the argument's unstated assumptions. Here the argument assumes that because __one way is impossible__ something is guaranteed to fail, a common pattern seen in __Flaw__ questions. To avoid the flaw, simply assume what really ought not be assumed, which Answer Choice (D) does. Remember, the conclusion here is that their rights will _never be protected by law_, and (D) eliminates law by eliminating those who make laws, legislators.

(D) Answer Choice (A) simply eliminates another possibility rather than declaring that there are _no possibilities_; Answer Choice (B) is a case of __but for one word,__ since the conclusion concerns the future, not just what is _currently_ the case; Answer Choice (C) is __reasonable but irrelevant__, since we don't know what being a _modification_ has to do with the patent process (unless we're relying on outside information, a big no-no); and Answer Choice (E) is more information __one step removed__ from the argument without some __real-world thinking__ covering an additional assumption.

22. The newly revised *Diagnostic and Statistical Manual of Mental Disorders* has only further complicated the controversy <u>about whether Asperger syndrome should be classified as a unique condition or if it is</u> one of the autism spectrum disorders.

(A) about whether Asperger syndrome should be classified as a unique condition or if it is

(B) about Asperger syndrome and if it should be classified as a unique condition or it is

(C) concerning whether Asperger syndrome should be classified as a unique condition or

(D) with respect to Asperger syndrome being classified as a unique condition or if it is more

(E) whether or not Asperger syndrome should be classified as a unique condition or it is

Issues: idiomatic construction (*controversy over* as well as *whether* versus *if*), **parallelism** (demanded by whether something is X or Y)

(C) The sentence is built upon a two-part construction that presents the classification of Asperger syndrome as a choice between two things, thus both options must be grammatically parallel. Answer Choice (C) fails to be parallel (*should be classified… one of*), as does Answer Choice (D) (*being classified… it is more*). The idiom used to create the construction is itself a fruitful decision point. The GMAT prefers *whether* for choices or options (*whether it rains or it snows)* and *if* for hypothetical situations (like *if it rains tomorrow)*, eliminating Answer Choices (A), (B), and (D). Answer Choice (E) fails the idiomatic requirement on a different level, as the GMAT considers *whether or not* to be the wrong idiomatic form because *or not* is redundant.

You might have also investigated the idiom used with *controversy*. Both *controversy over* and *controversy concerning* are acceptable—if a preposition is used to connect a description to *controversy* then *over* is the one to use; otherwise, descriptions without prepositions can be correct, too. Answer Choice (D)'s *with respect* is a big red flag, not always ungrammatical, but never the sort of thing the GMAT likes to see.

---

23. The recent spike in the cost of heating oil to heat homes this winter is due to a dramatic decrease in the supply of heating oil relative to demand. However, the total amount of heating oil available is greater now than it was last winter.

If the statements above are true, which of the following must also be true?

(A) The efficiency of oil-burning furnaces has not increased since the past winter.

(B) The number of homes that use oil for heating has decreased since the past winter.

(C) The demand for heating oil has increased since the past winter.

(D) The cost of transporting heating oil from refineries has increased since the past winter.

(E) The percentage of homes using oil for heating has increased since the past winter.

Facts: This **Inference** prompt might seem more appropriate for an **Explain** question, as it appears to contain a **violated rule**. According to the law of supply and demand (one of the *very few* pieces of real-world information that you are expected to know), when supply rises, price falls as long as demand doesn't fall and when demand rises prices rise as long as supply doesn't rise. The prompt indicates that in this case, compared with last winter, this winter the overall supply of oil has risen but the price has also gone up. Thus, demand must have also gone up, as Answer Choice (C) states.

(C) Answer Choice (A) eliminates one factor that might contribute to demand falling, which isn't the same as proving that demand is up. Answer Choice (B) is feinting with a **percent versus number** flaw, but this is irrelevant here, as this is, like Answer Choice (A), just one reason demand might be down. Answer Choice (E) tries the exact same move as (B); and Answer Choice (C) brings up a sort of **irrelevant comparison**, as we can't infer any *particular* way that demand is up, only that it is up.

The passage for questions 24–26 appears on page 685.

---

24. The author of the passage would most likely agree with which of the following statements?
(A) Cash-based societies are less prone to identity theft than cashless ones.
(B) Consumers who do not check their credit reports frequently are more likely to be poor managers of their money.
(C) It is less likely that those with a long-established credit history will have errors on their credit report.
(D) If someone has never applied for a line of credit, there would be no reason for one of the credit agencies to have a file on them.
(E) Even when a consumer has applied for a line of credit, it is possible for one of the credit agencies to fail to open a file.

Question: The phrase "most likely agree" indicates an Inference question. Unfortunately, this stem lacks any specific clue as to where the inference will be drawn from, making a firm prediction all but impossible. A process of elimination with the answer choices will be your best strategy.

Facts: The correct answer is drawn from the last sentence of the first paragraph, which states that "nearly every adult has a file with at least one of the three [credit agencies], if not all of them." Combine this with your knowledge from earlier that files are opened once someone has applied for credit, and you can infer Answer Choice (E): sometimes one or more of the three agencies will not open a file on someone who applies for credit (though at least one almost always does).

(E) Answer Choices (A), (B), and (C) are all **irrelevant comparisons**. Answer Choice (A) is the worst of the three, as "cashless societies" never even appear in the passage. Answer Choices (B) and (C) refer to things actually mentioned by the author, but go further than the information in the passage, making stronger claims than are warranted, **reasonable but unsupported** claims. Answer Choice (D) is **explicitly contradicted** by the passage, which does give a reason a report could be opened falsely (identity theft).

25. If the information contained in the passage is accurate, which of the following groups would be most likely to not have a file at one of the three credit reporting agencies?
- (A) Consumers who have never opened a legitimate line of credit
- (B) Consumers who have not applied for a form of credit for at least seven years
- (C) Consumers who have either been victims of identity theft or who have applied for credit themselves
- (D) Consumers who have never been the victim of identity theft nor applied for a form of credit
- (E) Consumers who have avoided opening lines of credit except when such credit was necessary

Question: Parse the **double negative** trickery and you'll see this question asks for a group that could possibly end up without a credit report. The correct inference draws on the same rules as before. We know that there is only one way that a credit report is opened: when someone (and it doesn't have to be the person whose name is used) applies for credit. Thus, people who have never had any credit applied for in their name ought not have a report, as Answer Choice (D) indicates.

(D) Answer Choice (A) forgets the identity thieves; Answer Choice (B) is something you might know from the **real world** that is not supported here; Answer Choice (C) is the **exact opposite** of the right answer, as both of these groups ought to have reports; and Answer Choice (E), like (A), forgets the identity thieves but also forgets that even necessary credit is credit.

---

26. Which of the following best describes the organization of the passage as a whole?
- (A) A financial practice is described; exceptions to the practice are presented; and recommendations to replace the practice are listed, but none are supported.
- (B) A financial practice is criticized; an explanation of the criticism is given; and the conclusion is advanced that the practice is, nevertheless, inevitable.
- (C) A financial practice is recommended; some considerations against the practice are given; and a rebuttal to those considerations is presented.
- (D) A financial practice is described; a consequence of that practice is given; and further explanation of that consequence is presented.
- (E) A financial practice is described; recommendations against that practice are given; and further details of that recommendation are provided as support.

Question: Sometimes a **Function** question is so global that it almost feels like a Main Point question. Rather than being asked about a specific part of the passage's function, this question asks us for the function of *all the parts* (which we would need to know if this were a Main Point question, regardless). Your noteboard notes probably helped you here to spot Answer Choicer (D) as the correct answer. The *practice* (that begins all the answer choices) is the existence of credit reporting agencies, the *consequence* is the need to check your credit report when you open a line of credit because of false reports, and the *further explanation* is all that business at the end explaining how identity theft works.

(D) Like a lot of **Function** questions the splits in the answer choices make for a quick process of elimination. Since credit reports are neither recommended nor criticized, only the neutral *described* will stand, eliminating Answer Choices (B) and (C) on the first past, then later Answer Choices (A) and (E), as the first also mentions a recommendation not made, the recommendation to *replace* the system and the second mentions similarly unmade *recommendations against.* The only recommendation in the passage is the recommendation that you check your credit report. (And you should, just not while taking the GMAT.)

The passage for questions 27–30 appears on page 686.

---

27. The passage implies which of the following things about representative plaintiffs in class action lawsuits?

(A) It is preferable that they share at least one quality with each member of the class, though not strictly required.

(B) It is both preferable and required that they share at least one quality with each member of the class.

(C) If they do not share any qualities with a substantial majority of the members of the class, the suit will be unsuccessful.

(D) Their similarity to other members of the class will have little to no effect on the ultimate success of the suit.

(E) The likelihood that they will be eventually proved unable or unwilling to continue the suit is a factor in their selection.

Question: Inference is by far the Reading Comprehension's favorite question type. This passage's first Inference question is built on what might seem like a throwaway detail, the explanation of why the UC system was chosen as a plaintiff. Of course, since so much of the information in this passage is **qualified** (lacking *always* and *never* rules), the correct inference, as in Answer Choice (E), is going to be of the **but that's too obvious!** variety.

(E) The incorrect answer choices are, for the most part, **definite** (but **irrelevant**) **comparisons** that can't be supported by the **qualified** information in the passage. Answer Choice (A), on the other hand, is **reasonable but unsupported**, because since we don't know if there are any definite requirements, we also don't know that there *aren't* any, either.

---

28. With which of the following evaluations of the civil law system would the author most likely agree?

(A) Although imperfect, the class action lawsuit is preferable to any other previously proposed solution to the problem of a selectively useable system of justice.

(B) Only in those cases where a criminal judgment is impossible should a class action lawsuit be used.

(C) Objections against a practice in civil law can sometimes be answered by appeal to concerns beyond the letter of the law.

(D) When one party accuses the other of injury, physical and financial damages should be rewarded before psychological or emotional ones are considered.

(E) If the financial barriers to entry in the system were relaxed, then the class action lawsuit would not be necessary.

Question: *Likely agreement* is just another way of asking for an Inference, and again the correct answer is a **but that's too obvious!** inference, built on the information at the end of the passage that indicates that the appeals to an extralegal principle were successful.

(C) Answer Choice (A)'s *preferable to any other solution* is **too extreme** for our qualified and hedging author, as are Answer Choices (B)'s *only* and (E)'s *not necessary*. Answer Choice D is out because it creates an **irrelevant** and unsupported **comparison**.

---

29. According to the passage, one reason that the University of California was chosen as lead plaintiff was that
    (A) its losses from its pension fund were at least as great as those from its endowment fund.
    (B) the award for damages would have been much less than $8 billion without its participation.
    (C) the expected duration of the suit would have been unduly burdensome upon other plaintiffs.
    (D) it was more likely to see the suit through to its final conclusion than some other plaintiffs
    (E) it was deemed to be the most similar to the largest percentage of parties to the suit.

Question: Detail questions just require us to track down information in the passage, and Answer Choice (D) can be found right there in the discussion of why the UC system was chosen, because they were more likely to stick with a long case (rephrased to more likely to stick with the case than other plaintiffs).

(D) Answer Choice (A) is a **distortion** of a detail (no comparisons are made between the pension and the endowment, just the total from both given). Answer Choices (B) and (C) are **reasonable but never stated**, and Answer Choice (E) is another **distortion** of the discussion of why the UC system was chosen.

---

30. The primary purpose of the passage is to
    (A) explain the factors that contribute to a plaintiff being selected to lead a class action suit.
    (B) compare strategies used in civil courts to those used in criminal courts.
    (C) illustrate the considerations involved in the development of a device used in civil courts.
    (D) describe the manner in which litigants in the Enron stock collapse were able to achieve success.
    (E) rebut the assertion that practical considerations should never be used to evaluate a legal practice.

Question: A vertical scan of these answer choices is in order, as they all begin with verbs.

(C) The author's overall tone was definitely neutral, more descriptive than argumentative, meaning our eyes should be drawn first to Answer Choices (A)'s *explain*, (C)'s *illustrate*, and (D)'s *describe*, as Answer Choices (B) and (E) have the **wrong tone**.

Answer Choice (A) is **part but not the whole**, something mentioned but not the main point, and Answer Choice (D) is a **distortion**, as the only thing we know about the Enron case is that the UC system was picked and that they ultimately succeeded; we're never told why, in a larger sense, they won.

---

31. Added to the tax bill that they already pay to fund their local fire departments, home owners in some cash-strapped municipalities are now being charged a hefty "accident tax."

(A) Added to the tax bill that they already pay to fund their local fire departments, home owners in some cash-strapped municipalities are now being charged a hefty "accident tax."

(B) Added to the property taxes that they already pay to fund their local fire departments, some cash-strapped municipalities are now charging home owners a hefty "accident tax."

(C) Some cash-strapped municipalities are now charging home owners a hefty "accident tax" to be added to fund their local fire departments with the property taxes that they pay already.

(D) In addition to the property taxes that they already pay to fund their local fire departments, some cash-strapped municipalities are now charging home owners a hefty "accident tax."

(E) In addition to the property taxes they already pay to fund their local fire departments, home owners in some cash-strapped municipalities are now being charged a hefty "accident tax."

Issues: modification (what is being *added* or is *in addition to* what), **idiomatic construction** (the choice between *added to* versus *in addition to*), **pronoun reference**

(E) The most obvious decision point is likely the split between Answer Choices (D) and (E)'s *in addition to* and Answer Choices (A) and (B)'s *added to*. Both are grammatically correct, but only *in addition to* is appropriate for the meaning of this sentence because the accident tax is something that the home owners are being *asked to **pay** in addition to what they have already **paid***. Here, *added to* creates a modification error, because *added to* only works as a description of nouns and because the entire first clause acts as a modifying phrase for whatever appropriate candidate follows the comma. So, technically, the *accident tax* is being added to the *home owners* in Answer Choice (A) and the *municipalities* in Answer Choice (B). Answer Choice (C)'s *added to* might have worked, but ultimately it just makes a nonsensical construction elsewhere, *added to fund … with* (which has one too many prepositions to work).

Of the two remaining answers, Answer Choice (D) creates a pronoun reference error by moving the *they* so that now the sentence seems to imply that it's the municipalities that are paying the taxes.

32. Fire prevention experts agree that inebriated and intoxicated people are more likely to cause fires—both accidentally and deliberately—than they are when sober. The damage done by such fires is exacerbated by the fact that the chemically impaired are also less capable at extinguishing fires they have started. Nevertheless, the damage from fires started by the sober far exceeds that done by fires started by intoxicated and inebriated people combined.

Which of the following, if true, best explains the discrepancy above?

(A) It can be difficult to determine who started a fire and in what condition they were in when it was started.

(B) Naturally occurring fires or those caused by accidents do more damage than those set deliberately.

(C) Most people who become inebriated or intoxicated do so for only a few hours each week.

(D) Many people prone to starting fires abstain completely from alcohol or other intoxicating chemicals.

(E) The sight of a burning fire often is sufficient to allow a person to temporarily overcome the impairment caused by intoxication.

Dilemma: the discrepancy here is a sort of **net calculation** or **percent versus number** issue that seems to be out of whack. On the one hand, (1) *damage* from fires caused by the sober is greater than *damage* from fires caused by the chemically altered, yet on the other hand (2) the sober are less likely to cause fires than the chemically altered. There are two ways we might increase the damage enough to overcome this reduced likelihood: either (1) increase the number of sober people so that even though they don't, on average, commit many fires, there's enough people that the low average still results in a lot of fires, or (2) increase the *damage* from the fires that are caused by sober people, however few those fires are. Answer Choice (C) does the former, by establishing that, most of the time, people aren't drunk. Thus for most of the week, drunk people aren't drunk, they're sober, inflating the number of sober people available to start fires.

(C) Answer Choice (A) is **reasonable but irrelevant** to our dilemma, as the comparison only concerns fires whose source can be identified; Answer Choice (B) is as well, since the dilemma doesn't concern natural versus manmade fires. If there were *enough* of these teetotalers mentioned in Answer Choice (D), it might inflate the number of the sober, as we need, but *many* on the GMAT only implies *at least one*. Answer Choice (E) doesn't affect the dilemma because the fire has already been started once the formerly intoxicated are suddenly sober.

33. The Tennessee Valley Authority brought electricity to rural Americans, <u>who had long been isolated due to its lack, and consequently no longer able to</u> operate at a complete remove from the national government.

(A) who had long been isolated due to its lack, and consequently no longer able to

(B) whose lack had long isolated them, due to their no longer being able to consequently

(C) who due to its lack had long been isolated, and was consequently no longer able to

(D) who had long been isolated due to its lack; consequently, they were no longer able to

(E) which had long been isolated due to their lacking it; consequently, they were no longer able to

<u>**Issues: connecting clauses**</u> (twice, between the first and second and first and third clauses)**, modification** (placement of *consequently*)

(D) As written, the sentence's *comma-and* should connect two *independent* clauses (with the *who*-clause serving dependent to the first independent clause), but the second half of the sentence lacks a noun to serve as the subject for the clause. Answer Choice (B) fixes this error, but Answer Choice (C) still suffers from it. The semicolon in Answer Choices (D) and (E) are also good solutions to how to connect the sentence's clauses up, removing the *comma-and* and making the clauses both *independent*.

Answer Choice (E), unfortunately, breaks the relationship between the middle dependent clause and the first clause. As a rule of thumb, *comma-which* is usually part of a wrong answer on the GMAT, but the answer is usually wrong for reasons other than the use of *comma-which* itself (the old restrictive versus nonrestrictive clause issue that confuses just about everyone). The trend holds here, as *which* is the wrong connecting word to use to connect the description …*had long been isolated* to the *rural Americans* (as they are people, not things).

Answer Choice (B) breaks the *dependent* second clause in a different way, stranding the word *lack* so that it's no longer clear who's lacking what. Moreover, moving the *consequently* makes the sentences nonsensical.

---

34. Because it has outgrown its current space and because that space cannot be expanded, the county animal shelter must be moved to a larger facility. Vacant buildings of sufficient size that are located near the current shelter are far more expensive than those found near the county line. Since the cost of rent is the biggest single cost associated with running the shelter, it would be cheaper to move the shelter to the county line.

Which of the following is an assumption made by the argument above?

(A) It is not possible to build an entirely new facility for the animal shelter.

(B) The animals that are currently housed in the shelter will be able to be moved to a new shelter.

(C) Volunteers who currently work at the shelter will not be dissuaded from continuing if the shelter moves.

(D) The possible sites for the shelter near its location do not require substantially less energy to heat and cool.

(E) City codes do not prevent the shelter from being placed in any of the buildings near its current location.

Argument: Many difficult assumption questions ask us what a *bad* or *flawed* argument would need to assume to be correct. Here, the argument is clearly flawed. One factor that would affect the **net calculation** is mentioned (rent), but no others are mentioned. Thus, the argument assumes that there are no other factors that would affect the overall costs associated with putting the shelter close to where it is currently or out by the county line. Answer Choice (D) is a **defending assumption** that eliminates a factor that might have altered the net calculation, heating and cooling costs.

(D) Answer Choice (A) is a **closed issue**, since the argument is only discussing which of two options is preferable, not suggesting that one option is the best of all possible options. Answer Choice (B) tugs at the heart strings but is irrelevant, **one step removed** from the evidence as we don't know if it'd be expensive to deal with these unmovable animals or not. Answer Choice (C) is also a **closed issue**, as the shelter is definitely moving, so these volunteers might be lost with either of the two proposed plans. Answer Choice (E) is tempting, but also a **closed issue,** as the argument does not need to assume that either of the two proposals is *definitely possible*, since its conclusion is limited only to a comparison of the costs of the plans if they are put into place.

---

35. The biotech companies that sell genetically modified foods have always claimed that their products are no more dangerous to eat than unmodified foods. In support of this, they have widely touted the results of research published by an independent study group, the Sunbelt Foundation. But it has recently come to light that the Sunbelt Foundation's chief scientist falsified data, likely because his family was heavily invested in biotech stocks. Clearly, there is good reason to worry that these purportedly safe foods are actually harmful.

The reasoning in the argument above is suspect because
- (A) the failure to prove a claim is taken as equivalent as proof that the claim has been disproven.
- (B) generalizes from a single case of wrongdoing to an insupportably broad conclusion
- (C) fails to consider the possibility that financial interest alone is not sufficient to discredit a party
- (D) takes the behavior of an individual as representative of a group to which the individual does not belong
- (E) assumes without justification that independent research is sufficient to establish safety

Argument: Again, we see the common nestled argument structure (with a little bit of **double negative** distraction mixed in for good measure). Someone argues for something, and the speaker argues that the original conclusion is false by providing other evidence, or **somebody says X (and they're wrong).**

Also, always beware of prompts that invoke the issue of bias, as this is almost always a distractor on the GMAT and not a live issue. Here, the flaw is actually another familiar pattern: **disproving an argument does not disprove a conclusion.** Just because one reason to believe these foods are harmful (the evidence from the Sunbelt Foundation) has been eliminated does not mean that the conclusion of the argument (that food is safe) is itself false. Answer Choice (A) states this in an oblique but acceptable way.

(A) Answer Choice (B) springs the bias trap, but remember which conclusion we're supposed to be dealing with, the speaker's, not the Sunbelt Foundation's. Answer Choices (C) and (D) likewise hint at bias, irrelevant here because the evidence already establishes that the Sunbelt Foundation was biased. As for Answer Choice (E), it's the **right idea**, **wrong person** as the speaker *does* assume that lack of a guarantee means lack of something entirely (no proof means no truth), but Answer Choice (E) is dealing with the conclusion of those who believed the Sunbelt Foundation, not the speaker's conclusion.

---

36. Economist #1: Rises and falls in the global economy correlate almost exactly with the amount of volatility in the currency market. Clearly, regardless of what politicians may think, the global economy's health is strictly a function of currency market volatility.

Economist #2: Absurd. Any true economist would know that in a system as complicated as the global economy, no single variable could account for its overall performance.

The second economist's rejection of the first economist's position employs which of the following argumentative strategies?
(A) Establishing by counterexample that a proposed rule is false as stated
(B) Supporting a conclusion about a specific case by appeal to a general rule
(C) Showing that an apparent correlation is actually the result of direct causation
(D) Rejecting a purely theoretical conclusion on the grounds that it has no practical value
(E) Suggesting that the argument against a conclusion is based on personal animus rather than logic

Argument: The key to identifying the responder's technique is to make sure you note which parts of the original argument the responder takes issue with and which are either explicitly or implicitly accepted. Here, the second economist never mentions the argument of the first at all, instead choosing to reject the argument's conclusion with a new argument based on a rule: *nothing as complicated (as the global economy) could be accounted for by a single variable (currency market volatility)*. Answer Choice (B) states this directly.

(B) No counterexamples are present, so Answer Choice (A) is out. Answer Choice (C) is the **exact opposite** of what we want, as it describes the first economist's position, not the second one's; Answer Choice (D) is a flaw that we often see, just not in this argument; and Answer Choice (E) is, once again, the old **bias trap**, always a possibility in a two-party prompt.

37. The tyrannical conduct of Tarquinius Superbus led to the abolition of the Roman monarchy, <u>which ruled for nearly three centuries and had claimed to trace their royal authority</u> to Romulus, legendary founder of Rome.

(A) which ruled for nearly three centuries and had claimed to trace their royal authority

(B) by which it was ruled for nearly three centuries and claimed to trace its royal authority

(C) ruled for nearly three centuries and which they claimed that royal authority traced

(D) which ruled for nearly three centuries and claimed to trace its royal authority

(E) who ruled for nearly three centuries and claiming to trace its royal authority

<u>Issues:</u> **modification** (who ruled?), **parallelism** (of the two-part construction created by *and*), **sequence of tenses** (for the verbs *led, claimed, traced*), **pronoun reference** (who ruled or claimed what?)

(D) The first part of the underlined section splits dramatically, offering a decision point over how to connect the modifying information to the original sentence, and in a twist we might expect from a difficult sentence correction question, all of the initial words (*which, by which, ruled, which, who*) in *certain contexts* could possibly work, requiring us to lean heavily on meaning to sort out the proper grammatical relationships. So who's ruling whom and how are they ruling? The answer should be *the monarchy*, but Answer Choice (C)'s version doesn't make this clear. Answer Choice (B) introduces a new pronoun error that makes the question unanswerable, since the antecedent for *it* is unclear (what or who was ruled?).

The *and* in the underlined section sets up a two-part construction of things that describe what the monarchy did, and such constructions must be grammatically **parallel**. The already eliminated Answer Choice (C) adds an extra *they* that breaks the parallelism with *ruled*; Answer Choice (E)'s *claiming* is also wrong. All that's left to eliminate is the original Answer Choice (A), disagreeable because of *comma-which*, but unacceptable because of the stranded pronoun *their* which has no clear antecedent.

Thus, in the end, this question breaks the *comma-which* rule of thumb in a way (which is why it's a rule of thumb and not a rule), as *comma-which* **is** part of the right answer; nevertheless, it remains the case that *comma-which* is not *itself* usually in error on the test. Remember that as questions get more difficult, the test maker will force you to "swallow a few lemons," accepting things you usually avoid.

38. If asked in 1600 to predict which nation would come to dominate North America, a reasonable person likely would <u>guess Spain, England, or France and be</u> absolutely wrong.

(A) guess Spain, England, or France and be

(B) guess Spain, England, or France and it would have been

(C) have guessed Spain, England, or France and been

(D) have guessed that it would have been Spain, England, or France and

(E) have guessed Spain, England, or France and would be

<u>Issues:</u> **sequence of tenses** (*asked, guess,* and *be*), **pronoun reference** (*it*), **parallelism** (around *...and...*)

(C) The initial split between *guess* and *have guessed* is a useful decision point, but if analyzed without the content of the sentence, it would have been less than useful. (Content is increasingly important as the difficulty of questions climbs.)

Essentially, the sentence describes a sequence of events. First, the reasonable person is *asked* to make a prediction. The person then makes a guess *after* the question and *before* the person is right or wrong about the guess—and all of these things happen back around 1600, meaning *in the past*.

The **present perfect** is a flexible tense, chronologically speaking, used to describe events that started happening at some point before the present, but might continue up to it, but also might have ended before the present tense starts or before some other past event began. The correct answer, (C), relies on this flexibility to put the guessing *after* the asking. The *been* in *been wrong* is also in the present perfect, sharing the helping verb *have* with *have guessed* (an acceptable way to handle the two-part construction around *and*).

Answer Choices (A) and (B) thus fail because the guessing happens in the present tense. Answer Choice (E) adds an extra *would*, ruining the parallelism around *and*, while Answer Choice (D) ruins the parallelism a different way, by dropping the second verb entirely (*and absolutely wrong* makes no sense).

---

39. Six out of every seven long-practicing doctors agree about one thing, the *Washington Post* health editor reports: the nation's insurance system, as currently constituted, cannot long endure.

(A) Six out of every seven long-practicing doctors agree about one thing, the *Washington Post* health editor reports

(B) Out of every seven, six doctors of long-standing practice agree about one thing, the *Washington Post*'s health reports

(C) One thing is agreed upon by six out of every seven long-practicing doctors, the *Washington Post's* health editor reports

(D) Six out of every seven long-practicing doctors agree upon one thing, the *Washington Post*'s health editor has reported

(E) Out of every seven doctors who have practiced for long, six agree about one thing, the *Washington Post* health editor has reported

Issues: modification, indirect and direct verbs (*agree, reports, endure*)

(A) Another trick reserved for the more difficult Sentence Correction questions is what some grammarians call a *garden path* sentence, a sentence in which one meaning is suggested at first, but that is unsupportable the longer you walk down the sentence's "*garden path*." At first it seems like *agree* is going to be the main verb of the sentence, but then the *Washington Post* health editor shows up to make things confusing, as the editor isn't agreeing with anything, but rather *reporting* the information in the first clause. Viewed that way, the first clause *six out of…etc.* works fine, even if it "sounds off."

Answer Choice (B)'s rearrangement of words creates two descriptive clauses where there was originally one, resulting in ambiguity as to what's being reported and what's out of seven (and *of long-standing practice* is itself incorrect)—a modification error.

Moreover, Answer Choice (C)'s *long-practice doctors* is a bit of nonsensical modification that ruins an otherwise OK sentence.

But the much larger error present is the relationship between the agreeing by the doctors, the reporting by the *Washington Post* health editor, and the enduring that the health system won't be able to do. For verbs like *report*, which can be used to present **indirect speech**—the statement that follows the original sentence's colon—it's acceptable to use either the *present* or the *past* tenses only (a rule that has only been tested *very* rarely on the GMAT). So *has reported* in Answer Choices (D) and (E) are out, leaving us with the original sentence, as odd as it might sound.

---

40. The manuscript tradition of Julian of Norwich's *Revelations* is fraught <u>by ambiguity with no surviving autograph, only one of the extant manuscripts being medieval, and we do not even know if</u> the work was ever disseminated in the medieval period at all.

- (A) by ambiguity with no surviving autograph, only one of the extant manuscripts being medieval, and we do not even know if
- (B) by ambiguity: with no autograph surviving, only one of the extant manuscripts is medieval and we do not know even if
- (C) with ambiguity; no autograph survives, only one of the extant manuscripts is medieval, and we do not even know whether
- (D) with ambiguity; without an autograph that survives, only one of the extant manuscripts is medieval; and we do not even know whether
- (E) ambiguously with no autograph surviving, only one of the extant manuscripts being medieval, and us not knowing whether or not

Issues: idiomatic construction (*fraught with* and *whether* vs. *if*), **connecting clauses, modification**

(C) This question is built on the somewhat obscure idiom *fraught with <noun>* (usually appearing in the melodramatic phrase *fraught with danger*). The *by* in (A) and (B) is not idiomatically correct, and (E)'s switch to *fraught with no autograph* is nonsensical. Of the two remaining answers, the deciding issue is **modification**—and not, as you might have worried, the correct use of the colon vs. the semicolon (which hardly ever appears on the GMAT as the single deciding issue that makes an answer right or wrong).

In (D), the phrase *without an autograph that survives* is a dependent clause, and thus must be used as some sort of description of *only one of the manuscripts is medieval*, but there's no sensible way to manage that.

Another place to start would have been the *whether* vs. *if* choice the GMAT so loves. Remember, *whether* is for choices and options (and doesn't get an *or not*), while *if* is for hypotheticals. No hypothetical is found here, so *whether* is preferred.

41. Ranked first among the emotions that Aristotle thought an orator must learn to manipulate <u>are moral indignation, used both to incite citizens against injustice and for punishing those who would rise</u> above their station.

   (A) are moral indignation, used both to incite citizens against injustice and for punishing those who would rise

   (B) are moral indignation to use inciting citizens against injustice and, for punishing, those who would be raised

   (C) is moral indignation, used both to incite citizens against injustice and punish those who would rise above their station

   (D) is moral indignation for both inciting citizens against injustice and used to punish those who might rise

   (E) are moral indignation, which was used both to incite citizens against injustice and punishment of those who would have rose

Issues: subject/predicate agreement, parallelism (for the *both... and...*)

(C) The inverted sentence structure (*ranked first is moral indignation,* instead of *moral indignation is ranked first*) is used to hide a simple subject/predicate agreement error in three of the answer choices. Indignation is singular, so plural *are* in Answer Choice (A), (B), and (E) disqualifies those answers. The choice between Answer Choices (C) and (D) is made most easily by checking to see that the elements following the *both... and...* are grammatically parallel (required by all coordinating idioms). Answer Choice (D)'s *for both inciting... and used* is not parallel.

EVALUATING YOUR SCORE

Tabulate your score for the Quantitative and Verbal sections of the Sample Test by giving yourself one point for every correct answer, and record the results in the Self-Scoring Table below. Then find your approximate rating for each score on the Self-Scoring Scale and record it in the appropriate blank.

SELF-SCORING TABLE

Section	Score	Rating
Quantitative		
Verbal		

SELF-SCORING SCALE—RATING

Section	Poor	Fair	Good	Excellent
Quantitative	0–12	13–20	21–29	30–37
Verbal	0–15	15–25	26–30	31–41

Study again the Review sections covering material in Sample Test 2 for which you had a rating of FAIR or POOR.

*Important note: Up-to-date scoring guidelines for all sections of the GMAT can be found at *mba.com.*

ANSWERS EXPLAINED

Index

NOTES

NOTES

NOTES